THE WORLD TODAY SERIES®

Russia, Eurasian States and Eastern Europe 1993

FORMERLY *THE SOVIET UNION AND EASTERN EUROPE*

24TH ANNUAL EDITION

M. WESLEY SHOEMAKER, Ph.D.

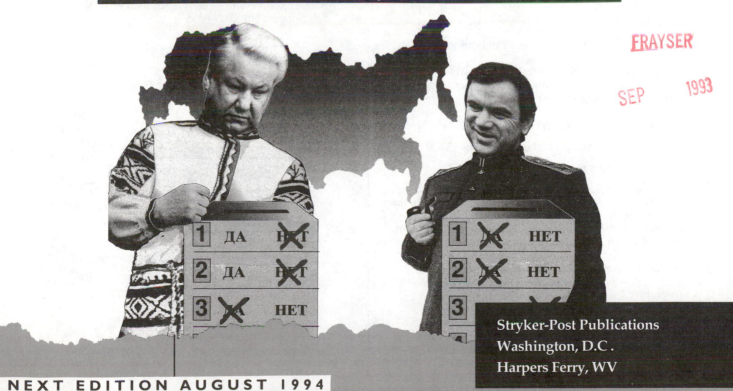

Stryker-Post Publications
Washington, D.C.
Harpers Ferry, WV

NEXT EDITION AUGUST 1994

M. Wesley Shoemaker . . .

Chairman, International Relations Program, Lynchburg College, Lynchburg, Va. B.A *Magna Cum Laude*, Waynesburg College (History); M.A. and Ph.D., Syracuse University (Russian History). Before he entered the teaching profession, he served for a number of years as a Foreign Service Officer with the Department of State. He had assignments in the European Bureau of the Department and abroad at the American Embassy in Kingston, Jamaica, the American Embassy in Bonn, Germany, and the American Consultate General in Stuttgart, Germany. He travels extensively in Eastern Europe.

Photographs used to illustrate *The World Today Series* come from many sources, a great number from friends who travel worldwide. If you have taken any which you believe would enhance the visual impact and attractiveness of our books, do let us hear from you.

First appearing as a book entitled
The Soviet Union and Eastern Europe 1970,
revised annually, published in 1970
and succeeding years by

Stryker–Post Publications
888 Seventeenth St., N.W., Washington, D.C. 20006
with executive offices at Harpers Ferry, W.Va. 25425
Telephones: 202–342–6055
           304–535–2593

International Standard Book Number: 0–943448–80–8

International Standard Serial Number: 1062–3574

Library of Congress Catalog Number 67–11537

Cover design by Susan Bodde
    The Russian weekly, *Arguments and Facts,* predicts the outcome of the April 1993 referendum. Pictured are President Yeltsin and Ruslan Khasbulatov, Chairman of the Russian Federation's Supreme Soviet.

Historical Research: Robert V. Gross

Cartography by William L. Nelson

Typography by Stryker–Post Publications
and Braun–Brumfield, Inc.

Printed in the United States of America by
Braun–Brumfield, Inc., Ann Arbor, Michigan

18th century Russian wedding feast. The new husband lifts the bride's veil.

contents

Political and economic conditions in the republics of the former Soviet Union are in a state of flux. The **Commonwealth of Independent States (CIS)** is probably just a transitional arrangement designed to manage the emergence of these new nations. Boundaries of some of the republics which seceded from the now defunct Socialist Federal Republic of Yugoslavia are in doubt, especially with the attempted dismemberment by its neighbors of multi-ethnic Bosnia-Herzegovina.

Russia, Eurasian States, and Eastern Europe 1993

One of the characteristics of revolutionary periods is the euphoria that results from the promise of change, and by definition change for the better if one is a supporter of the revolution. The Revolutions of 1989 in Eastern Europe produced such a euphoria and even the Revolution of 1991 that brought about the repudiation of communism and the collapse of the Soviet Union had some of that euphoria, even if it was actually the result of a failed *coup* whose purpose was to reaffirm old verities. It is, however, important to make this distinction between the two revolutions. In Eastern Europe, the repudiation of communism, which was at the core of the revolutions, was accompanied by a positive vision of an alternative society modeled on the rest of Europe. In the ex–Soviet lands, however, the repudiation of communism was a by–product of the failed *coup*—and those who opposed the *coup* were in most cases more motivated by nationalism or local control than they were by things like democracy or a market economy. For this reason, the evolution in the ex–Soviet lands has been different than it was in Eastern Europe.

That is not to say that there are no democrats in the ex–Soviet lands or that democracy and market economies have no chance to develop there. They will, over time, but they are not the things the new rulers—or even most of the people—value most.

Russia is a partial exception to the above, for a part of the reform wing of the communist party, those who supported President Yeltsin, has shown since 1991 that it really does favor democracy and an economy based on the principle of a market economy. Even so, many "nationalists" who supported Yeltsin in 1991 when he led the struggle against the *coup* have broken with him since and have even been willing to ally themselves with the remnants of the old communist power elite in an effort to call a halt to the dismantling of the old communist economic system. Two names that spring prominently to mind are Yeltsin's own

Vice President, Alexander Rutskoi, and Ruslan Khasbulatov, the Chairman of the Supreme Soviet. Khasbulatov stood at Yeltsin's side in August 1991, but he, and Rutskoi, have become two of the most powerful opponents of the government's program of economic reform. On the other hand, the Russian people, given the chance in the April 25 referendum to choose between Yeltsin and change or the Supreme Soviet's policy of retrenchment, opted decisively for Yeltsin and change. That increases the possibility that Yeltsin and his reformers will be able to continue the process of transforming Russia, but does not guarantee it. Yeltsin's opponents still occupy key positions in the government and their first reaction to the results of the referendum was to declare that it had no meaning.

But if Yeltsin has had to push his reforms against significant opposition, in the remainder of the ex–Soviet lands the problem has been finding anybody who is even pushing for reform. A partial exception is the Republic of Ukraine, where the new Prime Minister, Leonid Kuchma, has surprised nearly everybody by becoming a proponent of reform. But nearly everywhere else, leaders have been acting as though they feared some impending chaos and their efforts have been directed toward maintaining order in the economy and in the society. Repression has been more the order of the day than freedom and whatever economic changes have occurred have been either forced on them from outside or are marginal in nature. In Central Asia, even the issue of greater religious freedom has become intertwined with politics, and particularly so in the cases of Tajikistan and Uzbekistan, and the result has been a partial return to religious repression.

Developments in Eastern Europe are at the same time more pessimistic and more optimistic. The war for the creation of a Greater Serbia which has been raging in ex–Yugoslavia for nearly two years now has stymied all of the efforts of the rest of the world to negotiate a peace. It now

appears that the war will go on until the Serbs have achieved all of their goals, with the on–looking world providing as much humanitarian assistance to the victims as they are permitted by the Serbs to do. The peaceful separation of the Czechs and Slovaks into separate nations presents a more benevolent pattern for the resolution of the strains of nationalism, but the underlying economic causes of the separation are more likely to be exacerbated by this development than otherwise.

Finally, we have those countries where developments give us cause for optimism. The Czech Republic probably still fits into this category, although the separation from Slovakia has had some negative economic effects. The Czechs have enthusiastically endorsed a transformation to a market economy and they have been making excellent progress while managing to keep unemployment at just above two percent. Poland has also made progress in the past year. Prime Minister Suchocka has shown herself to be a strong and determined leader and she has managed to push through her economic reforms. She has also been helped by the fact that industrial production has begun to grow again. Hungary continues to be a success story. Although salaries are low and so buying power is also low, Hungarian industry is growing and the country continues to be the favorite insofar as foreign investment is concerned.

Thus we have a mixed picture. In general, change is continuing, even if much more slowly in some nations than in others. No where does there appear to be any significant sentiment for a return to communism, even among ex–communist officials leading the fight against greater change. And among the young everywhere, support for change remains extremely strong.

M.W.S.

Lynchburg, Virginia, June 1993

The Russian Federation

Area: 6.8 million sq. mi., or three–quarters of the territory of the former U.S.S.R.

Population: 147 million (as of 1989 census), not including former Soviet republics or Russians living in them.

Capital City: Moscow (Pop. 8.7 million).

Other Major Cities: St. Petersburg (5.1 million), Nizhny Novgorod—formerly Gorky (1.5 million), Ekaterinburg—formerly Sverdlovsk (1.4 million), Samara—formerly Kuibyshev (1.3 million), Omsk (1.2 million), Kazan, Perm (1.1 million each).

Climate: Russia lies within the temperate sub–arctic, and arctic zones. Most of European Russia is within the temperate zone, while most of Siberia lies in the arctic zone.

Neighboring States: (from the northwest) Norway, Finland, Estonia, Latvia, Belarus, Ukraine, Georgia, Azerbaijan, Kazakhstan, Mongolia, China, Japan. Kaliningrad (separated from the rest of the nation) is lodged between Lithuania (north and east) and Poland (south).

Official Language: Russian.

Ethnic Composition: Russian (83%), other 17%).

Principal Religions: Russian Orthodox and Protestant Christianity, Islam, Judaism. Until recently, religious worship was officially discouraged.

Chief Commercial Products: Russia is a major industrial power, abeit highly polluted, largely self–sufficient insofar as the domestic economy is concerned, but presently experiencing food shortages of unparalleled proportions. Exports have consisted primarily of petroleum, natural gas and other raw materials and manufactured goods, particularly military machinery. Imports include grains, tropical produce, manufactured goods, including consumer goods and machinery. Russia has more than 90% of the former U.S.S.R.'s oil reserves.

Currency: Ruble.

Former Political Status: Core of the Russian Empire for centuries to November 7, 1917. Russian Soviet Federative Socialist Republic, member of the Union of Soviet Socialist Republics from 1922 to 1991.

Federal Structure: The huge Russian Federation encompasses 16 autonomous republics and 64 subordinate political jurisdictions each with elected leaders and legislative bodies—and many with strong separatist movements, possibly an impending danger to the unity of the nation.

Chief of State: Boris N. Yeltsin, President.

National Flag: Three equal horizontal stripes of white, pale blue, and red (the same as used by the Russian Imperial Empire).

THE LAND AND THE PEOPLE

The Russian Federation, which became a separate, independent nation in December 1991 after the collapse of the Union of Soviet Socialist Republics, consists of the Russian–speaking core of that former union. Still the largest country in the world, it stretches 5,500 miles (9,200 km.) from the Kaliningrad enclave in the west to the Kamchatka Peninsula in the east, encompassing not only the lands of historic Russia west of the Ural Mountains, but all of Siberia. Expressed another way, the Russian Federation reaches 172 degrees around the globe (from longitude 19°39′E to 169° W).

Eleven time zones separate the Kaliningrad Region in the West from the Chukotka Peninsula in the East. Thus, even though fourteen republics broke away and established themselves as independent nations in 1991, the Russian Federation continues as one of the great nations of the world.

The heart of this enormous land is a seemingly endless plain that stretches from the Polish border in the west to beyond the Yenisei River in the east and into Central Asia in the south. This Eurasian plain, actually three interconnected plains partially separated by the low-lying Ural Mountains, is known as the Russian Plain west of the Ural Mountains. East of the Urals, it becomes the Western Siberian Lowlands. That part of the plain that extends across Kazakhstan and into Central Asia is known as the Turan Lowland.

The Russian Plain is part of the even larger East European Plain. It begins at the Baltic Sea in the North and extends to the Black Sea and the Caucasus Mountains in the South. Not totally flat, it is broken up by a series of higher elevations, the most significant of which is the Valdai Hills (also known as the Central Russian Upland), located in the northwest.

These somewhat higher elevations give rise to several large rivers which, flowing outward to the seas, connect most parts of the Russian Plain. Although the Valdai Hills only cover an area of approximately 100 square miles, they are the birthplace of four rivers, including the two largest rivers of the Russian Plain, the Dnieper and the Volga. The other two rivers are the Western Dvina (known in Latvia as the Daugava) and the Lovat.

Today, the Valdai Hills form part of the border between the Russian Federation

1

and the Republic of Belarus (formerly Byelorussia). However, this area, and the area of the Pripet Swamps to the south-west, is usually accepted as the birthplace of all the Eastern Slavs which include Russians. The Dnieper River flows west, then south, crossing the border into Belarus. It then continues southward, passing through the Republic of Ukraine before entering the Black Sea.

The Volga flows eastward, then southward, finally emptying into the Caspian Sea. The Western Dvina flows northward into Latvia, where it undergoes a name change and becomes the Daugava. It flows through Latvia into the Gulf of Riga, an arm of the Baltic Sea. The Lovat flows north into Lake Ilmen. When its waters leave the lake, they become the Volkhov, on which the historic city of Novgorod is located. The Volkhov, in turn, flows into Lake Ladoga. As they go from the lake, they become the Neva River. The Neva, on which St. Petersburg is located, flows into the Gulf of Finland, another arm of the Baltic Sea.

The origins of the Russian state are associated with a north–south water trade route that arose in the ninth century using the western part of this river system. The major river involved was the Dnieper, along whose middle reaches the city of Kiev is located. Kiev, capital of the Republic of Ukraine, was also the capital of Kievan Rus, the first Russian state. The other river system was the Lovat–Volkhov–Neva, and here the other important Russian city was Novgorod, located on the Volkhov at the northern edge of Lake Ilmen. These two cities guarded the trade route, and their unification under a single ruler marked the beginning of the then small Russian state.

There is one other river of the Russian Plain that needs to be mentioned, though its significance is more recent. The Don River lies between the Dnieper and Volga Rivers in the South. It flows into the Sea of Azov, an arm of the Black Sea. Because it is connected to the Volga by the Volga–Don canal, it provides a link between the Caspian and Black Seas.

The Western Siberian Lowlands, though nearly as large as the Russian Plain, have little of its importance, largely because of the climate. All of Russia lies quite far to the north, but most of European Russia benefits from weather patterns that give it a milder climate than its northern location would indicate. The warm waters of the Gulf Stream, pushing up through the English Channel and into the Baltic Sea, greatly modifies the climate of northern Russia. Other weather patterns associated with the Mediterranean Sea have a similar effect on the southern part of Russia.

The influence of these weather patterns are not found east of the Ural Mountains. Moreover, they are replaced by countervailing weather patterns whose effect is to make the climate even more severe than would be expected at similar latitudes. In addition, much of Siberia lies further north than the European part of the Russian Federation.

Nearly half of Siberia is situated north of the 60° parallel, the same parallel as St. Petersburg, and perhaps one–fifth of it lies north of the Arctic Circle. Another influence is that the land tends to slope downward from south to north, meaning that Arctic fronts can sweep unhindered southward across the landscape. This means also that Siberia's rivers flow from south to north—and their mouths in the north freeze earlier in the fall and thaw later in the spring than their more southerly upstream portion. The northern two–thirds of the Western Siberian Lowlands are, accordingly, a land of mixed evergreen forest and swamp.

This is the western third of that broad band of forest stretching from the Ural Mountains to the Pacific Ocean known as the Taiga. Agriculture is possible only in

To keep the map simplified, names of the former, now independent, Soviet republics, are not shown.

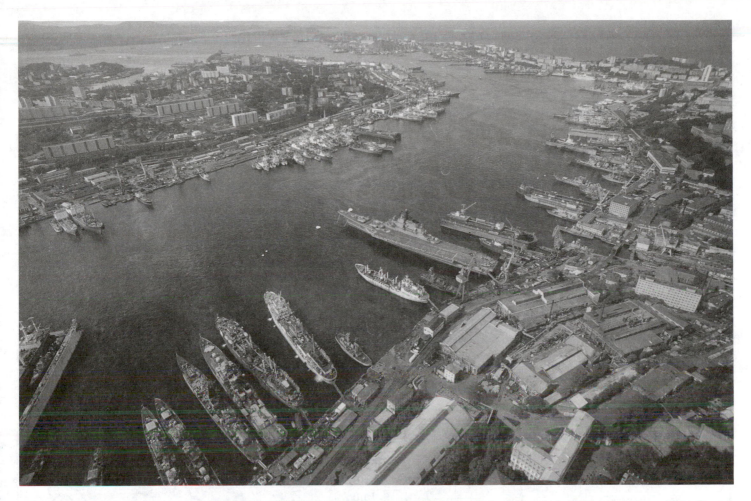

The first helicopter tour by an American journalist of the main harbor of Vladivostok (eastern coast of Siberia facing on the Sea of Japan) produced this aerial view. In the foreground is a naval shipyard now serving the Russian Pacific fleet, with the aircraft carrier Minsk (center) undergoing maintenance.

Photo by Bryan Hodgson © 1990 National Geographic Society

the south, in a fairly wide band just east of the Ural Mountains, but sharply narrowing as one travels eastward, ending west of Irkutsk. It is easy to locate this fertile band on a map for here are found all of the major cities of western Siberia, connected by the Trans–Siberian Railway, which passes through the region.

The Western Siberian Lowlands are dominated by two great river systems, the Ob–Irtysh and the Yenisei. The Ob–Irtysh drains the western and central part of the plain; the Yenisei drains the eastern part plus the western edges of the Central Siberian Plateau. Because they both flow northward, their economic usefulness is very limited.

To the east of the Western Siberian Lowlands, the land rises and becomes known as the Central Siberian Plateau. Here the land is still mostly flat or slightly rolling, but the climate is also much harsher, partly because of the higher elevation. In the North, the area is all treeless tundra, while the rest of the land is covered by evergreen forests, a continuation of the taiga. All of the plateau is classified as an area of permafrost—the land is permanently frozen to a depth of 50–60 feet and in the short Siberian summers only the top

3–4 feet melt. Subsistence agriculture is carried on in openings in the forests in the south, but this is generally not an area suitable for agriculture.

The Lena River, mightiest of Siberia's rivers, divides the Central Siberian Plateau from the Eastern Siberian Mountains. The southern, upstream portion of the Lena River Valley has been developed somewhat more because of extensive mineral deposits that have been found in the area. Yakutsk, capital of the Republic of Yakutsk–Sakha, which is located on the banks of the Lena River, boasts a population of over 200,000 inhabitants.

The Eastern Siberian Mountains are a series of ranges that run for 1,500 miles from west to east, up to the Bering Strait and the Pacific Ocean. Like the Central Siberian Plateau, this is an area of permafrost, with tundra in the north and taiga in the south. The tallest of these mountains is only about 10,000 feet in height, but the area is largely uninhabited except for wandering tribes of reindeer herders because of the extreme climate. Temperatures average above freezing for only about two months out of the year, partly because of the north-

ern location, but also because of the effect of cold Arctic ocean currents just offshore.

South of the Eastern Siberian Mountains, the Amur River forms the boundary between the Russian Federation and the People's Republic of China for a distance of about 700 miles before it turns northeastward and eventually empties into the Sea of Okhotsk. The Amur is the only major Siberian river to flow from west to east and the Amur River Valley is the only area of extensive cultivation in the eastern part of Siberia. The amounts produced are insufficient to supply the population, however, so this, like the rest of Siberia, is a net food–importing area.

The last major feature of the Siberian landscape is a series of very high mountain chains that stretch all along the southern border. These are, starting from the west, the Altai, Sayan and Yablonoi, plus the Stanovoi Mountains. The latter, which begin north of the Amur River, are separated from the Eastern Siberian Highlands by the Aldan Plateau. These are mostly high, rugged mountains that hem in the land and isolate Russian Siberia from its neighbors.

NATURAL VEGETATION

Legend:
- Subtropical Forest
- Broadleaf Forest
- Fertile Steppe
- Dry Steppe
- Taiga
- Tundra
- Desert

Natural Regions

The Russian Federation includes within its limits climatic belts varying from the temperate to the Arctic, stretching from west to east in wide bands across the country. Two of these, the tundra and the taiga, are found primarily in Siberia. The tundra stretches across the northern part of the land that borders on the Arctic Ocean from the Ural Mountains in the west to the tip of the Chukotka Peninsula in the east. It is almost entirely uninhabited and nothing but moss and swamp shrubs grow there. Migratory herds of reindeer graze briefly in the southernmost part of the tundra during the brief summer.

Immediately south of the tundra is the taiga, a zone of evergreen forest that begins at about Archangel in the west and gradually widens toward the east until it takes in an area as far south as Lake Baikal. The belt then bends somewhat northward before continuing on to the Sea of Othotsk.

To the south of the taiga is a zone of mixed forest which stretches from west to east across the entire country. West of the Urals, this takes in about two–thirds of the Russian Plain, reaching as far south as Kiev, capital of the Republic of Ukraine. On its southern edge, it gradually thins out, becoming mixed wooded steppe and grassy meadow. The northern slope of the Caucasus Mountains also belongs in this climatic zone.

The last vegetation zone is the steppe, or prairie area. The steppe begins as a 150–mile band north of the Black Sea and stretches eastward into Central Asia. It was originally a natural grassland, but today this area is mostly cultivated land. The chief city of the Russian steppe is Stavropol, the main city of the region where Mikhail Gorbachëv grew up.

Ethnic Diversity

The Russian Federation, with 83 percent of the population ethnic Russians, is relatively homogeneous. Nevertheless, it is home to numerous non–Russian ethnic groups and this is reflected in the fact that it includes 16 autonomous republics, five autonomous regions and ten autonomous areas. A number of these autonomous republics have declared their "sovereignty" vis–a–vis the Russian Federation. This is what happened in the case of the Tatar Autonomous Republic, which now calls itself the Republic of Tatarstan, and the Yakutsk Autonomous Republic, now the Republic of Yakutsk–Sakha.

In the area of the northern Caucasus, one group, the Chechens, seceded from the Chechen–Ingush Autonomous Republic to establish their own Republic of Chechen.

President Yeltsin attempted to reassert Russian authority over the Republic of Chechen in November 1991, but discovered he had neither the force nor the political support to carry it out. He backed down when the Russian Supreme Soviet refused to endorse his policy. Yeltsin's attempted move against the Republic of Chechen was an aberration, however. In general, he has taken the position that he favors the maximum grant of local sovereignty to the autonomous republics and other autonomous political subdivisions. There is opposition to this position in the Russian Supreme Soviet. In November 1991, it refused to consider a draft Russian Federation constitution submitted by Yeltsin's government, partly on this issue.

European Russia's Heartland
showing principal cities and railroads

History

The origins of both the Russian state and nation are found in the area north of the Black Sea and in the steppe lands to the north and east of that strategic body of water. Although there is evidence of human settlement in the area dating back to the neolithic period of the Stone Age, significant history begins with the Slavs. These people were and are identified by a common or similar language rather than by any other common features. The Russians are part of an Eastern Slav group, the other members of which speak Ukrainian and Byelorussian.

The Poles, Czechs and Slovaks belong to a second major group, the West Slavs. There is also a South Slav branch represented by the Bulgarians and the ethnic groups of Yugoslavia.

Little is known about the original home of the early Slavs and many theories have been developed and discarded by scholars. As early as the beginning of the Christian era, however, Slavic people were found throughout most of the Russian Plain west of the Dnieper River and in Eastern Europe as far west as the Vistula River in what is now central Poland. References to the Slavs are also found in the writings of the Greek and Roman historians of the early Christian

era, but very little is known about them in this time period. Essentially, they were cut off from classical civilization by the fact that they occupied only the center of the Russian Plain, the more southern part bordering the Black Sea not being suitable for medieval agriculture. The Slavs were traditionally agricultural people and left the grassy steppe of southern Russia to others.

The early political organization of the Slavs was basically tribal, with groups of self-governing villages cooperating in such areas as defense. By the 7th century, towns had begun to develop and trade between the tribes became more important. Kiev, later the capital, was founded at about this time and probably owed its existence to the trade that had started along the Dnieper River. Located high on the bluffs that overlook the western shore of the river, Kiev was ideally located to dominate all such trade.

Novgorod, located at the northern edge of Lake Ilmen, was established somewhat later. Begun as a trading post for amber and other products of the Baltic Sea area, it soon developed as a manufacturing center for jewelry, metals and wood products. Its chief significance, however, was as the northern terminus of the trade route known as the "Road

from the Varangians to the Greeks." It was the existence of the trade route that led to the creation of the first organized Russian state.

"Varangian" was the old Slavonic word for a Norseman or Viking. Ancestors of today's Scandinavians, the Vikings were great seamen and from about the seventh century onward, they had been pushing out of Scandinavia, carrying out raids and explorations in all directions. Eventually they established settlements in eastern England, northern France and along the southern coastline of the Baltic Sea. This brought them into contact with Novgorod. According to tradition, Rurik, leader of one of these Viking bands, established himself at Novgorod in 862.

The story of the coming of the Vikings is told in *The Primary Chronicle*, a 12th century compilation of history from unknown earlier sources. According to the *Chronicle*, Rurik and his band of Varangians were invited to set themselves up as the local rulers—"Our land is great and abundant, but there is no order in it; come rule and reign over us." It is more likely that the Novgorodian merchants hired Varangians as mercenaries and then Rurik decided to take complete control himself. Twenty years later, Oleg the

Norwegian, Rurik's successor, "set himself up as prince in Kiev." Since he retained control in Novgorod, he then controlled the two chief cities of the "Road from the Varangians to the Greeks."

Kievan Russia: This was the beginning of "Kievan Rus," the first organized Russian state. Oleg lived until 913 and he spent the rest of his life extending his control over neighboring Slavic tribes and building up the trade route upon which the prosperity of the new state was based. His most spectacular gesture, according to Russian sources, was an attack on Constantinople which he launched in 907. Byzantine sources make no reference to such an attack but they do record that in 907 the Byzantine Emperor signed a treaty with Oleg which granted access to Byzantine markets on very favorable terms. Oleg was succeeded by Igor in 913; the latter was either the son or grandson of Rurik and from that time onward the descendants of Rurik sat on the throne of Kievan Rus. This Rurikovichi ("sons of Rurik") dynasty later made the transfer when the capital was moved to Vladimir and, later to Moscow, so that it remained the ruling dynasty of Russia until 1598, when Fedor, son of Ivan the Terrible, died without an heir.

The first ruling family of Russia was thus Varangian in origin, but it must be emphasized that they became rulers of a land that had already developed an extensive "slavic" culture. The Varangians were fine warriors and good leaders, but the Viking culture did not replace the native Slav culture. In fact, the opposite happened—the Varangian rulers were soon enveloped by Slavic culture.

This can be seen in the names of subsequent rulers. Igor was killed in 945 while on an expedition to collect tribute from a neighboring Slavic tribe. He was succeeded by his wife, Olga, because his son was still only a child. But that son, who succeeded to the throne in 962, was named Sviatoslav—the third generation of Varangian rulers already had Slavic names and, one can reasonably assume, were speaking the local Slavic language.

The subject of early Slavic culture is complex; by this time it was indeed fairly well developed, but was centered around a belief in pagan Slavic deities. The trade connection between Kievan Rus and Constantinople meant that the Russians were exposed to Byzantine culture and religion.

Constantinople was the leading city of Europe, the capital of the Byzantine Empire and the home of the Patriarch of Constantinople, leader of Greek Orthodox Christianity. It was a center of wealth, power and culture. Further, the Orthodox Church was actively commit-

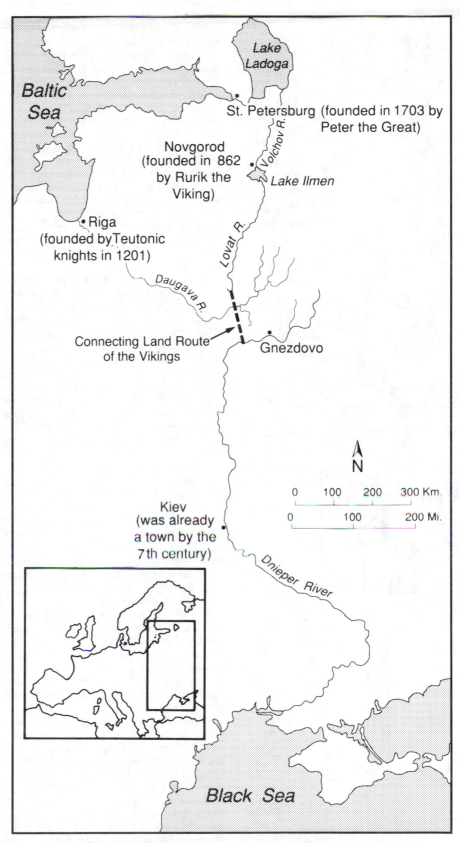

ROAD FROM THE VARANGIANS TO THE GREEKS

ted to a policy of conversion of the Slavs; its missions had been active among the Bulgarians for some time. Two Orthodox monks, Cyril and Methodius, had trans-

lated the *Bible* into Old Slavonic and in the process, created the Cyrillic alphabet designed to portray the *sounds* of Slavonic in characters different from the Roman alphabet. There thus was created the first written Slavic language.

Oleg permitted an Orthodox mission to open in Kiev, but the first breakthrough did not occur until 955 when Olga underwent Christian baptism by missionaries from Constantinople. But her son, Sviatoslav, never converted, and Christianity remained a minority belief. The largest conversion to Orthodox Christianity occurred during the reign of Sviatoslav's son, Vladimir (978–1015). It was somewhat ironic that Vladimir was responsible for the conversion to Christianity, since he assumed the throne as a champion of the old Slavic gods. Paganism was a dying force, however. Poland, Hungary and Bulgaria had already become Christian and the kings of Denmark and Norway were converted shortly after Vladimir's accession to the throne.

Thus, when the Byzantine Emperor found himself faced with revolts in various parts of the empire and called upon Vladimir for assistance, offering his own sister to Vladimir as a bride, the offer was irresistible—Vladimir sent help and looked forward to the added power his anticipated bride would bring. But he found that the marriage could only take place if he converted to Christianity. Without hesitation, with the intent of allying himself with the most powerful state of that age, he underwent baptism in 988. After the marriage arrangements had been completed, he ordered the mass baptism of the entire population of Kiev and began the construction of St. Sophia Cathedral, the first of the great Orthodox cathedrals that were built during the time of Kievan Rus. The Byzantine style of architecture was introduced into Russia in this manner, a style that would remain dominant until Peter the Great introduced the neo–classical style at the beginning of the 18th century.

Kievan Rus also officially adopted the Cyrillic alphabet at this time, and Vladimir ordered that schools be set up for the education of the sons of the upper classes. Kievan Rus had, in fact, completely opened itself to Byzantine influence and gradually, much of its culture was transformed.

Vladimir and his successor, Yaroslav (1019–1054), were responsible for much of this transformation, and it is for this reason that the combined reigns of these Grand Princes is known as the height of Kievan Rus. Influenced by the Byzantine example, the relationship of Grand Prince to the people changed and it was at this time that Kievan Rus first became a nation. Earlier princes had merely levied tribute on the various tribes and each

spring they had traveled about the country, collecting goods which were then traded in Constantinople. Vladimir replaced the tribute system with taxation. Yaroslav was responsible for having the Bishop of Kiev named a *Metropolitan*, meaning that he became the head of an autonomous Russian Church. The Patriarch of Constantinople still retained the authority to *name* the Metropolitan, but this made Kiev the religious as well as political capital of the state. Yaroslav's other important achievement is that he was responsible for the first Russian law code, the *Russkaya Pravda*.

After the death of Yaroslav there was a period of decline partly because of a system of inheritance which tended to break up the kingdom into separate principalities, and encouraged competition for the throne among brothers and cousins. Occasionally uncles and nephews entered the contest for the dominant throne of Kiev. New Asian invaders, the *Polovtsy*, appeared on the scene, contributing to the decline of Kiev. The city was attacked in 1169 by a contender for the throne and lost its position as capital of the Russian states for a time. It was almost completely destroyed in 1240 by a massive invasion of Mongols (Tartars) let by Batu, grandson of the renowned Ghengis Khan, founder of the empire of the "Golden Horde."

What came to be called the "Mongol Yoke" had to be endured by the Russians until it was finally overthrown in 1480 by Ivan III, Prince of Moscow. An earlier attempt in 1380 ended in failure, despite the dashing military exploits of the Russian forces led by Dmitri, also a Prince of Moscow.

The Effects of Mongol Occupation

Historians are in dispute concerning the exact significance of the period of Mongol (Tartar) occupation. Generally speaking, the division is between those who point to the catastrophic result of the Tartar rule, those who felt it was beneficial and scholars who feel that the importance of the occupation is exaggerated. In the view of the so–called Eurasian school, the Tartars contributed to the transformation of a number of small and disjointed states into a strong, centralized and autocratic unit, launching it on the way toward becoming a powerful, modern state. Some specific developments, such as the legal system, military organization, taxation and tax collection are listed (sometimes incorrectly) as positive results. Some scholars argue that the contemporary Russian style of behavior and other psychological attitudes are to be attributed to evil Mongol influence. They stress the bad aspects, such as the fearful destruction of cities and the wholesale murder of populations as well as forced migrations of people from the fertile

N.C.B.

1. Goddess
2. God of the Under-World
3. Hammer of a God
4. Sky God
5. Male God

Christian Orthodox (Byzantine) cross and pagan symbols

8

19th century drawing of a Mongol general

plains to the dense woodlands of the northeast. Of greatest importance, according to this group, is the disruption of contact between the Russian people and important centers of culture such as Byzantium and the developing European states to the west. One of the results of this isolation was the lack of beneficial influences provided by the European Renaissance and the Reformation.

The necessity of resisting the greedy Tartars affected the style of government life in Russia, encouraging cheating, evasion, corruption and violence. A lasting element of the modern Russian outlook is the sense of being threatened and exploited; some scholars charge that this attitude was founded in the harsh period of Tartar rule.

Regardless of what judgment is placed on the effect of Tartar rule, there is agreement on one incidental result: the growth and rise to power of a new center of leadership in the Russian lands: the state of Moscow. The emergence of this area as a leader compensated for the destruction of Kiev and the breaking away of other states which remained detached from Russia for centuries.

To understand the contribution of the Tartars to the growth of Moscow, it is necessary to know of the way the Mongols exercised their power over the conquered Russian lands. With few exceptions, the Tartars usually left the native princes on their thrones and converted them into collectors of tribute and taxes and also used them as law enforcement officials of their territories. First as pagans

and later as Moslems, the Tartars also left the Orthodox Church alone, and in fact increased its authority and power. Working for the Tartars was one of the many factors that helped to transform the insignificant village of Moscow, first mentioned in the year 1147, into the center of a future empire.

The Rise of Moscow

Moscow profited from its location close to frequently traveled river routes. Called *Moskva* in Russian, the city is located on a river of the same name that flows to the Oka River, the most important western tributary of the mighty Volga. The rise of the small principality of Moscow was helped by the traditional battles to determine the successor to the throne, as well as by the expansion through purchase and conquest, service agreements with lesser princes and, finally, clever dealings with the Tartar leaders that appeared to be part of a pattern of obedient behavior. Occasional military help was provided to the Tartars in their battles to suppress rebellious princes and populations.

According to one prominent historian, Moscow was the more or less deliberate choice for a grand–ducal position because of support from the large landowners, called *boyars* in Russian, and from the Church. The boyars suffered from the constant damage resulting from feuds among the lesser princes—they were looking for a suitable state that could enforce its authority and thus bring greater law and order to Russia. The Orthodox Church had transferred the

seat of the head of the Russian Church, known as the Metropolitan, from devastated Kiev. During the reign of the Grand Prince Ivan Kalita (whose name literally means "John Moneybags") the Metropolitan Theognostus settled in Moscow, making it the new spiritual capital of "all Russia."

The Prince of Moscow thus acquired the status of a national leader and was looked upon to protect the Russian lands against the Mongols.

As the power of the *Golden Horde* began to wane, the leading position of Moscow became more of less uncontested. The amount of territorial gain was tremendous—from the time of Ivan Kalita to the second half of the 15th century, the area of Moscow control expanded from about 600 to 15,000 square miles. In still further expansion, the ruler Ivan III ("The Great") added another 40,000 square miles by a combination of purchases, inheritance and conquest.

Ivan "The Great"

Ivan's most important military effort resulted in the capture of the powerful city of Novgorod, referred to in its own official title as "Lord Novgorod the Great." This was the most significant trading place in western Russia. It possessed a unique form of government. Although a prince was the head of state, he was required to keep his throne outside the city walls; the internal affairs of the city were managed by the *Veche*, a representative city council which could be summoned into session when any

An Italian map (1560) of the Principality of Moscow

Ivan IV—the boy and the man

Nell Cooke Byers

citizen rang the town bell. This early experiment in democracy came to an end when Novgorod was absorbed by autocratic Moscow.

Ivan III further achieved prestige in 1472 when he married Zoë, niece of the last of the Byzantine emperors who was killed when the Turks conquered Constantinople in 1453. The Moscow prince adopted the term *Tsar*, a Slavic contraction of the word *Caesar*, to refer to himself. Ivan started to behave like a direct heir to the Byzantine throne, adding also the titles *Autokrat* (Greek for "absolute ruler") and *Gosudar* ("sovereign") to *Tsar*. About this time, a scholarly Russian monk developed in his writings the concept of a "Third Rome," which identified Moscow as the true capital of Christendom, in a line of succession through Rome and the recently fallen Constantinople. In later centuries, this doctrine was interpreted as a call for imperial expansion, although it had only a religious significance when first expounded.

Ivan "The Terrible"

The "ingathering of lands" was continued by Ivan's successors. His grandson, Ivan IV (1533–1584) came to be known as "The Terrible." Actually the English word "terrible" is not an entirely accurate translation of the Russian word *grozny*, which is better described by the term "awe–inspiring." There is much to justify Ivan's nickname—he was a ruler impressive enough to inspire awe and he was undoubtedly cruel and unpredictable enough to be called "terrible."

Well–educated by comparison with other princes of his time, this shrewd man with a deep interest in theology was given to uncontrolled outbreaks of violence and cruelty. His pattern alternated between exaggerated acts of pious behavior and periods of unrestrained viciousness.

Ivan was a child of three in 1533 when his father died and he became the titular ruler of Russia. When his mother, Elena Glinskaya, died mysteriously five years later, Ivan found himself at the mercy of two competing *boyar* families: the Belskys and the Shuiskys. In their struggle for power, the two families paid public homage to Ivan, but ignored him in private. They exploited the state and pillaged the treasury. Ivan put an end to the situation in 1543 when, as a 13–year–old boy, he turned to his guards and ordered them to take Prince Andrew Shuisky away and kill him. A 13–year–old boy can't rule a state, but from that day onward, no one dared to oppose his will.

Ivan was crowned "Tsar of All the Russias" in 1547, the first ruler to assume the title at the time of his coronation. In this same year, he married Anastasia Romanova, daughter of a minor *boyar*

family. Ivan proved to be an energetic Tsar and the next years were full of his reforms and military conquests. The changes were intended to reduce the traditional powers of the *boyars*, but they also included a new code of laws, the *Sudebnik*, which was issued in 1550, and an attempt to reform the Church through the calling of a church council in 1551.

Ivan was also responsible for creation of Russia's first parliament, the *Zemskii Sobor* ("Assembly of the Land"), which he convened in 1550 and again in 1566.

Ivan also defeated and annexed the Khanate of Kazan in 1552, thus giving him control over the middle Volga. Four years later, he attacked and defeated the Khanate of Astrakhan, adding those domains to his realm. This gave him control of the entire course of the Volga River and access to the Caspian Sea. To celebrate his victory over the Tatars (Tartars), Ivan ordered the construction of St. Basil's Cathedral in what is now Red Square in Moscow.

Problems began in 1558 when he decided to launch an invasion of Livonia—modern Estonia and Latvia—in an attempt to gain access to the Baltic Sea. When Livonia disintegrated, Poland–Lithuania and Sweden moved in to pick up the pieces and Ivan found himself at war with both of these nations plus Denmark. The war dragged on until 1582 and left Russia all but depleted.

The war also was at least partly responsible for Ivan's creation of the *Oprichnina*, a separate administration which was intended to finally destroy the traditionally separate power of the *boyars*. During the Livonian war, some of the *boyars* engaged in open treason and joined the side of Poland–Lithuania. One of the most distinguished of the *boyars* was Prince Andrei Kurbsky, one of Ivan's army commanders. He defected to the enemy side in 1564 after having been defeated by Lithuanian forces. The event is remembered through a fascinating exchange of correspondence between the Tsar and the prince; the Tsar called the prince a traitor, while Kurbsky maintained that he "chose freedom."

Ivan became determined to deal with all "traitors" and he threatened to abdicate as Tsar unless he was given a free hand to deal with his enemies, both real and imagined, as he wished. His terms were spelled out in two letters he had delivered to the Metropolitan of Moscow. What Ivan proposed was to set up half of the realm as a personal domain, free from normal governmental administration and supervision by the "Chosen Council." In effect, half of Russia was to become Ivan's private property, and he would be free to take the lands of all the *boyars* located within the *Oprichnina*—"area set apart."

To enforce his will, he set up an

oprichnik army of 6,000 men. Black–robed and riding black horses, each *oprichnik* had a dog's head fixed to his saddle and carried a broom, all to symbolize the Tsar's determination to hound traitors and to sweep corruption from the land.

As Ivan obviously intended, the *oprichniki* struck terror throughout the land and the operation was successful from his viewpoint. The ability of the *boyars* to oppose the Tsar was destroyed completely. The purges lasted seven years and, its purpose accomplished, Ivan dissolved the *Oprichnina* in 1572, after executing some of the chief executioners.

The Time of Troubles

Two years before his death in 1584, Ivan quarreled with his eldest son and namesake and, in a fit of passion, struck and killed him. He was succeeded, therefore, by his second son, Fedor, who was mentally retarded. Under Fedor, actual power was exercised by a regency council headed by Boris Godunov. Fedor had no children, so the Rurikovichi dynasty came to an end when he died in 1598.

This left the throne vacant and meant that the Russian people had to choose a new tsar. There were a number of candidates but three men eventually emerged as serious contenders—Boris Godunov, Fedor Romanov and Basil Shuisky. Each had some connection to the previous ruling family. Boris Godunov was married to the sister of Fedor, Fedor Romanov was the son of Nikita Romanov, brother of Anastasia, Ivan IV's first wife; and Basil Shuisky was descended from the elder branch of the Rurikovichi line.

To give legitimacy to the choice, the Patriarch proposed calling a *Zemskii Sobor* and allowing this popular assembly to select the new tsar. It chose Boris Godunov, who took the throne as Boris I (1598–1605).

Boris's reign started out well but, when a combination of early frosts and droughts produced widespread crop failures, the superstitious Russian people began to believe that they had made a mistake in choosing Boris, and opposition mounted to his rule. He managed to hold on to power during his lifetime but things began to fall apart when he died suddenly in April 1605. Within a month, his son, who had succeeded him, was overthrown by the first would–be Dmitri, an impostor who claimed to be the youngest son of Ivan IV.

This marked the beginning of a period of great turmoil in Russian history known as the "Time of Troubles." Dmitri (1605–1606) survived for approximately a year before he was murdered by Basil Shuisky, who then ascended the throne as Basil I (1606–1610). Basil, who represented the interests of the old *Boyar* class, was unable to consolidate his control and was overthrown in 1610. Russia was once again without a tsar. In addition, a Polish army occupied Moscow while a Swedish army occupied parts of northern Russia. A number of Russian nobles proposed to offer the throne to Wladyslaw, the 15–year old son of Sigismund, the Polish king. Sigismund rejected the offer and claimed the throne himself.

This posed a basic threat to a major power: the Russian Orthodox Church. Sigismund was a Roman Catholic and probably would have tried to force a union of the Church with the Roman Church. The Patriarch of Moscow, Hermogen, called urgently for the Russian people to drive out the Poles. A national revival to save "Mother Russia" began, led by Kuzma Minin, a wealthy commoner from Nizhni Novgorod. Minin assembled an army representing all classes of Russian society from *boyar* to serf and the Polish army was driven out of Moscow. A *Zemskii Sober* was summoned and proceeded to choose Michael Romanov as the new tsar.

From Act I of Musorgski's opera Boris Godunov.

Michael

Alexis

Fedor

The First Romanovs

Michael Romanov (1613–1645) was a boy of sixteen when he was elevated to the throne of Russia. The *Zemskii Sobor* wanted Michael's father, Fedor Romanov, as tsar, but that proved impossible for two reasons. The first was that Boris Godunov, after his own election as tsar, had forced Fedor to become a monk. He did this in order to remove a potential rival to the throne since Fedor, as a monk, would be ineligible for the throne. The second reason was that Fedor, now the Metropolitan Filaret, was in prison in Poland.

He had gone to Poland in 1610 as a member of the Russian delegation sent to negotiate with the Polish king with regard to his son Wladyslaw's accession to the Russian throne. When Sigismund decided to claim the throne for himself, he threw the entire Russian delegation into prison. When Filaret was finally permitted to return to Moscow in 1619, he was named Patriarch of the Russian Church and made co–ruler with Michael. He effectively ruled Russia until his death in 1633. Thus Michael remained in the shadow of his father most of his life.

Michael was succeeded by his son, Alexis (1645–1676) who also was sixteen when his father died. Like his father, he was a gentle person easily dominated by those about him. Dominated in his youth by his tutor Morozov, he later fell under the influence of the Patriarch Nikon and, still later, by his last favorite, Artamon Matveev. Most of the accomplishments of his reign are more the product of these men than of Alexis.

Fedor III was the third Romanov Tsar (1676–1682), son of Alexis who came to

the throne as a boy of fourteen. An invalid, Fedor left most of the decision–making of the state to his advisors; he died after six years on the throne.

The first Romanovs were thus not very impressive, either as individuals or as rulers. Cautious and conservative, always looking to the past rather than the present or future, manipulated by those around them, their greatest contribution was that they survived. Yet this was a significant period since a number of things occurred during the reigns of these three tsars that would have an important bearing on subsequent Russian history.

The first thing is that the Russian state had to recover from the effect of the Time of Troubles and the Livonian War. The situation in 1613 was less than positive. The economy was in a shambles with large parts of the countryside going untilled and whole villages abandoned. Rebellious peasants and gangs of soldiers from the various disbanded armies roamed the countryside, robbing civilians and looting property. Novgorod was under Swedish occupation and Russia was still at war with Poland. Prince Wladyslaw of Poland continued to press his claim to the Russian throne.

Sweden agreed to return Novgorod in 1617 but, in that same year, Prince Wladyslaw invaded Russia at the head of a Polish army and laid siege to Moscow. The invasion actually helped Michael to establish his authority since he became identified with defense of the Russian homeland against the foreign invader. Wladyslaw's forces were driven out and a truce was signed between the two sides in 1618.

To further bolster his authority,

Michael kept the *Zemskii Sobor* in more or less continuous session in Moscow and all important decrees were issued under the joint authority of the Tsar and that body. This might have led to the creation of a permanent representative institution in Russia, but as he became more firmly established, Michael made less use of the *Zemskii Sobor*. A policy emerged whereby sessions were called only to discuss unusually important issues, such as whether Russia should go to war against Poland in the 1630's. A new *Zemskii Sobor* was also called to confirm Alexis' succession to the throne in 1645.

Alexis called two further sessions—in 1649 to issue a new law code and in 1651–1653 to address the question of war with Poland. It did not meet thereafter. The *Zemskii Sobor* was thus used to create and reinforce the authority of the Tsar at a time when that authority was not firmly established. When this purpose was fulfilled, it was allowed to evaporate.

Another major development had to do with the revolt of the Ukraine against Polish rule and its acquisition by Russia. The area of the Ukraine had originally become part of the Principality of Lithuania in the 14th century. Subsequently, a dynastic marriage brought Poland and Lithuania together under a single monarch and in 1569 they merged into a single state.

Poland was Roman Catholic and the Ukrainians were Russian Orthodox. Efforts to catholicize the Ukrainians were intermittent until 1589, when the Metropolitan of Moscow was raised to the rank of Patriarch and given authority over all Russian Orthodox believers. Poland refused to recognize the authority of the

Patriarch within any of its territories and attempted to force all its Orthodox subjects to join a new "Uniate" church that recognized the authority of Rome.

In addition, economic pressure was applied as the estates of upper class Orthodox were seized and redistributed to Polish nobles while attempts were made to turn the mass of Ukrainian peasants into serfs.

Bogdan Khmelnitsky, who had himself lost lands to a Polish nobleman, was elected *Hetman* (chief) of the Zaporozhian Cossacks, a group of adventurous independent soldiers and mercenaries. He became the leader for Ukrainian autonomy. Khmelnitsky was successful initially, but a defeat at the hands of Polish forces convinced him that the Ukrainians could not hope to maintain their independence for long. Believing that a victory by Poland would mean the end of the Orthodox Church and the enslavement of the people, Khmelnitsky offered to bring the Ukraine under Russian rule.

Tsar Alexis and his advisers discussed the matter for two years before accepting the offer because they recognized that if they did so, it would mean war with Poland. The *Zemskii Sobor* finally in 1653 decided to incorporate the Ukraine into Russia and declare war on Poland. The war lasted until 1667, ending with the Truce of Androsovo under the terms of which Russia obtained all of the Ukraine east of the Dnieper and was permitted to occupy the city of Kiev for two years. Russia never gave back Kiev, however, and in 1686 the terms of the truce were made permanent by a treaty of peace.

Another important territorial addition that occurred in the 17th century was the extension of Russian control over Siberia. The penetration of Western Siberia first occurred in the 16th century during the reign of Ivan IV when the famous merchant family of the Stroganovs became interested in Siberian furs. It was this family that hired Yermak, an *ataman* of the Volga Cossacks, to explore east of the Ural Mountains. He led an expedition to the Irtysh River, defeated the Siberian ruler and claimed Siberia west of the Ob and Irtysh rivers for Russia.

Territorial acquisition was resumed in the 17th century. The Stroganovs continued to be involved, but now they were joined by other enterprising types; these merchant traders and explorers advanced from the Ob to the Yenisei, then from the Yenisei to the Lena. As they advanced, they left fortified trading posts behind them. By the middle of the century, they had reached the Amur River and had come into contact with the Chinese. The Chinese attempted to starve out the Russians by withdrawing the entire population from the Amur River valley. The matter was resolved in 1689 by the Treaty of Nerchinsk whereby Russia gave up all

claims to the area of the Amur River Valley, but was conceded the rest of Siberia north of the Amur. Thus, by the end of the 17th century, Russian territory in the east extended to the sea.

The last development associated with the first Romanovs had to do with a church reform carried out by the Patriarch Nikon. Russian church books contained many errors that had crept in over the centuries as a result of mistakes of copyists. Nikon was determined to correct them according to the Greek originals. The changes were not very significant—correcting the spelling of the name Jesus, making the sign of the cross with three fingers instead of two, three Hallelujahs instead of two at a certain time during the worship service—but the old ways had been entrenched by tradition. Nikon found himself opposed by a significant element among the clergy who resisted the changes. Avvakum, the chief spokesman for the "Old Believers,"

called Nikon "a mocker of God and a heretic." Nikon retaliated by banishing the supporters of the old order.

A church council eventually approved Nikon's changes and Avvakum was sentenced to be burned at the stake. That, however, only resulted in a division in the church as the Old Believers continued to oppose the reforms. Since Tsar Alexis supported the measures, he became the "Anti–Christ" as far as the Old Believers were concerned, a term they applied to subsequent tsars as well. The government outlawed them as heretics but there were too many of them for this to be effective. Overall, the effect of the schism was to weaken the power of the church and to make it more dependent on the government for support. That soon became an important consideration, for it is unlikely that Peter the Great could have carried out many of his reforms against the united opposition of the church.

Nikon, Patriarch of Moscow

Peter I

Peter "The Great"

This man (1682–1725) is usually conceded to have been the greatest of Russia's rulers and to have had a greater impact on the Russian land and people than any of his predecessors or successors. Yet, his was a disputed succession to the throne and for seven years after he became co–tsar in 1682, there was a serious question whether he would be permitted to rule in his own right.

The problem was that his father, Alexis, had married twice and Peter was born of the second marriage. Alexis' first wife, Maria Miloslavska, had given him two sons, Fedor and Ivan, as well as several daughters, including the ambitious and strong–willed Sophia. When Fedor came to the throne in 1676, he chose his advisors from among the Miloslavsky family and shunted the relatives of his step–mother, Natalia Narishkina, aside. When Fedor died in 1682, the next in line for the throne was Ivan, Fedor's younger brother. Ivan, however, was mentally retarded, subject to fits and nearly blind.

The Narishkin clan proposed that the ten–year–old Peter become the next tsar. Sophia, recognizing that this would mean her total exclusion from power, appealed to the *streltsy*, the hereditary tsarist guard, to intervene on behalf of the weak Ivan, suggesting that his life was in danger. She promised pay increases to the *streltsy* to encourage their support. They invaded the Kremlin, killed a number of Peter's relatives and demanded a reordering of the succession to the throne. As a result, Peter and Ivan were named "co–tsars" and Sophia became regent and the real ruler of Russia. Peter and his mother were permitted to take up residence in a palace in the village of Preobrazhenskoe outside Moscow, and it was here that he spent the next seven years.

Moscow's "foreign quarter" was located in a suburb near Preobrazhenskoe, and Peter, bored with life in the village, soon made the acquaintanceship of a number of foreigners who had come to Russia to take service with the Russian government. These included a Swiss, Franz Lefort, a Scot, Patrick Gordon and a Dutchman, Franz Timmerman.

Another of Peter's diversions was to organize the young nobles assigned to him as playmates into opposing "toy regiments" and to have mock battles. He also discovered that a note dispatched to the Royal armory would bring him any piece of military equipment he asked for. So, he combined his two diversions, using Lefort, Gordon and Timmerman, who were all military men, as advisors.

Gradually Peter learned military engineering, artillery and even geometry as part of these war games, and the "toy regiments" became more and more proficient. Eventually the two regiments were given the names of Preobrazhensky and Semenovsky and became the nucleus of a new army that Peter later created.

When Peter was fourteen, he found an old English sailboat that was in storage. He had it brought out and launched on a nearby lake. Soon he found a Dutch shipmaster to instruct him, and he began building other boats, working alongside Dutch carpenters from the foreign quarter. Peter also liked to sit in the foreign quarter drinking with his friends, so it is not surprising that his first mistress was the daughter of the Dutch innkeeper Mons.

Peter's mother disapproved of Peter's choice of pastimes and decided that he needed a wife to settle him down. He was therefore married at the age of sixteen to Eudoxia Lopukhina, a rather pious and uninteresting young woman. Peter was distracted long enough for her to become pregnant, but within a few weeks returned to his military games and his boats. Some years later, Peter banished Eudoxia to a convent. His son, Alexis, was partly raised in that convent, and he grew up hating his father and all he stood for.

When Peter was seventeen in 1689, Sophia decided that she should become ruler of Russia in her own right and began making plans to dethrone both Ivan and Peter. Peter, learning of the plot, fled to the Trinity Monastery and called his "toy regiments" to his side. Sophia's support began melting away and she was forced to surrender power. Peter banished her to a nunnery.

Never particularly interested in the more ordinary aspects of governing, he turned the day–to–day control of Russia to his wife's relatives and returned to his military training. He participated in his first military campaign in 1695–1696 which resulted in the capture of a Turkish fortress at Azov, at the mouth of the Don River. It was to seek allies for a general war against Turkey that Peter next organized a "Grand Embassy" to travel to western Europe. Peter accompanied the embassy in the guise of an apprentice shipbuilder, Peter Mikhailov. He went to Brandenburg–Prussia, Holland, England and Vienna, capital of the Holy Roman Empire. He spent six months in Holland working as an ordinary shipbuilder. Although he learned a great deal, he found no potential ally for a war against Turkey. Charles XI of Sweden had recently died, however, and several countries—Poland, Brandenburg–Prussia and Denmark— were eager to go to war to despoil Sweden of territories won during the 17th century in the Baltic Sea area. This offered Peter an even better chance to gain a seaport, so he agreed to go to war against Sweden as soon as he could bring the war against Turkey to an end.

Peter was in Vienna when he learned of another revolt by the *streltsy*. Although the revolt had been quashed by the time he got back to Moscow, Peter took terrible revenge upon the mutineers. The leaders were beheaded and hundreds of others were tortured or killed and their bodies left to lie out on display as an object lesson for others. Sixteen *streltsy* regiments were ultimately disbanded; Peter had managed to destroy the political power of the *streltsy* but he also had left himself without an army.

Peter is remembered as the "Great Westernizer" and it is true that he introduced many things into Russia from the west, particularly dealing with culture and manners. Peter was not an uncritical admirer of the west, however, and his primary motivation for introducing western styles was to make Russians more acceptable to Europeans. Thus beards, which were out of style in the west, were forbidden at court and Peter personally took a pair of shears and cut the hair of his chief courtiers. Nobles who chose to keep a beard were required to pay a tax of 100 rubles and to wear a badge indicating that they had paid it. Peasants were permitted to keep their beards, but had to pay a fine of 1 kopeck each time they entered Moscow. Western–style clothing became mandatory for members of the upper classes. Women, previously kept in isolation, were now invited to public entertainments and dinners, and court balls were organized where men and women danced in the western manner.

Peter kept changing Russian ways of doing things all the rest of his life, but most of the other changes which he introduced might more properly be characterized as modernizations. He simplified the Russian alphabet, eliminating what he considered useless letters, and ordered that the new characters be used in all lay books. Church books continued to use the old style, which came to be known as Old Slavonic.

He also set up the first newspaper in Russia in 1703, established all sorts of technical institutes, laid the foundations for the Universities of Moscow and St. Petersburg, created the Russian Academy of Sciences, sponsored expeditions to explore the Kamchatka Peninsula, the Kuril Islands and the Bering Strait, carried out extensive administrative reforms, reorganized the government of the Orthodox Church, established an iron industry, a

munitions industry, textile factories, and in general encouraged the development of trade.

Peter also built a modern army and navy and he fought a long, 21–year war with Sweden for control of the southern shores of the Baltic Sea. The war was ultimately successful, and Russia became established as one of the "great powers" of Europe as a result, but it was extremely costly. Taxes had to be increased on the peasantry and other commoner classes, while a lifetime service obligation beginning at age 15 was instituted for the nobility. Peasants were also drafted into the military for the first time. Although military service became a lifetime obligation for them, it did have the advantage that they ceased to be serfs upon taking the military oath.

After Peter's death, the term of military service for both nobility and commoners was reduced to 25 years. His proudest achievement was the city he built at the mouth of the Neva River on land newly liberated from the Swedes. St. Petersburg, whose foundations were laid in 1703, was to be his capital, his chief seaport on the Baltic and his "window to the west." It was here—and at Tsarskoe Selo ("the Tsar's village"), twelve miles away—that he began the magnificent palaces which were to signify Russia's new great power status. His new capital was partly responsible for his death, however, for St. Petersburg was built on a swamp and was subject to periodic flooding. Peter died in early 1725 as the result of a chill he caught while helping to rescue victims of such a flood.

An Era of Palace Revolutions

One of Peter's greater disappointments was his son, Alexis, who in the normal course of events would have succeeded him. Alexis opposed everything that Peter stood for, however, and he made no secret of the fact that he planned to undo all of Peter's reforms if he came to power. He embarrassed his father further in 1716 by fleeing abroad and requesting sanctuary from the Holy Roman Emperor. Two years later, he returned home at his father's urging, where Peter forced him to renounce his claim to the throne, then had him put on trial for treason. He was found guilty and sentenced to death, but it was later announced that he had died while under interrogation.

Peter issued a decree abolishing succession of the oldest son or child of the tsar, which stated that the tsar would name his successor. He never got around to designating his own, however, and his sudden death left the succession unsettled. It was resolved by Prince Alexander Menshikov, one of Peter's close associates, who called upon the Guards regiments to support Catherine, Peter's second wife, as his successor. The Guards regiments, descendants of Peter's original "toy regiments," thus set a tradition of intervention which would continue throughout the 18th century. It was not until 1796 when the Emperor Paul came to the throne that Peter's succession decree was finally repealed and primogeniture was reinstituted as the method of succession.

The weird succession to the throne of Russia following the death of Peter the

The Winter Palace of the Tsars in St. Petersburg

Great at the age of 53 is best understood with the help of a diagram. The rulers between Peter the Great and Catherine the Great were as follows:

CATHERINE I, a peasant woman, Peter's second wife (two years)

PETER II, son of the dead Prince Alexis (three years)

ANNE, Duchess of Courland, half-niece of Peter I (ten years)

IVAN VI, half great-great nephew of Peter I (one year)

ELIZABETH, younger daughter of Peter I by his second wife (twenty-one years)

PETER III, son of Elizabeth's older sister Anna and the Duke of Holstein, grandson of Peter I. (Less than one year; deposed)

This peculiar succession reflects the sequence of intrigues, plots and *coups* by a series of advisers, court favorites and lovers. The amazing thing is that during this period Russia's international position did not decline because other powers failed to take advantage of the internal upheaval.

Of these rulers, only one, Elizabeth, made any important contribution to Russian development. She consciously took up Peter's reforms where they had been left hanging in 1725 and carried them forward. It was Elizabeth who completed the Winter Palace in St. Petersburg, who hired the famous Italian architect, Rastrelli, to rebuild the Peterhof at Tsarskoe Selo and who established Moscow University. She also emulated Peter's foreign policy by signing alliances with Paris and Vienna and by intervening in the Seven Years War against Frederick the Great of Prussia. She partially neutralized that accomplishment, however, when she named Peter III as her successor to the throne.

When he succeeded her at the beginning of 1762 he immediately set out to undo nearly everything she had accomplished. Although a grandson of Peter the Great, Peter III was completely German by upbringing and was Lutheran in religion. He was not at all happy about becoming Tsar of Russia, a position for which he was totally unfit, both physically and mentally. His marriage to the daughter of a minor German princely family, Sophie of Anhalt–Zerbst, had been arranged by his aunt, the Empress Elizabeth. It had been Peter the Great who had begun the practice of "arranged marriages" for political purposes (a pattern followed by German and other western European dynastic alliances) and she continued the policy. But the 1745 marriage remained "in name only" for nine years because the young Grand Duke had a physical disability which made it impossible for him to consummate the relationship. Peter eventually had an operation to cure his disability, but Catherine, as the young Grand Duchess, was known after her conversion to Russian Orthodoxy, had already been urged by Empress Elizabeth to take a lover in order to assure an heir to the throne. In her memoirs, Catherine identified the young lover, Sergei Saltykov, as the father of her son, Paul. Whether true or not, Peter III evidently believed it because, when he became Tsar in 1762, he decided to disinherit Paul and send Catherine to a convent. This led to his overthrow and to his death in a *coup d'etat* which installed Catherine as Empress of Russia.

ROMANOV DYNASTY

Catherine "The Great"

Catherine had no personal claim to the Russian throne, but she did win the support of the Guards regiments—partly because her latest lover, Gregory Orlov, was an officer of the Guards. For thirty-four years the growing Russian Empire was governed by a woman of great talent and even greater determination to excel in everything and to control all things. She was hard–working and devoted to matters of state. She saw herself as both a figure of the Enlightenment and as Peter the Great's successor. She had a lively correspondence with Voltaire and Frederick the Great of Prussia and at one point she invited Diderot, the French Encyclopedist, to St. Petersburg and set aside an hour each evening for conversation with him.

When she first came to the throne, she had great hopes for further reforms and she did a great deal to encourage culture and learning. At one point, she spent two years drafting instructions for a Legislative Conference which she called to draw up a new code of law. The instructions, heavily based on the writings of Montesquieu and other Enlightenment thinkers, were considered so radical that they were banned in France. The instructions were apparently also too radical for members of the Legislative Conference; they were unable to draft a new code based on them.

When Catherine first came to the throne, she expressed her dislike for serfdom. But she ultimately found that she could do nothing about it, for serfdom formed the economic basis of the nobility, the class that staffed the army and civil administration. In her role as an enlightened despot, therefore, Catherine didn't accomplish very much. On the other hand, she proved to be a good publicist whose writings and correspondence created a good impression of Russia in the West.

Something more should perhaps be said about her lovers. It is a matter of record that she had, over a period of many years, at least 21 lovers. In this regard, Catherine was not greatly different from other 18th century monarchs. The Empress Elizabeth, at whose court she grew up, had a succession of lovers who were given the official title of "Gentleman of the Bedchamber." Louis XIV of France was famous for his succession of official mistresses, known as "Ladies of the Bedchamber." The practice was so well accepted that one Prussian monarch had an officially appointed Lady of the Bedchamber even though he personally preferred men.

Catherine had more lovers than most, but only four had any significance insofar as Russian history is concerned. Two of these, the presumed father of Paul and the officer who helped her come to

Catherine II

power, have already been mentioned. A third was Stanislaw Poniatowski, a handsome Polish nobleman whom she later made King of Poland. The fourth was Gregory Potemkin (Poh–*tyom*–kin), who was responsible for a number of Russia's military victories during her reign, including the conquest and annexation of the Crimea. Potemkin became her lover and chief adviser—and there may even have been a private marriage ceremony. But when the two functions conflicted, he chose to remain her chief adviser—and over the next several years personally selected the young Guardsmen who became Catherine's "Gentleman of the Bedchamber."

Catherine deserves to be called "the Great" primarily because of her successful wars and because of Russia's extensive territorial expansion during her reign. Perhaps the most important of her territorial expansions is associated with her participation with Prussia and Austria in the partitions of Poland that resulted in an end of the Polish–Lithuanian state.

The liquidation of Poland brought into the Russian empire all the lands which had been claimed as "Russian" during earlier history. This was not the only success of Catherine—under her leadership the first major victory was scored against the Ottoman Turkish empire to the south, hastening the decline of a once–powerful foe. Russia obtained access to a considerable portion of the Black Sea in 1774 and secured the right of passage through the Turkish Straits into the Mediterranean. It was also recognized as the official protector of Orthodox Christians living under Turkish rule. Further expansion led to the acquisition in 1792 of a little–known fortress called Ochakov and the right to control the Crimean Peninsula. These events caused the first alarm in England over the possibility of Russian expansion into areas of interest to the British.

During the struggle between England and the American colonies, Russia played an important role in the League of Armed Neutrality. This was a group of nations that insisted on the right of passage of neutral ships across the Atlantic Ocean and other bodies of water in spite of

British objections. Catherine followed with interest the developments in Western Europe and broke off relations with France after revolutionaries executed King Louis XVI. She apparently intended that Russia would be part of an armed intervention in France. She also entertained a greater scheme for the creation of a Christian empire out of Greece and other Turkish possessions, but nothing came of this.

The French Revolution and Russia

For a century prior to the French Revolution, Russia had been governed by a series of rulers committed to the concept of a "revolution from above." In the process, the nobility and urban classes had been transformed, but the peasantry—90% of the people— remained the same. It was this obstacle that Catherine was unable to overcome and when the French Revolution popularized the ideas of "liberty, equality and fraternity" and announced the end of serfdom and legal distinctions based on class, this made the ideas of the French Revolution subversive within the Russian part of Europe.

An even greater difficulty was that Russian rulers from Catherine onward, educated in the Enlightenment traditions, agreed with many of the ideals of the French Revolution, but could not see how to achieve them in Russia without completely disrupting the very fabric of Russian society. All agreed, for example, that serfdom was a clearly seen evil and ought to be abolished, but none before Alexander II could bring himself to do so. As a result, the distance between convictions and actions widened, and the actions of Russian rulers became more and more conservative as the 19th century progressed. Half–hearted and partial reforms were still proposed and sometimes implemented, but they were never sufficient to transform the basic organization of the Russian society; the ideals of the French Revolution continued to be regarded as suspect and unworthy in Russia.

Further change was afoot in Western Europe—the Industrial Revolution—transforming social and economic relationships. As England, France and Germany industrialized, Russia, with a social and economic system incompatible with capitalism, fell further behind. In spite of all of its efforts, therefore, Russia's system of government and its role as a great power were both in decline throughout most of the 19th century, even as its rulers attempted to catch up. Russia remained "on hold."

Romanov Monarchs After Catherine

We continue to refer to monarchs after Catherine the Great as Romanovs even though she was a German, and if her memoirs are correct, they are all descendants of Catherine and Sergei Saltykov. Before the Romanov dynasty ended its historical role, a sprawling and multi–national Russia was ruled by six tsars— Catherine's son, Paul, his two sons, Alexander I and Nicholas I, Nicholas I's son, grandson and great– grandson—Alexander II, Alexander III and Nicholas II.

Paul, who succeeded his mother in 1796, had been alienated from her because he believed that she had usurped his rightful throne. He therefore spent the first part of his reign attempting to undo his mother's accomplishments. Possessing a military mentality and a foul temper, his was an unstable reign that ended after five years in a *coup d'etat* made on behalf of his son, who gave his advance approval. Paul was murdered during the *coup*, a fact that was said to prey on Alexander's conscience and may explain some of his otherwise unexplainable actions. As one historian has pointed out, this was the last "indoor" assassination—the Tsar was killed in his bedroom by an "inside" group of conspirators and officers of the Guards regiments. In the next century, "assassinations were to take place in the open street." With this last palace revolution, Russia drifted into the 19th century, loaded down with traditions of the past, with autocratic rule, a privileged upper class and with serfdom weighing as heavily as ever on the shoulders of the Russian people.

The first Alexander has presented a puzzle to both historians and psychologists. At first, he was inclined toward liberal ideas and was determined to continue efforts to westernize Russia. He ended up in a fanatically conservative and mystical stupor, dying in southern Russia apparently during an attempt to run away from it all. Typical for Russia, there was a legend that he didn't really die, but chose the life of a saintly hermit to ask forgiveness for his sins. His knowledge of the plot to kill his father may have been the sin that really bothered him.

At the beginning of his rule, Alexander asked the outstanding statesman, Michael Speransky, to plan basic reforms, including a constitution, a modern code of laws and an educational system. He even gave half–hearted consideration to abolishing serfdom, but the only result of this was a law of 1803 that permitted the voluntary emancipation of serfs by landlords. Needless to say, few were inclined to make use of this opportunity. On Alexander's orders, Speransky drew up a constitution which would have created a national legislature and guaranteed various civil rights. Most of the nobility opposed the plan, however, and Alexander, needing the nobility's support in his confrontation with France, was forced to dismiss Speransky. Alexander did carry out an administrative reorgani-zation, turning the Colleges he had inherited from Peter the Great into Ministries and organizing them into something analogous to a cabinet, called the Committee of Ministers. In addition, he created an appointed legislature called the Council of State, to draw up legislation for the Tsar's approval and increased the authority of the Senate. None of these changes or new institutions actually restricted the Tsar's authority, but they did regularize procedures and increase the size of the circle of advisers.

The War of 1812

The most famous achievement of Russia in this period was the spectacular defeat of Napoleon I of France when he tried to invade the endless land mass of Russia.

Russia had joined in the so–called Third Coalition to fight against Napoleon in 1805. It and its allies, Prussia and Austria, were beaten and had to submit to rather harsh conditions of the Treaty of Tilsit. A period of relative peace and cooperation with Napoleon, then the master of the European continent, followed. Russia profited from it by securing areas remote from Napoleon's control at the expense of Persia and Turkey. Georgia was annexed in the south; to the southwest, Bessarabia was added, giving rise to a greater Russian influence on the neighboring Balkan area of Eastern Europe. At the same time, Russia also seized Finland from Sweden, converting it into a Grand Duchy with the Tsar as ruler. It was also during this period that forts were established in "Russian America"—first in Alaska and then close to what is now San Francisco.

Mutual jealousy between France and Russia emerged in 1811–1812. Napoleon, swayed by his past successes, decided to invade Russia and did so on June 21, 1812, with an army of almost one–half million; the French constituted only about half of this force. A great number of Poles joined the effort, expecting Napoleon to liberate and restore to them all or most of the territory of the defunct Polish–Lithuanian commonwealth.

As in the past, the peasant masses, in spite of their grievances, rallied to the support of "Mother Russia." Another significant factor in turning Napoleon's invasion into a major defeat was the well-known Russian winter, which in 1812–1813 was unusually severe. This completely disrupted the extremely long supply lines of the French.

Hoping for a speedy surrender of the Tsar's forces, Napoleon rejected the advice to retreat to winter quarters and before long his glorious army was in tatters and without food. "Scorched earth" tactics and roaming bands of guerrillas were used against the invader by the Russian general, Mikhail Kutuzov.

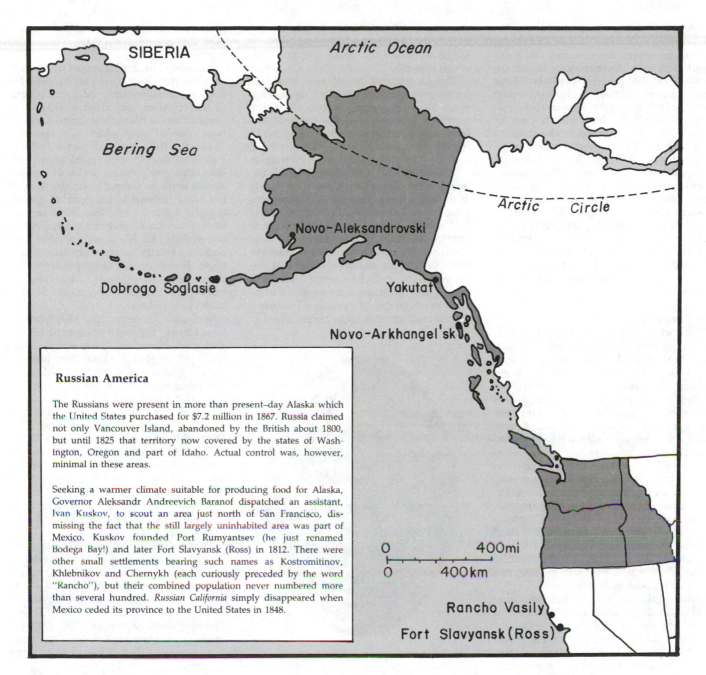

SIBERIA

Arctic Ocean

Bering Sea

Arctic Circle

Novo-Aleksandrovski

Dobrogo Soglasie

Yakutat

Novo-Arkhangel'sk

Russian America

The Russians were present in more than present–day Alaska which the United States purchased for $7.2 million in 1867. Russia claimed not only Vancouver Island, abandoned by the British about 1800, but until 1825 that territory now covered by the states of Washington, Oregon and part of Idaho. Actual control was, however, minimal in these areas.

Seeking a warmer climate suitable for producing food for Alaska, Governor Aleksandr Andreevich Baranof dispatched an assistant, Ivan Kuskov, to scout an area just north of San Francisco, dismissing the fact that the still largely uninhabited area was part of Mexico. Kuskov founded Port Rumyantsev (he just renamed Bodega Bay!) and later Fort Slavyansk (Ross) in 1812. There were other small settlements bearing such names as Kostromitinov, Khlebnikov and Chernykh (each curiously preceded by the word "Rancho"), but their combined population never numbered more than several hundred. *Russian California* simply disappeared when Mexico ceded its province to the United States in 1848.

0   400mi

0   400km

Rancho Vasily

Fort Slavyansk (Ross)

The departure of Napoleon's forces was not just a retreat—it was a rout.

Russia played a major role at the Congress of Vienna which was convened to settle the affairs of Europe. The supposed allies of Russia had some success in trying to contain the "undue" expansion of Russian political power in Europe. Great Britain and Austria in particular opposed the demands of Alexander I for reestablishment of a large Kingdom of Poland with himself as king under a constitutional govern ment with an independent Polish army.

Although such a kingdom was created, it was much smaller than desired by the Russians, and substantial portions of what used to be Poland were kept until after World War I by Austria and Prussia. While haggling over the boundaries of Europe in Vienna, the Russian Tsar tried to promote a scheme for a "Holy Alliance" of monarchs. This was to bind the rulers of Europe in a spirit of Christian brotherhood. It was a rather unclear plan that had no important practical results in the field of international relations. Of greater significance was the Quadruple Alliance, signed by Russia, Great Britain, Austria and Prussia, which made provision for periodic conferences to review matters of common interest and to assure continued peace. The consensus about what it meant to maintain the peace settlement did not last very long, however. The British wished to limit international cooperation to international attempts to overthrow the *status quo*, while Russia, Prussia and Austria argued for international cooperation to put down revolutionary movements within individual states. Great Britain broke with the other three nations on this issue in 1820, but Russia, Prussia and Austria continued to cooperate.

Alexander I put domestic policies on hold during the War of 1812. After Napoleon's attempt he turned his attention back to domestic affairs, but a large foreign debt and a budget deficit precluded major new programs such as had marked the earlier part of his reign. His antipathy toward serfdom continued, however, and in 1816 he abolished serfdom in Estonia. Another decree the next year ended serfdom in Courland, while a third decree abolished it in Livonia in 1819.

But Alexander I began to lose interest in secular change after he fell under the influence of a Russian monk known for his piety during the Napoleonic Wars. Another influence on him was Prince Metternich, chief minister of the Austrian Empire, who persuaded Alexander that revolutionary forces threatened the political stability of Europe. Alexander began to collect more conservative advisers about him and, increasingly, to act on their advice. The most influential of these was General Alexis Arakcheev, who drew up and implemented plans for "military colonies" in the western part of Russia. Recruits assigned to the military colonies helped to support themselves by growing most of their food. Hated by both soldiers and officers, the military colonies were abolished by Nicholas I after Alexander's death.

Alexander also appointed religious conservatives to major posts such as the Ministry of Education with predictable results. A new regime of censorship was imposed and religious instruction was given a more prominent place in the curriculum.

The Decembrists

The end of Alexander's reign in 1825 is associated with the first Russian revolution—that of the Decembrists. Although this was exclusively a revolt by army officers and lasted only one day, it is labeled a revolution because the leaders had specific plans about changing the nature of the Russian state and society and did not merely wish to change rulers. The Decembrists were all nobles who had served in western Europe and who wished to rid Russia of its backwardness. Their specific goals included the abolition of serfdom and the creation of a constitutional government. They were particularly aggrieved that Alexander I had granted a constitution to Poland and had permitted Finland to retain a constitution it had when it was annexed in 1809, but one was refused in Russia.

Organized into secret societies, they carried on discussions for a number of years, but were unable to agree on any specific action to take. They were galvanized into action by Alexander I's death, when no new Tsar was immediately sworn in as his successor. The confusion about the succession arose because Constantine, the nominal heir, had married a Polish countess and relinquished his claim to the throne—but this was not known. It was compounded by the fact that Constantine was in Warsaw, where he was regent and all communications were by mail.

By the time the matter was sorted out and Nicholas was ready to officially take over as Tsar, the Decembrists had decided "to refuse to take the oath of allegiance to Nicholas and . . ." But it seems that they had gotten no further than that for, on the appointed day, 3,000 troops, assembled on the Senate Square, refused to take the oath to Nicholas, but then did nothing further. Nicholas surrounded the square with 10,000 loyal troops and demanded their

surrender. When they refused, he ordered the artillery to fire on the insurgents, who then broke and ran. The revolt was over.

The Decembrist revolt was therefore only a minor affair. Five of the top leaders were executed, while approximately a hundred others were imprisoned and later exiled to Siberia. But what made it important was the myth that grew up about the Decembrists; Alexander Herzen, Russian revolutionary publicist, later took up the cause of the Decembrists and made them heroes to subsequent generations. Another importance of the Decembrist revolt was the breach it opened between the government and Russian liberals, who never forgave Nicholas for his harsh treatment of the Decembrists and remained alienated throughout his reign. Conversely, Nicholas was never able to overcome his suspicion that all liberals were potentially disloyal.

Nicholas I

Nicholas was 29 years old when he became Tsar and ruled Russia for 30 years until his death in 1855. He was not particularly well educated and he had no practical experience in administration before he succeeded to the throne. His background was entirely in the military, where he held the rank of brigade general. He liked the military and during his lifetime he surrounded himself with soldiers, preferring them as advisers and chief administrators.

He distrusted public opinion and did not believe that solutions could arise from among the people. He therefore prohibited public discussion of current problems, and books, journals and newspapers were censored. Since he also distrusted the bureaucracy but needed sources of information, he created "His

Majesty's Third Section" as his eyes and ears; this organization was no more than a secret police organization.

However, he kept a report of the testimony of the Decembrists on his desk and conscientiously attempted to meet some of the criticism contained in their statements. One of his early successes was the new code of laws which was issued in 1833—the first new code since 1649. He was also deeply concerned about serfdom and appointed a series of committees to work on the problem, but he could not bring himself to the point of abolishing the system. He did, however, improve the lot of the State Peasants by commuting all labor service into taxes and by setting up local government for them. Just over 50% of all peasants were State Peasants—people who lived on state land rather than on the land of individual nobles.

Nicholas I's reign has also been referred to as "the reign of outer repression and inner liberation" since it was during his tsardom that Russian literature and culture first attained international stature and recognition. Great Russian writers of this period included the poet Alexander Pushkin, the author of the first great Russian Novel *A Hero of Our Time*, Mikhail Lermontov and Nicholas Gogol, famous for novels, plays and short stories. Nicholas I, who attended the premiere of Gogol's play *The Inspector General*, a biting satire on Russian officialdom, afterwards commented "Everybody got what was coming to him and I got more than anyone."

Other Russian creative artists who began their work during the reign of Nicholas I included Ivan Turgenev, (*A Sportsman's Sketches*), and Mikhail Glinka, founder of Russian classical music and famous for his operas. The Bolshoi Theater, constructed in 1824, also provided a showcase for Russian ballet, comparable to that of France from where it came.

There were economic changes of some note as well, though the prohibitive tariff system adopted at the close of the Napoleonic Wars tended to isolate Russia from the momentous changes in Western Europe as a result of the spread of the Industrial Revolution. The continued existence of serfdom was another factor hindering change.

In spite of that, there was a dramatic growth in textile manufacturing in the province of Moscow and in and around the city of Lodz, in Russian Poland during the reign of Nicholas I. Most of the factories were primitive. Powered machinery only began to be introduced toward the end of his reign. This new industry was significant, however, because it was the first to make widespread use of free wage labor in Russia.

What made it even more interesting is

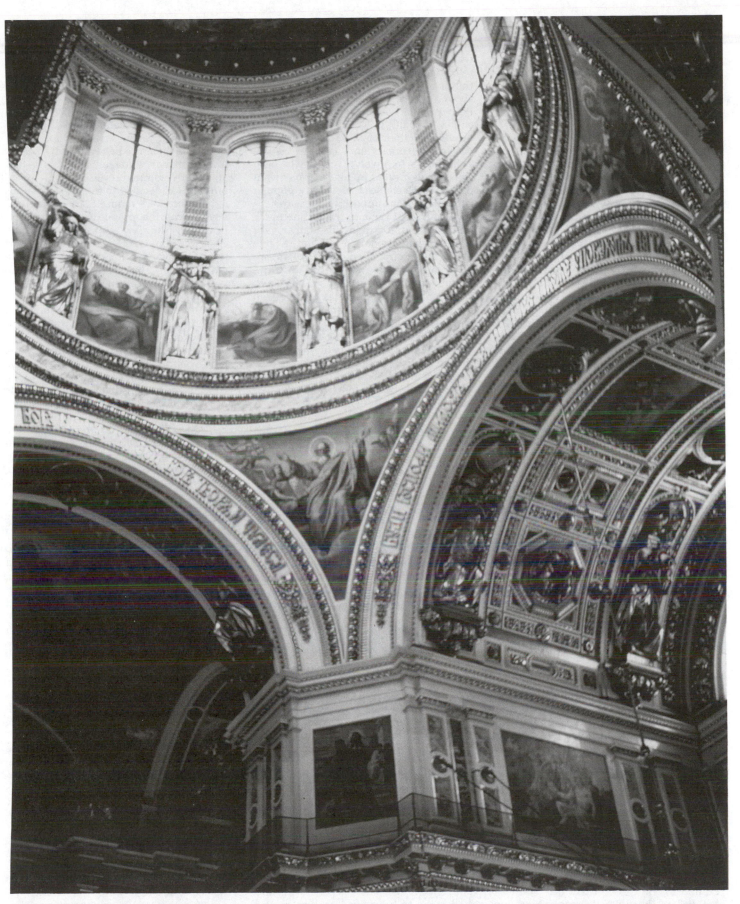

St. Isaac's Orthodox Cathedral in St. Petersburg was commissioned by Tsar Nicholas I. It was designed by French architect Auguste Montferrand and under construction from 1818–1858. The workers who applied the magnificent gold-mercury amalgam knew when they breathed the toxic fumes that they would die, often within 2 years.

Photo by Miller B. Spangler

that most of the workers were serfs who also compensated a master for labor services not performed in return for permission to take an outside job. The success of the new factories using wage labor foreshadowed the end of serfdom in Russia, for they established that free labor was more efficient than serf labor.

Nicholas I was also responsible for construction of the first railways in Russia, against the advice of his ministers. The first line, between St. Petersburg and Tsarskoe Selo, the royal palace complex located 12 miles away on the Baltic, was constructed as an experiment. The second line connected St. Petersburg with Moscow. Nicholas I authorized a third line linking St. Petersburg and Warsaw, but the Crimean War intervened and the project was put on hold.

In foreign affairs, Nicholas carried out a mainly peaceful policy, though he did fight a war against Turkey in 1828–29 which gave Russia the mouth of the Danube River and the eastern coast of the Black Sea. His troops were used again in 1830–31 to put down a Polish insurrection. The Poles were punished when Nicholas abolished their constitution and declared Poland an integral part of the Russian Empire. Troops were dispatched to Hungary in 1849 to end a revolt there and force the Hungarians back within the Austrian Empire.

Two years before his death, Nicholas involved the Russians in his first major war, the Crimean War. The basis of the original quarrel with Turkey—Russia's claim to be the protector of all Orthodox Christians under Turkish rule—would not have justified a war involving three great powers, but England and France intervened because England believed that Russia was attempting to partition Turkey. The war began with naval attacks against coastal Russian towns on the Baltic Sea, the White Sea and the Pacific Ocean, but the main attack came in 1854 when 60,000 allied troops began a siege of the Russian naval base at Sevastopol on the Crimean Peninsula.

Although faced with superior forces, the siege of the Russians lasted almost a year. One episode of the senseless loss of many lives is known to most pupils from Alfred Tennyson's "Charge of the Light Brigade." Tsar Nicholas died in the midst of the war, which was brought to an end by the Treaty of Paris in 1856. Russia had to surrender some territory, including Bessarabia, and give up the right to have naval forces or fortifications on the Black Sea.

The Tsar Emancipator

Alexander II (1855–1881), who succeeded to the throne upon the death of his father, Nicholas I, went down in history as the "Tsar Emancipator," the greatest westernizer since Peter the Great. Yet, he was not particularly well-liked during his reign, and he died the victim of a terrorist's bomb. The problem was that, though he saw the need for reforms, he wished to implement them in the form of another "revolution from above," in the manner of previous tsars. Perhaps that was inevitable, but the result was that, first, his reforms were modified in their application by a conservative bureaucracy and, second, his unwillingness to involve the newly educated elites created by his reforms meant that he lost a chance to develop a popular constituency to support his measures.

Alexander II came to the throne much better prepared than his father, for Nicholas had appointed him to the State Council (the appointed legislative assembly created by Alexander I) and the Committee of Ministers (the Tsar's cabinet, also created by his predecessor). He held a series of military commands and had also sat on a committee on serfdom appointed by Nicholas. At the conclusion of one session, Alexander petitioned his father to abolish serfdom. Nicholas said he recognized that serfdom was a present, existing evil, but to touch it might perhaps create greater evils.

Alexander II

Russia's defeat in the Crimean War convinced Alexander that Russia could no longer afford to do nothing; its continued existence as a great power was now at stake. The industrialization that had spread across Europe in the first half of the nineteenth century had largely left Russia untouched. Serfdom, with its mass of peasant workers tied to the soil, was incompatible with industrialization. Russia stood still while Europe progressed.

Moreover, serfdom, which had been abolished everywhere else in Europe, had come to be viewed as a moral evil whose continued presence in Russia excluded it from the company of civilized Europe. This moral revulsion toward serfdom had been an important factor in the harsh terms applied to Russia in the Treaty of Paris. Alexander II thus had two important reasons to move for the abolition of serfdom.

Alexander appointed his first committee to consider ways to abolish serfdom in 1857. Four years later, in 1861, he gave his approval to the emancipation manifesto which immediately freed all serfs from personal bondage. Since Russia had an overwhelmingly agricultural economy, it was decided to free the serfs with a type of land tenure. Since the land legally was the property of the nobles, however, the law stipulated that the ex–serfs would get the amount of land they had worked for themselves before emancipation, but they would have to pay for it. Since the ex–serfs had no money, the government arranged to pay the nobles for the land and to have the ex–serfs pay off their debt to the government over a period of 49 years.

Direct and personal ownership of the land was not given to the peasants; the so–called peasant commune was to be collectively responsible for the payments of its members and had the right to allot the land to peasant families. This was to be done according to the size of the family, and the allotments were open to revision every few years. Because of the financial responsibility, the commune hindered the attempts of the peasants to move away, causing overpopulation and land hunger in some areas.

Emancipation ended the control of the nobility over the serfs and necessitated the creation of local government and judicial institutions for the newly–freed peasants. Both of these reforms were carried out in 1864. The *Zemstvo* reform created elective councils at the district and provincial level and gave them responsibility for the local economy, health protection and education. Although voters were organized into three classes—nobles, townsmen and peasants—and voted separately, the *Zemstvo* assemblies were genuinely democratic institutions in which all classes participated. They became an important voice for rural interests.

The judicial reform was even more radical, because it abolished traditional Russian judicial practices and created an entirely new system that introduced trial by jury, public trials, defense attorneys and an independent judiciary, none of which had hitherto existed in Russia.

Cities were granted local government in 1870 along the lines of the *Zemstvo* reform. Elected city councils were created and an executive board was headed by a mayor. Although weighted voting systems meant that a relatively few large taxpayers could control the city council, the effect of the overall reform was positive.

THE GROWTH OF RUSSIA

Murmansk
1945
1795
Minsk
1793
Kiev
MOSCOW ★
1940
Igarka
Okhotsk
Petropavlovsk
Kazan
Yakutsk
Samara Ufa
1783
1864
Omsk
1810-29
1824 1822
Caspian
Sea
1804-30
1853
Irkutsk Lake
Baikal
1858-60
1873
1854 1881
1873
Vladivostock
1881
1871
1884
1895

Grand Duchy of Moscow and Russia in 1533
Year territory gained: 1533-98 1598-1689
1689-1725 1725-1801 1801-1945

0   200   400 mi
0 200 400 km

An army reform, introduced in 1874, initiated the principle that every man, regardless of class, was liable for military service. The ordinary term of service was reduced to six years, schools for officers were modernized and specific provisions were made to ensure that all enlisted men were taught how to read and write. Since illiteracy was quite high in Russia, the army thus became a significant adjunct to the nation's educational system.

Alexander also reorganized the secondary school system, granted autonomy to the universities and waived university fees for those too poor to pay. The *Zemstvos* had been given responsibility for primary education, but Alexander did approve a law calling for the establishment of a system of primary education throughout Russia. Many *Zemstvos* were slow to follow through on the Tsar's orders, but primary schools slowly came into existence; by 1914, *Zemstvos* were spending approximately one–third of their budget on primary education.

Alexander's economic reforms were—aside from serf emancipation—his most important measures, but they were more long–term and so took longer to show an effect. In addition, Alexander's commitment to industrialization was closely connected to his desire that Russia remain a great power. One of the major reasons for Russia's defeat in the Crimean War was the inability of the Russian government quickly to move men and supplies to the Crimean area. Because of the nature of the climate and the soil, getting about on land was nearly impossible for several months every year—roads turned into quagmires in the spring and fall. Russia's rivers were important transport links, but they were frozen during six winter months.

Alexander, whose mother and wife were both German and who visited Germany regularly, had been impressed by the extensive railway building in Germany in the 1840's and 1850's and the thrust this had given to German industrialization. The Tsar conceived of a similar program for Russia. But since there was little capital in Russia for investment and even fewer entrepreneurs—and the Russian government had no funds adequate for such railway construction—Alexander and his advisers set out to encourage the creation of private railway companies in Russia financed by foreign private capital investment.

Railway companies were permitted to bring in duty–free all equipment and material needed to construct a railroad; in addition, dividends and interest on stocks and bonds issued by the railway companies were guaranteed by the Russian government. Investors were, in effect, guaranteed against all losses.

The plan worked. By 1881, the time of Alexander II's death, approximately 7,500 kilometers of railroad had been constructed, metal–working and machine–building companies had sprung into existence and the beginnings of a modern iron and steel industry had been laid. It was still only a beginning, but railroad construction continued in the 1880's and 1890's and, after a financial and political crisis that lasted for several years, again began between 1907 and 1914. By 1914, European Russia was covered by an extensive network of railways and the Trans–Siberian Railway had been built across Siberia down to Vladivostok.

Alexander II was obsessed with Russia's defeat in the Crimean War and was determined to undo at least the more onerous clauses of the 1856 treaty. This became the main thrust of his foreign policy; his efforts to win over the French resulted in a friendship treaty between the two nations in 1857, but the Polish uprising six years later disrupted this relationship, since the French were sympathetic to the Poles. Alexander next turned to Prussia as a potential ally and this led to Russian support for German unification and a growing economic relationship between the two.

When the Franco–Prussian War broke out in 1870, the Russian government took advantage of the situation by denouncing the Black Sea clauses of the earlier treaty. England protested, but agreed to drop the offending clauses when it became clear that the new German government supported Russia.

Russia and the Austro–Hungarian Empire tended to be rivals in the Balkan area and their relations had been strained since the Crimean War. However, Russia, Germany and Austria signed an agreement in 1873—The Three Emperor's League—which brought them together in a quasi–alliance. It was Bismarck, the German Chancellor, who sponsored the agreement; he hoped to end the Russo–Austrian rivalry in the Balkans. Russia and Austria could, however, only agree to maintain the *status quo*, so when an uprising began in Bosnia in 1875 and quickly spread to Serbia and Bulgaria, relations between the two countries soured.

Russia and Austria signed the Reichstadt Agreement in 1876 whereby Austria agreed to remain neutral in case of war, while Russia agreed to a suitable territorial compensation for Austria and promised that it would not sponsor the creation of a single large Slavic nation. War broke out between Russia and Turkey in 1877; Russian armies were victorious. In the ensuing treaty, Russia got back southern Bessarabia plus three small towns east of the Black Sea; Turkey agreed to recognize the independence of Serbia, Romania and Montenegro. The remaining Slavic territories in the eastern Balkans would be organized into a single, autonomous state with an elected Christian Prince. No mention was made of any territorial compensation for Austria.

A bitter Austria threatened to go to war and England also objected to the terms of the treaty, sending its fleet into the eastern Mediterranean. War appeared imminent and Bismarck quickly agreed to host a conference of the powers in Berlin.

At the Congress of Berlin, the powers modified the terms of the treaty as follows: Bulgaria was reduced to one–third of its former size; another third was set up as the autonomous region of Eastern Rumelia and the final third, Macedonia, was returned to Turkey. Austria received the right to administer Bosnia and Herzegovina and was allowed to station troops in the Sanjak of Novibazar. England got Cyprus. Even as modified, the Treaty of Berlin was a triumph for Russia, for with the return of Bessarabia the last of the offending clauses of the 1856 treaty had been overturned. But instead, the Congress of Berlin was considered to be a humiliation for Russia and Alexander's foreign policy was judged to be a failure. The Three Emperors' League was dead; relations between Russia and Germany cooled and for three years Russia drew more and more into self–isolation.

Although at odds with most European powers, Russia was quite friendly with the United States of America. During the Civil War, the North was pleased to see squadrons of the Russian fleet appear both in New York and San Francisco. The Russians actually came to avoid being trapped inside their bases in the event of a European war—they were not really interested in helping the North. The abolition of serfdom was greeted in the U.S. as a move similar to the emancipation of the American slaves.

In the atmosphere of mutual friendship, it was possible for the United States to purchase Alaska in 1867 for the sum of $7.2 million. Although this turned out to be one of America's greatest bargains, it was denounced in the United States at the time as "Seward's Folly," a reference to the U.S. Secretary of State who arranged the purchase.

In spite of Alexander II's preoccupation with relations with the West, the Russian nation continued to expand in Asia during his reign. In the Far East, China was involved in a struggle with the western powers encroaching on its coastal areas. Taking advantage of this, Russia forced China to cede the regions around the Amur and Usuri Rivers. The city of Vladivostok, meaning "Ruler of the East," was founded in 1860 as a symbol of Russian power on the Pacific shores.

Central Asia was another area of expansion for Russia in the 19th century. This was Russia's southern frontier and as settlers pushed southward, they came increasingly into contact with central Asian peoples who resented their presence and showed this by carrying out periodic raids against Russian settlements. This would be followed in turn by punitive forays by the Russian army against central Asian settlements. As the raids continued, the army would begin building a new line of forts along the frontier and a new piece of territory would be added to the Russian empire.

By 1846, when a large part of Kazakhstan was incorporated into Russia, central Asia had been reduced to three independent Islamic khanates, Bokhara, Khiva and Kokand. Great centers of trade and export in the middle ages which had made them legends of wealth and power, all three khanates had subsequently declined in importance. By the middle of the 19th century, their main cities had been reduced to regional trading centers and the khanates were pale shadows of their former selves. Moreover, the writ of their rulers extended mainly to the larger settlements and they made no significant attempt to control the undisciplined tribesmen of the countryside or to stop them from carrying out raids on Russian settlements across the border.

In the 1860's, the Russian armies began a final conquest of the area. Kokand, with its ancient cities of Tashkent and Samarkand took three years to subdue. Its final conquest came in 1868. Bokhara fell the same year and Khiva was conquered in 1873.

Revolutionary Stirrings

While Russia was having general success in the area of international relations, the situation at home was deteriorating. Alexander II's promise of reforms brought a wave of enthusiasm among the people at the beginning, and even support from old revolutionaries such as Alexander Herzen in his exile in London. But disillusionment set in as implementation of the reforms began, for it became clear that, first, from the point of view of liberals, there were flaws in the legislation itself and, second, that a conservative bureaucracy would do its best to limit even further the benefits to come from the new legislation. Moreover, the very fact of reform from above brought a questioning of the *status quo* among educated Russians because it legitimated the question—"what further should be changed?" One writer who wrote on this theme was Nicholas Chernaevsky, whose novel, *What Is To Be Done?* became almost a bible for the questioning youth of the 1860's.

This questioning occurred mainly among the greatly increased numbers of young men streaming into the universities—as yet young women had to go abroad if they wanted a university education. Exposed for the first time to the latest scientific and philosophical theories from western Europe—revolution, positivism, French Utopian Socialism—many of these young people began questioning everything about Russian culture and the Russian way of life. Although women were denied access to the universities, some of them soon became important leaders in this new movement.

We speak of this movement as *nihilism* and it was perhaps best summed up by the great Russian novelist Turgenev in his novel *Fathers and Sons*. Turgenev saw the development as a kind of generation gap, a clash between the ideas of the "fathers and sons."

The *nihilists* of the 1860's were in general not revolutionaries, but there were some exceptions. In 1866, one such "student" decided to shoot the tsar and he actually went to the garden of the palace, walked up to Alexander II, pulled out his revolver and shot at him. What saved Alexander II's life at that moment is that a worker in the gardens, seeing what was happening, grabbed his arm.

By the 1870's the vague and somewhat negative revolutionary stirring of the previous decades merged into the so–called *Narodnik* (populist) movement.

The *Narodniki* were heavily influenced by the writing of the French Utopian Socialists. Appalled by what they thought of as the evils of industrialism, they advocated a kind of agrarian socialism based on the traditional Russian peasant commune. The leadership expected to stir the Russian masses by going among the simple people, teaching

Alexander III

NIHILISM

The following is an excerpt from Ivan Turgenev's *Fathers and Sons*. In this scene, Arkady, son of a large landowner, has just returned home from St. Petersburg, having graduated from the university. He is accompanied by a classmate, Bazarov, who has just gotten his medical degree. Arkady's father, Nikolai Petrovich and his uncle, Pavel Petrovich, both old liberals, ask about Bazarov:

"What is Bazarov?" Arkady smiled. "Would you like me, uncle, to explain?"

"If you will be so good, nephew."

"He's a nihilist."

"How?" inquired Nikolas Petrovich, while Pavel Petrovich lifted a knife in the air with a small piece on its tip, and remained motionless.

"He's a nihilist," repeated Arkady.

"A nihilist," said Nikolai Petrovich, "That's from the Latin, *nihil, nothing*, as far as I can judge; the word must mean a man who . . . who accepts nothing?"

"Say, who respects nothing," put in Pavel Petrovich, and he set to work on the butter again.

"Who regards everything from the critical point of view," observed Arkady.

"Isn't that just the same thing?" inquired Pavel Petrovich.

"No, it's not the same thing. A nihilist is a man who does not bow down before any authority, who does not take any principles on faith, whatever reverence that principle may be enshrined in."

them, but also learning from their supposedly pure and simple outlook which they allegedly had because they had not been "contaminated" by urban life. It became fashionable to "go to the people" to bring education and sanitary habits to the primitive, rural folk. Often the peasants repaid this by denouncing the uninvited tutors to the police.

Some of the populist leaders concluded that someone else would have to work for the peasants, because the masses were not mature and thinking enough to stage a general uprising against the Russian system. A decision was made to engage in acts of terrorism, the most spectacular of which was the attempt to kill the military governor of St. Petersburg. By the end of the 1870's, the revolutionary organization *Zemlya i Volya* (Land and Freedom) split into two major groups, one of which favored gradual change. The other, *Narodnaya Volya* (Will of the People) chose more terror in the somewhat questionable belief that removal of a few high personalities would change things in Russia. The Tsar was selected as the chief target for assassination. After several unsuccessful attempts, Alexander II was killed by terrorists in 1881. This apparently came on the very day when he was about to sign a new decree granting more political freedom to the people.

An Age of Reaction

The death of Alexander II brought to an end the age of reforms that originally began with Peter the Great. "Western" and "liberal" took on sinister meanings in the eyes of the government and upper classes. Alexander III (1881–1894), who was in narrow political terms a reactionary, believed that it was impossible to come to terms with the liberals and that his father's assassination had partly resulted from his attempts to do so. He made it clear that liberals could expect nothing from him when, in his accession address, he declared his "complete faith in the strength and truth of autocracy" and that " for the good of the people" he would "maintain and defend the autocratic power from attack."

He was 36 when he came to the throne. A great bear of a man, he referred to himself as the "peasant Tsar," and he was very proud of the fact that he could straighten horseshoes with his bare hands. He was honest and hard-working, but intellectually somewhat dull. He recognized his limitations, however, and left many decisions to his ministers, supporting them and keeping them in office even when he didn't understand what they were trying to do.

His most important political advisers were Constantine Pobedonostsev, Michael Katkov and Dmitri Tolstoy. Curiously enough, all had been supporters of Alexander II's reforms. Pobedonostsev had helped to draft the judicial reforms, for example, and Tolstoy had been Minister of Education in the previous regime. Katkov had been a well-known westernizer and liberal.

By 1881, however, they rejected their earlier admiration for foreign ideas and sought Russia's salvation in its own past. Alexander III, strongly nationalistic with Pan–Slav leanings, accepted their advice about the need to Russify the minorities and to bring the entire population into the Russian Orthodox Church. In Poland and in the Baltic provinces, Russian was made the language of instruction in the schools. Catholics, Protestants and Old Believers found themselves affected by government policies aimed at the conversion of these groups to Russian Orthodoxy. More affected were the Jews, for even more restrictive policies were applied to them. Laws forbidding their settlement in central Russia were tightened, and they were confined to an area called the "Pale of Settlement." Limitations were placed on the entry of Jews to universities; they were excluded from most government service and forbidden to acquire land in rural areas. In addition, agencies of the government were frequently engaged in stirring up violent outbreaks (*pogroms*) of the people against their Jewish countrymen. Repeated outbreaks caused a massive migration of Jews from the lands of the Russian empire. Many came to America.

The nature of Alexander III's reign was thus quite different from that of his father. Yet, though he disagreed with his father politically, he was loath to undo the work which his predecessor had begun. The substance of reform survived,

although the new Tsar did approve some amendments aimed at reducing popular participation. Provincial governors were, for example, given greater control over the *Zemstvo* assemblies and the franchise was changed to increase the representation of the nobility. The government also increased its administrative powers over the judiciary.

Alexander III shared his father's commitment to industrialization, so there was no essential change in economic policy. Government policy continued to encourage the construction of railroads, though more state–owned railroads were built in this period. Tariffs were also raised several times in order to encourage "infant industries." The policy worked in the sense that there was a good deal of foreign investment in Russia in the 1880's, but it also led to a tariff war with Germany from 1887 to 1893.

The policy of Alexander III toward the peasantry was probably his most important personal contribution toward the economic policy of his reign. Genuinely interested in the welfare of the peasantry, the Tsar set out to do what he could to improve their lot—at least insofar as that could be done within the framework of Russia at that time. The redemption debt was reduced in 1881 and again in 1884. Two taxes that weighed heavily on the lower class, the salt tax and the poll tax, were repealed. They were replaced by two taxes which applied mainly to the upper and middle classes: an inheritance tax and a tax on bonds.

The increase in population since emancipation had also reduced the average size of peasant allotments. To remedy this, the government set up a Peasant Land Bank to lend money. It also made loans to those who were willing to move to Siberia. In spite of these measures, the true state of Russia became evident in 1891 when crop failures led to famine in the countryside.

Although Russia remained at peace during the 13 years that Alexander III was on the throne, Russia's foreign relations were often abrasive, for, as one historian says of him, Alexander III attempted to obtain peacefully objectives that are usually obtained only as the result of a successful war. Russia's quarrels were primarily with Austria–Hungary and Germany and led to Alexander's decision to sign an alliance with France in 1892.

Alexander III's quarrels with Germany were of a two–fold nature, but they were exacerbated by his pan–Slav leanings. In the 1870's, Alexander III, then the heir to the throne, had supported pan–Slav aspirations in the Balkans and was deeply angered when Austria refused to accept the Treaty of San Stefano, negotiated at the close of Russia's victorious war against the Ottoman Empire in 1878. He favored a connection with Germany,

however, and, in 1881, accepted his foreign minister's advice that a renewal of the Three Emperors' League was the only way this could be arranged.

Things went smoothly until 1885, when the Bulgarians, at that time proteges of the Russians, decided to carry through a union with East Rumelia without consulting their Russian overseers. Alexander III "punished" the Bulgarians by withdrawing all Russian military advisers. When Austria took advantage of the situation to increase its own influence in Bulgaria, Alexander III felt betrayed and denounced the Three Emperors' League. His real quarrel, therefore, was with Austria. Alexander III still wanted a connection with Germany, however, and suggested a bilateral alliance with Germany in 1887, "not against Austria, but without Austria." This became the Reinsurance Treaty, which existed for three years, until 1890.

Alexander III also had a grievance with Germany having to do with economic relations between the two countries. In the 1880's, Germany was Russia's chief trading partner and the source of most foreign capital investment in the Russian economy. Russia had an adverse trade balance with Germany, which it attempted to solve by raising tariffs on the main goods coming in from Germany. This led a good number of German firms to open affiliates in Russian Poland as a way to retain the Russian market. However this large German commercial presence in Russian Poland became another problem, because Russian nationalists felt it threatened Russian political control in this borderland area. In 1887, the Russian Government issued a decree prohibiting foreigners from owning land in border areas such as Russian Poland, and Germany retaliated by an attack on Russian securities, known as the *Lombard Verbot*. Thus began an economic war that lasted until 1894 and brought the two nations as close to war as they were to come in the 19th century. It was these poor economic–political relations with Germany which led Alexander III to sign an alliance with France in 1892. That alliance, still in force in 1914, would bring Russia and France into World War I as allies against Germany and Austria.

Nicholas II and Alexandra

The Last Tsar

Alexander III has sometimes been referred to as the last Russian autocrat; whatever else can be said of him, it is generally agreed that he personified the policy of his reign. Nicholas II (1894–1914), by contrast, was a weak–willed individual who all his life was dominated by those about him. Moreover, he hated confrontations and got around them by seeming to agree with whomever he was talking. This made it extremely difficult for government ministers, for they never knew whether his approval of one of their suggestions was apparent or real. This also inclined him against strong–willed ministers, for that increased the possibility of disagreement. This trait became even more noticeable as he grew older, probably the result of the influence of his wife, Alexandra.

Alexandra, who also attempted to dominate him, called him weak–willed to his face and demanded that he stand up to his ministers. Other examples of her advice follow. Her baleful influence came primarily toward the end of his reign, however, as she undoubtedly saw the future crumbling.

Nicholas II was 26 years old when he succeeded to the throne. Professing his admiration for his father, he retained his father's ministers and promised to continue his policies. Meeting with representatives of the *Zemstvo* of Tver, for example, Nicholas told them that:

> "It has come to my knowledge that . . . there have been heard in some *Zemstvos* the voices of those who have indulged in senseless dreams that the *Zemstvos* might participate in the direction of the internal affairs of the state. Let all know that I shall devote my energy to the service of the people, but that I shall maintain the principle of autocracy as firmly . . . as did my father."

In spite of his promise, Nicholas did modify his father's policies in one area. He did not share his father's dislike for German culture and this showed up domestically in his reversal of his father's Russification policy as it applied to the Baltic Germans. It showed up internationally in the much better relations that developed with both Austria and Germany after 1894.

Russia was already in the midst of an economic boom when Nicholas came to the throne. The Minister of Finance was Sergei Witte (*Vit*–ay), a strong proponent of industrialization. Witte put the country on the gold standard, encouraged the inflow of foreign investment and pushed the construction of railroads. The boom lasted until 1899; by that time, the production of large–scale industry as a whole had doubled.

CATHERINE II
("THE GREAT" 1762–96)

PAUL I
(1796–1801)

ALEXANDER I
(1801–25)

CONSTANTINE

NICHOLAS I
(1825–55)

ALEXANDER II
(1855–81)

ALEXANDER III
(1881–94)

NICHOLAS II
(1894–1917)

One ominous sign on the horizon was the lack of domestic entrepreneurs, however. Of 14 new steel mills built during the 1890's, only one was Russian. The other 13 were foreign–owned and had foreign management. Other branches of industry dominated by foreign capital included the electric and electro–technical industry, the gas industry, chemicals and dyes. Many metal–working and machine-building companies were also foreign–owned and run. Using the terminology of Karl Marx, whose economic theories were to have such a dynamic impact on Russia, it was *creating* capitalism *but very few capitalists.*

The Revolution of 1905

The flow of new foreign capital into Russia was halted by a world–wide financial crisis in 1899, and brought about a wave of bankruptcies and mounting unemployment. Just as business was starting to recover, the economy was set back by crop failures in the countryside. A period of unrest followed, with strikes in the cities and peasant demonstrations in the villages. Illegal political parties began to appear and agitation for basic reforms increased.

Then came the Russo–Japanese War of 1904. It was badly fought, and the defeat of Russian forces at Port Arthur swelled the numbers of those who had come to believe that the government was unfit to rule.

In this tense atmosphere, the government made yet another blunder and set off the Revolution of 1905. Father Gabon, a Russian Orthodox priest who had started an organization for workers, was asked by them to lead them in a march to the Winter Palace to present a petition for redress of grievances to the Tsar. The peaceful crowd of workers, accompanied by their wives and children, were fired upon by the police as they approached the Winter Palace. Approximately a hundred people were killed and another hundred wounded. Although it had been one of the Russian Grand Dukes who had given orders to fire on the crowd—Nicholas II was not in residence at the Winter Palace at the time—Nicholas was blamed for what happened. Thus this event, which has gone down in history as "Bloody Sunday," had a significance beyond the immediate deaths and injuries. On that day, a myth died. The peasants had always thought of the Tsar as the "Little Father" who cared for his people. With the events of Bloody Sunday, that myth could no longer be sustained.

It triggered a wave of resentment and protests that continued throughout the spring and summer of 1905 and led, then, to a general strike that began in early fall. The general strike established that Nicholas II's government had lost the confidence of all Russian society, with the possible exception of the nobility and some of the military.

On the advice of Sergei Witte, Nicholas issued a manifesto promising constitutional government, civil liberties to all citizens and a national legislature (*Duma*). This was termed the "October Manifesto;" Nicholas also named Witte as his new chief minister.

Elections to the first *Duma* took place in March 1906. Nicholas showed his pettiness and lack of foresight by dismissing Witte as chief minister just before the legislature convened. The first *Duma* was dominated by a liberal group supported by Russia's professional classes, the Constitutional Democrats (*Kadets*). They clashed with the executive branch of government and when this division deepened, the *Duma* was dissolved. A second *Duma* was even more radical and it also was dissolved.

In calling for elections to a third *Duma*, Nicholas changed voting regulations to reduce the representation of troublemakers that had been voting for more radical candidates. He also appointed Peter Stolypin as his new Chief Minister.

The change in voting made the new *Duma* less representative, but it also produced a body willing to work with the Tsar and his ministers. Stolypin turned out to be a strong individual who managed for several years to save the Tsar from himself. Stolypin's name is particularly associated with a land reform which broke up the peasant communes and redistributed the land to the peasants as their private property. He hoped that, by giving the peasants something to lose, he would wean them away from their support of the radicals. But the reforms came too late and took too much time; by 1914 only about 25% of the peasants had managed to exchange their scattered strips for a single, contiguous plot of land. Stolypin was himself assassinated by revolutionaries in 1911 and with his strong presence gone, Nicholas II again began to exercise a greater say in the government.

World War I

The good relations which Nicholas had cultivated with Germany and Austria came to an end in 1908 when a new quarrel erupted between Russia and Austria over events in the Balkans. Austria's annexation of Bosnia began the dispute, but it soon spread and involved Germany—because of its support of Austria. Russia then became a patron of Serbia, which was anti–Austrian. The assassination of Archduke Francis Ferdinand, heir to the Austrian throne by a Serbian nationalist led Austria to declare war on Serbia. The general system of alliances transformed this Balkan war into World War I.

It was not long before the continent of Europe was aflame. At first the Russian

people responded to the call to arms with patriotic fervor, but this cooled considerably when the tides of battle turned. The Germans were pressing forward in France and soon threatened Paris; in order to take the pressure off, Russia invaded East Prussia. The army turned out to be ill–prepared and poorly equipped for a lengthy war, and Russia suffered a humiliating defeat. The government was incapable of enlisting the help of social organizations that were willing to assist in the war effort. Attention was focused mainly on the prospects of a glorious post–war seizure of coveted lands; especially attractive was the idea of taking Constantinople from the Turks, who had entered the war on the side of Germany. A victory would also have meant a Russian control over the straits that separate the Black Sea from the Mediterranean. However, while the government engaged in these dreams, German and Austrian forces actually occupied parts of Russian territory.

Tsar Nicholas made things worse for himself by assuming direct command of the armed forces. This kept him away

Nicholas II: A Prisoner at Tsarskoe Selo, 1917

from the capital and the result was that crucial matters of government were left in the hands of his German–born wife, the Empress Alexandra. She was extremely conservative, ambitious, hysterical and surrounded by advisers, some of whom may have been German spies. There also was another unbelievable influence in the palace—that of an illiterate, immoral and filthy peasant "Holy Man" named Rasputin who had wormed his way into the highest social circles of St. Petersburg. Empress Alexandra turned to Rasputin because of a tragic family problem, the incurable bleeding disease hemophilia. Her only son and heir to the throne, Alexis, suffered from this illness, inherited through his mother. Rasputin became a powerful figure at the palace, and extremely important matters of state were

soon "solved" according to his advice. Tsar Nicholas had become weak and sentimental and offered no opposition to his wife.

The effects of the war at first caused unrest mainly among the city dwellers who were suffering from fuel shortages and high food prices caused by disrupted supplies. Soon the countryside also became restive. The army command lacked skill—it tried to remedy Russia's lack of modern weapons by pouring seemingly endless millions of human bodies into the battle lines. The peasants provided the bulk of the manpower sent into what became a senseless slaughter; desertions became frequent.

The first move to remedy the alarming situation was a revolt from above; members of the highest aristocracy murdered Rasputin in December 1916. As the supplies of food decreased, food riots occurred more frequently in the cities, and workers went on strike. Troops summoned to restore law and order tended to side with the angry people. A half–hearted attempt was made to save the monarchy by having Nicholas abdicate in favor of his son, an incurably ill boy. However, the Tsar's brother, the Grand Duke Mikhail (Michael), refused to accept a regency under the circumstances, and overnight the Romanov dynasty ceased to govern Russia. The royal family was later put under arrest and finally gunned down by a gang of Bolsheviks in a cellar in Ekaterinburg, together with the family pet dog and the court doctor on the night of July 16–17, 1918.

An Experiment With Democracy

During the war years the *Duma* had

been totally ignored by the Tsar. As the end of the monarchy approached, it began to show signs of activity. When the tsarist regime "evaporated," the *Duma* organized a Temporary Committee. This contained all political groups except the extreme right and the extreme left; the Bolshevik representatives in the *Duma* were in jail or in Siberian exile. The Committee in turn produced a Provisional Government under the chairmanship of a liberal aristocrat, Prince George Lvov. It was intended that the Provisional Government would run the affairs of Russia until a Constituent Assembly could be elected by the people and write a constitution. The leadership of the Provisional Government later passed to a moderate socialist, Alexander Kerensky, who held power until overthrown by the Bolsheviks in October (November) of the same year—1917. In order to understand what happened in Russia after the Romanovs were deposed, it is important to know that on the very day that the *Duma* organized its Temporary Committee, there also came into existence the *Soviet* (Council) *of Worker's Deputies*. This was actually a revival of the institution that briefly functioned during the unsuccessful revolution of 1905. The Soviet was soon enlarged by adding representatives of the soldiers in revolt, and was led by moderate socialist members. These men believed that Russia, a rather backward country in terms of industrial development, would first have to "catch up" by going through a *bourgeois democratic* stage which would sweep away the remnants of the old feudal system. It was thought that the *bourgeois–democratic* administration would bring Russia to the level of a mature, capitalist nation which would then, and only then, be ripe for a socialist revolution. The workers, or *proletariat*, would grow in numbers in the democratic capitalist period and would become aware of their power and historical role and be the basis for another revolution that would usher in socialism.

The leftist parties, including the Bolsheviks prior to Lenin's return to Russia, gave their support to the Provisional Government, although at first refusing to serve in it. A peculiar pattern of power emerged; the Soviet enjoyed substantial support from the workers and soldiers, but refused to govern directly. It reserved for itself the position of being a critic and "watchdog" of the revolution. While the Provisional Government was the official governing body, it had no mass following and was forced to rely on the Soviet for support. This was particularly true in matters involving the army—the Provisional Government had nominal control of the armed forces, but the Soviet had ordered enlisted personnel to keep arms out of the reach of officers in order to prevent a counter–revolution.

Grigori Efimovich Rasputin

Lenin's Return

Events took a decisively new turn when Vladimir Illich Ulianov (Lenin), the leader of the Bolshevik faction of the *Social Democratic Party*, returned to Russia on April 3, 1917. A natural politician, Lenin understood how to appear faithful to Marxist ideals and at the same time to be flexible enough to deal with unexpected situations not covered by Marx. Lenin saw through the confused situation and brilliantly analyzed it as being one of "dual government." The Provisional Government held nominal authority but the *Soviet* enjoyed the support of the people. The way to eliminate this duality was to dominate the *Soviet* and then eliminate the "official" government.

Lenin was aware that at the moment his own group, the Bolsheviks, were a minority in the Soviet. It took him some time to win over the leadership of his own group. He added a new direction of thinking to the Bolsheviks—seizure of power. The Bolsheviks were able to win additional support because of the insistence of the Provisional Government that Russia had an obligation to continue to fight Germany, an idea that was becoming increasingly unpopular. Another factor was the failure of moderate elements to deal with pressing internal problems such as distribution of land to peasants and creating an orderly supply of food.

Propelled by Lenin's determined will and by simplified slogans directed to the people, such as "Peace, Bread and Land," the Bolsheviks began their quest for power. Because of his more flexible

---

FROM LENIN'S "APRIL THESES"

(A few days after his return to Russia, Lenin published on April 7, 1917, a set of brief "theses" stating his view of the situation in the war–torn country. He outlined a program for the "second stage" of the revolution. Below are some excerpts.)

1. In our attitude toward the war, which unquestionably remains on Russia's part a predatory imperialist war under the new government of Lvov & Company because of the capitalist nature of that government, not the slightest concession to "revolutionary defencism" is permissible.

The class–conscious proletariat can give its consent to a revolutionary war which would really justify "revolutionary defencism" only if (a) the power passes to the proletariat, (b) all foreign annexations be renounced in fact and not just in word, and (c) that a complete break be made in fact with all capitalist interests . . .

5. There should not be a parliamentary republic—to return to a parliamentary republic from the Soviets of Workers' Deputies would be a step backwards—there must be a republic of Soviets of Workers', Agricultural Laborers' and Peasants' Deputies throughout the country, from top to bottom.

There also must be abolition of the police, the army and the bureaucracy . . .

9. (c) (We must) change the Party's name. Instead of "Social Democracy," the world leaders of which have betrayed Socialism and deserted to the bourgeoisie . . . we must call ourselves a Communist Party.

10. There must be a new International. We must take the initiative in creating a new revolutionary International . . .

---

leadership they were not saddled with burdensomely rigid theories of government that handicapped the other socialist groups.

In July 1917, there was a Bolshevik–inspired uprising in Petrograd (the Russian version of St. Petersburg adopted in 1914) which was suppressed, and Lenin was forced to flee across the border to Finland. In spite of this temporary setback, the influence of the Bolsheviks grew steadily, particularly among the soldiers and sailors. The determined attitude of the Bolsheviks against continuing the war with Germany was especially helpful. The Provisional Government,

besides failing to solve internal problems, seemed to make no real effort to get out of the unpopular war because it felt bound by an agreement with Russia's allies not to make a separate peace.

An unfortunate decision to mount one more military offensive in the summer of 1917 contributed to the near collapse of army organization and morale. This played right into the hands of the Bolsheviks. The government, by this time quite desperate, tried to turn the anger of the people against Lenin and his followers, stating that the instigators of the July uprising were German agents.

Demonstration against the Provisional Government, July 1917

30

Lenin

Lenin was not widely popular throughout Russia nor within his own party organization. It was charged that he had spent the war years away from Russia, mainly in neutral Switzerland; that he was an "internationalist" who had opposed the war from its very beginning in 1914; that he had returned to Russia with the assistance of the German army's High Command, who arranged for his travel through Germany in a sealed railway car, and that he had been the recipient of sums of money from Germany since his arrival in Russia. Lenin never denied the first three charges and there is some evidence that the fourth accusation was true as well. But Lenin was never a German agent. The German army High Command helped Lenin to get back to Russia because he was a known opponent of the war and they hoped his presence in Russia would weaken the Russian resolve to continue the war. Any financial assistance they may have given Lenin was for the same reason. And Lenin was willing to take assistance from any source, provided it promoted his own particular goals.

Lenin was forced to remain in hiding because of these charges against him, but the Bolsheviks continued to grow in popularity, primarily because of bumbling and failures on the part of the Provisional Government and the other political parties. One such case of bumbling was the "Kornilov Affair."

Alexander Kerensky, who had been head of the Provisional Government since July 20, 1917, entered into negotiations with the recently-appointed commander-in-chief of the armed forces, General Lavr Kornilov. The exact nature of their understanding remains a matter of controversy to this day, but it appears that Kerensky turned to the general, a believer in "law and order," to obtain military assistance against the growing influence of the Bolsheviks. However, when Kerensky thought the general and

his troops were marching on Petrograd to stage a *coup* and possibly restore the old regime, he turned on Kornilov.

When the general refused to give up his post and issued a statement directed against the Provisional Government, Kerensky sought the help of the workers of the threatened capital, including groups that were known to be under Bolshevik influence. The end of the "Kornilov Affair" with the arrest of the general and his leading staff officer seemed for a while to strengthen Kerensky's position. In reality, the prestige of the Provisional Government had all but vanished.

Lenin's attitude at the time of the "Kornilov Affair" is reflected in his response to Kerensky's plea for support against Kornilov—"We will support him the way a noose supports a hanged man." Lenin apparently liked analogies about ropes and nooses, for on another occasion he characterized capitalists as being willing to "sell you the rope with which to hang them."

The Kornilov affair actually rehabilitated the Bolsheviks and prepared the way for their eventual seizure of power. In September, the Petrograd Soviet returned a Bolshevik majority; a week later, the Moscow Soviet did likewise. The new chairman of the Petrograd Soviet was Lev D. Bronstein, better known by his revolutionary name, Trotsky. Although a longtime revolutionary and radical ideologist, he had only joined the Bolshevik faction in the summer of 1917. With Lenin still in hiding, however, it was Trotsky who took charge and actually carried out the *coup d'etat* against the Provisional Government which was to go down in history as the "Great October Socialist Revolution."

Very little is heard about Trotsky in the Soviet Union today. This is because, after Lenin's death, there was a struggle for power between him and Josef Stalin and he came out the loser. Forced into exile, he became a bitter opponent of Stalin and his policies in the 1930's. He was eventually killed on Stalin's orders. But no amount of falsification of history can erase the key role Trotsky played in organizing the workers and winning over the soldiers and sailors to the side of the Bolsheviks. Trotsky was a fiery orator who could sway masses of workers and peasants to follow his advice. His leadership in the brief military operations which resulted in the overthrow of the Provisional Government was brilliant.

However, even Trotsky later conceded that Lenin was the one indispensable individual in the Russian Revolution. It was Lenin who was convinced that the time was ripe to move against the Provisional Government and who persuaded the Central Committee of the Bolsheviks to begin preparations for the seizure of power.

Trotsky accepted that decision and set about to implement it. He persuaded the Executive Committee of the Petrograd Soviet that a Military Revolutionary Committee needed to be created for the defense of the revolution. This Military Revolutionary Committee then sent "political commissars" to each of the military units stationed in Petrograd. Their instructions were to persuade the soldiers and sailors to accept no orders from their officers unless they were countersigned by the political commissar of the Petrograd Soviet. In this manner, Trotsky managed to neutralize the entire Petrograd Garrison.

After many hesitations, the attempt to seize power was timed to coincide with the sessions of the All-Russian Congress of Soviets called for November 7, 1917 (October 25 by the old calendar). However, events came to a head a day earlier—the government had been tipped off about the impending *coup* and began to move some loyal troops into position. It also ordered the soldiers to occupy the premises where the Bolshevik newspaper *Pravda* (Truth) was printed.

By this time the Bolsheviks were in control of the major military unit of the Petrograd garrison, and easily secured a number of important points. The seat of government in the Winter Palace was defended briefly by a detachment of military cadets and a women's battalion, but when the guns of the cruiser Aurora were trained on the palace, resistance ceased. Most members of the Provisional Government were put under arrest. Kerensky escaped in disguise in a car flying the U.S. flag. He died in New York in 1970; his writings blame everyone but himself for the events of 1917.

The Bolsheviks march into Moscow

THE COMMUNIST ERA (November 1917–August 1991)

Soviet Russia

Creation of the New Soviet Regime

Although the *coup d'etat* that brought the Bolsheviks to power was made in the name of the Second Congress of Soviets, it was actually carried out by the Military Revolutionary Committee of the Petrograd Soviet, and the Bolsheviks announced the overthrow of the Provisional Government before the Congress of Soviets convened on the evening of October 25/November 7. The Congress was dominated by the Bolsheviks and their allies, the Left Socialist Revolutionaries, however, so they accepted their new role and passed a resolution written by Lenin proclaiming the transfer of all power to the Soviets. Executive power was vested in a Soviet of People's Commissars (*SOVNARKOM*).

Lenin became chairman, and he filled the other positions on the *SOVNARKOM* (equivalent to a cabinet) with Bolsheviks. Thus the Bolsheviks managed to clothe themselves in the legitimacy of the Soviet movement and to use it to gain political power in Russia. The Congress of Soviets, having installed the Bolsheviks in power, had completed its usefulness. A Central Executive Committee was therefore elected, composed of 2/3 Bolsheviks and 1/3 Left Socialist Revolutionaries, and given full authority to pass legislation in the name of the Congress, which now adjourned. Just in case that wasn't sufficient, the *SOVNARKOM* was authorized to issue decrees which would have the force of law.

Soviets had sprung up spontaneously over all Russia after the February Revolution, but they only existed at the local level and were not universal. In December 1917, a decree of the *SOVNARKOM* called for the creation of Soviets at the local, district, regional and provincial level, these Soviets to replace the *Zemstvos* as organs of government. Soviet officials were in theory to be elected, but only workers and peasants had the right to vote.

Since the Soviets only recognized socialist political parties, all others had become illegal as of the creation of the new Soviet government. Mensheviks and Socialist Revolutionaries lost their representation when the Congress of Soviets adjourned and they soon found themselves subject to some repression as well. Menshevik newspapers were closed first, but this ban was soon extended to all opposition newspapers, By the spring of 1918, all opposition political parties had been outlawed and the *Communist Party* (the new name the Bolsheviks had adopted in March 1918) had become the sole legal party in Soviet Russia.

War Communism

The period of Soviet history down to March 1921 is usually referred to as the period of *War Communism*. Once it got itself organized, the new regime set out to communize the country—or at least those parts that recognized its authority, since at this time the various minority nationalities had broken away and were in the process of establishing separate governments.

First priority was given to the nationalization of the means of production. A decree on land, issued immediately after the takeover, abolished private property in land but permitted the peasants to continue to use the land, provided they did not make use of hired labor. Banks, railroads, shipping and foreign trade were nationalized almost immediately, and the Supreme Economic Council was set up to begin state planning. Another decree established worker control over production and distribution of industrial output. Lenin would probably have preferred to move more slowly with nationalization of the rest of the economy, but he found his pace forced by so–called "nationalizations from below" as individual workers expelled owners and seized control of factories on their own. By the spring of 1918, all industry had been nationalized and the government had taken control over all internal trade as well.

The Treaty of Brest–Litovsk

Of all the things Bolshevik propaganda had promised the people, peace had perhaps been the most significant. But the Bolsheviks also needed peace in order to have time to consolidate their government. They attempted a "Decree on Peace" on the very first day after seizing power, but that had no more than a propaganda effect. For real peace, they had to find a way to negotiate with those making war on Russia—the German Imperial General Staff. Preliminary negotiations resulted in the signing of a temporary truce in December. But when peace negotiations began in January, the German terms were so harsh that Trotsky, in charge of the negotiations, rejected them out of hand. Lenin argued that there was no alternative to acceptance of the German terms, but it was not until the Germans began a new advance that he could get his associates to agree. The Treaty of Brest–Litovsk on March 3, 1918, ended the state of war between Russia and the Central Powers, Germany and Austria.

By the terms of the treaty, the Soviet government obligated itself to recognize that Georgia (in southern Russia), the Ukraine (between Russia and Poland and Finland (to the northwest) were no longer parts of Russia. Poland and three small Baltic states, Lithuania, Latvia and Estonia, were conceded to be in Germany's sphere and control. The Aaland Islands in the Baltic Sea were evacuated, and the Turks, then allied with Germany, were given land in and near the cities of Kars, Ardahan and Batum.

Profiting from Russia's weakness, the Romanians occupied the province of Bessarabia which had been a part of southwestern Russia. Altogether, the terms of the treaty meant a loss of 1.3 million square miles of Russian territory. This represented about 32% of the agricultural land, about one–third of the factories and approximately 75% of the coal and iron mines of Russia.

Harsh as the terms of the Treaty of Brest–Litovsk were, they gave the hard–pressed Bolsheviks an opportunity to consolidate their power in areas outside the two main cities of the country. Trotsky undertook the gigantic task of building an army. The name of this new force was *Workers and Peasants Red Army*. The name "Red Army" continued to be used by some in the western world although the name had been changed to the more respectable *Armed Forces of the USSR*.

What is Communism?

Every human society claims to be guided by some basic set of rules—a philosophy, theory or ideology. With the Age of Enlightenment, there was an attempt to substitute for the traditional religious explanations for the origin and behavior of man a more "modern" description of (1) what man was, (2) why he was here and (3) where he was going. Further, there was an effort to explain why mankind thought the way it did.

This philosophic effort occupied several centuries and still persists, although now at a lower degree. The study of philosophy reached its heights in the 17th and 18th centuries in Europe—England, France, Germany, Switzerland and Rome, not necessarily in that order. The effort of philosophers was to discover, through the processes of science and thought, the reason, origin and destiny of mankind, independent of the teachings of religion.

The ideas and ideals of modern communism had their birth in the writings of Karl Marx (1818–1883), a German–born philosopher, social critic and revolutionary, who spent almost 35 years in England. His residency there was contemporary with the life styles described in the writings of Charles Dickens, which heavily influenced his thinking. His original work, *Das Kapital* (referring to capital) of which only the first volume was published during Marx's lifetime, was supplemented by others edited from his notes by his closest colleague, Friedrich Engels. The latter was a wealthy capitalist who had turned radical. The two founding fathers of communism are even better known for the *Communist Manifesto*, made public in 1847.

The theory (if a legitimate one ever actually existed) has undergone so much change that it is difficult to explain to the world today.

The first consideration was Marx's belief as to the origin of ideas. Borrowing heavily from the ideas of others, particularly the philosophers Hegel and John Locke, Marx accepted the idea of Hegel that human ideas—thought—arose from the interplay of two forces. A theory (idea) always had an opposite: the antithesis. From the two, there was a combination of the best features of both into a *synthesis*. But Marx went further—he rejected the proposition that man could think independently of things he had experienced with his five senses. All thought, he urged, was nothing more than a mirror of material things which had been experienced. This borrowed from the so–called "blank tablet" theory of John Locke. It is demonstrably wrong as has been repeatedly proved during the decades following Marx. Chemical elements of the *periodic table* were predicted far in advance of any opportunity to *see, hear, feel, touch or smell them*. Many of Einstein's theories of relativity remained to be experienced or proven until after his death.

But Marx doggedly persisted in his advancement of the "blank tablet" idea of Locke, and went further: he said in effect that human ideas, insofar as they would effect history, were determined by the *changes in the modes of production*. He further proclaimed that the "modes of production" had made people wealthy or poor. Applying his ideas to 19th century England, he labeled the times as "capitalistic" and proclaimed that the ruling class was the "bourgoisie" (boor–zwah–see). It was fashionable toe borrow terms from other languages, particularly French, at the time he wrote.

Marx correctly observed that capitalists were identified with the economic idea of "free competition" and that they had "historically played a most revolutionary part" and could not, in fact, "exist without constantly revolutionizing" (i.e. improving) the instruments of production.

But he then denounced the capitalist "class" as evil. He said that as a result

"the bourgeoisie, during its rule of scarce one hundred years, has created more massive and more collosal productive forces than have all the preceding generations together. Subjection of Natures' forces to man, machinery, application of chemistry to industry and agriculture, steam navigation, railways, electrical telegraphs, clearing of whole continents for cultivation, canalization of rivers, whole populations conjured out of the ground—what earlier century had even a presentiment that such productive forces slumbered in the lap of social labor?"

Marx saw three sinister laws associated with capitalism: capitalist accumulation, concentration of capital and increasing misery (of the lower classes). His laws were based on the conclusion that *human labor alone creates value,* and, accordingly, the profits of capitalists *are derived from unpaid labor time.*

Marx urged that competition results in more labor–saving machinery (or bankruptcy) and therefore increased unemployment and a general lowering of employee wages. The end result is monopoly capitalism—whereby all wealth is in the hands of a few capitalists and a countless mass of the people have been driven down into the ranks of "the proletariat."

The ultimate result, according to Marx, was "the more or less veiled civil war . . . break(ing) out into open revolution," overthrowing the bourgeoisie and raising the proletariat to the position of the ruling class. Once in power, the proletariat would nationalize all means of production and institute state planning to

Karl Marx

replace the discarded schemes of competition. The state—"nothing more than a machine for the oppression of one class by another"—will wither away and mankind will have entered the highest and last stage of development: Communism.

Marx claimed his to be a scientific doctrine which, having mastered the general laws that govern human society, could apply them to understand the future. The logical test of Marxism, of course, is whether his "laws" subsequently came true.

In fact, none came true. The total number of capitalists continued to grow throughout the remainder of the 19th and 20th centuries as inventions such as the electric dynamo, the internal combustion engine, the light bulb, the telephone, the aerosol valve, the silicone chip, radar, the computer (which is setting this typography) and a multitude of whole new industries came into being. As for Marx's "proletariat," living standards improved as wages began an upward spiral, the union movement took hold and living standards steadily improved. By 1900, it was generally conceded that Marx's law of "increasing misery" was not in operation and his followers made efforts to update and correct him.

Vladimir I. Lenin was not actually one of these "revisionists." He thought of himself as primarily a revolutionary, not a theoretician, but it was precisely for this reason that he wanted to know *why* the revolution had not yet occurred and what could be done to bring it about. He set forth his conclusions in *What Is To Be Done?,* a book he wrote in 1902. In essence, he argued that the revolution hadn't occurred because the proletariat wasn't capable of carrying out a socialist revolution—that, left to itself, it was only "able to develop trade union consciousness."

The revolution would be made by "a revolutionary youth, armed with Social–Democratic theory." What was needed, therefore, was an organization of full-time professional revolutionaries who, acting as "the vanguard of all the revolutionary forces," would bring about the revolution in the name of the proletariat.

Lenin thus presented an "organizational solution" to the question "what could be done to bring the revolution?" This "organizational solution" had additional implications, however, for it effectively excluded the proletariat (which it intended to benefit) from control of the revolutionary party. Only individuals trained in Marxist ideology would have the necessary "socialist consciousness" to be able to provide proper guidance to the proletariat.

Lenin's position on the nature of the party became the chief issue at the Second Congress of the Russian Social Democratic Labor Party when it met in 1903.

Lenin's supporters became known as Bolsheviks, while his opponents became known as Mensheviks. There was, in effect, a split in the party.

The Bolsheviks became a small band of professional revolutionaries, whose chief common characteristic was their personal loyalty to Lenin. Lenin's control was further reinforced in July 1917 when a Bolshevik party congress adopted the principle of *democratic centralism* as the basis of party organization. This is still the basis of Communist Party organization and it has meant in practice that subordinate party units are mere agents of the party leadership, bound to follow all instructions from above. When this is contrasted with Jefferson's ideals of democracy, one can see how it has been possible for the proletariat—anyone not in a position of leadership—to be subjected to almost anything.

Lenin made a somewhat broader contribution to Marxist theory in 1916 when he wrote *Imperialism, The Highest Stage of Capitalism.* Most of the thought of the book is not original, but it does contain an argument which tends to modify Marx's theory that the socialist revolution occurs in a country only after capitalism has been fully developed. According to Marx,

"a social system never perishes before all the productive forces have developed for which it is wide enough; and new, higher productive relationships never come into being before the material conditions for their existence have been brought to maturity within the womb of the old society itself."

According to Lenin, however, imperialism created a new situation which called for a modification of Marx's statement insofar as colonial or semi–colonial people were concerned. Under imperialism, monopoly capitalists exploit "backward, colonial peoples," first as markets and, second, as a cheap source of raw materials. This exploitation permits the capitalists to pay their own workers higher wages than they would otherwise be able to pay, and accounts for the improvement in the lot of the workers, contrary to Marx's theory. At the same time, it gave a new form to the *proletariat*—which came to include the "toiling masses of the backward countries."

Accordingly, every country that was subject to capitalistic exploitation was a suitable target for revolution *regardless of the extent of its industrial development.* Russia thus became a proper target for revolution although it had not entered the industrial stage required for revolution. The Russian Revolution of February 1917 further reinforced Lenin's conviction that Russia was ready for a socialist revolution. He returned to Russia in April 1917 to fulfill his fate with destiny.

Area and Latitude Comparison

Intervention and Civil War

Russia's departure from the war with Germany led to military intervention from the outside and to a civil war within Russia waged by elements opposed to the new regime. These anti–Bolshevik groups received some, but not enough outside support—"a wretched half– measure" as the late Sir Winston Churchill called it. The intervention was due to a number of reasons. There was fear that Germany, freed from the need to fight on the eastern front, would be able to move large numbers of troops to the western front. This would permit Germany to score a decisive victory before the impact of America's entry into the war would be felt. There were also arguments that large stores of military supplies in the far north of European Russia would fall into the hands of the Germans.

In France there was an outcry to protect the money of many investors who were holding tsarist Russian loan bonds. The Japanese were looking for an opportunity to establish themselves on the Asian mainland at the expense of a weakened Russia. This, in turn, stimulated U.S. participation in the intervention because the American leadership did not care for the idea of Japanese expansion in the Far East.

Technically, American intervention was also on behalf of the *Czechoslovak Legion*, a group of about 100,000 troops of the Austro–Hungarian army who had deserted or had been captured on the Russian front during the war. While moving across Russia to form a fighting force that was to assist on the western front, they clashed with the Bolsheviks.

The intervention was a series of badly coordinated military efforts. The foreign forces became tied in with the attempts of opposition groups to hold parts of the vast Russian territory and to form counter–governments in attempts to overthrow the Bolshevik regime. Various groups were sponsored and supported by foreign powers. There was a period of short–lived resistance by former tsarist generals in the winter of 1918, followed by a major effort of General Anton Denikin to deny the Soviet government access to the food and oil producing regions of the south.

Elsewhere, an uprising against the Bolsheviks was staged by the right wing of the *Social Revolutionaries* who were in favor of rejoining the war on the side of the Allies. They engineered the murder of the first German ambassador to Soviet Russia, Count Wilhelm von Mirbach. An anti–Bolshevik counter–government was established in the Siberian city of Omsk by socialist elements. This was quickly taken over by Admiral Alexander Kolchak, who proclaimed himself "Supreme Ruler" of Russia. In still another area in the Caucasus, General Peter Wrangel was fighting the Bolsheviks, largely with French support. The British were lending their support to General Denikin and Admiral Kolchak.

The civil war was marked by much heroism and cruelty on both sides, and dragged on until 1920. By that time, the allied intervention had come to an end and most of the anti–Bolshevik armies had been defeated. During the year, Russia signed peace treaties with Estonia, Latvia, Lithuania and Finland, recogniz-

ing their independence and establishing their boundaries.

Poland was another problem, however, for the Pilsudski government which was in control claimed Poland's "historic" boundaries and insisted that the Soviet government surrender all land west of the 1772 border—in other words, prior to the first partition of Poland. This included areas with significant Byelorussian and Ukrainian populations and the Soviets therefore refused this demand.

Pilsudski launched an invasion into the area of the Ukraine in the spring of 1920. He captured Kiev, but was unable to hold it. A Soviet counterattack then drove the Poles back into Poland and shortly thereafter a Soviet army was threatening Warsaw. But the tide of battled turned once again, and the Russian troops found themselves retreating and on the defensive. A compromise territorial settlement was then reached giving Poland part of what it wanted—though not the 1772 boundaries—and the Peace of Riga was signed in October 1920. The settlement left about 4.5 million Byelorussians and Ukrainians inside Poland, however, a factor that continued to influence Soviet–Polish relations until 1939.

In the autumn of 1920, the Soviets drove the last of the anti–Bolshevik armies out of western Russia. This led to the collapse of anti–Bolshevik governments in Georgia, Azerbaijan and Armenia and their replacement with socialist governments allied with Soviet Russia. Shortly therafter, the Central Asian provinces came back under Russian rule. This effectively brought peace to Russia. Only the area east of Lake Baikal remained outside of Soviet control—organized as a separate Far Eastern Republic. And, in late 1922, that territory also decided to rejoin Russia.

New Economic Policy

With the end of the civil war and the war with Poland, a new situation existed. The economy had deteriorated over the preceding three years to such an extent as to make a mockery of the Bolshevik claims to have improved the lot of the worker. Industrial output had fallen to 20% of its 1914 level and half of all industrial jobs had evaporated. Cities were being deserted as people fled to the countryside to find food. The population of Petrograd had declined from a pre–war total of 2.3 million to 900,000. Agricultural output had also declined significantly, partly because of the ravages of the civil wars, but also in response to the government's food requisition policy.

Neither the workers nor the peasants had supported the anti–Bolsheviks, but many were also unhappy with Bolshevik policies. They now felt free to put pressure on the government to change its policies. The result was peasant unrest, strikes by workers and, finally, a revolt of sailors at Kronstadt in early 1921. Lenin now recognized that some compromises were necessary and he announced a *New Economic Policy (NEP)* in March 1921.

The *NEP*, as it came to be called, reestablished a market economy in Russia. Food requisitions were to cease, to be replaced by a tax on agriculture to be paid with produce. After the peasant had paid the tax, he could dispose of the remainder of his crops as he saw fit. That meant that internal trade had to be within the private sector, otherwise the peasant would not have been able to dispose of his crops. An important feature of this era was the *NEP–Man*, the private trader who bought the peasant's produce and furnished him with the products he wanted to buy. In the cities, private ownership of the shops and factories employing fewer than 20 workers was to be permitted. Money, which had largely lost its value, came back into use and a new currency was issued with gold backing.

The "commanding heights"—all large factories, mines, steel mills, transportation, banking and foreign trade—remained in government hands. Eighty–five per cent of all industrial workers, therefore, continued to work in nationalized industry. Even the government plants were reorganized into separate combines or trusts, and ordered to operate on the basis of market principles. The government also invited foreign capital to invest in Russia and offered contracts to foreign technicians to come to Russia to teach their skillls to Soviet workers. The Ford Motor Company opened a tractor factory in Russia at this time, but in general, the attempt to secure foreign capital investment was unsuccessful.

The *NEP* brought new life to Soviet Russia. By 1927, agricultural production had surpassed the levels of 1913 and consumer goods were again in ample supply. Only the large nationalized plants had not regained their pre–war levels—but even they had made great progress.

The *NEP* was never intended to exist for any given length of time, however, and Soviet state planning for industrialization continued throughout the period of the NEP. The State Planning Commission *(GOSPLAN)*, which subsequently became responsible for the *Five Year Plans*, was actually set up on February 22, 1921, that is, immediately prior to the adoption of the *NEP*. Thus, one might say that Lenin ordered that planning would begin which would make it possible to eliminate the *NEP*, at the very same time he was approving the new program.

Constitutional Arrangements
It was also during the period of the *NEP* that the Union of Soviet Socialist Republics (USSR) came into being—though nearly all the territories included in the new USSR had been under Communist control since 1920. The first piece in the new constitutional structure was the *Russian Soviet Federated Socialist Republic (RSFSR)*, created in July 1918 when the Communists adopted the first Soviet constitution. As they extended their control to Byelorussia, the Ukraine and the Caucasus, these areas were given similar constitutions and the designation of Soviet Socialist Republic. Although they had signed treaties with the RSFSR, they remained technically independent republics. That situation created all kinds of legal and bureaucratic problems, so these four republics were brought together as the USSR in December 1922. The RSFSR institutions were then enlarged and somewhat modified to become "union" institutions. A new constitution for the USSR was drawn up and adopted in 1924. It was essentially a copy of the 1918 RSFSR constitution. These constitutional arrangements were extended to Central Asia in 1924 with the admission of the Turkmen and Uzbek Republics to the USSR. By 1936, five more republics had been created, raising the number of union republics to eleven.

In spite of these developments, it was interesting in 1945, when the United Nations was formed, the USSR insisted that Ukraine and Byelorussia were separate, sovereign nations, deserving a separate vote in the organization. The rationale given was that the Latin American nations were U.S.–"allied" (i.e. "puppet states") and the USSR should be allowed to balance this by espousing the theory that its areas were independent. Unwise minds acquiesced in this unreality at the time, but in 1991 it virtually became true.

CONSTITUENT REPUBLICS
OF
THE USSR

1. Russian S.F.S.R.	1922
2. Ukrainian S.S.R.	1922
3. Byelorussian S.S.R.	1922
Transcaucasian S.S.R.	1922
(Dissolved in 1936 into three	
constituent Republics, 4–6):	
4. Armenian S.S.R.	1936
5. Azerbaijan S.S.R.	1936
6. Georgian S.S.R.	1936
7. Uzbek S.S.R.	1924
8. Turkmen S.S.R.	1924
9. Tadzhik S.S.R.	1929
10. Kazakh S.S.R.	1936
11. Kirghiz S.S.R.	1936
12. Moldavian S.S.R.	1940
13. Lithuanian S.S.R.	1940
14. Latvian S.S.R.	1940
15. Estonian S.S.R.	1940

The Struggle For The Succession
Lenin was disabled by a major stroke in the fall of 1922, but lived on until January 1924, even returning briefly to his desk. The struggle for succession, however, began with his first stroke. The problem with succession in the Soviet Union was never (as some scholars insisted) certain. Rather, all power resided with the Communist Party, with all power concentrated at the top. The struggle was over who, if anyone or group, controlled the party.

Once Lenin's stroke removed him from the active leadership of the party, a struggle broke out among Lenin's chief lieutenants to determine who would succeed him. Lenin himself identified four possible successors—Trotsky, Kamenev, Zinoviev and Stalin. Trotsky appeared to be the most logical choice, for he was the only one of Lenin's associates whose contributions to the revolution rivaled those of Lenin. In fact, according to a document reported on by a Soviet historian, Lenin offered Trotsky the number two position in the government in 1922 but he turned it down. His reason, according to what he told the Central Committee in 1923, was that "we should not give our enemies the opportunity to say that our country was being ruled by a Jew."

As Lenin's deputy, Trotsky would have been in a good position to outmaneuver Stalin when Lenin's stroke set off a struggle for the succession. Instead, it was Stalin, Kamenev and Zinoviev who formed a *troika* (a three–member team) with the express purpose of excluding Trotsky from the leadership.

Trotsky had his own levers of power—he was Commissar for War and a member of the Politburo—and he decided to carry the battle to the Party Congress. As has been said, he was a great orator, and he expected to win over the delegates to his side. Two things made that impossible. First, Lenin had gotten the Party Congress to outlaw factions in 1921. This meant that Trotsky could not do any pre–Congress organizing. Second, Stalin had been made General Secretary in 1922, and this gave him control over selection of the delegates to the Party Congress. Trotsky found the battle had been lost before it had begun.

Stalin later fell out with Kamenev and Zinoviev and this led them in turn to form a "United Opposition" with Trotsky against Stalin. But Stalin's control over the administrative levers of the party allowed him to defeat all three. Trotsky was expelled from the Politburo and then from the party; in 1928 he was exiled to Siberia, then a year later deported to Turkey. Stalin rapidly filled the Politburo with his supporters and was well on his way to establishing his "dictatorship over the party."

The struggles between Stalin and Trotsky involved apparent differences over policy and these were also aired during the period. Trotsky was an advocate of world revolution and he also wanted to end the *NEP* and embark on a rapid, large–scale industrialization of Russia. Stalin developed a theory of "socialism in one country" and defended the *NEP*. These turned out to be differences without a difference, however, for Stalin adopted Trotsky's policy on industrialization immediately after eliminating Trotsky as a source of competition.

Foreign Policy During the NEP

When the communists first came to power in November 1917, their first consideration, as stated, was to end the war with Germany. They considered it an "imperialistic" war that they had opposed from the beginning, but mainly because Lenin recognized the need for peace in order to firm up his control over Russia. Because of Russia's withdrawal from the war under the Bolsheviks, France and England excluded Russia from the peacemaking at Versailles. Russia reciprocated by condemning the Treaty of Versailles and the League of Nations. Russia was thus hostile to the postwar settlement and the allies responded by attempting to isolate the new government of Russia, and all that it stood for, diplomatically.

This didn't bother the Russian communists too much, for it essentially coincided with their own perception that the capitalistic countries would inevitably be hostile to the new Soviet government. Further, Lenin was convinced that the world socialist revolution predicted by Marx would break out at any moment; he was primarily concerned with what the Russian communists could do to bring it about.

This led to the creation of the Communist International (*COMINTERN*) in March 1919 as a sort of coordinating body for the coming world revolution. Efforts such as these only convinced the British and French in their opinion that Soviet Russia was a radical nation that had to be quarantined internationally.

With the adoption of the *NEP* in 1921, however, the Russian policy began to change. The revolutionary tide in Europe had begun to ebb and Lenin opted for a policy which he called "peaceful coexistence." His emphasis was now on rebuilding the Russian economy and for that he wanted outside assistance. He therefore called for the establishment of trade and diplomatic relations with all countries willing to live in peace and offered to reopen the country to foreign capital investment.

The free market aspects of the NEP convinced many people that Russia was moving away from communism and that,

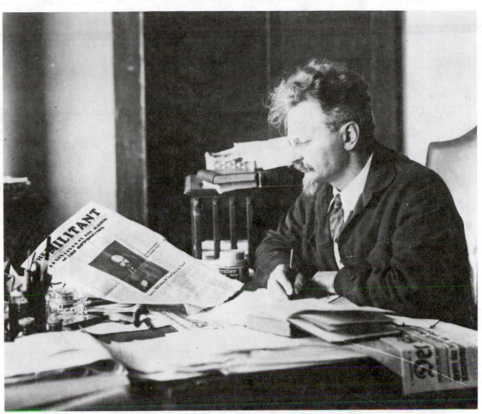

Leon Trotsky

too, had a good effect abroad. Trade talks took place with England and Germany in 1921, but neither nation wanted to be the first to open diplomatic relations with Russia.

The breakthrough came in 1922 when the allies called for an international conference to discuss reparations. The Soviets had to be invited because, according to the Treaty of Versailles, they were also entitled to reparations from Germany. The Genoa Conference failed to resolve the reparations issue, and this convinced the German delegates that they had nothing to lose by signing an agreement with Russia—particularly since the Soviets were willing to give up any claim to reparations from Germany. Over the weekend, the Russian and German delegates got together in the nearby town of Rapallo and signed an agreement reestablishing diplomatic relations between the two countries.

The Rapallo Agreement became the basis for a Russo–German relationship that was to continue throughout the 1920's and to serve the interests of both countries. What they had in common is that both were outcast nations who opposed the post–World War I settlement. Germany used the Russian connection to obtain concessions from England and France; for Russia, it served the purpose of ending its diplomatic exile. A major British trade delegation led by ex–Prime Minister Baldwin visited Russia in 1923, and this was followed by the resumption

of diplomatic relations between the two countries in 1924. Italy, Austria, Greece, Norway and Sweden followed almost immediately thereafter and before the year was out they had been joined by China, Denmark, Mexico and France. Of the major countries, only the United States continued to withhold diplomatic recognition. Although there were fairly extensive trade relations between the two countries, formal recognition did not come until 1933.

Building Socialism—The Five–Year Plans

Marx had written that "new, higher productive relationships never come into being before the material conditions for their existence have been brought to maturity within the womb of the old society itself." Lenin's revolution had brought the communists to power in an, at best, imperfectly industrialized country, one that obviously lacked the material conditions for communism, however. There could be no real guidance in Marx as how to remedy the lack, for he had never anticipated that this situation would arise. Lenin, guided by a reference in the *Communist Manifesto* to increasing "the total of productive forces as rapidly as possible" and, elsewhere, by references to **state planning** as the mechanism that would replace free competition as the driving force within a society under communism, did create the *Supreme Economic Council* in 1917 and the *State Planning*

Stalin: Ruler of Russia

duction was to go from 4.2 million tons to 10 million tons; coal from 35 million to 150 million tons; electric power from 5 million to 22 million kilowatt–hours. Some of these higher levels were to come from increased production at already existing plants, but it mostly involved new productive capacity.

In all, the plan called for the creation of 1,500 new enterprises and a capital construction budget of 64.5 billion rubles. Such funds were not available to the state under the conditions of the the *NEP* market economy. Stalin's solution was to phase out the NEP and to replace it with a "Command Model" which gave the state direct control over all economic activity. For the urban sector, this meant a return to the situation as it had existed under War Communism; for the villages it meant an end to individual agriculture and the forcible creation of collective farms.

The Collectivization of Agriculture

Collectivized agriculture had come to be considered an integral aspect of the economic system of almost all communist countries even though Marx, concerned with his proletariat and industry, had little to say about the organization of agriculture under communism. Some of the more pertinent references are to be found in the *Communist Manifesto*, where he referred to

> the bringing into cultivation of wastelands, and the improvement of the soil generally in accordance with a common plan . . .
> Establishment of industrial armies, especially for agriculture [and] . . .
> Combination of agriculture with manufacturing industries; gradual abolition of the distinction between town and country, by a more equitable distribution of the population over the country.

After the revolution, the communists took over the estates formerly owned by the Imperial family and organized them into state farms (*sovkhozy*).

These units, owned and operated by the state, were run like "factories in the field," with the peasants receiving daily wages. The object was to turn the peasants into proletariat in line with Lenin's theory, expressed in *The Agrarian Program of Russian Social Democracy*, that hired agricultural workers belonged to the "working class." The communists also had in mind to create examples of good farming methods which the peasants could follow.

The *sovkhozy* represented—and until Gorbachëv's agricultural reforms continued to represent—the communist ideal for organization of the countryside, but the obligation to pay year–around wages means that they are expensive to run. The communists therefore developed a

Commission (GOSPLAN) in 1921; he also linked the creation of large–scale industry with the electrification of the country. But he favored government efforts in this direction within the context of the *NEP*.

The policy of "socialist" industrialization was first proclaimed at the 14th Party Congress in late 1925 and was the first victory for Stalin's "socialism in one country." The measure did not come into effect immediately, however, for there were serious disagreements at the time as to how the industrialization was to be carried out. Two years later, the Party Congress ordered *GOSPLAN* to prepare a Five–Year Plan for expansion of the national economy. This first Five–Year Plan went into operation in 1928.

The purpose of the plan was to carry out a large–scale, state–directed rapid industrialization. The priority was on heavy industry. Specifically, the government embarked on the construction of steel mills, the opening of coal mines, building dams for production of hydro–electricity, building plants for the manufacture of tractors, agricultural machinery, automobiles, chemicals and a host of other products. The goals for increased production were impressive: steel pro-second type of farm organization which they called the *kolkhoz*. This, in theory, is a cooperative organization formed on a voluntary basis by a group of peasants. Land, livestock and farm machinery are pooled and then become the property of the *kolkhoz*.

The unit is farmed collectively by the group of peasants, and all income after expenses and taxes is shared on the basis of the total number of workdays performed by each member of the collective. The farmers were permitted an individual "private plot" of not more than an acre for use as a garden. They also could keep a cow, pigs and chickens.

In the 1920's, the government offered special subsidies and favorable tax treatment to those who would join a *kolkhoz*, but they were not popular with the peasants and, by 1928, only about one peasant in 60 had joined.

The first Five Year Plan called for 17.5% of the cultivated land to be organized into *kolkhozy*, which would have entailed persuading between 4 and 5 million peasants to join collective farms. There was strong resistance to the collectivization, however, and even the offer of seed, credit and the use of state–owned machinery brought a meager response, primarily among poorer peasants having little to lose. The communists, recalling how the peasants had frustrated them during the period of War Communism, decided to force the issue. Peasants opposing collectivization were labeled *kulaks* and were declared to be class enemies. Communist squads from the cities were sent into the countryside to seize the grain of the *kulaks*. Committees of poor peasants were also set up to cooperate with the government and report on their wealthier neighbors. In effect, the communists deliberately promoted class warfare in the countryside. At first, Stalin made it look as if the new measures of the government and party were only directed against the *kulaks* who were said to constitute less than 1 million out of a total of over 25 million peasant families. It was not long, however, before the bulk of the peasant population was involved. The progress of collectivization is shown by the following figures:

Year	Per Cent Collectivized
1928	1.7
Oct. 1929	4.1
Jan. 1930	21.0
Mar. 1930	58.0

A temporary halt was called in early 1930. Collectivization was slowed down and many *kolkhozy* were dissolved and the land was returned to individuals. This was done on Stalin's order after he criticized in a famous article the "dizziness with success" of those carrying out the forced collectivization. But the program was soon fully resumed and by the end of 1932, the percent collectivized had grown to 61.5. By the end of 1938, the 25 million peasant households were almost completely gathered into some 240,000 collective farms.

Because of extensive resistance, the former voluntary nature of the *kolkhoz* ceased and the farm manager, formerly elected by the membership, was selected by and subordinate to the higher Communist Party authorities. In addition, Machine–Tractors Stations (MTS's) directly controlled by the state, were set up in the countryside. The MTS got all the new farm machinery that was being manufactured and, using its own crews, it performed all of the mechanical labor on the collectives. It usually also contained the local Communist Party cell, so it exercised a control function in rural areas.

At the end of the harvest, each collective farm first delivered a set amount of its total production to the state at a controlled price, then paid off the MTS. Any remaining production was divided among the peasants. In many years, the amount remaining to be divided was relatively small and the peasants had to rely on produce raised on the garden plots to feed themselves.

In the 1950's the government began a program of consolidation of the collective farms and in the process many were transformed into state farms (*sovkhozy*). This process of transformation has continued. As of January 1987 there are 22,900 *sovkhozy* and 26,300 *kolkhozy*, with slightly over half the land being organized as *sovkhozy*. The MTS's were phased out in 1958 and since that time both the *sovkhozy* and the *kolkhozy* have had their own agricultural machinery.

The most recent innovation in agricultural organization is the "agro–industrial complex," which was introduced in the early 1970's. Today, there are more than 9,000 of them in existence. Most tend to specialize in the producing and processing of a single crop, such as grapes—which are then processed into wine or raisins. They have always been considered experimental, however.

There were several important reasons for the collectivization of agriculture, but the most important was that it allowed the Communist Party to gain control of the countryside in a predominantly rural nation and to force the peasantry to serve the interests of the Communist State. In one of his moments of candor, Stalin explained that since Russia had no colonies to exploit, it could only find the funds for industrialization by taking them from its own people. And, this is what was done.

During the period of the first Five–Year Plan, overall living standards diminished by an estimated 35%, with the peasantry suffering a greater drop than the urban population. But by pouring 35% of the gross national product into new productive facilities, the government managed to more or less meet the goals of the plan.

Second and third Five–Year Plans followed and continued the process of industrialization. Nearly all of the investment continued to be in heavy industry, however, so the Soviet people saw very little change in their standard of living. But the heavy pace wore out the country, and criticism of Stalin's harsh policies increased even among his supporters. His reaction was to launch a purge—massacre—that eventually enveloped all parts of Russian society.

Terror and Purges

Stalin resorted to terror not only to deal with temporary emergencies; terror became a permanent and prominent feature of his style of governing. Lenin and other Bolshevik leaders had used terror on a smaller scale, and they had employed a special organization to combat "counter–revolution"—the Cheka. It came into existence soon after the Bolsheviks seized power. The name of the organization was changed several times; known by its Russian initials, it has been the GPU, OGPU, NKVD, MVD, MGB and KGB. Its function was always the same—a highly secret police snooping into the private lives of the people and looking everywhere for saboteurs, spies and counter–revolutionaries. Abroad, it came to be used as a highly active espionage organization; more often than not, members of the Russian diplomatic corps were members of the organization. In this sphere of operations, agents had been "cultivated" for years to gain positions of prominence enabling them to spy on virtually every government in the world, particularly the U.S. and western powers. Bribes were commonplace, and the organization systematically tried (frequently with great success) to obtain technological advances of western nations through this method.

Stalin made the secret police a major instrument of ruthless purges. These mass "liquidations" of people were calculated to uproot every possible source of opposition to him and his dream of transforming Russia's social, economic and political structure.

The first targets of a systematic series of purges were the non–communist technicians and specialists, both Russian and foreign, who had been enlisted to help in the first Five–Year Plan. They were convicted with the help of manufactured evidence and forced confessions. This had the effect of terrorizing the people into redoubled efforts and at the same time provided an excuse for failure to achieve some of the goals of the plan. Another group subjected to terror and liquidation were those peasants who were accused of sabotaging the collectivization drive. The action was officially known as the "liquidation of the *kulaks* as a class," but it actually affected millions who could by no stretch of the imagination be called "rich" peasants. Besides the million or so who suffered death, there were others who filled forced–labor camps and were used in digging canals, mining gold and other enterprises under unbelievably inhuman conditions.

What is known as the *Great Purge* lasted from 1934 to 1938 and differed from earlier periods of Stalinist terror. This time it was directed against the leaders of the Communist Party. In Soviet terms, "purge" technically means removal from the party, not necessarily followed by criminal prosecution, exile or death. In reality, these severe consequences followed, especially in the *Great Purge*. The orgy of purges was triggered by the assassination of Sergei M. Kirov, a rising star in the party leadership and boss of the Leningrad (formerly Petrograd) party organization. It is now known that Stalin probably engineered the murder because Kirov was questioning the wisdom of continuing the break–neck tempo of change in Russia. He also was seen as a possible leader in a move to unseat Stalin, whom many were beginning to suspect of having lost his mind.

Purge at the Top

Although Stalin professed grief at Kirov's death, he used the occasion to unleash a vicious purge of party members, and particularly, party leaders. Most significantly, the Society of Old Bolsheviks, whose members had worked closely with Lenin, was dissolved in mid–1935. A "verification" of party membership cards was ordered, and some 10% were expelled; by 1936 at least one–quarter of the membership had been dropped from the party. A series of trials was held, and in 1936 sixteen Old Bolsheviks, including Zinoviev and Kamenev, were

convicted and executed. Michael P. Tomsky, leader of the trade unions, committed suicide. In early 1937, seventeen prominent communists, diplomats, economists and writers, including Karl Radek, who had closely collaborated with Lenin, were tried as alleged German and Japanese spies. They were also charged with other crimes that were ridiculous and most unlikely. At the trials, an attempt was made to "expose" Trotsky and to condemn his activities abroad as being directed against the USSR. Thirteen of the accused were shot and the other four sentenced to long prison terms—they were never heard from again. There was a brief press announcement in mid–1937 which told of the secret trial and execution of Army Marshal Michael Tukhachevsky and seven other leading generals of the Red Army. This was followed by a mass purge of officers which undoubtedly contributed to the poor showing of the Russian forces during the first part of Russia's involvement in World War II.

The climax of the purge trials came in 1938 when several former Politburo members, Nikolai Bukharin, Alexei Rykov and N.M. Krestinsky and distinguished provincial party leaders were liquidated. For good measure, Stalin included Yagoda, former head of the secret police and himself a major purger; he was executed as a spy. The period known as the *Yezhovschina*, after Yezhov, the new head of the secret police, lasted until late 1938, when Lavrenti Beria was named in turn to replace Yezhov (who simply disappeared).

One observer has aptly called this period "a reign of terror without parallel in Soviet history" in which "no sphere of Soviet life, however lofty, was left untouched." The destructive madness can only be explained by the assumption that Stalin was determined to eliminate once and for all any possible challenge to his personal power within the party leadership. He evidently believed that terror was a most useful instrument of power because it made sure that there were no entrenched or safe positions and therefore discouraged organized opposition to the will of the leader.

Many westerners, while accepting the fact of the purges, have been loath to believe that Stalin was directly responsible for them. They argued that the purges must have been the product of over-zealous subordinates who carried out the executions on their own. A new book published in the Soviet Union in 1989, *Stalin: Triumph and Tragedy*, answers those doubts. According to a review in the *Economist*, the author, Dmitri Volkogonov, "examined Stalin's personal papers and found his marginal comments or initials on thousands of execution lists and reports of mass repressions. His

scribbled remarks invariably call for harsher measures."

Forced Movements

Stalin, however, had a great talent for calling a sudden halt to the orgies of brutality unleashed by himself, to blame and liquidate his own agents and pose as a man of moderation, justice and mercy—a sort of father–protector. The start of World War II also made it possible for him to whip up patriotic fervor and to divert attention from his grisly pursuits.

During the second World War, the security organization was busy uprooting whole groups of the population whose loyalty to the Soviet regime was in question. Thus, the Crimean Tatars and the Volga Germans were forced to abandon their homes and move to Siberia. As the war progressed, other ethnic groups that had shown a willingness to collaborate with the Germans, or to engage in massive desertions from the Red Army, were also affected.

After the war, the main task of the NKVD, as it was then called, was to screen and "brainwash" Soviet citizens who had spent some time in Germany as prisoners of war or as forced labor. Many people also were deported from the areas acquired by the Soviet Union during and after the war.

Renewed watchfulness, rather than relaxation became the policy of Stalin as the memory of the war began to recede into the background and the "Cold War" became a reality. Following the death of A.A. Zhdanov, a close collaborator of Stalin, in 1948, a new purge was launched, particularly in Leningrad. A vicious campaign was launched against intellectuals, especially those of Jewish origin who were accused of being unpatriotic, "rootless cosmopolitans." Several Jewish writers were executed without a trial in 1952. Toward the end of Stalin's life, a monstrous general purge was apparently in the making. It began with the ominous "discovery" of a "Doctors' Plot" allegedly aimed at killing or undermining the health of leading Soviet officials.

In a "secret" speech in 1956, the Soviet leader Nikita Khrushchev stated that the doctors' plot was fabricated from beginning to end. Apparently it was part of a major scheme to eliminate the entire top rank of the party leadership, including such old faithfuls as V.M. Molotov and Marshal Klementi Voroshilov. As Khrushchev put it so dramatically, whenever he was summoned by phone to the Kremlin, he wasn't sure whether this meant promotion or death. This simple statement revealed the main purpose of Stalin's terror: to implant uncertainty.

Death of a Commissar (1928)   K. S. Petrov-Vodkin

Stalin's Cultural Counter–Revolution of the 1930's

Marx had very little to say about the implications of his philosophical system insofar as the performing and creative arts were concerned, though it follows that, since the creative arts must be part of the superstructure of society, they must, according to Marx's general theory, reflect the social and economic environment in which they appear. Marx did indicate that the proletariat would take over that which was good in the previous bourgeois society, but he also stipulated that much would be discarded—and he made a specific attack on the bourgeois family. In most respects, however, Marx had conventional tastes in art and literature.

Lenin was also rather ordinary in his tastes, but he never attempted to enforce his personal viewpoint on the new communist state and his first Commissar for Education specifically proclaimed the right of individual creation. Lenin never permitted the printing of anything anti–revolutionary or anti–communist, but with that limitation, there was considerable artistic freedom in Russia under Lenin. Among the excellent works produced in the 1920's were Alexander Blok's *The Twelve*, Mikhail Bulgatov's *The Master and Margarita*, Mikhail Sholokov's *Quiet Flows the Don*, poems by Boris Pasternak and Vladimir Mayakovsky and, finally the music of Dimitri Shostakovich.

In the schools, all sorts of experimental ideas were tried out—such as abolishing discipline—and courses in mathematics and chemistry, geography and physics were phased out in favor of vocational education. Traditional family values also came under attack as divorce became a mere registration process and the emancipation of women from home life was stressed. Religious training, traditionally also a function of the family, came under attack.

All of this came to an end in 1929 when Stalin, launching his Five–Year Plan, decided that the creative arts had to be mobilized in support of the industrialization program of the Communist Party.

Publishers were instructed on the types of books they were to publish. Specific "proletarian" goals were announced for art, music and literature. Experiments in style were condemned and creative workers were informed that what they produced had to be intelligible to the masses. Themes suggested to the creative artists included industrial construction, the fight against external aggression and internal subversion and the glory of life on collective farms.

Schools were reorganized and traditional courses reinstated. Examinations were reintroduced, and teachers were again given control in the classroom. Family life was again emphasized and the parents were instructed that they were responsible for training and disciplining their children.

Socialist Realism

Stalin also developed a specific theory for the arts which he called Socialist Realism—in his definition, a portrayal of reality in its revolutionary development

41

Militarized Communist Youth (1933)

A. N. Samokhvalov

in order to remake and re–educate the workers in the spirit of socialism was the goal of the state. What this meant in practice is that artists were to depict Soviet reality *as it would be, or should be,* rather than as it was. As one historian has expressed it, it was Communism with a smiling face. No morbid or pessimistic themes were allowed; music was to be melodic and life was to be portrayed as good and getting better.

The effect of these restrictions was pre- dictable. Soviet paintings tended to be either poster art in the revolutionary style or Soviet versions of *Saturday Evening Post* covers. Favorite themes were portraits of Lenin and Stalin; scenes from the Russian Revolution and Civil War; and land-

Kolhkoz Festival (1937)

S. V. Gerasimov

scapes that included factories or glamorized collective farms. Modern dance and jazz were outlawed and Soviet ballet returned to classical style. Composers such as Shostakovich and Prokofiev began to base their compositions on folk music. Abstract and semi–abstract art were out, and this led to a purge of paintings in Russian museums. Artists whose works were now labeled decadent included Vincent Van Gogh, Paul Gauguin, Georges Seurat, Henri Matisse, Pablo Picasso, Marc Chagall and Vasili Kandinsky. Their paintings were taken down from display and locked away in storerooms.

Soviet Foreign Policy In The 1930's

The Soviet Union established friendly relations with Germany as a result of the Rapallo Pact in 1922 and those relations continued after Stalin came to power. Trade between the two countries actually increased after 1928 as the Soviet Union began its Five–Year Plan. Political relations also remained good and in 1931 the two nations signed an agreement prolonging the Berlin Treaty on neutrality which the two nations had signed in 1926. The Soviet Union was willing to continue good relations even after Adolf Hitler came to power in 1933; it was Hitler's decision, not Stalin's, that changed the course of German–Soviet relations—and eventually led to a change in overall Soviet foreign policy.

The change of course by Hitler and his extreme anti–communist speeches convinced the Soviet Union that it would have to seek new friends. Russia had always been an opponent of the League of Nations, but when Nazi Germany left the League, the Soviets decided to join. Stalin appointed Maxim Litvinov, a Jew, as the new Soviet Foreign Minister—a move that must have been intended to irritate Hitler. Litvinov became a familiar figure at Geneva and the Soviet Union became a leading advocate of "collective security."

Although it appeared that the Soviet Union was interested in active opposition to Nazism and Fascism, Stalin's actual policies at the time can best be described as isolationism with a substantial amount of appeasement. This reflected his caution and his obsessive fear of having to fight alone against a united capitalist world. Appeasement was also shown towards Japan when it decided to assert its strength on the Asian mainland. Although Stalin encouraged the Chinese nationalists and communists alike to resist the Japanese, he was unwilling to expose the USSR to direct Japanese attack. To lessen the threat of conflict, he agreed to sell the Russian share in the Chinese Eastern Railway to the Japanese conquerors of Manchuria (technically to the puppet state of Manchukuo set up by the Japanese).

Lenin's Tomb, Red Square, Moscow

Although Stalin was determined to find allies in the West to oppose the growing menace of Nazi Germany, he proceeded here, too, with caution, to avoid involving the USSR too early in a conflict with Hitler. Attempts to enter into mutual assistance treaties to protect eastern Europe against German aggression failed mainly because of the objection of the independent–minded and then excessively self–assured Poles.

Stalin then turned to more distant potential allies. He signed agreements with France and Czechoslovakia in 1935. In the Spanish Civil War (1936–1939), the Soviet Union supported the loyalist side against the insurgents led by General Francisco Franco. At the same time, pressure was brought to bear on the Spanish communists not to adopt a radical program of reforms in order to avoid discouraging public opinion in the West, especially in France.

When Germany demanded that it be given a part of Czechoslovakia in 1938, France, following the appeasement–minded lead of England, made no move to assist the Czechs in spite of treaty obligations. The treaty between Russia and Czechoslovakia was worded in a way that obligated the USSR to give assistance only if France did likewise. In a meeting at Munich, the Western Powers yielded to Hitler's demands.

Attempts at closer and friendlier relations turned out, from Stalin's viewpoint, to be frustrating and unproductive. The leading Western governments were turning away from the League of Nations and the policy of collective security. They were tolerating one violation after another committed by Hitler, such as the reintroduction of the military draft and

occupation of the Rhineland Province which was supposed to remain demilitarized. The willingness of Great Britain and France to deal with Hitler at Munich, and their willingness to exclude the Soviet Union from those discussions, showed that the Western Powers were not taking Russia's power or its interests seriously. In addition, there was an extremely negative reaction in the West to the gruesome purges that Stalin was then conducting in the Soviet Union. Stalin probably realized that this Western revulsion would make any close cooperation between the Soviet Union and the Western democracies extremely difficult.

The actions of the Western Powers may have also led Stalin to suspect that they were hoping to encourage Hitler to attack the Soviet Union and thereby remove the threat from themselves. Some groups in the West did indeed nourish such hopes, although it was a crude falsification when Soviet propaganda claimed that this was the official and deliberate policy of the Western governments.

The seizure of the rest of Czechoslovakia by Germany in March 1939 created a serious crisis. Neither Great Britain nor France took any action, even though both had guaranteed Czechoslovakia's remaining territories. On the other hand, Britain's Prime Minister Chamberlain did make it clear in his Birmingham speech of March 17 that his country would resist any further act of aggression by Germany. The position of the Soviet Union was spelled out by Stalin in a famous speech to the 18th Party Congress in which the Soviet dictator declared that the Soviet Union was not willing to "pull the chestnuts out of the fire" for the benefit of others.

Hitler could expect war with Great Britain, and possibly France, if he pursued his objectives on Poland, but this did not deter him. On the other hand, the position of the Soviet Union now became all important. Germany would need to come to an understanding with the Soviet Union before it could invade Poland.

As the crisis deepened, the Soviet Union became involved in two sets of negotiations: with the French and British on one hand and with Nazi Germany on the other. Stalin had to ask himself whether an alliance with Great Britain and France would deter Hitler—or whether it would only mean that the Soviet forces would be exposed to the fury of a German attack from the very beginning of an armed conflict.

The Nazi–Soviet Non–Aggression Pact

An offer from the German side looked much more interesting: the division of Poland between Germany and Russia. From Stalin's selfish point of view, this offered the opportunity to stay out of the war and to be rewarded by Hitler with part of soon–to–be defeated Poland. The Germans were also willing to recognize the Baltic area as belonging to the Soviet Union's "sphere of influence."

The agreement between the Soviet Union and Germany was announced on August 23, 1939, and came as a shock and surprise to the world. It was, however, the most logical choice among the alternatives facing Stalin at the time. Soviet–Polish relations had never been particularly good, and the Soviet Union had no substantial reason to come to Poland's assistance. Moreover, what Stalin feared most of all was to be dragged into a war against Germany by Great Britain and France, and then be forced to bear the brunt of that war while those countries sat on the sidelines. Hitler's invasion of Poland came on September 1, 1939, its purpose, in the language of the war order, "to destroy Polish military strength and create, in the East, a situation which satisfies the requirements of defense." The end was not long in coming. The Polish forces collapsed under the onslaught of the first German *Blitzkrieg*. The fighting was mostly over by September 17 when Soviet troops entered from the east to claim the Soviet share of the spoils. The last member of the Polish Government had already left the country to seek refuge abroad. Stalin then claimed that his troops were entering a no–man's land and even had the

nerve to suggest to Hitler that he be permitted to state that Soviet troops were entering the former Polish territory in order to save the largely Ukrainian and Byelorussian population of the area *from the Germans!*

The Soviet side also suggested a change in the terms of the secret agreement. They wanted less of the territory of Poland than originally was given them in the deal, and asked instead to have Lithuania included in the Soviet "sphere" along with the other Baltic republics, Latvia and Estonia. They soon imposed agreements on the three providing for the stationing of Soviet troops on their territory.

Similar pressure was exerted on Finland, but here the Russians encountered determined opposition to their demands and had to resort to war in the winter of 1939–1940. Although the Finns first managed to stop the Soviet offensive and in doing so inflict embarrassing losses, the small country was eventually forced to make peace with the Soviet Union and to submit to some of its demands.

The use of military force by the biggest country in the world against the proud and popular Finns added to the bad reputation the Soviet Union had in the West, where resentment had been aroused by the Soviet deal with Hitler. Unrealistic ideas of coming to the assistance of Finland almost resulted in the involvement of France and England in war *against the Soviet Union*, which was then looked upon as an "ally" of Adolf Hitler. Actually, Stalin was fighting his own war, with an eye toward the future, taking up military positions directed against possible German aggression.

German troops swept across France, Belgium and the Netherlands in record time in the spring of 1940. This swift military success in the West disturbed Stalin, who would have preferred to see a long involvement of German troops on the Western front. He began nervously to tighten his hold on the areas gained in 1939. The Baltic republics were forced to join the Soviet Union. Romania was asked to cede the province of Bessarabia, taken from Russia during World War I, and parts of Bukovina, about which there had been no clear arrangement with the Germans in 1939. The Russians protested the entry of German troops into Finland and domination of the remaining Romanian territory. Hitler, flushed with success, began to feel that he had paid too high a price in 1939 for Stalin's neutrality.

Soviet Entry Into World War II

In late 1940 and early 1941, relations between the Soviet Union and Germany acquired an air of unreality. Stalin, frozen with fear, was alternately appeasing and teasing Hitler, while the *Führer*, already scheming to crush the Soviet Union, tried to lull the latter into believing that he was willing to share the spoils of the British Empire, soon to become available. The Soviet Foreign Minister, V.M. Molotov, was presented with such a proposal during a visit to Berlin in late 1940, but the Soviets took the position that it was too early to discuss the cutting up of the hide of the British lion.

By the autumn of 1940, Hitler was in a quandary. His invasion of England, Operation Sea Lion, had to be aborted when his air force was unable to gain control of the air over England. Now America was throwing its support behind England, and that support was sure to grow. There was no immediate threat in the west but also no chance to bring the British to the negotiating table. Was this the time to turn on the Soviet Union and, in another lightning onslaught, destroy his long-term foe in the east? On December 18 he answered that question by signing Operation Barbarossa "to crush Soviet Russia in a quick campaign even before the end of the war against England." This was contrary to the advice of his top military advisors, who foresaw that Germany would be stretched too thinly to be successful on *all* fronts.

It mattered very little what the Russians did at that point. However, Stalin's behavior immediately prior to the German attack was erratic, alternating between appeasement and provocation. It has been said that Stalin refused to believe the reports of an impending German invasion supposedly because he "liked" and "trusted" Hitler. This cannot be taken seriously because Stalin neither liked nor trusted *anyone*. His problem was serious—the Soviet Union had damaged its reputation in the deal with Hitler in 1939. It could now be accepted as an ally of the West only if it became the victim of unprovoked aggression by Hitler. Therefore, Stalin was forced to let the Germans fire the first shot. Nevertheless, his unwillingness to prepare for battle later caused millions of unnecessary Russian deaths.

His failure to improve the combat readiness of the Soviet armed forces exposed millions of soldiers to slaughter and capture in the very first weeks of the war launched by Hitler on June 22, 1941. Even Soviet sources now admit that Stalin "failed to take full advantage" of the time gained by the Soviet Union as a result of the 1939 agreement.

Ally of the West

Hitler's fateful decision to attack the Soviet Union changed Russia's international position literally overnight. England's Winston Churchill, though a life-long enemy of communism, welcomed the Soviet Union as an ally of isolated and threatened England. With admirable precision and honesty, he stated "If I heard that Hitler invaded Hell, the least I could do would be to say a few nice words about the Devil." The United States, not yet engaged in the war, also promised aid to the Soviet Union. However, there were serious doubts in the West about Russia's ability to resist Hitler's offensive for a very long time. The speedy advance of German troops seemed to justify gloomy predictions. Although it was felt that Russia should be supported in its struggle against Germany because it was tying down masses of German troops, the Soviet Union appeared not to be an important factor to reckon with at the time.

In this period the Russians yielded to British pressure to reestablish relations with the Polish government–in–exile located in London. However, even at the darkest time of their military fortunes, the Russians made it clear that their postwar plans included retention of all the territorial gains made during the period of "friendship" with Hitler from 1939 to 1941.

The German offensive consisted of three attacking forces whose destinations were Leningrad, Moscow and the Caucasus. It achieved tremendous successes at the beginning as Soviet defense units at the border disintegrated and German mechanized armies swept into Russia, surrounding and conquering whole Russian armies. Stubborn Russian defenses temporarily halted the German armies at Pskov and Smolensk, but reinforced German armies eventually overcame the Soviet defenders and continued their advance eastward. In the meanwhile, Kiev was captured on September 19th. In the north, the siege of Leningrad also began in September; but the Germans were not able to cut off the city entirely, so that it continued to be reprovisioned from outside. The siege eventually lasted for 600 days before it was broken by a German retreat.

The 1941 offensive ended with the German Central Front just 35 miles west of Moscow, while in the south, the German armies had overrun the entire Ukraine and reached as far east as the Donets River. Hitler was not satisfied with the extent of the advance, however. Enraged that neither Leningrad nor Moscow had been captured, he dismissed his chief generals and assumed personal command himself.

This was a gift for the Russians—Hitler, although occasionally capable of brilliant insights, was not a military strategist. In 1942, for example, he held his forces on the north and center on the defensive while he attempted to make a breakthrough in the south. His original goal was the oil of the Caucasus, an entirely logical one under the circumstances. But in June he turned his armies directly east and opened a drive toward Stalingrad (since renamed Volgograd), a city of no particular strategic significance. Stalingrad was reached in September 1942, after slow progress in the face of heavy Russian resistance.

In late 1942 a new offensive began. It brought disaster to the German forces apparently made worse by panic among Hungarian, Romanian and Italian troops fighting alongside Hitler's armies. The German Sixth Army was soon encircled, but Hitler ordered the 285,000 men trapped by the Soviets not to retreat. Attempts to relieve the army failed and the 90,000 survivors of the battle of Stalingrad finally surrendered to the Russians on January 30, 1943. This was one of the major turning points of the war.

Hitler did not realize or didn't care that he had fallen into the same trap as did Napoleon when he attempted to take Russia. The faithful ally of the Northern slavs had again come to the rescue— "Mother Winter." Not only did this friend cause countless deaths by freezing among the German troops, few of whom had buildings in which to take refuge, when the spring thaw came, the whole land turned to a sea of mud in which a mechanized army could only become bogged down.

After Stalingrad

The reversal of Soviet military fortunes created an entirely new political situation. Stalin made the utmost use of the delays in Anglo–American plans to open a western front in Europe. A promise had been made to Stalin that this would happen in 1942, but he was soon informed that there would be no second front during that year or the next. Lend–lease supplies began to flow into Russia in very large amounts from the United States at the cost of many lives lost to German submarines. However, the Russians developed the feeling that they had managed to live through the darkest moments of the war largely by their own efforts and that their Western allies were deliberately dragging their feet.

As soon as the military situation eased, Stalin began to test the intentions of his allies. The question of the status of Poland was used for this purpose and the Polish government–in–exile actually played into Stalin's hands.

The Germans announced the discovery of a mass grave in the Katyn Forest in the spring of 1943, containing the bodies of thousands of Polish army officers who had fallen into the hands of the Russians in September 1939. They had been shot in the back of the head, a standard method of execution practiced by the Soviet secret police. Alarmed by the discovery, the Poles in London asked for an investigation by the International Red Cross. Stalin accused the Polish government–in–

"The Big Three:" Stalin, Roosevelt and Churchill at Tehran

exile of aiding German propaganda and broke off diplomatic relations. Soon a new organization, the Union of Polish Patriots, was formed from among Polish refugees in the Soviet Union. This became the nucleus of the Soviet–sponsored Lublin Government, which was installed in power by the Soviet army after the liberation of Poland.

Wartime Conferences and the Occupation of Eastern Europe

The Soviet military occupation of Eastern Europe and the Soviet decision to set up communist governments in the area are usually considered to be important factors in the origins of the Cold War that developed between the Soviet Union and its western allies after World War II. The matter is somewhat more complex, however.

First of all, there were always differences between the Soviet Union and its allies over Soviet territories obtained as a result of the Non–Aggression Pact which Stalin signed with Hitler in 1939. In particular, neither the United States nor Great Britain ever recognized the incorporation of Latvia, Estonia, Lithuania and Bessarabia into the Soviet Union.

When the United States and Great Britain drew up the Atlantic Charter in 1941, setting forth their wartime goals, they stipulated there were to be no territorial changes without the freely registered approval of the people involved.

They also promised to respect the right of all peoples to determine the form of government under which they would live. When, six weeks later, the Soviet Union gave its approval of the Atlantic Charter, American policymakers accepted that as a basis for cooperation. Toward the end of 1941, although the United States was not yet at war, it extended a billion dollar "lend–lease" grant to the Soviet Union for the purchase of supplies in the United States. By the end of the war, the United States had shipped to the Soviet Union approximately $11 billion worth of equipment and supplies.

Presumably the Soviet Union signed the Atlantic Charter because it wanted the "lend–lease" agreement with the United States and it would have been for the same reason that it agreed to the incorporation of the Atlantic Charter into the Declaration of the United Nations which the U.S., Great Britain, the U.S.S.R. and 23 other nations signed on January 1, 1942. That it never intended to apply the terms of the Atlantic Charter to territories annexed in 1939–1940 can be seen by the fact that it continued to pressure the U.S. and England to recognize the incorporation of these territories into the U.S.S.R. after signing the Atlantic Charter.

Another factor was Franklin D. Roosevelt's opposition to balance of power politics and spheres of influence. The United States was committed to allowing the peoples of Eastern Europe to set up their own freely elected government and FDR attempted to bind his allies to a similar position. What he forgot, however, is that Nazi Germany's defeat would bring about a power vacuum in Eastern Europe and, *one way or the other*, that power vacuum would be filled. But perhaps the most important factor influencing American foreign policy at this juncture was FDR's belief that Stalin didn't want anything for himself in Eastern Europe. As he commented to Ambassador Bullitt just prior to the Tehran Conference, "I have just a hunch that Stalin doesn't want anything but security for his country, and I think that if I give him everything I possibly can and ask nothing in return, *noblesse oblige* he won't try to annex anything and will work for a world of democracy and peace."

Roosevelt's "hunch" seemed to be confirmed when he, Churchill, and Stalin met in Tehran in November 1943, for it was here that the "Big Three," in a general declaration which they drew up, promised an enduring peace in which "all the peoples of the world may live free lives untouched by tyranny and according to their varying desires and their consciences."

In delineating spheres of military operations, however, Romania, Bulgaria, Hungary, Yugoslavia, Czechoslovakia, Poland and Finland were designated areas of Soviet operations. If Roosevelt was right about Stalin, it wouldn't matter; but if he was not, he was putting his stamp of approval on whatever policy Stalin chose to carry out in Eastern Europe. Churchill, recognizing the potential danger in such an arrangement, pushed for an allied invasion up through the Balkans, but he was overruled.

Soviet troops began entering Eastern Europe in August 1944; by the time of the Yalta Conference in early 1945, Soviet armies occupied Romania, Bulgaria, Poland and parts of Hungary and Czechoslovakia. The Yalta Conference was primarily concerned with the problem of Germany, and it was at this time allied zones of occupation were established. The Soviet Zone would eventually become the German Democratic Republic.

Poland was also considered. Its eastern and western borders were established; the Communist Provisional Government was to be enlarged by the inclusion of democratic leaders from abroad, and the broadened Provisional Government was to hold "free and unfettered elections as soon as possible on the basis of universal suffrage and secret ballot. The rest of Eastern Europe was covered by a general declaration that other people of the region would be encouraged to

> form interim governmental authorities broadly representative of all democratic elements in the population and pledged to the earliest possible establishment through elections of governments responsive to the will of the people.

It has often been charged that the United States essentially yielded to Soviet demands concerning territorial matters and the composition of the government of postwar Poland because it was eager for Soviet military assistance in the Far East. It is true that Stalin agreed at Yalta to enter the war against Japan within 90 days of victory in Europe. It is also true that an American military study had estimated that, without Soviet assistance, the war against Japan would last until 1947 and might mean another million American lives. The study obviously did not take the atomic bomb development into consideration, and it is possible that Roosevelt didn't either. On the other hand, the essential fact is that the American armies were only approaching the Rhine River at the time when Soviet troops were in western Poland and approaching the German border at a point much closer to the main prize: Berlin. Political and strategic decisions made much earlier meant that the United States could only hope that the Soviet Union shared American perceptions about the future of Eastern Europe.

The Cold War

The Cold War essentially began when the Soviet Union, in occupation of East-ern Europe, began to implement its intentional misunderstanding of the various wartime agreements. The problem arose over the differing Soviet and western Allied understandings of such terms as "democratic," "free elections" and "governments friendly to the Soviet Union." The United States, recognizing the Soviet Union's concern for its security, agreed that the Russians could demand governments "friendly to the Soviet Union" in Eastern Europe. The problem was that Stalin believed that any non–communist government would be *hostile* to the Soviet Union. The same thing applied to such terms as "democratic" and "free elections." According to communist dogma, both terms applied only to states in which communism prevailed.

Stalin was probably not certain that his Western Allies would permit him to communize Eastern Europe. He also recognized that it was necessary to mobilize as much popular support as possible for the new regimes he was installing. That is why "Popular Front" governments were installed nearly everywhere in Eastern Europe in the beginning and why they were normally headed by a non–communist. This transition phase lasted approximately three years. In the meantime, Soviet–Allied relations worsened as it became clear just what Stalin was doing.

It is difficult to pinpoint an exact date for the beginning of the Cold War, but revisionist historians who suggest that President Truman's suspension of "lend–lease" assistance to the Soviet Union in May 1945 was motivated by anti–Soviet feelings place it too early. Actually, Truman was merely following the mandate of Congress, which in passing the original legislation, specified that it would continue only for the duration of the war. Moreover, a quarrel over the political make–up of the new Polish Government was resolved just prior to the Potsdam Conference (July 1945) when the U.S. and Great Britain extended diplomatic recognition in return for Stalin's promise to add non–communist elements to it.

At Potsdam (a suburb of Berlin), the U.S. and Great Britain threatened to withhold recognition from the communist–dominated governments of Romania and Bulgaria unless they were enlarged to include a broader political spectrum. But on the major topic, Germany, the Big Three were in general agreement on policies of disarmament and de–Nazification. The U.S. and Great Britain also agreed that the Soviets were entitled to reparations from Germany, although they insisted that the Soviets extract them primarily from their own zone of occupation. That may have been hard on the East Germans, but did not affect the Soviets unduly.

Averill Harriman, who was U.S. Am-bassador to Russia at the time, dates the beginning of the Cold War to a conversation he had with Stalin in the fall of 1945. Stalin had apparently just come from a meeting of the Politburo, and he told Harriman that "we have decided to go it alone." Stalin expanded on this theme in a speech which he gave in early 1946, just prior to new elections to the Supreme Soviet. It was a long speech, but its essence was that the alliance between the Soviet Union and the western democracies had been for limited purposes—to defeat fascism—and now that the purpose had been accomplished there was no longer any basis for cooperation. From now on, the emphasis would be on strengthening the "Soviet social order," which had established its superiority over any non–Soviet form of social organization.

If we place Stalin's comments into the context of the widespread destruction that occurred in the Soviet Union during World War II, they take on a more specific meaning. Large parts of the country had been occupied by foreign troops, and the effects of the actual fighting plus the Soviets' *scorched earth* policy during the retreat of 1941 and the willful destruction of the Germans as they retreated in 1943–44, left very little intact in the western part of Russia. In addition, an estimated 20 million Soviet citizens had died during the war—seven million of them in action. Even though the blame for much of this destruction is historically that of Stalin, it was realized that the rebuilding of Russia would require tremendous sacrifices on the part of the Soviet people. Some who lacked a sufficient "proletarian consciousness" might be *seduced* by capitalist promises of a better life. This explains why, as Alexander Solzhenitsyn has documented, hundreds of thousands of Soviet soldiers and prisoners of war were shipped off to labor camps in the GULAG Archipelago rather than being treated as heroes. They had become ideologically contaminated because they had seen and might bear witness to what Soviet propaganda endlessly continued to deny—*that even in devastated Germany the people were better off than those living in the land of the victorious proletariat.*

It also helps to explain Stalin's policy toward Eastern Europe. If these economies could be tied to the Soviet economy, exploitation would make the rebuilding much easier. To accomplish this, trade agreements and mutual friendship and alliance treaties with the Eastern European countries were forged as soon as new governments were formed, with the purpose of reorienting their trade toward the Soviet Union. By 1947, a third of Russia's imports were coming from Eastern Europe, and the figure continued to grow thereafter. Slowly, Eastern Europe was being cut off and isolated from Western Europe. When Winston Churchill made his famous speech stating that a curtain of iron had been erected between East and West by Stalin in 1946, he was partly referring to this occurrence.

Though disturbed by developments in Eastern Europe, the United States continued to maintain an ambivalent attitude toward the Soviet Union. Something of a break in that pattern came in March 1947 when President Truman, in a speech to Congress, enunciated a policy toward Greece and Turkey that subsequently became known as the "Truman Doctrine." The Greek government was fighting a communist insurgency supported by Bulgaria and Yugoslavia, while Turkey was under pressure from the Soviet Union to cede certain frontier districts. In Truman's words, it was to be "the policy of the United States to support free people who are resisting attempted subjugation by armed minorities or by outside pressure." Neither communism nor the Soviet Union was mentioned, but the meaning was clear.

Three months later, Secretary of State George Marshall, speaking at the Harvard commencement, offered a broader response, insisting that:

> . . . Our policy is directed not against any country or doctrine but against hunger, poverty, desperation and chaos . . . governments, political parties or groups which seek to perpetuate human misery in order to profit . . . politically will encounter the opposition of the United States . . .

He thus spelled out a policy which later became known as the "Marshall Plan." The purpose of this was to assist Europe in the restoration of its destroyed economies, and it was to be open to all European nations. For a short while, it appeared that the Soviet Union was interested in the American offer, and Foreign Minister Molotov even attended a preliminary meeting in Paris to discuss details. Czechoslovakia and Poland also expressed their interest. Then Molotov abruptly denounced the Marshall Plan as an attack on the sovereignty of Europe and announced that the Soviets would not participate after all. Czechoslovakia and Poland withdrew their applications as well. As American economic assistance began to pour into Western Europe, the gulf between East and West widened even further.

The Soviet Union, recognizing that a resurgent Western Europe might prove such an attraction that it would weaken the Soviet hold over Eastern Europe, decided to tighten its controls by organizing the Council for Mutual Economic Assistance (CMEA). While Stalin was alive, the CMEA was used primarily as a tool to exploit the Eastern European economies. After 1953, however, it became more of a coordinating body to facilitate economic planning and effort.

A second reaction to the Marshall Plan was the creation of a successor organization to the COMINTERN, which had been dissolved in 1943. The Communist Information Bureau (COMINFORM) came into being in the fall of 1947 with its headquarters in Belgrade, Yugoslavia. This turned out to be a poor choice—a scant year later, Yugoslavia was expelled from the COMINFORM upon Stalin's orders. Its offense: Marshal Tito's objection to Moscow's intermeddling in Yugoslavia's domestic economic affairs.

Stalin would have driven Tito from power had he been able to. But Stalin had no Soviet troops stationed in Yugoslavia and the Yugoslavian Communist Party remained loyal to Tito. And, compounding his treason, Tito turned to the United States for support; Stalin did not dare risk sending in his armies. Concerned that there might be other Titos, Stalin ordered a purge of other communist parties of Eastern Europe. Individuals suspected of "national deviationism"—putting the interests of one's own country above the interests of the Soviet Union—were removed from office and sometimes put on trial and executed. As the number of executions grew, the American distaste for what was going on inevitably also grew, and so American–Soviet relations deteriorated even further.

The year 1948 also brought a direct Western–Soviet confrontation over Berlin, when Stalin cut off all land access routes between West Germany and Berlin. The Western response was an "airlift" that kept West Berlin supplied with food and fuel for nearly a year until Stalin lifted the blockade.

The Berlin Blockade was a double failure, for it, plus the communist *coup d'etat* in Czechoslovakia, convinced the West that a more long–term response was needed. The North Atlantic Treaty Organization (NATO) came into being in April 1949 with General Dwight D. Eisenhower as Supreme Commander of the Allied Forces in Europe. Agreement was also reached on merging of the three western zones of occupation of Germany, and in May 1949 the Federal Republic of Germany came into being. Conceding defeat, the Soviet Union ended the Berlin Blockade in May 1949. Five months later, it organized a separate government for its own zone of occupation, which became the German Democratic Republic.

As the European situation turned into a stalemate, Soviet interest began to turn to the Far East. Here, the victory of Mao Zedong's communists and the establishment of the People's Republic of China seemed to open new vistas for communist expansion. In mid–1949, *Pravda*, the Soviet Communist Party newspaper, carried a long article by Liu Shaoqi, one of the main leaders of the Chinese revolution, reporting on Asian communist parties. The article explicitly endorsed armed struggle as the primary tactic to be pursued by them. Since the article was followed by several similar articles, it was evident that the party line on armed struggle had changed. Thus, when the communist government of North Korea launched an invasion of the south in June 1950, the United States assumed that it was operating under Soviet direction. The United States, therefore, brought the matter before the Security Council of the United Nations, which declared the North Korean invasion to be an act of aggression and called upon all members of the United Nations to join in a united "police action" to defend South Korea. This action was possible because the Soviet delegate had been boycotting meetings of the Security Council since January 1950 in protest of the failure to seat communist China.

The Korean "police action" turned into a full–scale war that lasted until after Stalin's death in March 1953. It soon became obvious that neither side would be permitted to resolve the issue by force, but too much prestige had been invested on both sides to allow for a compromise. News of the gray–haired old dictator's death was therefore greeted with relief, for it was hoped that a compromise now might be reached. The armistice came approximately four months later—on July 27, 1953.

The Post–Stalin Era

The Struggle for Succession

The announcement of Stalin's death came on March 5, 1953. It was a strange announcement, for it spoke of the need to prevent "any kind of disorder and panic." The disarray in the leadership which this indicates derived from the fact that Stalin had never permitted his lieutenants any independent authority and squelched any discussion of who his successor would be; now, for the first time, they were on their own. In his memoirs, Nikita Khrushchëv reminisced about this period:

Right up until his death Stalin used to tell us, "You'll see, when I'm gone the imperialistic powers will wring your necks like chickens." We never tried to reassure him that we would be able to manage. We knew it wouldn't do any good.

The disorder did not last very long, but it did result in some policy reversals in the first few days. Georgi Malenkov, who was silently looked upon as Stalin's logical successor, was permitted to succeed to both of Stalin's positions—General Secretary of the Central Committee of the Communist Party and Chairman of the Council of Ministers—but after one day he gave up the position of General Secretary for unexplained reasons. Nikita Khrushchëv unofficially got the top party position. It was obvious that the *Presidium* (the new name for the Politburo, adopted at the 19th Party Congress in 1952), was attempting to end the rise of a new "sole leader," and had decided to split the top party and state offices. Malenkov chose to remain as Chairman of the Council of Ministers— apparently because he believed that the more immediate power position lay with that title. For awhile, it appeared that he had made the correct choice, for in the party, collective leadership of the entire Presidium was stressed while Malenkov was treated in the Soviet press as spokesman for the regime.

A recent Soviet history characterizes this period as one of "restoration of Leninist norms and the collective principle in the work of the Party and state." There was actually a great deal of agreement in the Presidium about the need for modifications in the system. Some of these changes were inevitable. Stalin had concentrated all decision–making in his own hands—now, some decentralization was in order. The Central Committee, which had fallen into disuse, was revived and regular meetings scheduled. The various ministries were given a greater say in decision–making and there was a great deal of talk about streamlining and rationalizing the ministerial and planning bureaucracies.

In foreign affairs, the turn away from confrontation that led to an armistice in Korea also had an effect on Eastern Europe. In East Germany, the political leadership, concerned about the lack of domestic support, announced a "New Course" aimed at reducing popular dissatisfaction. But before the "New Course" could be put into action, worker demonstrations and strikes broke out in East Berlin and in other cities. When Soviet tanks were brought in to quell the demonstrations, the workers rebelled and had to be put down with force. June 17th, the date of the workers' rebellion in East Berlin, is still commemorated as a legal holiday in the Federal Republic of Germany.

In July 1953 the Central Committee met in a plenary session to hear that Lavrenti Beria, head of the Secret Police and a top member of the party leadership since 1939, had been arrested and subsequently executed. The charge was that he had been attempting a bid for total power based on his control of the Secret Police. To forestall such an attempt in the future, the Secret Police were brought firmly under party control by taking them out of the Ministry of the Interior and creating a separate Committee for State Security (KGB) directly accountable to the Presidium. The powers of the KGB were also somewhat restricted by the issuance of new regulations specifying when arrests could be made. Beria was to be the last leading communist to be physically eliminated after losing in a struggle for power. Since then, the maximum penalty has been expulsion from the party and subsequent "non– person" status. Ironically, following his execution, Beria, a well–known ruthless, cold–blooded killer, was lamented by some of the more naïve U.S. press as a "good guy" who was an innocent victim of ruthless communists.

The Beginning of the Khrushchëv Era

In September, the first indication that Khrushchëv might be a claimant for power came when it was announced that the title of the chief party post had been changed from *General* Secretary to *First* Secretary and that Khrushchëv had been confirmed in this office. He now became a vigorous advocate of strength ening the party after years of Stalin's neglect.

The first sign that there were policy differences between Malenkov and Khrushchëv also appeared in September—though in the carefully phrased way in which Party speeches are made, but this was easy to see only in retrospect. In

Nikita Khrushchëv

August, Malenkov had addressed the Supreme Soviet setting forth the future direction of the regime. Bidding to reverse Stalin's traditional emphasis on heavy industry, Malenkov set forth a program calling for additional investment in the areas of consumer goods and agriculture. His theme was that people had a "right to demand consumer goods of high quality."

Khrushchëv, addressing a plenum of the Central Committee of the party after having been installed as First Secretary, argued that something had to be done for agriculture, but rejected a change in investment priorities to finance it.

The battle continued in 1954 and, in fact, became clearer. Khrushchëv wanted to retain the priority of heavy industry and wanted to pour additional funds into modernizing defense—while greatly increasing agricultural production. He proposed to accomplish this through what later became known as the "virgin lands" program. This involved opening up for cultivation huge quantities of steppeland in Kazakhstan in Central Asia that had traditionally been considered too dry for normal agriculture. Khrushchëv's program was approved by a Central Committee plenum in March 1954; it was started in that year, but primarily was carried forward in 1955.

In the meantime, Khrushchëv had continued his attacks against Malenkov and managed to get him removed as Chairman of the Council of Ministers in early 1955. His replacement was Marshal Nikolai Bulganin. Khrushchëv had won a victory, but it was only partial. Bulganin belonged to the same faction on the Presidium as Malenkov.

Although it is largely coincidental, the period of joint leadership by Bulganin and Khrushchëv is associated with a number of breakthroughs in the foreign policy area. Calling for a resurrection of the old Leninist doctrine of "peaceful coexistence," the team of "B and K," as they became known to the West, engaged in a number of spectacular trips abroad, the most notable of which was a trip to Belgrade, Yugoslavia, to heal the breach with Marshal Tito. In a gesture to the West, the Soviet Union also agreed to end the joint military occupation of Austria, which regained its independance in 1955. This was the first withdrawal of Soviet troops without leaving a communist regime behind since World War II.

The good feeling engendered by the Soviet action in Austria was an important factor in producing the first meeting of major heads of government since the Potsdam Conference in 1945. This was the Geneva Summit of 1955. No specific agreements were reached but there was an exchange of views on German rearmament and reunification, European security, disarmament and the improve-

ment of East–West contacts. The major Soviet proposal dealt with the opposing military alliances. It offered to disband the newly created (in May 1955) Warsaw Pact in return for the disbanding of NATO and the withdrawal of all "foreign troops" from the European continent. The proposal was so obviously one-sided that the West was unwilling to even consider it seriously. The summit was valuable from the Soviet point of view, however, for it signified that the West was willing to accept the Soviet Union as an equal in diplomatic discussions.

The 20th Party Congress, which met in February 1956, represented a new high for Khrushchëv, for it confirmed that he had taken control of the party apparatus. It also represented a new foreign policy departure, for it was here that Khrushchëv first articulated the view that war between capitalism and communism was no longer "fatalistically inevitable"— the view *always* held by Stalin. Khrushchëv justified his position on the basis of the emergence of socialism into a world system which made possible a world-wide peaceful transition to communism.

It appears, however, that the real basis for the change was Khrushchëv's recognition that the existence of nuclear weapons had changed the basic nature of war and rendered it no longer "thinkable."

De–Stalinization

Khrushchëv's most important speech at this Congress did not take place in the public session, however. In a separate "secret" session of the Congress, Khrushchëv launched a major attack on the record of Stalin and what he called the "cult of personality." The speech set forth in great detail the many crimes of Stalin. Its content soon became known in the Soviet Union, however, and the actual text, first available in the West, has since been made public.

Khrushchëv gave the speech to smash the "Stalin myth" and so to free himself to carry out wider changes in the system than conservatives favored. Khrushchëv and his supporters apparently believed that it was possible to condemn Stalin's "errors" and at the same time maintain and even strengthen their own position. This was an effort to make communist rule more respectable by moving back toward older, "Leninist" norms. It signaled no basic change in the nature of communist rule, but it did suggest an end to harsh, terrorist tactics.

The impact of Khrushchëv's speech went far beyond what he had obviously intended. Stalin had defined the nature of communism for so long that the move to repudiate him unleashed forces which threatened the very foundations of Soviet power. Only weeks after the Congress, riots in Tbilisi, the capital of Soviet Geor-

gia, resulted in the deaths of over a hundred persons.

The most serious and direct consequences of de–Stalinization occurred in Eastern Europe, however. In the Polish cities of Poznan and Warsaw, armed clashes occurred between the workers and police. In Hungary, university students demanded, and obtained, an end to compulsory Russian language instruction.

The situation continued to build in both countries. In October, a Polish Party plenum elected Wladislaw Gomulka as First Secretary and called for internal reforms. In Hungary, the clash between university students and the Hungarian secret police led to large-scale fighting and, when it was ordered to intervene, to the disintegration of the Hungarian army.

The Soviet Ambassador to Hungary, Yuri Andropov, met with the new Hungarian Government and arranged for the withdrawal of Soviet troops from Budapest on October 28. One week later, on November 4, they returned and put down the uprising. The Soviet intervention in Hungary brought revulsion abroad and a wave of resignations among prominent foreign communists. Jean-Paul Sartre of France and Howard Fast of the United States were among those who turned in their party cards at this time.

Khrushchëv began now to downplay de–Stalinization, but he had lost the confidence of a number of the leading members of his own party. In June 1957 the Presidium voted seven to four to dismiss him as First Party Secretary. Khrushchëv refused to accept the decision of the Presidium, however, and demanded that the full Central Committee be convened to vote on the matter. Khrushchëv won in the larger forum and managed to obtain the removal of his opponents from full membership on the Presidium. Malenkov was sent to manage a remote installation in Central Asia while Molotov was named Soviet Ambassador to Mongolia. Nine months later, in March 1958, Khrushchëv assumed the additional office of Chairman of the Council of Ministers (head of government).

One of those who benefited from Khrushchëv's victory was Leonid Brezhnev, who became a full member of the Presidium in June 1957. Three years later, in May 1960, Brezhnev became Chairman of the Presidium of the Supreme Soviet (titular head of state). That same month, Alexei Kosygin and Nikolai Podgorny were promoted to full membership in the Presidium.

The 22nd Party Congress met in Moscow in October 1961. Its major theme was de–Stalinization. Following the Congress, Stalin's body was removed from alongside Lenin in the mausoleum on Red Square and buried outside the Kremlin wall. The city of Stalingrad had its name changed and became Volgograd, and other cities named after Stalin had their names changed as well. Yevgeni Yevtushenko, already well–known because of his poem about Babi Yar (where the Nazis carried out a massacre of Soviet Jews during World War II), now produced his poem entitled "The Heirs of Stalin" in which he spoke of those who

"from rostrums, even heap abuse on Stalin
    but, at night, hanker after the good old days"

and warned that

"As long as the heirs of Stalin walk this earth,
    Stalin, I fancy, still lurks in the mausoleum."

This was followed in November 1962 by the publication of *One Day in the Life of Ivan Denisovich*, Alexander Solzhenitsyn's bold novel about life in Stalin's concentration camps.

Writings with a specific political content were not published in the Soviet Union except with approval from high up, and it was said that Khrushchëv authorized publication of Solzhenitsyn's book. But this was the surface reality. None of the "heirs of Stalin" denounced as criminals at the 22nd Party Congress suffered anything more than verbal abuse. They kept their jobs and bided their time. And in October 1964 they took their revenge by casting their votes for Khrushchëv's ouster from power.

De–Stalinization was only one of several factors involved in Khrushchëv's dismissal from power, however. Foreign policy was an issue and in particular, the Cuban missile crisis. It was an American who characterized Khrushchëv's foreign policy as one of "overextension followed by capitulation" but this appears to have been the opinion of some of those on the Presidium itself. One of the few specific charges brought against Khrushchëv in October 1964 was that he had caused a Soviet defeat at the time of the Cuban missile crisis. The theme of overextension was specifically taken up by Brezhnev the following month when he asserted that, in the future, Soviet foreign policy would take into consideration the "military power of the countries of the socialist camp."

The other chief issue was domestic. Khrushchëv had staked a great deal on economic development and he had promised the Soviet people that the U.S.S.R. would catch up with the United States economically by 1980. He had carried through a partial economic decentralization in 1957 when he created 105 new regional Economic Councils (*sovnarkhozy*). In November 1962 he announced a division of the party into separate industrial and agricultural sections, the object to turn the party into an economic administrative apparatus. This move threatened the power position of the regional first party secretaries and created a great deal of dissatisfaction throughout the party.

In the end, it was probably the failure of Khrushchëv's agricultural policies that did him in. After the initial success of his "virgin lands" program, agricultural production stagnated and the country began to suffer chronic food shortages. The 1962 division of the party was an attempt to deal with the problem administratively, but it was a failure. In August 1964, Khrushchëv announced yet another reorganization of agriculture which he intended to submit to a November party plenum. But by this time the other members of the Presidium had had enough. On October 15, 1964, Moscow's TASS (the official news "wire") announced that Khrushchëv had been relieved of his duties as First Party Secretary and Chairman of the Council of Ministers, and that Leonid Brezhnev had been elected First Party Secretary in his place. Alexei Kosygin became Chairman of the Council of Ministers. Anastas Mikoyan, who had succeeded Brezhnev as Chairman of the Presidium of the Supreme Soviet (titular head of state) in July 1964, retained that position until his retirement in December 1965; he was succeeded by Nikolai Podgorny, who continued to serve in that position.

Soviet Foreign Policy under Khrushchëv

Of key importance to the leadership of the Soviet Union was the problem of relations with the United States, the country which, after World War II, was the leader of the Western alliance. Stalin, knowing that he could not both keep control over Eastern Europe and continue good relations with the United States, chose confrontation. His successors, perhaps frightened at the turn that confrontation had taken and more aware of the threat that nuclear weapons represented, attempted to reach an accommodation with the West while retaining Stalin's empire. This led to some easing of tensions and to increased diplomatic contacts. A Geneva Summit Conference in 1955 after Stalin's death represented the culmination of this trend. No significant agreements were reached, but the "spirit of Geneva" continued to influence relations between the two powers for about five years.

The United States' refusal to accept Soviet domination of Eastern Europe always remained a factor in U.S.–Soviet relations, however, and when, as in 1956, the Soviet Union resorted to the use of force to retain its control, bilateral relations suffered. Not all of the Soviet Union's problems with regard to maintaining control were amenable to the use of force, however. One such case was Berlin, established under separate four–power occupation in 1945. In the 1950's, West Berlin (representing a union of the three western zones of occupation) was a free enterprise, democratic island in the middle of a communized East Germany and it had become a place of refuge for East Germans fleeing communism. Determined to put an end to the constant drain of manpower, Khrushchëv demanded in November 1958 that the occupation of West Berlin be terminated and that it be turned into a "free city" within the territory of the communist German Democratic Republic. Khrushchëv's position, put in the form of an ultimatum, created the Berlin Crisis of 1958.

First Secretary Khrushchëv and President Kennedy, Vienna

It is difficult to determine whether Khrushchëv expected his viewpoint to prevail, but it did result in a four–power Foreign Ministers' conference in Geneva in May 1959 and an invitation to Khrushchëv to visit the United States in September. Khrushchëv stayed for 18 days, which included three days spent at Camp David in private conversation with President Eisenhower.

Though the talks produced only an agreement for additional summit level negotiations, the Soviets subsequently referred to them as having created the "spirit of Camp David." When Khrushchëv returned to Moscow, he publicly characterized Eisenhower as a man who "sincerely wants to liquidate the cold war and improve relations between our two great countries." That also led Khrushchëv to suggest, in early 1960, that the Soviet armed forces would be reduced by about one–third.

This was the high–water mark in U.S.–Soviet relations under Khrushchëv. But in May, the Soviets shot down an American U–2 photo–reconnaissance plane that had penetrated Soviet air space. Khrushchëv demanded an apology from Eisenhower and, when it was not forthcoming, he torpedoed a Summit Meeting scheduled to take place in Paris in mid–May. This also was one of the factors that explains Khrushchëv's extraordinary performance at the United Nations General Assembly in September when he took off his shoe and banged it on his desk to show his disapproval of one of the speeches.

A meeting between Khrushchëv and President Kennedy in May 1961 proved to be unproductive and, in fact, Khrushchëv resurrected the Berlin Crisis by demanding a settlement by the end of the year. Further, he coupled this with a statement that the Soviet defense budget would be *increased* by one–third. Then, on August 13, 1961, the Soviet Union instituted a unilateral solution to the Berlin Crisis by beginning to build a wall between West and East Berlin. Since the wall was being built on the territory of East Berlin, there was little that the United States and its allies could do other than to issue a diplomatic protest—but it obviously had a negative effect on U.S.–Soviet relations. Barriers were later placed to totally divide East Germany from West Berlin. This was the first time in history that a fortified wall had been erected to keep people *in* instead of *out*.

The next test of wills came in October 1962—the Cuban missile crisis. In his memoirs, Khrushchëv relates that:

"It was during my visit to Bulgaria (May 14–20, 1962) that I had the idea of installing missiles with nuclear warheads in Cuba without letting the United States find out they were there

until it was too late to do anything about them."

But the United States found out what the Soviet Union was up to as the missiles were being installed and demanded their removal. Khrushchëv had to acquiesce, but he attempted to save face by claiming that he had preserved world peace and obtained (an oral) guarantee for Cuba's Fidel Castro against any future attempts to overthrow him by troops launched from the U.S. In fact, he did have some gains to show. In the final settlement, the United States confined its objective to the withdrawal of Soviet missiles, thereby conceding Castro's right to remain a Soviet ally and to retain a communist form of government if he wished. This was a tacit repeal of the Monroe Doctrine. In addition, the U.S. soon afterwards began removing its intermediate range ballistic missiles from Turkey, which Khrushchëv could claim as an additional victory on his part.

Moreover, in retrospect, the United States was as appalled as the Soviet Union at how close the two nations had come to all–out war and the result was further steps toward *détente*. This led to the installation of a Washington–Moscow "hot line" and the signing of a limited test ban treaty in 1963.

Domestically, however, Khrushchëv drew different conclusions from the Cuban missile crisis and in March 1963 he pushed through a revision of the last two

years of the Seventh Five Year Plan to allow for a large–scale deployment of Soviet ICBMs. As he records in his memoirs, "the experience of the Caribbean crisis also convinced us that we were right to concentrate on the manufacture of nuclear missiles."

The Brezhnev Era

During the years that followed Khrushchëv's ouster, the Soviet Union was governed by a relatively stable coalition of leaders that included Brezhnev, Kosygin and Podgorny, but also included Michael Suslov, the party's chief ideologist, as well. Brezhnev gradually consolidated his position as first among equals, however, and, starting in the late 1960's, he became the dominant figure in foreign policy. Brezhnev's style of leadership was undramatic, however, and both his successes and his failures tended to be associated more with the system than with the man.

The immediate period following Khrushchëv's departure was characterized by a reversal of many of his policies. Most importantly, the November 1962 division of the party into separate industrial and agricultural units was reversed and a unitary party structure was recreated. The regional Economic Councils created in 1957 were also gradually phased out and replaced by centralized ministries.

Leonid Brezhnev

View of Moscow and the Moscow River

In 1965 at a Central Committee plenum, Brezhnev announced a change in agricultural policy which, he said, would place the emphasis on farm autonomy. The real thrust of the new program was *not* farm autonomy, however, but increased incentives—diffused in such a way that they probably had little economic effect. Ever since their creation in the 1930's, collective farms had been required to deliver a set quota of grain to the government at artificially low prices. Brezhnev now lowered that quota by 11 million tons and increased the price that the government would pay for above-quota deliveries. The price of various types of agricultural equipment was also lowered at this time. These changes increased retained earnings for the collective farm administrations, but they did not filter down in a meaningful way to the individual peasant. Two other reforms did, however; peasants for the first time became eligible for old age pensions and were guaranteed a minimum monthly income. In addition, there was an attempt to encourage the production of more fruit, vegetables and meat for sale in the free peasant markets of the big cities by easing restrictions and reducing taxes on small private plots. All of these changes under Brezhnev had the effect of blurring the distinction between state and collective farms.

Major changes in the industrial sector were also experimented with at this time. These experiments, collectively known as the *Liberman Plan*, were actually suggested in 1962 when a Kharkov (Ukraine) University professor by the name of Yevsei Liberman wrote an article for *Pravda* setting forth general principles for economic reform. Under the Soviet economic system, manufacturing enterprises operated on the basis of detailed instructions drawn up by planning experts in centralized ministries. Liberman proposed that much of this planning be dismantled and that individual plant managers be given authority to run their enterprises themselves, subject only to overall production figures and fulfillment of delivery dates. Profitability, rather than the meeting of production norms, would be the new test of the efficiency of an enterprise, and supply and demand would replace the exchange of goods on the basis of pre-planned indexes. Wages and salaries would also be tied to the profitability of individual enterprises.

The Liberman article in *Pravda* had been personally approved and endorsed by Khrushchëv, and in August 1964 the first test of the *Liberman* ideas began with an experimental tryout of the system in two textile plants. After Khrushchëv's fall, Alexei Kosygin made the Liberman Plan his own and ordered that a reform program be drawn up for the entire economy. The new program was put into effect beginning in September 1965. There was considerable opposition from among those who believed that it would tend to decrease the role of the party in the economy, however, and Brezhnev apparently aligned himself eventually with this group. As a result, the Central Committee plenum that instituted the reform also reinstituted central industrial and technical ministries, at least partially negating the reform from the very beginning. *Libermanism* was subsequently adopted by many Eastern European regimes, most notably Hungary, but in the Soviet Union it was phased out beginning in 1970.

Another program reversal that followed the ouster of Khrushchëv was the gradual end of de-Stalinization, accompanied by a generally harder line on the cultural front. A *Pravda* article in 1965 by Professor Sergei Trapeznikov, chief of the Central Committee's department of science and education, characterized the Stalin era as "one of the most brilliant in the history of the Party and the Soviet State" and suggested it as a pattern for the theoretical and practical activity of the Party.

A month earlier, in September 1965, A.M. Rumiantsev, editor of *Pravda*, had been dismissed after he came to the defense of Andrei Voznesensky, a Soviet writer who had been accused of nihilism. In that same month, Andrei Sinyavsky and Yuri Daniel were arrested and tried for publishing abroad works critical of the Soviet Union. They were sentenced to 7 and 5 years at hard labor.

The 23rd Party Congress of 1966 appeared to confirm the trend toward re-Stalinization. The Presidium again became known as the Politburo while the First Party Secretary resumed the title of General Secretary. Both names dated from the Stalinist era and had been dropped by Khrushchëv.

The Dissident Movement

De–Stalinization was accompanied by the rise of a dissident movement that grew in numbers and in significance in the late 1960's. In 1966, an underground journal, *Phoenix 61*, began to appear. Four writers associated with the journal were arrested at the beginning of 1967 and later sentenced. This, in turn, led to several public and private petitions of protest, signed by increased numbers of distinguished Soviet intellectuals. The situation was further worsened when Stalin's daughter, Svetlana Allilueva, defected in April 1967 and in a subsequent book, *Twenty Letters to a Friend*, expressed her solidarity with the Soviet intellectuals in their struggle for intellectual freedom. Also, about this time, two of Alexander Solzhenitsyn's novels, *First Circle* and *Cancer Ward*, were published abroad—without Solzhenitsyn's permission, to be sure, but the mere fact of publication abroad was considered to be an act of dissidence *by him*.

As the dissident movement continued to grow, it gained a widening circle of recruits. In July 1968, Andrei Sakharov, a distinguished physicist and father of the Soviet Union's hydrogen bomb, allowed a manuscript of his entitled *Thoughts on Progress, Peaceful Coexistence and Intellectual Freedom*, to be published abroad. Sakharov had joined the ranks of active dissidents two years earlier when he wrote a letter to Brezhnev protesting the arrest of four persons whose crime was that they had protested against the trial of Sinyavsky and Daniel. Since Sakharov was a prominent member of the Soviet Academy of Sciences and a recipient of both the Stalin Prize and the Lenin Prize, nothing had happened then or subse-

quently when he signed a letter to the Party warning against a resurgence of Stalinism. In August 1968, however, Sakharov was removed from all secret work and transferred to another academic institute in Moscow; he and his wife were later sent to the official detention city, formerly named Gorky.

The Soviet invasion of Czechoslovakia in 1968 brought both renewed protests and a harsher crackdown on dissidents. One of the seven individuals who staged a brief demonstration in Red Square against the invasion was Pavel Litvinov, grandson of Maxim Litvinov, Stalin's Foreign Minister in the 1930's. Litvinov was sentenced to five years internal exile in a Siberian village. After his return to Moscow in 1973, Litvinov and his wife applied for exit visas as Jews and shortly afterwards emigrated.

One of the more interesting developments of the Brezhnev era was the adoption of a policy of allowing Jewish emigration. There are a little over two million Jews in the Soviet Union and the large majority of them consider themselves to be assimilated and at home. In 1970 for example, only 17.7% of all Jews listed either Hebrew or Yiddish as their mother tongue. There has always been some anti–Semitism in Russia, but the Soviet Union, to its credit, has seldom encouraged the attitude. In 1967, however, following Israel's defeat of the Soviet Union's Arab clients, Egypt and Syria, the Soviet Union unleashed a violent anti–Zionist campaign. For some of the Russian public, the distinction between anti–Zionism and anti–Semitism was too fine a difference to draw. As a result, an increasing number of Jews began applying for visas to emigrate to Israel; even-

tually over 100,000 Jews applied to emigrate. In 1968, the Ministry of Interior notified a few Jewish families that, if they still wanted to leave, they could. The flow of Jewish emigrants grew steadily thereafter, and by 1973 an average of 30,000 Jews were leaving every year. This abated by the end of 1975, but since 1988 the pace has quickened with the encouragement of Israel. Actually their preferred destination is the U.S.

The question of Jewish emigration became a foreign policy matter in 1974 when the U.S. Congress, following the leadership of Senator Henry Jackson of Washington State, approved an amendment to the 1972 trade agreement on "most–favored–nation" status for the Soviet Union which made approval contingent on increased Jewish emigration from the Soviet Union. The Soviets, calling the Jackson Amendment an interference in their domestic affairs, rejected the trade agreement in 1975.

Jewish emigration continued at a decreased level for awhile after 1975, but then began growing again. By 1979, an average of 4,000 Jews were departing monthly. Then came a policy reversal. From a peak of 51,320 in 1979, the number of emigrants declined to 2,688 in 1982, the last year of Brezhnev's regime.

Non–Jewish dissidents did not, in general, have the right to apply for emigration but the Brezhnev regime rediscovered, in the period of the 1970s, that emigration or expulsion sometimes provided a suitable alternative to imprisonment for individuals too prominent to treat as ordinary criminals. Alexander Solzhenitsyn, expelled in February 1974, remains the most famous of these, but the list of those given permission to go abroad temporarily who thereafter had their Soviet citizenship withdrawn is much longer. Thus by the end of the Brezhnev regime in 1982, most individuals who had joined the ranks of the dissidents in the 1960s or early 1970s were either living abroad, in prison, a psychiatric hospital, or in internal exile.

A few new dissidents did appear in the late 1970's, particularly in association with attempts to demand implementation of the human rights provision of the Helsinki Accord, signed in 1975. They were small in number, however, and quickly rounded up. There was also some dissident activity in connection with the 1980 Summer Olympics and again at the time of the 1980–81 Madrid follow–up conference to the Helsinki Conference on Security and Cooperation in Europe.

Yet the movement, although troublesome because of its international ramifications, was never more than an annoyance to the regime. The actual number of dissidents was always quite small. A recent Western study which attempted to identify all those who were in any way involved in the dissident movement was able to come up with names of only 3,400 persons for the period 1956 to 1975. The disturbing element from the point of view of the regime was that the dissidents originated in a social base that consisted essentially of the scientific–cultural intellentsia. Their significance was that they *said* aloud what other intelligent people could only think.

A Regime In Crisis

A more serious problem in the long run was that the Soviet economy, which began a slowdown by 1970, continued in that pattern to the end of the Brezhnev era and, in fact, the pattern is yet to be reversed. Moreover, wage increases granted to the workers after 1965 exacerbated the situation for they had not been accompanied by an equivalent increase in consumer goods.

The Five Year Plan for 1971–1975 attempted to deal with this situation by calling for vast investment in agriculture and increased investments in consumer industry. For the first time in Soviet history, consumer goods were to be favored over heavy industry. But by the end of 1972, the planners had to admit that their priorities did not permit the planned investments in consumer goods and the plan was revised to renew the emphasis on heavy industry. The Tenth Five Year Plan (1976–1980) continued the revised priorities of the preceding plan. These targets were also not met.

The 11th Five Year Plan (1981–1985) called for a slightly larger growth in consumer industry than heavy industry. Some of its goals, particularly those with regard to agriculture were unrealistic, however, and were never met. The essential problem—and it is a continuing one—is that Soviet productivity slowed to a negligible rate in the 1960's and all the tinkering with the economy since that time did nothing to reverse that trend. Any effective economic reform would have had to decrease the role of the cadre of the Communist Party in the economy. Under Brezhnev, this was always unacceptable.

The Brezhnev era has one last characteristic worth mentioning. The Soviet Union had a huge bureaucracy which ran all things under the guidance of the Party. Khrushchëv had feared that the bureaucracy was becoming ingrown (which it was) and in 1961 he had sponsored a new Party statute which attempted to deal with the problem. Under the terms of the statute, there was to be a normal turnover of personnel on each of the Party committees, with a certain percentage of the membership to be replaced at each election. There was considerable opposition to this policy among Party bureaucrats and, at the 23rd Party Congress in 1966, the policy was reversed.

Although a general clause was added stressing the intention of the Party to promote "energetic and competent young cadres," this was generally ignored in the period of the 1970's.

The result was an unparalleled continuity in office at all levels of government, and an aging Party and government elite. One can see how this operated with regard to membership on the Central Committee. In 1966, 76% of those elected at the 24th Party Congress were already full members. The percentage of full members reelected subsequently remained at this level. In fact at the 26th Party Congress in 1981, the figure was actually 75%; it would have been much higher, but the Central Committee was also growing during these years, having increased by 44 since the previous Congress.

Soviet Foreign Policy under Brezhnev

When Brezhnev replaced Khrushchëv as Party chief in October 1964, a subtle change occurred. Without repudiating *détente*, Brezhnev began to speak about the necessity of maintaining Soviet defense potential at the highest possible levels. In July 1965, he spoke of a five–year defense plan to "increase the defensive might of the U.S.S.R." The subsequent 1966–1970 Soviet defense budget nearly doubled defense spending; it continued to grow in the period of the 1970's, though a CIA report issued in the middle 1980s indicated that the annual growth rate may have dropped somewhat for the period 1979–1982.

Brezhnev's push for increased defense expenditures was, from the Soviet point of view, entirely compatible with a policy of *détente* and, in some respects, a precondition for it. Cooperation between the two super powers was made somewhat more difficult because of the United States' increasing involvement in Vietnam but, in spite of this, a treaty to ban nuclear weapons in outer space was negotiated in 1967. This was followed in 1968 by a treaty on the non–proliferation of nuclear weapons.

Negotiations to limit the size of both countries' strategic nuclear forces were to begin in 1968, but were canceled by President Johnson after a Soviet invasion of Czechoslovakia. The Strategic Arms Limitation Talks (SALT) concept was revived by President Nixon, however, and this led to a visit by President Nixon to Moscow in May 1972 and the signing of the SALT–1 accords. SALT–1 primarily limited the deployment of antiballistic missiles (ABMs) but it also contained a five–year interim agreement freezing the number of land and sea–based missiles. In late 1974, President Ford met with Brezhnev in Vladivostok and there the two leaders agreed on general guidelines for a SALT–2 pact which would deal with strategic nuclear missiles. SALT–2 was finally initialed in 1979, but President Carter later withdrew the treaty from consideration by the United States Senate after a Soviet invasion of Afghanistan.

Military Intervention in Afghanistan

A group openly claiming to be Marxist–Leninist came to power in Afghanistan in a bloody *coup*. in late 1978. The U.S. government recognized the new regime, but became more and more disquieted by subsequent events. A large number of

Presidents Carter and Brezhnev exchange signed copies of the SALT II Treaty agreement, Vienna, June 1979

Mujahidin resistance fighters look down on a village after a Soviet aerial attack. At left are terraced crop fields.

AP/World Wide Photos

"advisers" were imported from the Soviet Union and the regime began an attempt to bring about a social revolution within the country. This produced strong resistance among the Afghan population, however, and it wasn't long before armed uprisings throughout the country threatened the very existence of the regime. In late 1979 therefore, the Soviet Union intervened with 80,000 Soviet troops to prop up the faltering Afghan communist regime. But Afghanistan is mostly rugged mountain country with a population of about 20 million people; the Soviet troops were only sufficient to keep the communist regime from being overthrown, but not enough to put down the rebellion.

Soviet intervention in Afghanistan had an adverse effect on the Soviet Union's relations with most of the rest of the world, however. A number of countries, including the United States, boycotted the 1980 Moscow Olympics.

President Carter also announced a partial embargo on the sale of grain to the Soviet Union and began negotiating an agreement with Pakistan to provide military support to the *mujahidin,* the Afghan resistance. In addition, the Carter Administration reversed its earlier position on the adequacy of American military power and began a new buildup of U.S. forces. Further, it sponsored resolutions in the United Nations condemning the Soviet military presence in Afghanistan.

The Reagan Administration continued and intensified most of these policies. Agreement with Pakistan was reached and significant aid began flowing to the *mujahidin..* Military budgets were greatly enlarged and the administration openly boasted about beginning a new arms race which they expected to win. The B–1 bomber aircraft, canceled by the Carter

Administration, was reinstated and a number of new weapons systems, including the multiple–warhead MX and the Trident submarine, were proposed.

This was the stick. At the same time, the Reagan Administration stipulated its willingness to negotiate arms reductions and symbolized this by changing the name of the arms negotiations process from SALT—Strategic Arms Limitation Talks—to START— Strategic Arms Reduction Talks.

The START negotiations began in June 1982. The American position, set forth by President Reagan, called for a reduction of missile launchers to 850 each (down from 2,000 for the USA and 2,700 for the USSR) and a reduction of nuclear warheads by about a third. No more than half of the missile launchers could be land–based. Agreement on these points would lead to a second round of talks aimed at reducing other elements of the two nations' "balance of terror."

Brezhnev rejected Reagan's proposal in May 1982, apparently disturbed by its proposed limits on land–based ICBMs. His own proposal called for a two–thirds reduction in nuclear warheads, a ban on the development of new types of strategic weapons, and a freeze on strategic weapons at current levels, to begin concurrently with the negotiations. The United States rejected the freeze on the basis that it would codify existing Soviet advantages, but welcomed Brezhnev's willingness to negotiate.

The USA and USSR were at least talking with each other in the area of strategic weapons. One other area of American concern, that of theater nuclear weapons in Europe, remained totally stalemated. The problem dated from 1977, when the Soviet Union began installing SS–20 missiles in Eastern Europe. A mobile missile

with three warheads, the SS–20 caused great concern among Western European leaders and they began pushing for NATO to match these missiles.

In 1979, therefore, NATO voted for the emplacement of American Pershing II and Cruise missiles in Europe, if talks with the Soviet Union did not produce another solution. The Soviets refused to discuss the removal of their missiles, however, so President Reagan offered his Zero Option— if the Soviet Union would pull its SS–20s out of Eastern Europe, then the USA would refrain from installing Pershing IIs and Cruise missiles in Western Europe—in a public speech in September 1981. The Soviet Union had not yet responded as of November 1982, when Brezhnev died.

Pravda announces Brezhnev's death

Government Transition

November 1982–March 1985

Prior to Brezhnev's death in November 1982, there was a widespread feeling that the last years of his regime had been ones of stagnation and even decline. Many felt that what was needed was a strong, vigorous, but tested leader who could get the country going again.

Konstantin Chernenko was Brezhnev's protégé and therefore represented continuity; Yuri Andropov, who had been head of the KGB for 15 years, was a man from outside Brezhnev's inner circle, and therefore represented change. The choice fell to Andropov. It turned out, however, that Andropov was a frail reed on which to lean. He was personally honest and hard–working, and he had attached to himself a number of younger individuals committed to change. But he was also suffering from a heart condition and diabetes, and was temporarily incapacitated only five months after becoming General Secretary. Moreover, although a majority of the Politburo had chosen him over Chernenko, it soon became clear that there was no firm majority for reform. As a result, there were only three major policies associated with Andropov's name. The first of these was his campaign against corruption and slack labor discipline. There was undoubtedly corruption and slack discipline, but if western observers were correct that these things were only symptoms and that the major problems were systemic—arising from or pertaining to the system *itself*, then Andropov's campaign was relatively meaningless.

Andropov was also interested in renewing the leadership of the Party by retiring older individuals and promoting younger men in their places. He succeeded to a certain extent at secondary levels, but the average age of the Politburo was well past the usual age of retirement.

He also introduced two economic "reforms," a system of brigades for farm workers that permitted some wage differentiation based on actual production, and an experiment, limited to five ministries, in which work teams were set up in factories and encouraged to compete with each other. The factory reform was begun as of January 1, 1984. Both reforms constituted "tinkering with the system" and therefore made no significant contribution to higher productivity. They did represent Andropov's commitment to economic reform, however, and provided a beginning upon which Gorbachёv could later build.

Foreign relations under Andropov deserve comment. He essentially represented a hard–line faction in this area, but he was extremely vigorous in his negotiating stance. Thus it was Andropov who issued the first formal reply to President Reagan's "Zero Option" speech of September 1981. In November 1982, shortly after becoming General Secretary, Andropov gave a speech in which he proposed to reduce the number of SS–20s in Eastern Europe to the same number of missiles held by Great Britain and France if, in return, NATO would cancel deployment of Pershing IIs and Cruise missiles in Western Europe. The offer was unacceptable because the British and French missiles, being part of their "national" arsenals, were not under NATO control. It did open the way for formal negotiations to begin, however.

The United States continued to push its Zero Option until March 1983. Then President Reagan gave another speech in which he introduced his "Interim Proposal." He proposed that the USA and the USSR agree to an equal number of theater nuclear warheads on each side, with the expectation that talks on an eventual Zero Option would continue. The Soviets rejected this proposal.

Negotiations nevertheless continued and there was at least the possibility that an agreement would have been reached, except for the unfortunate circumstances of the Soviet shooting down of a commercial airliner, South Korean Flight 007, in September 1983. The mutual recriminations that followed that event doomed the Theater Nuclear Weapons discussions.

In order to preserve their real or imaginary advantage, the Soviets embarked on a vigorous campaign to drive a wedge between the USA and its Western European NATO allies through mountains of propaganda describing the horrors of nuclear war. This did, in fact, succeed in attracting the sympathies of a substantial number of people in Western Europe and led to numerous anti–nuclear demonstrations. However, in November 1983, with no agreement in sight, the United States began delivering the first of the Pershing II and Cruise missiles to Western Europe. The Theater Nuclear Force discussions were then abruptly recessed by the Soviets in December 1983. They announced that they would not return to the negotiating table unless the United States agreed to withdraw all nuclear missiles emplaced in Western Europe.

Andropov fell ill at just about this point. He was last seen in public shortly before the downing of the airliner, and it is not known what role, if any, he had in foreign affairs during those last five months when he remained sequestered from the world.

This is the record which the members of the Politburo had to evaluate when they met to choose Andropov's successor

***Izvestia* announces Andropov's death**

in February 1984. The promise he represented had been largely unfulfilled, but even the pallid reforms instituted had been negatively received by a large part of the bureaucracy. In particular, Andropov's attempts to weed out incompetents and to promote younger persons to positions of higher responsibility threatened the security of the tenure of the "old guard" Party cadre, and they mobilized their forces accordingly. Chernenko, passed over once precisely because he represented the politics of the waning years of the Brezhnev era, became their candidate.

The other two candidates were Mikhail Gorbachёv and Grigori Romanov. Gorbachёv and Romanov represented the younger generation of the Politburo and tended to be classified as economic specialists because both probably favored greater experimentation in the area of the economy. The Politburo chose Chernenko—although it appeared that Gorbachёv moved into a clear number two position and was the heir apparent.

And how did Chernenko change things after becoming General Secretary? Serge Schmemann, Moscow correspondent for The New York Times, wrote, quoting from an interview he had with a knowledgeable figure in Moscow:

> "We have come to peace with Mr. Chernenko. He has contributed nothing new, the pace has slowed, the results are humble, but at least he has not turned back the clock."

Chernenko was a transitional figure, chosen to hold the fort a little longer before transferring power to a new generation. As such, his initiatives, or lack of them, reflected the will of a majority of the Politburo. When he first took over,

General Secretary Konstantin Chernenko of the U.S.S.R.

there apparently were high–level disagreements on a number of policy issues,
most importantly, on foreign policy. The
result was several months of hibernation,
exemplified by a Soviet boycott of the
1984 Summer Olympics in Los Angeles
and a cancellation of a visit to China by
Ivan V. Arkhipov, Vice Chairman of the
U.S.S.R. Council of Ministers.

But Chernenko, who suffered from
emphysema and a weak heart, disappeared from view for two months in
mid–1984 and reportedly was brought
back to Moscow in a wheelchair. It was
shortly afterwards that Foreign Minister
Gromyko agreed to a meeting with President Reagan. The seriousness of Chernenko's illness had apparently broken
the stalemate in the Kremlin and a new
majority favoring negotiations with the
U.S. had emerged. At the beginning of
November, it was announced that new
high–level economic talks would be held
in Moscow in January 1985. Two weeks
later, Gromyko and Secretary of State
George Shultz agreed to meet in Geneva
in early January to discuss resumption of
arms talks. It was also at about this time
that Moscow announced that Arkhipov's
delayed visit to China would take place in
December.

The Moscow talks were inconclusive,
but there was agreement to resume arms
talks in Geneva beginning March 12, 1985.
Arkhipov's visit to China also resulted in
some improvement in Soviet–Chinese relations.

These events occurred in Chernenko's
absence, for he had disappeared from
sight on December 27 and had not

been seen again in public. In February
it was officially confirmed that he was
ill. A short television clip showed him
voting in the Republic elections on February 24th, but it appeared to have
been "doctored," since its background
matched another clip reported to be at
another time and place. Fifteen days later
his death was announced. According to
the official medical report, his death resulted from a combination of factors
which included emphysema, a heart condition and chronic hepatitis which had
developed into cirrhosis. Evidently his
death was quite expected, for the Central
Committee had already met and decided
on his successor.

THE GORBACHEV ERA

A new General Secretary

The story of Gorbachëv's formal installation as General Secretary is well–
known—how Gromyko made the nominating speech at the meeting of the
Central Committee and how he concluded his remarks with the observation
that "Comrades, he has a nice smile, but
he has iron teeth." No other candidates
were presented to the Central Committee
and acceptance was therefore assured.

In March 1987, however, a somewhat
different report surfaced about a secret
Politburo meeting which took place prior
to the Central Committee meeting that
installed Gorbachëv as General Secretary.
This report, which appeared in a Finnish
newspaper, *Svomen Kuvalehti*, was based

on an interview with Mikhail Shatrov, a
Soviet playwright and Gorbachëv adviser. According to Shatrov, nine persons
were present at the Politburo meeting.
With Gromyko as chairman and abstaining, the vote was tied four to four between Gorbachëv and Viktor Grishin,
Moscow party leader. Gromyko then intervened to cast the deciding vote.

The story can't be directly confirmed,
but Gromyko was later named Chairman
of the Presidium of the Supreme Soviet
(head of state) and Grishin and three
other members of the Politburo did
shortly afterwards lose their seats on the
Politburo. Moreover, the story has a plau-
sibility in that Grishin was logically the
leader of what was left of Brezhnev's
faction after the death of Chernenko.

Born on March 2, 1931, Gorbachëv was
at the time the youngest man on the
Politburo. He was also the best educated,
having graduated from Moscow University in 1955 with a degree in law. He later
would add a second degree when he
earned the qualification of "agronomist–
economist" from the Stavropol Agricultural Institute in 1967.

It was at Moscow University that Gorbachëv first began to take an active interest in politics. He became the head of the
Moscow University branch of the *Komso-
mols* (Young Communists) and it was
at this time that he joined the Communist Party. After graduation, Gorbachëv
joined the Stavropol Agricultural Institute. East of the Black Sea, this is an important agricultural district in southern
Russia. It was also Gorbachëv's home region, so he probably had political contacts
there. He began work as a researcher,
agronomist and economist, but he soon
moved over into full–time party work. By
his thirty–fifth birthday, he was Stavropol
party chief; four years later, he had become the party chief of the entire region.

Gorbachëv was brought to Moscow in
1978 to become a member of the Central
Committee Secretariat with responsibility
for agriculture. A year later, he was made
a candidate member of the Politburo; in
1980 he became a full member.

When Andropov became General Secretary in 1982, he apparently began
grooming Gorbachëv as a possible successor. The first evidence of this came in
May 1983 when Gorbachëv made a visit
to Canada. This was his first official trip
outside the Communist Bloc and he
acquitted himself very well. A trip to
England in December 1984 was equally
successful. Domestically, Gorbachëv had
been in charge of the Secretariat since
at least October 1984. By March 1985, it
was clear that Gorbachëv was well–
qualified to handle the General Secretary
position.

In making his acceptance speech at the
CPSU Central Committee meeting on
March 11, 1985, Gorbachëv broke no new

ground but he did make a number of points which gave some indication of his thinking. First of all, he referred to "enhancing the independence of enterprises, raising their interest in the end product of their work." This implied a commitment to greater economic reform. Second, he made the assertion "we want a real and major reduction of the arms stockpiles." Although again somewhat vague, it appeared to be a commitment to pursue arms reductions talks with the United States with a definite goal in mind rather than simply exploring areas of disagreement.

Manipulation of the Politburo

The first order of business of the new leader was to consolidate his power base. He began the process a little over a month later, on April 23, at a special session of the Central Committee. Three men, all obviously Gorbachëv allies, were promoted to full membership on the Politburo and one other individual was made a candidate member. The elevation of Viktor Chebrikov, the KGB chairman—who was already a candidate member—came as no surprise. But the promotions of Yegor Ligachëv and Nikolai Ryzhkov were different, because both were elevated to full membership without having to go through the intermediate step of candidate member. Moreover, both worked in the Secretariat under Gorbachëv and were closely tied to him personally. The other promotion, that of Minister of War Sokolov to non–voting candidate membership, was probably an effort to appease the "old guard" and military at the same time. Sokolov, already 74, was viewed at the time as an interim appointee.

The April 1985 changes gave Gorbachëv a firm majority and he used it to begin remaking the Politburo and the government. At the regular plenary session of the Central Committee on July 1, 1985, Georgi Romanov—another of Gorbachëv's rivals for the position of General Secretary—was retired from the Politburo "on health grounds." His Politburo seat went to Eduard Shevardnadze, First Secretary for the Georgian Republic. Gorbachëv's promotion and Romanov's retirement had also created two vacancies in the Secretariat and these were filled by Boris Yeltsin and Lev Zaikov.

Some additional reasons for the changes became evident the next day when the Supreme Soviet met. One of its tasks was the selection of a new Chairman of the Presidium (often referred to in the West as the Soviet President), vacant since the death of Chernenko. It had been thought that Gorbachëv would assume this position but, in a switch, he announced that, having been requested to devote all of his time to Party affairs, he was nominating Andrei Gromyko to the position. He then added that Eduard Shevardnadze would replace Gromyko as Minister of Foreign Affairs. Gromyko thus got the honor of becoming head of state, while Gorbachëv got a new Minister of Foreign Affairs, untainted by any connection with previous Soviet foreign policies.

When he took over his new job, Shevardnadze was totally without experience in foreign affairs. He did have a reputation for being honest and hard–working, however, and had, it was said, waged an energetic and effective campaign against corruption and laziness in his native Georgia. Shevardnadze's appointment suggested that Gorbachëv intended to have the principal voice in foreign affairs. That indeed proved to be the case, although Shevardnadze earned high marks during his tenure as Foreign Minister.

Gorbachëv continued his rebuilding in the fall of 1985. In September, Nikolai Tikhonov stepped down as Chairman of the Council of Ministers and was replaced by Nikolai Ryzhkov. A Gorbachëv ally now occupied the office responsible for implementing economic reforms approved by the Politburo.

Additional changes occurred in Octo-

Gorbachëv speaks at the Kremlin's Palace of Congresses

ber when Tikhonov retired from the Politburo and Nikolai Talyzin became a candidate member. Talyzin, a telecommunications specialist, became head of GOSPLAN at the same time. Now an individual closely associated with Gorbachëv was also in charge of economic planning. The move was particularly significant, since Gorbachëv had already rejected the draft Five Year Plan drawn up by Nikolai Baibakov, the man whom Talyzin replaced at GOSPLAN. But Talyzin proved to be the wrong choice. At the mid–1987 meeting of the Central Committee, he was singled out for criticism by Gorbachëv for failure to embark upon economic change with sufficient rapidity. Somewhat later, he was replaced at GOSPLAN and named Permanent Representative to the Council for Mutual Economic Assistance.

Economic leadership changes were particularly important to Gorbachëv. As he made clear at the 27th Party Congress in February 1986, the Soviet leader intended an economic transformation of his country and was well aware of the human factor in any such transformation. This almost certainly is why he forced the resignation of the relatively young Georgi Romanov, an economic specialist, but also a conservative on programs of economic reform. Tikhonov, 81, and Baibakov, 75, on the other hand, were probably replaced primarily because of advanced age.

Having promoted four of his allies to the Politburo within six months of becoming General Secretary and accepted the resignation of two others, it is clear that Gorbachëv had carried out a rapid transformation of this ruling body. As it turned out, however, the transformation was not complete. In January 1986, Viktor Grishin resigned his Politburo seat and simultaneously turned over his position as Moscow City First Secretary to Boris Yeltsin. One month later, a number of other personnel changes were announced. Lev Zaikov became a full member of the Politburo while Boris Yeltsin and Nikolai Slyunkov became candidate members. Two candidate members, Boris Ponomarev, 81, and Vasily Kuznetsov, 85, were edged into retirement.

There were also two interesting additions to the Secretariat at this time. The first of these was Anatoli Dobrynin, who had served as Soviet Ambassador to the United States since 1962. Gorbachëv, probably hoping to make use of his extensive personal knowledge of the United States, appointed a new ambassador to replace him in Washington and added him to the Secretariat. The second addition was Alexandra Biryukova, who thus became the highest ranking woman in the Soviet Communist Party. Biryukova, whose background was that of a national trade union leader, had been a member of the Central Committee since the early 1970's, but this marked her transition to full–time party work.

Gorbachëv's extensive changes since becoming General Secretary placed a new generation of leadership in power in the Soviet Union. At the 27th Party Congress in February 1986, this new leadership committed the Soviet Union to a Five Year and a Fifteen Year Plan whose goal was to triple the rate of productivity growth by the year 2000 and at the same time double living standards. The goals for the five years 1986–91 were less ambitious—basically an increased growth of approximately one percent over what had taken place during the previous five years. As the end of that plan came, it became clear that it had not been achieved.

Gorbachëv's greatest problem was that while the top leadership favored reform, the working level bureaucrats who had to implement any reform remained unconvinces, particularly whe it might have involved loss of their jobs. It was this opposition in both the party and administrative bureaucracy that explained why Gorbachëv began waging a major public relations campaign following the 27th Party Congress designed to generate support for reform, going over the "heads" of the bureaucracy with a direct appeal to the people.

Glasnost, Perestroika and Democracy

In the process, Gorbachëv introduced three slogans, glasnost, perestroika, and democracy, which came to symbolize for the West what he wanted to accomplish in the Soviet Union. However, none of

The legendary summer palace—*Tsarskoe Selo* ("The Tsar's Village"), 15 miles south of Leningrad

these words has the same meaning in Russian that they have in the West. For example, we have translated *glasnost* as "openness." The actual root of the word is "voice," thus a more appropriate translation might be "speaking out." That was what Gorbachëv was stating when he used the term—that people who support what he was trying to do should speak out to make their support known. His campaign resulted in a greater openness within Soviet society, but that was a by–product of what he sought to accomplish.

Gorbachëv's second key word, *perestroika*, is usually translated as "restructuring." Again, the translation here is adequate, but also does not really reflect what is understood by the term within the Soviet Union. When Gorbachëv first used the term, he meant it in the purely economic sense of reorganizing economic activity to make it more productive. At that point, the principles associated with it were "socialist" and "self–financing." But its meaning has been endlessly extended since that time and people now apply it to all aspects of the society, speaking of the restructuring of science, the media or even politics. Thus it has become a synonym for general societal change.

Democracy, Gorbachëv's third slogan, is perhaps the most difficult word to explain in the Soviet context. At least in the beginning, it did not mean democracy in the sense of political democracy and it was not meant to challenge the monopoly of the *Communist Party of the Soviet Union* as the directing agent of Soviet society. Yet Gorbachëv did mean greater popular participation in decision making at the local and possibly even up to the Republic level. Partly, this was once again an attempt to mobilize popular support behind his reform program, but it was also an attempt to give the people a feeling that they had a real stake in their country's future. Because more than one candidate was to be nominated for each position, it had also given the people somewhat more control at the local level and now appeared to be moving toward something like genuine democracy.

Additional Politburo and Leadership Changes

This campaign was accompanied by changes in the Politburo related to Gorbachëv's campaign for reform. The first such change came in December 1986, when Dinmukhamed Kunaev was dismissed as First Secretary for Kazakhstan. Accused of corruption, he lost his Politburo seat in January 1987. Kunaev may have been corrupt for it was the policy of the Brezhnev regime to co–opt non–Slavic leaders by not paying too much attention to what they did within their own jurisdictions (including thievery) so

long as they remained loyal supporters of Moscow's policies nationally. On the other hand, he was dismissed primarily because he was an oldline conservative unable to adjust to Gorbachëv's new technocratic vision.

But Gorbachëv's decision to put his own man in charge backfired in this case. When word reached Alma Ata, the Kazakh capital, that Kunaev had been dismissed and that he was being replaced by Gennady Kolbin, an ethnic Russian, violent rioting broke out and several persons were killed. Kolbin's appointment violated a long–standing tradition that the first secretary of a republic is always of the dominant group (i.e., in this case, a Kazakh). Kolbin was later reassigned and a Kazakh was appointed First Secretary in his place.

The next changes came at a plenary session of the Central Committee on June 26, 1987. Three men, Aleksandr N. Yakovlev, Nikolai Slyunkov and Victor Nikonov, were added to the Politburo, while Dmitri Yazov, the new Defense Minister, became a candidate member. Yakovlev, who had served for a number of years as Ambassador to Canada, quickly established himself as a strong voice for reform. Nikonov, a member of the Secretariat, had picked up the agriculture portfolio from Gorbachëv when he became General Secretary. Slyunkov, who had been First Secretary of the Republic of Byelorussia, was considered to be a protege of Ryzhkov's.

These additions to the Politburo must have strengthened Gorbachëv politically, even though two stalwarts of the Brezhnev era, Geidar Aliyev and Vladimir Shcherbitsky, retained their positions.

Geidar Aliyev announced his resignation three months later, in October, ostensively because of ill health. Although there were some rumors earlier that Aliyev had suffered a heart attack, it is still not clear whether Aliyev left voluntarily or was pushed out. What was significant, however, is that Aliyev was the last Central Asian on the Politburo and his departure left Foreign Minister Shevardnadze as the sole non–Slav on the ruling body.

If Aliyev's departure may have been voluntary, the dismissal, in the same month, of Boris Yeltsin as First Secretary for Moscow was clearly not. His dismissal, after a speech criticizing the pace of reform, came as something of a shock because he had been closely associated with Gorbachëv up to that time. His "crime" was apparently that he favored a more confrontational approach with the bureaucracy than Gorbachëv and wanted to force the pace of reform even against growing opposition. He was subsequently accused of holding the "political illusion" that reform "could be achieved through vigorous and honest guidance

Boris Yeltsin

from above alone, that is, by using 'purified' but still high–handed methods."

It appears that Yeltsin fell victim to an emerging split in the top leadership ranks over the issue of how quickly economic reform should be implemented. Everyone in the top leadership accepted the necessity of economic reform but several wanted the reform to be as narrow and technical as possible. At this time, Ligachëv, Chebrikov and Yazov were the most outspoken exponents of this point of view. All three publicly criticized aspects of the reform. Gorbachëv obviously felt that he needed their general support, however, and when Yeltsin took a confrontational position and attacked Ligachëv and others, Gorbachëv abandoned him and he lost his leadership position in the party.

Even though Yeltsin was subsequently made First Deputy Chairman of the State Construction Committee, meaning that he was not totally disgraced, his dismissal had a chilling effect on the more outspoken reformers. In February 1988, Yeltsin lost his seat as an alternate member of the Politburo, though he retained his membership on the Central Committee.

However, the same Central Committee meeting that dropped Yeltsin also added two persons as alternate members of the Politburo. They were Yuri Maslyukov, 50, a defense expert, and Georgi Razumovsky, 52, an agricultural expert. Maslyukov subsequently replaced Nikolai Talyzin as head of GOSPLAN. Razumovsky, who was supposed to have close ties to Gorbachëv, became a member of the Secretariat with responsibility for personnel.

The *da*s have it: Gromyko is voted out as Chairman of the Presidium of the Supreme Soviet. He sits dejected while Ryzhkov and Gorbachev vote "yes".

And a New Definition of Democracy

The next event of significance in 1988 was the 19th All–Union CPSU Conference, which met in Moscow on June 28–July 1. Gorbachëv, who presided over the conference, encouraged an atmosphere of open expression and, occasionally, debate among the delegates. The delegates eventually voted to accept six resolutions, the most important of which called for "Democratization of Soviet Society and the Reform of the Political System."

The resolution provided only a bare outline of a new political system, but it did put the party on record as favoring a restructuring of the political system. Not everyone was happy with the resolutions, however. In August, two Politburo members, Yegor Ligachëv and Viktor Chebrikov, gave speeches critical of the direction Gorbachëv was taking the party.

Gorbachëv responded by calling a meeting of the Central Committee which met at the end of September. The meeting led to a major reshuffle within the top leadership, several retirements, and some promotions. Among those retired were Andrei Gromyko, who also stepped down as Chairman of the Presidium of the Supreme Soviet (informally, President), and Mikhail Solomentsev. Vladimir Dolgikh, and Pyotr Demichev, who had been alternate members of the Politburo, were retired at the same time. The meeting also nominated Gorbachëv as Gromyko's successor as Chairman of the Presidium of the Supreme Soviet, and this was subsequently confirmed by the Supreme Soviet.

Yegor Ligachëv retained his seat on the Politburo, but he lost his position as chief ideologist and his informal position as Second Secretary, by virtue of which he had chaired meetings of the Secretariat. He gained the title of Chairman of the Agricultural Commission. Chebrikov was removed as head of the KGB and made Chairman of the Legal Affairs Commission. Both moves were considered to be demotions.

Vadim Medvedev, considered to be an ally of Gorbachëv, was added to the Politburo and made chief ideologist. His official title is Chairman of the Ideological Commission. In addition, Aleksandra Biryukova, Aleksandr Vlasov, and Anatoly Lukyanov were made alternate members of the Politburo. Biryukova thus became the first woman on the Politburo since the Khrushchev era.

In yet another change, Anatoli Dobrynin was relieved of his duties as secretary of the Central Committee and sent into honorable retirement. Increasingly, Gorbachëv's chief adviser on relations with the United States would be Aleksandr Yakovlev.

Although these personnel shifts helped Gorbachëv to further consolidate his power, structural changes adopted at the same time may have an even more important long–term significance. Essentially, the Central Committee voted to abolish the old Secretariat in the form in which it had previously existed—that is, as a body charged with implementing Politburo decisions. Instead, secretaries of the Central Committee were appointed as chairmen of six newly created commissions. In addition to those mentioned above, commissions were created for Party Building and Cadre Policy (Razumovsky), Socioeconomic Policy (Slyunkov), and International Policy (Yakovlev).

The secretaries thus became responsible for longer–term policy planning, while shorter–term decisions became the prerogative of persons occupying state positions. The obvious purpose of the change was to remove the party from the day–to–day supervision of affairs and to have it concentrate on matters of broad policy. Similar instructions—that is, to stop interfering in the day–to–day affairs of the Soviets and the economy—were sent out to party secretaries at subordinate levels at this same time. The continuing evidence indicated that it had little effect on how party secretaries operated, however.

A Legislature?

The party had, in fact, long decided everything. If it were to be restricted to long–term planning, then a power vacuum would be created unless the governmental institutions were strengthened. This was the thrust of the reorganization plan which Gorbachëv submitted to the Supreme Soviet in late November. An elaboration of the outline approved by the party conference in June, it created a 2,250-member Congress of People's Deputies, to be elected on the basis of a competitive ballot. The new Congress, when it met, would elect a Chairman of the U.S.S.R. Supreme Soviet (informally, President), plus a two chamber standing legislature, the U.S.S.R. Supreme Soviet.

In effect, Gorbachëv had redesigned the political system to allow for at least a partial transfer of power from the *Communist Party* to popularly elected legislative bodies. In addition, by creating strong executive ties to the new legislative bodies, he had partially freed himself from having to consult constantly with other members of the Politburo.

Elections to the Congress of People's Deputies took place on March 26, 1989, with the most interesting part being the campaign that preceded the actual election. Every candidate had to present an election platform, so the voters were able to choose between candidates based on issues. Most seats were contested. Of 1500 seats, only 384 had a single candidate; the rest had two or more. Seven hundred and fifty other seats were filled by various officially recognized organizations, including 100 filled by the *Communist Party*. But, although only this small number were elected directly by the *Communist Party*, it is significant that 82% of all the candidates were members of the *Communist Party* and the party endorsed candidates in most of the districts.

Approximately 80% of those endorsed by the party won. The party was, therefore, in no way repudiated. However, a number of individuals who, a few years ago, were considered to be dissidents were among the winners. These included Andrei Sakharov and historian and writer Roy Medvedev. A third individual who won running against a candidate endorsed by the party was none other than Boris Yeltsin, who got almost 90% of the vote in a Moscow at–large seat. There were also some prominent losers. The highest ranking of those was Yuri Solovyev, First Secretary for the Leningrad area, who failed to muster 50% of the vote, even though he was running unopposed. As a result, he eventually lost both his position as First Secretary and his seat on the Politburo.

The new Congress was scheduled to convene at the end of May but, before that occurred, Gorbachëv called a meeting of the Central Committee at the end of April and asked for the retirement of 110 people, or approximately one–third of the membership of that body. In turn, 24 persons were added to the Central Committee. In one sense, this was not a purge, however, as most of those who were retired from the Committee had already retired from the jobs that had earned them entry to the Central Committee in the first place. As one official associated with Gorbachëv expressed it, since there was to be a genuine working legislative body for the first time, Gorbachëv needed a Central Committee which was also made up of currently active individuals.

The Congress, when it did meet, proved to be lively but, ultimately, Gorbachëv dominated the session. The Congress first grilled Gorbachëv, then proceeded to elect him Chairman of the U.S.S.R. Supreme Soviet (informally, President). The new U.S.S.R. Supreme Soviet, the smaller, standing legislature, was then elected, and remained in session over the summer.

Although Gorbachëv set the agenda and tended to dominate discussions, it established itself as a genuine independent voice and a valuable forum. The second session showed itself to be even more independent and less subject to Gorbachëv's control.

Gorbachëv's greatest problem was to find groups who were not only loyal but were also committed to his programs. Again and again he made it clear that commitment to his goals came even before loyalty. This was shown once again in 1989, when he directed another major reshuffle. Three members of the Politburo, Viktor Nikonov, Viktor Chebrikov and Vladimir Scherbitsky, were "relieved of their duties" as Politburo members. They were joined in retirement by two alternate members, Yuriy Solovyev and Nikolay Talyzin.

Shcherbitsky was the last remaining member of the old Brezhnev Politburo (except for Gorbachëv) and his dismissal had been long predicted. Chebrikov, Nikonov, Solovyev and Talyzin, on the other hand, were early allies of Gorbachëv who had shown a general lack of commitment to reform.

The additions were equally telling. Vladimir Kryuchkov, head of the KGB, and Yuriy Maslyukov, head of GOSPLAN, had both been early Gorbechëv supporters. Their promotion to full membership appeared to Gorbachëv two strong allies on the Politburo. The two new alternate members, Yevgeniy Primakov and Boris Pugo, were also viewed as Gorbachëv loyalists though they later would turn on him. Primakov, chairman of the Council of the Union of the U.S.S.R. Supreme Soviet, was also an academician of the U.S.S.R. Academy of Sciences with a doctorate in economics. Pugo, chairman of the Party Control Commission, and a former head of the Latvian Communist Party, was also a deputy of Latvia's Supreme Soviet.

Nationality Problems

The major agenda topic at the Central Committee Plenum at which these political changes were made was nationality policy. The *Communist Party* had always boasted that it had solved the nationality problems in the U.S.S.R. but, in fact, the problems were merely suppressed.

Gorbachëv's policies, which among other things encouraged people to get involved and to demand reform, and which also tolerated the creation of unofficial groups and promised economic autonomy to the individual republics, had led to the creation of national fronts in nearly every republic and other groups organized along ethnic or nationality lines whose function was to air grievances and demand redress. In the Caucasus region, this had eventually led to a state of virtual war between Armenia and Azerbaijan over the mixed area called Nagorno–Karabakh and autonomy movements in the Baltic republics, in Moldavia, and within Western Ukraine (where the Ukrainian Catholic Church is predominant).

At the Central Committee Plenum, Gorbachëv, arguing that "the need for profound changes is long overdue in ethnic relations," promised a new federation under which "the right of each ethnic group to enjoy all the fruits of sovereignty and to decide all issues of its development—economic, political, and cultural," would be guaranteed.

Although Gorbachëv's position was endorsed by the Central Committee Plenum, the subsequent collapse of communist governments throughout Eastern Europe in the last three months of 1989—even though in one sense orchestrated by Gorbachëv—changed the equation and brought calls for greater change.

A Distressed Economy

In addition, the domestic economic situation had been deteriorating for some time and this added to the pressures as shortages of consumer goods continued to grow worse, producing greater public dissatisfaction. Reform–spirited communists, now organized into the *Democratic Platform*, threatened to split the party unless they got their way. Conservatives, on the other hand, reacted by urging a slowing down in the pace of reform.

In December, Nikolai Ryzhkov, Chairman of the USSR Council of Ministers, brought in a new draft five–year plan that represented a clear retreat from economic change. It looked like the planners would remain in charge for another five years.

As had become his practice, it was at this moment that Gorbachëv opted for more political reform. First of all, he accepted the idea of a multi–party system and formally proposed that the constituioin be changed to delete the *Communist Party's* leading position. This was accomplished in January–March 1990.

Next he proposed that, under the new circumstances, what the Soviet Union needed was an executive President, able to take action in an emergency without consultations with other bodies such as the Presidium of the Supreme Soviet.

This led, in March, to creation of the office of President of the U.S.S.R., to which Gorbachëv was subsequently elected. It also led to creation of a Presidential Council, which appears to have

been an attempt to create a Soviet version of a National Security Council or, possibly, a "super cabinet." Its membership, originally 16, included the foreign, interior, and defense ministers, the head of the KGB, other government and party officials, plus two prominent writers, Valentin Rasputin and Chingiz Aitmatov. In addition, the Chairman of the Council of Ministers sat as an ex–officio member. It didn't work out and was later disbanded.

The first challenge which the new President had to handle came from Lithuania. Following multiparty elections which were won by *Sajudis*, the Lithuanian national front, the Lithuanian legislature installed Vytautas Landsbergis as President and passed a declaration of independence. Similar declarations were adopted by Latvia and Estonia, although in a somewhat different form. Gorbachëv condemned all three as illegal and initiated a partial economic blockade of Lithuania. He then offered that, if the three republics suspended their declarations, talks leading to independence within two years could begin.

Gorbachëv also said that he would not use force against the would–be breakaway republics. Since he was scheduled to meet with President Bush on May 30,

that obviously acted as a restraint on his actions. Although President Bush raised the subject, he apparently did not press it with vigor. The United States found itself in an awkward position at this time. The three republics had been incorporated into the Soviet Union as a result of the Nazi–Soviet Non–Aggression Pact signed in August 1939. In the Pact, Hitler had recognized these nations as being in the Soviet sphere of influence in return for a Soviet promise of neutrality when Hitler invaded Poland.

The United States had never recognized the incorporation of the three republics into the U.S.S.R. and its legal position was that they were still sovereign nations. In fact, embassies of the three republics were still to be found in Washington, D.C. At the same time, the United States favored closer relations with the Soviet Union.

However, the Soviet position articulated by Gorbachëv was even more awkward. Although the Soviet Government had repudiated the Nazi–Soviet Non–Aggression Pact and considered it invalid, it continued to maintain that the three republics were factually a part of the U.S.S.R. and therefore had to apply for and receive permission to leave.

Just weeks before his dream collapses, a giant portrait of Lenin, father of modern communism, rises in front of KGB headquarters in Moscow.

Photo by Steve Raymer © National Geographic Society

Rumblings of Change

Gorbachëv also had other concerns. In the spring of 1990, elections in the Russian, Byelorussian, and Ukrainian republics produced a strong showing for the radical reformers, who won majorities in the largest cities, including Moscow and Leningrad. In Moscow, Gavriil Popov, a member of the Congress of People's Deputies and one of the leaders of the radical inter–regional group in the USSR Supreme Soviet, was elected mayor on the promise to move Moscow quickly toward a market economy.

Mayor Gavriil Popov of Moscow

Perhaps more important, Boris Yeltsin, was elected Chairman of the RSFSR Supreme Soviet (popularly, Russian President) on the third ballot in May. Gorbachëv thus lost control of the all–important Russian Republic.

Essentially, all of this happened because the party had split into three factions, conservatives, Gorbachëv supporters and democrats. The democrats wanted to move more quickly on reforms than Gorbachëv did, and threatened to leave the party and form a new political party if Gorbachëv didn't go along. Gorbachëv, citing the need for party unity, urged them to stay. The conservatives, on the other hand, urged the democrats to leave.

This was the background to Gorbachëv's other concern, the party congress which was scheduled to take place in late June/early July 1990. Gorbachëv decided to use the party congress to remake the party, getting rid of the Politburo and replacing it with a larger, less powerful Presidium, the majority of whose members would be ex officio—the party chairman and his deputies plus the 15 republic party secretaries. Gorbachëv intended the new Presidium to concentrate on coordinating the activities of the party. Broad policy functions would then become the prerogative of the Soviet Government.

The draft made no mention of the office of General Secretary but it did specify that there would continue to be a secretariat. The leader of the party would be the "chairman," and he was to be elected by the party congress as was the case under Lenin.

The draft was modified at the Party Congress but Gorbachëv got most of what he wanted. The office of General Secretary was retained, but he was elected by the party congress. The Politburo was retained, but its membership and function were modified as Gorbachëv desired.

The delegates also adopted a document called "Toward Humane, Democratic Socialism." Although the word socialism is in its title, the document actually moved the party a long way toward a rejection of what traditionally has been understood as Marxism–Leninism. Instead, the document spoke of the ideology of the party being based on "the legacy of Marx, Engels and Lenin, freed from dogmatic interpretation."

This document broke with traditional ideology in two basic ways. Socialism, it declared, should be based on individual, not collective, interests; and "private ownership...must have a place in the system of forms of ownership" of equal validity with collective ownership. What this meant is that the *Communist Party* was now claiming to represent the interests of Soviet citizens as individuals, not as members of a class or socio–economic grouping. Thus Marx's entire class–based analysis was discarded. And granting private property equal status with collective property flaunted Marx's premise that ownership of the means of production provided the basis for exploitation of man by man. In ideological terms, this programmatic statement moved the *Communist Party* a long distance from Marxist–Leninist orthodoxy. It could still claim to be a socialist party, of course.

Two other issues preoccupied Gorbachëv in 1990–91, the economy and the negotiation of a new union treaty. The two issues were intricately linked to each other, since one of the demands of the republics was control over economic activity and natural resources. An economic plan that would devolve authority to the republics would go a long way toward meeting this demand.

That is why the Shatalin Plan, which proposed transforming the Soviet Union to a market economy in 500 days, had the support of fourteen of the fifteen republics. Proposed in August 1990 as an alternative to the government's plan to retain the old system of state orders for another 18 months, it even got Gorbachëv's backing for a short while.

But Gorbachëv backed down when Ryzhkov, Chairman of the Council of Ministers, threatened to resign rather than take responsibility for implementing a plan he disagreed with. Gorbachëv then proposed that Ryzhkov take the two approaches and combine them. The result, which turned out to be mainly the Ryzhkov plan, was accepted by the Supreme Soviet in November. As a result, however, nearly every one of Gorbachëv's economic advisers left to work for Boris Yeltsin and the Russian Government.

Gorbachëv did get one good bit of news in October when he learned that he had been awarded the Nobel Peace Prize. Even that could not distract from worry about the economy, however. As Georgi Arbatov, the traditionalist director of the U.S.A. and Canada Institute, commented at the time, "I am sure that he deserves the Peace Prize. I wouldn't think he has deserved the Nobel Prize for economics."

In late 1990, under prodding from the Supreme Soviet, Gorbachëv changed the organizational structure once more. The Presidential Council and Council of Ministers were abolished and their place was taken by a strengthened Council of the Federation (created in March 1990) and a streamlined Cabinet of Ministers. There continued to be a Chairman who headed up the Cabinet, but he was made directly subordinate to Gorbachëv. These provisions were more or less implemented while some other provisions, such as Gorbachëv's suggestion that the Congress of People's Deputies be replaced by a directly elected Supreme Soviet, were not.

Gorbachëv lost his most valuable ally in December 1990 when Foreign Minister Eduard Shevardnadze resigned after charging that the Soviet Union was headed toward a dictatorship. He was replaced by Alexandr Bessmertnykh, whose previous position had been Soviet ambassador to Washington. After his resignation, Shevardnadze became head of a new independent foreign policy research institute, the Soviet Foreign Policy Association.

Gorbachëv lost a second adviser in December when Nikolai Ryzhkov suffered a heart attack and resigned as Chairman of the newly created Cabinet of Ministers. He was replaced by Valentin Pavlov, who had been Ryzhkov's Finance Minister. A conservative, Pavlov's first major action was to attempt to reduce the money overhang by a partial repudiation of the currency. All 50 and 100 ruble notes were withdrawn from circulation, with individuals given three days to redeem a limited amount related to monthly salary. Pavlov's overall economic program was a

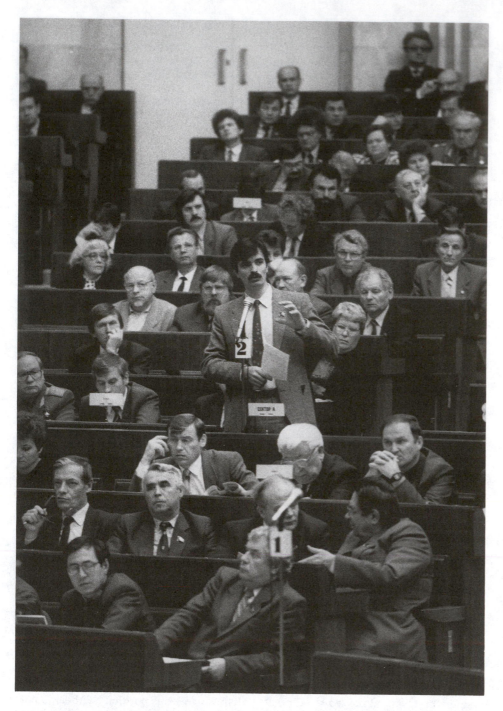

The Supreme Soviet of the USSR discussing problems of stabilizing the national economy and transition to a market system, October 1990.

continuation of the Ryzhkov program. Gorbachëv also dismayed many people when he appointed Gennadi Yanayev, a Communist Party bureaucrat, as his Vice President.

The Baltic Republics became the center of attention once again in January 1991, when Ministry of the Interior troops stormed the Lithuanian press center and a building occupied by the Lithuanian civilian militia on January 13, killing 14 persons. Gorbachëv's role in all this was ambivalent. He did not repudiate the attack, but claimed to have found out about it only after it happened. The fol-

lowing weekend, five more persons were killed when Ministry of Interior troops seized the Latvian Ministry of Interior building.

The European Parliament then moved to block $1 billion in food aid to the Soviet Union, and a number of European nations began threatening other sanctions. In Washington, the Bush administration began discussing postponement of an upcoming summit meeting, which was in fact postponed, though publicly it was because of the Iraq conflict. Responding to this international pressure, Gorbachëv backed down in early February and

agreed to appoint a commission to consult with the Baltic Republics about their demands for independence.

Gorbachëv's great concern was the national referendum on the question of the future of the USSR which was scheduled for March 17, 1991. The question asked of the Soviet people was whether they considered it "necessary to preserve the Union of Soviet Socialist Republics as a renewed federation of equal sovereign republics, in which human rights and the freedoms of all nationalities will be fully guaranteed?"

Six republics refused to participate in the referendum, and four other republics modified the question in some way. Gorbachëv nevertheless claimed a victory on the basis of the 76% who voted "yes" among those who participated.

The next month, Gorbachëv and the heads of the nine republics who had participated in the referendum announced their agreement on an outline for a new union treaty that would create a Union of Sovereign Soviet Republics. The draft called for a great deal of decentralization, particularly in the economic area, plus a remaking of the national government, including new elections for a national legislature and President. In early May, Gorbachëv agreed to turn coal mines over to the Russian Government as part of a deal to end a miners' strike.

Later in the month, Gorbachëv also endorsed a new plan for economic reform drawn up by Grigory Yavlinsky, who had also contributed to the Shatalin Plan. This new plan called for significant international economic assistance to act as a "shock absorber of social costs and shocks" as the Soviet Union moved to a market economy.

Events tumbled on at a faster and faster rate. In May–June there was a resolution of differences over the CFE Treaty and a new immigration law was passed by the Supreme Soviet. It was announced that President Bush would travel to Moscow for a Summit meeting sometime during the summer. And, in a new test of public opinion, Boris Yeltsin won 60% of the popular vote in his run for the newly created office of President of the Russian Federation. The official communist candidate came in a dismal third. Gorbachëv, reversing his previous position, warmly embraced Yeltsin's victory.

Communist conservatives, evidently alarmed by this development, began to plot a "constitutional *coup*" against Gorbachëv in late June. It took the form of a request by Premier Pavlov that the Supreme Soviet transfer from Gorbachëv to him the power to rule by decree. The President, Pavlov explained, was "overworked." Pavlov's request was supported Defense Minister Yazov, KGB Chairman Vladimir Kryuchkov and Minister of Interior Boris Pugo. Forewarned of Pavlov's attempt to strip away some of his powers, Gorbachëv counterattacked and defeated the move. In the process, however, Gorbachëv did two things that he would later rue. He permitted all four of his treasonous subordinates to retain their positions of power, while he attacked their political arguments. He told these four representatives of the military–industrial complex that the Soviet Union was overmilitarized and that "we have to remove this burden and turn the economy over to the people. Otherwise my mission will be useless and I will have to resign." The attempt failed.

Gorbachëv had a busy summer. In July, he traveled to London to meet with the "Group of Seven" (USA, Great Britain, Canada, Germany, France, Italy and Japan). His purpose in requesting the meeting was to try to get a promise of economic assistance. He basically used the Yavlinsky Plan as the basis of his discussions. He got no promises of cash, though the Group did offer the Soviet Union some technical assistance and a "special associate status" with the IMF and World Bank.

President Bush came to Moscow at the end of July. The summit meeting included two days of discussions and a ceremonial signing of the completed START agreement. Gorbachëv then left for a vacation in the Crimea with his family.

He planned to return to Moscow on August 19 since, the following day, he and the leaders of nine of the republics were to sign a new union treaty that conceded significant powers to the individual republics. Instead, Gorbachëv was placed under house arrest on the evening of August 18. The next day, the world learned that a *coup d'etat* had been launched by conservative communists in the top echelons of government—their goal to preserve the Soviet Union and the communist system. Among the top leaders were Pavlov, Yazov, Kryuchkov, and Pugo, the four participants in the attempted "constitutional *coup*" against Gorbachëv in late June. They were joined this time by Vice President Gennadi Yanayev. These five, plus three other conservatives, took control as the "State Committee for the State of Emergency."

The *coup* lasted approximately 60 hours

Soviet President Mikhail Gorbachëv joins the Group of Seven leaders in London. First row (l. to r.) President Bush, Gorbachëv, British Prime Minister Major, French President Mitterrand, German Chancellor Kohl. Second row: EC President Jacques Delors, Italian Prime Minister Andreotti, Canadian Prime Minister Mulroney, Japanese Prime Minister Kaifu, Dutch Prime Minister Lubbers.

Reuters/Bettmann

presided over the demise of the CMEA and the Warsaw Pact, thus formally dissolving the ties that bound the various countries of Eastern Europe to the Soviet Union. And, of course, he presided over a series of military negotiations that helped to bring an end to the Cold War.

Changing Relations with Eastern Europe under Gorbachëv

The pattern of foreign relations established by Stalin with Eastern Europe after World War II was one of almost total subordination on the part of the communist leaderships of those countries, exemplified after 1948 by Stalin's campaign to remove from office those communist leaders who showed any independence whatsoever. During this period, Soviet ambassadors acted as virtual proconsuls, whose orders had the force of law.

Poland's Wladyslaw Gomulka, one of those who resisted and, as a result, was purged, described this phenomenon:

"In this bloc of socialist states, it was Stalin who stood at the apex of this hierarchic ladder of cults. All those who stood on lower rungs of the ladder bowed their heads before him. . . . The first secretaries of the central committees of the parties of the various countries who sat on the second rung of the ladder of the cult of personality, in turn donned the robes of infallibility and wisdom."

Soviet–East European relations were thus, for Stalin, an extension of domestic Soviet politics.

All of that began to change after Stalin's death. The new Soviet leadership, which had been subject to the same treatment during Stalin's lifetime, committed itself to a "New Course" in intrabloc relations. Modifying the previous relationship, they allowed Eastern European leaders greater independence and encouraged them to develop policies designed to win them greater popularity among their people. This was, they concluded, the best way to ensure the long–term success of communism in Eastern Europe.

There were limitations to this independence, of course. All were required to join the Warsaw Pact when it was established in 1955 and even Khrushchëv, chief spokesman for this viewpoint, didn't hesitate to intervene militarily in Hungary in 1956, when the communist leadership there began to lose control. Khrushchëv's decision to allow Gomulka to take power in Poland in 1956 was another part of this loosening of control.

Khrushchëv sought to further integrate the Soviet and East European economies, but he permitted Romania to opt out when that country opposed the international division of labor proposed by the

President-Elect Bush, President Reagan and General Secretary Gorbachëv check out their "where to stand" marks for a photo-taking session at Governor's Island, NY., December 7, 1988.

AP/Wide World Photo

and eventually failed, thanks primarily to Boris Yeltsin and supporters of reform and democracy throughout the country. But the complicity of the Communist Party in the *coup* was so great that there were few objections when Boris Yeltsin, on the morning after the *coup* was defeated, banned Communist Party activities in the Russian Republic. Two days later, Gorbachëv resigned as General Secretary and called upon the Central Committee to dissolve itself. He then issued a decree suspending the activities of the party and seizing all party property. After 74 years, the Communist Era had come to an end.

Foreign Policy Under Gorbachëv

Soviet foreign policy had been changing since 1985, not only with regard to the United States, but also with regard to the Third World and Eastern Europe. Soviet support for a settlement in southern Africa led to an agreement to pull Cuban troops out of Angola. It was also Soviet pressure on Vietnam that caused that country to pull its troops out of Cambodia. It also eventually halted the shipment of military equipment to Nicaragua and then tacitly supported the free elections that resulted in a non–Communist government coming to power there in April 1990.

When Iraq invaded Kuwait, Gorbachëv gave his support to the various UN Security Council resolutions demanding that Iraq pull out of Kuwait and then those authorizing the use of force against Iraq, even though Iraq had been a long–time ally of the Soviet Union. Gorbachëv also

Soviet Union. Khrushchëv also did nothing when, in April 1964, Romania claimed the right to develop its own policies. Romania would later go on to develop its own, independent foreign policy, though it always remained an orthodox communist party domestically.

Brezhnev intervened in Czechoslovakia in 1968 when that country's communist party moved to give up its monopoly of political power. He also put strong pressure on the Polish communist leadership to reverse its decision legalizing the independent trade union *Solidarity* in 1981. But he quietly permitted Hungary to implement ever more far–reaching economic reforms without interference. Gorbachëv's attitude toward Eastern Europe when he became General Secretary in 1985 appeared to be relatively orthodox, though from the beginning he tended to treat individual communist leaders as though he considered them partners in a common enterprise. His first plans for economic reform relied heavily on Eastern Europe as a source of new technology and he confidently expected them to join him in implementing similar reforms in their own countries. The Soviet Union already got many of the more sophisticated products that it imported, such as computers, computer software and machine tools, from Eastern Europe, and he expected that they would want to upgrade their technology and become a source of ever more sophisticated technology.

He was disappointed by the first response to his reform ideas. Only Hungary, already well along in its own reform program, was enthusiastic. For a while, he attempted to lead by example and by persuasion, speaking of his economic reform and pointing out its advantages on visits to Eastern Europe, but making no effort to coerce communist leaders into adopting the same approach. On the other hand, the Soviet Union did chide Eastern European leaders for the poor quality of their exports and it put behind the scenes pressure on them to upgrade the quality and technological level of their products, though with little success. Czechoslovakia and the German Democratic Republic, the Eastern European countries with the most developed economies, were both led by conservative leaders who believed that a program of economic reform would undermine their own legitimacy.

Gorbachëv slowly came to realize that the Eastern European countries weren't going to provide the significant assistance in the area of technology that he had been counting on to help him with his own *perestroika*. Their unreformed economies simply weren't up to it. Finland, the only non–communist neighbor, proved to be much more valuable as a source of technology than any of the communist countries of Eastern Europe.

Meanwhile, the Soviet Union was providing Eastern Europe with energy supplies and raw materials below world prices, while receiving shoddy consumer goods and old technology in return. The question Gorbachëv had to ask himself was whether the conservative and unreformed communist leaderships were more of a burden than an asset. Was Finland a better model? A number of articles appeared in the Soviet press at about this time discussing the merits of a "Finlandization" of Eastern Europe.

The 1989 Revolutions

Thus we come to the events and decisions of 1989, when communism collapsed nearly everywhere in Eastern Europe. In country after country, ruling communist parties were first forced to compromise with their opponents and then, in most cases, to relinquish part or all of their power to them. Communism, a doctrine imposed from the outside by Soviet armies after the defeat of Nazi Germany, never was popular among the people of Eastern Europe. Yet the communist elites remained in power, partly because they controlled a monopoly of

October 1989: On a stone lion in front of parliament a Hungarian youth hoists the flag of his country—with the hammer and sickle surgically removed. AP/Wide World Photos

Bucharest, Romania, Christmas Eve 1989. A Romanian soldier points his rifle at enemy positions during street fighting.
AP/Wide World Photos

power and partly because they could always count on the support and backing of the Soviet Union, spelled out after 1968 in the "Brezhnev Doctrine."

So no one predicted the events of 1989, precisely because no one expected that the Soviet Union would permit such changes to occur in Eastern Europe. And that points out the most important difference about 1989—that the Soviet Union did not merely acquiesce in these changes; it was, in fact, an active agent in bringing them about. In hindsight, it was predictable. The Soviets had become economically exhausted and their only choice to continue control in Eastern Europe was military, which would have enraged world opinion.

Gorbachëv had several times said things that sounded like a repudiation of the Brezhnev Doctrine after becoming General Secretary, but no one was certain whether he meant it. It was his intervention in Poland in the latter part of 1988 that gave the first indication that he meant what he had said.

After outlawing *Solidarity* in December 1981, General Jaruzelski and the ruling *Polish United Workers' Party* introduced a program of economic reform to remake the Polish economy and to deal with the conditions that had brought *Solidarity* into existence in the first place. That attempt at economic reform from above was unsuccessful and the government, under challenge from the official trade unions, collapsed in September 1988.

It was at this moment that the first indication of a reversal of Soviet policy occurred, in the form of a series of articles in the Soviet press portraying Lech Walesa and *Solidarity* in a favorable manner. This led to formal talks between the Polish Government and *Solidarity* and the now famous April 1989 agreement relegalizing *Solidarity* and setting new elections for June 4.

Those elections provided for only 35% of the seats in the *Sejm* (lower house of parliament) to be freely contested, but did include elections to a new Senate, all of whose seats were competitive. *Solidarity* took 99 out of 100 seats in the Senate, plus all of the open seats in the *Sejm*. In addition, most of the top communist leadership, running unopposed for *Sejm* seats, were rejected because they failed to get 50% of the valid votes. These seats, reserved for communists, were filled in a second round of voting only because *Solidarity* instructed its supporters to endorse the new candidates.

The failure of the communists at the polls meant that they were in practice unable to form a government. Their allies, the *United Peasants' Party* and the *Democratic Party*, refused to support the communist candidate for Chairman of the Council of Ministers and opened discussions with *Solidarity*. This led Lech Walesa to propose a *Solidarity*–led coalition government which would include communists. Now came a second decisive Soviet intervention. After Mieczy-

slaw Rakowski, the new head of the *Polish United Workers' Party*, announced his opposition to such a coalition, he got a 40 minute telephone call from Gorbachëv, the essence of which was that Gorbachëv expected the Polish party to accept a *Solidarity*–led coalition government.

The psychological effect on the rest of Eastern Europe of the installation of a non–communist government in Poland was enormous; and even more important, it was known that Gorbachëv not only gave his support to the change but actually intervened to help bring it about. This was seen as making change possible all over Eastern Europe. Surprisingly, Gorbachëv continued to support change in Eastern Europe, even as those changes led to the collapse of communist governments throughout the region.

After Poland, the next development occurred in Hungary, where a reform communist leadership had been installed in May 1988. Over the next year, opposition political parties were legalized and free elections were scheduled. New laws were also passed guaranteeing Hungarians the right to travel abroad and to emigrate. And in March 1989, Hungary signed a United Nations protocol on refugees in which it obligated itself not to force refugees to go back home. In signing the protocol, the Hungarian Government obviously had in mind Hungarian–speaking Romanians who were infiltrating across the border from Romania. By August 1989, however, tens of thousands of East German citizens had gathered in Hungary, drawn there by Hungary's decision to begin dismantling the barbed wire on its border with Austria. Refusing to return to East Germany, they wanted to go west.

The problem was a treaty that Hungary had signed with the German Democratic Republic in 1968 under which the Hungarian Government promised to obtain clearance from the GDR before permitting GDR citizens to travel from it to a third country, a permission that was not forthcoming. The Hungarian Government now decided to let the East Germans go, but there was some concern about the Soviet reaction. When informal sounding established *that the Soviet Government would not object*, Hungary opened the border for the East Germans on September 10.

The third break occurred in the German Democratic Republic, largely as a result of the decision of the Hungarian Government to allow East Germans to depart for the west. After the Hungarian action, other East Germans, unable to obtain visas to Hungary, began traveling in large numbers to Czechoslovakia, where no visa was required. Gathering in Prague, they began to inundate the grounds of the West German Embassy. Here they were given West German passports, but they still needed permission to depart Czechoslovakia for the west. The Czechoslovakian Government, not wanting to be caught in the middle, requested clearance from the GDR Government. The GDR eventually gave in and began arranging for trains to carry its citizens directly to West Germany.

The flight of hundreds of thousands of East Germans began to have repercussions at home, however. Protest demonstrations which were already occurring in a number of East German cities grew in size and number. The most organized of the demonstrations occurred in Leipzig. At first, the regime tried to handle the situation through the use of force. In addition to its usual riot police, it called out special "battle groups" of its party militia and fighting teams of the state security police, equipped with water cannons and armored cars. And on October 3, the East German Government closed its borders with Czechoslovakia.

The matter came to a head on October 9 in Leipzig, when the local party leadership rejected orders from East Berlin to put down demonstrations scheduled for that day and instead called for a dialogue, promising to "use our full power and authority to ensure that this dialogue will occur, not only in the Leipzig area but with our national government."

At the Politburo meeting called to discuss the Leipzig decision, Egon Krenz, the number two man in the party, supported the Leipzig leaders over Erich Honecker's objections. This led to a Central Committee meeting eight days later and to Honecker's ouster as General Secretary on October 18.

Egon Krenz took over as General Secretary and promised reforms. He reopened the borders with Czechoslovakia and promised East Germans 30 days a year travel abroad. The flight through Czechoslovakia immediately resumed. Krenz next gambled that he could stabilize the situation by granting all citizens the right of unrestricted travel to the west, symbolized by the opening of the Berlin Wall on November 9, 1989. He accompanied this with promises of freer elections, economic liberalization, and power–sharing with other parties. Within a week, an estimated one–third of all East Germans had visited either West Berlin or West Germany.

After the initial euphoria, however, the pressure for change continued. On November 17, Hans Modrow, Dresden party chief, who had a reputation as a reformer, became the new head of government. Modrow proposed roundtable discussions with the opposition and these began on December 7.

In the meanwhile, Egon Krenz and the other members of the Politburo submitted their resignations and a caretaker committee was appointed to run the party. At a special party congress that began five days later, Gregor Gysi, an attorney who had made his reputation as a defender of critics of the state and people caught fleeing the country, was appointed the new party leader. The delegates also voted to change the name of the party and to set the goal of the party as "democratic socialism."

At the congress, Hans Modrow spoke in favor of a confederation between the two Germanys. Helmut Kohl, the West

November 11, 1989: With the Reichstag in the background, young Germans sit on the Berlin Wall in its final hours.

Foreign ministers meet in Bonn, West Germany, May 1990. Third from left is Foreign Minister Shevardnadze

German Chancellor, had proposed a ten–point plan for unification in November, but this was the first time that any East German leader had endorsed the concept. Unification received another boost when Chancellor Kohl paid an official visit to East Germany on December 19. Kohl spoke in Dresden to cheering crowds and then he and Modrow joined the mayors of West and East Berlin in a ceremony opening a pedestrian crossing at the Brandenburg Gate.

Reunification was the big issue in the elections on March 18 and they were won by the conservative "Alliance for Germany," led by the GDR *Christian Democratic Union*. On April 12, Lothar de Maizere, leader of the *Christian Democratic Union*, became the first non–communist head of government, leading a "Grand Coalition" of the main non–communist parties, including the *Social Democrats*.

The new government immediately began preparing for German reunification. For a while, Gorbachëv maintained that the Soviet Union would not agree to German unification, unless Germany either suspended its membership in NATO or maintained its membership in the Warsaw Pact as well. After negotiations with the Federal Republic, however, he accepted continued German membership in NATO. An economic, social and currency union went into effect on July 1 and final unification took place on October 3, 1990.

Czechoslovakians had not reacted to the large numbers of East Germans fleeing west by way of their country, but subsequent events in East Germany did lead to the beginning of massive demonstrations in Prague. On November 17, three thousand young people gathered near Wenceslas Square in Central Prague and began demanding free elections. The Government reacted by ordering the police to put down the demonstration by force. It was a fatal mistake. The Czechoslovak people, aroused by the government's brutality, went into the streets in great numbers, singing, chanting, and demanding the ouster of Milos Jakes, the party General Secretary who had approved the police action. It was at this moment that Michael Gorbachëv intervened by sending a message that the Soviet Government would not tolerate violence.

As the demonstrations continued and grew in size, a Central Committee meeting was called for November 24 and Milos Jakes and his entire Presidium resigned. The party had begun to crumble. Prime Minister Ladislav Adamec opened negotiations with the opposition, now organized as the *Civic Forum*. But Adamec, who wanted to retain a communist–dominated government, was forced to resign on December 6. His replacement, Marian Calfa, organized a new government in which the communists were in a minority.

The Czechoslovak parliament was subsequently purged and on December 28 Alexander Dubcek, leader of the 1968 Prague Spring, was elected chairman. The next day, Vaclav Haval, the Czech playwright whose opposition to the previous regime had landed him repeatedly in prison, was elected President. Czechoslovakia thus had its first non–communist president since 1948. *Civic Forum*

won the multiparty elections that took place on June 6, 1990 while the communists were reduced to a tiny remnant.

Change also came to Bulgaria, though in the beginning at least it was engineered to a greater extent from above. On November 9, Todor Zhivkov was forced out as communist party leader and replaced by Petar Mladenov. Zhivkov had been in power for 36 years. Mladenov, who had served as Bulgarian foreign minister for the previous 19 years, immediately instituted a policy of liberalization that soon led to legalization of opposition groups and the beginning of demonstrations in the streets. Broad–based talks began in January between the party and the opposition and a few days later the parliament voted to end the party's monopoly of power. At a hastily called party congress, the party voted to change its name and to become the *Bulgarian Socialist Party*. Mladenov also stepped down as party leader in April, after he had been elected to a new executive Presidency.

Multi–party elections that took place in June were won by the ex–communists, but they had lost in the cities and the opposition, emboldened by this, continued their attacks on the government. In July, Mladenov was replaced by Zhelyu Zhelev, a leader of the opposition. After continued demonstrations, Dimitar Popov, a non–communist, was appointed Prime Minister. There was never any direct Gorbachëv intervention in the political events occurring in Bulgaria in 1989–90. However, Gorbachëv's responses with regard to events in other parts of Eastern Europe were well known in Bulgaria and undoubtedly were a factor influencing events in Bulgaria as well.

Romania experienced perhaps the greatest change of any country in Eastern Europe in 1989 when Nicolae Ceaucescu, who had ruled the country since 1965, was overthrown in a violent uprising that ended in Ceaucescu's death by firing–squad on December 25. Ceaucescu, who was proud of his independence from Moscow, had rejected Gorbachëv's policy of reform and made every effort to isolate his countrymen from events going on elsewhere in Eastern Europe. In November 1989, he had reaffirmed his policies at a party congress and had been reelected head of the party for a further five–year term. It was probably this reaffirmation of policies that was responsible for his downfall, for they had been responsible for a significant decline in the standard of living of Romanians over the previous nine years.

The revolt, which actually began as an ethnic dispute in the city of Timisoara, in the western part of Romania, spread to Bucharest, the capital, when Ceausescu called a mass meeting for December 21 to denounce the events in Timisoara. Instead, the people began shouting "freedom" and "democracy" and Ceausescu stalked off. That afternoon, the streets were full of people demonstrating against Ceausescu. That evening, Ceausescu ordered the secret police to begin firing on the people. A similar order to the army brought a refusal from General Milea, the Defense Minister. General Milea was executed the next morning, but the army now joined the revolution. Ceausescu and his wife fled the capital, but they were captured, brought back to Bucharest, and summarily tried and executed.

The *Securitate*, Ceausescu's secret police, fought on for a few days more but the army gradually managed to restore order. In the meantime, a group calling itself the *National Salvation Front* emerged as the new political leadership in the country. The *Front*, at first made up almost exclusively of former establishment figures who had fallen out with Ceausescu, was enlarged within a few days to take in various non–communist elements. It then began referring to itself as the *Council of National Salvation*. In the third week of January, the *Council* announced that multi–party elections would take place in May and that it intended to run its own candidates. This brought a condemnation from the leaders of the three largest opposition parties. After a series of negotiations, the *Council* agreed to make room for representatives of other parties. On February 1, the *Council* brought the representatives of 29 other political parties into the government coalition.

By this time, it had grown to approximately 180 members. It also underwent a name change and became the *Provisional Council for National Unity*. A new ten member Executive Committee, headed by Acting President Ion Iliescu, also came into existence now. Meanwhile, the original *National Salvation Front* reorganized itself as a political party and announced that it, not the *Council*, would field candidates in the upcoming May 20 elections. As its candidate for President, it nominated Ion Iliescu. Most of the leadership of the *Front* had been members of the old *Romanian Communist Party* and the local branches of the *National Salvation Front*, set up at the time of the revolution, were largely made up of ex–officials. Thus, while the old communist party structure had collapsed, a large percentage of its membership transferred their loyalties to the *National Salvation Front*.

Eventually, some 80 political parties came into existence, though only three of them had any significant political support in the country. Two of these, both parties that were outlawed when the communists took over, are the *Liberals* and the *Peasant Party*. The third, the *Hungarian Democratic Union*, represents the interests of ethnic Hungarians. Although the opposition attacked the *National Salvation Front* because of its high component of ex–communists, there was, in fact, little to differentiate between them as far as programs were concerned. All were committed to the creation of a multi–party democracy and a market economy.

In the May elections, Ion Iliescu was elected President with approximately 83% of the vote while the *National Salvation Front* took 66% of the seats in the National Assembly. Election observers announced that there had been some irregularities in the voting but that, overall, the election was free.

An Overview

The events of 1989 and 1990 transformed eastern Europe and laid the basis for a new relationship with the Soviet Union. In the beginning, all of the new governments promised to remain in the Warsaw Pact and the Council for Mutual Economic Assistance, but the basis for those organizations no longer existed. The CMEA was changing in any case, having agreed to carry on all trade in dollars as of January 1, 1991. This turned out to be so destabilizing that the CMEA effectively ceased to exist after the change-over and was formally dissolved on July 1, 1991. The military aspects of the Warsaw Pact were phased out in April after Hungary had announced that it intended to resign its membership; on July 1, 1991, the Warsaw Pact was also dissolved.

The Soviet Union pulled the last of its troops out of Hungary and Czechoslovakia in June 1991. It also signed an agreement with Germany to withdraw all Soviet troops by 1994 and gave a similar promise to Poland.

The various East European countries had begun to reorient their exports toward hard currency areas and away from the Soviet Union, a process that speeded up after the Soviet Union canceled standing orders with eastern European companies because of an inability to pay for the products in the now required hard currency. In a curious twist, the Economic Community actually helped to recreate some of those ties in 1991 as part of an agreement giving Hungary, Czechoslovakia and Poland associate membership status in the EC. France, concerned about agricultural imports from eastern Europe, persuaded the EC to buy a part of the production from these countries for delivery to the Soviet Union.

U.S.–Soviet Relations
Under Gorbachëv

In 1985, the overriding factor in U.S.–Soviet relations was the military rivalry between the two superpowers and how it was managed. Arms negotiations had occurred at intervals since the 1960s. There had been the occasional, successful negotiations, but the period 1979–85 was basically one of stalemate. The two sides had continued to talk, but no agreements were reached. Meanwhile, the size of the arsenals continued to grow on both sides. Gorbachëv's first policy speech after becoming General Secretary outlined a traditional Soviet position, but even that speech contained the phrase, "we want a real and major reduction of the arms stockpiles." The sticking point was President Reagan's Strategic Defense Initiative, launched in March 1983.

The SDI was a proposal to use emergent technology to develop a shield to stop incoming missiles, using a combina-

Presidents Gorbachëv and Bush at dinner aboard the Soviet Ship *Gorky*, off Malta, December 1989

tion of laser beams, computers, satellites and radar. SDI promised to reduce the threat of Soviet missiles to the United States. The failure of international negotiations gave it much of its political support, for it promised to achieve unilaterally what could otherwise be achieved only by successful negotiations.

The threat of having its missile force neutralized alarmed the Soviet leadership, and led to a Soviet proposal for talks on space weapons in mid–1984. The first discussions actually took place on March 12, 1985, one day after Gorbachëv succeeded Chernenko as General Secretary. The beginning Soviet position was that the USA cease *research* on development of a SDI system.

Officially, the Soviet opposition to American development of an SDI system was based on the premise that a successful one would give the United States a first strike capability *since it would not have to worry about retaliatory Soviet missiles.* The actual reasons for this opposition are far more complex, but are associated with Soviet weakness in the area of technological innovation and a Soviet recognition that the western world is experiencing a technological revolution in the areas of computers and automation that is leaving the Soviets further and further behind.

This new computer technology has significant military applications and, in fact, must be at the heart of any successful SDI system. The Soviets thus fear SDI for the emerging technology it could produce. There is also the possibility of SDI "spin–offs" which could revolutionize conventional warfare, thus reducing Moscow's huge advantage in this area. (Consider, for example, the effect of a lethal beam effective at a distance of five miles on the vast Soviet tank fleet.) It is no coincidence that Gorbachëv's opposition to SDI internationally has been coupled with a domestic program aimed at giving the Soviet Union mastery of advanced technology.

Although arms negotiations talks continued in Geneva, no progress was possible because of the deadlock over SDI. To break this, Reagan and Gorbachëv decided to hold a summit conference in Geneva in November 1985. The talks were relatively cordial, and the two spoke privately for about five hours. There was no breakthrough on SDI, but Gorbachëv did accept an invitation extended by Reagan to visit the United States in 1986.

Negotiations at Geneva continued in 1986. They were serious, and differences were narrowed, but a final agreement still remained beyond their grasp—because of SDI differences. When Gorbachëv, as a consequence, postponed his visit to the United States, it was decided to hold a "pre–summit" in Reykjavik, Iceland. The two leaders met on October 11–12, 1986 for what turned out to be wide–ranging discussion of the entire field of arms control.

No accord was reached, but the astonishing thing is how close they came, considering the topics discussed during that historic weekend. Insofar as intermediate range ballistic missiles stationed in Europe, Gorbachëv agreed to the U.S.–proposed "zero option." On strategic offensive weapons, the two sides agreed to 50% cuts in five years and elimination of *all* such weapons in ten years.

Negotiations with regard to SDI proved to be most intractable, but even here progress in resolving differences was made. Thus, the Soviet position was that each side agree to adhere to the ABM Treaty for ten years; that during this time all SDI testing be confined to the laboratory, and that the two sides negotiate about SDI stationing at the end of ten years. Prior to the summit, the United States had been offering not to withdraw from the ABM Treaty for a term of 7-1/2 years. At Reykjavik the U.S. agreed to adhere to the ABM Treaty for ten years if, during that same time period, strategic nuclear ballistic missiles were reduced to zero.

The two sticking points were the question of confining SDI testing to the laboratory and the question of whether the United States could begin deploying SDI at the end of ten years without further negotiations with the Soviet Union. When agreement could not be

President Reagan and General Secretary Gorbachëv, Reykjavik, Iceland, October 11, 1986

reached on these two points, the negotiations fell through, because the Soviet position was that the arms talks proposals were a single package, and agreement on any part of the package depended on acceptance by both sides of the *entire* package.

The first reaction to the Reykjavik summit was one of disappointment, but as both sides began looking back at what *had been accomplished*, the many areas of agreement became clear. In January 1987 the Soviet Union indicated its desire to continue discussions by naming a new chief Soviet negotiator at Vienna, Yuli Vorontsov, who holds the rank of First Deputy Foreign Minister.

Because of the lack of breakthrough, Gorbachëv launched a new initiative on February 28. Reversing his position at Reykjavik, he called for urgent negotiation of a separate agreement on intermediate–range nuclear missiles. He accompanied this with the promise that once agreement on intermediate–range missiles was reached, the Soviet Union would withdraw its shorter–range missiles from East Germany and Czechoslovakia. In April, he further modified his proposal by indicating that the Soviet Union would eliminate all shorter–range missiles from Europe as part of an agreement on intermediate–range missiles. He was also quoted by TASS at this time as saying that he was ready to meet Reagan in order to "conclude" a treaty on intermediate–range missiles and to reach agreement on "key provisions" regarding strategic offensive arms, space defense, arms and nuclear tests. Negotiations between the two countries continued over the summer of 1987 but became stalled when the Soviet side insisted that West Germany's 72 Pershing 1A missiles (with U.S.–controlled warheads) had to be included in the deal. This obstacle was removed in August when West German Chancellor Kohl agreed conditionally to dismantle the Pershing 1A missiles. It took a visit to Washington by Foreign Minister Shevardnadze in September and a visit of Secretary of State Shultz to Moscow in October, but the result was a draft agreement banning intermediate–range (and Soviet shorter–range) missiles, known as the INF agreement. It was this INF agreement that General Secretary Gorbachëv signed when he made his first visit to the United States on December 8–11, 1987.

The successful conclusion of the INF treaty did not, as it turned out, provide enough momentum for agreement on strategic arms in time for President Reagan's visit to the USSR on May 29–June 2, 1988. As a result, the Moscow summit was largely ceremonial, though not less important for that reason.

Negotiations on strategic arms contin-

ued, but no agreement was reached, partly because of the change of American administrations and partly because of the complexity of the subject. There were other major developments in this area, however. The most important of these came in December 1988, when Gorbachëv, during an address to the United Nations General Assembly, announced that the U.S.S.R. would make unilateral cuts of 500,000 troops and 10,000 tanks, with 50,000 troops and 5,000 tanks to be pulled out of Eastern Europe. He also promised that, in addition to the tanks, other equipment used in an attack, including river–bridging equipment would also be withdrawn. Some troops and tanks have already been pulled out.

The new Conventional Forces in Europe (CFE) talks—the enlarged version of the old MBFR talks—also began in Vienna in March 1989. The talks went very well from the beginning for it was the Soviet Union which proposed eliminating "imbalances and asymmetries" over a period of two years. Since they have an overwhelming advantage in ground equipment, their proposal meant that the Soviet Union would have to eliminate about 10 tanks for each tank eliminated by NATO.

The Soviet plan also suggested "equal collective ceilings which would be 10 to 15 percent lower than the lowest level possessed by either of the politico–military alliances." The ceiling proposed by NATO had been only slightly higher than this.

Finally, the Soviets also acknowledged the need for "the most stringent and rigorous verification, including inspections without right of refusal," thus meeting yet another of NATO's concerns.

There were still some major differences between the two sides at this point, but they have significantly narrowed since that time. In May 1989, Gorbachëv agreed that the Warsaw Pact was prepared to withdraw from Eastern Europe 40,000 of 58,470 tanks, 42,000 out of 70,330 armored vehicles and 47,000 our of 71,560 artillery pieces, and finally that it was willing to "make similar reductions in manpower and other types of weaponry." This was precisely the area of NATO's greatest concern and, therefore, Gorbachëv's offer was accepted with enthusiasm.

Two weeks later, President Bush, at a NATO summit in Brussels, proposed an equal ceiling of 275,000 troops which the two super–powers would be permitted to station in Europe outside their own territory and suggested that the CFE talks be expanded to include helicopters and land–based combat planes. He further called for demobilization of all troops to be withdrawn and for destruction of all equipment thus removed. Bush also sug-

gested that it would "be possible to reach agreement in six months or even a year." Since the Soviets had earlier suggested troop reductions and had wanted to include combat aircraft in the discussions all along, they welcomed President Bush's proposals. The CFE talks subsequently became stalled, however, partly because of the political changes that occurred in Eastern Europe in 1989. With non–communist leaderships in power throughout the region and with the German Democratic Republic moving toward unification with the Federal Republic of Germany, the old political basis of the Warsaw Pact no longer existed. In addition, the Soviet Union had agreed to withdraw its troops from Hungary and Czechoslovakia by the end of 1991.

President Bush, responding to these changes, proposed lowering the total number of troops on each side to 195,000 in the area of Central Europe. It is unlikely that the Soviet Union will be able to keep that many troops there. It has already agreed that its troops will be out of both Germany and Poland by 1994.

The CFE Treaty was initialled in November 1990 at a meeting of the CSCE. Shortly afterwards, the Soviet armed forces leadership reclassified three divisions as naval forces and claimed that these divisions were not covered by the CFE, since naval forces had not been included in the discussions. The United States and other western nations objected and the treaty was put on hold. The disagreement was resolved in May 1991 when Gorbachëv sent General Moiseyev, the chief of the Soviet Staff, to Washington, D.C. to work out a compromise. The compromise stipulated that the three divisions could be excluded from overall figures, provided commensurate reductions were made in forces not originally covered by the agreement.

Two months later, the USA and the Soviet Union announced that they had reached agreement on a START Agreement and that it would be signed at the end of July when President Bush traveled to Moscow for a Summit Conference with President Gorbachëv. The agreement, signed on July 31, 1991, required the two signatories to reduce the number of nulear warheads to 6,000 each, though an involved method of counting raised this figure by about one–third. Nevertheless, it was the first treaty to achieve actual reductions in the number of nuclear weapons on each side. This was, it turned out, Gorbachëv's swansong. Less than three weeks later, conservative communists tried to oust him in an attempted *coup*. Although the *coup* was defeated, it discredited the Communist Party and led to the collapse of the Soviet Union. Gorbachëv resigned as President of the USSR on December 25, four days after eleven of the republics had formed the Commonwealth of Independent States at Alma Ata.

An Independent Russia is Reborn

Gorbachëv still thought to save the union, even if under another name and with reduced powers, but it was not to be. By the end of August, nine of the fifteen republics were committed to independence. With the three Baltic Republics already receiving international recognition, Gorbachëv called a special session of the Congress of People's Deputies for September 2. After three days of debate, the Congress accepted Gorbachëv's proposal for the creation of a new interim government whose chief purpose would be to negotiate a new union treaty.

Gorbachëv remained president of this new interim government, but final executive authority was lodged in a State Council made up of Gorbachëv and the leaders of the participating republics. A separate Interrepublic Economic Committee, appointed by the State Council, assumed the economic functions of the former Council of Ministers. Finally, a two chamber legislature was established, the membership of the second chamber to be appointed by and represent the governments of the individual republics. In this chamber, voting would be by delegation, with each republic having one vote.

From the beginning, only ten of the republics participated in the interim government. The first act of the State Council was to recognize the independence of the Baltic Republics. Moldova refused to participate at all and Georgia sent only observers. In addition, over the next several days, all of the remaining republics other than the Russian Federation, Kazakhstan and Turkmenistan declared their independence. Later, even Kazakhstan and Turkmenistan would join the list.

Gorbachëv knew that his new interim government existed on sufferance and that Boris Yeltsin's support was the first requisite. Gorbachëv therefore dismissed all of his former advisers and accepted Yeltsin's advice on the make–up of his new government. He thus surrounded himself with liberals. He even appointed Ivan Silayev, Prime Minister of the Russian Federation, as Chairman of the Interrepublic Economic Committee, a post that effectively made him the caretaker Prime Minister of the union government.

Determined to save some form of union, he asked the reform economist Grigori Yavlinsky to draw up a plan for economic union and he and the State Council began working on a plan for a new political union. Yavlinsky's draft for a new economic union was submitted to the State Council in late September and won general approval. It was then submitted to the individual republics in October.

Most of the republics accepted the language of the economic union treaty, but the big exception was the Republic of Ukraine. Opposition was centered in the Ukrainian parliament, which drew up two pages of objections. The parliament demanded the right to set up an independent Ukrainian national bank, to issue a separate Ukrainian currency and, in general, to control its own fiscal policy. Later that same month, the Ukrainian parliament withdrew the mandate from its delegates to the USSR Council of the Republic and instructed them to participate as observers.

It came as no surprise, then, when the Republic of Ukraine decided to boycott the November 14 session of the State Council, called to consider Gorbachëv's draft for a new union treaty. In the event, only seven republics gave their preliminary approval to a new treaty creating a "Union of Sovereign States." Two weeks later, the State Council met again, supposedly to initial the draft agreement. Instead, they voted to submit it to the individual republic legislatures for ap-

Inside St. Petersburg's nuclear power plant

Courtesy: NOVOSTI

proval, a process that put the proposed treaty into severe jeopardy.

Up to this point, Boris Yeltsin had consistently maintained that he favored a continuation of the union. But he had also said that he could not envisage a union without the Ukraine. Yet Leonid Kravchuk, the Ukrainian leader, said on November 12 that he would "never sign" a treaty which contained "even the slightest hint of certain governing central bodies" and he had refused to participate in discussions in the State Council on the new union treaty.

Yeltsin's own actions during this time indicate that he was also having second thoughts about the advisability of maintaining a strong center. At the end of October, he took over as his own Prime Minister and then announced that Russia would unilaterally begin a sweeping program of economic reform that included freeing prices, privatizing industry and land, and creating a strong Russian currency. He requested the Russian parliament to grant him the power to suspend Soviet laws that "hamper economic reforms." He also announced that, effective November 15, the Russian Government would no longer finance union ministries which it did not utilize. Yeltsin's program got the Russian parliament's endorsement on November 1. Two weeks later, he assumed control of Soviet diamonds and gold production and took charge of issuing oil export licenses. He followed this up with another decree taking over the remaining structures of the Soviet finance ministry, including its controls over foreign currency. This was accompanied by an announcement that Russia would no longer be responsible for any new debts incurred by the union government.

In effect, Yeltsin had begun a unilateral dismantling of the central government. This was carried a step further at the end of the month when Yeltsin stepped in and offered to finance the Soviet payroll after the central government had run out of funds. An integral part of the agreement was that Yeltsin henceforth controlled the union budget. He used his new power to order most central ministries to be closed.

Very little of the central government remained on December 1 when the Ukrainian people went to the polls to elect a new president and to vote on a referendum on independence. Leonid Kravchuk won the presidential race with 61.5 percent of the vote. Nearly 90 percent of all Ukrainians voted yes on independence. "The independence of the Ukraine is a new political reality," commented Boris Yeltsin upon receiving the results of the Ukrainian vote. Yeltsin recognized that the draft union treaty drawn up by Gorbachëv was dead, but he still felt that

some kind of coordinating mechanism was necessary to handle the many problems of the now–separating republics. He therefore contacted President Kravchuk and Stanislav Shushkevich, President of Belarus, and suggested that the three presidents meet the following weekend to discuss the future. Shushkevich agreed to host the meeting and offered the use of a hunting lodge located not far from the Belarusian city of Brest. "We came to the conclusion," Shushkevich commented after the meeting, "that we had to sort out the concept of the kind of union we are capable of building."

The three leaders talked for two days, December 7–8. At the end of the second day, they returned to Minsk, where they signed an agreement creating a "Commonwealth of Independent States." Its most significant clause stated that "the USSR has ceased to exist as a subject of international law and as a geopolitical reality." This was, in effect, the Russian Federation's declaration of independence. Eight other republics—the sole holdout was Georgia—joined the CIS at a conference in Alma Ata on December 21. Gorbachëv resigned as President of the U.S.S.R. on December 25, turning the Kremlin and authority over the Soviet Union's nuclear arsenal to Boris Yeltsin. The Russian Federation succeeded to the Soviet Union's membership in the United Nations and its seat on the security council.

Boris Yeltsin launched his economic reform on January 2, 1992. Over the next several months, his government was mainly occupied with the implementation of that program, assuming the Soviet Union's international obligations, including its various diplomatic missions abroad, and carrying on negotiations with the other members of the CIS over economic relations and the future of the Soviet military forces. The republics had agreed to maintain strategic and nuclear forces under a single command, but three republics, Ukraine, Moldova and Azerbaijan, opted from the beginning to establish their own national armies. Plans for a unified command under the CIS for the remaining forces were gradually discarded as the remaining republics moved toward creating their own national armies.

The original CIS agreement called for the republics to maintain a single economic space, but that has proved impossible in practice. One problem is that the other republics would like to buy more from Russia than it needs to buy from them. As a result, Russia had built up a positive balance of 1.2 trillion rubles with the other republics by the end of 1992. The Russian Government abandoned its commitment to maintaining a single ruble zone for the CIS about the middle of 1992.

In view of the growing trade imbalance coupled with Moscow's perception that the governments of the other republics were not doing enough to control spending, the Russian Government began limiting the amount of rubles they were willing to make available to the other republics and it began encouraging the other republics to develop their own currencies. Most eventually moved to do so, though in a number of cases "coupons" rather than a new currency were authorized.

A number of the other republics complained about the speed of Russia's economic reform, particularly the wide–ranging freeing of prices, but most grudgingly went along with it. At home, however, Yeltsin soon found that a majority of the members of the Supreme Soviet were also appalled at the speed of the reform. Even though they had, in December 1991, granted Yeltsin the right to rule by decree for the period of one year, by June 1992 they were strongly attacking his program and doing what they could to frustrate it or slow it down. Between June and December, they undermined his economic reform mainly through an enormous increase in credit, accomplished through taking control of the Russian State Bank. And in those same months, Speaker Khasbulatov emerged as the chief spokesman for the anti–reform majority in the Supreme Soviet.

This raises an important question, for Khasbulatov had been elected Chairman in 1991 with the support of reformers associated with Yeltsin; further, he had stood at Yeltsin's side in August 1991 in opposition to the attempted coup. Why did he now abandon his former allies and throw in his lot with many of the same individuals he had opposed in August 1991? It appears clear that he did it, not primarily for ideological reasons, but because his own position was threatened. Khasbulatov was elected in 1990 to represent the autonomous republic of Chechenya. Since that time, Chechenya had declared its independence and was attempting to secede from Russia. An extremely ambitious individual, Khasbulatov's one chance for continued power on the national level was if secessionist movements were put down resolutely.

Thus he made common cause with a coalition of ex–Communists and Russian nationalists dreaming about a restoration of the old Soviet Empire. Because he is an able man and a facile speaker, his joining the parliamentary opposition to President Yeltsin has given that grouping more success than it would have been able to achieve on its own.

That became clear in December 1992, when the Congress of People's Deputies met to decide what policy to take toward

President Boris Yeltsin shares microphones with Chairman Ruslan Khasbulatov

President Yeltsin and his reforms. At issue was whether to extend President Yeltsin's power to name his own government ministers and to issue decrees with the force of law. Under the leadership of Speaker Khasbulatov, the Congress failed by a narrow four votes to pass a constitutional amendment that would have stripped President Yeltsin of most of his powers. The Congress then voted a resolution condemning Acting Prime Minister Yegor Gaidar's reform program and calling his methods of work unsatisfactory. They subsequently rejected Yegor Gaidar as Prime Minister.

President Yeltsin then stalked out of the Congress and threatened to organize a referendum on his policy of economic reform. Apparently frightened by the possibilities inherent in such a referendum, the Congress leadership proposed additional talks with Yeltsin. Valeri Zorkin, chairman of Russia's constitutional court, also intervened at this time, offering his services as an honest broker during any talks. The result was a compromise whereby Yeltsin would retain his decree–issuing powers for another four months while a nation–wide referendum on a new constitution would be scheduled for April. In return, President Yeltsin agreed to nominate as Prime Minister a person acceptable to the

Congress. The Congress's choice fell on Viktor Chernomyrdin, a centrist who had been vice prime minister for oil and gas production since July. Chernomyrdin was undoubtedly a disappointment to the Congressional majority, however, for he continued the basic thrust of Gaidar's economic program.

Frustrated in its attempts to put an end to economic reform, the Supreme Soviet continued its attacks on Yeltsin and his government. In addition, a majority of the Supreme Soviet began having second thoughts about a referendum which might lead to a new constitution and new elections which might see them removed from office. Things came to a head in February 1993 when Speaker Khasbulatov denounced the idea of a referendum. A few days later, Valeri Zorkin added his voice in opposition to a referendum. In addition, the leaders of Russia's regional governments, meeting with Yeltsin on February 9, told him that a referendum might lead to an explosion in the country. Faced with this wide–spread opposition, Yeltsin backed down and agreed to postpone the referendum indefinitely, provided a power–sharing arrangement could be reached with Khasbulatov and the Supreme Soviet. Yeltsin and Khasbulatov finally reached an agreement of sorts, subject to approval by

the Congress of People's Deputies, which was reconvened on March 10.

But the full Congress was not in a mood to compromise. Rejecting Khasbulatov's efforts, the Congress voted to severely limit Yeltsin's right to rule by decree and canceled the referendum scheduled for April. Yeltsin temporized for seven days, then went on national television on March 20 to announce that he would organize his own referendum to take place on April 25. The Russian people would be asked to cast a vote of confidence on his presidency and to approve a new constitution that would serve as a basis for new elections. In the meantime, Yeltsin added, he planned to ignore the Supreme Soviet and rule by decree.

Vice President Rutskoi and Valeri Zorkin, Chairman of Russia's constitutional court, immediately denounced Yeltsin's plan as unconstitutional. On the other hand, at an emergency meeting of the Supreme Soviet the next day, the prime minister and the defense, security and interior ministers all threw their support behind Yeltsin. The Supreme Soviet then requested the Constitutional Court to rule on Yeltsin's plan. The Court declared Yeltsin's decree to be unlawful on the basis of his television speech, since it had not yet received a copy of the decree itself. On that basis, Khasbulatov call for Yeltsin's impeachment and the Supreme Soviet voted to convene the Congress of People's Deputies on March 26.

A motion to impeach was supported by a majority of the Congress members voting, but fell 72 votes short of the two–thirds vote necessary to convict. Having failed to impeach Yeltsin, the Congress agreed to the idea of an April 25 referendum, but demanded that four questions be submitted to the people instead of Yeltsin's two: "Do you have confidence in the president? Do you approve of the socioeconomic policy carried out by president and government in 1992? Do you think early presidential elections are necessary? And do you think early parliamentary elections are necessary?"

The Congress further stipulated that Yeltsin would have to win the votes of a majority of all registered voters on the first two questions in order to claim a popular mandate. Such a stipulation would have been almost impossible to obtain. In 1991, Yeltsin won 57 percent of all votes cast but that constituted only 42 percent of registered voters. The Constitutional Court subsequently ruled that Yeltsin could claim a victory on the first two questions if he won a majority of votes cast, but that the last two questions were constitutional and required the support of a majority of all registered voters to be binding.

In the event, Yeltsin won a 57.4 percent approval on the first question and 53.7 percent on the second. On the third question, 49.1 percent favored immediate presidential elections; however, 70.6 percent voted in favor of immediate parliamentary elections. Nevertheless, this constituted only 44.8 percent of the registered electorate, so was not legally binding.

But Yeltsin had won only a battle, not the war. Speaker Khasbulatov dismissed the voting results as meaningless and divisive and announced that neither he nor the Congress of People's Deputies were prepared to accept the results as decisive. Vice President Rutskoi, for his part, argued that:

"there can be no talk of overall popular support. Those who said 'no' or remained silent are also Russian citizens, and we have to ask ourselves why they did so."

Rutskoi later added:

"There is no popular support. That is why all these reform policies should be changed."

Yeltsin's reaction to his victory was predictably different.

Saying that the referendum had created "a fundamentally new political situation," which required a new constitu-

tion, he summoned the political leaders from Russia's regions and republics to Moscow on April 29. Here he presented them with copies of a new draft constitution to replace the old Communist–era constitution dating from the Brezhnev era. The new constitution provided for a new, French–style presidency, with a prime minister and cabinet appointed by the president and confirmed by the legislature. The legislature would consist of two chambers. The upper house, representing regions and republics, would be called the Council of Federation. The lower house, elected by electoral districts, would be called the State Duma. Yeltsin thus deliberately evoked the pre–communist experiment in democracy of the period 1906–1917. Yeltsin proposed that each region and republic examine the draft constitution and submit their comments to him by May 20. He asked them also to appoint two delegates to a constituent assembly which would convene in late May or early June to complete work on the constitution.

This procedure, not specified anywhere in the current constitution—which bestows the power to amend to the Congress of People's Deputies—challenges the present Congress of People's Deputies, which is not expected to acquiesce meekly in its own demise. It is thus a high risk gamble on Yeltsin's part. Given the circumstances, however, it appears to be a necessary one.

Foreign Policy of the Russian Federation

The now independent republics have agreed to honor all arms agreements signed by the now defunct Soviet Union. President Yeltsin, to whom Gorbachev turned over control of nuclear missiles after he resigned, has ordered that ICBMs be retargeted away from American cities.

In his State of the Union speech on January 28, 1992 President Bush proposed the USA and the former republics of the Soviet Union eliminate all multiple–warhead missiles and reduce the number of permitted nuclear warheads to 4,500. President Yeltsin countered by an offer to end production of all new nuclear warheads and to reduce the total number of long–range warheads to 2,500 on each side. A few days later, Yeltsin suggested, in a speech at the United Nations, that the USA and Russia jointly construct a global anti–missile shield. And in a breathtaking break from the past, Yeltsin proclaimed that he considered "the United States and the West not as mere partners but as allies." Yeltsin recognizes that the collapse of the Soviet Union also threatens the collapse of the unified Soviet armed forces, in spite of commitments by most CIS member republics to maintain a unified command.

This puts the successor republics in a potentially dangerous position and raises the question whether they will be able to defend their borders from attack. Russia, thinking particularly about its long border with the People's Republic of China, wants the reassurance of American and Western support should such a threat arise.

Yeltsin paid an official visit to the United States in June 1992. The highlight of the visit was the signing of an agreement in principle setting a new limit of 3,000 3,500 nuclear warheads on each side. This agreement in principle was then codified into the START–2 agreement, which the United States and Russia signed in Moscow in December 1992. Both the United States and Russia have ratified the START–1 agreement, but implementation cannot begin until the Government of Ukraine ratifies it. One factor delaying Ukrainian ratification of START–1 is that Ukraine maintains that it does not have the money to begin dismantling the missiles. The U.S. Congress voted to provide $800 million to help defray the cost of dismantling nuclear missiles in the four ex–Soviet Republics, but Ukraine maintains that its cost alone will be $1.5 billion. In the meantime, START–2 remains on hold.

The United States Government also announced, shortly before the Yeltsin visit, that the Peace Corps would begin operating the area of the former Soviet Union. Plans called for 250 Peace Corpsmen to be dispatched to Russia, Ukraine, Armenia and one Central Asian country. A separate program applied to the three Baltic republics.

Also during the Yeltsin visit, the United States and Russia worked out the broad outlines for an agreement for joint space flights beginning in 1993. The detailed agreement was finally signed in October 1992. Under the agreement, a Russian cosmonaut would participate in a U.S. shuttle flight in 1993, while a U.S. astronaut would be aboard a 1995 research mission which involved the U.S. shuttle docking with the Russian space station Mir.

In other developments, Russia supported sanctions against Serbia after the beginning of the war in Bosnia. Since that time, however, it has maintained a rather ambivalent policy, sometimes refusing to support further actions against the Serbs. Even so, the Russian policy has come under strenuous attack from conservatives and nationalists who favor supporting the Serbs.

Russia's relations with Japan remain somewhat cool. Yeltsin had planned a visit to Japan this Spring, but postponed it again. The issue between the two countries remains the four islands taken by the Soviet Union at the end of World War II which Japan insists on getting back.

Government of the Russian Federation

A presidential bodyguard salutes Russian President Boris Yeltsin and Italian President Francesco Cossiga at the Quirinale Presidential Palace on December 19, 1991.

The Government of the newly independent Russian Federation is again currently in a state of transition and at the moment does not even have a current constitution. President Yeltsin's Government submitted a new constitution to the Supreme Soviet and Congress of People's Deputies in November 1991, but the Congress of People's Deputies ordered the Supreme Soviet to rework it and resubmit it to the next session of the Congress of People's Deputies in April 1992. One of the areas of controversy is the status of autonomous republics and regions under the new constitution. Yeltsin apparently proposed to devolve considerable authority on such units, but a number of people in the legislature balked at this point. The problem is that Russia is really a unitary

state except for the subdivisions specifically designated as "autonomous." This has not mattered in the past because all such grants of autonomy were really theoretical. Now that such grants would take on real meaning, some people in the legislature have argued that they ought to be more restrictive.

Although there have been a number of significant amendments to the constitution in the past couple of years, the structure is still that of the old Russian Soviet Federative Socialist Republic. Under the old RSFSR constitution, sovereignty resided in the legislature, which consisted of a Congress of People's Deputies, which met twice a year for but a few days, and a two–chamber Supreme Soviet, which remained in session most of the year.

Under the original procedure, the Congress of People's Deputies elected a Chairman of the Supreme Soviet, who was assisted by a Presidium, also elected by the Congress. There was also a Council of Ministers, with its own chairman, confirmed by and responsible to the legislature. The first significant amendment, approved in May 1991, abolished the office of Chairman of the Supreme Soviet and created an executive President of the Russian Federation, to be directly elected by popular vote. The election took place in June 1991 and, as been said, the winner was Boris Yeltsin.

The Chairman of the Supreme Soviet had been something of a figurehead, but the Supreme Soviet granted President Yeltsin the right to legislate in a number

80

of areas by decree, thereby transferring a portion of their legislative authority to the President.

Another of the powers of the President is to appoint the Chairman of the Council of Ministers (informally, Premier), subject to confirmation by the Supreme Soviet. In the aftermath of the failed August 1991 *coup*, however, Yeltsin's Premier, Ivan Silayev, was appointed the head of the Inter–Republican Economic Committee. He eventually resigned as Russian Premier, but Yeltsin was unable to find a replacement that he found satisfactory.

As a result, he decided in October to head up his own government. At the same time, he modified the old system by creating a State Council directly under himself and gave it control over the Council of Ministers. The State Council consists of nine cabinet ministers, including defense, finance, and foreign affairs, a State Secretary, Gennady Burbulis, who acts as Yeltsin's deputy, and six state counselors. It thus has some of the features of a cabinet plus some of a Policy Planning Staff. There has been speculation that Yeltsin would allow the Council of Ministers to wither away, but that has not happened. Instead, the State Council is being used to make policy while the Council of Ministers has the task of implementing it.

Yeltsin has also created three additional bodies, a Security Council to deal with emergencies such as ethnic violence, a Council of the Federation and Territories, to give autonomous republics and regions a voice at the center and to bind them to the Federation, and a Control Department, a sub–unit of the State Council, whose job is to supervise local government.

These bodies obviously reflect Yeltsin's style of governing, but it is impossible to determine whether the government will continue in this form when the new constitution is drawn up and approved. Some of the new bodies created by Yeltsin have the look of *ad hoc* bodies at the moment, but it may be that Yeltsin is moving toward creation of a Russian Government modeled on that of the French Fifth Republic. It is clear that he favors a strong Presidency, though it is not clear that the Congress of People's Deputies will endorse such an approach on a permanent basis.

The Court System

One of the first things that Lenin did after coming to power in 1917 was to abolish the old Russian court system and create new people's courts staffed by communists and other revolutionaries. The Russian court system, created by Alexander II in the 1860s, was modeled on western judicial practices. It incorpo-

Midnight, with the Russian tri–color floating over the Kremlin after 74 years. St. Basil's Church is in the foreground.

Courtesy: NOVOSTI

rated the concept of "equal justice under the law" and included an independent judiciary, trial by jury, public trials, and defense attorneys.

The Soviet court system was specifically created to defend the revolution. Judges and prosecutors were required to be members of the Communist Party and to be loyal implementers of the party line. Trials by jury were abolished. Guilt or innocence was determined by a judge, assisted by two ordinary citizens who were referred to as lay assessors. Their function was to support the prosecution. Defense attorneys existed, though their role differed from that of attorneys in western countries. With no presumption of innocence, a long legal tradition developed against an acquittal–oriented defense. The function of the defense attorney was therefore to negotiate for the most lenient sentence rather than to get the client off. This was reinforced by the fact that, under the law, defense attorneys had a lesser status than representatives of the state. Acquittals were almost unknown.

Attitudes toward the law began to change after Gorbachëv came to power in 1985, particularly after he endorsed the concept of a "nation of laws." The first practical manifestation of this changed thinking came in December 1989, when a law on judicial procedure went into effect giving individual republics the authority to increase the number of lay assessors on the bench. This was viewed by some as a move toward creation of a jury system. Defense attorneys were also permitted to establish a national Union of Advocates and the number of acquittals began growing slightly.

Gorbachëv's main goal was to free the legal system from outside political interference. He wanted to create courts where fairness and objectivity were the rule and cases were decided exclusively on the basis of evidence presented in court. He made some progress, but most of the authoritarian system originally created in the 1920's and 1930's continued to exist even after his reforms.

The repudiation of communism and the emergence of an independent Russian Government have created a new situation, however, and Moscow is full of talk about reforming the entire legal system. One of the reformers is Boris Zolotukhin, chairman of the subcommittee on reform of the Russian Supreme Soviet. Zolotukhin advocates making judges and lawyers independent and more attuned to the rights of the accused. He favors lifetime appointments for some judges. He also speaks of the need for higher salaries, higher status, and more training for judges. Other things being considered are reestablishing a presumption of innocence and trial by jury. But, Zolotukhin points out, his

proposals are moving slowly. There is considerable opposition from prosecutors, who stridently oppose change.

Ordinary citizens often support the *status quo* as well, and the recent spurt in crime in Russia has increased demands for more "law and order," not less. For many ordinary Russians, a conviction rate of 99 percent is fine, since that indicates that "justice is being done."

This attitude is found even among lawyers. Elena Bariknovskaya, a St. Petersburg lawyer who recently set up a Lawyers Committee for Human Rights, said

"I'm not sure I want such wide rights as American lawyers have. If lawyers have broader rights during investigation, I'm afraid justice will not be served at all. Lawyers will just teach the defendants to lie. I think it is no problem for us to lie, to save our life or to get lost."

There is thus no general groundswell for judicial reform in Russia; yet it will come. Specifically, there will be a depoliticalization of the system, inevitable now that communism has been repudiated. If the Russians are lucky, the system should eventually come to resemble the system abolished in 1917.

THE YELTSIN DRAFT CONSTITUTION

The latest draft of President Yeltsin's proposed new constitution, published in *Izvestiya* on April 30, 1993, supersedes a earlier draft published in 1992. The Russian Supreme Soviet, controlled by Yeltsin opponents, rejected it in May 1993, then produced its own, competing draft. The greatest difference between the two drafts is that the Yeltsin constitution creates a strong Presidency and limits the legislature largely to legislative functions. The Supreme Soviet draft envisages a ceremonial Presidency and places the fultrum of power in the legislature.

Article 1. The Russian Federation—Russia is a democratic rule–of–law secular federative state whose highest values are the individual and his dignity and inalienable rights and freedoms. . . .

Article 4. State power in the Russian Federation is based on the separation of the legislative, executive, and judicial powers. . . .

Article 6. No ideology or religion may be established in Russia as a state or compulsory ideology or religion. No party or church may be under the patronage or control of the state.

Article 9. Everyone is equal before the law and the courts. Equality of rights and freedoms is guaranteed by the state. . . .

Article 14. Everyone is guaranteed the right to freedom of conscience, spiritual freedom, freedom of religion, religious or atheistic activity, freedom of thought and expression of opinions and convictions, and free development of the personality. . . .

Article 16. Everyone has the right to freedom of movement and to the choice of his place of sojourn and domicile throughout the territory of the Russian Federation. Everyone may travel freely outside the Russian Federation. . . .

Article 21. Everyone is entitled to own property and to enjoy, use, and dispose of it. . . . The right of private ownership is a natural human right.

Article 22. Everyone has the right to economic freedom and the free utilization of his capabilities and property in pursuit of any economic activity that is not prohibited by law.

Article 26. No one may be deemed to have committed a crime or subjected to punishment until his guilt is proven in accordance with the procedure laid down by law and established by a court verdict. Detention in custody and deprivation of liberty are permitted solely on the basis of the law and by a court decision. No person may be held in detention for more than 36 hours without a court hearing. . . .

Article 35. No one is obliged to bear witness against himself, his spouse, or his close relatives as defined in law. . . .

Article 52. The defense of the fatherland is the citizen's duty. . . . A citizen whose beliefs or faith are at odds with the performance of military service, or in other cases as laid down by law, has the right to perform alternative civilian service instead.

Article 70. The president of the Russian Federation is the head of state. The president is the guarantor of the Constitution and of the rights and freedoms of the citizens. Within the procedure established by this Constitution he adopts measures to protect the sovereignty of the Russian Federation and its independence and state integrity and ensures the coordinated functioning and interaction of all state organs. As head of state the president is the state's highest official representing the Russian Federation inside the country and in international relations.

Article 71. The president of the Russian Federation is elected for five years. The same person cannot hold the post of president for more than two consecutive terms. . . .

Article 73. The president of the Russian Federation makes direct appointments to the highest state posts or submits to the Federal Assembly condidacies for election or appointment to such posts. The president of the Russian Federation:

submits to the Federal Assembly a candidacy for appointment to the post of chairman of the Government of the Russian Federation; puts to the Federal Assembly questions of confidence in the Government of the Russian Federation or its dismissal; submits to the Federal Assembly a candidacy for appointment to the post of chairman of the Central Bank of the Russian Federation;

on the recommendation of the chairman of the Government of the Russian Federation and after consultation with the Federation Council, makes appointments to the posts of federal ministers and leaders of federal departments and releases them from their posts;

submits to the Federation Council candidacies for appointment to the post of justice of the Constitutional Court of the Federation, the Supreme Court of Arbitration of the Federation, and the Superior Court of Arbitration of the Federation; candidacies of federal justices for appointment to the Superior Judicial Office of the Federation; and also the candidacy of the general prosecutor of the Russian Federation; . . .

Article 74. The president of the Russian Federation:

calls Federal Assembly elections;

after consultation with the chairmen of the Federation Council and the State Duma, effects the early dissolution of the Federal Assembly in the event that the Federal Assembly does not adopt the decision necessitated by Article 106 of the present Constitution for the formation of the Government of the Russian Federation and in other instances when a crisis of power cannot be resolved on the basis of the procedures established by the present constitution;

calls a nationwide referendum;

submits draft laws to the Federal Assembly on his own initiative; sends an annual message to the Federal Assembly on the implementation of Russia's domestic and foreign policy;

signs and promulgates federal laws after their adoption.

Article 84. The Federal Assembly–Parliament of the Russian Federation is the highest representative federal organ of the Russian Federation.

Article 85. The Federal Assembly consists of two chambers: the Federation Council and the State Duma. Two deputies from each component of the Federation are elected to the Federation Council. Additional deputies are elected from republics within the Russian Federation, autonomous oblasts, and autonomous okrugs according to representation norms laid down by federal law in such a way to ensure that deputies from these components of the Federation make up at least 50 percent of the Federation Council. The State Duma consists of 300 deputies elected from territorial electoral districts on the basis of uniform representation norms.

Article 86. The Federation Council and the StateDuma are elected simultaneously for a four–year term. . . .

Article 94. At the submission of the president of the Russian Federation the Federation Council appoints the chairman of the Government of the Russian Federation and decides the question of confidence in the government or of its dismissal.

Article 99. The State Duma:

exercises legislative regulation on questions within the charge of the Russian Federation;

establishes federal taxes and levies;

exercises control over the emission of money; . . .

Decisions of the State Duma are adopted by a majority of the total number of deputies, unless some other decisionmaking procedure is laid down by the present Constitution or federal constitutional law.

Article 106. The chairman of the Government of the Russian Federation is appointed by the Federation Council within two weeks of the submission of a candidacy to it by the president of the Russian Federation;

If the Federation Council rejects the candidacy . . . the president . . . submits the question of appointing the chairman of the government for fresh examination by the Federation Council. If the Federation Council again rejects the candidacy . . . , the question . . . is referred . . . for joint examination by the chambers of the Federal Assembly. In this case the appointment of the chairman of the government must be made no later than one month from the day of the president's submission. If the chairman of the government is not appointed . . . within this time, the president can adopt a decision on early dissolution of the Federal Assembly and appoint an acting chairman of the government.

Article 115. Judges are irremovable. A judges's powers may be terminated or suspended only on the grounds and according to the procedure laid down by federal law.

Article 117. Judges are independent and are subordinate only to the Constitution and the law. If in the examination of a case a judge establishes that a legal act of a state organ or other organ is at variance with the law, he makes his decision n the basis of that law.

The grand staircase in the Winter Palace (now part of the Hermitage Museum in St. Petersburg.) In 1732 Tsarina Anna commanded Italian architect Bartolomeo Rastrelli to build a four-storied Winter Palace of extravagant design and furnishings; it was built during the reign of Tsarina Elizabeth (1741–62).

Photo by Miller B. Spangler

Culture

The repudiation of communism following the failure of the August 1991 attempted *coup*, followed by the collapse of the Soviet Union, have created a situation of an independent Russian Federation committed to the goals of pluralism, democracy, privatization and a market economy. That marked an end to official Soviet culture, but seventy years plus of indoctrinating the people with the philosophy of Marxism–Leninism will not be overcome overnight. Proletarianism and socialism are still defining ideas for many people, and even terms like "socialist realism" have their supporters among conservatives.

At least two other cultures always co–existed with the official version of Soviet culture, however, and the repudiation of communism means that, in the future, they will define Russian culture. The first is the great cultural contribution of Russians of the pre–Soviet era; the second is non–official Soviet culture. To these must be added religious culture, which survived in spite of official disparagement by the state, and today again flourishes.

How much of Soviet culture will persist? Some "proletarian" authors and artists will undoubtedly continue to write or paint, although the Russian people have very little taste for political art after a steady diet of it for 70 years. But the fact is that there never was very much purely

"Soviet" art and what there was of it was usually tied to specific political campaigns that became outdated. Such art has a historical interest, of course, but it was by definition not made to transcend the age in which it was produced, and so it now lacks artistic interest.

Some of the work by revolutionary artists and novelists in the 1920s was an exception to this, but even that period had its darker aspects. Many artists, stifled in the new conformity, fled abroad. Others, like the poets Vladimir Maiakovsky and Sergei Yessenin, committed suicide.

The Association of Proletarian Writers was an annoyance in the late 1920's because of its intolerant attitude toward those who did not share its "proletarian" outlook, but that period appeared mild in retrospect after Stalin had instituted his authoritarian cultural controls and enforced his "socialist realism." Most of the great works of the 1920s were banned as unproletarian in the 1930s. These included the novels of Mikhail Bulgakov, author of *The Master and Margarita* and *Heart of a Dog*, and the paintings of Andrei Malevich, who even in the 1920s had been forced to give up his earlier, abstract style.

Dmitri Shostakovich, the composer, and Sergei Eisenstein, the film producer, were two exceptions who managed to produce great works in the 1930s, but both of them came under criticism in the periods of the 1940s and either had to revise their works or couldn't get them released at all.

But the fact is that most "Soviet" culture was actually pre–Soviet culture. There never were that many revolutionary artists, and most of these eventually found themselves stifled by the regime's tight controls. So the great novels that people continued to read or the great artists that they admired were mostly pre–revolutionary. In effect, except for elements considered anti–revolutionary, the regime appropriated Russian culture to itself. Thus poets like Alexander Pushkin and Michael Lermontov continued to be published throughout the Soviet period, along with short story writers like Nikolai Gogol, novelists like Ivan Turgenev, Fedor Dostoyevsky, Leo Tolstoy and Maxim Gorky, and playwrights such as Anton Chekhov.

Russian ballet, one of the "glories" of Soviet culture, continued to be dominated by classical French choreography. There were some experiments with modern dance after Stalin's death but, because they usually expressed revolutionary themes, they seldom rose to the level of art. Most Russian operas performed throughout the Soviet era were pre–revolutionary. All of this gave Russian culture the eerie aspect of being a museum of the past.

Things did get better after Stalin's death, but artists had been repressed so long by that time that very few of them were capable of great art. Still, some of these works are interesting for historical purposes. Ilya Ehrenburg's novel, *The Thaw*, is not a very good book, but everyone read it because of its message of hope. To a certain extent, this period of liberalization was associated with the personal fortunes of Nikita Khrushchev. Although vocal in his own dislike for modern, especially abstract, painting, he encouraged writers who wrote works critical of the "distortions" of the Stalin era. He personally defended the book *Not By Bread Alone* by Vladimir Dudintsev. It was also he who authorized the publica-

tion of Alexander Solzhenitzyn's *A Day in the Life of Ivan Denisovich*.

Cultural controls were tightened again after Khrushchev's departure. This produced a great outpouring of unofficial Soviet culture. Some painters had always found their art to be unacceptable to the regime, so they had to find ways of supporting themselves by other means. The number of individuals able to afford paintings increased considerably after the death of Stalin, however, so artists, though shut out of official exhibits, were able to find customers for their unofficial art.

The situation for writers was somewhat different. Unable to get works published, some resorted to circulating them in

manuscript form. This was referred to in Russian as *samizdat*—literally, self–publication. Others, seeking a wider circulation, contrived to have a manuscript smuggled abroad, where it would be published, usually in translation. Having an unapproved manuscript published abroad was legally an anti–Soviet act, however, and a number of writers were imprisoned for this offense. Because of the Soviet Union's policy of "socialist realism," nearly every great work of Soviet literature written after 1930 had to be published abroad and almost every Soviet Nobel Prize winner for literature was labeled a dissident.

In the early 1970s, the Brezhnev regime added a refinement when it began expel-

"Family":——**D.D. Zhilinsky (Grand themes tended to give way to scenes of daily life in the 1960s)**

ling Soviet artists or stripping them of their citizenship while abroad. The most famous of those was Alexander Solzhenitsyn, expelled from the Soviet Union in 1974. A number of other artists who had been given permission to travel chose to live and work abroad. The pianist Vladimir Ashkenazy chose to live in England. The renowned cellist–conductor Mstislav Rostropovich and his talented wife settled in the United States. Several top ballet performers defected while touring abroad, while others, like the Panovs, emigrated after long delays in waiting for permission to leave Russia.

The beginning of the Gorbachëv era, with its emphasis on *glasnost,* widened the area of the permissible and brought the publication of previously banned works. Thus writings of Anna Akhmatova, Boris Pasternak, Alexander Solzhenitsyn, Mikhail Bulgakov, Vladimir Nabokov, Osip Mandelshtam and Marina Tsvetaeva were all published. A selection of Akhmatova's poems was put out by the journal *Oktyabr.* Moscow's Taganka Theater brought a play about Pasternak and his novel, *Dr. Zhivago,* to the Soviet stage, and the novel itself, for which Pasternak received the 1958 Nobel Prize for literature, was published beginning in January 1988 by the journal *Novy Mir.*

Another example of greater freedom for the arts under Gorbachëv was the new play by Mikhail Shatrov, *The Brest Peace.* Shatrov's play gives a detailed and fairly sympathetic treatment of Lev Trotsky and Nikolai Bukharin. Trotsky's name had been anathema in the USSR ever since his expulsion by Stalin in 1929; Bukharin was executed in 1938 as part of the Stalinist purges. What is perhaps most interesting about the play is that it was written in 1962, but the author had previously been unable to get it performed or published. Gorbachëv eventually put his personal stamp of approval on this new trend:

"There should be no forgotten names or blanks. We must not forget names and it is all the more immoral to forget or pass over in silence large periods in the life of the people."

As Gorbachëv apparently intended, part of this new "openness" turned into an attack on Stalin. Thus a novel by Anatoly Rybakov published in 1986, *Children of the Arbat,* depicts Stalin as pathologically suspicious and politically obtuse. Like Shatrov's play, *The Brest Peace,* Rybakov's novel was written in the 1960's but he was not able to get it published earlier.

New plays with similar themes also began to appear by 1988. The best known was another play by Mikhail Shatrov, entitled "On, On, On," which was published in the January 1988 issue of the literary monthly *Znamya.* A controversial play, it is full of suppressed details of Soviet history and is harshly anti–Stalinist. Interviewed about the play, Shatrov commented that "If you read my plays you will see that all of them are in essence about one thing: Stalin is not Lenin's heir. Stalin is a criminal of the kind the world has never had. He is not a Communist for me, because if he is a Communist, I have to leave the party immediately."

Many Soviet intellectuals who shared Shatrov's point of view began pressing the party for a total repudiation of Stalin and a rehabilitation of his victims. Gorbachëv was, in general, sympathetic but other members of the leadership, including Ligachev, Chebrikov and Yazov, spoke out against what they termed the "one–sided" evaluation of Stalin. While willing to condemn such things as the 1930s purges, they argued that Stalin should be given credit for such things as industrialization and collectivization and the USSR's victory in World War II. In essence, their view of Stalin was that he was a good Communist who had made mistakes.

The resulting division led to a battle in the Soviet media in which Shatrov, in particular, was accused of "inaccuracies," "juggling with the facts," and "departure from the truth." What more conservative reformers like Ligachev apparently feared is that excessive criticism of the past would weaken popular faith in the party. In the summer of 1990, after the final defeat of Ligachev at the 28th Party Congress, Gorbachëv ended the controversy by issuing a decree rehabilitating Stalin's victims.

After 1990, artists were basically free to write or compose or paint what they wanted, free of party tutelage. Thus, with few exceptions, Gorbachëv had brought an end to the long period of official supervision of the arts by the cultural affairs section of the Communist Party. These last few exceptions ended in August 1991 with the failure of the *coup* to unseat Gorbachëv and reinstate a new orthodoxy. The complicity of the Communist Party in the *coup* led to its repudiation and Boris Yeltsin subsequently issued a decree in effect banning the party.

The collapse of the Soviet Union and the emergence of an independent Russian Federation with Boris Yeltsin as President mark the beginning of a new era in which Russian culture, free finally of all state controls, will develop as Russians wish it. This ought to bring major changes over the next several years. On the other hand, the old Soviet regime subsidized art as well as controlled it. Many of the literary magazines which have published new artists will probably cease publication when they lose their subsidies. How Russian society will adapt to meet this new situation is still

His Holiness Patriarch Aleksiy of Moscow and All Russia

very much up in the air. *Pravda,* the party newspaper, is now closed down for lack of funds.

Religion in the Russian Federation

Religion had a peculiar status in the now defunct Soviet Union. There was an officially declared separation of church and state, and Soviet citizens had a constitutionally guaranteed freedom of worship. But communism, the ideology of the only legal political party, was militantly atheistic, so the constitution guaranteed the right of anti–religious propaganda as well.

Official opposition to religion had its roots in the basic materialistic philosophy of Marxism, which held that spiritual matters were merely a reflection of material things and conditions. Karl Marx, in a famous phrase, stated that religion was being used by the ruling classes as an opiate, or drug, which dulled the ability of the masses to know their real problems and find the solution for them. Claiming to derive their views from scientific knowledge, communists saw themselves as secular and "this world" minded and opposed religion as "unscientific" and false. Since communists held that their value system represented "truth," they were extremely intolerant of all religious teachings, because of their competing claims to truth. In fact, communism had a comprehensive world outlook and set of beliefs which made it a sort of "religion" itself. It even promised paradise, though it was to be here on earth rather than in another world.

Communist theory held that communism represented a new "consciousness" on the part of mankind. To reach the stage of communism, therefore, it was necessary to "transform" the thinking of the people through a process of consciousness–raising or indoctrination. This process was to result in the emergence of a "New Man," conditioned to living in a communist society.

Communists attached particular importance to the "educational" functions of the party. They were especially concerned with shaping the basic beliefs of the younger generation, since young people were still untainted with the corruptions of the previous system. Religious bodies, since they represented the values of the previous system, were forbidden to proselytize or to carry on any public functions other than the worship service itself. Churches, synagogues, and mosques were barred from all areas of education, including Sunday schools and catechism classes. Organized acts of charity were also forbidden and religious marriage ceremonies were banned. For a time, even the ringing of bells was forbidden.

Beyond that, the regime tended to differentiate in its treatment of individual religions depending on the total number of adherents and the role accorded it in pre–revolutionary Russia. The Orthodox Church, to which most Russians, Ukrainians and Byelorussians belonged, had been one of the mainstays of the old system and a loyal tool of the tsarist governments. Moreover, the Orthodox Church adopted a strongly anti–Bolshevik position during the revolutionary

upheaval of 1917 and the civil war that followed. Thus the Orthodox Church became a particular target. During the civil war, many members of the clergy, including the Patriarch, were arrested and quite a number were executed. All church buildings were nationalized and many were closed. In the 1920s, the party created an organization known as the *League of Militant Atheists* to carry on the battle against religion. Members of the league, lavishly supported by the regime, engaged in all sorts of anti–religious propaganda. One of the things they did was to turn Kazan Cathedral in St. Petersburg, a beautiful, neoclassical church built in the 18th century, into the Museum of Atheism.

Islam came under similar restrictions. Islam was considered to be even more dangerous than Christianity in some respects, since it recognized no distinction between the secular and the religious. In addition, the Moslem clergy were strong defenders of the traditional way of life, and so opposed most of what the communists were trying to do. Communists therefore did their best to stamp out Islam in Central Asia. Religious schools and mosques were closed and many of the Islamic clergy were imprisoned.

Nor did this cease after the regime had consolidated its power. In the 1930s, Stalin ordered churches, synagogues and

mosques closed all over the country and he had a number of Moscow's historic churches torn down as a part of his rebuilding of the center of the city. Most of the remainder were turned into museums or converted to other secular uses.

As conditions became stabilized in the late 1930's, the Stalin regime adopted a somewhat less militant position toward religion. A dramatic turn occurred after the German invasion of the country in June 1941. The *League of Militant Atheists* was dissolved and its printing facilities were actually turned over to the Russian Orthodox Church. Stalin had come to the conclusion that, in a crisis, the communist regime could make use of the support of the Church with its deep roots among the masses.

The regime tightened its control again after the end of the war, but this was mainly to guarantee that the church continued to serve the goals of the state. Internationally, members of the higher Orthodox clergy were frequently used as delegates to various international peace congresses. Domestically, the Patriarch and other members of the hierarchy were expected periodically to speak out in support of Soviet policy. The Islamic clergy, by this time tamed, was also used occasionally for diplomatic missions, mainly to the Middle East.

Faithful Moslems gather for Friday prayer at the central mosque in Kazan, capital of the Tatar autonomous region on the Volga River.
Photo by Steve Raymer © 1991 National Geographic Society

Even so, about 10,000 additional churches were closed between 1959 and 1964—about half the remaining total in the Soviet Union. In 1960, the Archbishop of Kazan was tried and sentenced to prison. That same year, the Metropolitan Nicholas of Krutitsy was deprived of his offices. And in Central Asia, historic mosques, sitting unused, fell further into disrepair. This policy of repression, associated mainly with the regime of Nikita Khrushchev, came to a partial end in 1964. The Brezhnev regime later permitted 500 of the closed churches to be reopened. Mosques were not reopened, but the most historic ones were given the classification of national treasures and the first efforts at restoration were begun.

The Brezhnev regime remained officially atheist, but it was a conservative regime that tended to accept religion as part of the status quo. Russian nationalism enjoyed something of a revival at this time as well, and that was often extended to include the Orthodox Church. As a result, it was the best–treated of all the organized religious groupings in the U.S.S.R. under Brezhnev and saw even a modest growth in its nominal membership to more than 30 million. In the last years of the Brezhnev regime, church services were overflowing and, in a change from the past, many young people began attending services. Since most of this growth occurred in the period now known as "the era of stagnation," it was partly a symptom of the loss of faith in communism that was then only beginning to manifest itself.

Brezhnev died in November 1982, but the era of stagnation really lasted until March 1985, when Mikhail Gorbachëv was appointed General Secretary. Although it was not immediately apparent, Gorbachëv had an entirely different attitude toward religion than his predecessors as leader of the Communist Party of the Soviet Union. Although not a believer, his attitude may have been influenced by the fact that his mother is. But whatever the reason, Gorbachëv set out rather systematically to end the party's traditional hostility toward religion. One of the points he made in justifying this change of position was that people needed moral values and that religion had an important contribution to make in this area. In 1988, official celebrations marking the millennium of Russia's conversion to Christianity symbolized this changed attitude on the part of regime.

In September 1990, the USSR Supreme Soviet passed new legislation prohibiting the government from interfering in religious activities. Another law required the state to reopen a place of worship on receipt of a petition signed by at least 20 believers. Some 4,000 new parishes opened between 1985 and 1991.

In another indication of this change, when Patriarch Pimen died in May 1990, one of those who spoke a eulogy at his funeral service was Anatoliy Lukyanov, Chairman of the USSR Supreme Soviet. And in 1991, Boris Yeltsin, the President of the Russian Federation, and Valentin Pavlov, the Soviet Chairman of the Cabinet of Ministers, were among those attending Easter services at Epiphany Cathedral in Moscow. Easter services were also held at St. Basil's Cathedral on Red Square, even though it was still officially a museum.

Gorbachëv's changed policy eventually came to be applied to Moslem areas as well, though somewhat later because the Iranian revolution and the war in Afghanistan had created fears of an Islamic fundamentalism sweeping through Central Asia. The Soviet troop pullout from Afghanistan and the death of Iran's Khomeini reduced that threat, and paved the way for a changed policy toward Islam.

This brought the beginnings of a religious revival. Mosques were reopened all over Central Asia. In 1990, fourteen new mosques were opened for services in Kokand, some while still under construction. For decades, a single mosque had served a Moslem population of 150,000 in that city. Elsewhere, mosques were being opened at the rate of almost one a day. In Uzbekistan, over 200 new mosques were opened in 1989–90. Hundreds of students were enrolled in theological colleges and millions of copies of the Koran were distributed. And more than 1,500 Soviet Moslems made the pilgrimage to Mecca in 1990, the largest number in recent memory. As Muhammad Yusuf, the grand mufti of Tashkent and Central Asia's senior Moslem leader said, "at first Moslems were rather passive and did not react quickly to what was happening elsewhere in the country. Now we are demanding the same privileges accorded to other religions."

Judaism represented a somewhat different situation because, under Soviet law, Jews were viewed as both a religious group and a nationality. Various factors made the situation complex, including a pre–revolutionary tradition of anti–Semitism which Lenin combated as being a tool of reaction. Stalin reversed this position in the late 1940s with his campaigns against "rootless cosmopolitan writers," and his later "Doctors' Plot." Anti–Zionism survived Stalin and continued to justify anti–Semitism under his successors.

In the past, religious practices of Soviet Jews were limited by the government, but the Gorbachëv regime's changed attitude toward religion brought about a basic change of attitude toward Jews as well. In general, the restrictions on the practice of Judaism were abolished. Jews were authorized to set up religious schools and seminaries and to begin giving religious instruction to young people. One problem was the lack of trained rabbis. That was partially solved by bringing in rabbis from abroad. Hasidic organizations from the United States and Israel have also been actively providing assistance of all sorts.

The failed *coup* of August 1991 created a new situation by bringing a repudiation of the Communist Party and a break up of the Soviet Union. The newly independent Russian Federation closed down the Communist Party and rejected its ideology. Religion is now considered to be a matter of conscience and as such beyond the purview of the state. In December 1991, President Yeltsin symbolized this new approach by issuing an appeal to heads of religious faiths and believers in which he condemned "the policy of spiritual genocide" of the previous regime and promised to "eliminate the consequences of the profoundly unjust policy of the many–year–long communist dictatorship with regard to believers [and] to hand over religious shrines, churches, and cloisters to those to whom they should rightly belong."

Christian churches still have a job of rebuilding after the years of repression, but they have already begun the task. The Moslems of the Soviet Union, located mainly in the six republics of Central Asia, now have their own independent governments to look after their interests. Moslems living in the Russian Federation constitute a tiny percentage of the population. They have been guaranteed the same rights as other believers, but they have another guarantee as well, since they are mainly to be found in the autonomous republics or other autonomous regions and so have their own governments to represent their interests. They are mainly found in the Volga River Valley and in the area of the north Caucasus.

The greatest current threat to Jewish culture in the Russian Federation today is probably the large emigration currently going on, approximately 400,000 in the period 1990–91. If that rate of emigration continues, there will soon be few Jews left in Russia. That would be unfortunate, since the Jews have made many great contributions to Russian culture in the past. In fact, emigration seems to be declining somewhat following the collapse of the Soviet Union and there are increasing indications that Jews are reconsidering leaving. A number of new Jewish high schools, newspapers and theaters have been opened in the past two years, and an increasing number of individual Jews are speaking about the newly independent Russian Federation as a place that offers bright prospects for Jewish life.

The Smolny Cathedral and Convent of St. Petersburg, under the Soviet Union used as a Museum of History of that city.

Photo by Miller B. Spangler

Photo by Miller B. Spangler

Education

Russian education, like almost everything else in Russian society, is currently in a state of transition. The failure of the August 1991 *coup* has brought about a repudiation of Communism and the subsequent collapse of the Soviet Union itself. As a result, the regimentation in the area of education enforced by that old system has also disappeared. The Government of the Russian Federation has not rushed in to assume the authority of the old center, so individual school districts find themselves very much on their own. The result is that individual schools are beginning to make changes and institute programs that, increasingly, set them off from other schools. Some school authorities fear that this is producing a fragmented, localized system, but others see this as another example of increasing pluralism in the society.

One of the changes already evident is an abandonment of the school uniforms worn by all school children under the old system. Most children continue to wear the uniforms, or parts of them, but they now also wear a variety of sweaters and jackets. Some schools have also begun offering classes in religious education. In other schools, educational reformers are asking how school systems can be changed to make them better able to serve the needs of a market economy.

Education in Russia saw many changes in the 74 years following the Russian Revolution of 1917. In the first years after the revolution, "Progressive" methods were tried on all levels, with an almost total elimination of classroom discipline. Teachers were subjected to the rule of committees of pupils; there was much noisy activity and very little learning.

When the revolutionary fervor faded, education was reestablished along traditional lines, with uniform studies for all schools of the huge country and a strong emphasis on the sciences and mathematics. Elective courses were abolished in favor of a standard curriculum throughout the Soviet Union. Teaching was conducted in the native languages of the various Union Republics, but the content was centrally determined in Moscow.

A major problem of pre–revolutionary Russia was that more than 60% of the people could not read and write. This high illiteracy rate was vigorously attacked by the Soviet government and as a result, by 1928, more than half of the citizens were literate. The figure rose to 81% in 1939 and is now almost 100%.

For a while, the state–controlled school was looked upon as a counter–balance to the "reactionary" influences of traditional family ties; at the height of the purges, children were encouraged to report "subversive" activities of their own parents and other relatives. In the late 1930s, this approach was abandoned in favor of an emphasis on the Soviet family as the source of "correct" values. The events of August 1991 have reinforced this approach.

Because increasing numbers of Russian women were drawn into the work force in the 1930s, a wide network of nurseries and kindergartens—usually run by individual factories—was created to take care of children of working mothers. These facilities have often been crowded and not particularly well run, and in recent years privately–operated day care centers have come into existence. That trend is expected to increase as the Russian privatization program progresses over the next several years. In addition, many factories will begin running their day care centers as commercial ventures, making them available to anyone who wants to use them, not just their own factory employees. The Russian Supreme Soviet has already set fees at "20 percent of the cost of maintaining the child" as of April 1, 1992.

Regular schooling lasts for 8, 10 or 11 years, depending on where the student lives and his or her academic achievement. Children attend school six days a week, though the school day for primary students is relatively short, consisting of four 45–minute lessons. Additional after-school supervision is offered to children of working mothers. Such children are organized into "extended–day" groups and they remain at school until their parents come to take them home. After-school supervision is an area that is likely to feel the pinch of tight budgets which are scaling back the amount of money going into education.

There are basically two types of secondary schools—general and technical—but a movement began in the late 1970s to merge the two. In 1978, for instance, the time reserved in the school curriculum for machine–shop practice was doubled. Senior pupils were also required to spend four hours a week at a factory or on a farm, receiving on–the–job training.

A new reform decree, issued in early 1984, carried this evolution further. Beginning in 1986, children started school at age 6, one year earlier than previously, and they began to receive greater vocational training as an integral part of their schooling. Each student was now expected to master at least one basic mechanical skill before graduating, even though enrolled in an "academic course." Compulsory vocation courses will probably disappear under the new system that is beginning to evolve, though vocational education for those who opt for it is likely to become more available in the future.

There were great fears even before August 1991 that Gorbachëv's move to a market economy would have an adverse effect on the university system. Thus far, the collapse of the union government has had no such effect, because the Russian Government has taken over responsibility for institutions of higher education and has continued to fund them.

The likely scarcity of funds over the next several years and the policy of the Russian Government that societal institutions should, to the maximum extent possible, be self-supporting will undoubtedly bring about changes. Most universities will probably have to institute tuition fees to cover part of the cost of education. The Russian Government has also authorized the creation of new schools and universities and some non-state educational institutions, including church schools and private schools, have already come into being. Some of the current state universities have raised the possibility of turning themselves into private institutions. A distinct growth of pluralism is thus beginning within the system, though the process will continue to be gradual.

The area of culture most favored under the old system was that of the natural sciences, mainly because the regime came to the conclusion that keeping scientists in a strait-jacket in harmony with official dogma hampered Russia's ability to compete with nations with superior technology. Scientists were some of the most independent people in the Soviet Union and some of them spoke out courageously against the official pressures and Party-imposed limitations. One has only to think of Andrei Sakharov as an example.

The life sciences such as biology always had to put up with greater tutelage than the natural sciences, but even here the party eventually withdrew as an arbiter. The social sciences remained under official tutelage until 1985, but gained almost total freedom under Gorbachëv. Sociology, not even recognized as a separate discipline until recently, was also freed by Gorbachëv.

Opinion polls began to play an increasing role in the society. Even history, always the most controlled of the social sciences, underwent the beginnings of a renaissance when Gorbachëv called for new histories of the Communist Party and new school books that would restore names and historical periods that had been cloaked in official silence. "There should be no forgotten names or blanks either in history or literature," he said, adding that "history must be seen for what it is." In fact, Gorbachëv's policy of *glasnost* had brought about so many changes in this area by 1988 that the history exams had to be canceled that year, since all of the history books were completely out of date.

Thus the older system of control was greatly weakened even before the attempted *coup* of August 1991 brought that whole system down completely. Still, it had a major effect for the Communist Party apparachniks were expelled from their previous positions of power, and centralized controls disappeared. Much that existed down to August 1991 had nothing to do with Communist ideology as such, however, and reflected traditional Russian cultural mores. The new leaders of Russian society are working to purge the last remnants of communist ideology from the system, but a great deal is likely to continue to look and operate the way it always did. The difference is that there will be a great deal more pluralism in the system that is now being created.

A St. Petersburg school specializing in English. Russian students present Tom Sawyer, Becky Thatcher, and the fence painted white—with the dialogue all in English!

Photo by Miller B. Spangler

Democratic groups march through Moscow in September 1990 to demand immediate steps towards a market economy

The Changing Economy

The old command economy created by Stalin in the 1930s had already been seriously undermined—though not eradicated—by Gorbachёv's policy of *perestroika* even before the failed *coup* in August 1991 brought about a repudiation of communism and a collapse of the Soviet Union. The end of the Union and the emergence of an independent Russian state have transformed the situation completely. With the Union abolished, the old centralized bureaucracy which had dominated the economy for so long lost their jobs and their authority. Control of the economy now rests with the Government of the Russian Federation and President Boris Yeltsin, a man committed to eradication of the command system and the creation of a market economy based on private enterprise.

The Russian Federation came into existence as an independent state only in December 1991, so this process of transformation is only barely beginning. Moreover, the last two years of Gorbachёv's *perestroika* were a disaster insofar as the economy was concerned, so the

Russian Federation inherited a system that was in collapse. Some of the symptoms were a hyperinflation in which the ruble, officially valued at about $1.75, actually traded at about one cent; a state trading system which was unable to provide the public with any goods because they could obtain almost no goods at the low fixed prices they were authorized to pay—and much of what they did obtain was siphoned off for sale at a large mark–up on the black market; and a budget deficit that was over half the size of the overall budget. Overall industrial production was also down approximately 10% over the preceding year as individual enterprises found it more and more difficult to obtain raw materials and component parts.

President Yeltsin launched his program to begin the transformation to a market economy and private enterprise on January 2, 1992. His first step was to abolish state–set prices for most goods. Prices jumped an average of 300–350% percent, reflecting the hyperinflation of the preceding months but, by the end of January, more goods began to appear in the shops and prices started to drift downward, reflecting the increased supply and resistance among consumers to the

higher prices. In the cities and towns, lively street vending is rampant.

The price increases permitted the government to begin phasing out subsidies to industry and agriculture, and allowed it to draw up a budget for the first three months of 1992 with a deficit reduced to 4.4% of the Gross Domestic Product. The government later lowered the Value Added Tax, which the Yeltsin Government had instituted to replace the old turnover and sales taxes, from 28 percent to 15 percent as a way to lower costs to consumers. The ruble continued to stabilize, however, then actually began to increase in value as demand for the ruble grew—in effect a vote of confidence in the government's program. The shortage of foreign "hard" currency became acute.

Freeing prices and moving toward a balanced budget were necessary first steps. President Yeltsin's government was also committed to achieving ruble convertibility as soon as possible and had negotiated with the International Monetary Fund for a ruble stabilization fund, like the one created in 1990 to support the Polish currency. As an interim step, he announced that the Russian Central Bank would set a single official value for the

92

ruble based on the results of weekly currency auctions. Yeltsin hoped that the stabilization process could begin in the summer of 1992, after Russia was admitted to the IMF and World Bank.

Yeltsin also moved forward on other aspects of his economic reform. In February 1992, he announced plans to privatize 25% of state property by the end of the year. Under the plan, 25% ownership in state firms would be turned over to current employees, while the remaining 75% would be sold at auction.

The government also decided that, in order to maintain a tightened fiscal policy, it would have to phase out most remaining subsidies. Even in this first stage of reform, however, approximately 90% of consumer goods and 80% of industrial goods were freed of direct administrative regulation. Controls were maintained over twelve basic food products, certain communal services, certain fuels and some semi–finished products. The government also announced that it would begin a liberalization of fuel prices after the winter heating season was over. Fuel prices were then to begin rising in steps until they reached world prices at the end of 1993. The government predicted that the economy would continue to decline until sometime in 1993, when a turnabout was expected.

In retrospect, the government's predictions on the amount of inflation that would be unleashed with the freeing of prices turned out to be unduly optimistic. By June 1992, the exchange rate for the ruble had declined to about 100 + to the dollar, there were money shortages throughout the country and many individuals had not been paid for weeks. Other disruptions were occurring as well. Many of the state stores had closed down, while others had almost nothing to sell. Overall, more goods were available, but they were mainly sold from kiosks erected along the sidewalks, since most of these new, private entrepreneurs operated on a small–scale and, in any case, the state–owned buildings were still not available for private entrepreneurs to rent. Many of the items sold were imported also, since the state companies continued to deal only with other state companies. Some private shops did manage to find local suppliers, but it wasn't easy. The result was that ordinary individuals were ambivalent in their attitudes. There was still support for Yeltsin, but almost everybody had their complaints.

In this atmosphere, the Supreme Soviet, which five months earlier had granted President Yeltsin the power to rule by decree for one year, emerged as a center of opposition to Yeltsin's reforms. Under the leadership of Arkady Volsky, Chairman of the Union of Entrepreneurs

of Russia, and with the cooperation of Vice President Rutskoi and Ruslan Khasbulatov, Chairman of the Supreme Soviet, the Supreme Soviet became the forum for blistering attacks on President Yeltsin's economic policies.

In a series of measures taken during the month of June, the Supreme Soviet voted down two separate attempts to pass a bankruptcy law, rejected a land reform law which would have permitted greater private ownership, then refused to consider the draft constitution submitted by President Yeltsin. It also began putting extreme pressure on the government to loosen up on credit to state enterprises. About 25 percent of the members of the Supreme Soviet and the larger parent body, the Congress of People's Deputies, are managers of state enterprises, but this was not viewed as a conflict of interest. In their rhetoric, in fact, the enterprise managers portrayed themselves as protectors of the workers' livelihoods.

Industrial production had dropped by about 15 percent over the preceding year and President Yeltsin now recognized that something would have to be done to prevent further declines. Accordingly, the government promised to provide industry with an extra 320 billion rubles in credit. In addition, President Yeltsin issued a decree at the beginning of July canceling the accumulated debts of all state enterprises, a sum amounting to approximately 1.9 trillion rubles. The government also agreed to postpone scheduled increases in energy prices.

The conservative majority in the Supreme Soviet was not satisfied with these governmental actions, however. Yeltsin was still committed to his program of economic reform and other decrees had continued that process. For example, a decree issued at the beginning of July established a process for bankruptcy for enterprises defaulting on debts incurred after July 1. Yet another decree ordered the privatization of all state–owned enterprises, except state farms and certain defense and energy firms deemed vital to the country, by July 1, 1995.

Coincidentally, the Supreme Soviet

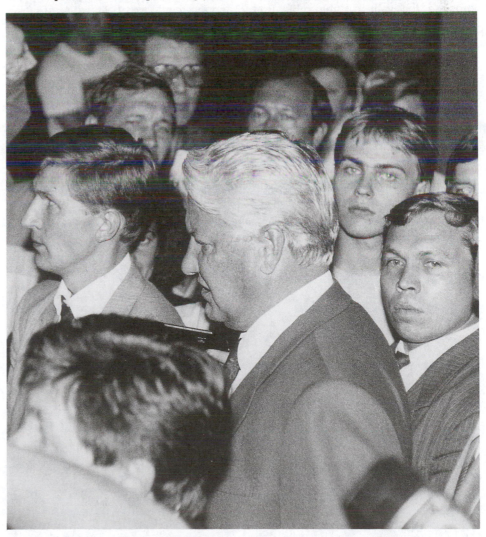

President Yeltsin with alert bodyguards

Courtesy: NOVOSTI

was presented with an opportunity to further undermine economic reform when Georgy Matyukhin, head of the Russian State Bank, resigned toward the end of June. Taking advantage of the fact that the old Communist Era constitution designates the parent Congress of People's Deputies as the highest authority within the system and makes the State Bank Chairman accountable to the Supreme Soviet, Speaker Khasbulatov and the Congress appointed Viktor Gerashchenko, former head of the USSR State Bank, as the new Russian State Bank Chairman.

Gerashchenko immediately began issuing large amounts of credit to state enterprises. This policy, which Gerashchenko later said he had instituted at the behest of the Supreme Soviet leadership, had the full and vocal support of the members of the Supreme Soviet. The alternate, argued individual speakers, was massive layoffs of workers. Over the next five months, the State Bank Chairman flooded the country with massive new credits, setting off an inflation that dropped the value of the ruble from about 100+ to the dollar to about 750 to the dollar.

Then in December the leaders of the Supreme Soviet convened the parent Congress of People's Deputies and used this forum to challenge Yeltsin directly. Here they attempted to strip him of most of his powers; though they failed, they did manage to oust Yegor Gaidar as Deputy Prime Minister and to force Yeltsin to accept a man of their choice, Viktor Chernomyrdin, as Prime Minister. Prime Minister Chernomyrdin turned out to be a disappointment to the parliamentary leadership, however, for he shortly became a convert to Yeltsin's overall economic reform.

Parliamentary opposition to Yeltsin and economic reform has continued, however. In March 1993, the Congress of People's Delegates narrowly failed to impeach Yeltsin, then structured the referendum he had requested into a four question query designed to undermine him. The referendum, held on April 25, actually provided a vote of confidence in Yeltsin and his economic program. Meanwhile, the parliamentary attacks continue.

Yeltsin's political struggle with the legislature has undoubtedly consumed a great deal of his time but, surprisingly, his overall reform appears to be more or less on track. Anatoly Chubais, the minister in charge of privatization, announced in March 1993 that 46,815 firms had been privatized in 1992. Most of these were small firms, but 18 large firms were privatized in December 1992 in exchange for privatization vouchers and this new procedure is being greatly expanded in 1993. In March, another 249 firms were to be privatized using the privatization voucher, among them the automobile manufacturing company Zil. Zil, with 103,000 workers, is important not only because of it size, but because the privatization is supported by the management and employees of the company.

Other economic news is even more encouraging. According to the latest statistics, overall production, which had fallen to 72% of its December 1991 level by August 1992, has since reversed itself and by March 1993 had climbed to the 82% level. Inflation, which had been running at 27% a month in January 1993, had also dropped to 21% by March. In addition, a deal struck between the Russian State Bank and the Russian Government in April 1993 give the government greater control over credit creation. Although Gerashchenko, head of the State Bank, has said that he agreed to the restraints because he believed that the government would not be able to live within the new restraints, the government at least has the opportunity to prove that it can do so.

The government will also benefit from an additional $43 billion which the west promised to Yeltsin in the run–up to the April 25 referendum. A large part of that package actually includes things such as a variety of loan facilities conditional on further reform, debt relief that will provide no new cash, and aid already promised earlier and not yet delivered, but it has a large psychological significance and undoubtedly will make a net material contribution as well. Russia is by no means out of the woods, but things are starting to look better.

What is Being Changed

The most distinctive feature of the now defunct Soviet economic organization was the reliance on a rigid central plan for the national economy. This is in contrast to a *market* economy, which relies on the independent, or semi–independent decisions of many producers. In theory, a rigidly planned economy was supposed to avoid the ups and downs—inflation and depression—of a free market economy. Marx and Engels charged that a market economy amounted to "anarchy of production."

In practice, centralized planning proved to be difficult. For many years, economic targets and goals were met by lavish investments of capital and labor. Progress was identified with the rate of growth of specific key industries—coal, steel and heavy industry in general—and a high percentage growth rate for overall industrial production. Quantity was stressed over quality.

Such a growth strategy produced an economy that led the world in the production of a long list of industrial products, including coal, steel, cement, manganese and chrome ores, locomotives,

The ice cream vendor in St. Petersburg is a highly popular figure even in winter.

Photo by Miller B. Spangler

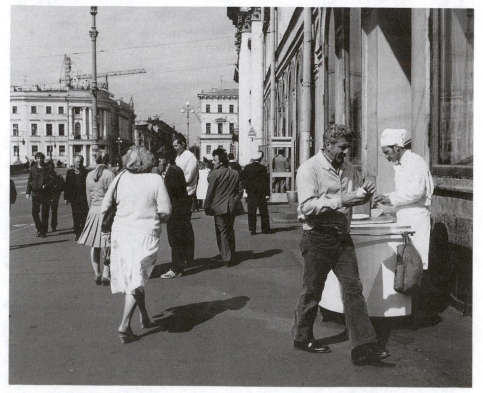

metal–cutting lathes and mineral fertilizer. Yet it also produced an economy that, from the point of view of the consumer, was an economy of scarcities. Some consumer goods were not manufactured at all while others were obtainable only after a long waiting period. Still, there were important improvements in the availability of consumer goods over the years. Today, most Russian families have a color television set, for example.

Although the Soviet standard of living improved between 1960 and 1985, it was still only about 37% of the level of the United States—and probably falling. Moreover, it was even below the level of the neighboring countries of Eastern Europe. From the point of view of the consumer, an even more important problem was that Soviet goods were of such poor quality that they could not be sold abroad.

Gorbachëv was already aware of the weaknesses in the system when he came to power in 1985. During his first year as General Secretary, he put together a team of younger and better–educated individuals and, at the 27th Party Congress in February 1986, he put the party on record as favoring economic reform. He then began to give substance to this commitment.

It soon became clear that many party members objected to any major modification of the economic system on ideological grounds, however. As Gorbachëv pointed out at the 27th Party Congress:

Unfortunately, there is a widespread view that any change in the economic mechanism is to be regarded as virtually a retreat from the principles of socialism.

Gorbachëv was faced with a major contradiction. Gorbachëv's own chief source of authority was his leadership of the party. Moreover, since the party controlled the levers of power, economic reform was possible only with the party's support. Yet how could he use the party to direct his program of economic reform if the party was itself the chief opponent of that reform? Gorbachëv's twofold answer was to remake the party in terms of personnel, organization and ideology while, at the same time, restructuring the system so that the party was no longer in direct control.

The process began in 1987 with the introduction of three slogans which came to symbolize his campaign for reform—openness (*glasnost*), restructuring (*perestroika*), and democracy. Unfortunately, his successes in political reform were not matched in the economic area.

In June 1987, Gorbachëv outlined future economic plans to a Central Committee Plenum. Here he called for "cardinal reform" in the *financing and credit systems*. He also spoke of the need for "develop-

For a century (in importance, if not quality), the GUM Department Store flanking Red Square has been the Macy's of Moscow.   Photo by Miller B. Spangler

ment of self–management," and "fundamental change in the style and methods of work." Factories should, he urged, be "self–financing" and more efficient so as to reduce their work force.

That same Central Committee session approved a "Law on the Socialist Enterprise" which went into effect on January 1, 1988. Under the terms of the law, 60 percent of Soviet industrial and agricultural production began working under a new system of "economic accountability" in which individual enterprises became responsible for obtaining their own raw materials and fuel and were expected to compete with other enterprises for business.

While they now had the right to dispose of any profits earned by the enterprise, they also became responsible for replacing obsolete machinery and paying the wages of their employees. Subsidies to money–losing enterprises were supposed to be phased out and such enterprises were to be permitted to go bankrupt, if they could not begin turning a profit. Companies were also to be able to get rid of surplus workers, so unemployment became another possibility. All of this was supposed to be in effect by the end of the 1986–90 Five Year Plan.

The system was never fully implemented, however. In 1988, 90 percent of the output of factories was still produced for "state orders." Two years later, state orders still controlled nearly 90% of industrial production. The state was also supposed to gradually withdraw from direct control of most economic activity with GOSPLAN relinquishing its control over individual enterprises and concentrating on long–term planning. Some of that happened. In 1987, for example, the number of centrally planned indicators was reduced from 46,000 to 22,000. It was supposed to be further reduced to 3,500 indicators in 1988, though it cannot be verified that this second reduction took place. Ministries and departments were supposed to be reduced by approximately one–third and there was supposed to be a drop of approximately 100,000 in personnel. Again, reductions occurred but not in those magnitudes.

One problem was that the economic program had two major goals—a short–term goal of accelerating the growth rate of national income and a long–term one of promoting innovation and reconstruction—and they were in basic conflict with each other. The first goal required all out production, while the second goal could only be met by things like closing down assembly lines while obsolete machinery was being replaced by modern technology and enforcing higher quality standards by rejecting goods that failed to meet the new standards. That conflict, obvious by 1989, got considerably worse in 1990–91, with the result that neither goal was met.

A second problem had to do with decentralization of decision–making author-ity within the system. Essentially, enterprises were given authority to set wages but no responsibility for paying them. As a result, they granted wage increases far in excess of increases in productivity, and the state had to make good the difference. It did this through the expedient of printing additional money. The increase in money in circulation first produced shortages as individuals used their higher wages to buy more goods. In a capitalist system, that would have led to inflation as prices increased to reflect additional demand. But all prices were controlled, and so could not increase. What happened instead was a loss of faith in the banking system and the currency itself.

The result was well summed up in February 1990 by N. N. Slyunkov, a member of the Politburo, in remarks he made at the Central Committee Plenum:

"The situation has deteriorated especially in the consumer market as regards both food and essential goods over the past two years."

A similar picture of the state of the Soviet economy is to be found in a poll published in the Moscow *Ogonek*, also in February 1990. Seventy–three percent of all respondents said that they "constantly or quite often" experienced difficulty in locating food that they needed, while 60% reported that they spent over half of their income on food.

All of this economic distress put the government under extreme pressure. Everybody agreed that *something* had to be done but there was no consensus on what that something should be. The radical reformers wanted to push forward rapidly, while conservatives urged pulling back. Gorbachëv fell somewhere in the middle. The draft Five Year Plan submitted in December 1989 by Nikolai Ryzhkov, Chairman of the Council of Ministers, represented a distinct pulling back, but there continued to be strong pressures to move more quickly.

Ryzhkov submitted a later version of his plan in May 1990. Saying that the state of the economy and the mood of the people did not permit any immediate changes, he proposed a continuation of the policy of state orders for another 18 months coupled with what he called price reform. They were, in fact, just price increases, since prices were not to be freed but simply raised. He characterized his program as "a transition to a regulated market economy." Radicals attacked his proposals and Gorbachëv called them absurd, though he added that people were unprepared for market economics.

Economic reform was on the agenda at

On Moscow's Arabat Street, models pose in some of the latest fashions

the 28th Party Congress in July 1990. After heated discussions, the party adopted a document called "Toward humane, democratic socialism," one of whose major points was that private property did not contradict communist ideology. Reflecting this change, Ryzhkov, in a speech given on July 20, spoke of moving toward a market economy. All references to the word "regulated" were dropped.

Then in August came the Shatalin Plan for a 500 day transition to a market economy. It had the support of Boris Yeltsin and the other radicals and was actually accepted by the Russian Supreme Soviet in early September. Gorbachëv rather reluctantly endorsed the plan, but it came under attack by conservatives and Ryzhkov threatened to resign if the plan were adopted. Eventually the USSR Supreme Soviet turned it down. Essentially the Soviet Union had no plan for economic reform.

Ryzhkov suffered a heart attack at the end of December and was replaced by Valentin Pavlov in January 1991. Pavlov, who had been Finance Minister under Ryzhkov, was a conservative. One of his more notorious "reforms" was to attempt to reduce the fiscal overhang by withdrawing 50 and 100 ruble notes from circulation. Since individuals were limited in the amount of bills they could redeem, Pavlov in effect reduced the overhang by expropriating a portion of the public's wealth. Its most important effect was to further reduce faith in the currency.

Real GNP fell by ten percent in 1990 and shortages were even more pervasive than they were in 1989. Yet the stalemate continued. Conservatives were convinced that further moves in the direction of a market economy would disrupt the economy even more, while reform advocates argued that any action was better than no action. Gorbachëv, no economist, didn't know what to believe. A joke he told reporters in November 1990 illustrated his position.

"They say that Mitterrand has 100 lovers. One has AIDS, but he doesn't know which one. Bush has 100 bodyguards. One is a terrorist, but he doesn't know which one. Gorbachëv has 100 economic advisers. One is smart, but he doesn't know which one."

By May 1991, Gorbachëv had lost confidence in Pavlov's economic program and he began seeking outside advice. Grigory A. Yavlinsky, who had helped draw up the Shatalin Plan, now proposed a new plan whereby the western nations would provide substantial aid to the Soviet Union to help in its economic transition. Gorbachëv endorsed this plan and used it as a basis for his meeting with the "Group of Seven" nations in July 1991.

George A. Cohon, Vice Chairman of Moscow-McDonald's and President/CEO of McDonald's Restaurants of Canada Ltd., with Russian crew members at McDonald's on Pushkin Square.

Though no specific overall sums were mentioned, Soviet economists talked about the need for $30 billion a year in grants and loans. The G–7 nations gave a cool reception to the general idea, though they promised assistance once transition to a market economy had begun. Before any further progress could happen, the August 1991 failed *coup* brought an end both to the Soviet Union and Gorbachëv's leadership.

Agriculture

The failure of the August 1991 *coup*, although it gave Mikhail Gorbachëv four more months as President, actually marked the beginning of the breakup of the Soviet Union and the emergence of Boris Yeltsin as head of an independent Russian Federation. What this means insofar as agriculture is concerned is that the reforms that Yeltsin has been demanding for two years are finally being implemented.

This has a two–fold significance. First of all, the demise of the Soviet Union has definitely ended all of the central control mechanisms of the old regime. For the first time since the early 1930s, Russian peasants are on their own. Amazingly, the peasants managed to plant even more winter wheat following the collapse of the Ministry of Agriculture than they had when it was telling them what to plant and when.

The old system still exists, of course. Nearly all peasants are still employed on the collective and state farms. It will, in fact, take years to dismantle the old system. But Yeltsin is committed to giving land to those peasants that want it, and the process is already underway. Commissions have been set up nearly everywhere to begin the process of dismantling the old system. This dismantling will be voluntary, however. Peasants are themselves to decide whether they want to retain the collective or state farm structure or to transform their old collectives into peasant farm associations, joint–stock companies, or cooperatives. A preliminary survey of fourteen *oblasts* showed seven percent opting for the *status quo*. Another 40% decided to establish peasant farm associations, 32% joint–stock companies and 21% cooperatives. All peasants are to have made their decision before spring. Some peasants have already begun receiving documents entitling them to a share of the land.

What is Being Changed

When the Soviet Union introduced the collectivization of agriculture as part of its first Five Year Plan, it was considered to be the first step in the creation of a modern, scientifically–organized, mechanized agricultural system. Distinctions between city and the countryside were to be abolished and peasants were to become "proletarians in the fields." Until 1953, this remained largely a dream, although Khrushchev's plan for the creation of *agrogoroda*—loosely, "agricultural cities"—which he first put forward in 1950, showed that the dream had only been postponed, not abandoned.

Khrushchev, as he consolidated his power after 1953, gave a great deal more emphasis to agriculture than had Stalin. Agriculture was placed much higher on the Soviet list of priorities and additional investments were directed into this area. In the late 1950's, in a move that was to have great consequences, Khrushchev decided that the Soviet Union should greatly increase meat production in the country. There were large increases in the numbers of livestock and poultry, and a greatly increased demand for grain for use as animal feed. Between 1960 and 1980, the amount of feed grains used for livestock and poultry tripled, going from 40 million tons to 120 million tons.

Grain production also increased during this period, but it could not keep up with the constantly growing demand. In 1963, after a relatively poor harvest, the Soviet Union imported its first grain. It imported grain only intermittently during the remainder of the 1960's, but after 1972 it become a regular customer on the world grain market.

This concerned the Soviet leadership and under Brezhnev huge sums of money were poured into the agricultural sector. Capital investment in the 1970's was over 300 billion rubles, which was 2.3 times what had been invested in agriculture in the previous decade. Most of the investment went into creation of a large artificial fertilizer industry.

None of this did any good. Grain harvests from 1979–1985 were uniformly dismal, averaging between 40 and 50 million tons below annual targets specified in the Five Year Plan. As a result, the Soviet government stopped publishing overall grain production figures in 1980. No overall figures were published again until October 1986, when it was announced that the grain harvest for 1985 totaled 191.5 million tons. Although this figure was 47.4 million tons less than the target, it actually was an improvement over the trend for the period 1981–1985, when production averaged only 179.5 million tons.

Grain figures for 1987 and 1988 were higher, at 210 and 211.3 million tons, but dropped in 1989 to 195 million tons. The 1990 harvest, on the other hand, was magnificent, reaching 247 million tons, though a significant amount was lost before reaching the Soviet public. The 1991 grain harvest was a disappointing 180–185 million tons.

The important thing, however, is that the Soviet Union, year after year, imported an average of 40 million tons of grain because Soviet collective and state farms fell that much short in meeting the demands of the economy. Even in the bumper year of 1991, the government imported approximately 28 million tons of grain.

Western agricultural experts have believed for a long time that the basic problem was in the system itself, that a basic conflict existed "between a centrally planned and controlled agriculture and the evolution of a modern, highly productive agriculture." Before Gorbachёv,

Soviet planners always rejected this point of view and tended to blame it on Russian weather.

Western experts also point out three other problems which they feel contributed to the failure of Soviet agriculture. The first is that Soviet farm equipment is always breaking down. This is partly because Soviet tractors don't last very long and partly because there is never a sufficient supply of spare parts for them. This is an unsolved problem. A report in February 1992 indicates that 200,000 tractors are standing idle because of a lack of spare parts.

The second problem is the lack of adequately trained and motivated labor in the countryside. Young, better educated individuals have been leaving the collective and state farms and seeking work in the cities for a long time. In the 1970s, 15 million workers left for the cities and that trend, though diminished, continued in the 1980s. The reason is that young people see no opportunity for advancement on the collective or state farm. A large number of persons are still employed in agriculture, but many of these persons are women and lesser educated, older men, precisely those elements which are least productive and least amenable to change.

The third problem is related: there is a terrible shortage of food–carrying railroad cars and storage facilities. Because of this a substantial part of annual production fails to reach city markets, but simply rots. When properly used, food–carrying cars, refrigerated and unrefrigerated, properly become a place of storage as they move over large distances.

Gorbachёv had held the agriculture

portfolio in the secretariat for a number of years before becoming General Secretary. There were some reforms he had been urging for a number of years, and he began implementing them after 1985. In his keynote speech to the 27th Party Congress, Gorbachëv spoke of the need to significantly extend "the independence of collective and state farms," and he proposed a two–fold plan for agriculture. State and collective farms would be assigned fixed annual quotas that would not be altered. All production in excess of the quotas could be used as the farms saw fit, including selling it "in fresh or processed form at the collective farm market or through cooperative trade."

Gorbachëv described his proposal as "the creative use of the Leninist idea of a tax in kind"—a reference to Lenin's *New Economic Policy*. The idea had great potential, for it could have been manipulated to create a major free market for agricultural produce if the level of fixed deliveries were set low enough. In addition, 100% of the production of state farms has traditionally gone to the state. Including them in the proposal was a departure from past practice and a genuine decentralization as far as state farms were concerned. Including them was also important because slightly over 50% of all agricultural land belonged to state farms. The potential was never reached, however, largely because so many people were opposed to any general loosening of control, and they managed to sabotage the reform.

Another of Gorbachëv's innovations was to suggest that the "brigade" or "team" system in agriculture might be extended by making them available at the level of families. Under this setup, a group of workers "contracted" to perform certain agricultural tasks as, for example, to cultivate a specified acreage or run a dairy. Remuneration, divided according to the individual contributions of the members of the brigade or team, was based on the productivity of the unit. Gorbachëv's innovation was approved, but the problem was in the implementation. Some family contracts were certainly written, but anecdotal reports indicate that the idea was not widely implemented.

This is the background that produced a Central Committee Plenum on Agriculture that took place in March 1989. In his speech to the Plenum, Gorbachëv argued that "the essence of economic change in the countryside should be in granting farmers broad opportunities for displaying independence, enterprise and initiative." To accomplish this, he proposed turning collective and state farms into "a supreme type of cooperative."

To accomplish this, he proposed that land, equipment and buildings be leased out to individual farmers for periods up to 50 years. The state and collective farms would continue to exist as some sort of coordinating agency, but would not directly control production.

Although conservatives such as Ligachev spoke up for lesser reforms, Gorbachëv's plan was approved in principle. The Plenum also voted, once again on Gorbachëv's initiative, to abolish *Gosagroprom*, the super–ministry for Agriculture that Gorbachëv had created in 1985.

In April 1990, the Supreme Soviet actually passed a new law allowing the leasing of land, equipment, buildings and other property for 50 years. Private farms were now a possibility. A few braver peasants moved to take advantage of it. They often had difficulty with the management of their collective or state farm, but there were an estimated 100,000 private farmers in Russia by the beginning of 1992.

Boris Yeltsin launched his economic reform on January 2, 1992. Since that time, his government has been kept busy implementing that program, assuming the Soviet Union's international obligations, including its various diplomatic missions abroad, and carrying on negotiations with the other members of the CIS over economic relations and the future of the Soviet military forces. The republics have agreed to maintain strategic and nuclear forces under a single command, but three republics, Ukraine, Moldova and Azerbaijan, have begun to establish their own national armies. Current plans call for a unified command under the CIS for the remaining forces.

Russia's economic relations with the other members of the CIS absorb a significant part of the government's time at the present because the members of the CIS are committed to maintain a single economic unity, but are also trying to take charge of their own economies. Privatization programs and development of market economies in the individual republics will eventually take care of this problem, but that is 2–3 years off. Meanwhile, the governments spend a great deal of time negotiating agreements about such things as oil and gas deliveries.

Yeltsin is essentially building on what Gorbachëv already accomplished while President. Last summer, even before the collapse of the USSR, Yeltsin persuaded the Russian Supreme Soviet to establish the right of private property. This was a significant step beyond Gorbachëv's concept of leasing land. Gorbachëv, of course, always had his problems with party conservatives who opposed any breakup of the collective and state farms. They are gone now from position of influence, so Yeltsin's job will be that much easier.

Russians line up in front of McDonald's in Moscow for a "Beeg Mak."

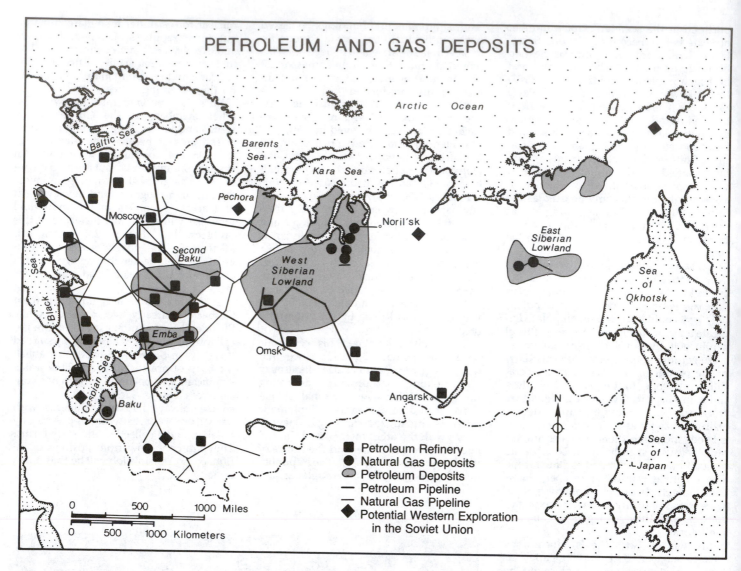

PETROLEUM AND GAS DEPOSITS

Legend:
- ■ Petroleum Refinery
- ● Natural Gas Deposits
- ▒ Petroleum Deposits
- — Petroleum Pipeline
- — Natural Gas Pipeline
- ◆ Potential Western Exploration in the Soviet Union

Natural Resources

The Russian Federation is well supplied with most of the raw materials necessary for industrial production, although the major source of minerals is Siberia. European Russia is less well supplied. The area of the Russian Plain has bauxite and lignite deposits, while anthracite and iron ore are found mainly along the western slopes of the Ural Mountains. The northern Caucasus has a petroleum field, an extension of the famous petroleum field centered on the city of Baku, in the Republic of Azerbaijan. Oil is also produced in the area between the Volga River and the Ural Mountains.

In Siberia, on the other hand, there are found some of the largest reserves of coal, petroleum and natural gas in the entire world, plus gold, silver, diamonds, platinum, copper, lead, zinc, chromium, cobalt, tungsten, manganese, and uranium. Beginning in the west, there are the iron ore and anthracite coal deposits of the eastern Urals that are exploited by the cities of Magnitogorsk and Yekaterinburg (Sverdlovsk).

To the northeast is Russia's largest oil field, centered on the city of Raduzhny, in Tyumen Province. The Tyumen Field, located in the southern part of the West Siberian Plain, produces 6.1 million barrels of oil a day, more than any country other than the United States and Saudi Arabia. Small fields are found in the vicinity of Pechora, far to the north on the Barents Sea, and further to the east in an area known as the East Siberian Lowland. Both are extremely isolated areas and production costs are thus higher.

The rest of the Russian Federation produces another 2.13 million barrels a day, making current Russian production 9.23 million barrels a day. That is down approximately 1.3 million barrels a day over 1990.

One reason is that, until March 1992, the Russian Government continued to sell petroleum for the equivalent of less than a dollar a barrel, not only domestically but to the former Soviet republics as well. Oil exported to Europe brought $18 a barrel, but oil companies only got 25 percent of the resulting revenues, the rest going to the government as a royalty payment. At those prices, particularly with the virulent inflation raging in the country, the state companies producing the oil are not getting a sufficient return to replace worn out or broken equipment. In March, the Russian Government partially freed oil prices and coupled this with a 50 percent royalty tax. Energy usage was expected to drop by 10–15 percent, which would allow Russia to increase its oil exports. Fuel prices are expected to rise to world levels by the end of 1993.

Most Russian oil is either used within the republic itself or exported to the other republics of the former Soviet Union. It does have long–term contracts, negotiated by the now defunct Soviet Union but which it has agreed to honor, to export to both Eastern and Western Europe. The Soviets had built over 60,000 kilometers of main oil pipeline, including one that reaches into Poland, Czechoslovakia, Hungary and Germany. Most of these countries are totally dependent on Russia for oil.

It also has large reserves of natural gas, also located in Siberia. Most of the natural gas is found in West Siberia, in the northern part of Tyumen Province. These are the Urengoi Fields. Some natural gas also comes from the area of the East Siberian Lowland. The production of natural gas has grown greatly in importance in recent years as new fields have been found and exploited. Production is down from a daily output in the 1980s of 1,000 million cubic meters—equivalent to 29% of total world output in 1981—but Russia remains the world's leading exporter of natural gas. Most of Eastern Europe is almost totally dependent on this supply and Western Europe is becoming increasingly dependent.

One of the Soviet Union's larger and more controversial industrial projects in the 1980s was a 3,400 mile pipeline constructed from the Urengoi fields of Siberia to Western Europe. The pipeline was largely constructed with Western technology and credits, with the Western European countries that have financed it—Great Britain, France, Germany and Italy—receiving payment in future gas deliveries. The first gas began to flow to Western Europe in December 1983. The collapse of the Soviet Union has brought no change in this arrangement.

The Russian Federation, and the Republics of Kazakhstan and Ukraine together contain almost 20% of the world's known reserves of coal and lignite and the three republics today account for nearly a quarter of all coal mined in the world. The Ukraine's main coal field is in the Donbas region, while Kazakhstan's coal is found in the region surrounding the city of Karaganda. Russia's two largest coal fields are located in Siberia. Both were developed by the Soviet Government after 1917. Pechora, the first Siberian field developed, is in the far north at the beginning of the Ural Mountains, along the Barents Sea. More interesting—and more challenging—is a major new coal field located in the southern part of the Republic of Yakutsk–Sakha (formerly the Yakutsk Autonomous Republic), which the Soviet Union began developing in 1974 in a joint project with Japan.

The Republic of Yakutsk–Sakha in eastern Siberia has large deposits of gold, diamonds, gas and tin, in addition to coal. But it is also one of the coldest inhabited places on earth, with temperatures known to plunge to –60°C (–108°F.). It is also extremely remote from the major populated areas of Russia.

This provides a problem for any form of development, but presents a specially difficult one in the case of a low value, bulk item like coal. As early as the 1930s, Soviet scientists had identified deposits of high grade coking coal in the vicinity of

the city of Neryungri, estimated to be as large as 300 million tons. It is an isolated area, however, and the Soviet government poured its limited development funds into more accessible areas. Then, in 1974, the Soviet Government negotiated a joint project with a number of Japanese companies to develop the coal field. The Japanese companies provided the necessary technology and equipment, while the Soviet Union built a spur rail line to connect Neryungri with the Baikal–Amur

Railway (BAM), a new railway completed in the 1980s that runs parallel but to the north of the Trans–Siberian Railway. The Japanese payment was in the form of deliveries of coal.

The project went forward and was eventually completed, though capital costs turned out to be four times the level of European Russia, and the project took several years more to complete than originally planned. As a result of the development, however, Yakutsk, the regional

BASKIN 31 ROBBINS

ПЕРЕЧЕНЬ ВКУСОВЫХ СОРТОВ МОРОЖЕНОГО

САМОЕ ПОПУЛЯРНОЕ МОРОЖЕНОЕ В АМЕРИКЕ

ВАНИЛЛА	Сливочное ванильное мороженое.	П
СТРОБЕРРИ	Клубничное мороженое с кусочками клубники.	П
ЧОКЛАТ	Шоколадное мороженое.	П
ЧОКЛАТ АЛМОНД	Шоколадное мороженое с жареным миндалем.	П
ЧОКЛАТ ЧИП	Ванильное мороженое с шоколадной стружкой.	П

Times are changing! Baskin Robbin's offers Moscovites a "List of Ice Cream Flavors"—"The most popular ice cream in America" . . . beginning with Vanilla, Strawberry, Chocolate, Chocolate Almond, Chocolate Chip, etc. (Courtesy of David Hertzberg)

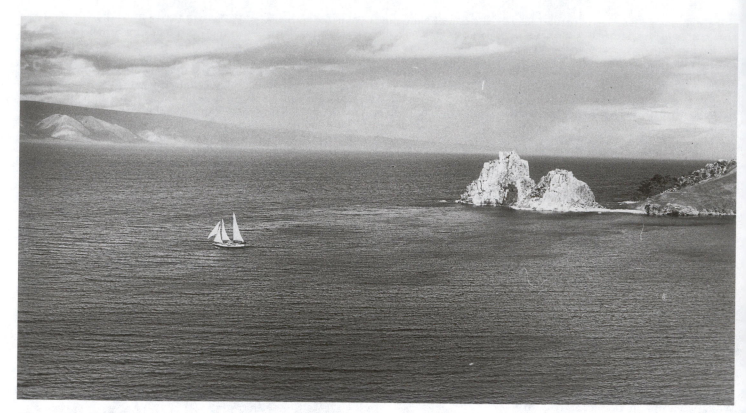

View of Lake Baikal

NOVOSTI photo

capital, has grown from a small settlement to 200,000 people. The potential for further development in this area is very great, but most projects are on hold at the moment.

Russian deposits of iron ore are found, first of all, in the Ural Mountains and, secondly, in the mountains that form the southern border of Siberia, particularly in the area around Lake Baikal. There are vast deposits around Lake Baikal, but the iron mines of the Urals are extremely old and largely worked out, having been originally developed in the 18th century. But Russian iron ore deposits are lower in ore content than those of the Republic of Ukraine, particularly those of Krivoy Rog, where the pure iron content runs as high as 68 percent. Russia will continue to get much of its iron from the Ukraine for the next several years, but development of the iron deposits of the Lake Baikal area is a good possibility for the future.

With respect to other ferrous metals, the Russian Federation is remarkably endowed; it is the world's largest producer of manganese and chromium and has substantial reserves of nickel, titanium and vanadium. On the other hand, there is a relative shortage of such important metals as cobalt, molybdenum and tungsten, all of great importance in steel production.

Insofar as non–ferrous metals are concerned, copper mining resources, developed primarily since World War II, now produce about 12% of the world total. Tin is in relatively short supply; lead and zinc are available in relatively large quantities. Russia is the world's second–largest producer of gold, though production is down and the mines, at the moment still all state owned, have been having labor problems. The production of light metals such as aluminum is steadily growing; the known deposits of aluminum ore are estimated to be adequate for at least forty years.

In discussing the natural resources of this country, mention must be made of the extensive system of waterways. Because of the difficulty in building roads in some areas, waterways played an important role in past centuries. The network of navigable inland waterways, totaling some 75,000 miles, is still of importance in reaching certain otherwise almost inaccessible areas, but the total volume of goods now carried by water is no more than 10% of the total. Practically no rivers remain open all year, and those that do suffer from seasonal shortages of rainfall which makes them too shallow.

The water resources of the Russian Federation have been used to construct hydroelectric power stations, including some of the largest in the world. An intricate system of canals, developed in the past, is still maintained and continues to play a significant economic role.

Paved roads continue to be scarce and the number of all–weather roads suitable for trucks is limited, so people and goods are still carried primarily by railroad. The Soviet Union was the first country to use jet airplanes for passenger traffic and certain remote areas can still be reached only by air; thus the network of air routes gets much use. Flights tend to be irregular and many times are simply cancelled. Railroads have been designated a "Commonwealth" interest, and the newly independent republics are committed to maintaining the integrated network that had existed under the now defunct Soviet Union.

Nuclear Power

Until the nuclear accident at Chernobyl in April 1986, the Soviet Union had been committed to nuclear power as a major source of electric power. At that time, the USSR had a capacity of 17.5 million kilowatts generated from this source and it had 18 more nuclear power stations under construction. In addition, Russia had produced two prototype industrial fast breeder–reactors, plus two nuclear heat supply stations, each of which was designed to produce enough heat for a city with a population of about 400,000. The most important reason for this ambitious program was the severe lack of alternate energy sources in the area of European Russia.

The nuclear accident at Chernobyl changed all that. Under growing public pressure, most of the nuclear power stations under construction were put on hold, then canceled entirely.

Chernobyl is a small town about 60 miles north of Kiev, in the now independent Republic of Ukraine. The plant had four reactors, two with "containment" buildings and two without. An experiment was underway using one of the unprotected devices when a sudden burst of power surged through the reactor, causing a steam leak. This led to the formation of hydrogen gas, which then exploded, demolishing the roof of the plant and killing two workers. Unrestrained by containment, the released radioactive gases quickly spread into the atmosphere, leading to widespread contamination not only of Soviet territory, but of neighboring nations as well.

The world found out about the accident two days later when the Swedes, detecting increased radiation in the atmosphere, began making inquiries. After first denying that anything untoward had occurred, the Soviets finally admitted the fact of the accident. It is now known that the reactor which got out of control was an unusual type that made use of graphite in its core. The graphite caught fire when overheating occurred. There was at least a partial "meltdown" and the reactor continued to spew out radiation for about two and a half weeks before it began to be controlled.

About 300 radiation victims were brought to Moscow hospitals; thirty five of these had suffered severe radiation exposure. Emergency bone marrow transplants were performed under the direction of an American surgeon. The death toll from radiation quickly reached 19 out of the 35; *The Times* of London reported that the figure had grown to 31 and that 209 others "remained in hospitals or sanatoria suffering from various degrees of radiation sickness." Dr. Gale, the American surgeon who performed the emergency bone marrow transplants gave as his own estimates that there were "about 50,000 to 100,000 individuals who have received at least some dose [of radiation] that may be of long–term concern. Soviet delay in the matter and failure of communication was, at best, shabby. Primary blame was placed on local officials who "didn't have a true assessment of the accident."

The Soviet Union did carry out major modifications of the 14 other graphite–core nuclear reactors which it operated. It also announced that future reactors would have containment buildings and would be pressurized. That was not enough for an increasing number of Soviet citizens, however. Protests grew around the Soviet Union and, increasingly, republic governments began putting pressure on the central government to cancel nuclear reactor building programs in their republics. The Soviet Government canceled the two reactors it had

been planning to build at Chernobyl, and later stopped construction on a number of other plants in southern Russia, Armenia, and elsewhere, but it never abandoned its commitment to nuclear power. In particular, it continued to discuss construction of at least three more reactors in the northeast by the year 2000. This area produces gold, and other minerals and new sources of energy will be required in the future to exploit this mineral wealth.

The Russian people were not among the major protesters against nuclear power in the past, but there is an increasing movement in Russia urging that the government phase out nuclear energy. The government has already drawn up plans to convert one of the nuclear heat supply stations to alternate fuels. There are, on the other hand, the continuing energy shortages in the area of European Russia which the government has to take into consideration.

The Russian Government also has its privatization program and its conversion to a market economy to keep it busy, plus the problem of disposing of tons of radioactive plutonium and enriched uranium from warheads now being disabled because of the CFE and START agreements. Disposing of the warheads alone is estimated to cost billions of dollars, money the Russian Government doesn't have. The U.S. Congress has authorized $400 million to help pay the cost of dismantling the missiles, but much more will be needed. In view of these problems, it is likely the Russian Government will put the entire nuclear energy problem on hold for the next several years. So this may be one decision that is made by inaction. Current nuclear plants will continue to be used, but no new ones will be constructed.

THE FUTURE

The failure of the August 1991 *coup*, leading as it did to the repudiation of communism and the disintegration of the Soviet Union, removed many of the obstacles to progress in the now independent successor republics, though most probably don't have the leaders necessary to take advantage of it. The Russian Federation appears to be an exception, and actions taken by President Yeltsin since independence which became a fact in December 1991 supports that conclusion.

The Commonwealth of Independent States is probably just a transitory mechanism, but Yeltsin's support for that organization should help to make the transition to independent statehood smoother for most of the republics. This is less of a problem in the case of the Russian Federation, since it is a nation of over 147 million people, and no one today questions that it is entitled to independent status.

Yet even the Russian Federation is having, and will continue to have, a rough time for several years as it continues to transform its economy. It is receiving fairly significant international assistance, but the very size of the country and the magnitude of the problems faced mean that this assistance can, at best, be marginal.

Russia is potentially a wealthy nation, however, and the Russian people are in some ways better equipped to deal with adversity than most, having experienced so much of it in the past. Provided they are able to retain the political will, Russians now have the possibility for a rather bright future.

The Commonwealth of Independent States

Five of the plotters: Interior Minister Pugo and Vice President Yanayev (third and fourth from left)

THE COLLAPSE OF THE SOVIET UNION

It was early in the morning in Moscow on Monday, August 19, 1991, when Soviet television issued its news bulletin. Mikhail Gorbachëv, alleged to be unable for health reasons to perform his duties, had been relieved as President. His powers had been transferred to his vice president, Gennadi Yanayev, who was to exercise them in consultation with an eight–member *State Committee for the State of Emergency*, composed of himself, the Prime Minister, the Ministers of Defense and Interior, head of the KGB, two individuals representing the military–industrial complex, and the chairman of the Farmers' Union of the USSR.

A state of emergency was announced throughout in the country, demonstrations and protest meetings were banned and independent newspapers were closed. Subsequently it was revealed that Gorbachëv had actually been in military custody since the preceding evening.

Although portrayed as an ordinary transfer of power resulting from the inability of the Soviet President to fulfill his duties, this was actually the beginning of an attempted *coup d'état*, a fact that became clear as soon as one looked more closely at what was happening. First of all, if Gorbachëv had really been ill, his vice president could have temporarily assumed his duties without further ado. It

was not necessary either to declare a state of emergency or create a "State Committee for the State of Emergency" to supervise it.

Secondly, not only was every member of the State Committee for the State of Emergency a prominant conservative, this was the second attempt by four of them to assume Gorbachëv's powers. Two months earlier, the Prime Minister, Valentin Pavlov had asked the Supreme Soviet to give him the right to issue decrees that would not require Gorbachëv's signature; his request had been supported by the Ministers of Defense and Interior plus the head of the KGB. Gorbachëv had to personally and energetically intervene to defeat this first maneuver of the conservatives. In retrospect, Gorbachëv should have dismissed Pavlov and the other plotters at that time, but he evidently thought he could continue to control them and he desired to rule by consensus without breaking with the more conservative members of his government.

Now the plotters were trying again. They decided to make their move because Gorbachëv, vacationing in the Crimea with his family, was due to return to Moscow that morning. A second consideration was that Gorbachëv was scheduled to sign a new union treaty the next

day that would transfer considerable powers to the republics. Communist traditionalists opposed the new union treaty and were determined to stop it.

That the pending union treaty was a major factor in the timing of the *coup* was made clear by the plotters when they issued their first statement announcing the removal of Gorbachëv. Here they listed their aims as "overcoming the profound and comprehensive crisis, political, ethnic and civil strife, chaos and anarchy that threaten the . . . territorial integrity, freedom and independence of our fatherland" and referred specifically to the March 1991 "referendum on the preservation of the Union of Soviet Socialist Republics." Further, Yanayev's first action after assuming power was to cancel the treaty–signing ceremony. The question was, could the *coup* succeed?

In theory, it should have. The leaders controlled all of the traditional instruments of force within the country. Marshal Dmitri Yazov controlled the military as Minister of Defense; Vladimir Kryuchkov was head of the KGB and Boris K. Pugo controlled both security troops and the police as Minister of the Interior. They demonstrated this control by ordering tanks, troops and armored vehicles into the major cities at the beginning of the attempted *coup*, ringing republic government buildings with troops and tanks, and seizing control of television and radio facilities.

Moreover, the *coup* leaders included, in addition to the Prime Minister, the First Deputy Chairman of the Defense Council (Oleg Baklanov), the president of the Association of State Enterprises and Industrial, Construction, Transport and Communications Facilities of the USSR (V. A. Staradubtsev) and the chairman of the Farmers' Union of the USSR (A. I. Tizyakov). Further, they had the support of the *Communist Party* and a significant percentage of officials throughout the country.

It must be noted that the *coup* would probably have succeeded two or three years earlier. What the leaders overlooked, however, was the significant democratization, coupled with extremely damaging revelations of past history and mismanagement, that had taken place over the preceding years. These moves had produced new leaders such as Boris Yeltsin, elected President of the Russian Federation in June 1991, and Anatoly Sobchok, Mayor of Leningrad. An order was actually issued for the arrest of Yeltsin, but no attempt was made to take other democratic leaders into custody or even to dismiss them from their positions.

The attempt to arrest Yeltsin was bungled. Eluding his would–be captors, Yeltsin made it to the Russian Republic Parliament building by 10:00 a.m. and immediately began organizing opposition to the *coup*. His first step was to call a press conference to question the authority of the "State Committee for the State of Emergency." He followed this up with a decree ordering all Russian Republic citizens to obey the orders of the Russian Republic Government, rather than the orders of the unconstitutional "Committee."

In perhaps his grandest gesture, he then went outside where tanks ringed the parliament building, climbed up on top of one of the them, and called for an "unlimited general strike" and mass civil disobedience. The soldiers, apparently devoid of orders about what to do in case of opposition, allowed Yeltsin to then climb down and go back into the Parliament building. Subsequently, thousands of Yeltsin supporters gathered around the structure and, forming a human shield, made it impossible for the *coup* leaders to move against Yeltsin and his democratic supporters without inflicting major casualties.

The *coup* leaders overlooked many things, but perhaps their greatest failure was in communications. They took the traditional action of seizing control of the radio and television stations (which abruptly acquired an air of unreality).

They did close down opposition newspapers, but they never gained control of telephone lines or stopped foreign reporter's from filing their dispatches with their home organizations.

As a result, the democrats built up their own internal communications using computers and modems (a means for communication by telephone line from one computer to another). News of the *coup* and growing opposition to it was broadcast to the Soviet Union by the BBC, Voice of America, and the rest of the international media. The Soviet people also learned thereby of the nearly universal condemnation of the attempted *coup* by world

leaders. Western nations suspended aid programs and otherwise made it clear that its leaders would find themselves isolated internationally if they won.

What the leaders also forgot to take into account was the possibility that parts of the military and the KGB might be weaned away from loyalty to the attempted *coup*. In fact, however, as popular demonstrations grew, many individual commanders adopted a passive stance or actively threw their support to Yeltsin and the forces of democracy. In Leningrad, 200,000 demonstrators gathered in the square outside the Winter Palace, while in Siberia coal miners an-

August 20: A heavily-armed bodyguard watches over Russian President Boris Yeltsin inside the Russian parliament.   Reuters/Bettmann nounced a protest strike. Gradually, one after another of almost all of the Republic leaders came out against the *coup*.

When it became clear to the *coup* leaders that the Soviet people (1) would not accept their rule peacefully and (2) that they could win only through a ruthless use of force and (3) a continuing regime of oppression that would leave the Soviet Union isolated internationally, one after another of the *coup* leaders lost his nerve and the move began to collapse. After approximately 60 hours, Gorbachëv was freed, the troops were ordered out of Moscow, and an order went out for the arrest of the *coup* leaders.

Boris Pugo, Minister of the Interior, committed suicide as later also did Marshal Sergei Akhromeyev, Gorbachev's chief military adviser, who was implicated in the attempted *coup*. Aleksandr Bessmyrtnikh, the Foreign Minister, was fired because of questionable loyalty despite his protests of innocence which were even expressed by live satellite TV in the United States.

The Return of Gorbachëv and Collapse of the Union

Gorbachëv arrived back in Moscow Thursday morning to loud cheers but, though he claimed to be in complete control of the Soviet Union, it soon became clear that the three–day attempted *coup* had rung a death knell to the old system. Even as Gorbachëv defended the *Communist Party* and promised to work for its renewal, Yeltsin issued a decree banning party activities in the Russian Republic and specifically prohibited party cells in military units, police units of the Ministry of Interior and in the KGB.

Abruptly, on Friday, Gorbachëv, speaking to the Russian Parliament, abandoned his earlier defense of the party and referred to the Central Committee as "traitors." On Saturday, he followed this up by resigning as General Secretary and calling on the Central Committee to dissolve itself. He then issued a decree suspending the activities of the party and seizing all its property. This about–face created a serious problem of credibility.

The Soviet Union, which Gorbachëv still hoped to save, was crumbling around him. Estonia had declared itself independent on August 19 and Latvia followed the next day. In the week following the defeat of the *coup*, four more republics followed with their declarations of independence: the Ukraine on August 25, Byelorussia (now Belarus) on August 25, Uzbekistan on August 26 and Moldavia (now Moldova) on August 27. Armenia set a referendum for a vote on independence for September 16.

Several of the other republics also promised to hold plebiscites to confirm their declarations. The most important of those was the Ukraine, which set its referendum for December 1. Thus the situation was that, including Lithuania and Georgia which had declared their independence even before the attempted *coup*, nine of the fifteen republics were committed to independence. If the republics really meant their declarations of independence, no viable union was possible. It was unclear whether their declarations of independence were real or only bargaining tools in preparation for negotiations on a new union treaty.

The Rise of Boris Yeltsin and Attempts Toward Union

Crucially, Boris Yeltsin, President of the Russian Federation, still favored some form of union, and on August 28 he sent a delegation to the Ukraine to see what could be worked out. What he got was a provisional economic and military alliance which, the Russian and Ukrainian Governments announced, other "former subjects of the U.S.S.R." were welcome to join.

The next step came on September 2 when a special session of the Congress of People's Deputies met in Moscow, with the leaders of ten of the republics in attendance. Here Gorbachëv proposed the creation of a new interim government to replace the discredited one over which he presided. After three days of debate, the Congress voted, in effect, to dissolve itself and transfer authority to a new executive council and legislature controlled by the participating republics.

Gorbachëv remained President, but final executive authority was lodged in a State Council made up of Gorbachëv and the leaders of the participating republics. A separate Inter–republic Economic Committee, appointed by the State Council, assumed the functions of the former Council of Ministers. Finally, a two chamber legislature was established, the membership of the second chamber to be appointed by and represent the governments of the individual republics. In this chamber, voting would be by delegation, with each republic having one vote. This clearly interim government was to govern until a new union treaty could be signed by the individual republics bringing into being a proposed "Union of Sovereign States."

The first act of the State Council was to recognize the independence of Lithuania, Latvia and Estonia. It can be argued that recognition had become inevitable by this time, since most of the world, including the United States, had already recognized the independence of the Baltic Republics. Nevertheless, this was the first formal step in the breakup of the Soviet Empire. Even at this time, only ten of the twelve remaining republics were supporting the interim government. Moldavia refused to participate at all and Georgia sent only observers. Neither appeared likely to sign a new union treaty. In addition, over the next several days, all of the remaining republics other than the Russian Federation, Kazakhstan and Turkmenistan declared their independence. Later, even Kazakhstan and Turkmenistan would join the list.

The next three months were to prove decisive. Gorbachëv, determined to save some form of union and, recognizing that Boris Yeltsin's support was absolutely vital, dismissed all of his former advisers and accepted Yeltsin's advice on the make–up of his new government, surrounding himself with liberals and even appointing Ivan Silayev, Prime Minister of the Russian Federation (i.e. the Russian state), as Chairman of the Inter–republic Economic Committee, a post which effectively made him the caretaker Prime Minister of the union government. He then asked the reform economomist Grigori Yavlinsky to draw up a plan for economic union which he presented in draft form to the State Council in September.

The leaders of ten of the republics attended the meeting and gave their general approval to the plan. The two missing republics were Moldova (formerly Moldavia) and Georgia. Former President Gamsakhurdia of Georgia had made it clear that his government was pursuing a policy of complete independence and wanted nothing to do, even economically, with a union. The Moldovan Government was undecided whether to participate in an economic union and so chose to abstain.

The other key republic was the Ukraine, led by Leonid Kravchuk, the former head of the Ukrainian *Communist Party*, who had repudiated the party and become a convert to democratization and a market economy. Kravchuk himself supported the idea of some form of continued union at first, but he came under increasing pressure from the Ukrainian parliament, which opposed supranational ties as a limitation on Ukrainian independence. In October 1991, the Ukrainian parliament drew up two pages of objections to the pending economic treaty, after which the Ukrainian Government announced that it would not sign the agreement without significant changes in the language. Among the changes that the parliament was demanding was the right for the Ukraine to set up its own national bank, issue its own currency, and, in general, to control its fiscal policy.

The Ukrainian parliament then decided that the deputies selected to represent the Ukraine in the Union Supreme Soviet would participate only in the Council of the Republic and only as

The presidents of Ukraine, Belarus, and Russia: (l. to r.) Leonid Kravchuk, Stanislav Shushkevich, and Boris Yeltsin in Minsk, Belarus, December 8, 1991.

observers. It came as no surprise, therefore, when the Ukraine joined Georgia and Moldova in boycotting sessions of the State Council called to talk about a new union treaty.

Thus, only seven republics agreed, on November 14, to establish a new "Union of Sovereign States." The additional two republics not signing were Uzbekistan and Armenia. Two weeks later, when the State Council met again, supposedly to initial the draft agreement, seven republics were again present but, this time Uzbekistan was represented while Azerbaijan was missing. And instead of initialling the treaty, they decided to submit it to their republic parliaments for approval, a process that put the proposed treaty into severe jeopardy.

By this time, Leonid Kravchuk had dropped his earlier general support for some continuation of the union. Having said on November 12 that the Ukraine would "never sign" a treaty which would contain "even the slightest hint of certain governing central bodies," because "the center has fully exhausted itself," he added two weeks later that he would "take no part in the . . . talks on signing a new Union Treaty" and "all allegations that I meant to join the treaty later are nothing but fiction."

All of that might have become more or less academic, had the December 1 referendum on Ukrainian independence gone differently. In fact, nearly 90 percent of all Ukrainians voted *yes* for independence. At the same time, Kravchuk proved himself to be in line with Ukrainian thinking and a popular politician by winning 61.5 percent of the vote in the concurrent race for the newly created office of Ukrainian President.

"The independence of the Ukraine is a new political reality," commented Boris Yeltsin upon receiving the results of the Ukrainian vote. And what Yeltsin meant when he used the phrase "new political reality" was that Gorbachëv's draft for a political union was now dead. The Ukraine would not join and, as Yeltsin had already said, he could not conceive of a political union that did not include the Ukraine. As far as that goes, Gorbachëv had said much the same thing, although he apparently still hoped that the Ukraine might still be persuaded to reverse its stand. Yeltsin had no such hopes.

Yet Kravchuk had said on a number of occasions that he favored some kind of coordinating mechanism to handle the many problems of the now–separating republics. The question was what sort of political structure the Ukraine was willing to accept to achieve that coordination. Yeltsin decided to find out. He contacted Kravchuk and Stanislav Shushkevich, President of Belarus, and suggested that the three presidents meet the following weekend to discuss the future of the union. Shushkevich agreed to host the meeting and offered the use of a hunting lodge located not far from the Belarus city of Brest. "We came to the conclusion," Shushkevich commented after the meeting, "that we had to sort out the concept of the kind of union we are capable of building."

So the three leaders talked for two days and, in the end, they produced the agreement, which they signed late in the day on December 8, 1991, in the Belarusian capital of Minsk, calling into being the "Commonwealth of Independent States."

COMMONWEALTH OF INDEPENDENT STATES

The suddenness of the December 8th agreement probably shocked a lot of people, but two aspects of the agreement caused some disquiet in the beginning. The first was that the three signatories were the heads of the three Slavic republics of the old union, suggesting to some that they were creating a "Slavic Commonwealth," even though the agreement specified that membership was open to "all member states of the former U.S.S.R," plus "other states that share the goals and principles of the present agreement." The second cause for concern was that the agreement also specified that "the USSR has ceased to exist as a subject of international law and as a geopolitical reality."

The first issue was defused rather quickly when the leaders of the five Central Asian Republics met in Ashkhabad, Turkmenistan, and there signed an agreement to become co–founders of the Commonwealth of Independent States. This led to a conference in Alma Ata, Kazakhstan, on December 21, 1991 which was attended by the presidents of eleven of the republics, with former President Gamsakhurdia of Georgia the sole hold out. Even Georgia sent an observer, however. The three Baltic Republics were not represented, having made it clear earlier that they would not join any new political union.

At Alma Ata, the eleven presidents signed a protocol making all eleven republics co–founders of the Commonwealth of Independent States. An additional protocol and two accords were also

Air Marshal Shaposhnikov arrives in Alma Ata, Kazakhstan, December 20, 1991

signed dealing with subsidiary matters. They also signed a resolution supporting Russia's claim to the USSR's United Nations membership, including its permanent membership in the Security Council. They further agreed to meet again in Minsk on December 30.

The December 30 meeting was actually the first "session" of the executive bodies of the Commonwealth of Independent States and included separate meetings of the heads of state and heads of government. A total of 15 documents was negotiated and signed at these meetings, fleshing out the structures of the CIS and establishing certain forms of cooperation. Since the CIS was seen as a coordinating body, there was to be no "center" as such—no president or prime minister, no ministries and no legislature. Instead, using to some extent the structure of the European Community (EC), the leaders drew up documents creating a Council of the Heads of States and a Council of Heads of Government.

Another agreement created a "working group" as a sort of secretariat to "prepare organically and technically the holding" of the meetings of the two councils. Unlike the EC, however, they did not create the presidential commission and cadre of bureaucrats that plays such an important role in Brussels. In fact, possibly to underline that point, the CIS Heads of State agreed that the the job of drawing up proposals on how this working group should be structured

would be handled by a conference of CIS foreign ministers meeting in Minsk in early January.

ARMED FORCES

Perhaps the most important topic discussed at the Minsk meeting was the future status of the armed forces. Immediately prior to the meeting, the defense ministers and chairmen of the committees for defense questions of the 11 member states had met in Moscow with Air Marshal Yevgeniy Shaposhnikov, named Soviet Defense Minister following the August attempted *coup* and designated temporary commander of the union forces at the Alma Ata meeting.

An earlier proposal to maintain a unified armed force became moot when it became clear that the Ukraine, Azerbaijan and Moldova wanted to have their own armies. Thus the agreement that actually came before the CIS heads of state was based on the concept of joint CIS armed forces. The signed agreement stipulated that each republic had the right to establish its own army; but it also provided for continuation of a unified army under CIS command which republics could participate in if they wished. National armies were to be limited to conventional forces, however; all 11 republic heads of state agreed that nuclear forces would remain under unified command. Nuclear weapons were at

that time based in four different republics—the Russian Federation, Ukraine, Belarus and Kazakhstan. All except for the Russian Federation had stated that they intended to go "non–nuclear"—that is, eventually to get rid of all nuclear weapons on their soil. In the meanwhile, it was agreed that the President of the Russian Federation would have primary authority over nuclear weapons with the other three republican presidents having a veto power on their use.

The Ukrainian Government immediately set about creating its own armed forces, and also moved to extend its control over the Black Sea fleet as well. Azerbaijan also moved to take control of the Caspian Sea fleet.

Marshall Shaposhnikov, who also participated in the military discussions at the Minsk meeting, was named commander–in–chief of the CIS armed forces. A council of republic defense ministers was also created and charged with elaborating a common defense policy.

The CIS Heads of States also touched on the subject of foreign policy. In addition to a general commitment to coordinate policy, they signed an agreement which provided for the division of the former USSR's property held abroad, including embassy and consulate buildings.

Other agreements signed in Minsk included one that called for joint activities in the exploration and use of space, plus several that dealt with a number of regional issues which the various heads of state agreed to treat as matters requiring CIS cooperation. These included the problems of the Aral Sea, the consequences of the Spital earthquake [centering in Armenia], preservation of fish stocks in the Caspian Sea, and elimination of the consequences of the Chernobyl nuclear power station disaster. Though he had very little confidence in the viability of the Commonwealth of Independent States.

President Gorbachëv recognized it as a *fait accompli*. He therefore agreed to a wind up of the old union by December 31 and the transfer of the Kremlin and the state bank to Russian control. Yeltsin, meanwhile, issued a series of decrees taking control of all union ministries other than defense and atomic energy. Gorbachëv himself resigned as President of the USSR on December 25. Separately the USSR Supreme Soviet held its own last session on December 26. The handful of deputies present, far less than a quorum since most of the republics had already withdrawn their deputies, recognized the Commonwealth of Independent States before voting itself out of existence.

Thus the Union of Soviet Socialist Republics officially disappeared and the Commonwealth of Independent States came into being. The CIS did not, if fact, replace the USSR, since the individual independent republics see themselves as the collective heirs to the USSR. The CIS is not even a sovereign entity, but rather a coordinating body for the independent republics which make up its membership. Its significance, and even its viability, remain matters of conjecture. In addition to Gorbachëv, among those who have publicly questioned whether the CIS has any chance for long–time survival are Edward Shevardnazde, former Soviet Foreign Minister, U.S. Secretary of State James Baker, and Henry Kissinger.

Their criticisms are to the point. The CIS does have a weak structure at the moment and the newly independent republics are faced with mammoth tasks in the months and years ahead. It will be extremely difficult for the CIS to contribute much toward the solving of those problems. On the other hand, the CIS came into existence precisely because the apparachniks of the old center acted as a major force holding back and frustrating necessary reforms. Creation of the CIS has already made the positive contribution of getting rid of most of that particular countervailing force.

Perhaps the greatest weakness of the CIS is that some of its members, Ukraine in particular, fear continued domination by Moscow. As this fear recedes in the future and as the republics see the need for greater coordination, they can begin to strengthen the institutions of the CIS and to bestow on them additional responsibilities. What is clear in any case is that the most important problems facing the republics over the next several years are economic and they are best solved at the lowest level possible. The commitment of the members of the CIS to a market economy, private enterprise and to popular participation in government represents the best long–term guarantee that they will be able to solve their problems.

ECONOMY UNDER THE CIS

The economy of the old USSR was designed and built as a single economy, with all important decisions coming out of Moscow. In addition, the first principle of the planners was economies of scale which translated into "bigger is better." Since all enterprises were owned and run by the Soviet state, they deliberately set out to create monopoly situations in every part of the economy, since these were considered to be more efficient. Accordingly, all over the Soviet Union, single, large factories were built, designed to serve the needs of a large part of the country or even, sometimes, the entire Soviet economy.

Such factories, being part of the "union" economy, took their orders from their supervising ministry in Moscow; the republic government exercised no control whatsoever. This made for a highly integrated economic system, though it also made it highly vulnerable, since a single, badly–run factory could disrupt a complete sector by failing to deliver acceptable products in good time. Two further factors were possible time delays and added transportation costs.

All of these factors were magnified tremendously in 1991 in the situation of a collapsing Soviet Union. As the individual republics moved to establish their political independence, they also moved to take control of their own economies. But when they tried to do so, they found that, in many cases, a significant part of their industry was totally dependent on deliveries of raw materials and parts from other republics and could not operate without these continued deliveries. Moreover, the same was true with regard to factory output. Worst of all, in many cases, too, the customers were factories located in other republics.

Just how complicated this could get was explained in November 1991 by V. Razumov, Deputy Minister of the former U.S.S.R. Ministry of the Chemical and Petroleum Refining Industry, just after the ministry had been abolished on November 15. Razumov used the example of the plastic that goes into making refriger-

ators. "One of the many things that could make our life a little easier today," commented Razumov, is refrigerators. But you can't make them in, say, Belarus, if you have no polystyrene, which is made in Kazakhstan. Kazakhstan cannot produce polystyrene unless ethylbenzene is supplied from Tataria. They cannot make ethylbenzene in Tataria if they have no benzene. And benzene is made from petroleum, which is extracted mainly in [the] Tyumen [region].

That is roughly the system that is currently just [barely] managing to supply plastic for refrigerators. It could easily be destroyed. The people of Tyumen will sell independently a little more of their petroleum, the refinery workers a little more of the benzene produced from their supply of petroleum, and so on, with the quantities being reduced at each stage of the production of plastic. And it could easily turn out that the end result is that we get no refrigerators."

Razumov was speaking as a planner worried about the collapse of a system that, with all of its faults, managed to produce refrigerators. In the short run, his criticism has some validity, because it will take some time to create the market links necessary to replace the collapsing command economy.

Razumov was dealing with a single example. Just how serious is this problem for the overall CIS economy? A Moscow Interfax "Soviet Business Report," issued on October 31, 1991, looked at the overall problem based on 1989 data, the latest obtainable. What the report established was that 20.3 percent of all domestic trade was inter–republic in 1989. What the report also pointed out, however, is that the smaller republics were most closely bound into the old command economic system, while larger republics like Russia and Ukraine were far less dependent on inter–republic trade.

Soviet Republics' Individual Share in Inter–Republic Trade (from 1989 data)

	Imports	Exports	Average
Russia	12.2%	13.0%	12.6%
Ukraine	26.2%	26.6%	26.4%
Kazakhstan	36.6%	20.6%	28.6%
Azerbaijan	23.6%	41.6%	32.6%
Uzbekistan	40.5%	28.8%	34.5%
Georgia	34.4%	40.3%	37.4%
Kyrgyzstan	42.8%	32.5%	37.7%
Turkmenia	40.2%	35.5%	37.9%
Armenia	39.7%	37.2%	38.5%
Tajikistan	48.9%	32.8%	40.9%
Belarus	37.5%	46.3%	41.9%
Moldova	43.3%	43.3%	43.3%

There was clearly some deterioration in inter–republic trade in 1991, but the number of alternate producers in the USSR/CIS is so limited that there is almost no likelihood that these figures have changed significantly. What they make clear is that, except for the Russian Federation, there is a high level of mutual economic dependence among the republics which would lead to an almost total disruption if they were unable to work out some form of continued economic cooperation. A number of republics have negotiated bilateral trade agreements, but these have not worked very well, since suppliers and customers are seldom from a single republic or even from the *same* republic. An even more important problem is the matter of prices.

In the old Soviet Union, prices were largely symbolic, set by the state for reasons such as to encourage development of individual industries or to discourage consumption, and having little or nothing to do with the international value of the articles. All of this was possible because it was then a closed system. In general, the prices of food, fuel and raw materials were kept low, while the prices of most consumer goods were above world prices. The movement to world prices, now well underway, has tended to disrupt interrepublic trade, since some of the poorer republics are unable to pay the greatly increased prices for food and fuel, while other republics do not want to pay world prices for merchandise that does not meet world standards. But an even more important factor is that the suggestion that all of the republics would be able to continue using the ruble as their own currency has failed in practice. The former union–wide banking system having collapsed, the individual republics were unable to come to an agreement at the CIS level on the transfer of funds between the republics. The result was a rapidly growing mountain of debt until the Russian Government restricted credit to the other republics, then effectively forced them off the ruble standard. Most republics have now developed their own currencies, but the CIS continues to lack adequate mechanisms for the transferal of funds between republics. As a result, inter–republic trade had dropped by as much as 70 percent in some cases.

The CIS heads of state and heads of government have met several time since December 1992 and some agreements have been signed. However, even those who were optimistic about the possible contribution of the CIS at the beginning have since become pessimistic. The CIS has not yet shown that it can handle the major economic problems facing the newly independent republics.

This is a transitional problem, of course, related to the fact that most economic activity in the CIS is still state–run. The real, long–time solutions lie in privatization and movement to a market economy. The various republic leaders are committed to move in this direction, but the movement has been extremely slow for most republics thus far. Russia and, surprisingly, Ukraine are making faster progress, but it will take even these republics from five to ten years to make the transition. The real question, then, is whether the political will and/or popular support exist for such a program.

Production was already down an average of 12 percent across the old Soviet Union in 1991 and that rate of decline may have accelerated somewhat in 1992. Interrepublic and international trade also dropped, partly in response to the move to world prices and partly because of the lack of adequate banking mechanisms. Trade with Eastern Europe, which collapsed in 1991, continues to be a negative factor as well. Many Soviet consumer goods manufacturers, making products such as refrigerators, washing machines and electric sewing machines, have been trying to find domestic suppliers for the engines or other components they had been importing from Eastern Europe but the collapse of the Soviet Union has further exacerbated that situation by cutting ties between manufacturers located in different republics. In addition, individual republics have begun prohibiting the export of scarce items in order to protect their own citizens, while cutting imports from other republics in order to hold on to precious hard currencies. All of this helps explain the further contraction of the economies of the various CIS states in 1992. The only optimistic development is that new, private enterprises have begun to come into existence and they have begun to meet the needs of companies cut off from their suppliers by the new restrictions.

There are also some bright spots in the overall CIS economy. The most important one is that there has been some progress made in freeing industrial activity from state control. The latest CIS economic figures date from October 1991, but even those indicate the trend. Although 72.9 percent of all workers were still employed by state enterprises and organizations at that time, this represented a decrease of 5.8 percent over 1990. Looking at some of those now employed outside the state sector, we find that as of October 1991 there were 10.7 million persons, or 7.8 percent of the total labor force, working for leased enterprises, joint stock companies or other business associations. In addition, 6.5 million persons, comprising 4.8 percent of the working force, were listed as self–employed. This included the category of private farmers. A further 17.6 million persons comprising 13 per-

cent of the working force were employed on collective farms. Since centralized control has collapsed, these collective farmers will, in effect, be required to take control of decision–making and they will also, if they wish, have the right to break up the collective farms completely, something which is already happening in places such as Georgia and Armenia and something Yeltsin is encouraging in Russia.

Moreover, the Yeltsin reforms, instituted as of January 1, 1992, have forced the other republics to institute similar reforms. Clearly they would have been less costly and less painful if instituted earlier, but the political will did yet exist at that time. Though painful in the short run, they represent the best promise of all for the future.

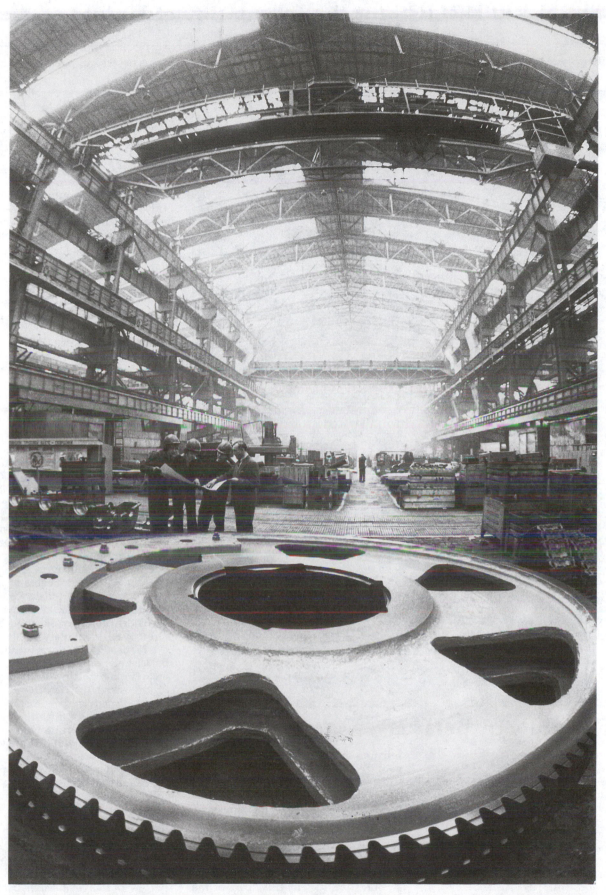

Uralmach, the biggest Russian machine-building plant, which makes equipment for both Russian and foreign nations. The plant is located in the city of Ekaterinburg.

NOVOSTI photo

Due to their shared histories as well as frequent geographical and cultural similarities, there is necessarily some repetition from one entry to the other.

Showing principal cities and railroads

The Republic of Belarus

(Pronounced *Bee–ella–roose*)

Area: 83,040 sq. mi. (207,600 sq. km., about the size of Minnesota).

Population: 10.2 million (estimated).

Climate: Temperate.

Neighboring States: Russia (east), Latvia, Lithuania (northeast), Poland (west), Ukraine (south).

Languages: Belarusian, Russian.

Ethnic Composition: Belarusian (78%), Russian (13%), other (9%).

Principal Religions: Orthodox Christianity, Roman Catholicism. Until recently religious worship was officially discouraged.

Chief Commercial Products: Grain, potatoes, cattle, agricultural machinery, motor vehicles, machine tools, oil, electricity, steel, coal and metal production.

Currency: Belarus Ruble.

Recent Political Status: Part of the Russian Empire until 1917, became the Byelorussian SSR in 1919, part of the USSR (1922-1991).

Chief of State: Stanislav Shushkevich, President.

The Land

The Republic of Belarus is the ultimate independent successor state to the Byelorussian Soviet Socialist Republic, established on January 1, 1919. It is located in the northwestern portion of the Russian Plain, just southwest of the Valdai Hills. The northern part of the republic is made up mostly of low, rolling hills. Dzyarzhynskaya Mountain, the loftiest point in the republic, is only 1,135 feet high. Most of the southern part of the republic is covered by a lowland area known as the Prypyats (Pripet) Swamp. Much of this area is a mixture of swamp and forest with a very low population density.

Four major rivers flow through Belarus. In the north the Western Dvina River, which begins in the Valdai Hills, enters from the east and then flows in a mainly northwestern direction until it crosses into Latvia, there becoming the Daugava. The Dnieper River also enters Belarus from the east, then flows in a southern direction a short distance west of the eastern border. It actually forms the eastern border for a short stretch before entering Ukraine. The third of the rivers is the Prypyats, which enters from the south from Ukraine, then flows eastward just north of the southern border. It crosses into Ukraine shortly before emptying into the Dnieper.

The last of the rivers is the Nyoman [Nemunas], which begins in northwestern Belarus, a short distance west of the capital city of Minsk, and flows west and then north before crossing the border into Lithuania. A tributary of the Nyoman, the Neris (Villia), starts in northwestern Belarus just north of Minsk. It flows in a meandering northwestern direction before crossing the border into Lithuania. Originally covered in forests and fens, today Belarus is a mixture of forests and fields. Reclamation projects in the south have reclaimed about 6.25 million acres of swampland, thereby increasing the agricultural potential of this area, particularly for pasturage, although hemp is another major crop. The south also has over six thousand peat deposits.

The People

The population of the Republic of Belarus was 10,200,000 as of the 1989 census. Belarusians constitute about 78 percent of this total. Russians, the largest minority group, are around 13 percent of the population. Other minorities include Poles (4.2%), Ukrainians (2.4%), Jews

Belarus

(1.4%), and Lithuanians. Belarusian belongs to the eastern Slavic family of languages. It is fairly modern in origin and arose primarily for historical reasons. Its ancestor is Slavonic, which had been spoken by all eastern Slavs as late as the thirteenth century. This area became part of the Grand Principality of Lithuania in the fourteenth century. After the Lithuanian Union with Poland in 1569, the upper classes became heavily Polonized and this, plus the several centuries of separation, eventually produced a language that was different from either Russian or Ukrainian. As a result of the industrialization of the twentieth century, about half the population now lives in urban areas.

History

The area of the Pripet Swamp, in southern Belarus, is believed to be the original home of the eastern Slavic peoples. Spreading out from that point, they eventually occupied most of the Russian Plain. The first organized Slavic state, Kievan Rus, came into existence as a trading state which controlled the "road from the Varangians (Vikings) to the Greeks." That "road" was the water system that permitted travel from the Baltic Sea in the north to the Black Sea and Constantinople in the south. The most important of those rivers was the Dnieper, which flows south through the eastern part of Belarus.

Kievan Rus was destroyed by an invasion of the Mongols in 1238–41. The collapse of that first Slavic state left the northwest in a state of anarchy which ended in the first half of the fourteenth century when Gedaminas founded the Grand Principality of Lithuania. It had its capital at Vilnius but the state extended southward as far as the Black Sea, including all of present–day Belarus. The majority of the people living in this state were Slavs and the language used at the court was old Slavonic, the language of Kievan Rus.

This situation continued until 1569 when Lithuania became part of the Polish Kingdom as a result of the Union of Lublin. From that time onward, the upper classes became increasingly Polonized. When an independent Patriarchate was established at Moscow a few years later, the Polish King separated the Orthodox Church in Lithuania from Moscow and forced it to recognize the Pope as the head of the church, thereby creating the Uniate Rite of the Church. That situation continued for over thirty years before the Orthodox Church was again allowed to begin operating again. After about 1625, therefore, you had a situation where the upper classes were Polonized and increasingly Roman Catholic and the peasants were Orthodox and enserfed.

The southern portion of the Orthodox lands broke away in 1654 and joined Russia; this became the Ukraine. But the northern Orthodox lands remained part of the Polish Kingdom until the three partitions of Poland in 1772, 1793 and 1795. These gave the area of present day Belarus to Russia. From 1795 to 1918, therefore, these lands were part of the Russian Empire. Russia did not recognize Belarusian as a separate language, however, so Russian became the language of government while Belarusian was merely the local dialect of the peasantry.

The Russian Revolution brought about a collapse of the old Imperial Government and the various parts of the empire began to set up autonomous governments. On March 25, 1918, anti–communist leftists established the independent Belarusian Democratic Republic. Lenin and his Bolsheviks in Moscow refused to recognize the new republic and it was later overthrown by the Red Army. On January 1, 1919, the communist victors set up the Byelorussian Soviet Socialist Republic.

One of the few buildings to survive World War II when most of the city of Minsk was destroyed, an Orthodox Church holds a lonely vigil as it stands surrounded by modern office and apartment buildings.
Photo by Miller B. Spangler

Belarus

The then Byelorussians accepted their inclusion in the new Soviet regime and they remained loyal and subservient citizens throughout the Soviet era. In return, Moscow transformed the country industrially over the years. In addition, the republic was greatly enlarged in November 1939 when significant territories taken from Poland as a result of the Nazi–Soviet Non–Aggression Pact were added to the republic.

Gorbachëv's program of *glasnost* and *perestroika* brought some changes in Byelorussia, but the majority of the communist leadership was conservative. A *Byelorussian Popular Front* was established but, harassed by the leadership of the republic, it found it difficult to build up support and it remained a minority movement. The infamous Chernobyl nuclear accident in April 1986 created great fear throughout the republic, but the accident had actually occurred across the border in the Ukraine, so Belarusian officials were only blamed for not doing enough. They, in turn, blamed Moscow and otherwise helped keep a tight lid on news of the event.

When the attempted *coup* against Gorbachëv began in August 1991, Nikolas Dementei, the first secretary of the *Byelorussian Communist Party*, made the mistake of supporting the *coup* leaders. When the attempt collapsed, therefore, Dementei was ousted from his position as Chairman of the Supreme Soviet. On August 25, the Byelorussian Supreme Soviet also declared the republic's independence, adopting the name *Belarus* (initially spelled Belorus). It then suspended the activities of the communist party.

Stanislav Shushkevich was elected chairman of the Belarus Supreme Soviet on September 20, 1991. He previously had held the position of first deputy chairman of the Supreme Soviet. He is a nuclear physicist by training, however, and "headed laboratories and departments of nuclear physics in various Minsk higher educational institutions." He was also a member of the USSR Supreme Soviet where he was a member of the liberal Interregional Deputies Group. He favors "the speediest introduction of market relations and private ownership," but the Belarus Supreme Soviet, still filled with ex–communists, is much more conservative. Because Shushkevich has attempted to govern by consensus, economic change has been very slow.

Shushkevich supported a continuation of some form of union as long as that appeared a viable option. After the December 1 referendum and elections in the Republic of Ukraine, however, Shushkevich joined with Presidents Yeltsin and Kravchuk in creation of the Commonwealth of Independent States on December 8. Shushkevich had hosted the meeting at his hunting lodge and the agreement was signed in Minsk, the capital of Belarus.

Foreign Policy

The Government of Belarus has adopted an official stance of international neutrality. To that end, it has signed the Nuclear Non–Proliferation Treaty and, in February 1993, its legislature ratified the START–1 agreement. There are currently 81 nuclear–armed SS–25 missiles stationed in Belarus. These missiles are to be shipped to Russia for dismantling by the end of 1994 according to an agreement which Belarus negotiated with the Russian Federation.

Belarus is an active supporter of the Commonwealth of Independent States and has, in addition, negotiated agreements with the three Baltic Republics. Its relations with its western neighbors are also good. Belarus has otherwise played a rather reticent role internationally.

Nature of the Regime

Belarus is the only CIS member which has not changed its political system as yet but, instead, has retained the system in existence when it was a constituent member of the Union of Soviet Socialist Republics. The head of state is the Chairman of the Supreme Soviet, currently Stanislav Shushkevich.

The prime minister, who is appointed by the Chairman of the Supreme Soviet and confirmed by the Supreme Soviet, overseas the day–to–day affairs of government and presides over his cabinet; the current prime minister is Vyacheslav Kebich.

A draft constitution, originally circulated in December 1991 but still not yet approved by the legislature, provides for a presidential form of government with the president to be elected by popular vote. The legislature will continue to be called the Supreme Soviet, but its membership will be only 160 persons, or half the current membership. The new draft constitution also authorizes republic and local referendums on "the most important problems affecting the republic's life."

Of the political parties, the *Belarus Popular Front* supports the current government, while the *United Democratic Party* has called for new elections to form "a government independent of the conservative Supreme Soviet, one that would start with decisive reforms without having to wait for the parliament's reelection."

Culture

Belarus has one prominent architectural monument from the period of Kievan Rus, the Cathedral of St. Sophia in Polotsk, which dates from the eleventh century. There are also two church–fortresses dating from the period of the Lithuanian Grand Principality, Maloye Mazheykava and Synkavichy. The seventeenth century saw the introduction of the Baroque style. The Jesuit church at Grodno exemplies this new style and also the growing presence of Roman Catholicism, officially fostered by the Polish Government at this particular juncture in time.

Polotsk was long a center of learning and there are a number of names associated with it. Frantsyk Skaryna produced the first Belarusian translation of the Bible in the first quarter of the sixteenth century. The two editions of the Bible were actually printed in Prague and Vilnius. Symeon of Polotsk was a seventeenth century poet who wrote in Belarusian.

Maksim Bahdanovich was an important poet of the late nineteenth century. Three poets of the early Soviet period are Ales Harun, Yanka Kupala, and Yakub Kolas. Kupala also produced a play, *Natives*, which was first produced in 1924. Kolas also produced a three volume novel, *On the Crossroads*. Maksim Haretski was a novelist who wrote *The Quiet Current*. His diary was also published under the title of *On the Imperialist War*.

There was, in fact, a great outpouring of literature in the period of the 1920s. These included poets (Uladzimir Dubouka and Yazep Pushcha) and writers of fiction (Kuzma Chorny and Kandrat Krapiva). Stalin's introduction of socialist realism in 1930 brought a decline in the level of Belarusian writing, although some writers continued to be published. After World War II, a number of good composers appeared in Belarus. Dzmitry Lukas produced his first opera, *Kastus Kalinouski*, in 1947. Ryhor Pukst produced three operas between 1947 and 1955. Yauhen Hlebau produced an opera, *Your Spring* in 1963 and a ballet, *Alpine Ballad* in 1967. Yauhen Tsikotski and Yury Semyanyaka also wrote operas at this time. Belarus has both a conservatory of music and a philharmonic society. There is, in addition, the Belarusian State Theater of Opera and Ballet in Minsk, plus a state dramatic theater.

Belarus has a well–developed system of higher education. There are 33 institutes of higher education scattered throughout the republic, plus another 138 technical colleges. The Belarusian Academy of Sciences also has 32 scientific institutes in various parts of the republic. There is a comprehensive system of primary and secondary schools. In 1989, 71 percent of all eligible children were in preschool institutions.

The republic also publishes approximately two hundred daily newspapers, 130 of which are in Belorusian and the rest in other languages.

Economy

Belarus has a fairly well balanced economy, with an agriculture capable, in general, of feeding its population and a well developed industrial base. The problem with its agriculture is that about two–thirds of the peasants are still organized into collective farms, with most of the remainder in state farms. A few private farms were set up after that became possible, but the treatment they received from the state sector has discouraged others from trying. The Belarusian Government now says that it favors a changeover to private agriculture, and the Council of Ministers decided in November 1991 that farmers could receive up to 150 acres of land. The land was to be made available by March 1, 1992, but there have been no reports as to whether this was actually carried out.

The weakness of Belarusian industry is two–fold. It has to import most of its raw materials from other republics and most of its energy.

Agriculture in the northern part of the republic concentrates on cattle raising, both beef and dairy cattle. The farms produce their own fodder and hay and otherwise, except for those set aside for growing flax, the land is in pasturage. In the center of the republic, the farms concentrate on pig breeding. The most important crop grown in this area is potatoes. In the south, there are once again many farms that specialize in cattle raising, either for milk or beef. Hemp is also grown in this area. Grain is grown throughout the republic with 6.9 million tons produced in 1988. Some grain is imported into the republic, but mainly to be used as cattle feed.

Belarus has very little heavy industry. It produces about 1.1 million tons of steel a year and it manufactures machine tools, agricultural machinery and motor vehicles. It also manufactures chemicals, paper, and bricks. There is also a branch of industry that manufactures consumer goods such as watches, radios, televisions and bicycles. Most of the rest of its industry is associated either with textiles or processing of agricultural products. It manufactures artificial fibers as well as natural fibers. There is a flax-spinning industry and another that manufactures artificial silk. Shoes and boots are also made. Agricultural end products include sugar processing and the making of preserves. Domestic energy supplies are limited mainly to peat, which is widely used in industry. In 1988, Belarus produced 2.3 million tons of peat briquettes.

One drag on the economy is the continuing cost associated with the 1986 Chernobyl nuclear disaster, now estimated at 17 billion rubles a year. The southern part of Belarus was badly hit by nuclear fallout and many of the estimated 2 million victims live in Belarus. This was listed as a continuing problem to be handled by the Commonwealth of Independent States, but so far only Russia has confirmed its intention to pay a share of the expenses. In the meanwhile, the Belarus Government instituted an 18 percent wage tax in January 1992 to help raise the necessary money to pay for medical treatments and scientific research.

Belarus has also decided to issue its own currency. The republic began paying 40 percent of workers' salaries in coupons in January 1992. As of April 1, it began issuing rubles carrying a Belarus sign on them to replace the coupons. The Supreme Soviet also authorized one million rubles for construction of a mint to print a new Belarusian currency, to be called the *Taller*, in January 1992. Production was originally scheduled to begin sometime in 1992, but it appears that the government may now be having second thoughts about the matter.

The Future

The collapse of the Soviet Union, and the breakup of centralized control over most economic activity, has been hard on the people of Belarus, for the republic's industry depends heavily on inputs of raw materials and energy supplies from other republics. The government is committed in theory to creation of a market economy and private enterprise, but ex–communists still control the legislature and they are not really in favor of change. Belarus's head of state, Stanislav Shushkevich, is more liberal and appears to be quite competent. Even the most optimistic scenario presupposes that living standards will drop for at least a couple years, however.

The Republic of Ukraine

Kiev, capital of Ukraine, on the Dneiper River on a cold, damp February morning

Photo by Miller B. Spangler

Area: 240,000 sq. mi. (621,840 sq. km., twice the size of New Mexico).

Population: 52.2 million (estimated).

Capital City: Kiev (Pop. 2.6 million, estimated).

Climate: Temperate.

Neighboring States: Russia (west, south), Belarus (northeast), Poland (northwest), Czechoslovakia, Hungary (northwest), Romania, Moldova (west).

Languages: Ukrainian, Russian.

Ethnic Composition: Ukrainian (74%), Russian (12%), others (5%).

Principal Religions: Ukrainian Orthodox and Roman Catholic Christianity. Until recently, religious worship was officially discouraged.

Chief Commercial Products: Grain, potatoes, fruit, vegetables. Ukraine has some of the richest land in the former USSR. Highly developed fuel and power resources, iron and manganese ore, metal production, engineering, chemical production, gas, processed food, building materials. The nation has 60% of the former USSR's coal reserves.

Currency: Currently "coupons" issued by Ukraine; a new currency, the *hryvna*, will be issued once inflation is under control, probably in late 1993.

Recent Political Status: Part of the Russian Empire until 1917, Ukrainian Republic (1917-1922), Ukrainian Soviet Socialist Republic (1922-1991).

Chief of State: Leonid Kravchuk, President.

The Land

The Republic of Ukraine is the independent successor to the Ukrainian Soviet Socialist Republic, a constituent republic of the Union of Soviet Socialist Republics. Ukraine declared its independence on August 24, 1991 and this was confirmed by a popular referendum that took place on December 1, 1991. The Republic of Ukraine also has included the Crimean Autonomous Republic (created in 1991), which in early May declared *its* own independence from Ukraine. The matter basically involves control of the former USSR Black Sea naval fleet.

The Republic of Ukraine lies in the southwestern part of the Russian Plain. The chief feature of the landscape is the Dnieper River, which flows down through the center of the republic. There are two upland regions, a series of rolling hills in the southeast and the Volyn–Podol Plateau, which stretches from the

Polish to Moldovan border in the west. The only large mountainous area is along the western border, where the northern ridges of the Carpathian Mountains cross the republic. The southern tip of the Crimean Peninsula (the status of which is now open to question) also has a small mountainous area, a western extension

116

of the Caucasus Mountains. Mountains make up only about five percent of the total land surface of the republic.

Because so much of the republic consists of a level plain, the differentiation between the various parts is based on the amount of rainfall that each gets. The most rainfall occurs in the north and diminishes to the south. The northern part of Ukraine is actually a large swampland, called the Pripet Marsh, the major part of which lies across the border in Belarus. The Dnieper Lowland dominates the central part of the republic. It is flat in the west and gently rolling in the east. Its chief feature is the Dnieper River and its tributaries. This is the traditional grain basket of the republic, which extends as far south as the city of Dniepropetrovsk, on the Dnieper River. Here the rainfall is adequate to support wheat and other grains without irrigation. In the area south of Dniepropetrovsk, on the other hand, irrigation becomes necessary.

The area immediately north of the Crimean Peninsula is known as the Nogai Steppe. This, plus the northern part of the Crimean Peninsula, referred to as the Crimean Lowland, were once grassy steppes, homelands of the Nogai and Crimean Tatars and pasturelands for their animals. Today a huge artificial lake on the Dnieper provides water for irrigation.

The southern shore of the Crimean Peninsula has a mild Mediterranean–type climate, with average January temperatures of 39° F. Summers are hot and dry. The northern shore of the Black Sea is much colder, with average January temperatures of 26° F. Spring comes early, however, usually at the end of January. Average January temperatures in Kiev are 18° F. Temperatures are also lower in winter and higher in summer in the eastern part of the republic.

Soils vary somewhat throughout the republic, but rich *chernozems* (black earth soils), which cover the entire central part of the republic, make up about 65% of the total. To the north of the *chernozems* area are found mixed gray *podsol* and black earth soils, and eventually pure, gray *podsol* soils, which are less fertile and also acidic. South of the *chernozems* belt is an area of chestnut soils, not as rich as *chernozems* and tending to be saline as one nears the Black Sea. The vegetation also reflects this soil division. Forests are found only in the north, in the area of the gray *podsols*. Mixed forest and grassy steppe cover the *chernozems* area. Desert and semidesert plants grow in the chestnut soils of the south.

The People

The population of the Republic of Ukraine as of the 1989 census was 51,704,000. The majority speak Ukrainian as their first language. Russians, the largest minority, make up another 12% of the population. There are nearly a hundred other ethnic groups, but the only two larger groups are Jews (1%) and Belorusians (.8%). Ukrainian belongs to the eastern Slavic family languages, the other two of which are Russian and Belarusian. Ukrainian is derived from Old Slavonic, the language spoken by all eastern Slavs during the period of Kievan Russian history from the 10th century or before. Ukrainian evolved after the split caused by the Mongol invasion in 1240. After 1240, the area of the Ukraine was ruled directly by the Mongol Empire for a hundred years, then was incorporated into the Grand Principality of Lithuania. The area east of the Dnieper River merged with Russia in 1654 and the rest of the Ukraine was added in the eighteenth century. It was this historic separation, and the connection with Lithuania and Poland between 1341 and the end of the eighteenth century, that resulted in the Ukrainian language. The word Ukraine means "the border" and describes Ukraine's position *vis–à–vis* Moscow. Historically, the Ukrainians have spoken of their land as *Malaya Russiya*, or "Little Russia."

History

Archaeological evidence indicates that the first settlement at the city of Kiev, capital of modern–day Ukraine, was made in the seventh century. Kiev, built on the bluffs overlooking the western bank of the Dnieper River, commanded traffic on the river and soon became a regional trading center. At the end of the ninth century, then, it became the capital of the first organized Russian state when Olaf the Norwegian conquered it and moved his headquarters here from Novgorod. Kiev remained the capital of this first Russian state until 1169, when Iuri Dolgaruki, Prince of Vladimir, became Grand Prince but decided to move the capital to his own city of Riazan. Although Kiev lost its political preeminence at this time, it remained an important trading center until 1240, when it was sacked and virtually destroyed by the Mongols. All of southern Kievan Rus was then incorporated into the new Mongol Empire and ruled from its regional capital of Sarai, located on the eastern bank of the Volga River, just north of the Caspian Sea. Kiev itself became a ghost city when the craftsmen who had not been killed in the sack of the city in 1240 were rounded up and sent to Sarai.

The Golden Horde, as the Russians called the Mongol Government, appointed new Grand Princes to govern in the north, but the weight of the Mongol yoke brought a collapse of this line by the early fourteenth century. Slowly, then, Moscow rose in the northeast and built its leadership, all the time acting as agent for the Golden Horde.

In the northwest, however, a new leadership rose, based on freeing as much of the area as possible from the Mongol yoke. The leader of this new state was the Lithuanian Prince Gediminas (Gedymin in Russian), founder of the Jagellon dynasty, but the majority of the subjects of this new Grand Principality of Lithuania were eastern Slavs and their language, Old Slavonic, became the official language of the court. Gediminas extended his control southward and in the process freed Kiev and the western territories as far south as the Black Sea from Mongol control.

One effect of the Mongol control had been that most of the area of southwestern Kievan Rus was virtually depopulated. Since this area remained subject to periodic attack from the Mongols, for another two hundred years it remained a borderland where only the brave or the desperate dared to live. Increasingly, however, communities of Slavic speakers fleeing from oppression in either Lithuania or the Moscow area settled this area, adopting many of the habits of nomadic neighbors, particularly the use of the horse and methods of fighting.

These became the Cossack communities of the southern steppe, one of the most important of which was the Zaporozhian Cossacks, with their settlements south of the cataracts on the Dnieper River.

These Cossacks had to fight constantly for their freedom, against nomads to the east and against encroachments from governments to the north. After the Grand Principality of Lithuania was merged with the Kingdom of Poland in the Union of Lublin in 1569, the combined Kingdom of Poland–Lithuania attempted to control this southern borderland area. The fighting prowess of the Cossacks was such, however, that the government was often willing to sign a treaty recognizing their status as Cossacks in return for military service to the Polish–Lithuanian state. At the same time, however, the government was giving out land to Polish noblemen and encouraging their settlement in this borderland area. These Polish noblemen brought the institution of serfdom with them—and there were constant efforts to enserf individual free peasants of the steppe.

A second issue, religion, arose at the end of the sixteenth century. The Cossacks were Russian Orthodox, while the Polish nobility moving into the area were Roman Catholic. When the Patriarch of Constantinople recognized Moscow (Muscovy) as a separate Patriarchate at the end of the sixteenth century, he recognized

Ukraine

the Russian Patriarch's jurisdiction over all Russian Orthodox, including those of the southwest under Polish–Lithuanian control. For political reasons, the Government of Poland–Lithuania refused to recognize this jurisdiction and outlawed the Russian Orthodox Church within the area of its jurisdiction. Instead, it created the Uniate or Eastern Catholic Church, which used the traditional Orthodox service and the Old Slavonic language but recognized the spiritual leadership of the Pope.

Thus the free peasants of the Ukraine found themselves under a three–pronged attack in the first half of the seventeenth century—encroaching serfdom, Polonization pushed by the increasing numbers of Polish nobility establishing estates in the area, and attempts to destroy the independent Orthodox Church. The man who now rose to the leadership of the Ukrainian forces was Bodgan Khmelnitsky, a Ukrainian landowner elected Hetman (head) of the Zaporozhian Cossacks. Khmelnitsky defeated the Polish forces a number of times and for a while apparently dreamt of creating an independent Ukraine. But it soon became apparent to him that the Ukrainian forces were not strong enough to sustain an independent Ukraine. Believing that a victory by Poland would mean the end of the Orthodox Church and the enserfment of the free peasants of the Ukraine, he turned to Muscovy and offered to bring the Ukraine under Russian control.

Tsar Alexis, then ruler of Muscovy, hesitated for some time before accepting the offer because he recognized that it would mean war with Poland. He finally accepted in 1653, however. This led to a war between Poland and Muscovy that began in 1654 and ended with the Truce of Andrusovo in 1667. Under the terms of the truce, Poland recognized Muscovite control over all lands east of the Dnieper River, plus temporary control of the city of Kiev. Russia never gave Kiev back, however, and the terms of the truce were confirmed by a peace treaty signed in 1686. Russia got the remaining parts of the Ukraine during the partitions of Poland in 1772 and 1793. Thus the destinies were tied with those of Russia primarily over the issue of religion, i.e., loyalty to the Orthodox Church. Cossacks also retained their freedom from serfdom, though there was some encroachment in this area in the eighteenth century.

Russian–Ukrainian relations were not always smooth, however. For example, Ivan Mazepa, who was elected Hetman of the Zaporozhian Cossacks in 1687, concluded an alliance with Charles XII of Sweden in 1708 under which the Ukraine was to become an independent nation under Mazepa's leadership. It was only Peter the Great's victory over Sweden at the battle of Poltova that put an end to that dream. There were three further Hetmans in the eighteenth century, all Russian nominees. The last Hetman was Kyrylo Razumovsky, younger brother of Empress Elizabeth's "Gentleman of the Bedchamber." Catherine the Great accepted his resignation in 1764.

Catherine the Great incorporated the Ukraine directly into Russia by dissolving separate Cossack bodies and dividing the area into *guberniyi*. In 1793, when the remaining territories occupied by Ukrainians were taken from Poland in the second partition, the name Ukraine was dropped and all of the territory simply became part of Russia.

Ukrainian nationalism resurfaced in the nineteenth century when the secret Brotherhood of Saints Cyril and Methodius was founded in Kiev in 1846. The membership of the Brotherhood included two historians, Mykola Kostomariv and Panteleimon Kulish, plus the Ukrainian poet Taras Shevchenko. It was suppressed in 1847 and its thirty members were exiled to other parts of the empire.

Tsar Alexander II authorized the publication of a journal, *Osnova* (The Outset) in Ukrainian in 1861. In 1876, however,

Cossacks of yesteryear hunt on the open Ukrainian plains

Alexander II prohibited the publication of journals or books in the Ukrainian language and closed all Ukrainian language schools. Thereafter, Ukrainian nationalists migrated abroad, either to Lvov in Austrian Galicia or to Switzerland. The Austrian Government permitted a Shevchenko Scientific Society to be founded there in 1872 and in 1890 a chair in southeastern European history was established at the University of Lvov.

The first man appointed to fill the position was Myhailo Hrushevsky, a Ukrainian historian. Hrushevsky eventually published a ten-volume *History of Ukraine-Rus*, whose major thesis was the continuation of Kievan Rus–Ukrainian history and the separate development of the history of Muscovy–Russia. After the Revolution of 1905, when the Russian Government lifted its ban against the publication of journals and books in Ukrainian, Hrushevsky moved back to Kiev.

After the Russian Revolution of 1917, Ukrainian nationalists held a National Ukrainian Congress in Kiev in April and elected a Rada (Council) headed by Hrushevsky. The Ukrainian Rada proclaimed an autonomous Ukrainian republic on June 23 with Hrushevsky as President, and within days Volodymir Vinnichenko as premier and Symon Petlyura as minister of war.

After the Bolshevik *coup d'etat* in November, the Ukrainian Rada called for convocation of a freely elected Ukrainian Constituent Assembly. Opposing this, the Bolsheviks announced formation of a Ukrainian Soviet Government on December 26. On January 22, 1918, the Ukrainian Rada proclaimed a "free and sovereign" Ukrainian Republic. The Central Powers signed a separate peace treaty with this government at Brest–Litovsk on February 9, but the Bolsheviks managed to seize Kiev on February 8. The Rada fled to Zhitomir and German and Austrian troops moved in and occupied most of the Ukraine. The Rada and the Central Powers now came into conflict, whereupon the Central Powers overthrew the Ukrainian Rada on April 24 and appointed Pavlo Skoropadsky as Hetman of the Ukraine.

After the collapse of Germany in November 1918, a five-man directorate took over in the Ukraine, with Volodymir Vinnichenko as chairman and Symon Petlyura as commander in chief. A separate Republic of the Western Ukraine was proclaimed in Lvov. Lvov was occupied by the Poles about three weeks later, however, so this government fled to Ivano–Frankovsk. In January 1919, a union of the two Ukraines was proclaimed, but a Red Army occupied Kiev the same day. On March 14, 1919, a Ukrainian Soviet Socialist Republic was formed under the leadership of Khristian

Rakovsky. The whole of Galicia remained in Polish hands and the Bolsheviks lost control of Kiev to the anti–Bolshevik forces under General Denikin in September 1919. However, Denikin and the Ukrainian nationalists fell out over the issue of a separate Ukraine. Denikin was defeated in December and most of the Ukraine fell under communist control.

Communist Control

In December 1919, Lenin recognized the equality of the Russian and Ukrainian peoples and proposed an alliance. The Ukrainian nationalists couldn't bring themselves to come to terms with the Bolsheviks, however. Instead, Petlyura allied himself with Pilsudski, the Polish leader, which led to a Polish invasion of the Ukraine in April 1920. The Poles occupied Kiev on May 7. Pilsudski now began dreaming of a reconstructed Polish–Lithuanian–Ukrainian Commonwealth. But that vision was not acceptable to Ukrainian nationalists and the Polish forces were soon forced out of the Ukraine. In December 1920, Lenin and Rakovsky, head of the Ukrainian Soviet Socialist Republic, signed an alliance uniting Soviet Russia and the Ukraine. A peace treaty with Poland was signed on March 18, 1921. Under the terms of the treaty, Poland got to keep Eastern Galicia and Volhynia.

In December 1922, an All–Union Congress of Soviets representing the Russian, Ukrainian, Byelorussian and Transcaucasian Soviet Socialist Republics agreed to form the Union of Soviet Socialist Republics. A constitution for the new union was adopted in July 1923.

In the Ukraine, a Language Act of August 1, 1923 established the priority of Ukrainian over Russian. Hrushevsky was appointed president of the Ukrainian Academy of Science, founded in 1918. This period of Ukrainization came to an end in 1928 when Stalin forced the government to introduce Russian as the second official language. Two years later, "nationalist deviation" became a crime punishable by death when 45 intellectual leaders were put on trial and charged with treason. Thirteen were sentenced to death and the rest were deported. Hrushevsky, though not one of the 45 accused, was also deported. As part of Stalin's grisly purges, additional trials were held in 1931 and 1933. Being a member of the *Communist Party* was no defense. Yury Kotsiubinsky, deputy premier, was shot in 1933; in 1937, Panas Lyubchenko, an ex–premier, was also shot; and in 1939, yet another premier, Vlas Chubar, was shot.

Ironically, an undetermined but substantial number of Ukrainians were willing to join Hitler in his invasion directed against the Russians in World War II, but

the deranged German simply ignored them. When the outcome of the campaign in Russia is considered, his actions may have affected it.

The territory of the Ukraine was considerably enlarged as a result of World War II. Those parts of Poland where Ukrainians lived, essentially eastern Galicia and Volhynia, were occupied by the Red Army beginning in September 17, 1939 and incorporated into the Ukraine later that year. Romania ceded Bessarabia and northern Bukovina to the Union of Soviet Socialist Republics in June 1940. Northern Bukovina and the Bessarabian districts of Hotin and Izmail went to the Ukraine. On June 29, 1945, Czechoslovakia ceded Sub–Carpathian Ruthenia to the USSR, and this area was also incorporated into the Ukraine.

The last addition to the Ukraine came in February 1954 when Nikita Khrushchev marked the 300th anniversary of the Russo–Ukraine union by transferring the Crimea to the Ukraine. In 1991, the Ukrainian Government decided to grant the Crimea the status of an autonomous republic. But in early May, it declared, through its parliament, its own independence.

The Gorbachëv program of reform instituted after 1985 found no immediate response in the Ukraine, for Vladimir Shcherbitsky, first secretary of the *Ukrainian Communist Party*, was a Brezhnev stalwart who was quick to slap down any signs of dissent. He was removed in September 1989 and died soon afterwards. His successor, Leonid Kravchuk, although he had come up through the party apparatus, quickly established himself as more "liberal" than his predecessor and more willing to make concessions on nationalism.

This made good political sense, since the Ukraine had by this time a national front movement, *Rukh*, that was challenging the communists for the political leadership of the republic. Kravchuk managed to turn back the *Rukh* challenge in the March 1990 elections by stealing a number of their positions. After the communists had managed to hold on to 239 out of the 450 seats in the legislature, Kravchuk sponsored a declaration of republican sovereignty, which was adopted in July 1990.

In March 1991, Kravchuk agreed to hold a referendum on a new union treaty, but insisted on rewording it to make it clear that the Ukraine was unwilling to give up its claim to sovereignty. As Gorbachëv negotiated for a new union treaty in the summer of 1991, Kravchuk worked to insulate the Ukraine from Gorbachëv's economic policies, suggesting in July, for example, that the Ukraine intended to issue its own currency. The Ukrainian legislature also began taking more nation-

Ukraine

President Leonid Kravchuk

alistic stances, for example repealing a series of Soviet tax and foreign–trade laws.

When conservatives launched their *coup d'etat* to overthrow Gorbachëv in August 1991, Kravchuk compromised by refusing to recognize the authority of the leaders while, at the same time, not condemning them publicly. After it collapsed, he resigned as first secretary of the *Ukrainian Communist Party* and banned the party from the republic. On August 24, he got the Ukrainian legislature to declare the Ukraine independent, subject to a popular referendum to take place on December 1, 1991.

At this point, it was believed that Kravchuk favored some form of continued union, and Ukrainian delegates cooperated in creating the new interim government that the Supreme Soviet approved on September 5. Nationalist pressures continued to grow, however, and by October Kravchuk was beginning to sound as though he wanted a completely independent Ukrainian state. By November, the Ukrainian legislature voted to "decertify" the Ukrainian deputies to the USSR Supreme Soviet; henceforth they were to participate as observers only. Meanwhile, Kravchuk had stated that the Ukraine also intended to create its own national army.

The December 1 referendum and popular election for the office of President of Ukraine became the culmination of this increasing trend. Over 90% of all voters cast their ballots in favor of Ukrainian independence, at the same time giving 61% of their votes to Kravchuk to make him the first president of an independent Ukraine. Eight days later, Kravchuk met with the presidents of Russia and Belarus

to declare the Union of Soviet Socialist Republics dead and create the Commonwealth of Independent States. Eight other republics joined the CIS on December 21, and Gorbachëv resigned as President of the USSR on December 25.

Since December, there have been difficulties as the members of the CIS attempt to use the mechanism of the CIS to work out continued means of cooperation, while at the same time dividing up the remaining parts of the old Soviet Union and elaborating their own independent structures. Economic cooperation agreements between republic leaders have been signed again and again, only to find that promised goods haven't been delivered because individual firms have ignored their government's instructions.

The members of the CIS also committed themselves to a unified CIS strategic force at the time of the break–up. The Republic of Ukraine continues to support that position, but made it clear from the beginning that it intended to take control of all conventional forces stationed in Ukraine, including naval forces. There has been no problem with the army. The Government of Ukraine has not attempted to take control of strategic missile forces and in other units Russian officers have been willing, as required, to take an oath of allegiance to the Government of Ukraine. However, a quarrel with Russia did arise over the Black Sea Fleet, headquartered in the Crimea. Kravchuk first claimed the entire Black Sea Fleet, then only the conventional portion of it. But Russia argued that dividing it would destroy it. Yeltsin and Kravchuk eventually worked out an arrangement for joint supervision of the Black Sea Fleet until they could figure out how to divide it.

Another problem has been the status of the Autonomous Republic of Crimea. Crimea, with a population of about 2.5 million, is about 67% Russian with an additional 26% being Crimean Tatars. Ukrainians are actually a 26% minority. A majority of the Crimea population voted for Ukrainian independence in December 1991, but Russian nationalists in the Crimean legislature later pushed for a vote of independence from Ukraine. The Crimean legislature has actually been ambivalent on the issue, voting for independence and then modifying the vote to indicate that Crimea was a part of Ukraine. The issue has also been fueled by Russian nationalists in Russia, in particular Vice President Rutskoi and his allies, who have argued that Crimea ought to be returned to Russia, to which it belonged until 1954. In May 1992, the Russian Supreme Soviet actually passed a resolution declaring the 1954 transfer to be invalid. The Yeltsin Government repu-

diated the resolution, but the Supreme Soviet's vote was seen by Ukrainian nationalists as another example of Russia's traditional tendency to bully and dominate.

All of this has become tied up with the question of how much the Government of Ukraine is willing to cooperate with the CIS. Ukrainians, busy creating an independent state, have been wary of any significant cooperation. Their apparent fear is that Ukraine could find itself dominated once again from the outside, this time by the CIS. President Kravchuk, working hard to create nationalist credentials for himself, has also taken a hard line toward the CIS. In May 1992, shortly before departing for an official visit to the United States, Kravchuk said of the CIS that "today it is evident that the CIS is not capable of resolving those problems faced by its constituent countries." Asked if he wanted to destroy the CIS, his reply was that "you can only destroy something that exists."

Part of the problem at this time was that Kravchuk's Prime Minister, Vitold Fokin, was an old–line communist bureaucrat who found himself beyond his depth in the new circumstances of a collapse of the old communist system. Ukraine's economic circumstances continued to grow worse over the next several months, but the government was unable to come up with any programs to tackle the problems. By September 1992, inflation was outpacing even the Russian rate so Ukrainian coupons were trading at a ratio of 3 coupons to 2 rubles, and in spite of seemingly unlimited easy credit to industry, economic activity was down 18% over the preceding year. Faced with that situation, even the Supreme Soviet, dominated though it was by ex–communists, was unwilling to continue to put up with Fokin's policies. On September 30, he and his cabinet were forced to resign.

President Kravchuk's first choice as his successor was another former communist boss, Valentin Simonenko, but he was unacceptable to the Supreme Soviet. President Kravchuk then settled on Leonid Kuchma, a member of the Supreme Soviet who had also been Director of *Yuzhmash*, Ukraine's largest producer of nuclear missiles, since 1986. Although a long–time member of the *nomenklatera*, Kuchma had a reputation for being hard–driving and competent. Moreover, he took office with a mandate to step up the pace of economic reform if he so wished. In confirming him, the Supreme Soviet also gave him the power to rule by decree until May 1993.

Kuchma has since launched a major economic reform that promises to address most of Ukraine's problems and move the country toward a market economy. Surprisingly, Kuchma has managed to maintain strong support in the Supreme Soviet for his reforms.

The Government of Ukraine withdrew from the ruble block in November 1992, at the prompting of Russia. Its currency continues to be the coupons that the government began issuing in the spring of 1992. The government has a new currency, the *hryvna*, already printed up, but Kuchma says that he will not release the currency until after the government has gotten the deficit and inflation under control.

Nature of the Regime

The Republic of Ukraine has a presidential–parliamentary system with a popularly elected president who acts as spokesman for the nation and sets general policy. He also appoints a prime minister, currently Leonid Kuchma, who handles day–to–day activities of the government and presides over the cabinet. The Ukrainian Supreme Soviet has its own internal organization which is independent of either the president or the prime minister. Since the *Ukrainian Communist Party* was banned, a majority of the legislators belong to no party, but they have normally been responsive to President Kravchuk's wishes. Political parties are permitted, but play a relatively small role thus far. *Rukh*, the Ukrainian popular front organization, is the strongest organizationally, but its greatest strength is in the western part of the republic, which puts it under suspicion in other parts of the republic. In addition, it split in late 1992 over the issue of how much cooperation there should be with President Kravchuk and the former communists. One faction argued that this cooperation was necessary because the most important issue was creating a strong Ukrainian state. Finding itself outvoted on the issue, it broke away and formed a new organization called the *Congress of National Democratic Forces*. *Rukh* is now more clearly a part of the opposition. Its current position is that democracy and a strong economy are necessary prerequisites for statehood. It has recently formed a loose coalition with another oppositionist grouping called *New Ukraine*.

Culture

There is a rich cultural life in the Republic of Ukraine, but most of it belongs to a larger Slavic culture, except for a traditional Ukrainian folk culture. Ukrainians are different from Russians, but it is a matter of degree. Ukrainian houses tend to be painted or whitewashed with traditional decorations worked into the wood trim and around the windows. Ukrainians plant many more flowers in their yards. The Ukrainian folk costume is often highly embroidered, with bright colors worked over white or black. Ukrainian villages also tend to be more prosperous looking and better cared for, reflecting the richer soil found in most of the Ukraine. Historically, the Ukrainian Orthodox clergy has had greater contacts with the Greek Orthodox Church and so is closer to the Greek original. Church music of the Ukraine was patterned on Byzantine and Bulgarian models, which set it off from the music of Russia. The Ukraine also developed its own distinct choral music, which also came to influence Russian music in the seventeenth century.

The Ukraine has produced many writers, poets and historians over the years, a number of whom were mentioned in the historical section above. On the other hand, Ukrainian intellectuals were always getting into trouble because of their Ukrainian nationalism, and often found themselves unable to get their works published. This has been true in the Soviet period as well.

The Ukraine began to develop a secular music in the nineteenth century. There are a number of nineteenth century operas with specific Ukrainian themes, such as Semen Hulak–Arte-

A country wedding day—complete with troubadours

Ukraine

St. Sofia Cathedral, Kiev, the city's oldest structure dating back to the times of the Kievan Rus
NOVOSTI photo

movsky's *A Cossack Beyond the Danube*. Mykola Lysenko was an early twentieth century composer who wrote the opera *Taras Bulba*. Two other composers of this period were Kyrylo Stetsenko and Mykola Leontovych. Lev Revutsky and Borys Lyatoshynsky were two composers of the early Soviet period. The cultural regimentation of the 1930s led to a cultural decline, but there was a revival of sorts after Stalin's death. Contemporary composers include Kostyantyn Dankevych, Yuliy Meytus, and the brothers Yuriy and Platon Maiboroda.

The Ukrainian theater is primarily a twentieth century phenomenon, primarily because censorship laws would not allow works in the Ukrainian language before 1905. Three pre–Soviet Ukrainian playwrights are Lesya Ukrainka, Volodymyr Vynnychenko and Oleksandr Oles. All wrote before 1905, but their works were not available in the Ukraine until after that time.

There was a flowering of Ukrainian theater in the period of the 1920s, the so–called period of Ukrainization. Mykola Kulish, who used expressionist techniques, was perhaps the most famous. As in opera, the introduction of socialist realism led to a decline in drama. A contemporary Ukrainian playwright of some fame is Oleksandr Korniychuk.

The Ukraine has great cultural poten-tial for the future, however, since the Soviet era left it with plenty of facilities. There are currently six opera theaters, numerous symphony orchestras, 60 professional theaters, plus a Ukrainian motion picture industry.

Economy

The Ukraine has been the historical "bread basket" of Russia and, although industry today plays a larger role in the economy, agriculture continues to play an extremely important role. In recent years, the Ukraine produced about 20 percent of all Soviet food. Grain, in the form of wheat and corn, is the most important crop, but others include potatoes, vegetables, fodder crops, fruits and grapes. Sugar beets are the most important industrial crop.

Cattle are raised for both milk and meat. Other important animals raised include pigs, sheep and goats. Honey is another important product, as are silkworms. All of this was, of course, disrupted by the Chernobyl nuclear explosion, the effects of which will remain for years.

Most of the land has been controlled by collective farms, but in January 1993 the Ukrainian Government began working on a decree aimed at breaking up the collective farms and turning the land over to private farmers. The new Prime Minister, Leonid Kuchma, who had announced soon after assuming office that he firmly believed in the private ownership of land, promised that the collective farms would be disbanded by spring planting time.

The development of industry in the Ukraine goes back to the end of the nineteenth century when fourteen steel mills were built on the steppe north of the Black Sea. Even today, the center of Ukraine's heavy industry is a belt that stretches from Krivoi Rog in the west to the border of the republic in the east. Here the republic produces cast iron, steel and rolled steel, and steel pipe. Other allied manufactures include diesel locomotives, freight cars, automobiles, giant airliners, seagoing vessels, electric generators, thermal and gas turbines, metallurgical equipment, and tractors.

Iron ore reserves are found in the Krivoi Rog, Kerch, Belozyorka, Kremenchug and Mariupol regions. Some of the richest manganese–bearing ores in the world are also found in Ukraine. The Donets Basin has huge reserves of anthracite and bituminous coal, while brown coal is found in the Dnieper Basin. Petroleum is produced in the Ciscarpathian, Dnieper–Donets, and Crimean regions. The republic also produces titanium, bauxite, cinnabar, nephelites, ozokerite, potassium salt, rock salt, phosphates, and sulphur. There is a chemical industry that produces mineral fertilizers, coke products, synthetic fibers, caustic soda, petrochemicals, photographic chemicals, pesticides, and sulfuric acid.

The Ukrainian food–processing industry includes the processing of granulated sugar, vegetable oils, and wine. Light industry includes textiles, the manufacture of ready–to–wear garments, and shoes. The preponderant weight of heavy industry in the Ukraine has meant that a large percentage of its production was shipped to other republics—amounting to approximately 25 percent of the republic's gross domestic product. In return, it imported natural gas, some raw materials, and a good percentage of its consumer goods. Unless it can maintain many of those markets, the switchover to a market system will be extremely painful for its citizenry.

For the first ten months after achieving its independence, very little was done about the economy and the result was a disaster. By October 1992, inflation was running at 30% monthly, economic activity was down 18% over the preceding year, and the budget deficit was running at 44% of GNP. Prime Minister Fokin was forced out at the end of September and replaced by Leonid Kuchma. Since becoming Prime Minister, Kuchma has proven himself to be the reformer that Ukraine needs. One of his first acts was to raise the central bank lending rate to 80% and to announce that the government would no longer provide inefficient state enterprises with soft credit. In November, he submitted an ambitious, market–oriented reform program to the Supreme Soviet which called for a tight budget, a temporary wage freeze in state–owned enterprises, cuts in social welfare payments, a law forbidding the government to finance the budget deficit by printing money, and a commitment to begin large–scale privatization. Kuchma also announced recently that enterprises that cannot be made efficient will be broken up and their pieces sold on the auction block. It is clear now that Kuchma intends a complete restructuring of the Ukrainian economy. Thus far, he continues to have the full support of the Supreme Soviet, which makes his task somewhat easier than that of Yeltsin, though obviously still daunting.

The Future

The Republic of Ukraine has a very strong agricultural–industrial base which gives it a great potential for the future, once it makes a transition to a market economy. Its population of over 52 million, most of whom are well–educated and adapted to an industrial economy, adds to that potential. Thus, from the moment of its birth, the Republic of

Ukraine becomes one of the more important European countries. Some question whether the political leadership is adequate to fulfill the potential that is obviously there, but the appointment of Leonid Kuchma as Prime Minister in

October 1992 helped to allay some of those doubts. Kuchma has now launched a comprehensive economic reform that should lead to a thorough restructuring of the economy over the next 2–3 years.

A young Ukrainian economist NOVOSTI photo

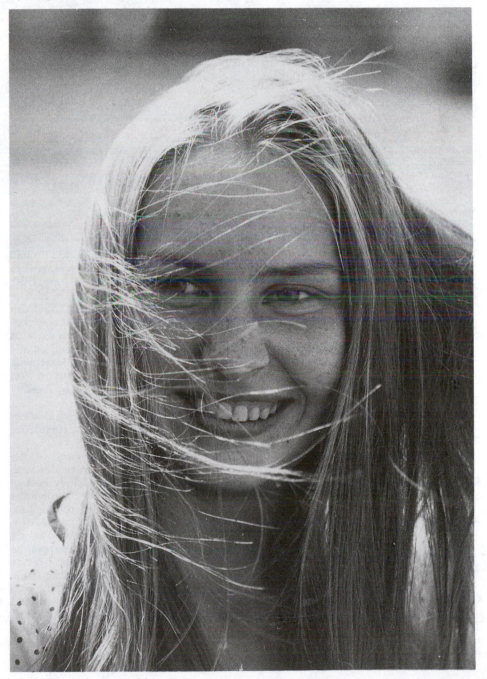

The Republic of Moldova

A wheat–growing area of Moldova

Courtesy: NOVOSTI

Area: 13,000 sq. mi. (33.700 sq. km., a little larger than Maryland).

Population: 4.5 million (estimated).

Capital City: Chisinau (pronounced *Kee–sih–now*, Pop. 700,000).

Climate: Continental, with moderate rainfall.

Neighboring States: Romania (west). Ukraine surrounds the country on the other sides.

Languages: Moldovan, Russian, Ukrainian.

Ethnic Composition: Moldovan (64%) Ukrainian (14%), Russian (13%), others (9%).

Principal Religion: Orthodox Christianity. Until recently, religious worship was officially discouraged.

Chief Commercial Products: Grain, livestock, silk, honey, processed foods, wine and cognac.

Recent Political Status: Formed in 1940 by union of the Moldavian SSR, previously an autonomous republic within the Ukrainian SSR, and most of Bessarabia, transferred to the USSR by Romania in 1940.

Chief of State: Mircea Snegur, President.

The Land

The Republic of Moldova is the independent successor state to the Moldavian Soviet Socialist Republic. The Moldavian SSR was created in August 1940 when Stalin merged Bessarabia, which he had forced the Romanian Government to cede to the Soviet Union in June 1940, with the autonomous republic of Moldavia, which was then part of the Ukrainian SSR. He gave it constituent republic status. In 1941, after Nazi Germany invaded the Soviet Union, Romania (then an ally of Nazi Germany) reclaimed Bessarabia. Soviet troops retook the territory in 1944 and the Moldavian SSR was reestablished.

The republic was renamed Moldova in 1990. Moldova declared its independence on August 27, 1991.

The Prut River, a tributary of the Danube, forms the western border with Romania. The area immediately east of the Prut is somewhat elevated, with a flat highland in the north and rolling hills interspersed with deep flat valleys further south. The highest elevations are about 1400 feet. The southern part of the republic is a low plain. The chief feature of the eastern part of the republic is the Dnestr River, which originates in the Carpathian Mountains to the northwest and flows southward across western Ukraine, then forms the border between Moldova and Ukraine for some distance. At this point, the border shifts eastward, while the Dnestr continues south and into Moldova. A major feature of the river is the 60–mile–long Lake Dubossary, created when a dam for producing hydroelectric power was built on the Dnestr. The Dnestr crosses back into Ukraine again shortly before it empties into the Black Sea. On its western side, the Dnestr has a high bank, formed by the eastern slope of the Dnestr Up lands. Trans–Dnestr, the small strip of territory east of the Dnestr, is a low plain.

124

Rainfall in the republic varies considerably but averages between 18 and 22 inches. Most of it falls in summer. Moldovan soils are mostly rich, black *chernozem* soils. About 40% of the land is covered by forest, most of it in the uplands.

The People

The population of Moldova as of the 1989 census was 4,341,000. Most Russians live in the Trans–Dnestr region. Other minorities include Gagauzi (4%) and Jews (2%). The Gagauzi are a non–Moslem, Turkic speaking people. Both they and the population of Trans–Dnestr are threatening to secede from Moldova.

History

Moldova's history is really the history of Bessarabia, the historic name for the area between the Prut and Dnestr Rivers. In the first century B.C., this area, and the area of present–day Romania formed the Roman province of Dacia. Rome soon lost control, however, and the area knew many masters over the following centuries. The eastern part of the area was incorporated into Kievan Rus in the tenth century. Later, independent Galician princes ruled. After 1240, it became part of the Mongol Empire for about one hundred years. The Genoese built fortified commercial outposts on the Dnestr in the fourteenth century, though they never attempted to rule the area.

In the fifteenth century, an independent Principality of Moldavia came into existence which included the northern part of present–day Romania and all of Bessarabia. The Ottoman Empire soon extended its control over most of the area, however, along with the second Romanian Principality of Wallachia. In 1711, Peter the Great occupied part of Bessarabia during a short war with Turkey. He was forced to abandon the territory after his army fell into an ambush, however. Russia occupied the territory three more times in the eighteenth century, each time relinquishing it to the Turks. In 1812, however, Russia occupied Moldavia and Wallachia when war broke out between the two countries. This time, Russia forced Turkey to cede Bessarabia to it in the Treaty of Bucharest.

As a result of Russia's defeat in the Crimean War, it was forced to cede Bessarabia to Moldavia, at that time an autonomous principality under the Ottoman Empire, in 1856. After its victory in the Turkish War of 1877–78, Russia took Bessarabia back and kept it until 1918. After the overthrow of the Tsar in 1917, a National Moldavian Committee was organized in Bessarabia in April. Its program included autonomy, use of the Romanian language, and land reform. After the Bolshevik *coup d'etat* in November, a government was established in Bessarabia, called the *Sfatul Tarei*. On December 2, 1917, the government proclaimed Bessarabia to be an autonomous constituent republic of the Federation of Russian Republics. The Bolsheviks occupied the capital, Chisinau (Kishinev) on January 5, 1918. Two weeks later, they were driven out and the Bessarabian Government then proclaimed itself an independent Moldavian Republic. Two months later, it voted for a conditional union with Romania. Unconditional union was voted on December 9, 1918. The Union of Bessarabia with Romania was recognized by the Treaty of Paris, signed by Great Britain, France, Italy, and Japan, on October 28, 1920.

The Union of Soviet Socialist Republics never recognized Romania's right to the province and refused to establish diplomatic relations with Romania until 1934. In the meantime, the frontier along the Dnestr was closed.

Under the terms of the Nazi–Soviet Non–Aggression Pact of August 23, 1939, Hitler recognized Bessarabia as being in the Soviet sphere of influence. The Soviet Union revived its claim to Bessarabia, but Romania rejected the claim until after the fall of France in June 1940. On June 27, the Soviet Union demanded the immediate cession of Bessarabia, plus the additional territory of northern Bukovina as "compensation for Romanian misrule in Bessarabia." Without an ally, Romania had to submit. Troops of the Red Army entered Bessarabia on June 28.

The central districts of Bessarabia were merged with part of the Moldavian Autonomous Republic and in August it became the Moldavian Soviet Socialist Republic. Ukraine was compensated for the loss of the Trans–Dnestr territory by receiving the Khotin district in the north and the Cetatea Alba and Izmail districts in the south.

Romania declared war against the Soviet Union in July 1941. Its war goal was to reclaim Bessarabia and to reincorporate it back into Romania. This was accomplished by December 1942. Soviet forces reentered Bessarabia in 1944 and its forces occupied all of Romania as well. Bessarabia was formally ceded back to the Soviet Union by the peace treaty signed between the two countries on February 10, 1947.

After Gorbachëv launched his programs of *glasnost* and *perestroika*, a nationalist movement arose, which called itself the *Popular Front of Moldavia*. The ultimate goal of the front was union with Romania. In 1989, the legislature abolished use of the Cyrillic alphabet (see Russia), and restored the Roman alphabet which had been used prior to the republic's incorporation into the Soviet Union. On July 29, 1989, Mircea Snegur was elected president of the presidium of the Moldavian Supreme Soviet. Snegur was at that time first secretary of the *Moldavian Communist Party*, but he represented the democratic–nationalist faction of the party. In June 1990, the legislature adopted a declaration of republic sovereignty and changed the name of the republic to Moldova.

In March 1991, the Government of Moldova refused to participate in a referendum on continuation of the Soviet Union. It also refused to take part in subsequent discussions on a new union treaty. When conservatives launched their attempted *coup* against Gorbachëv in August 1991, Moldova became a target also. The local military commander surrounded the capital of Chisinau (Kishinev) with troops and threatened to use them against the republic government. President Mircea Snegur refused to recognize the *coup* committee, however, and called on the people of Moldova to demonstrate in support of democracy and freedom; over 100,000 persons demonstrated in the capital. Following the collapse of the Russian *coup*, Moldova declared its independence on August 27. It also formally outlawed the *Communist Party*.

Moldova now began to have its problems with the Trans–Dnestr region, an area with a population of about 600,000, only a third of whom are Romanian speakers. This area rejected Moldovan independence because it felt it was merely the first step to merging with Romania. As far back as 1989, a separatist movement had been organized in this area after the republic government had declared its intention to move toward independence. In August, the "Dniester Moldavian Republic" declared its independence. A referendum on independence on September 2 showed that a majority of people of the area supported the policies of the breakaway republic. Igor Smirnov was elected head of the new republic. Its capital was established at Dubossary.

Some violence occurred when the Moldovan Government tried to reestablish its control east of the Dnestr. The situation calmed down after President Snegur threatened to resign if the Moldova Supreme Soviet insisted on using force to restore control. The government also repudiated the idea of immediate union with Romania. This led to the opening of talks between the two sides. In October, the "Dniester Moldavian" leader said that he would be willing to join a federal Moldova, together with Moldova and Gagauzia. In 1990, the Gagauz, a non–Moslem, Turkic–speaking minority, had proclaimed a separate republic in southern Moldova. Like "Dniester Moldavia," they objected to the idea of merging with Romania.

Moldova

In October, President Snegur publicly broke with the leadership of the *Popular Front of Moldova* and said that he favored an independent Moldova. "A union with another state is out of question," he said. "At present Moldova promotes a policy pursuing the assertion of our independence internationally." Snegur also supported continued economic ties with the former Soviet republics.

The Moldova presidential elections had been set for December 8, 1991 and the question of independence versus merging with Romania became the major issue. In addition to President Snegur, there were originally two other candidates, Grigori Eremei, the former first secretary of the *Moldovan Communist Party* and Gheorghe Malarciuc, a writer. The other two candidates withdrew in the middle of November, however. The *Popular Front of Moldova* did not nominate a candidate because the head of the front, Mircea Druc, did not meet the residence requirements. Instead, the front urged voters to boycott the election. The leadership of "Dniester Moldavia" adopted the same position.

"Dniester Moldavia" and the "Republic of Gagauzia" held their own separate elections on December 1. Igor was confirmed as president of "Dniester Moldavia" and Stepan Topal was elected president of Gagauzia. Neither area permitted voting in the December 8 republican elections.

President Snegur was running unopposed in the December 8 elections, so the fact that he got 98% of the vote was unsurprising. On the other hand, the vote count indicated that 83% of all registered voters actually voted in the election, thereby rejecting the *Popular Front of Moldova's* call for a boycott of the election. This gave President Snegur a great deal more leeway in dealing with the front than he had had before.

Later in the month, the president broke his long–standing opposition to any form of political agreement with the former Soviet republics by going to Alma Ata on December 21 and taking Moldova into the Commonwealth of Independent States. Moldova did not agree to maintain a CIS military command, however, and has already begun to create its own national army. Current plans call for it to be a cadre army of about 12,000 persons, with a larger number of citizens serving in an army reserve.

The Moldovan Government has been unable to resolve its differences with either "Dniester Moldavia" or Gagauzia. On December 11, the parliament formally nullified the results of the December 1 elections in the two breakaway republics. Later, President Snegur offered to establish a free economic zone in "Dniester Moldavia" if it would withdraw it declaration of independence. So far, neither carrot nor stick has worked. The main issue is still the question of Moldova's merging with Romania. Even though President Snegur has said that he favors an independent Moldova, the leaders of "Dniester Moldavia" and Gagauzia are convinced that union with Romania remains on the agenda.

In March 1992, a weekend of clashes that left 23 dead caused President Snegur to issue an ultimatum to "Dniester Moldavia" to lay down their arms or face the use of force against them. Igor Smirnov, leader of "Dniester Moldavia," then declared a state of emergency, closing the enclave to outside contact. "Dnieser Moldavia" reportedly has organized a 10,000 man militia to defend the enclave.

Meanwhile, the unstable political situation was contributing to what was in any case a deteriorating economic situation. This led on June 1 to the resignations of the Prime Minister, Valeriu Muravsky, and his cabinet. President Snegur then nominated Andre Sangheli, outgoing Agriculture Minister, as the new Prime Minister.

But President Snegur has been more concerned about establishing political control throughout all of Moldova than about the economy. Fighting with Dniester Moldova flared up again in June 1992 when President Snegur's troops tried to take control of the city of Bendery. It appeared for a while that Moldova might find itself involved in a confrontation with Russia when elements of Russia's 14th Army, stationed in eastern Moldova, supported the "Dniester Moldavia" forces. It turned out that it was only rogue elements of the 14th Army that were involved, however. Moldova has been quiet in recent months, but that is mainly because President Snegur has refrained from further attempts to extend his authority outside the ethnic Romanian areas. Meanwhile, the political instability continues to have a negative effect on the economy.

Nature of the Regime

The Republic of Moldova has a presidential–parliamentary system, with the executive president recognized as spokesman for the nation and also responsible for setting general policy. The president appoints a prime minister who must be confirmed by the legislature. The prime minister handles day–to–day policy and presides over meetings of the cabinet.

There is also a Supreme Economic Council, created in October 1991, which is headed by the prime minister. The presidential decree that created the council gave it the task of defining "the main direction of state economic policy under the conditions of the transition to a market economy." It has two foreign economists, a Romanian and a Britisher, among its membership.

The Moldovan political system is in theory committed to political pluralism, but political parties have only begun to develop. The largest political force in the republic is the Popular Front of Moldova, headed by Mircea Druc, an ex–prime minister. On the other hand, President Snegur is the strongest political leader, and he belongs to no political party.

Culture

The Republic of Moldova is primarily an agricultural society, with about two-thirds of the population still living in the countryside. On the other hand, Moldovan villages are large, averaging over a thousand inhabitants, and fairly modern. All have electricity, for example, and most are supplied with natural gas as well. Because of the ethnic identity of most Moldovans, the culture of Moldova is similar to that found in Romania. Most people think of themselves as members of the Orthodox Church and that has become more important since all restraints on religion were lifted three years ago.

The border with Romania is also now open, so that reinforces the connection.

Most Moldovans are literate, and there is a comprehensive system of primary and secondary schools throughout the republic. Around 70% of the children go to preschool before entering primary school. The most prestigious institute of higher education is the State University at Chisinau (Kishinev), but there are eight other institutions of higher education in other parts of the republic. There are also

51 technical schools scattered throughout the republic. The Moldovan Academy of Sciences was established in 1961. It has 17 research institutes under its jurisdiction.

Economy

The Moldovan economy is still predominantly agricultural, with approximately two–thirds of the people still employed on the land. Its equable climate and fertile soil, plus the extensive mechanization that has taken place since 1940, mean that agriculture is fairly productive, in spite of the fact that most land is still organized into collective or state farms.

Winter wheat and corn are the main grain crops grown. Wheat is consumed within the republic, while some of the corn is exported to other republics. Average grain production is about three million tons. Other crops that have traditionally produced surpluses for export include sugar beets, tobacco, and sunflower seeds. Moldova also produces significant quantities of fruits, vegetables, berries, grapes and walnuts, all of which have been exported to other republics in the past.

Moldova has a diversified industry, though the most significant branch is food processing. These include sugar refining, wine making (including champagne and brandy), oil pressing, canning and the processing of essential oils. All of these branches have traditionally exported to other parts of the Soviet Union. Flour mills, dairies, meat processing and candy making industries also exist, but these serve the domestic market.

Other light industry includes things such as the processing of pelts for fur coats, footwear, and textiles, particularly knitting and the processing of silk. There is relatively little heavy industry, though the republic does have some machine–building, including tractors, and it also manufactures building supplies, including bricks, tiles, cement, slate, and concrete blocks.

The Department for Privatization submitted a draft privatization program to the Supreme Economic Council in January 1992, but it was rejected as being too narrow in scope. Cabinet members who participated in the discussion favored an alternate program drawn up by government experts. The disagreement appears to be more political than economic. The parliament created the Department for Privatization as an agency separate from the cabinet, but several cabinet members believe that the cabinet ought to be in charge of privatization. Parliament, which wants privatization to start immediately, opposes this.

The Moldova parliament has passed legislation creating a Moldovan currency, to be called the *leu*. This has caused some problems also, since that is what the Romanian currency is called.

The Future

Moldova is suffering the same sort of economic difficulties found elsewhere in the ex–Soviet Union as it begins to move toward a market economy. This is intensified by the political controversy over whether to merge with Romania or not and the actions of "Dniester Moldavia" and Gagauzia to separate from Moldova, essentially because of this controversy. How this dispute is resolved will determine how quickly, and how painlessly, Moldova can make the transition to a market economy.

An aerial view of Chisinau

Courtesy: NOVOSTI

TRANSCAUCASIAN REPUBLICS (of the former Soviet Union)

Due to their shared histories as well as frequent geographical and cultural similarities, there is necessarily some repetition from one entry to the other.

Showing only capital cities and political boundaries

The Republic of Armenia

Area: 11,503 sq. mi. (29,804 sq. km., slightly smaller than Maryland).

Population: 3.5 million (estimated).

Capital City: Yerevan (Pop. 1.2 million, estimated).

Climate: Dry and continental.

Neighboring States: Georgia (north), Turkey (west), Nakhichevan Region of Azerbaijani (southwest), Azerbaijan (east), a slender border with Iran (southeast).

Language: Armenian.

Ethnic Composition: Armenian (94%), Azerbaijani and others (6%).

Principal Religion: Armenian Orthodox. Until recently, religious worship was officially discouraged.

Chief Commercial Products: Livestock, chemicals, textiles, wine, grain, footwear.

Currency: Ruble (de facto).

Recent Political Status: The Armenian S.S.R. was established in 1920; from 1922 to 1936 it was joined with Georgia and Azerbaijan into the Trancaucasian S.S.R., but reverted to status as a constituent republic of the former USSR. It declared independence on August 23, 1990.

Chief of State: Levan Ter–Petrossian, President.

The Land

Modern Armenia, which emerged as an independent state as a result of the collapse of the Union of Soviet Socialist Republics in 1991, is located in a land-locked area south of the Caucasus Mountains. The ancient empire of which it is a remnant included Turkish Armenia, an area of about 57,999 square miles (147,000 sq. km.) across the western border in present–day Azerbaijan.

Today, it consists of 11,503 square miles (29,800 kq. km.). It borders on Turkey to the west, Iran to the south, Georgia to the north and Azerbaijan to the east. Its principal cities are Yerevan, the capital, and Khodjent (formerly Leninabad).

All except about ten percent of Armenia is extremely mountainous. Its "lowlands" are over 3,000 feet high, while the average height above sea level for the entire country is slightly over a mile high; its highest mountains are in the northwestern part of the country. Mt. Aragats, the highest peak, is 13,418 feet high. The northern part of Armenia consists of a series of ranges and elevated volcanic plateaus, into which deep river valleys have been cut.

In the east, the dominant feature is a high mountain lake surrounded by mountains. Lake Sevan, which is 525 square miles in size, lies at 6,200 feet, while the surrounding mountains soar to 11,800 feet. In the south is the Ararat Plain, only the northern half of which belongs to Armenia. The Ararat Plain is divided by the Aras River, which forms Armenia's southern border.

Armenia's rainfall varies considerably, with over 300 inches in the high mountains and an average of 80 inches on the Ararat Plain. Most of this precipitation falls in the form of heavy rains in the autumn and as snow in the winter.

Armenia's many rivers arise in the mountains in the north and west. Because of the sharp drop in elevation, they tend to be short and turbulent, with many waterfalls and rapids. Armenia accordingly has great hydroelectric power potential, estimated at nearly 22 billion kilowatt–hours a year. Four of these rivers—the Akhuryan, the Razdan (which flows out of Lake Sevan), the Arpa, and the Bargushat—provide water to irrigate the Armenian half of the Ararat Plain before emptying into the Aras River, itself a tributary of the Kura River, which flows into the Caspian Sea.

Since it lies at the northern edge of the subtropical zone, Armenia has long, dry, hot summers with long, mild, sunny autumns. Because of the elevation of most of the land, it also has a winter with average temperatures below freezing, though only the plateau and mountains in the north have really inclement weather.

In spite of its small size, Armenia has an unusually large variety of landscapes. Because of a combination of location and variation in altitudes, it possesses five different vegetation zones: semidesert, steppe, forest, alpine meadows, and high–altitude tundra. The semidesert landscape is found in the south at altitudes below 4,600 feet. This region, unless irrigated, produces only a scanty vegetation of mostly sagebrush and similar drought–resistant plants.

The land between 4,600 and 6,600 feet is mostly steppe, and here, if not watered, mainly drought–resistant grasses grow. The forest zone is found mostly in the southeast at altitudes between 6,200 and 6,600 feet, and in the northeast, at altitudes between 7,200 and 7,900 feet. Oak grows mainly in the southeast, while beech grows in the northeast.

The alpine zone lies above 6,600 feet, where thinning forests give way to mountain meadows. Such meadows are used as summer pastures for goats and sheep. Finally, above the alpine zone is the area of tundra, where little grows other than cushion plants such as moss.

The Ararat Plain produces fruits such as figs, grapes, pomegranates, apricots, peaches and melons. The plateau and the mountain valleys produce cereals and grains, tobacco, vegetables, and orchard crops such as cherries, apples, pears, almonds, and hazelnuts. Higher altitudes produce potatoes, grain and fodder grasses.

The population of Armenia was 3,283,000 as of the 1989 census and is now probably close to 3.5 million. The republic is extremely homogenous, 94 percent of the population being Armenian. There are another 1.5 million Armenians living in the other former republics of the Soviet Union. The remaining six percent of Armenia's population is made up of Azerbaijanis and Russians, with smaller numbers of Ukrainians, Kurds and other groups. Many Azerbaijanis left

Armenia and moved to Azerbaijan in the period 1989–91 because of the quarrel between the two republics over the Nagorno–Karabakh, the majority– Armenian enclave in Azerbaijan which wanted to become part of Armenia. Similarly, many Armenians living in Azerbaijan have moved back to Armenia.

History

Armenians, who refer to themselves as the Hayk, are an Indo–European people who migrated into the area in the 7th century B.C., overrunning and conquering an earlier, high civilization. They subsequently came under the influence of the Medes, Persians and Greeks as they became part of these empires. The first Armenian Empire came into existence during the period of the rise of the Roman Empire. As the Roman Empire became ever more powerful, however, this empire disintegrated and Armenia became a sort of buffer zone between Rome and the Parthian Empire. The people of Armenia converted to Christianity about 300 A.D.; the Armenian Orthodox Church is known for its ancient and rich liturgy. Under communism, the role of the Church was severely limited but there has been a resurgence in recent years, and today the Church is playing an important role, particularly in the cultural sphere.

An independent Armenian state first emerged around 190 B.C., but it was not until the middle of the first century B.C. that a united Armenian state was created under Tigranes I the Great (c.94–c.55 B.C.). The first capital of this state was

Artaxata, located on the Aras River not far from modern–day Yerevan. This kingdom lasted for almost 500 years and it reached its pinnacle under Tigranes, who extended his kingdom eastward to include parts of modern–day Iran and westward to encompass Syria. His conquests brought him to the attention of the Roman General Pompey, who defeated him in battle in 66 B.C. Tigranes was forced to relinquish Syria and become an ally of Rome.

For the next 120 years, Armenia remained a buffer state between Rome and Parthia, each manipulating Armenia to achieve its ends. The area was annexed by the Emperor Trajan in 114, but abandoned by his successor, Hadrian. An army of Marcus Aurelius destroyed Artaxata in 163. Caracalla attempted to annex Armenia in 216, but his successor, Macrinus, abandoned the attempt and recognized Tiridates II as King of Armenia. The resurgent Persian Empire then began pressing Armenia from the east. In 238, it conquered Armenia and established it as a vassal state holding it for fifty–some years later before another Roman Emperor, Diocletian, intervened and restored Tiridates III, son of Tiridates II, to the throne.

The reign of Tiridates III is extremely important for Armenian history, for this is when Armenia was converted to Christianity. Tiridates III was himself converted by St. Gregory the Illuminator and he made Christianity the official religion of the realm in 300 A.D. From this time onward, the Armenian patriarchate also became an important symbol of Arme-

President Levan Ter–Petrossian of Armenia

Armenia

nian unity, holding the people together in periods of political instability.

Tiridates was later assassinated by his own court chamberlain in league with local nobles and Armenia split into two parts, with the smaller part gradually being absorbed into the Byzantine Empire. The larger part came under Persian domination in 428 when the Armenian nobility deposed their king and requested a Persian governor. The religion of Persia at this time was Zoroastrianism and the Persian ruler made the mistake of attempting to impose it on the Armenians. An Armenian revolt in 451 caused the Persians to declare that they would not attempt to impose Zoroastrianism by force. A second revolt in 481–484 won Persian recognition of a native Armenian ruler and a Persian promise to honor Armenia's political and religious freedom in return for Armenia's agreement to provide military assistance to Persia when called upon.

The Armenians asserted their religious freedom even further in 554 when an Armenian Church Council got into a quarrel with the rest of the Christian Church over a minor point of dogma, the dyophysite formula enunciated by the Council of Chalcedon in 451. The Armenian Church, by rejecting this formula, isolated itself from the rest of Christianity and turned the Byzantine Empire into an enemy.

Armenia came under attack from the Arabs beginning in 640. Thirteen years later, Armenia came under Arab control as an autonomous region under its own native ruler. This situation continued for the next three hundred years. In the tenth century, however, a resurgent Byzantine Empire invaded from the west, effectively destroying Armenia politically. The final blow came in the 11th century when Armenia was invaded from the east by the Seljuk Turks. The Seljuk Turk conquest was complete by 1071, although a few minor Armenian kingdoms survived for a time in the more remote mountains. In the 12th century, part of northern Armenia was annexed to the Georgian Kingdom. However, Armenia was overrun again in 1236–42 by the Mongols.

Most of Armenia eventually became part of the Ottoman Empire and, after the fall of Constantinople in 1453, the Armenian bishop of Bursa was transferred to Constantinople and appointed leader of the Armenian Church in the Ottoman Empire. The eastern area fell to the Ottoman Empire in 1516, but it soon became a battlefield as Persia and the Ottoman Empire fought for control. Persia gained control of the regions of Yerevan, Karabakh, and Nakhichevan as a result of the peace of 1620. In the mountainous region of Karabakh, however, five Armenian princes managed to assert their independence at the beginning of the 18th century. The Ottoman Empire occupied the area in the 1730s, but were driven out by the Persians.

Amid the swirling events that ultimately resulted in the end of the Ottoman Empire, Armenians claim that 1.5 million of their people were mercilessly slaughtered by the Turks in the late 19th and early 20th centuries. Many fled, and a substantial number were admitted to the U.S.

Armenia under Russian–Soviet Rule

The Russians began to focus their attention on the area of the Caucasus at the beginning of the 19th century. A war between Russia and Persia beginning in 1809 gave Russia Georgia, northern Azerbaijan and Karabakh. In 1828, Yerevan and Nakhichevan were added. A large part of traditional Armenia still remained under Ottoman control, but the area that was to become modern Armenia had become part of the Russian Empire.

The Russian Government tended to treat Armenians as co–religionists throughout most of the 19th century and being part of the Russian Empire meant that Armenians had greater access to western ideas than before. The 19th century therefore ushered in a cultural renaissance in Armenia.

This changed toward the end of the

Armenians fleeing Turkish lands in the early 20th century

century, however, when the government of Nicholas II began to get worried about Armenian nationalism and introduced repressive measures to stamp it out. In 1897, hundreds of schools and libraries were closed and Armenian newspapers were banned. And since the Armenian Orthodox Church was closely associated in people's minds with Armenian nationalism, the government moved in 1903 to confiscate all property of the Armenian Church.

Armenian nationalists joined with Georgians and Azerbaijani to form the Transcaucasus Federal Republic in April 1918, but the new state collapsed in just over a month. An independent Armenia was then declared on May 26, 1918. The republic, which lasted until March 1922, had a bumpy independent existence as it attempted to secure as much of the lands occupied by Armenians as it could. It fought short wars with Georgia and Azerbaijan—the latter over the area of Nagorno–Karabakh—and a war in 1920 with Turkey. The loss to Turkey in 1920 led to a change in government and the creation of the Soviet Republic of Armenia in December 1920.

The new government was established as a coalition of communists and nationalists, but the nationalists were soon eliminated and it became a purely communist government. In March 1922, this new government joined with Georgia and Azerbaijan to form the Transcaucasian Soviet Federated Socialist Republic. On December 30, 1922, it became a part of the Union of Soviet Socialist Republics.

The Transcaucasian Soviet Federated Socialist Republic was dissolved in 1936 when a new Soviet constitution was adopted and Armenia at that time became the Armenian Soviet Socialist Republic. Armenia did relatively well as a part of the Soviet Union. Quite a bit of industry grew up around Armenia's chief cities, and individual Armenians held important positions in industry and the professions in major cities throughout the Soviet Union. Yet Armenia was one of the first republics to "explode" after Gorbachëv launched his program of *glasnost*. The most important reason for this was the Nagorno–Karabakh Autonomous Republic, the Armenian enclave in the neighboring republic of Azerbaijan. The situation in Nagorno–Karabakh is treated in greater detail under the Republic of Azerbaijan (See page 120). Suffice to say here that this became a galvanizing issue for the vast majority of Armenians when the Nagorno–Karabakh regional council petitioned in February 1988 to become part of Armenia.

Within weeks, the Armenian political leadership had endorsed the Nagorno–Karabakh position. The Azerbaijani lead-

ership angrily rejected Armenia's claims on Nagorno–Karabakh and began to encourage popular demonstrations in support of its position. The demonstrations got out of control, however, and turned into an anti–Armenian move in the Azerbaijani city of Sumgait. Within weeks, an incipient state of war existed between Armenia and Azerbaijan.

Gorbachëv dismissed the *Communist Party* leaders of both Azerbaijan and Armenia in May 1988, on the grounds that they had not acted quickly enough to control the situation. The new first secretary of the Armenian Communist Party leader was Suren Arutunyan, a Gorbachëv loyalist who had spent the previous several years working in Moscow. He tried his best, but he was constantly caught between Moscow loyalists on the one side and nationalists organized as the Karabakh Committee on the other. In the process, the Armenian Communist Party lost much of its authority.

Armenia was hit by a natural disaster in December 1988, when a major earthquake killed over 25,000 persons and injured thousands more. Other thousands were left homeless. International aid poured in, but Armenians lost further faith in both the Armenian and union

leadership when help was slow in coming.

The people applauded in January 1989 when Gorbachëv announced that he had decided to suspend Azerbaijan's control over Nagorno–Karabakh and put the autonomous republic under Moscow's direct control. They suffered when the Azerbaijan Popular Front instituted its road and rail blockade against Armenia, but they refused to give in. They were, therefore, extremely angry when Gorbachëv gave in to the Azerbaijan Popular Front's blackmail and requested the USSR Supreme Soviet to relinquish control back to Azerbaijan. Armenian delegates refused to participate in that vote.

Armenians now turned conclusively against the Communist Party. By the spring of 1990, there were an increasing number of armed clashes between Armenian nationalists and Soviet troops. In July, Gorbachëv ordered all such vigilante groups to be disbanded, but then the Armenian Supreme Soviet defied Gorbachëv, declaring that his order "contradicts the Armenian people's natural right to self–defense." In August 1990, the Armenian Supreme Soviet elected Levan Ter–Petrossian to the top post in the republic, Chairman of the Supreme

Armenia

Soviet. Ter–Petrossian, a leader of the Karabakh Committee, was Armenia's first post–communist leader. On August 23, 1990, the Armenian Supreme Soviet followed this up by passing a declaration of Armenian independence.

Ter–Petrossian turned out to be a cautious leader in practice. He did not attempt to challenge Moscow, but, again, his quarrel was not really with Moscow. The confrontation with Azerbaijan continued and Armenia continued to suffer from an Azerbaijani blockade of fuel and most other supplies, but it would not cede on the political question. In the spring of 1991, it boycotted discussions about a new union treaty. Armenia took advantage of the *coup* attempt against Gorbachëv in August 1991 to reiterate its declaration of independence. This was followed by a popular referendum that received overwhelming approval. The Armenian Supreme Soviet also created the office of President to be elected by popular vote. The election took place on October 16 and Ter–Petrossian won 83 percent of the votes. He formally assumed the office in December 1991.

Armenia accepted Russian–Kazakh mediation of the Nagorno–Karabakh dispute with Azerbaijan in September 1991 and agreed to yield its claims over Nagorno–Karabakh at this time. It subsequently recognized the independence of the Republic of Nagorno–Karabakh, however, so its confrontation with Azerbaijan continues.

Armenia agreed to join the Commonwealth of Independent States at the December 1991 founding meeting. Unlike Azerbaijan, it opted to not establish a separate republic army at that time, even though large numbers of Armenian "freedom fighters" were already involved in the fighting in Nagorno–Karabakh. Partly this was because it hoped to win CIS backing for its position on Nagorno–Karabakh; partly it was because the Azerbaijani blockade had been successful and its economy was in terrible shape.

As a result of strains between individual CIS members and a continuing fear of being dominated by Moscow, however, most CIS members began to create national armies in 1992. Armenia created a Ministry of Defense and an Armenian army and began to equip these forces with heavier equipment such as tanks, transferred mainly from Soviet forces.

The war between Azerbaijan and Armenia widened somewhat in the spring of 1992, when forces within Nagorno–Karabakh extended their control over areas formerly occupied by Azerbaijani forces. These same forces then overran Azerbaijani territory lying between Nagorno–Karabakh and Armenia, creating a corridor connecting the enclave

with Armenia at the point where the two territories are the closest together. This had a military significance, since Armenia, which had been shifting supplies in by air up to this point, could begin bringing supplies in by truck.

Azerbaijan was going through a great deal of domestic political turmoil at this point, at least partly because of its military defeats. Azerbaijani forces in the enclave of Nakhichevan (cut off from Azerbaijan by a strip of Armenian territory), then began shelling Armenian villages across the border. This led to an Armenian attack on the enclave city of Sadarak, and so the war widened further. Fighting continued intermittently over the summer and into the fall, in spite of a series of truces negotiated with the assistance of international third parties; however, no further significant changes in the military situation occurred. But Azerbaijan maintained its blockade of Armenia, so the economic situation within Armenia deteriorated further.

The situation within Armenia became desperate in January 1993 when the sole gas pipeline leading into the country through Georgia was blown up. A new temporary pipeline was opened in February and some gas is once again flowing from Georgia. It is difficult to imagine the situation improving very much, unless an end can be brought to the continuing war with Azerbaijan, however. But even with almost all Armenian factories closed because of a lack of energy, there was no sign that Armenians were ready to compromise or lessen their support for fellow Armenians in Nagorno–Karabakh. Demonstrations in Yerevan calling for President Ter–Petrossian's resignation and for new parliamentary elections did occur in February 1993, but many of the demonstrators were critical of the President precisely because he had not pursued the war against Azerbaijan firmly enough.

The Nature of the Regime

The Armenian governmental setup is very similar to that of the Russian Federation. An executive President sets policy and makes major appointments, while a prime minister and cabinet handle the implementation of policy. The Armenian Supreme Soviet has considerable authority, but generally takes its lead from the President. Armenia is beginning to create a multiparty system, but the major political force at the moment is the Karabakh Committee, Armenia's version of a Popular Front. The dominating ideology at the moment is nationalism.

It has fairly good relations with all of its neighbors with the exception of Azerbaijan, though its relations with Turkey are likely to remain cool, since Armenia refuses to renounce its traditional claim to Armenian Turkey.

Armenia has received general international recognition and was admitted to the United Nations at the same time that the other members of the Commonwealth of Independent States were admitted. It has also been admitted to the Council for Security and Cooperation in Europe and membership in the IMF and World Bank.

Culture:

Traditional Armenian culture has deep historic roots that reach back as far as the 5th century when the first written literature began. Two works that date from that period are Moses of Khorem's *History of Armenia* and Erzik Koqhbutsi's *Refutation of the Sects*. The two themes represented by the works, history and religion, continued to be important in subsequent centuries, but they gradually began to be expressed in new forms.

Gregory Nare Katzi, who lived in the 10th century, was Armenia's first great poet. A deeply religious man, his mystical poems and hymns heavily influenced the Armenian Orthodox Church and led to his canonization after his death.

A secular tradition began to emerge in the 16th–18th centuries with the appearance of popular bards (troubadours). Known as *ashugh*, they produced numerous love songs which are now known by the people. The 19th century saw the emergence of both the novel and the short story. Famous Armenian novelists include Hakob Paronian, Ervand Otian and Hakob Maliq–Hakobian, whose pen name is "Raffi." Paronian also wrote plays, as did Gabriel Sundukian.

The communist era had a negative effect on Armenian culture; it rejected nearly every theme associated with traditional literature. Pre–revolutionary novelists and playwrights continued to be read and performed, but modern writers were required to conform to communism's "socialist realism," a requirement which turned them into party hacks. It is no surprise that the 20th century produced no great Armenian literature, but it did produce its first great composer, Aram Katchaturian, probably because it was hard for Moscow authorities to apply "socialist realism" to classical music.

Communism did leave behind an established society which will help Armenian culture to develop further in the future. There is both a state radio and television broadcasting system with studios in Yerevan. The city is also the site of a State Academic Theater of Opera and Ballet. Several drama theaters also exist, a national dance company, several orchestras and a film studio.

Old folk arts such as dancing, singing and artistic crafts were left undisturbed by communism. Thus, the new non–communist government has a firm basis on which to build. An Armenian Academy of Sciences runs a number of research institutes throughout the country.

Economy

Armenia today is overwhelmingly an urban and industrial society, with agriculture perhaps accounting for a fifth of the national income. Three fifths of the country's industries are located in and around the city of Yerevan, however, and because so many of them are types of heavy industry which heavily pollute, Yerevan today is one of the most polluted cities of the former Soviet Union. These include factories which produce synthetic rubber, fertilizers, chemicals, nonferrous metals, machines and equipment. It also produces other polluting minerals; all of these have badly polluted large areas of the countryside. The government will probably deal with this problem in the coming years.

It also has light industry—textiles, carpet–weaving, food processing, wine-making, fruit, meat–canning and creameries. Medium industries include electrical equipment, precision instruments and machine tools. It is also a large producer of cement, marble, pumice, volcanic basalt and fireproof clay.

Industry is in extremely poor condition at the present, primarily because of Armenia's political quarrel with Azerbaijan over the Armenian–populated enclave of Nagorno–Karabakh. Azerbaijan has maintained an almost continuous siege against Armenia for the past three years, and Armenian industry is thus starved for the energy and raw material supplies necessary to operate at its usual level. It has attempted to establish alternate sources of supply via Georgia, but because of the unstable political situation in that republic has been only minimally successful.

An economic turnaround will probably have to await a political settlement over Nagorno–Karabakh.

Agriculture contributes far less to the economy than industry, but it continues to support employment for almost half the population, together with related processing industries. As elsewhere, it had been organized into state and collective farms, but one of the first decisions of the non–communist government was to begin phasing them out.

As a result, Armenia had begun creating a privatization of agriculture even before it attained independence in 1991. The most valuable resource is probably grapes, from which famous wines, brandies and champagnes are made. Orchard crops are next in importance—peaches, apricots, apples cherries, pears, pomegranates, walnuts, hazelnuts and almonds are abundant. Tobacco is another important cash crop. Extensive mountain pastures support a significant dairy industry, plus many sheep for wool and meat. Pigs and poultry are also raised.

The Future

Armenia's future is clouded by its continuing quarrel with the Republic of Azerbaijan. So long as the Nagorno–Karabakh situation remains unsettled, Armenia will find it difficult to do much about its economy. This is unfortunate, since Armenia was among the first of the republics to take advantage of Gorbachëv's restructuring and begin the privatization of its economy. There is no political crisis, since the overwhelming majority of the people support the policies of the government, but there is an economic crisis which is unlikely to be overcome unless and until a political accommodation is achieved with Azerbaijan.

Looking down the main boulevard in Yerevan

Courtesy: NOVOSTI

The Republic of Azerbaijan

A view of Baku with the Adjarbek mosque

Area: 33,430 square miles (86,000 sq. km., about the size of Maine).

Population: 7,029,000 (1989 census).

Capital City: Baku (Pop. 1.8 million, excluding non–urban areas under its jurisdiction).

Climate: Generally dry, sub–tropical.

Neighboring States: Russia (north), Georgia (northwest), Armenia (west and east where the Nakhichevan Region is separated from the rest of the country), Iran (south).

Language: Azerbaijani.

Ethnic Background: Azerbaijani (78%), Armenian, mainly within the enclave of Nagorno–Karabakh which lies within its borders (8%), Russian (8%), others (6%).

Principal Religion: Islam, principally Shi'a.

Chief Commercial Products: Agriculture—grain, cotton, rice, grapes. Industry—oil, concrete, carpets, processed food (fish and caviar), wine, processed meat, cheese.

Currency: Ruble (de facto).

Recent Political Status: Azerbaijan S.S.R. was founded in 1920. Part of Transcaucasian Federation (1922–1936), Constituent republic of the USSR (1936–1991).

Chief of State: Abulfaz Elchibey, President (as of June 1992).

The Land

The Republic of Azerbaijan, which was one of the 15 Soviet republics before the collapse of the Union of Soviet Socialist Republics in 1991, is located in an area south of the Caucasus Mountains along the western shores of the Caspian Sea. It covers an area of 33,430 square miles (86,600 sq. km.). Iran lies to the south, Armenia and Georgia to the west, and the Russian Federation to the north. It also includes two autonomous republics, the Nakhichevan Autonomous Republic, occupied mainly by Azeri but separated from the rest of Azerbaijan by the southeastern part of Armenia, and the Nagorno–Karabakh Autonomous Republic, mainly occupied by Armenians.

More than 40 percent of Azerbaijan is lowlands, most of which are in the Kura

134

River valley, which runs in a northwest direction beginning at the Caspian Sea and ending in the mountains of Georgia. The Kura River actually originates in the Small Caucasus Mountains, which stretch along the border between Georgia and Turkey. It flows down through the high valley of central Georgia before crossing the border into Azerbaijan. The Aras River, a southern branch of the Kura, originates in the Aras Mountains of Turkey. It forms the southern boundary between Armenia and Turkey, between the Nakhichevan Autonomous Republic and Turkey and Iran, and between Azerbaijan and the Iranian province of Azerbaijan. It then turns northeast and joins the Kura River. The remaining lowland areas include the Lenkoran Lowland in the southeast, plus a strip of land beginning at the Apsheron Peninsula, which juts out into the Caspian Sea to the north of the mouth of the Kura River, and then running north along the western shores of the Caspian.

To the northeast of the Kura River Valley, the chain of the Great Caucasus Mountains runs southeast, ending just before the Apsheron Peninsula. Here the highest mountains are over 14,000 feet, though most of the territory is covered by foothills running perpendicular to the line of the higher mountain ridge and varying in height from 1,300 to 4,900 feet. Southward across the Kura River Valley, the ground again flows upward, becoming foothills then rising to become the Small Caucasus Mountains, which mark the border between Azerbaijan and Armenia. The Karabakh upland, where the Nagorno–Karabakh Autonomous Republic is situated, is also in this area.

The annual rainfall of the Kura–Aras Lowland varies from 8 to 16 inches and so has the plant life of the steppe and the semi–desert. A well–developed system of dams and canals means that most of the lowland is irrigated, however, and today most of the area is devoted to the cultivation of cotton. The largest of these dams is the Mingechaur, built in 1953 along the Kura River in northwestern Azerbaijan. Mingechaur Dam, which is also a major hydroelectric station, forms a lake that covers an area of 234 square miles and has a storage capacity of 565 trillion cubic feet.

The Kura River Valley has a dry, subtropical climate with hot summers and mild winters. Southeast Azerbaijan, which receives the most rainfall of any part of the republic, has a humid, subtropical climate. Here the annual rainfall is about 50 inches, which falls mainly in the winter. The Nakhichevan Autonomous Republic, with altitudes between 2,300 and 3,300 feet, has a dry, continental climate, with cold winters and dry summers. The Caspian Sea shoreline has a Mediterranean type climate, cool in winter and dry in summer. Forests are found on the upper slopes of the Great Caucasus and Small Caucasus Mountains. The main trees are beech, oak and pine.

The People

Azerbaijan's population as of the 1989 census was 7,029,000. Azeris or Azerbaijani, who make up about 78% of the population of the republic, are a Turkic–speaking people. They migrated into the area in the 11th century as part of the Oguz Seljuk migrations. There are another million Azeris living across the border in the province of Iranian Azerbaijan. Russians, the largest minority in the republic, make up about 8% of the population, and Armenians, who are about 7.9% of the population, come second. Most Russians reside in the major cities, particularly Baku, the capital and largest city, and Sumgait, an industrial city located 22 miles to the north. Daghestanis make up another 3.4% of the population. Other, smaller minorities include Iranians, Ukrainians, and Kurds.

History

After the Bolsheviks came to power in Moscow, national groups in Azerbaijan, Armenia and Georgia got together and established the Transcaucasian Federal Republic on April 22, 1918. It collapsed after one month. In Azerbaijan, a National Council of the Tatars, dominated by the *Mussavat (Nationalist) Party*, announced the birth of the Azerbaijanian Democratic Republic on May 28, 1918. This government continued to exist until April 1920, when it was overthrown by the Red Army. The communists established the Azerbaijan Soviet Socialist Republic on April 28, 1920.

This was the beginning of Azerbaijani political history. Prior to that time, the Azerbaijani were an undifferentiated Islamic people, first under Persian then under Russian rule, of the area of the Transcaucasus. Peter the Great was the first Russian ruler to take an interest in the area, when he occupied Baku in 1723. The coastal region actually became Russian in 1813 by the Treaty of Gulistan, under which Persia ceded the lands bordering the western shores of the Caspian Sea from the Lenkoran Lowland northward to Derbent. The interior was annexed by Russia in 1829.

Although Azerbaijan came under communist control in 1920, it remained theoretically independent until March 1922. It was then merged with Armenia and Georgia to form the Transcaucasian Soviet Federated Socialist Republic. The Transcaucasian SFSR became a formal part of the Union of Soviet Socialist Republics in December 1922. Fourteen years later, under the terms of Stalin's 1936 Constitution, the Transcaucasian SFSR was dissolved and the Azerbaijan Soviet Socialist Republic reemerged.

Azerbaijan was a pliant republic under the communists until Gorbachëv's policy of *glasnost* began to challenge the old *status quo*. The situation had been building up over a number of years, however, in connection with jobs in the modern, industrial sector. Azerbaijanis were traditionally either nomads or farmers, so when the Baku oil industry was developed, most of the jobs went to Armenians or Russians. After the Russian Revolution, literacy campaigns gradually carried education to the countryside where most Azerbaijanis lived.

As more and more Azerbaijanis became educated, they began to be recruited for positions in industry and government. For a long time this was nominal, but the Brezhnev leadership, in particular, encouraged the development of native elites in the republics. This new Azerbaijani leadership founded numerous institutes of higher education and, increasingly, favored a policy of edging out non–Azerbaijanis and replacing them with Azerbaijanis. Thus there was a very distinct bias among the Azerbaijani political leadership to favor Azeri speakers. Armenians were a particular target of this policy.

Many Armenians had taken jobs in the Baku area in the past. When they found themselves edged out of a job, however, they could always return to Armenia. This presented a different problem for the Armenians of the Nagorno–Karabakh Autonomous Republic, however, since this was a relatively poor area without significant industry. The Armenians of Nagorno–Karabakh also felt that the leadership at the republic level ignored needs of the autonomous republic. Thus they formally requested to be transfered to Armenian jurisdiction in February 1988. When the Armenian Republic leadership supported Nagorno–Karabakh's request two weeks later, apparently spontaneous riots broke out in the Azerbaijani city of Sumgait which turned into a slaughter of Armenians. When this was followed by retaliatory moves against Azerbaijani living in Armenia, the result was a dual stream of refugees, Armenians fleeing to Armenia and Azeris fleeing to Azerbaijan.

This first, open manifestation of Azerbaijani nationalism was exacerbated when Gorbachëv dismissed the first secretaries of the Azerbaijani and Armenian Communist Parties in May 1988 for allowing the situation to get out of hand. The Azerbaijani educated classes, up to this time loyal supporters of the party, now began to think of the party as Moscow–dominated. Gorbachëv aggravated the situation even further when he announced in

Azerbaijan

January 1989 that he was suspending Azerbaijan's authority over Nagorno–Karabakh and putting the autonomous republic under direct Muscovite control.

That summer the *Azerbaijan Popular Front* was founded for the specific goal of safeguarding Azeri national interests. And the national interest was defined as meaning the territorial integrity of Azerbaijan. In a challenge to the Communist Party, the front launched a series of mass demonstrations and labor strikes in August.

In September 1989, the front organized a road and railroad blockade of Armenia. With 85 percent of Armenia's freight entering the country by way of Azerbaijan, this action brought Armenian industry almost to a halt. The success of the blockade also brought the front a political victory over the *Azerbaijan Communist Party*. On September 13, Abdul Vezirov, the first secretary, signed a protocol with the front in which he agreed to call a special session of the Supreme Soviet to pass a law on sovereignty. The law was passed ten days later. Meanwhile the front threatened to maintain its blockade of Armenia until Moscow dissolved its special commission and allowed control over Nagorno–Karabakh to revert back to Azerbaijan. On November 28, the USSR Supreme Soviet voted to end Moscow's direct rule over Nagorno–Karabakh. The rail blockade was eased, but not lifted entirely.

A new 1990 series of killings of Armenians broke out in Baku, the Azerbaijani capital. The government declared a state of emergency to handle the matter. Gorbachëv then sent in Soviet troops to restore order and to forestall a *coup* by the Azerbaijani Popular Front against the Azerbaijan Government. Soviet Defense Minister Yazov later said that the Soviet troops were sent in "to destroy the organizational structure" of the *Azerbaijan Popular Front*. The Azerbaijan Communist Party leadership was changed as well. Ayaz Mutalibov, who had been Prime Minister up to this time, was installed as the new party leader and head of state.

Azeris were extremely angered by Gorbachëv's actions. Elmira Kafarova, chairman of the Azerbaijani Supreme Soviet, referred to the events of January 1990 as "a gross violation of Azerbaijani sovereignty." More than a million people turned out for the funeral of the approximately one hundred Azerbaijanis killed when Soviet troops entered Baku.

There were also rallies when *Communist Party* membership cards were burned, but Gorbachëv kept the troops in Baku and eventually order was restored. Mutalibov survived as party first secretary, though he never dared to lift the state of emergency declared in January 1990.

Mutalibov was abroad on a visit to Iran while an attempted *coup* against Gorbachëv was going on. He never condemned the the attempt, but, after it failed, he resigned as head of the party and issued a decree banning party cells in government and industry. The party later dissolved itself.

Mutalibov announced Azerbaijan's independence on August 30. He then had the Azerbaijan Supreme Soviet modify the constitution by creating a popularly elected, executive Presidency. He was later elected President in an uncontested election.

Mutalibov remained under intense pressure from a growing political opposition, however. In September 1991, he created an 8–member Defense Council and appointed members of the *Social Democratic Party*, the *National Independence Party* and the *Popular Front* to it. By this time, Tamerlan Karayev, leader of the *Azerbaijan Popular Front* had been elected deputy head of the Supreme Soviet.

The front demanded that the Supreme Soviet be replaced by a temporary "National Council" which would prepare for new elections. When Karayev threatened to resign his post as deputy leader in October, Mutalibov agreed to the creation of a National Council and to a second demand that Azerbaijan establish its own army.

On October 18, 1991, the Supreme Soviet passed a law formally reestablishing Azerbaijan's independence. It declared the present government the legitimate successor to the Azerbaijanian Democratic Government, overthrown by the communists in April 1920. The law further declared that "all acts and treaties concluded by the republic since April 1920" were considered invalid.

In early November, Mutalibov closed down the gas line to Armenia, cutting off the delivery of gas. Later in the month, when an Azerbaijani helicopter was downed over Nagorno–Karabakh, Mutalibov announced that he was calling an extraordinary session of the Supreme So-

At prayer in the Mashtagin mosque

viet and would request them to dissolve the Nagorno–Karabakh government. At the same time, he cut all railway links with Armenia. The Azerbaijani Supreme Soviet endorsed Mutalibov's actions on November 26. By this time, Azerbaijan had its own defense minister and had created a military force of about 25,000. Mutabilov ordered his defense minister to restore order in Nagorno–Karabakh. Something approaching full–scale war existed in the area.

The Azerbaijan National Council met for the first time on November 29. Its first act was to pass a law putting all of Azerbaijan's borders under state control, to be guarded by Azerbaijani border guard troops. The purpose of the legislation was to give Azerbaijan control of its border with Armenia.

Meanwhile, the Armenian political leadership in Nagorno–Karabakh had declared the area to be an independent republic. A referendum, held on December 10, brought overwhelming popular approval.

The war between Azerbaijan and Nagorno–Karabakh continued for the next two months. All of Nagorno–Karabakh's connections with the outside were cut off and Azerbaijani troops carried out raids into the area from the east. There were reports that the city of Stepanakert had been virtually destroyed, but the Armenian leadership of Nagorno–Karabakh refused to give in. They were also being assisted by elements of the Armenian National Army, which had opened a corridor between Armenia and Nagorno–Karabakh.

When Mutalibov said that he was still seeking a political solution to the problem, the *Azerbaijan Popular Front* demanded his resignation on February 20, 1992, charging that the course of military actions in Nagorno–Karabakh was detrimental to Azerbaijan. As Azerbaijani nationalists continued to press the government to step up the fighting against the Armenians in Nagorno–Karabakh, Mutalibov resigned as President on March 6.

The *Azerbaijan Popular Front* never accepted Mutalibov's conversion to nationalism, and they never forgot that he was installed by Moscow after Soviet armed forces had been used against the front. Under their prodding, an Azerbaijani legislative commission, appointed to investigate the events of January 1990, had concluded that Moscow had deliberately chosen Azerbaijan as a test case to see whether an independence movement could be crushed through the massive use of force. Forcing Mutalibov's resignation was therefore part of their revenge for the events of January 1990. They did not take any personal revenge against him, however. In addition to a grant of immunity against prosecution and a 10–

View of the port area of Baku

Courtesy: NOVOSTI

man bodyguard, the legislature provided him with a pension of 10,000 rubles a month and a villa in the countryside.

Following his resignation, the legislature transferred presidential authority to the newly elected Chairman of the legislature, Yagub Mamedov. One of the first acts of the new government was to launch new attacks against Nagorno–Karabakh. Their target was the city of Askeran, located not far from the capital city of Stepanakert. They were driven back by Armenian forces, however.

Ordinary Azeribaijanis reacted by calling for greater efforts to reclaim Nagorno–Karabakh. Mamedov, however, called for diplomatic efforts to get negotiations under way.

In March, the prime minister, Hasan Hasanov, said that "the chance of the conflict erupting into an all–out war and the chance of a political solution are 50–50. This depends on how much world public opinion realizes that the Armenian state terrorist army must immediately leave the occupied territory of Azerbaijan. If it continues its occupation of Nagorno–Karabakh, the chances of a military outcome will greatly increase."

In fact, Azerbaijani attempts to extend their control in Nagorno–Karabakh were unsuccessful. In May, forces of the Nagorno–Karabakh Defense Council managed to capture the Azerbaijani stronghold of Shusha and drive most Azerbaijani forces out of the enclave. Even as the Armenian and Azerbaijani Governments continued discussions aimed at bringing an end to the fighting, the Nagorno–Karabakh Defense Council forces captured a corridor across the

Azeri territory separating Nagorno–Karabakh and Armenia, thereby creating a ground connection with Armenia.

Later in May, the war widened when fighting broke out along the border between Armenia and the Azerbaijani enclave of Nakhichevan, separated from the rest of Azerbaijan by a strip of Armenian territory. According to Armenian reports, the fighting began after Armenian villages were shelled from across the border. Armenians retaliated by launching attacks on the Azeri villages of Sadarak and Lachin. Both Turkey and Iran protested the Armenian "aggression" at this point, however, and a sort of quasi–truce settled in along the border.

The next development came on June 7, when the Azerbaijani population went to the polls to elect a new president. There were five candidates, but the easy winner was Abulfaz Elchibey, leader of the *Azerbaijan Popular Front*, who won 60 percent of the vote. Elchibey, 53 years old at the time of his election, is a noted historian. He was also one of the founders of the *Azerbaijan Popular Front*. Though the *Popular Front* came into existence as part of a popular response to Nagorno–Karabakh's demand that it be permitted to become part of Armenia, it claimed democratic credentials and was determined to break the old–line Communist leadership's hold on power. Strongly nationalist, it also opposes cooperation with the other former Soviet republics in the CIS.

One of Elchibey's first acts as President was to announce that Azerbaijan would withdraw from the Commonwealth of Independent States and that Azerbaijan would deal with the other republics only

Azerbaijan

on a bilateral basis. Elchibey was particularly incensed that several of the CIS members had negotiated a mutual security pact which included Armenia, though he had been cool to the CIS from its first inception.

Aside from that, however, Elchibey has been relatively moderate in his actions since becoming President. This may be partly because he looks to Turkey as a model for his own government and the Turkish Government has been urging that course on him. He is committed to an economic reform based on free market principles, but little has actually been done in that direction, partly because of the Azerbaijan Government's continued preoccupation with Nagorno–Karabakh. Azerbaijan has not suffered the bad economic effects suffered by Armenia as a result of the struggle over Nagorno–Karabakh, but it appears to almost preclude Azerbaijani leaders from thinking about anything else.

Recent news has not been good for Azerbaijan's leadership, however. In April 1993, Armenian forces overran the northern part of the strip separating Nagorno–Karabakh from Armenia, capturing the Azerbaijani regional town of Kelbajar and in the process bringing about ten percent of Azerbaijan's territory under Armenian control. This represented a severe defeat for President Elchibey, even though his forces are expected to regain control of the overrun territories in subsequent fighting. It is also not known what effect this development will have on continuing mediation efforts currently being sponsored by the Council for Security and Cooperation in Europe.

Nature of the Regime

Azerbaijan has completed its transition to a pluralistic political system in principle, but the political situation associated with Nagorno–Karabakh has tended to polarize the society and to make moderate political stances suspect. The old–line Communists are, indeed, out of power, but the old Communist ideas have been replaced by a new orthodoxy based on the political positions of the Azerbaijan Popular Front. The government has attempted to quell dissent but has not been very successful. In one sense, Azerbaijan may have an excel of "democracy." Currently there are over 30 political parties, though most are quite small. The three largest political groupings are the *Azerbaijan Popular Front*, the *Social Democratic Party* and the *National Independence Party*. The *National Independence Party*, led by Ikitbar Mahmedov, had been part of the *Azerbaijan Popular Front* until 1992. It split off amid accusations that the *Azerbaijan Popular Front* was abusing its power. One problem is that the present legislature was elected during the previous regime

and it is a rump body of 50–members consisting of ex–communists and their opponents. It cannot be considered to be representative. President Elchibey nevertheless opposes new elections as long as Azerbaijan remains at war.

Although the Popular Front is publicly committed to creation of a free market economy, relatively little has been done in this area because of the government's continued preoccupation with Nagorno–Karabakh. The April 1993 Azerbaijan defeat at Kelbajar produced an estimated 100,000 new refugees for the Azerbaijani Government to cope with. Because of the refugee problem and the bad way the war is progressing, economic reform is likely to get short shrift for the foreseeable future.

The Azerbaijan Government

Azerbaijan's government resembles that of the French Fifth Republic. There is a popularly elected President who is considered to be the spokesman for the nation . He is responsible for general policy, but has a Prime Minister who handles day–to–day affairs of government. The President is Commander–in–Chief of the armed forces. He also presides over the State Council and the Defense Council.

The Prime Minister and members of the cabinet are appointed by the President, but must be confirmed by the legislature.

NAGORNO–KARABAKH

Nagorno–Karabakh, which declared itself an independent republic in December 1991 after a referendum earlier in the month had received overwhelming approval, was for many years an Armenian enclave located in Azerbaijan with the status of an Autonomous Republic. Around 180,000 Armenians live here and make up approximately 90% of the population of the republic.

They have organized their own 81 seat legislature (with 11 seats reserved for Azeris). The new head of state (whose position is chairman of the legislature) is Arthur Mkrtchyan, a man in his mid–30s who formerly had been a museum director.

Azerbaijan abolished Nagorno–Karabakh's autonomous republic status in November 1991 and has had the republic under siege since that time. It is receiving some support from Armenia, but is otherwise on its own. All CIS troops have been removed from the enclave.

Nagorno–Karabakh's current problems began in February 1988 when its regional council, feeling itself discriminated against by the Azerbaijani Government, asked that the region become part of the Armenian SSR. The matter quickly became an inter–republic dispute after Armenia endorsed Nagorno–Karabakh's re-

quest. Popular demonstrations in Azerbaijan and Armenia soon turned to violence, producing hundreds of thousands of refugees on both sides.

In January 1989, with the situation as bad as ever, Moscow announced that it was suspending both Azerbaijan's control over Nagorno–Karabakh and the local provincial committee and instituting "a special form of administration" for the rebellious autonomous republic, thus putting it under Moscow's direct control.

This led to the creation of the *Azerbaijan Popular Front*, which demanded the return of Nagorno–Karabakh to Azerbaijanian jurisdiction. To back up its demand, the front organized a blockade of railway traffic going into Armenia. Moscow then gave in to the pressure and returned Nagorno–Karabakh to Azerbaijanian control in November 1989.

Russia and Kazakhstan attempted to mediate the dispute between Azerbaijan and Armenia in September 1991, but without any lasting success. Armenia and Azerbaijan signed a ceasefire agreement and Armenia gave up its claim to the enclave in return for a promise by the Azerbaijan leadership that it would allow free elections in Nagorno–Karabakh and bestow additional autonomy on the enclave. The agreement also called for the disarming of illegal local militias and the resettling of Armenian and Azeri refugees in their homes. But President Mutalibov of Azerbaijan never implemented the agreement for fear of the nationalist opposition. Mutalibov had little popular support and deliberately appealed to nationalism in an attempt to outflank his nationalist opposition. When an Azerbaijani helicopter was downed in November 1991, President Mutalibov suspended talks with Armenia and called an emergency session of the Azerbaijan legislature. The legislature abolished Nagorno–Karabakh's autonomous republic status.

Both Turkey and Iran have attempted to mediate the dispute and at least six truce agreements have actually been signed. None has held, however. Negotiations were also begun in 1992 under the auspices of the Conference on Security and Cooperation in Europe. The peace talks appeared to be near success at one point in 1992 and eight nations agreed, at that time, to provide unarmed observers to monitor a ceasefire. The CSCE has continued its mediation effort, but they have been unable to achieve agreement between the parties on a ceasefire.

Culture

The Azerbaijani are historically a Shiite Moslem people, unlike their Moslem neighbors in Central Asia, who are mostly Sunni. This probably results from the fact that the area of Azerbaijan was for several centuries part of the Persian Empire. It became a part of the Russian Empire at the beginning of the 19th century, however, and the Azerbaijani became merely one of the Moslem peoples of Russia.

There was no sense of national Azerbaijani identity until fairly recently, but there have been a number of famous Azerbaijani thinkers, poets and scientists. Abul Hasan Bakhmanyar, who lived in the 11th century, wrote a number of books on mathematics and philosophy. Abul Hasan Shirvani, a later contemporary, left behind a book on astronomy. Nezami was a later poet and philosopher.

The Azerbaijani have an ancient musical tradition which has survived. Musicians improvise the words to songs as they play a stringed instrument called a *kobuz*. There are also vocal and instrumental compositions that have been kept alive in a folk tradition.

They also have modern composers with international reputations. Two of these are Uzeir Hajjibekov, author of a number of operas, and Kara Karayev, who writes ballets. The Baku Film Studio also has an international reputation. *Little Vera*, a recent film, tells a depressing story of a young girl growing up as a member of a working-class family in Baku.

Although a large part of the population was still illiterate in 1917, modern Azerbaijan now has 16 institutes of higher education with a student population of over 100,000. The largest of these is the Azerbaijan Institute of Petroleum and Chemistry.

In January 1992, the Azerbaijan National Council passed a law adopting the Latin script for the Azerbaijani language. It acted on the basis of a recommendation from a special commission, appointed two years ago, to look into the question. The commission, made up of a number of linguists, historians, and literary specialists, concluded that the Azerbaijan language's phonetic "peculiarities are best 'superimposed' on the Latin script." Azerbaijan had used the Latin script in the 1920s but, under pressure from Moscow, went over to the Cyrillic script at the end of the thirties. The changeover will be implemented over the next two years.

Economy

Baku, now the capital and largest city, was the center of the oil industry of Imperial Russia. In 1901, the Baku fields produced over 11 million tons of oil, which was 50 percent of the world's oil production at the time. The fields have lost much of their earlier significance, but the region still produced three percent of the Soviet Union's oil in 1991. Baku is still surrounded by oil derricks, though natural gas has come to rival petroleum in

significance in recent years. Once a beautiful city that spread out along natural terraces running down to a gulf of the Caspian Sea, Baku today is a grimy industrial city with terrible pollution problems.

Sumgait, a city located 22 miles north of Baku, is Azerbaijan's second most important industrial center. It has a major chemical industry and was the primary manufacturer of oil–drilling equipment in the now defunct Soviet Union. Three other cities with significant industry are Mingechaur, Gyanja (formerly Kirovabad), and Stepanakert. Mingechaur manufactures appliances and instruments and electrical equipment of all kinds, plus textiles, shoes and other consumer goods. Gyanja and Stepanakert also manufacture consumer goods, including textiles, and things like knitwear and souvenirs.

Most of Azerbaijan's industry was developed to process its petroleum and natural gas supplies. Thus it has refineries producing gasoline, herbicides, industrial oils and kerosene and also manufactures chemical fertilizers, synthetic rubber and plastics. It is also a major producer of electric power and traditionally has exported electricity to neighboring republics. There is a handicraft industry in southern Azerbaijan along the border with Iran. Here the Talysh, an Iranian people, live in their mountainous villages and support themselves by weaving rugs and carpets by hand in the traditional way.

Fishing is another industry that makes a major contribution to the gross domestic product, though it has declined in importance in recent years. The Caspian Sea is famous for its sturgeon, and Azerbaijan is a major source of caviar. But the sea is being rapidly polluted and the caviar supplies are quickly diminishing.

Agriculture is less significant than industry insofar as total value is concerned, but it still provides employment to over a third of the population. Cotton is the most valuable crop, followed by tobacco, grapes, vegetables, fruits and nuts. Most of the grapes are used to produce wine. There is also a small silk industry.

The Lenkoren region in southern Azerbaijan produces subtropical crops such as citrus and tea. It also produces rice and tobacco and is a major source for winter and spring vegetables.

The Nakhichevan Autonomous Republic has a semi–desert climate, but irrigation allows it to raise grapes, cotton and grain. It is also famous for its mineral water springs, which is bottled and sold as far away as Moscow.

The Future

Faced with a war with Armenia over Nagorno–Karabakh and all the problems associated with a collapse of the old Soviet command economy, Azerbaijan's future necessarily looks bleak. It must solve the dispute over Nagorno–Karabakh before it can expect any outside assistance, but it is not certain that the Azerbaijani people will accept a solution acceptable to the Armenians of Nagorno–Karabakh.

Offshore oil extraction near Baku   Courtesy: NOVOSTI

The Republic of Georgia

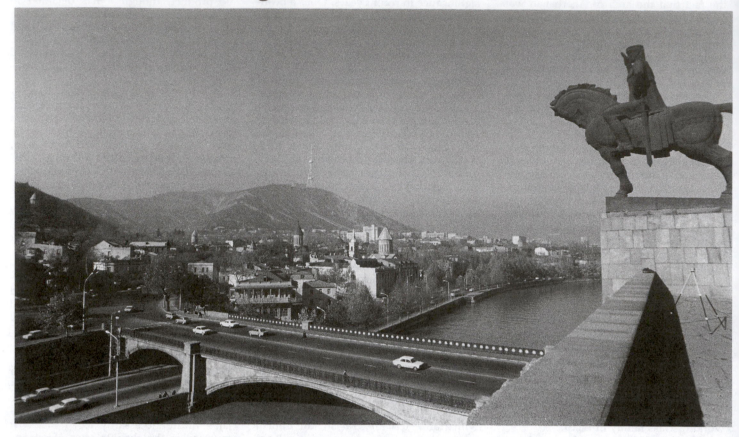

The Vorontsov Bridge across the Kura River, Tbilisi

Courtesy: NOVOSTI

Area: 26,903 sq. mi. (69,700 sq. km; half the size of Wisconsin).

Population: 5.5 million (1989 census).

Capital City: Tbilisi (Pop. 1.2 million).

Climate: Humid, subtropical.

Neighboring States: Russia (north), Turkey, Armenia (south), Azerbaijan (southeast).

Official Language: Georgian.

Ethnic Composition: Georgian (69%), Armenian (9%), Russian (7%), Azerbaijanis (5.1%), others (9.9).

Principal Religions: Georgian Orthodox. Until recently, religious worship was officially discouraged.

Chief Commercial Products: hydroelectric power, mining, electrical equipment, metals and alloys, automobiles, electrical manufactures, instruments, Wines, fruits, tea, vegetables, livestock.

Currency: Ruble (as of June 1992).

Recent Political Status: Soviet Republic (1921), part of Transcaucasian SSR (1922–1936), Republic of the USSR (1936-1991).

Chief of State: Eduard Shevardnadze, Chairman of the State Council.

The Land

The Republic of Georgia is the independent successor state to the Georgian So-viet Socialist Republic, which was one of the fifteen republics of the Union of Soviet Socialist Republics. The Georgia Supreme Soviet announced the republic's intention to separate from the Soviet Union in November 1990, but it was the August 1991 failed *coup* against Mikhail Gorbachëv that created a situation of *de facto* independence for Georgia. Georgia covers an area of 26,903 square miles (69,700 sq. km.) It includes The Abkha-zian and Adjarian Autonomous Republics, plus the South Ossetian Autonomous Region.

Georgia lies at the eastern end of the Black Sea, just to the south of the Great Caucasus Mountains. Eighty–five percent of the country is mountainous, the exception being a small area in the west bordering on the Black Sea known as the Kolkhida Lowland. This is the site of ancient Colchis, where Jason and the

140

Argonauts sought the golden fleece. The Kolkhida Lowland is a delta region formed by the deposits of three rivers that flow through the area, the Inguri, Rioni, and Kodori. It was once mostly swampland, but drainage projects have turned it into a major producer of subtropical crops and winter vegetables. Here winter temperatures average 41° F. and there is a plentiful year–round rainfall.

Behind Kolkhida, the land rises until it reaches two saddle ridges which connect the Great Caucasus and the Little Caucasus Mountains. Beyond that is a high plateau which runs eastward to the border of Azerbaijan. This high plateau, known as the Kartalinian Plain, is the heartland of Georgia. Most of it is covered by a loess type soil. Drier than the western coast, it nevertheless gets sufficient rainfall to sustain agriculture. In addition, the Kura River flows down out of the Little Caucasus in the southwest and then eastward across the plateau, providing plenty of water for irrigation. Open to the warm, moist air from the Black Sea and protected on the north by the wall of the Great Caucasus Mountains, the Kartalinian Plain has winters warm enough that citrus groves thrive. The high mountains to the north and south of this plateau are covered with forests of oak, chestnut, beech, ash, linden, alder, and Caucasian fir. Fruit trees also abound, including apples, pears, and various kinds of nuts. Dairying is practiced on the lower slopes of the mountains and on parts of the plateau. Vineyards are also widely cultivated. Grapes are sold fresh or turned into wine, brandy, or champagne. The eastern part of the country consists of the Alasari River Valley plus a saddleland to the south between that valley and the Kara River Valley. This area receives only between 16 and 28 inches of rainfall and therefore makes use of the water from the Alasari River for irrigation.

The People

Georgia's population as of the 1989 census was 5.5 million. In addition to the above nationalities, Ossetians constitute 2%, and Abkhazians (2%). Georgia is an ancient center of civilization. Archaeological excavations place the beginning of the bronze age here as early as 3,000 B.C. The ancestors of the Georgian people emerged for the first time in the first millennium B.C. in the annals of the Assyrian Empire. The Georgian language itself is classified as one of the Caucasian languages, meaning that, as far as is known, the Georgians originated here. Among the Georgian tribes were the Kulkha (Colchians), who once dominated most of the eastern shores of the Black Sea. Their city, Colchis, was known for its fabulous wealth and gave rise to the legend of Medea and the golden fleece. Colchis was later colonized by Greeks and still later incorporated into the Roman Empire.

History

Georgia converted to Christianity about the year 330. Over the next three centuries it became a battlefield between the Byzantine Empire and Persia. However, in 654 it fell to the Arqab caliphs, who established an amirate in Tbilisi. In reaction to the Arab presence, the various Georgian tribes united around a princely family long prominent in the affairs of Armenia, and this family eventually brought most of Georgia under its sway. King Bagrat III (975–1014) ruled all of Georgia except for the Tbilisi amirate, and that was conquered in the year 1122 by one of his descendants, King David II ("the Builder"). The Georgian Kingdom reached its zenith under Queen Tamara (1184–1213), when it included most of the Caucasus.

The end came in 1220 with the appearance of the Mongols from the east. Eastern Georgia became part of the Mongol Empire, with only the area west of the mountains along the Black Sea maintaining its independence. The decline of the Mongol Empire brought part of the high central plateau back under Georgian con-

An artist's concept of the medieval fortress of Queen Tamara in the towering Caucasus Mountains

Georgia

trol, but the new kingdom was destroyed by a fresh onslaught by Tamerlane, who created a great empire stretching across Central Asia.

The fall of Constantinople to the Ottoman Turks in 1453 isolated Georgia. In the sixteenth century, it, too, was incorporated into the Turkish Empire. The Turks were in turn driven out by Shah Abba I (1587–1629) ruler of the Persian Empire. In the process, thousands of Georgian Christians were transported to distant parts of the Persian Empire. There was a brief respite after 1658, when the Persians installed the House of Mukhran as viceroys at Tbisili, but this was brought to an end by a fresh Turkish invasion in 1722. The Persians expelled the Turks twenty–two years later. Another kingdom based on Georgia was installed by the Persians and lasted until near the end of the eighteenth century.

In 1783, Erekle, the Georgian king, signed the Treaty of Georgievsk with Catherine the Great, whereby Russia guaranteed Georgia's independence and territorial integrity in return for Erekle's acceptance of Russian authority. When Georgia was invaded by Persia in 1795, however, Russia offered no assistance. Tbilisi was sacked in 1795 and Erekle died three years later. His son, George XII, offered the kingdom to Paul, the Russian Tsar. Paul died before the treaty could be signed, so it was Alexander I who incorporated Georgia into the Russian Empire. In spite of the treaty of 1783, Alexander I then deposed George XII and replaced him with Russian military governors. Erekle's kingdom had included only the areas of Kartalinia and Kakhetia, so other parts of Georgia were incorporated in the Russian Empire between 1810 and 1864. The Black Sea ports of Poti and Batumi were added at the time of the Russo–Turkish War of 1877–78.

Georgia's incorporation into the Russian Empire provoked a number of popular uprisings at various times, but it did have the merit of ensuring the corporate survival of the Georgian nation. Georgia also benefited economically and culturally from its connection with Russia. A railroad connecting Tbilisi with Poti on the Black Sea opened in 1872 and mines, factories and commercial farms were established with Russian and foreign capital. Alexander II's reforms also included the end of serfdom and the spread of education. Alexander III's policy of Russification fostered nationalism among the middle–class intelligentsia, however, and marked the beginning of a national revival.

A number of illegal nationalist groups were founded in the 1890s, the most important of which was the "Third Group," a Marxist party. In 1898, the Third Group recruited Joseph Dzhugash-

vili, who later changed his name to Joseph Stalin ("Steel"). Stalin found himself in the minority after the national party split into Bolsheviks and Mensheviks at the second congress of the Social Democratic Party. After 1903, the Georgian Marxist party was Menshevik. Stalin was a Bolshevik.

Georgia saw widespread disturbances and guerrilla fighting during the 1905 Russian uprising, but these were put down by Cossacks in 1906. After the 1917 Revolution, an autonomous Transcaucasian committee was established under the authority of the Provisional Government. After the Bolshevik Revolution in the fall, however, this Transcaucasian committee, which was dominated by Mensheviks, broke with the national government and established the Transcaucasian Federal Republic on April 22, 1918. When this collapsed a month later, the Georgian National Council set up the *Georgian Social Democratic Republic*. The republic was under German protection for a while, but then was occupied by the British. The Georgians refused to cooperate with the British, however, and the latter departed Batumi in July 1920.

Georgia had signed a treaty with the Russians in May 1920, and this allowed the Bolsheviks to dispatch a mission under S. M. Kirov to Tbilisi. Kirov's task was to undermine the Menshevik regime and prepare for a Bolshevik *coup*. It received diplomatic recognition from the Allies in January 1921. One month later, a Red Army under the control of two Georgian Bolshevik leaders, Joseph Stalin and G. K. Ordzhonikidze, entered Georgia. A Soviet regime was installed on February 25.

Georgia was incorporated into the Transcaucasian Soviet Federated Socialist Republic in March 1922. This became a part of the Union of Soviet Socialist Republics on December 30, 1922.

Stalin, who was People's Commissar for Nationalities in the Moscow government, was determined to stamp out nationalist tendencies among his Georgian compatriots and carried out a purge of active nationalists, including even members of the *Georgian Communist Party*.

The Transcaucasian SFSR was formally dissolved in December 1936 when the Union of Soviet Socialist Republics adopted a new constitution and the Georgian Soviet Socialist Republic became one of the constituent republics in its own right. It was at this time that another Georgian Communist, Lavrenti P. Beria, rose to prominence when he was named head of the Soviet secret police, at that time known as the NKVD. Beria remained a top member of the CPSU until after Stalin's death in March 1953. He was then accused of planning a *coup* against

the rest of the party leadership and was executed.

Georgia certainly derived some benefits from its participation in the Union of Soviet Socialist Republics. Illiteracy was wiped out, schools of higher education were set up, a Georgian Academy of Sciences was established, and a great deal of industry was built. Yet the price was conformity to Marxist–Leninist ideology and a suppression of traditional Georgian culture.

When Gorbachëv launched his policy of *glasnost* after he took over in 1985, therefore, one of his early supporters was Eduard Schevardnadze, first secretary of the Georgian Communist Party from 1972 to 1985. Schevardnadze, made a full member of the Politburo and Minister of Foreign Affairs, became a strong voice at the center urging on Gorbachëv the necessity for further reforms. Although Schevardnadze no longer had any direct control over developments in Georgia, he had a well–earned reputation for scrupulous honesty.

Gorbachëv's reforms were endorsed and exploited as much in Georgia as any part of the Soviet Union. The *Georgia Communist Party* soon found itself outbid by Georgian nationalists, who did not have to worry about loyalty to Moscow. When Gorbachëv decided to permit real elections in 1989, the nationalists were given their chance. A seven party coalition called *Round Table–Free Georgia* managed to win 62% of the seats in the October 1990 republic elections. They took control of the Georgian Supreme Soviet, then elected a longtime nationalist dissident and anti–Communist, Zviad Gamsakhurdia, as Georgia's head of state. At the same time, they changed the name of the country to the Republic of Georgia and announced the beginning of a transition to full independence. Gamsakhurdia, founder of the Georgian Helsinki Group, had been jailed in 1977 by the former Brezhnev regime. He was imprisoned again in 1989, after Soviet special forces fired on peaceful demonstrators outside the parliament building, killing more than 20 persons.

In April 1991, the Supreme Soviet declared Georgia's independence, then changed the constitution to create a popularly elected, executive President. In the elections that took place on May 26, 1991, Gamsakhurdia won 86.5 percent of the vote. Valerian Advadze, who accused Gamsakhurdia of planning to turn Georgia into a personal dictatorship, came in second with 7.6 percent of the vote. Jimmy Mikeladze, head of the Georgia Communist Party, got 1.6 percent. Two other candidates polled less than two percent of the vote. It appeared that democracy had triumphed in Georgia.

Almost immediately after this overwhelming vote of confidence, however, Gamsakhurdia began to take actions that lent credence to the charge that he indeed wanted to create a personal dictatorship. A law signed by Gamsakhurdia made "maligning" the president a crime punishable by six years in prison. Gamsakhurdia also accused reporters of lying and had them thrown out of a news conference. And he began an attempt to remove the political autonomy enjoyed by Moslem South Ossetians in the north of the country.

When the attempted *coup* against Gorbachëv failed in August 1991, Gamsakhurdia promised *coup* leaders that he would cause no trouble in Georgia and then issued an appeal to Georgians to remain calm; this caused a split in the government coalition. Tengiz Sigua, the prime minister, and Gyorghi Khoshtaria, the foreign minister, opposed the *coup* and may have been privately critical of Gamsakhurdia's policy of inaction. As a result, Gamsakhurdia dismissed both of them in the days following collapse of the *coup*. When the two dismissals led to popular demonstrations in the main square of Tbilisi on September 2, Gamsakhurdia ordered the national guard to fire on the demonstrators.

But when Gamsakhurdia ordered Tengiz Ketovani, commander of the national guard, to use force against subsequent demonstrations, the latter refused. Gamsakhurdia then attempted to fire him also, but he refused to recognize the dismissal. In the meantime, the situation in South Ossetia deteriorated after Gamsakhurdia abolished its autonomous status. By September, there had been over a hundred deaths in the area and 50,000 Ossetians had fled over the mountains to North Ossetia, in the Russian Federation.

As daily demonstrations against Gamsakhurdia continued in Tbilisi, members of the government coalition began to go over to the opposition. Gamsakhurdia then had Georgi Chanturia, leader of the opposition *National Democratic Party*, arrested. The charge was that he and Eduard Shevardnadze were plotting a *coup* to overthrow the government.

This brought additional demonstrations, now led by Tengiz Sigua and Tengiz Ketovani, demanding Gamsakhurdia's resignation. On September 22, anti-Gamsakhurdia demonstrators seized control of the government radio and television station. They were later joined by members of the Georgia national guard. Following this, more than ten thousand demonstrators marched on government house to demand President Gamsakhurdia's resignation. Meanwhile, Gamsakhurdia supporters harassed the demonstrators from the sidelines. Later, they, in turn, occupied the opposition party offices.

Centenarian dancers of *Narta'u* go to give a concert　　　Courtesy: NOVOSTI

The next three months were punctuated by a series of riots, shootings and demonstrations. Through it all, Gamsakhurdia remained penned up in the parliament building. In late December, then, a major battle broke out. After two weeks, Gamsakhurdia fled the country on January 6, going first to Armenia, then making his way to western Georgia. Here, where he had lived prior to coming to power, he rallied his supporters and attempted, without success, to force his way back to power. He continued to have some support in the country, but not enough to return.

Meanwhile in Tbilisi the victorious opposition set up a Military Council to govern the country. Tengiz Sigua was installed as provisional Prime Minister while Tengiz Ketovani continued as commander of the national guard.

Soon after that, rumors began that Eduard Shevardnadze would return to Georgia and reenter Georgia politics. Schevardnadze refused to either affirm or deny the rumors, but he did congratulate Georgians "on this victory" after Gamsakhurdia fled Tbilisi. In February, however, he agreed to serve as honorary chairman of an opposition unbrella group called the *Democratic Union*. The Military Council then publicly announced that it would welcome Shevardnadze's return. In early March, the Military Council called a meeting of the legislature and relinquished power to that body. The legislature created a governing State Council to run the country until elections could take place. On March 10, Shevardnadze was elected chairman of the State Council.

In another apparent break with the policies of the Gamsakhurdia regime, the Georgia defense minister, Levan Sharashanidze, was sent as an observer to the February 14 meeting of the CIS. Georgia has since continued its contacts with the CIS, but has made no application to join the organization.

Shevardnadze's installation as chairman of the State Council brought formal recognition by the United States. An embassy was opened in April and Secretary of State Baker paid an official visit to Tbilisi in May.

Shevardnadze has not been able to bring peace to the country, however. It is estimated that up to a third of the population continues to support Gamsakhurdia and they control parts of north–western Georgia, in particular significant parts of Abkhazia. Gamsakhurdia's supporters even organized a *coup* to overthrow Shevardnadze in June 1992, though they only managed to seize the television tower and were easily routed by Georgia national guard troops.

In addition to the opposition supporters of Gamsakhurdia, Shevardnadze has had to deal with two secessionist movements inherited from his predecessor. The first of these, South Ossetia, is tied in with North Ossetia's wish to separate from Russia. Tengiz Ketovani, Defense Minister and head of the Georgian National Guard, ordered an attack on

Georgia

Tskhinvali, the capital of South Ossetia in May 1992. Shevardnadze preferred a negotiated settlement, however, and responded favorably when President Yeltsin offered to mediate the dispute. This eventually produced a negotiated ceasefire and a joint Russian–Georgian–Ossetian force to police the peace.

The second, Abkhazia, began originally in 1990 when Abkhazian nationalists demanded greater local autonomy. An alliance between these forces and Gamsakhurdia forces seems to have come into being in 1992, however. In August 1992, the Abkhazian legislature voted to reinstate the region's 1925 constitution, in effect asserting its independence. In addition, several Georgian officials were kidnaped in the Abkhazia area, presumably by supporters of Gamsakhurdia. In August, Shevardnadze sent in a force of 3,000 men armed with tanks and helicopter gunships to take control of the capital city of Sukhumi. There was resistance and approximately 10 Abkhazians were killed in street fighting. More were killed somewhat later. The Abkhazian Government, headed by Vladislav Ardzinba, fled the capital and Georgia faced the possibility of a long period of guerrilla warfare. Shevardnadze responded favorably when Yeltsin again offered to mediate this dispute, however, and in September Shevardnadze and Vladislav Ardzinba signed a cease–fire agreement.

The cease–fire did not hold, however. Fighting broke out again in October and the Abkhazians, this time supported by other mountain tribes of the Caucasus plus some Russian Cossacks, managed to gain control over a large part of northwest Abkhazia. The Abkhazia area has continued to fester since that time and Shevardnadze has claimed that the Abkhazians have received support from elements of the Russian army still stationed in the area. It is clear that at least some Russian forces were involved, for Georgian forces shot down a Russian plane in March 1993. These appear to be rogue elements not controlled by Moscow, however.

New Parliamentary elections were carried out in October 1992 and these involved also elections for the office of speaker of the State Council. Shevardnadze won this latter position, but the election was less significant because he ran unopposed. Shevardnadze is not an all powerful figure in Georgia, however, He continues to have to share power with His Prime Minister, Tengiz Sigua, and his Defense Minister, Tengiz Ketovani, the two men who arranged for his installation as chairman of the State Council in the first place.

Nature of the Regime

Georgia still has the governmental setup created at the time of the overthrow of President Gamsakhurdia; that is, it is being ruled by the governing State Council, a body set up in March 1992 by the legislature. Gamsakhurdia has not resigned, so technically he remains President. The governing State Council has the support of the legislature and the national guard, however. The men of the Military Council who deposed Gamsakhurdia, and who continue to be the real force behind the present government—almost all former associates of Gamsakhurdia—call themselves nationalists and democrats. New elections to the legislature and for the office of chairman of the State Council were held in October 1992. The newly elected legislature is supposed to produce a new constitution soon.

Culture

Georgia is a land of ancient culture, a surprising amount of which has survived, considering that it was for centuries a battleground between the Persian and Byzantine Empires and, later, the Ottoman Empire. Georgian architecture is particularly interesting because of the role it played in the development of the Byzantine style of architecture.

Picking citrus fruit on a state farm near Batum, Georgia   Courtesy: NOVOSTI

Georgia has also had a written language since the fifth century A.D., and there are a number of great works which have survived. The earliest of these is an epic masterpiece from the twelfth century by the poet Shota Rustaveli, called *The Knight in the Tiger's Skin*. A cultural renaissance at the end of the nineteenth century produced a number of poets, including Ilia Chavchavadze, Akaki Tsereteli, Vazha Pshavela, novelists such as Alexander Qazbegi, and writers like Mikheil Javakhishvili, Paolo Iashvili, Titsian Tabidze, Giorgi Leonidze and Irakli Abashidze.

Most of these artists were later executed by Stalin when he decided in the 1930s to stamp out Georgian nationalism in his native state. Georgia has also produced important painters (Niko Pirosmanashvili, Irikli Toidze) and composers (Zakaria Paliashvili, Meliton Balanchivadze). Vakhtang Chabukiani was the founder of the Georgian national ballet. There is also a vibrant Georgian theater and film industry. *Resurrection*, a recent surrealistic film about a Stalin–like dictator, was one specifically Georgian contribution to *glasnost*.

Nor should one forget Zviad Gamsakhurdia, the first anti–communist leader of the country, elected in 1990 and forced out as President at the beginning of 1992. Gamsakhurdia, the son of Georgia's best–known modern novelist, is a leading Georgian author in his own right, as well as a translator. Among the authors he has translated are Shakespeare and Baudelaire. Tengiz Sigua, currently the provisional Prime Minister, was a professor before he entered politics, while Tengiz Ketovani, is a sculptor.

Georgia has one major university, Tbilisi State University, which was founded in 1918. In addition, the Georgia Academy of Sciences, established in 1941, consists of a number of scientific institutions which conduct research throughout the republic. There is also an extensive library system.

Economy

Georgian industry has four main branches—mineral extraction, machine-building, chemicals and textiles. Extensive coal deposits have been developed along the southern slopes of the Great Caucasus Mountains, particularly at Tkvarcheli and Tkibuli. Georgia also has petroleum and some natural gas. Other minerals include manganese and talc.

The machine–building industry produces railway locomotives, heavy vehicles, several types of planes, and earth moving equipment, but it also produces things like lathes and precision instruments. The chemical industry produces pharmaceuticals, synthetic fibers and mineral fertilizers. The textile industry

Farmers graze flocks high up in the Caucasus mountains   Courtesy: NOVOSTI

produces cotton, woolen and silk fabrics and some clothing.

Agriculture contributes importantly to the economy, in spite of the fact that agricultural land is in short supply and much of it is located along mountain slopes. Major crops tend, therefore, to be labor intensive—and with a higher cash value—such as citrus fruits, tea and nuts. Georgia produced 97% of the citrus fruits and 92% of the tea of the now defunct Soviet Union. Georgia was also a major exporter of wines, brandy and champagne to other parts of the Soviet Union, though here Armenia is a major competitor and Azerbaijan produces wines as well. Georgia was also a significant exporter of dairy products and canned foods. Other major agricultural products include sugar beets, tobacco, perfume oils, poultry, bees and silkworms. With independence and the collapse of the Soviet Union, Georgia's problem now will be how to retain those markets for its traditional agricultural surplus.

This state has great potential for tourism. It already has several resorts and sanatoria located on the Black Sea coast, some of which are famous for their mineral springs. In the interior, there are many monasteries and churches which qualify as architectural monuments. In recent years, restoration and preservation efforts have led to an increasing number of tourists, both from other parts of the former Soviet Union and from abroad.

The current condition of the economy is terrible, however. Industrial output has dropped by 60% in the past two years and inflation is currently running at 1,500%. Georgia was forced out of the ruble zone in late 1992 and since that time Georgians have been making do with "coupons" issued by the state, no new currency having been created. A new Georgian currency is being printed in France, though it is not clear when it will be issued.

The Future

Georgia's greatest problem is its lack of political stability. As long as civil wars rage in parts of the country, there is little hope for significant improvement in the economy. The problem is two–fold—the nationalist movements in South Ossetia and Abkhazia and the continued opposition of Gamsakhurdia supporters. The nationalist movements might be defused by greater grants of autonomy, though important elements within the present government oppose that approach. It is also difficult to see what might persuade Gamsakhurdia and his supporters to make peace with the government. As everybody says, Georgia has great potential as an independent country, provided it can work out its political problems. But no one says how the leadership might go about doing that.

CENTRAL ASIAN REPUBLICS (of the former Soviet Union)

Due to their shared histories as well as frequent geographical and cultural similarities, there is necessarily some repetition from one entry to the other.

Showing principal cities and railroads

The Republic of Kazakhstan

Area: 1,049,155 sq. mi. (2,717,300 sq. km., almost twice the size of Alaska, second largest state in the former USSR).

Population: 17 million (estimated).

Capital City: Alma–Ata (Pop. 1.2 million, estimated).

Climate: Continental, with very hot summers and extremely cold winters.

Neighboring States: Russia (north), Turkmenistan (southwest), Uzbekistan, Kyrgyzstan, China (south).

Principal Languages: Kazakh and Russian.

Ethnic Composition: Russian (40.8%), Kazakh (36%), Ukrainians (6.1%), other (17.9%).

Principal Religions: Islam, Christianity (Orthodox). Until recently, religious worship was officially discouraged.

Chief Commercial Products: Agriculture—grain, livestock production. In-

dustry—Oil. Kazakhstan was the second–largest oil producer in the former USSR. The republic is also very rich in mineral resources.

Currency: Ruble.

Recent Political Status: The Kazakh SSR was formally a part of the Russian Soviet Federative Republic (RSFFR) but in December 1936 it was proclaimed a separate constituent republic of the former USSR, remaining in that status until 1991.

Chief of State: Nursultan Nazarbayev, President.

The Land

The Republic of Kazakhstan, successor government to the Kazakh Soviet Socialist Republic, declared its independence on December 16, 1991. The Kazakh Soviet Socialist Republic had existed only since December 1936. Its predecessor was the

Kirghiz (later renamed Kazakh) Autonomous Soviet Socialist Republic, which had been founded in August 1920 as an autonomous republic of the RSFSR by which it is bounded on the west and the north.

In spite of its size, Kazakhstan is geographically rather homogeneous. Essentially it is a great tableland, with lowlands, plains and plateaus making up approximately 80 percent of the landscape. Mountainous regions in the east and southeast make up the remaining parts of the land.

Kazakhstan is actually a Eurasian land, with its western border beginning at the northern end of the Caspian Sea, just east of the mouth of the Volga River. It then turns slightly west and runs northward just east of the Volga River before bending northeast and skirting the southern edges of the Ural Mountains. East of the

146

Urals, it zig–zags north until it passes the Russian city of Magnitogorsk before turning eastward. After passing just south of the city of Omsk, it turns southeastward and pushes to the top ridge of the Altai Mountains. It then turns at a sharp angle and runs in a southwestern direction along the ridges of the Tarbagatay Range and the Ulu–Tau Mountains until it passes just south of the republic's capital of Alma–Ata. Here it turns westward and runs along the foothills, crossing the Syr–Darya River, until just north of Samarkand. It then crosses the Kyzylkum Desert and passes through the center of the Aral Sea, bending from there southward to reach the center of the Caspian Sea.

The western portion of the republic is dominated by the Caspian Depression. The Mogodzhar Hills, a southern extension of the Ural Mountains, separates the Caspian Depression from the Turan Plain, which stretches west–east just north of the Aral Sea. To the east of the Aral Sea is the Kyzylkum Desert. To the northeast of that, separated by the valley of the Syr–Darya River, is an area called the Hunger Steppe. These areas in the south are all desert and only the presence of the Syr–Darya River makes any agriculture possible. The northern part of Kazakhstan is known as the Kazakh Steppe, however, and here there is sufficient rainfall to support grasses. The northern part of Kazakhstan is an area of farms that concentrate on growing wheat and other cereal crops.

Some irrigation is also possible in this northern area, using water from the Ural River in the west and the Irtysh River in the east. Two smaller rivers, the Ishim and Tobol, also provide water for irrigation. Overall, the republic has over 7,000 streams and rivers, plus about 48,000 small lakes. Kazakhstan also has 1,450 miles of coastline along the Caspian Sea.

Temperatures in the southern part of Kazakhstan are much milder, however, but temperatures average in January from 23–29%dg F. Average July temperatures are 68° in the north and 84° in the south. The area of the north has rich, black soils. South of that, soils are chestnut–brown but still fertile. Southern soils tend to be infertile, alkaline soils or sandy desert. Woodlands, found mostly in the mountains, make up only 3 percent of the total land surface.

The People

The population of Kazakhstan as of the 1989 census was 16,538,000; it since has grown. Although Kazakhs are designated as the "core" people of the republic, they are a minority in their own country. Russians outnumber them slightly. The birthrate among Kazakh speakers is higher than that among Russians, however, so the Kazakh percentage of the population is growing. Ukrainians and nearly a hundred nationalities make up the other 17 percent, among them Germans, Tatars, Uzbeks, Belarusians, Uighurs, Dungans

Kazakhstan's capital of Alma–Ata as seen from Mt. Kok Tyube

Courtesy: NOVOSTI

Kazakhstan

The dam in the Maly Almaatinsky Gorge at Medeo

and Koreans. The Kazakh people speak a Turkic language, but are Mongol in physical appearance. They are mainly Moslem.

History

The first reference to Kazakhs living in Central Asia is found in a Russian source dated 1534. Subsequently, the Russians referred to these people as Kaisak–Kirgiz or simply Kirgiz. Undoubtedly, the reason for this is that the Russian word *Kazaky* means Cossacks and it describes Russian peasants living on the frontier. It appears, in fact, that modern Kazakh are descendants of the old Kipchak tribes, which were part of the East–Central Asian "Golden Horde."

In the 15th century, there was a Kazakh Empire that controlled the steppe land to the east of the Caspian Sea and north of the Aral Sea stretching as far east as the western approaches of the Altai Mountains. This empire lasted until the beginning of the 18th century, but then was weakened by attacks from a revived Oyrat Empire to the east. The Kazakhs were at this time organized into three principalities, the "Little Horde," "Middle Horde" and Great Horde.

When the Russians began their advance into this area in the 18th century,

the Kazakhs decided to accept Russian protection against their enemies to the east. The "Little Horde" accepted Russian protection in 1731, followed by the Middle Horde in 1740 and the Great Horde in 1742.

The Kazakhs began to fear Russian control, however, and this led to a series of uprisings toward the end of the 18th century. As a result, Russia began to suppress the autonomy of the Kazakh Khans. The Khanate of the "Middle Horde" was suppressed in 1822, the "Little Horde" in 1824; and the "Great Horde" in 1848. In 1854, the Russians founded the fortress of Verna, which eventually became the modern capital of Alma–Ata. The area was administratively divided into four areas. In the latter part of the 19th century, there were large–scale settlements of Russian peasants established in the northern part of the territory.

A small Kazakh nationalist movement came into existence at the beginning of the 20th century, and a number of Kazakh deputies were elected to the first and second legislatures. The first Kazakh newspaper began publication in 1910. In 1916, a revolt broke out when the Russian Government ordered the mobilization of all persons between the age of 19 and 43. It was put down harshly.

After the Bolshevik seizure of power in November 1917 in Moscow, Kazakh nationalists demanded full autonomy for Kazakhstan. A Kazakh nationalist government was formed, but was suppressed in 1919–20 when the Red Army occupied the area. The Bolsheviks did sponsor creation of the Kirgiz Autonomous Soviet Socialist Republic in August 1920, however. In 1925, the name was changed to Kazakh. but in 1929, the capital was established at Alma–Ata. Kazakhstan became a Soviet Socialist Republic in December 1936.

The *Kazakh Communist Party* was established in 1937 and during World War II, Zhumabay Shayakhmetov became its first head. He was replaced in 1954 by P. K. Ponomarenko, a Slav, because of insufficient support for the Moscow-sponsored newly–launched Virgin Lands campaign. Ponomarenko was later replaced by Leonid Brezhnev, who remained first secretary of the *Kazakh Communist Party* until 1956. After he became General Secretary, Brezhnev appointed another Kazakh party hack, Dinmukhamed Kunaev, as first secretary of the *Kazakh Communist Party*. He held that position until December 1986, when he was removed by Gorbachëv and replaced by another Slav, Gennady Kolbin.

When word reached Alma–Ata that Kunaev had been dismissed and was being replaced by an ethnic Russian, violent rioting broke out and several persons were killed. Gorbachëv, recognizing that he had to be more sensitive to nationalist sentiments, later reassigned Kolbin and replaced him with another Kazakh.

When hardliners launched their *coup* against USSR President Gorbachëv on August 19, 1991, President Nursultan Nazarbayev condemned the action and called for Gorbachëv's return. After failure of the *coup*, Nazarbayev severed all ties with the *Kazakh Communist Party*, then banned all political activity in government, the courts and police. The *Kazakh Communist Party* disbanded, then subsequently reconstituted itself as a Socialist Party. The Socialists held their first congress at Alma–Ata in December 1991. They do not appear to have much influence, however.

Nazarbayev strongly supported some form of continued union of the republics and, almost alone among the republic leaders, he did not press for a declaration of independence until it became clear that the old union was dead. This made sense from the point of view of Kazakhstan, for it is a large republic with a relatively small population and its economy is heavily tied to Russia. Most people still live in the countryside and support themselves from the land. The only industry is mineral extraction, most of which is shipped to other republics for further processing. In addition, a significant percentage of the population has ethnic ties to Russia or one of the other republics.

Nazarbayev has been active in inter–republic relations. In September 1991, he joined Boris Yeltsin in a mediation effort between Azerbaijan and Armenia. The mediation effort produced an agreement, but it was never fully implemented. After the Presidents of Russia, Ukraine and Belarus agreed to formation of the Commonwealth of Independent States (CIS) on December 8, Nazarbayev was active in getting other republics to join and actually hosted the Alma–Ata meeting where the general agreement was signed.

In early May, President Nazarbayev, who had earlier said that he wanted Kazakhstan to become nuclear–free, asked for security guarantees from the U.S., Russia, and China in return for agreeing to give up Kazakhstan's nuclear weapons. He was asking for the pledge, he said, because some Chinese textbooks showed parts of Kazakhstan as being part of China. There was also other evidence to show that at least some Kazakh officials were having second thoughts about the merits of going nuclear–free. As one of Nazarbayev's advisers pointed out, Kazakhstan would not be receiving the attentions of Secretary of State Baker and

high–ranking officials of other countries, if it didn't have nuclear weapons. Nazarbayev paid an official visit to Washington later in May, however, and here he reversed himself once again and agreed to the withdrawal of nuclear weapons from Kazakhstan within seven years. Kazakhstan has since signed both the START–1 agreement and the Non–Proliferation Treaty.

The pace of change, fairly rapid just after Kazakhstan received its independence in 1991, has slowed in recent months. Foreign investment is still being encouraged, but there has been some retrenchment on market–oriented economic changes introduced in 1991 and early 1992. In addition, terms like "pluralism" and "moving toward democracy" are not heard much any more. Nazarbayev is now being characterized as an "authoritarian modernizer" who is putting economic development before political liberalism. In fact, Nazarbayev is an ex–communist who is actually rather pragmatic. He sees the opposition generated by Yeltsin's economic reforms in Russia and he doesn't want that to happen in Kazakhstan.

Nazarbayev is aware of growing nationalist currents within the country. He is sensitive to those feelings, but he is also aware that there are approximately as many Russian speakers in the country as there are Kazakh speakers. Moves in this area have accordingly been moderate. For example, the amount of instruction in the Kazakh language has been increased in the schools, but Russian is still the medium of instruction. Kazakhstan's new constitution, which recently went into effect, designates Kazakh as the national language, but Russian is described as the language of inter–ethnic communication. The constitution also requires the President to have a good command of the Kazakh language, but does not stipulate that he be an ethnic Kazakh.

Nature of the Regime

Kazakhstan has a presidential–parliamentary system modeled rather closely on that of Russia. A popularly elected, executive presidency was created after the failure of the *coup* against Gorbachëv. Nazarbayev ran unopposed for the position. One of the strange things in Kazakhstan is the almost total lack of any political opposition to Nazarbayev. No-

President Nursultan Nazarbayev of Kazakhstan

Kazakhstan

Sazgen, **the folk music quintet, shown at the Old Instruments Museum in Alma–Ata**

Courtesy: NOVOSTI

body has challenged him at the executive level and the locals have remained compliant to his wishes. Yet Nazarbayev has not acted in a dictatorial manner and appears to favor the development of political pluralism. The ethnic split in the republic may be part of the explanation. Nazarbayev is one of the few individuals who has managed to win significant support from both Kazakhs and Russians.

Culture

It is difficult to identify a separate culture for Kazakhstan. Kazakhs are basically a rural people who, until recently, played very little public role. Nearly all are Moslems, but there never has been a major center such as can be found in the Central Asian republics to the south, such as Tashkent, Samarkand, or Bukhara. Thus it affects the lives of the people, but in an easy–going way. There is a specific Kazakh style of clothing or interior decoration but there are no specifically Kazakh foods. Women still tend to wear a long, wide dress with a stand–up collar and bloomers gathered at the ankle, particularly in the countryside. Elderly men wear wide, white shirts, wide trousers and woolen or cotton robes. Young people of both sexes tend to wear European clothes.

Kazakh homes exhibit specific Kazakh

designs in stucco work and wall facings, while floors are covered with carpets.

There is a small national literature as well, most of it recent in origin. Abay Ibragim Kunanbayev, a 19th century humanist and poet, is usually considered to be the father of Kazakh written literature. Early twentieth century writers include Aqmet Baytursinuli, an author and newspaper editor, and Jambil Jabayev, a folk poet. The best known of the Kazakh literary figures of the Soviet period is Mukhtar Auezov, a playwright and novelist. His long novel, *Abay,* deals with Kazakh steppe life in the 19th century. It has been translated into English.

The population of the northern part of the republic is mostly Russian or Ukrainian and the culture here doesn't differ significantly from Russian areas across the border. The presence of significant numbers of Koreans and "Volga" Germans does introduce a greater element of cultural diversity, but these are mostly rural peoples who practice mainly a village culture.

Alma–Ata is the largest city and the center for most higher education. The Kazakh S. M. Kirov State University is located here, as is the Abay Teachers College. Alma–Ata also has polytechnical, agricultural and veterinary institutes. Karaganda has a medical institute and a

teachers training college. Other institutes of higher learning are also found in regional centers.

There is a Kazakh Academy of Sciences, founded in 1945. This has particularly encouraged scholarship in ethnographic studies of the Kazakh language and the history of Kazakh literature. It also finances industrial and agricultural research.

Economy

A majority of the residents of the republic support themselves from agriculture or stock raising. The northern part of Kazakhstan is a major grain growing area, with supplemental crops like fruits, vegetables, grapes, sugar beets and potatoes grown. Stock raising is concentrated in the dryer area to the south of the grain belt, in the area of the grassy steppe. Cotton, tobacco, grapes, and mustard are grown in the Syr–Darya and Ili River Valleys.

Kazakhstan had already instituted a number of reforms in agriculture during the Gorbachëv era which began to break down the old system of command control. For example, a 1987 law abolished all restrictions on the number of animals that a farmer could have. This led to an increase of about 2.5 million in the sheep and goat population and about a million additional cattle. Meat sales in the cooperative sector also quadrupled in that time. In addition, 890,000 families received plots of land in 1991 and 46,000 private houses were constructed with state assistance.

In February 1992, Nazarbayev signed a decree on privatizing the property of enterprises in the agro–industrial complex, apparently intending to end the collective and state farm system. At the time, Nazarbayev commented that Kazakhstan did not need loss–making farms. "Private farming works because it is private," he was quoted as saying. There was bitter resistance to this approach at the local level, however, and it appears that most agricultural land is still controlled by collective and state farms. While President Nazarbayev continues to favor a conversion to private farming, he recognizes that it will only work if it is done on a voluntary basis.

Kazakh industry is mainly of the extractive variety. Most industry is located in the northeastern part of the republic, in and around the cities of Karaganda, Zelinograd and Semipalatinsk. It has large deposits of coal and iron ore. It also produces lead, zinc, copper, chromite, nickel, molybdenum, tin, antimony, cadmium, bauxite, gold, silver, phosphates, and oil. In addition to the processing of ferrous and nonferrous metals, it has chemical, machine–building, cement, and textile industries. Light industries associated with agriculture include food processing and leather.

In September 1991, the government approved a program for the "first stage of destatization and privatization" of state property. The program, which included a coupon mechanism, proposed privatization in trade, public catering, construction, motor transport, agriculture, consumer services and small enterprises. Medium and large enterprises were to be converted to joint–stock companies, collective enterprises or partnerships. The program has apparently not been implemented, however. In a speech to the legislature in January 1993, Nazarbayev spoke of mistakes associated with free–market reform in Russia and Kazakhstan and declared that a significant decree of state control and regulation would be necessary in the future. He indicated that major enterprises would be run along commercial principles, but most would remain in state hands. Privatization would be gradual. As a spokesman for Nazarbayev said, "we can't get ahead of Russia; we're too closely linked to the Russian economy."

One colonial leftover that the Kazakhs are rather ambivalent about is the massive space complex at Baikonur Cosmodrone. There is no question but that the space program has given tremendous stimulus to the advancement of hi–tech education, but it has been almost exclusively Russians, not ethnic Kazakhs, that have benefited from the program. Another problem is that the complex continues to be run by Russia. The Government of Kazakhstan, which favors close cooperation with Russia, has made it clear that it does not want the complex closed down, but it would like ethnic Kazakhs to be able to benefit more from its presence.

Kazakhstan is one of the few ex–Soviet republics to have attracted significant interest among foreign investors since independence. The reason for this is that Kazakhstan has some of the largest unexplored oil, gas and mineral deposits on earth. Most of the investment interest thus far has been in oil. In April 1993, the Chevron Corporation and the Government of Kazakhstan officially established a 40–year, $20 billion joint venture to develop the Tengiz and Korolev oil fields on the northeastern coast of the Caspian Sea. The joint venture expects to invest more than $1.5 billion over the next 5–7 years to develop the oil field. It will also have to construct a pipeline in order to move the oil to a port for export.

The Future

Kazakhstan is a relatively poor republic without a particularly developed infrastructure. It is heavily dependent on Russia, particularly, for manufactured goods. On the other hand, the majority of the people live on the land and so are able to feed themselves. They also have what appears to be an astute political leadership in President Nazerbayev. Kazakhstan, like the other ex–Soviet republics, can look forward to several years of painful transition, but that transition should be easier than it is likely to be in several of the other republics.

Drying astrakhan pelts of the new–born Persian lambs, used like fur for garments

Courtesy: NOVOSTI

151

The Republic of Kyrgyzstan (Formerly Kirghizia; roughly pronounced *Keer–zhee–stan*).

President Akayev at dinner with his wife and children

Area: 76,640 sq. mi. (198,500 sq. km., slightly smaller than Nebraska).

Population: 4.3 million (estimated).

Capital City: Bishtek (formerly Frunze, named for an early Soviet army commander; original name restored in 1991).

Climate: Hot, dry valleys; cold, high deserts.

Neighboring States: Kazakhstan (north), Uzbekistan (west), Tajikistan (west, southwest), China (southeast).

Languages: Kyrgyz, Russian.

Ethnic Composition: Kyrgyz (52%), Russian (22%), Uzbek (12%), others (14%).

Principal Religion: Islam. About 25% of the people are nominally Orthodox Christian.

Chief Commercial Products: Livestock, cotton and cotton oil, vegetables, sugar beets, refined sugar, hides, flour mining enterprises, metals, textiles.

Currency: Ruble.

Recent Political Status: Autonomous Republic within the USSR (1926), Constituent Republic of the USSR (1936–1991).

Chief of State: Askar Akayev, President.

The Land

The Republic of Kyrgyzstan is the independent successor state to the Kirghiz Soviet Socialist Republic. Situated on a western spur of the Tien Shan Mountains, it is a mountainous country surrounded by more mountains; most of its borders run along mountain crests. Thus it is separated from Tajikistan by the Turkistan and Zaalay Ranges. The Kokshaal–Tau Range, a part of the Tien Shan, forms the border with the People's Republic of China.

The exception is in the southwest, where the border dips down to cross the upper reaches of the Fergana River Valley. Apart from the Fergana Valley, the only lowland areas are the downstream parts of the Chu and Talas River Valleys along the northern border. The capital, Bishtek, is located in the Chu River Valley. These lowland areas make up about 15 percent of the total surface of the republic.

Kyrgyzstan's most unusual geographical feature is Lake Issyk–Kul, a high mountain lake found in the eastern part of the country. Set in a massive hollow much like the Fergana Valley in western Kyrgyzstan, it is surrounded by mountains with a high, alpine plateau to the west. A deep clear lake, it is rich in fish and supports fishing communities around its edges.

The People

The population of Kyrgyzstan is very mixed, with Kyrgyz speakers constituting only 52% of the population. Russians, the largest minority, are about 22% of the population. Other minorities found in the republic include Uzbeks (12%), Ukrainians (3%), Tatars (2%), Chinese Moslems, Germans, and Dungans. The Kyrgyz language belongs to the Turkic group of languages.

History

The Kyrgyz have lived in the Tien Shan Mountains at least since the 16th century and some Soviet ethnographers postulate that they arrived as early as the 12th century. Since they had no written language until recently and continued to live as a nomadic people until modern times, archaeological evidence provides most of what we know of them.

They came under the nominal control of the Kokand Khanate until about 1850, when this area became a major region of Russian colonization. Since the Kyrgyz, as nomads, had no permanent claims on

152

the land, the Russian colonists moved in and took most of the best land, leading to an uprising in 1916, which was put down with great force.

After the Russian Revolution, this area became a part of Soviet Turkistan. In 1921, it then became part of the Turkistan Autonomous SSR of the Russian SFSR. In 1924, it was separated from the Turkistan ASSR and given the status of an autonomous *oblast* (area) of the Russian SFSR. Two years later, it became the Kirgiz Autonomous SSR of the Russian SFSR. It was not until December 1936 that it became a constituent republic of the USSR as the Kirgiz Soviet Socialist Republic.

Much changed during the Soviet years. The nomadic life of the people ended when they were settled on collective and state farms. Some mechanization was also introduced in the countryside, and irrigation projects increased cultivated land in the lowlands. The exploitation of minerals found in the mountains has increased the number of jobs in industry and drawn more of the Kyrgyz people into cities and modern life. Most have preferred to remain in stock raising or farming, however, so the overwhelming majority of people in industry and in the urban areas are non–Kyrgyz.

Gorbachëv's *perestroika* left the republic untouched until 1990, when ethnic riots broke out in the Fergana Valley along the border with Uzbekistan. The riots left 200 people dead and damaged the reputation of Absamat Masaliev, the *Kyrgyz Communist Party* leader. Masaliev tried to repair the damage by calling on the republic's Supreme Soviet to create the office of President, to be elected by that body.

Masaliev's political opposition in the Supreme Soviet organized themselves into a new party, called *Democratic Kyrgyzstan*, and elected Askar Akayev instead. Akayev, who is a physicist by training, worked for twenty years in St. Petersburg before returning to Kyrgyzstan.

In August 1991, there was an organized attempt to depose President Akayev as part of the attempted *coup* against Gorbachëv. The local military commander threatened to send tanks into the street and the local KGB chief attempted to arrest Akayev. The president's loyal troops surrounded the *Communist Party* headquarters and then had the KGB chief arrested. He subsequently banned the *Communist Party* from government offices. When the *coup* failed, the *Kyrgyz Communist Party* dissolved itself. After his own return to power, Gorbachëv asked Akayev to come to Moscow to become his vice president. He turned it down, saying that he wanted to stay in Kyrgyzstan.

As part of the further democratization of the country, the Kyrgyz Supreme Soviet modified the constitution to make the presidency an elective office and called for new elections on October 12. Akayev's position was so strong by that time that no candidate bothered to oppose him. His reputation as a genuine democrat has caused some problems with neighboring states, all of which are still ruled by ex–communists. The partial exception is Kazakhstan, whose President, Nursultan Nazarbayev, although an ex–communist, has gained a reputation for pragmatism. The U.S. Government showed its own support for Akayev when the first U.S. Embassy in Central Asia was opened in Bishtek on February 1, 1992.

Nature of the Regime

Kyrgyzstan has a presidential–parliamentary form of government with the president responsible for general policy and a prime minister, responsible to the Supreme Soviet, handling implementation of policy. The president is advised by a State Council, while the prime minister presides over his cabinet.

The republic legally has a multiparty system. Though *Democratic Kyrgyzstan*, the party that supports the president, it has become the dominant political force since the *Kyrgyz Communist Party* dissolved itself in 1991.

Culture

Most Kyrgyz are Moslems, and continue to live a largely traditional life within the context of changes forced on them during the Soviet period. An oral tradition among the people has kept alive epic cycles and lyric poetry. This has saved much that would otherwise have been lost, for the written language has been in three different forms in the twentieth century. The first written language used the Arabic script, but that was abandoned after World War I and the Roman script was introduced. In 1940, Stalin forced all of the Central Asian republics to adopt the Cyrillic alphabet. Now it is likely that they will switch back to the Roman script.

Kyrgyzstan has produced two writers of note in modern times, the playwright and novelist Chingiz Aytmatov and the playwright Kaltay Muhamedjanov. Aytmatov is the author of *Tales of the Mountains and Steppes*, which has been translated into English. It won the Lenin Prize in 1963. The two collaborated on the play *The Ascent of Mt. Fuji*, which has also been translated into English and was performed on stage in Washington, D.C. in 1973. Its theme is the moral compromises that people had to make under Stalin.

Newspapers and magazines are published in both Russian and Kyrgyz and radio and television broadcasts are made in both languages. National broadcasts are also received from Moscow by way of relay lines. The Russian cultural influence is, therefore, very strong. The State University of Kyrgyzstan is located in Bishtek; in December 1991, it opened a business school, support for which came partly from IBM, which donated a roomful of personal computers.

Economy

The Kyrgyz were once mainly nomads who pastured their herds in summer on the alpine–like slopes of the mountains where 30–40 inches of rainfall annually provide lush meadows for grazing. During the Soviet period, they were settled into villages and made part of collective or state farms. Livestock includes sheep, goats, cattle and horses. Mare's milk is the source for *koumiss*, the local fermented drink. Pigs, bees and rabbits are also raised in the mountains. Agriculture, practiced mainly in the lowland areas, is dependent on irrigation, since these areas receive an average of 7 inches of rainfall a year. The main crops include sugar beets, cotton, tobacco, opium poppies and cereal grains. Approximately two–thirds of the population is still engaged in agriculture or stock raising.

The number of people involved in industry has grown greatly in recent years. Extractive industries are important and Kyrgyzstan is a major source of antimony and mercury ores. Lead and zinc are also mined. It also has large coal reserves, which have begun to be exploited. Hydroelectric power provides about half the energy needs of the republic. It also produces petroleum and natural gas. Food processing and light industry have been developed, and the republic also manufactures machinery and instruments.

Kyrgyzstan is still a poor land, however, with a standard of living that is perhaps 65% of the former Soviet average. The reporter Georgie Anne Geyer, who visited the capital, Bishtek, in February 1992 to be present at the opening of the first U.S. Embassy in Central Asia, described it as "horrendously poor." "This isn't the end of the world, but you can see it from here," quip westerners, commenting on its isolation. The average monthly wage is still only 150 rubles, understandable in a poor, agricultural society, but still too low to permit Kyrgyzians to afford imports from other republics, let alone the west.

The Future

A large part of the Kyrgyz republic budget has been subsidized from Moscow in the past. Without outside assistance, drastic cuts in spending will be necessary to provide a balanced budget. Whatever economic progress comes is therefore not likely to be fast. The two–thirds of the population that lives on the land is largely self–sufficient, however, so at least they won't starve.

The Republic of Tajikistan

Grandfather shows his newly–fashioned whistles to his grandson and friend

Courtesy: NOVOSTI

Area: 57,250 sq. mi. (143,100 sq. km., slightly smaller than Illinois).

Population: 5.25 million (estimated).

Capital City: Dushambe (Pop. 5.25 million, estimated).

Climate: Continental, with sharp changes depending upon altitude.

Neighboring States: China (east), Pakistan, Afghanistan (south) Uzbekistan (west and north), Kyrgystan (north).

Principal Language: Tajik.

Ethnic Composition: Tajik (62%), Uzbek (23%), Russian (7%), other (8%).

Principal Religion: Islam. Until recently, religious worship was officially discouraged.

Chief Commercial Products: Mining, food processing, textiles, clothing and silk; fruit and livestock. The Ghissar sheep is famous for its meat and Karakul sheep produce wool and glossy, curly lamb pelts. The Republic has tremendous existing and potential hydroelectric resources.

Currency: Ruble.

Recent Political Status: Autonomous Republic within the former USSR (1924) as part of Uzbek S.S.R. Constituent Republic of the former USSR (1929–1991).

Chief of State: Imamali Rakhmonov, Acting President.

The Land

The Republic of Tajikistan is the independent successor state to the Tadzhik Soviet Socialist Republic. It declared its independence in September 1991.

Tajikistan is a small land, which includes the autonomous region of Gorno–Badakhshan. It is located in the extreme southern part of Central Asia.

It is also a mountainous land, with more than half of its territory lying above 10,000 feet. The northern border forms a loop around the western part of the Fergana Valley, running along the top ridges of the Kuramin Range in the north before turning south, crossing the valley, and then tracing its way westward along the foothills of the Altai Range. Here the western and eastern borders almost meet before turning south. The western border continues south, turning somewhat westward, while the eastern border bends sharply eastward and runs along the southern slopes of the Altai Range, continuing until it reaches the China border.

The center of the republic is dominated by the Turkistan Range and the slightly lower Zevavshan and Gissar Ranges. In the east are the Pamirs, which contain the highest peaks found anywhere in Central Asia. In the south, a series of transverse ridges and river valleys slope down to the Pyandzh River in Afghanistan.

Valleys make up about ten percent of the land of the republic. In addition to the western part of the Fergana Valley, there are the smaller Gissar, Vakhsh, Yavansu, Obikiik, Lower Kafirnigan and Pyandzh valleys in the south. There are also a number of small lakes in the eastern part of the country, in the Pamir Mountains. There is a dense river network. These include the stretch of the Syr–Darya that flows through the western part of the Fergana Valley and the upper reaches of the Amu Darya. Most rivers flow northward into Central Asia.

Tajikistan has two climatic zones. The valleys are subtropical, with average July temperatures in the eighties and January temperatures hovering around freezing. Annual rainfall in the valleys is only 6–10 inches, so agriculture depends entirely on irrigation. In the highlands, average January temperatures are 0° F. or below. The mountains get very little precipitation in the summer, but the high ranges get 30–60 inches in the form of snow in the winter. In the highest ranges, there are also huge glaciers that partially melt in the summer, only to be replenished in the winter. The spring and summer run-off from the mountains provides water for irrigation on the lower slopes and in the valleys.

The People

Tajikistan's population as of the 1989 census was 5,112,000. Uzbekis are found mainly in the northwestern part of the republic. Other minorities include Russians (7%), found mainly in urban areas, Ukrainians, Tatars, Germans, Kyrgyz, and Jews.

Tajik belongs to the southwest group of Iranian languages, which set the Tajiks off from the rest of their Central Asian neighbors. It is also spoken in the Hindu Kush area of northeast Afghanistan, where it is called Farsi. Because of the nature of the terrain, Tajiks actually speak a variety of dialects, depending on which part of Tajikistan they live in. The two most important sub-groups are Pamir Tajik, which also includes Bartang, the language spoken in the Gorno–Badakhshan Autonomous Region, and Yaghnabi, the modern version of the language spoken in the ancient Kingdom of Sogdiana.

History

The Tajiks are the descendants of Iranian–speaking people who entered Central Asia as early as 2,000 B.C. They were incorporated into the Persian Empire and the subsequent Empire of Alexander the Great. The ancient kingdom of Sogdiana, conquered by the Arabs in the eighth century, was Tajik–speaking. In the tenth century, an invasion of Turkic–speaking peoples overran Central Asia. Many Tajiks were assimilated at this time, with Tajik culture surviving mainly in the mountains.

The Tajiks were later brought under the control of the Emirate of Bukhara. In the eighteenth century, Afghanistan extended its control over the area. The Russian Empire gained control over this area in the 1860s. Bukhara became a Russian protectorate in 1868.

After the Russian Revolution, part of the area occupied by the Tajik people was incorporated into the Turkistan Autonomous Soviet Socialist Republic, established in April 1918. When the Red Army took over Bukhara in 1920, it also claimed most of the territory of modern Tajikistan. The Red Army captured Dushanbe early in 1921. The Basmachi revolt, which began in 1922 and lasted to the summer of 1923, was an attempt to throw off communist control, but it was ultimately unsuccessful. In 1924, the communist authorities decided to divide up Central Asia along ethnic lines. This led to the creation of the Tadzhik Autonomous Soviet Socialist Republic, at the time made part of the Uzbek SSR. In December 1929, the Tadzhik Autonomous SSR was separated from the Uzbek SSR and made a constituent republic in its own right.

Mountainous and isolated and divided into different tribes that had a long history of rivalry, the Tadzhik SSR was run throughout most of the Soviet period by officials sent out by Moscow. Even as late as 1990, Tajiks were a minority in the *Tajik Communist Party*. Gorbachëv's programs of *glasnost* and *perestroika* changed that. By 1988, Tajik officials had recognized the opportunity offered by the Gorbachëv reform program and had begun to implement Tajik solutions to local problems. This led the Tajik Supreme Soviet to assert Tajikistan sovereignty in August 1990.

After the attempted *coup* against Gorbachëv collapsed in August 1991, Kakhar Makhkamov, who had supported the *coup*, resigned as party leader and Chairman of the Supreme Soviet. He was replaced by Kadriddin Aslonov. Upon taking office, Aslonov resigned his membership on the Politburo of the *Tajik Communist Party* and issued a decree banning the *Communist Party of the Soviet Union* on Tajik territory.

This irritated a majority of the members of the Tajik Supreme Soviet, 95 percent of whom were communists. Accusing him of "unconstitutional actions," they ousted him as Chairman of the Supreme Soviet. In his stead, they elected Rakhmon Nabiyev, who had been first secretary of the *Tajik Communist Party* before Makhkamov. At about this time also, the Dushanbe party leader gave permission for a statue of Lenin to be torn down. He, too, was ousted and a state of emergency was declared in Dushanbe. In a related development, a hastily called congress of the *Tajik Communist Party* "dissolved" the party and established a new *Socialist Party* in its stead.

This combined set of developments appeared to political opponents to prove that the communists were determined to retain power. They organized a series of protest rallies in Dushanbe where they demanded that the state of emergency be lifted, the Supreme Soviet be dissolved and new elections called, and that Nabiyev resign as Chairman of the Supreme Soviet.

On September 30, after the rallies had continued for several days, the Supreme Soviet voted to lift the state of emergency in Dushanbe. Two days later, the Supreme Soviet suspended the activities of the officially dissolved *Tajik Communist Party* and its successor, the *Socialist Party* "until the party's participation in the *coup* attempt is estimated." Finally, Nabiyev submitted his resignation as Supreme Soviet Chairman on October 6. Akbarsho Iskandarov took over as acting chairman.

Spectators watch horses and riders at a popular equestrian event   Courtesy: NOVOSTI

Tajikistan

Famous woodcarver Sirodzhitdin Nuritdinov in his studio

The opposition had won every one of their points.

In September, the Supreme Soviet had created a new popularly elected presidency. That election had been set for October 27. The election date was postponed until November 24. As the presidential contest began, there were ten candidates, including Rakhman Nabiyev. Three later withdrew. There were also a number of political parties active, some registered and some not. Registered parties included the *Democratic Party of Tajikistan* and the *Popular Movement Rastokhez (Revival)*. The *Islamic Revival Party* was still in limbo at this point.

The government first banned all religious–oriented parties, then lifted the ban on October 22. At this point, a number of organizations had nominated Akbar Turadzhonzoda, head of the Spiritual Administration of Moslems of Tajikistan, for president. Turadzhonzoda's subsequent statement was therefore significant. "I support a secular parliamentary state with a free economy. Religion should be separated from the state so the sins of society cannot be attributed to Islam, which is what happened to the

Communist Party." Turadzhonzoda did not stand as a candidate for the presidency.

When the election was finally held on November 24, Rakhman Nabiyev won with 56.9% of the vote. His chief opponent, Davlat Khudonazarov, who had been supported by the united opposition, won 30.7 percent of the vote.

Nabiyev's victory in the elections did not put an end to the struggle, however. In the early spring, the Islamic–led opposition, organized as the *Union of Popular Forces*, launched a campaign demanding multi–party elections and more freedom of religion, though their real purpose was to drive Nabiyev from office. Responding to the threat, the Tajik parliament attempted to strengthen Nabiyev's hand by giving him the power to rule by decree. As demonstrations continued, Nabiyev declared a state of emergency. Instead of calming the situation, this brought calls for Nabiyev's resignation. In early May, opposition forces seized control of Dushambe, the capital, and declared the creation of a revolutionary council. In a compromise, Nabiyev then lifted the state of emergency and agreed to form a

"government of national reconciliation." In the new government, eight seats were assigned to an opposition coalition consisting of democrats and moderate Islamics, plus the *Islamic Revival Party*, whose program calls for the creation of an Islamic state.

Nabiyev's compromise calmed the situation briefly, but there was no reconciliation. Not only did the two disparate groupings find it difficult to work with each other; Nabiyev also found himself under attack from ex–communist allies in the northern part of the country who accused him of ceding too much power to the opposition. In addition, the government began to lose control of the country as ex–communists took control of local governments in the north and Islamics took control of local governments in the south and east. Then fighting broke out between regions, eventually resulting in about one thousand deaths.

To restore order, Nabiyev negotiated an agreement with the Commonwealth of Independent States for the dispatch of peacekeeping troops to the country. The opposition reacted by declaring an open rebellion and seizing control of Duchambe. Nabiyev, taken prisoner by demonstrators as he fled to the Dushambe airport, was forced at gunpoint to resign as President. The Islamic–democratic coalition then declared itself to be the new government and named Akbarsho Iskandarov as Acting President.

The Islamic–democratic coalition was unable to consolidate its control over the country, however. The northern, and most developed, part of the country was controlled by ex–communists associated with Nabiyev and they would have nothing to do with the new government. Meanwhile the situation in Dushambe remained so unstable that the new government was unable to convene a new session of the parliament. This government lasted two months and then resigned on November 12, turning power over to an interim council. Meanwhile the parliament, meeting in the northern town of Khojand, accepted President Nabiyev's voluntary resignation, then elected Imamali Rakhmonov, an ex–communist, as Chairman of the legislature. On December 10, forces loyal to the former president took control of Dushambe and at this time Rakhmonov was designated Acting President. Islamics fled to their strongholds in the mountains of eastern Tajikistan, pursued by elements of the Tajik army. Other Islamics sought refuge across the border into Afghanistan.

Thus far, the government, which does not yet control eastern Tajikistan, remains determined to stamp out opposition. Moderate Islamics, now ready to come to terms with the government, have found their overtures rebuffed.

Nature of the Regime

Most of the people in power were formerly leaders in the now disbanded *Tajik Communist Party*. Before the series of *coups* and counter–*coups* of 1992, Tajikistan appeared to be evolving toward an institutionalized pluralism. Some experts speculated that this was because the *Tajik Communist Party* had always had its organized political factions, based on differences between regional clans, and this was now coming out in the open. That trend suffered a severe setback in 1992 as first one side, then the other, resorted to force to get its way. Now the coalition of democrats and Islamics that held power briefly in 1992 has shattered and many of its members have fled into hiding, either in the mountains to the east or in Afghanistan.

There appears to be no place for political pluralism at the moment. Yet it is likely that this, too, is a temporary situation. Because the different parts of the country are so disparate, regional loyalties will continue to be important. If the government wants to establish real control over the eastern part of the country,

it will have to allow that region to be represented at the national level.

Because the current government seized power by force, it is not yet clear whether they intend to honor the constitution. On the other hand, since most of those now in power are political associates of those who wrote the constitution, it is probably in their interest to accept it as valid. The constitution designates the government as a presidential–parliamentary system. The president acts as spokesman for the nation and establishes general policy. He appoints a prime minister who must be confirmed by the legislature. The prime minister and his cabinet are responsible for the day–to–day operation of government. The Supreme Soviet represents the sovereignty of the nation. It is responsible for all legislation. It also has final authority over the budget. Most top government officials must also be confirmed in office by the Supreme Soviet.

Culture

Traditional Tajik festivals have always featured songs and dances and there is also a long tradition of theatrical and circus performances. Tajik circuses specialize in tightrope walkers, conjurers, singers and musicians. There is also a vigorous folk literature which is still being collected.

The Tajik National Theater was founded in 1929. It has nine separate theaters, performing operas, ballet, musical comedy and puppetry. There is also a Tajik film studio which makes both feature films and documentaries. Dushanbe has had its own television center since 1960.

Two pre–Soviet Tajik cultural figures are Abdalrauf Fitrat, author of *Last Judgment*, and Sadriddin Ayni, famous for two novels, *Slaves* and *Dokhunda*. His autobiography is titled *Bukhara*. Tajik writers of the Soviet period include the poets Abu ol–Qasem Lahuti and Mirzo Tursunzade. Tursunzade won the Lenin Prize in 1960 for his poem *The Voice of Asia*.

The Tajik State University, located in Dushanbe, is the largest of ten institutes of higher education. There are also 41 technical colleges. A Tajik Academy of Sciences was established in 1951. It now has sixteen institutions and oversees 61 research institutions located in various parts of the republic. The Pamir research station, located in the Pamir Mountains in the eastern part of the country, is a major regional meteorological observatory.

Most Tajiks are Sunni Moslems of the Hanafi school, although there are some Shiite communities among the Mountain Tajiks. Throughout the Soviet era, Islam was a barely tolerated religion and there were few mosques. But Islam is as much a way of life and a culture as it is a belief, so it survived in the villages in spite of

official hostility. There has been a clear revival of Islam since about 1989, with many mosques being built, but it does not appear to have a great political significance.

Economy

Tajikistan is primarily an agricultural economy and its most significant crop is long–staple cotton. Cattle raising (including sheep and goats) is also important, as is the growing of fruits, grain and vegetables. Fruits grown include apricots, pears, apples, plums, quinces, cherries, pomegranates and figs. Grapes and almonds are other major crops.

Tajikistan's light industry mainly involves processing agricultural products, such as cotton and silk processing, fruit canning and wine making. Related industries include knitted goods, shoes, leather working and carpet making. Light industry manufacturing plants tend to be small.

Its larger industry is either ore extraction or non–ferrous metallurgy. Tajikistan is rich in mineral deposits. It mines coal, iron, lead, zinc, antimony, mercury, gold, tin, and tungsten. Its mountains are the source of a number of non–metals, including salt, carbonates, fluorite, arsenic, quartz sand, asbestos and precious and semiprecious stones. Petroleum and natural gas have also been discovered and are beginning to be exploited, though it still imports natural gas from Afghanistan by means of a pipeline constructed in 1974. There are a number of large hydroelectric stations plus a number of thermal electric stations. Tajikistan exports some its electricity to other republics.

Gold is mined at two sites in the northern part of the republic. Current production is fairly small, only 3.79 tons in 1991. A major new gold combine is currently under construction, however, and gold production is expected to double after it becomes operational.

Tajikistan manufactures a number of engineering or metalworking products, including looms, power transformers, cables, and agricultural and household equipment. There is also a nitrogen fertilizer plant, built in 1967. Most workers in industry are non–Tajiks.

The Future

Tajikistan has the lowest per capita income of all the former Soviet republics. Most Tajiks still work in agriculture, however, so they are able to grow a considerable part of their own food. The government is committed to the development of a market economy, but this will be a slow process. Privatization is another eventual goal, but it will take even longer. In the optimistic scenario, living standards will drop over the next couple years, then stabilize.

The Republic of Turkmenistan

Inside a typical Turkmen home in Ashkabad

Area: 186,400 sq. mi. (488,100. sq. km., as large as California and half of Oregon).

Population: 3.6 million (estimated).

Capital City: Ashkabad (Pop. 400,000, estimated).

Climate: Hot and dry summers, very cold in winter.

Neighboring States: Kazakhstan (northwest), Uzbekistan (north, northeast), Iran, Afghanistan (south).

Language: Turkmen.

Ethnic Composition: Turkmen (68%), Russian (13%), Usbek (9%) Kazakh (3%) others (7%).

Principal Religion: Islam. Until recently, religious worship was officially discouraged.

Chief Commercial Products: Oil, natural gas minerals, cotton, jute, fruits (grapes), vegetables, sheep, goats.

Currency: Ruble.

Recent Political Status: A republic was formed in 1924, but in 1925 it was incorporated into the former USSR and remained so until 1991.

Chief of State: Saparmurad Niyazov, President.

The Land

The Republic of Turkmenistan, independent successor state to the Turkmen Soviet Socialist Republic, declared its independence following the collapse of the attempted *coup* against the USSR's Gorbachëv in August 1991. October 27 has been established as the official independence day.

Turkmenistan is a land of deserts and oases. The entire central part of the republic is occupied by the largest of these, the Kara Kum or Black Sand Desert. Topographically, it is also the southern part of the Turan Plain. Only in the south are there foothills and mountains. The Kopet–Dag forms the border with eastern Iran, while northern–reaching spurs of the Pamir–Alay Mountain Ranges form the border with Afghanistan and the

158

southern part of the border with Uzbekistan. On the northeast, the Amu Darya River flows along the border with Uzbekistan. It borders on the Caspian Sea in the west.

Three other rivers, the Tedzhen, Murgab and Atrek, flow north out of the southern mountains and provide water for irrigation. In the 1950s, the Kara Kum Canal was constructed from Kerki on the Amu Darya northwestward across the southern part of the Kara Kum to the city of Merv and Ashkhabad, the capital. It is the world's largest irrigation and shipping canal. Oases exist along the rivers plus in the foothills of the Kopet–Dag Mountains. The rest of the country is desert.

Turkmenistan has a strongly continental climate, extremely hot in summer (average of 95° F.), and bitterly cold in winter (temperatures as low as −27° F.). Precipitation averages 3 inches a year in the northwestern desert and 12 inches in the southern mountains. Except in oases areas, only desert vegetation grows.

The People

Turkmenistan's population as of the 1989 census was 3,534,000. Other minorities include Kazakhs, Tatars, Ukrainians, Armenians, Kara Kalpaks, and Azeris. Russians are found mainly in urban areas. About half the people live in urban areas, the rest in rural settlements and villages. Most Turkmens live in rural settlements and villages. Turkmen is, as its name implies, a Turkic language.

History

The Turkmens were mostly nomads up to the time of the Russian Revolution, though some had settled in oases and taken up agriculture. Divided up into a number of tribes, their main loyalty was to their tribe or clan, with almost no sense of a Turkmen identity. The creation of the Turkmen Soviet Socialist Republic in October 1924 provided a strong impetus toward creation of a Turkmen nation. Turkmens are the most distinctive of the Turkic peoples of Central Asia. Their language is closer to that of the Ottoman Turks and Azerbaijani than it is to the other Turkic peoples of Central Asia. Their origins are disputed, however. They have apparently been Moslems since the tenth century but, because they were desert tribes, the only record of their past is oral. Their main tribes were the Tekes, Ersaris, and Yomut. There were bitter rivalries between the tribes. Thus when the Tekes were fighting a struggle to drive back the Russians in the 1860s and 1870s, the other tribes offered no assistance whatsoever.

In 1869, a Russian military force landed on the eastern shore of the Caspian Sea and founded a settlement at the location of present-day Krasnovodsk. Five years later, the Transcaspian military district was established. This became the Transcaspian oblast in 1881. There was fierce resistance to the Russian advance, but it was broken at the battle of Geok–Tepe in 1881. In 1899, the area was incorporated into the Governor Generalship of Turkistan.

Turkmenistan was the scene of intermittent fighting during the Russian civil war that followed the Bolshevik Revolution. Red Army troops conquered Ashkhabad in July 1919 and Krasnovoksk in February 1920. The Bolsheviks organized the western part of present–day Turkmenistan as a separate oblast of the Turkistan Autonomous SSR. The remaining parts were included in the Bukharan and Khorezmian Soviet Socialist Republics. In 1924, a Turkmen Soviet Socialist Republic was formed, which took in all three Turkmen–inhabited areas. The Turkmen SSR was formally incorporated into the USSR in May 1925.

The life of the Turkmen people changed almost completely during the seventy years of the Soviet period but, through it all, the Turkmen SSR remained one of the most obedient of the constituent republics of the USSR. This began to change somewhat after Gorbachëv became General Secretary in 1985 and launched his program of glasnost and perestroika. In August 1990, the Turkmen Supreme Soviet passed a declaration of sovereignty, though there was still no real challenge to Soviet authority. However, Saparmurad Niyazov, first secretary of the Turkmen Communist Party, had the Supreme Soviet create the office of president and he was elected to that office in October 1990.

The attempted coup against Gorbachëv in August 1991 changed this situation again. Following the collapse of the it President Niyazov issued a declaration of Turkmen independence and called for a referendum on the question, which took place on October 26. When the referendum received a 94% favorable vote, President Niyazov declared October 27 Turkmen independence day.

He confiscated all assets held by the Communist Party of the Soviet Union within the republic, but he remained first secretary of the Turkmen Communist Party. and on November 18-19, the Central Committee of the party held a plenum to consider the future. It called a party congress for December 16 and recommended that the party be renamed the Turkmen Democratic Party. This recommendation was implemented by the party congress when it met in December. President Niyazov was elected chairman. According to the program of the Democratic Party, it is "oriented towards market reforms, sale of the state's property and support of all forms of property."

On November 15, Niyazov, who had appointed his prime minister as the chief of a newly formed Turkmen Railroad, decided to take on direct leadership of the government himself. His assumption of the duties of the prime minister was temporary, according to a government spokesman. There was no question of abolishing the office of prime minister. By January 1992, it appeared that the deputy prime minister, Nazar Suyunov, had become the de facto head of government, much as has also happened in Russia.

In April 1993, President Niyazov signed a decree approving a new alphabet of the Turkmen language based on Latin. This change, to be implemented as of January 1, 1996, will mark the third alphabetic reform for the Turkmen language since the beginning of the century.

Nature of the Regime

Turkmenistan still maintains the unreformed system left over from the Soviet era, except that President Niyazov has increased the powers of the presidency. In February 1992, he submitted the draft of a new constitution to the Supreme Soviet. It calls for a political system comprising a president, a majlis (legislature), a constitutional court, a supreme court, and a government. The president will be head of both state and government. He will serve for five years. The majlis will also be elected for a term of five years.

The draft also proposes creation of an additional entity, referred to as the Halk Maslahaty (People's Supreme Council). The Halk Maslahaty appears to be some kind of supreme consultative body. Its membership will include the president, the majlis deputies, the chairs of the constitutional, supreme and economic courts, the prosecutor–general, members of government, heads of local government, plus representatives from various political parties, public organizations and the clergy.

Culture

Prior to the Russian Revolution, most educated Turkmens were graduates of one of the several seminaries located in Bukhara. Perhaps the most famous of these was Abdulhekim Qulmuhammed–oghli, a writer, editor, researcher and cultural organizer, who eventually joined the Communist Party. He was killed in 1937 at the time of the great Soviet purge. The level of literacy increased greatly during the Soviet era, but the strait–jacket of socialist realism, instituted by Stalin in 1930, has meant that most work has been written "for the masses." In addition, many Turkmen writers' works were in Russian. This is true also of films, television, radio and theater, which appear in Russian.

Turkmenistan

Economy

The Soviet era brought about major changes in the lives of the Turkmen people. Prior to the Russian Revolution, most Turkmens were nomads who constantly moved from place to place in search of forage for their herds. Beginning in the 1930s, great engineering projects were launched to increase the irrigated areas. These irrigated lands were organized into state farms and the Turkmen people were settled on them, their nomadic life at an end.

Cotton became the chief crop grown throughout the area. New engineering projects in the 1950s and 1960s, in particular the Kara Kum Canal, brought additional lands under cultivation and increased Turkmenistan production of cotton even further. Local reports of increasing salinity in the soil or the constant drop in the level of the Aral Sea as a result of the new engineering projects were ignored by the central planners in Moscow.

After 1985, however, Gorbachëv's reforms allowed for greater local autonomy. Beginning about 1987, Turkmenistan began an attempt to restructure its agricultural economy. Moscow was asked to lower its cotton quota somewhat, and some land was removed from cotton production and switched to other crops. Turkmenistan began to grow more grain and feed, and the number of livestock grown also increased. This improved the situation somewhat, but the republic has not yet been able to restructure its economy. This is the likely direction for agriculture in the future, however.

President Niyazov has endorsed the idea of private property, but he has said that he favors transforming money–losing state farms into smaller collective farms and then allowing leasing and creation of rural cooperatives. Some degree of centralization will continue to exist in any case, because all farming depends on irrigation, which must remain centralized.

Turkmenistan is the least industrialized of all the Central Asian republics, with only 14.4 percent of material production provided by industry. What industry it has is mainly extractive. The petroleum industry began to be developed in the 1930s and Turkmenistan now comes third after Russia and Azerbaijan in the production of oil. Natural gas was also found and exploited and Turkmenistan now has a surplus which it sells to neighboring republics. Turkmenistan has begun raising its natural gas prices toward world prices, and this has caused some difficulty with its traditional customers in the ex–Soviet republics. Ukraine, for example, complained at one point that it could not afford the higher prices. The war between Azerbaijan and Armenia has also had an effect on sales. Armenia was once a large customer, but the pipeline from Turkmenistan to Armenia passes through Azerbaijan and that republic has refused to allow deliveries to Armenia.

Otherwise, economic changes in the republic have been few thus far. President Niyazov promised that privatization in the industrial sphere would begin in 1992. Some privatization of small enterprises has apparently occurred, but very little has changed as yet.

The Future

As one of the poorer societies of Central Asia and the least developed, Turkmenistan's evolution over the next several years is likely to be painful. Its chances of evolving into a democracy must also be rated rather low. The one positive thing that Turkmenistan has going for it is that it is a net exporter of energy supplies. If it can begin selling its oil and gas at world prices, that would help to finance the transition in the rest of the economy.

A catch of wild carp is hauled from the Kara Kum Canal

Courtesy: NOVOSTI

The Republic of Uzbekistan

Tashkent, the ancient capital of Uzbekistan shows its modern face

Courtesy: NOVOSTI

Area: 186,400 sq. mi. (447,400 sq. km.; as large as New York, Pennsylvania, Ohio, West Virginia, New Jersey, Maryland and Delaware combined).

Population: 20 million (estimated).

Capital City: Tashkent (Pop. 2.3 million).

Climate: Very hot and dry with average annual rainfall of only 8 inches.

Neighboring States: Kazakhstan (west and north), Kyrgystan, Tajikistan, Afghanistan (east and south), Turkmenistan (south and southwest).

Principal Languages: Uzbek and Russian.

Ethnic Composition: Uzbek (69%), Russian (11%), Kazakh (4%), others (12%).

Principal Religion: Islam. Until recently, religious worship was officially discouraged.

Chief Commercial Products: Cotton, livestock, melons, fruit, vegetables, wheat and rice, all due to vast irrigation. Textiles, food processing and construction materials.

Currency: Ruble.

Recent Political Status: The republic was proclaimed in 1924 and became part of the former USSR in 1925, which it remained until 1991.

Chief of State: Islam Karimov, President.

The Land

The Republic of Uzbekistan, independent successor of the Uzbek Soviet Socialist Republic, declared its independence on August 26, 1991. Its large area stretches from west of the Aral Sea to the Fergana Valley in the east.

Uzbekistan takes in parts of the Amu Darya River Valley plus the southern half of the Kysyl–Kum Desert. In the east, the republic includes the Fergana River Valley up to the foothills of the Tien Shan Mountain Range, which surrounds the valley on three sides. It is almost exclusively a landscape of deserts and dry steppes, with fertile oases formed by rivers flowing across the dry plains from out of the mountains to the south and southeast.

That part of Uzbekistan which lies west of the Aral Sea is known as the Ust–Urt Flatland. This area is a dry steppeland, flat and sun–baked and useful only for certain types of grazing. The Aral Sea, which Uzbekistan shares with Kazakhstan, was once the world's fourth–largest body of inland water which supported a large fishing industry. In the last 30–40 years, however, the sea and the land bordering on it have become an ecological disaster area. Since 1960, the Aral Sea has lost 60 percent of its water by volume and the level of the water has dropped nearly 50 feet. Each year, it drops another 9–10 inches.

The problem is that it receives its water from two main rivers, the Amu Darya and the Syr Darya, and those two rivers flow through 600 miles of desert and semi–desert before emptying into the Aral Sea. They form natural oases along their banks, but these cultivated areas were greatly extended in the Soviet era

161

Uzbekistan

through new irrigation projects. Uzbekistan today has 10.75 million acres of land under irrigation, mainly along the lower reaches of the Amu Darya. There are another 8.25 million acres of irrigated land in Turkmenistan, the Fergana River Valley of Krygyzstan and Kazakhstan. To stabilize the Aral Sea at its present level, the republics would have to agree to cut water usage sufficiently to allow the annual flow into it to grow from 11 million cubic kilometers to 35 million cubic kilometers per year. To raise it to its 1960 level, the republics would have to agree to cut out all water usage for three decades. Neither alternative is practical, so the Aral Sea will continue to shrink. Its salinity is steadily increasing.

The People

Uzbekistan, is the largest of the Central Asian republics in terms of population. Since 1936, Uzbekistan has also included the Kara–Kalpakia Autonomous Republic, located along the southern shores of the Aral Sea in the delta region of the Amu Darya River. Kara–Kalpakia has a population of about 1.2 million, with Kara–Kalpakians, Uzbeks and Kazakhs each constituting a little less than a third of the population. Both Uzbek and Kara–Kalpakian are Turkic languages.

History

The area where modern–day Uzbekistan is situated was an ancient center of civilization, beginning with ancient states like Bactria and Sogdiana. It was incorporated into the Persian Empire of Darius the Great and the Empire of Alexander the Great. In the eighth century, it was invaded by Arab forces and Islam was introduced for the first time. It became part of the Mongol Empire in the thirteenth century, then of the Empire of Tamerlane.

The Uzbeki people were late–comers to the area, however, arriving probably sometime in the fifteenth century. They are believed to be subordinate tribes of the Kipchak Khanate who called themselves Uzbeks in honor of the greatest Kipchak Khans, Uzbek or *Uzbeg*. Originally settled in the area of the Irtysh River, they began to move southeastward in the fifteenth century under their ruler Abu al–Khayr Khan. His grandson, Mu-

hammad Shaybani, conquered Samarkand and most of the Syr–Darya River Valley and the land south of it up to the Amu Darya.

The Shaybani dynasty ruled at Samarkand until 1598, with a collateral branch ruling in Khiva (called Khwarezm until the eighteenth century). Another dynasty, the Janids, ruled a portion of the country until the eighteenth century, when a reinvigorated Persia invaded and conquered Bukhara and Khiva.

The area between the Amu Darya and Syr–Darya was dominated by three khanates by the beginning of the nineteenth century—Bukhara, Khiva and Kokand. More city–states than empires, they exercised very little control over the nomadic tribes of the desert and semi–desert. These tribes subsisted by raids on settlements to the north.

As Russian settlers pushed into the area, raids became more frequent and a problem for the Russian military which was charged with protecting the area. Building first a line of forts along the frontier, they then began retaliatory raids. Finally they began annexing the border areas. Kokand was attacked in

A metro station in Tashkent

Courtesy: NOVOSTI

Uzbekistan

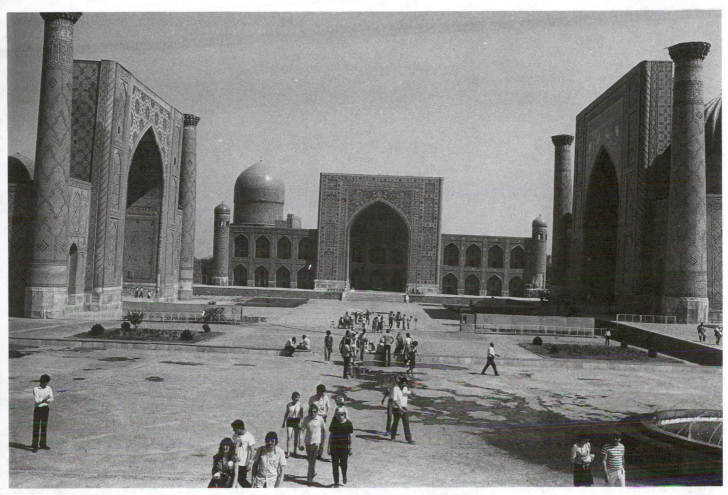

Registan Square in Samarkand

1864–65 and the emir was forced to cede Chimkent and Tashkent. In 1868, Bukhara was forced to accept the status of Russian vassal. Khiva fell in 1873. Kokand was formally annexed in 1876. The Imperial Russian Government referred to the areas it had annexed as Russian Turkistan. Bukhara and Khiva continued to be semi–independent khanates.

At the time of the Russian Revolution, a Turkistan Committee of the Provisional Government was set up in Tashkent, but it was soon replaced in April 1918 by the Autonomous Soviet Socialist Republic of Turkistan. Lenin extended his direct control over this organization in the fall of 1919. In 1920, the semi–independent Khanates of Khiva and Bokhara were conquered by the Red Army and made into People's Republics. Khiva was transformed into a Soviet Socialist Republic in 1923, Bokhara in 1924.

A fundamental redrawing of Central Asian boundaries along ethnic lines took place in 1924. The republics of Khiva, Turkistan, and Bukhara were abolished and five new republics were created. As a result, the Uzbekistan Soviet Socialist Republic was created in October 1924. It included a large part of the Samarkand region, a large part of the Fergana Valley, part of the upper reaches of the Syr–Darya River, including Tashkent and the surrounding area, plus the western plains of Bukhara. Between 1924 and 1929, it also included the Tadzhikistan Autonomous SSR, Tadzhikistan became a republic in its own right in 1929.

Uzbekistan received certain parts of Kazakhstan in 1956 and 1963, including part of the Hungry Steppe. Some of that land was returned in 1971.

Soviet rule imposed many changes on Uzbekistan, but perhaps the greatest change was the development of huge state farms that use irrigation to make Uzbekistan one of the principal producers of Central Asian cotton. Most people are, in effect, state employees and they have been mostly docile. Throughout the entire Soviet era, the *Communist Party* monopolized political power, so there was little chance for a political opposition to grow. The *Uzbek Communist Party* did begin making nationalist noises after several years of Gorbachëv's perestroika and in June 1990 the Uzbek Supreme Soviet adopted a resolution of sovereignty.

The leader of the *Uzbek Communist Party*, Islam Karimov, remained silent in August 1991 until it had become clear that the *coup* against Gorbachëv was failing. He then joined in condemning it and banned communist party cells in the armed forces, police and civil service. He declared Uzbekistan independent on August 31. In mid–September, Karimov called a congress of the *Uzbek Communist Party* and the name of the party was changed to the *People's Democratic Party*. There has, however, been no change in the personnel running the government, though Karimov began allowing some criticism in the Uzbek Supreme Soviet.

Karimov adopted Uzbek nationalist slogans, but he said publicly that Uzbekistan was not ready for democracy or a market economy. Later, he attempted to give himself a democratic aura by having the Uzbek Supreme Soviet provide for a popularly elected presidency and elections were set for December 29, 1991. Other political parties were legalized, but they were not able to operate freely. The Uzbek popular front *Birlik*,, potentially the largest opposition grouping, was not permitted to field a candidate. The *Islamic Renaissance Movement*, which advocated an Islamic state, was banned. Only the

Uzbekistan

Erk Democratic Party, which split from *Birlik* in 1990, was permitted to field a candidate. Karimov won 86% percent of the popular vote. His opponent, Mohamed Salikh, got 12.4%. In a separate referendum, 98.2 percent cast their votes in favor of Uzbek independence.

When U.S. Secretary of State James Baker visited Tashkent in January 1992, he met with Abdurahmin Pulatov, co–chairman of *Birlik*. Pulatov urged Baker to recognize Uzbekistan independence, but he admitted that there was no democracy in Uzbekistan. "Politically, we have no freedom at all. The totalitarian regime has been destroyed in Moscow, but in Tashkent it continues to exist."

Very little has changed since January 1992 and current reports out of Uzbekistan indicate that the government still tolerates very little dissent. One reason may be the very volatile nature of the Uzbeki people. In January 1992, for example, riots broke out in Uzbekistan after price increases, and calls were heard for the resignation of President Karimov. Developments in neighboring Tajikistan over the past year are probably a larger factor, however. Karimov is determined that a similar situation will not be permitted to develop in Uzbekistan. For that reason, political demonstrations are not permitted, religious–oriented political parties have been banned, and numerous members of the political opposition have been arrested and imprisoned. In January 1993, the activities of *Birlik*, the main opposition movement, were suspended and since that time a number of *Birlik* leaders were arrested. Even the registered opposition party, *Erk* (Freedom), has suffered tremendous harassment from the government, its newspaper shut and its bank accounts seized. Economic change is also coming slowly, though there has been some movement toward a freer market. Thus far, the economy continues to worsen and inflation is bad, though the government continues to subsidize basic items such as bread, butter, rice, and cooking oil.

Nature of the Regime

Uzbekistan has created a presidential–parliamentary system similar to those found in the other ex–Soviet republics. It is different from other republics in one major respect, however. The *Communist Party* continues to exist here, even if under a new name. But Islam Karimov, who had been head of the *Uzbek Communist Party*, remains head of the *People's Democratic Party*, which continues to exercise the dominant political role in the republic.

The Uzbek Supreme Soviet remains subservient, approving whatever is submitted to them by President Karimov.

There is a Prime Minister, Abdulhasim Mutalov, who presides over the cabinet, but he has no independent political role. He is appointed by the president and confirmed by the Supreme Soviet.

In January 1992, a law on the reorganization of the local authority bodies created a new executive official at the region, district and town level. These *khokim* report to the republic president and to the legislative body over which they also preside. The decree did not specify whether the *khokim* were appointed or elected. They would appear to exercise authority similar to that of a prefect in the French system.

Culture

Uzbekis are among the most traditional of the Central Asian peoples and national costumes are still often worn. Men wear a robe striped with bright colors and an embroidered skullcap. Women wear bright silk dresses with a shawl over the head. Rugs cover the floors of Uzbeki houses and often folk art decorates the walls. There are also traditional Uzbeki festivals in various times of the year when the people dress up in their finery and there is singing and dancing. Another specialty of the festivals is horse dancing. This is also the time for games

At *Uzbekistan Restaurant* in Tashkent, chef Bikhadyr Iskhakov prepares a traditional Uzbek dish—*lagman*, pasta with mutton
Courtesy: NOVOSTI

and tests of strength, dexterity and skill. And of course food plays a role. Some of the distinctive foods include *d'ighman* (meat with pastry in a strong broth), spicy chopped meat wrapped in a thin dough, and *plov* (rice with meat, vegetables, spices and dried apricots).

Religion also plays a great role in the lives of the Uzbeki people, and attendance at the Friday mosque service has been increasing in recent years. Uzbekis are Sunni Moslems of the Hanafi school. Sufism is also practiced by some, and there is a famous Sufi school, the Naqshbandi or *tariqat–al–Khwajagan*, in Bukhara.

The government has taken an ambivalent attitude toward Islam. Moderate leaders have been wooed, but when 400 Moslems tried to hold a congress in Tashkent, the leaders were arrested and non–Uzbekis were expelled from the republic. On the other hand, no effort is made to discourage the practice of Islam, and new mosques are being built every day. New Islamic seminaries have also been opened.

Tashkent is the Islamic center for Central Asia. The "Spiritual Department of Moslems of Central Asia," headed by the Mufti of Tashkent, is located here. It is allowed to receive large sums of money from Saudi Arabia, which has also donated a million *Korans* for distribution in Central Asia. It also publishes a newspaper, *Dawn of Islam*, and a magazine, *Islamic Faith*.

Uzbekistan has produced a number of writers in the twentieth century. Perhaps the best known is Abdullah Qadiri, famous for two historical novels, *Days Gone By* and *Scorpion from the Pulpit*, published in the 1920s. Qadiri was later killed in the Soviet purges of the late 1930s. *Sisters*, the novel of Asqad Mukhtar, has been translated into English. Uzbeks have also made some original contributions in modern graphic arts. Some of the ancient skills such as ornamental wall painting, wood carving and fabric printing have also been kept alive. There is an Uzbek film studio where films in the Uzbeki language are made, and the republic also has its own radio and television facilities. The Navoi Theater of Opera and Ballet in Tashkent is also famous for its productions.

Economy

Uzbekistan has what is traditionally referred to as a commercial single–crop agricultural economy. What this means is that the republic is heavily dependent on the production of a single agricultural product, cotton, which is mainly exported outside the republic. In fact, Uzbekistan is by far the largest producer of cotton in what was Soviet Central Asia, being responsible for two–thirds of all cotton production.

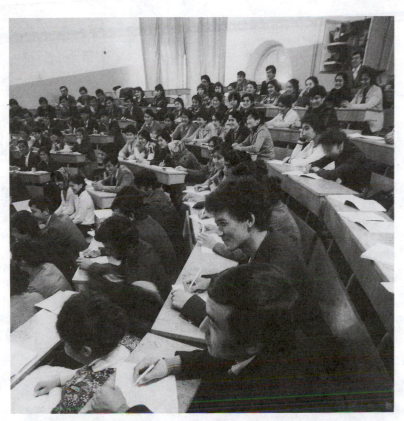

Students at Alisher Navoi University in Samarkand listen to a lecturer
Courtesy: NOVOSTI

Almost all agriculture is dependent on irrigation, and practically all irrigated land is now organized into huge state farms whose sole product is cotton. The majority of the people are employees of these huge state farms.

Silkworms are raised in the Fergana Valley, with mulberry trees planted along the streets and irrigation canals. Orchards of apricots, peaches, figs, and pears, and vineyards, used to produce table grapes, raisins and wine, are found in the Fergana Valley, the Zeravshan oasis and the Chirchik and Agren Valleys. Farm wages are low. Uzbekistan has a standard of living that is just half of the old Soviet average. Moreover, the republic has the second highest birth rate of Central Asia, which has resulted in a surplus rural population. The unemployment rate in the republic was over ten percent even before the collapse of the Soviet system.

Uzbekistan has large reserves of natural gas, petroleum and coal. Most local industry use natural gas. Gas is also exported to Russia via a pipeline that runs from Bukhara to the area of the Urals and then on to European Russia. Petroleum is being produced in the Fergana Valley, in the area around Bukhara, and in the area south of the Aral Sea. The Angren coal field produces coal for local use, but coal deposits have not been developed to any great extent.

Plentiful energy supplies are used to support some industry as well. Uzbekistan produces machines and heavy equipment, its specialty being machinery for cotton cultivation and harvesting. Machinery for irrigation projects and road construction are also manufactured, plus some for the textile industry.

Uzbekistan also mines copper, zinc and lead ores, plus tungsten and molybdenum. It also produces fertilizers, cement, cotton textiles, coke and chemicals.

The Future

Uzbekistan has two problems which appear unsolvable—the shrinking Aral Sea and a standard of living that has been dropping for a number of years. Both of these are related to an overdependence on the production of cotton using irrigation. Greater industrialization is a possibility that could provide more jobs for Uzbekis, but they have been reluctant to leave the land. Even today, a majority of jobs in industry are held by ethnic Russians.

All of this puts a great strain on government and helps explain why the president feels that Uzbeki are not ready for democracy or a market economy. Yet Uzbekistan must find a new direction, or suffer continued declines in the standard of living and a further degradation of the environment. The future is not optimistic.

EASTERN EUROPE

The Danube River at Budapest, Hungary

EASTERN EUROPE

... in 1877

... in 1914

. . . in 1921

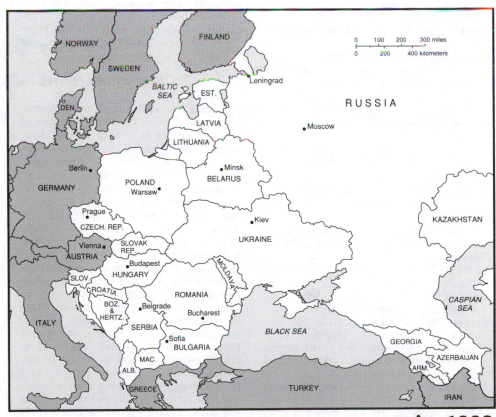

. . . in 1993

The Republic of Albania

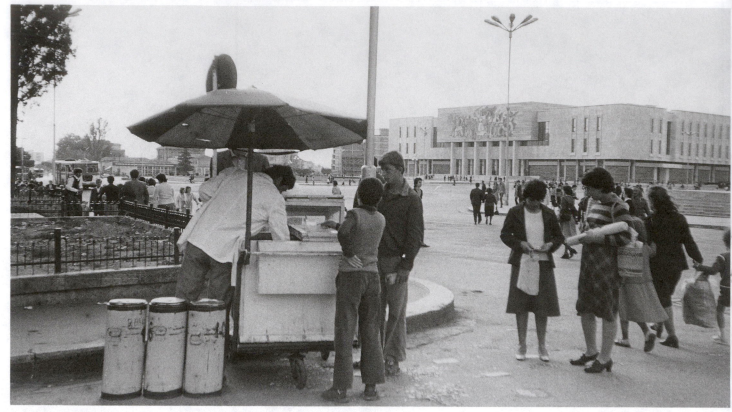

An ice–cream vendor in Tirana's traffic–free central Skanderberg Square

AP/Wide World Photo

Area: 28,749 sq. km. = 11,000 sq. mi.

Population: 2.97 million (projected)

Capital City: Tirana (Pop. 240,000, projected).

Climate: Mediterranean, with wet winters and hot, dry summers on the coast. The interior is colder in the winter.

Neighboring Countries: Yugoslavia (North. East); Greece (South).

Official Language: Albanian.

Other Principal Tongues: Greek

Ethnic Background: Illyrian, an ancient Indo–European group, mixed with Slav, Greek and Turkish ancestry.

Principal Religions: Islam (70%); Eastern–rite Orthodox (20%); Roman Catholic (10%).

Chief Commercial Products: Tobacco, cigarettes, timber, wood, dairy products.

Currency: Lek.

Chief of State: Sali Berisha, President of the Republic.

Head of Government: Aleksander Meksi, Chairman, Council of Ministers.

Former Political Status: Part of the Roman and Byzantine empires; conquered by the Ottoman Turks in the 15th century and under Turkish control until 1912, following which there were six years of conflicts and change associated with the Balkan Wars and World War I. Communist state between 1945 and 1991.

National Day: November 28, Independence Day.

National Flag: Red, with a black, two–headed eagle topped by a five–pointed star.

THE LAND AND THE PEOPLE

Albania is a small, largely mountainous land located along the eastern shores of the Adriatic Sea. In spite of its small size, it has a widely varied climate, the major factor being the mountains. About one–seventh of Albania consists of a series of small plains running north to south down along the coastline. Here the climate is hot and humid in the summer and relatively warm in most winters. Semi–tropical crops such as citrus can be produced, but other crops include figs, wine grapes and olives. Further inland, the plains are at increasing elevations and are correspondingly cooler—the average temperature in July is 63°F. in these regions. Here the chief crop grown is grain. As the elevation rises even further, the green foliage of rolling pastures gives way to sparse evergreens and scattered brush, which in turn is replaced by gray and brown craggy peaks rising steeply to the sky. The air is thin, cold and clear—this is the home of the eagle, where few sounds interrupt the stillness.

In this setting the people continue the isolated life they have experienced for centuries. There are some settlements that have little or no contact with the rest of Albania because of their inaccessibility. The few towns that exist are usually the result of a need for a place to trade agricultural goods. Fishermen ply the cool waters of Lake Shkodër in flat–bottomed boats. Although there is mineral wealth, it is almost impossible to extract it profitably because of the lack of transportation.

170

Albania

Most of the Albanians of today are remote descendants of the Illyrians, an ancient people of the Indo–European group; at one time, they were to be found throughout most of the Balkan Peninsula, but they were either gradually absorbed or driven out as successive waves of Slavs moved into the area; now they are found only in the western part of the Balkans. Even so, they spill across borders and are found in Serbia, Macedonia, and Greece. There are also colonies of Albanians in Italy, but that is the result of past migrations. In addition, there are about 600,000 persons of Albanian descent living in the United States.

HISTORY

Early Albanian Governments

The Kingdom of Illyria came into being in the 3rd century B.C., centered around an ancient city on the site of present–day Shkodër. Conquered by the Romans in 167 B.C., the area remained a part of the Roman Empire for the next five centuries. When the Empire dissolved in the 4th century A.D., Illyria became a part of the Eastern Roman—later Byzantine Empire.

As the Slavs arrived in the Adriatic region in the 6th and 7th centuries, most of the Illyrians were absorbed; the rest settled along the southern Adriatic coast where Albania is now located. During the centuries which followed, Albania was conquered and reconquered by various eastern and western armies. The most lasting influence was that of the Serbs and the Venetians (Italians).

The Albanians were conquered by the Ottoman Turks in the 15th century and incorporated into their Empire. Although the Albanians had put up stiff resistance to the Ottoman conquest, once they had been absorbed politically, they allowed themselves to be absorbed culturally as well. Albania was the only part of the Balkan Peninsula where the majority of the population converted to Islam.

Albanian nationalism was awakened by the decisions of the major powers at the Congress of Berlin which was held after the Russian–Turkish war of 1877–1878. The great powers awarded to Montenegro (now a part of Yugoslavia) and Greece territories which the Albanians claimed as their own.

They formed the *League of Prizren* to protest the division of lands they felt should not be given to neighboring countries, but this effort was not successful. They also demanded local control within a reformed Turkish Empire rather than independence which would have put them at the mercy of other foreign powers. Both Italy and Austria–Hungary had been showing interest in the area. Although the Turks supported the *League* in its protest against the expansion of neighboring states, the demand for local control was turned down. The Turks suppressed the *League* in 1881, and banned use of the Albanian language in 1886.

The *League* was a means of expressing the first national feelings of the Albanians in their native land, and when it and Albanian liberty were crushed, the national movement was taken up by Albanian communities living in Italy and the United States. Oppression by the Turks continued and there was a series of rebellions from 1909 to 1912 which resulted in Albanian control of almost all of what is now that country.

The remaining Turkish power was eliminated in the First Balkan War of 1912, and on November 28 of that year, a national assembly met at Vlore and proclaimed Albania's independence. Ismail Qemal headed the first provisional government.

The Birth of a Modern Albania

The Treaty of London ending the First Balkan War (1912) left the question of Albania to a conference of the major powers' ambassadors. They agreed with the demand for independence, but as might have been expected, they redrew the map of the region. Shkodër, demanded by Montenegro, was left to Albania; Kosovo, inhabited by a large number of Albanians, was given to Serbia, creating a problem that lingers to this day. In the south, the powers gave part of northern Greece to Albania, but with Greek support, the people revolted.

The great powers also provided a hand–picked ruler for Albania—William of Wied, a German Prince. Italian–supported Essad Pasha, successor of Ismail Qemal, was actually the most important man in the country. The years 1912–1914 were turbulent—there were rebellions in the north and south where borders were disputed and general dissatisfaction throughout the country. Prince William fled at the outbreak of World War I.

Four years of utter anarchy followed, with the armies of Serbia, Montenegro (now both part of Yugoslavia), Greece, Italy, France, Austria and Bulgaria occupying parts of Albania. At the end of the war, Albania was occupied by Italy, with Serbia holding the northeastern region and Korcä in the possession of the French.

On December 25, 1918, delegates from all parts of Albania met at Durrës to elect a provisional government and to send a delegation to the Paris Peace Conference to present a demand that Albania's 1913 borders be restored. Greece, Italy and Yugoslavia had made a secret deal to divide Albania between them. This was firmly rejected by U.S. President Woodrow Wilson—his action and the determination of the Albanian leaders saved the tiny nation.

In order to understand events that followed World War I, it is necessary to remember that Albania was still a primitive country. Although unique and interesting culturally, it was backward—there

Albanians under the Turks (1910), and as an independent kingdom (1912).

Albania

was no written Albanian language and no education system. There were only a few miles of road and one bridge. There was no industry in the whole country. Albania was divided into many localities along social, religious and geographic lines and the basic unit of power was the clan. Government control was at best scanty.

A parliamentary and cabinet system of government emerged in 1920. Italy, preoccupied with its own problems, reluctantly recognized Albania's government. The border questions were finally resolved by the major powers in 1926. Two political parties were organized, the *Progressive Party* dominated by Moslem leaders and the *Popular Party* headed by a liberal Greek Orthodox Bishop, Fan S. Noli, who had a U.S. college degree.

Ahmed Bey Zogu, one of the leaders of the *Popular Party* became Albania's premier in 1922 when he stayed to defend the capital against a revolt after the rest of the government had fled. Two years later, he resigned and fled to Yugoslavia when an angry band of demonstrators marched on the capital. Noli, his successor, hoped to introduce a reform program which would literally drag Albania into the 20th century. This could not be done without massive outside aid or internal unity. Noli could muster neither. Zogu returned with the support of Yugoslav troops; the National Assembly proclaimed Albania a republic and elected Zogu president for 7 years.

Ruthless and determined, Zogu had a constituent assembly proclaim Albania a "democratic, parliamentary and hereditary kingdom" in 1928 with himself as King Zog I. He sought financial assistance from Italy; by the mid 1930's this ripened into Italian control of Albania's economy. The fascist Italian dictator, Benito Mussolini, sent an invasion force which swept Albania on April 7, 1939; Victor Emmanuel, figurehead King of Italy also became King of Albania. Italy mounted an invasion of Greece through Albania; it was repulsed by Greek and Yugoslav armies which were able to occupy much of Albania until a German attack in 1941.

Albania Reborn as a People's Republic

Resistance groups were organized in 1941–42 by communists and non–communists. The *Albanian Communist Party* was founded in 1941 with Yugoslav help; among its leaders was Enver Hoxha, a young man educated in France and Belgium and considered one of the "intellectuals" in the party. The party set up the *National Liberation Movement (LNC)*, which for a time included the clan chief Abbas Kupi and his guerrilla fighters.

Another resistance group, the *National Front (Balli Kombetär)* had an anti–royalist and strongly nationalistic outlook. The two groups came close to joining in 1943,

King Zog I

but the *LNC*, on the advice of the Yugoslav communist leader Tito, backed out and soon the two groups were fighting each other. A provisional government headed by Enver Hoxha was formed in October 1944, moving to Tirana as the government of Albania upon withdrawal of the German forces.

Albania was proclaimed a People's Republic in 1946. The absence of political parties and assistance from Yugoslavia's communists enabled Hoxha to assume power with relative ease. After World War II, the Yugoslavs desired to assume the role the Italians had before the war. An economic treaty providing for a customs union, coordination of economic planning, currency equalization and the formation of "joint companies" was entered into in 1946. Yugoslav advisers appeared in greater numbers, and there was even talk of union between the two nations.

The Yugoslavian embrace was apparently too stifling for Hoxha, but there was little he could do about it at the time. In the meantime, the Yugoslavs threw their support to Koci Xoxe, who as Minister of the Interior controlled the police and security forces. What saved Hoxha was the

Enver Hoxha

Soviet–Yugoslav split which occurred at this time. Accusing Xoxe of being a supporter of Tito, Hoxha had him and his followers purged at the First Congress of the Albanian Party of Labor in November 1948; Xoxe was later executed.

Hoxha clearly dominated the *Albanian Labor Party (APL)* but he was not without his critics. The next major challenge came in the early 1950's, this time from moderates who objected to dislocations caused by a policy of industrialization and collectivization. After 1953, they also began calling for de–Stalinization as was occurring in Russia. The spokesmen for this point of view were two members of the Politburo, Bedri Spahiu and Tuk Jakova. With Stalin dead and the Soviet leadership moving cautiously toward de–Stalinization, Hoxha could not simply purge these critics.

He actually made a gesture toward the moderate wing of the party in 1954 when he gave up the position of Chairman of the Council of Ministers, though he turned it over to one of his own supporters, Mehmet Shehu. A year later, he managed to get both Spahiu and Jakova expelled from the Politburo.

Yet another challenge came in 1956 at the Third Party Congress, but this came from middle–ranking bureaucrats and military officers; Hoxha crushed it rather easily.

The last contest occurred in 1974–75. It appears not to have been a direct challenge to Hoxha, but rather to some of his policies. Now wielding absolute power, Hoxha purged the dissenters. Between July and December 1974 he removed the entire top level of the military establishment, including the Defense Minister, Beqir Balluku, who was also a member of the Politburo. His dispute with the military was apparently over the extent of party control in such areas as military training and discipline. He followed this ouster with a purge of the nation's top economic and managerial elite when they challenged the role of the party in their areas.

An ailing and tired Hoxha died in early April 1985 at the age of 77. He was succeeded by Ramiz Alia, whom Hoxha had been grooming as successor. Alia, born in 1925, had been a long–time associate of Hoxha, though it was only in 1982 that he became the designated successor.

Although 17 years younger than his mentor, Alia nevertheless belonged to the first generation of Albanian communist leaders. He became a member of the party in 1943 when it was still only an aspirant to power and became a full Politburo member and a member of the powerful Secretariat in 1961. When he was appointed President of the Presidium of the People's Assembly (titular head of state) in 1982, he retained all of his party posts. Thus, he was already a member of the Secretariat at the time of

Albania

Enver Hoxha makes a point to elderly villagers, while Ramiz Alia (left) listens attentively.

additional 25,000 persons were issued passports and left the country legally.

In the cities, demonstrations began occurring periodically and some people took to wearing crosses and shouting anti–communist slogans in the streets. Occasionally, violence erupted when officials of the secret police ripped the crosses off people's chests.

Meanwhile the government continued its program of liberalization. Collective farmers were told that they could have private plots and that they would be permitted to sell excess produce in local open–air markets. Cultural controls were also relaxed. At Enver Hoxha University in Tirana, a disco began playing rock music every Saturday night. The prohibition against individuals owning private automobiles was also lifted, though that change had little practical significance since almost no private individual could afford to own an automobile.

These gestures on the part of the party leadership probably only emboldened people to demand more, however. Nearly all of the protests were in the cities and overwhelmingly made up of young people, particularly young men. Then in December, about two thousand students at Enver Hoxha University organized a protest demonstration demanding greater democracy. After three days, the ruling *Party of Labor*, meeting in emergency session, gave in and endorsed "the creation of independent political organizations" and scheduled new elections for February 10. Albanian communists, like their fellow party members in Eastern Europe and the Soviet Union, had been persuaded to give up their monopoly of political power. The next day, the first oppositional political party, the *Democratic Party*, was organized. Approximately 80,000 people attended the rally for the new party.

By January 1991, three additional oppositional parties, the *Republicans*, the *Forum for Human Rights*, and the *Ecological Party*, had come into being. Charging that an election date of February 10 would not give them adequate time to prepare, they demanded that the elections be postponed until a later date. The government gave in and rescheduled them for March 31.

The period January–March was filled with demonstrations, political rallies, additional student strikes, and some violence. Oppositional newspapers also began appearing. At Enver Hoxha University, students decided that Hoxha's name should be stricken from the university's official title and organized a strike which later was turned into a hunger strike. The authorities allowed the strike to continue for twelve days, then surrounded the university with special troops. Demonstrations in support of the

Hoxha's death and only had to assume the additional duty of First Secretary.

Although no one challenged Alia for the office of First Secretary, it soon became clear that the other members of the Politburo considered him to be not more than a first–among–equals. Since the Politburo was dominated by hard–liners, he was extremely cautious in initiating changes for the first few years. No additions were made to the Politburo, even though that body had three fewer members than in 1982. Alia did make two lesser appointments—the addition of one person to the Secretariat and the replacement of the Chairman of the State Planning Commission.

At the Ninth Congress of the *Albanian Party of Labor* in November 1986, Alia had fulsome praise for Hoxha, to whom, he said, Albania owed boundless gratitude. At the same time, the new Five Year Plan adopted at the congress put much more stress on foreign trade than in the past. Alia indicated that he wanted exports to increase by nearly half over the period.

The new emphasis on trade was accompanied by a slow, and extremely cautious, movement away from the old Hoxha system in general. But that movement remained glacial until March 1990 when Alia, probably responding to the recent extraordinary changes elsewhere in Eastern Europe, launched his own campaign of "democratic" change. Among other things, Alia promised contested elections by secret ballot, including within the *Albanian Labor Party*; limits on terms of office; a decentralization of decision–making authority to district officials and individual enterprises; some price decontrol; and the introduction of economic incentives in industry and agriculture.

Subsequent changes were, in some ways, even more significant. In April, the assembly approved a law lifting criminal penalties for attempts to escape across the frontier and this was followed up in May by a new law explicitly granting citizens the right to travel abroad. The Assembly also lifted the old laws outlawing the practice of religion and declared religious belief to be a matter of individual conscience. Finally, it created the office of Justice Minister, and gave him the task of creating a new system of courts and defense attorneys. None of this represented a basic change in the system, however, for there was no change in the monopoly role of the party.

The May 1990 law granting citizens the right to travel abroad obviously raised expectations among the Albanian populace which were subsequently frustrated by Albanian officialdom. Toward the end of June, some 5,000 Albanians took refuge in a dozen foreign embassies in Tirana and demanded to be allowed to leave the country. After several days, the Albanian authorities gave in to the demands and the refugees were allowed to leave. Over the next four months, an

173

Albania

students erupted in urban areas across Albania and in two cities, Tirana and the port city of Durres, statues of Hoxha were toppled. The government again backed down and agreed to remove Hoxha's name from Tirana University.

Ramiz Alia, under attack from hard–line party members, decided to dismiss Adil Carcani, the hardline Chairman of the Council of Ministers, and assume personal control of the government apparatus by creating a "temporary presidential council." Named head of the new government was Fatos Nano, an economist who had been made Deputy Chairman of the Council of Ministers in January. Alia's actions made clear what up to that time had been only suspected—that the communist *Party of Labor* had split into two factions, orthodox Marxist–Leninists who wanted to stamp out dissent and reformers who supported Ramiz Alia.

Meanwhile, thousands of Albanians again began fleeing the country, first to Greece, and then, at the beginning of March, in commandeered ships to Italy. Many appeared to be fleeing the violence and bloodshed that were accompanying the street demonstrations. The government declared martial law in the port city of Durres in an attempt to stop the exodus, but about twelve thousand Albanians eventually made it out of the country anyway. They were not well–received in Italy, however, and many later returned home.

The March 31 elections were something of an anticlimax. The political opposition won in the cities, but the *Party of Labor*, managing to retain its hold over the countryside, won two–thirds of the seats in the People's Assembly. Ramiz Alia lost his own race in the city of Tirana, but was reelected Chairman of the Presidium of the People's Assembly on April 30. Fatos Nano was reappointed as Chairman of the Council of Ministers.

But as the *Party of Labor* very quickly learned, electoral majorities do not necessarily create a mandate to rule, particularly if, as in this case, that majority might have been the result of intimida-

tion and fraud. At least, those were the sort of charges hurled by the political opposition against the party, though no evidence was ever produced to substantiate the claim. But no evidence was really necessary. The party's almost total repudiation in the cities meant that it had lost the support of the workers, the very class it claimed to represent, and therefore its political credibility.

As it turned out, the new mandate lasted just over one month. After two weeks of verbal sparring between the government and the political opposition, a group of newly–formed, independent trade unions called for a general strike. With almost total worker support, the strike made clear, as nothing else could, that the party's claim to be the party of the workers was a fraud. During the three–and–a–half weeks that it continued, the general strike brought industrial production to a complete halt and established conclusively that the party had lost control of the cities. On Skanderberg Square in central Tirana, where demonstrators had torn down a huge statue of Enver Hoxha in February, 50,000 demonstrators battled police with rocks, bottles and fire bombs on May 29, leaving the front steps of the Palace of Culture on the Square shattered and fire–blackened.

The political opposition demanded the resignation of the communist government and the formation of an new interim government which would include representatives of the opposition parties. The workers demanded that their wages be doubled and the 48–hour work week be reduced. The party gave in and acceded to all demands in the first week of June. Fatos Nano, in submitting his resignation as Chairman of the Council of Ministers to the legislature, warned of food shortages and the threat of famine. "You have no idea how bad the situation is," he told the legislators.

The new cabinet, which was sworn in on June 12, was headed up by Ylli Bufi, a member of the *Party of Labor* but whose training was as an engineer, not a party apparatchik. His reputation was that of an open–minded reformer. Half of the 24–member cabinet was selected by the communists, while another 12 members came from the opposition. In theory, this government of national unity was supposed to be a government of technicians, with members selected as individuals, without reference to party. In fact, seven of the 12 opposition cabinet seats went to members of the main opposition party, the *Democratic Party*, the other five seats were allotted to the smaller *Republican, Social–Democratic,* and *Agrarian* parties. Sali Berisha, head of the *Democratic Party*, was one of the opposition leaders entering the cabinet. Two other members of his party named to important posts were

Gramoz Pashko, who became first deputy premier and minister of the economy, and Genc Ruli, who became minister of finance.

The Tenth National Congress of the *Party of Labor* was scheduled to take place on June 10–12. Prior to the beginning of the congress, President Ramiz Alia submitted his resignation as head of the party, so the keynote address was given by Xhelil Gjoni, the new party secretary. The speech probably shocked some of the delegates with its attacks on Enver Hoxha's collectivization of agriculture and his "brutal pursuit of 'class struggle,' under which intellectuals and churchgoers were persecuted and jailed, some merely for listening to foreign radio broadcasts or reading the Bible." The congress had its surreal moments as well, as when Hoxha's widow, Nexhmije, asserted that, if her husband were still alive, he would be a supporter of democracy and Albanian membership in the European Community. At the conclusion of the congress, the party voted to become the *Socialist Party of Albania*, hoping apparently that a change in name might help to stem a further decline in popular support.

The task of the new government was not an enviable one. Shops were empty and the people were angry. Industrial production was down drastically and exports were down by 50% over the previous year. In the countryside, communists and anti–communists quarreled about whether to break up the collective farms, while peasants held off on planting.

The government tried to solve the land problem first. In July, the legislature passed a law authorizing peasants to obtain small parcels of land from the collective farms. That helped, though communists in the legislature insisted on a clause forbidding peasants to sell any of their newly acquired land. In addition, because the legislation was passed so late in the crop year, a good percentage of the land never did get planted. The fall harvest would be much smaller.

The new government did get some good news, however. The aid already being provided from Italy, the United States and Turkey would continue and be expanded. The European Community offered a trade and co–operation agreement that would allow additional sales of such Albanian products as chromium to the EC and make Albania eligible for technical assistance. In addition, the EC promised Albania 50,000 tons of wheat.

None of this was enough, however. The food situation grew worse over the summer and unemployment continued to grow, reaching over 35% by August. As a result, an estimated 10,000 Albanians commandeered a freighter, the Vlora, and sailed for Italy. Five months earlier, the Italian Government, faced

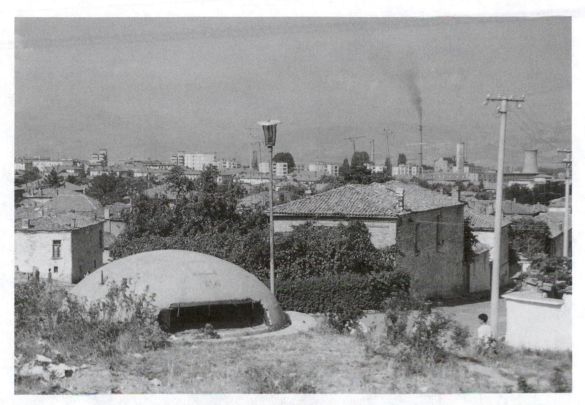

This once isolated nation had built bunker fortifications (which are still in place) along the entire coast.
Courtesy: James V. Elias

with 24,000 refugees on its hands, had tried to persuade them to return to Albania. About half went willingly.

Most of the rest remained in Italy, unemployable because they were unskilled. This time, the government decided it would use different tactics. When the Vlora arrived, its passengers were taken in hand by riot squads and locked up in a sports stadium. Five days later, most were given $40 in cash, a T–shirt and a pair of jeans, and flown back to Albania. If the treatment was rather brisk and perhaps a little harsh, the Italian Government did counterbalance this with an offer of $85 million in food aid and another $50 million to purchase imported materials to keep the factories running.

The Albanian Government, grateful for the aid, agreed to try to stop future mass departures by placing its ports under military control and instituting joint coastal patrols with Italian warships. Barbed wire was later strung around the port of Durres to keep would–be stowaways out of the port area.

The government announced a privatization program in September which called for 25,000 state businesses to be sold, but this brought protests from the unions that up to 100,000 jobs would be lost as a result. They demanded that the government guarantee unemployed workers 80 percent of their usual salary and this was actually written into law in November. The average worker's salary was less than $30 a month, but, even so, there was a question where the government would get the money to pay the unemployed workers. The budget deficit was already over 20% of GDP, and climbing.

Meanwhile, in the countryside, the people had gotten tired of waiting for the government to make up its mind about the collective farms and they had begun sharing out land and livestock on their own. These "spontaneous privatizations" produced a sort of anarchy in the countryside as looters stripped farm buildings of floors, window frames, roof tiles and even bricks. There were also reports of embittered ex–farm directors dynamiting greenhouses and farm buildings on their way out and farmers burning fields they claimed as their own rather than let a rival family have them.

Ylli Bufi visited the United States in November and thus became the first Albanian prime minister to visit Washington. He had high level conversations with officials at State, Treasury, Commerce and Agriculture, plus meetings with the House Foreign Affairs and Senate Foreign Relations committees.

Shortly after his return, however, the Democratic Party pulled out of the government coalition and it fell. Sali Berisha, head of the Democratic Party, accused the Socialists of hindering economic and political reforms. While the charges were true—the Socialists were chary of market economy solutions to problems and did force the Democrats to compromise with them—the real reason for the pull–out was that new elections were supposed to take place in May and the Democrats wanted them to take place as early as February. When the People's Assembly refused to agree to move up the elections, the Democrats withdrew from the cabinet. It is also likely that the Democrats wanted to fight the elections from outside the government.

The Democratic Party's withdrawal from the government coalition more or less coincided with new food riots which broke out in December 1991, apparently triggered by a comment by Bufi that food reserves would last only a week.

Bufi submitted his resignation as Chairman of the Council of Ministers at this point and was replaced by Vilson Ahmeti. Ahmeti was to preside over a caretaker government which would prepare for new elections. On December 23, President Alia announced that the elections would be moved up after all and take place on March 22.

The period between December and March was a trying time for Albania. With the population barely surviving on foreign humanitarian assistance, there were once again attempts to flee the country, followed by food riots as thousands of people stormed warehouses and seized what goods they found there.

Albania

An Albanian street vendor hawks his products.

With anarchy spreading, it became unsafe to go out at night as armed groups of young men roamed the streets attacking people.

During the election campaign, there were also disturbing signs that Albanians were being given an exaggerated idea of what the world could do for them. For example, one journalist quoted "ragged peasants in the countryside" as saying that Albania's *Democratic Party* leaders and U.S. Secretary of State Baker "will be bringing them shoes and food." A common shout at election rallies was "America will save us."

The *Democratic Party* won 62% of the vote in the March 22 elections, giving them an absolute majority in the People's Assembly. Including the votes of the *Republican* and *Social Democratic* parties, the opposition actually got three–quarters of all votes cast. The big losers were the *Socialists* with their 25% percent of the vote, down from 67% a year earlier. Since the *Democrats* had made it clear that they would remove Ramiz Alia as President if they and their allies won a two–thirds majority in the People's Assembly, Alia saved them the trouble and submitted his

resignation on April 3. The People's Assembly then elected Sali Berisha, leader of the *Democratic Party*, as the new President of the Republic. Berisha appointed Aleksander Meksi as Chairman of the Council of Ministers. Meksi said that he would include representatives of the *Republican* and *Social Democratic* parties in his cabinet.

Sali Berisha is a French–trained cardiologist with very little political experience. Aleksander Meksi graduated from Tirana University with a degree in engineering. Most of his experience has been with the Institute for Cultural Monuments and the Institute of Archaeological Excavations as a "restorer and student of monuments of medieval architecture." These two men have taken control of a country that is the poorest in Europe, that is suffering from a breakdown in political and economic life, and with an unemployment rate that approaches 50%. The electoral campaign also raised exaggerated hopes among the populace. Albania opted for democracy in the March 22 elections but, if the new leaders cannot deliver on their promises, democracy may not survive long in Albania.

Foreign Policy

Because of Albania's small size, foreign affairs have always played an extremely important role. Between 1945 and 1948, it was Yugoslavia which played "Big Brother" and attempted to dominate Albania. When Hoxha rebelled, he had no choice but to throw Albania into the arms of the Soviet Union. This marriage lasted as long as Stalin was alive, but Hoxha had no difficulty switching his loyalty to the new Soviet leadership in 1953—at least for awhile. The country entered the Council for Mutual Economic Assistance (CMEA), the Soviet–dominated economic organization for Eastern Europe in 1949 and the Warsaw Pact in 1955. Almost all foreign trade was with Russia and other members of the CMEA.

Signs of a Soviet–Yugoslavian reconciliation in 1955 gave Hoxha a degree of apprehension. Apparently Hoxha feared that the Soviets might accept his removal as the price for Yugoslavia's renewed friendship. But the situation was saved for Albania by an international crisis—Soviet intervention in Hungary in 1956, which led to a decided cooling in Russian–Yugoslavian relations.

Further, the Soviet leader Khrushchëv continued to push "de-Stalinization" after 1956, which was at cross-purposes with Hoxha's desire to retain absolute, one-man power. He also was disturbed by Russia's proposal in the CMEA for an "international socialist division of labor," for it appeared that Albania's role would be to furnish the CMEA with foodstuffs and raw materials. That would spell the death of Hoxha's cherished industrialization program. When it became evident that China was also becoming disgruntled with the Soviets' leadership, Hoxha decided to sound out the possibilities of becoming a Chinese protégé. Toward the end of 1959, Albanian speeches were already assuming a Chinese slant on political issues. The Chinese were delighted to have at least vocal support in their disputes with the Russians.

The new direction of Albanian policy became clear at a meeting in Bucharest, Romania in mid–1960 when the Albanian delegation backed the Chinese. The next occasion for a confrontation came in November at a Moscow conference of 81 communist parties. In spite of, or perhaps because of, Soviet pressure in the intervening months—including a denial of wheat deliveries at a time when famine threatened Albania—Hoxha attacked Russia's Khrushchëv in language which outdid even the Chinese criticism.

The dispute clearly was brought into the open in late 1961 when Khrushchëv attacked the Albanian party and they, in turn, denounced Khrushchëv. When the Chinese countered with an attack on Yugoslavia, the style of the dispute was set until the later open break between Moscow and Peking in 1963.

Diplomatic relations between Moscow and Tirana were broken in 1961. Albania also refused to participate in the Council for Mutual Economic Assistance (CMEA) or the Warsaw Pact after the break.

Albania accepted Chinese "guidance" in party and state affairs after its break with the Soviet Union in 1961 and between 1960 and 1975 received approximately half a billion dollars in interest–free credits from China. With almost 2,000 Chinese technical experts, Albania was able to set up some thirty new industrial projects, chiefly for the production of energy, irrigation and processing of raw materials. Albania was even exporting modest amounts of oil to Greece, with which it had concluded a trade agreement for the first time since World War II.

When Russia invaded Czechoslovakia in 1968, Albania announced officially its withdrawal from the Warsaw Pact. Apparently concerned about its security, it also launched an effort to improve relations with neighboring countries; for the first time since 1948, Albania began to cultivate better relations with Yugoslavia. This policy began to bear fruit in 1970. Trade between the two countries increased; Yugoslav tourists were permitted to enter Albania and cultural exchanges between the University of Tirana and the University of Pristina (in Kosovo Province) were approved. The two countries raised their diplomatic staffs to embassy level shortly thereafter.

The presence of 1.6 million ethnic Albanians living in Yugoslavia, so often in the past a basis for disagreements between the two countries, for a time helped contribute to a healing as cultural contacts between the ethnic Albanians on both sides of the border increased in frequency. Relations worsened again in 1976, however, as a new wave of unrest and Albanian "unity" activity began in the Kosovo region of Yugoslavia.

A number of violent demonstrations occurred among the students at Pristina University in 1981, accompanied by demands to exclude Kosovo from its program of cultural cooperation with Albania when the program came up for renewal in 1984. In retaliation, the Albanian Government accused Yugoslavia of practicing a policy of "cultural genocide" against ethnic Albanians living within its borders and broke off talks on a new cultural exchange agreement in October 1984. Yugoslavia continued to be Albania's chief trading partner but the level of trade dropped somewhat after 1984 and then stagnated at that lower figure. Economic factors probably played a role in this development, but political factors were clearly dominant. The Serbian Government's subsequent actions against ethnic Albanians in the province of Kosovo, in particular the destruction of that province's autonomy in 1990, only

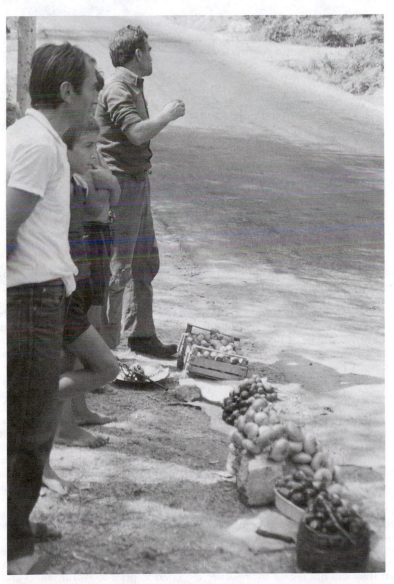

Albanian farmers selling their fruits and vegetables along the roadside.   Courtesy: James V. Elias

Albania

Rural Albanian transportaion.   Courtesy: James V. Elias

decreased the possibility of improved relations between the two countries.

The situation was further compounded in 1991, when Albania extended diplomatic recognition to the self–proclaimed independent "Republic of Kosovo."

Albania's relations with the People's Republic of China soured in the late 1970's, apparently because of a change that occurred in China's foreign policy at this time. Hoxha disapproved of the warming trend in Chinese–American relations that had begun in the early 1970's, but he was particularly angered when the People's Republic extended an invitation to Marshal Tito to visit China. Albania launched an anti–China campaign in mid–1977 and this led to a break in Chinese–Albanian relations in 1978. China discontinued all economic and military assistance to Albania and withdrew all of its technical experts.

Diplomatic relations were resumed in 1979, but they did not regain their earlier warmth, largely for ideological reasons. This time the reason was the economic

reform which Deng Xiaoping launched when he came to power in 1978. Hoxha disapproved of Deng's move and considered him to be a revisionist. Relations began to improve after Hoxha's death in 1985, however. Albania does not have extensive relations with the People's Republic of China, but they now would be considered good.

Albania continued to reject diplomatic relations with either the United States or the Soviet Union so long as Hoxha was alive, but it did come out of its self–imposed isolation to a limited extent in the early 1980's. There was an improvement in relations with Greece, Italy and France, and Albania opened talks with Great Britain and the Federal Republic of Germany in an attempt to resolve bilateral differences that prevented the establishment of diplomatic relations.

British–Albanian differences were over an Albanian gold reserve placed in London prior to World War II and British demands that Albania pay compensation for sinking a British ship off the Albanian

coast in 1946. The sticking point in Albanian–West German relations was Albania's demand for $2 billion in reparations from the Federal Republic for damage done in Albania during World War II.

The Federal Republic was unwilling to concede the principle of reparations, but did suggest the possibility of a loan or credits to finance a major industrial plant in Albania. Some improvement in relations became evident in 1984 when Franz Joseph Strauss, Premier of Bavaria, made a private trip to Albania. In spite of the unofficial nature of the visit, Strauss was received by Manush Myftiu, a Deputy Prime Minister and member of the Politburo. Strauss's presence was also reported in the Albanian press.

This process speeded up somewhat after Enver Hoxha died in April 1985. His successor, Ramiz Alia, though committed to a general continuation of Hoxha's policies, supported a policy of opening up more to the rest of the world. For example, Reiz Malile, the Albanian Foreign Minister, attended the 40th session of the United Nations General Assembly in 1985 and while there, held meetings with the foreign ministers of 16 other countries, including Italy, Greece, Turkey and Austria. In addition, Tirana played host to high–level diplomatic delegations from Italy and France as well as trade delegations from West Germany and Japan during 1985–86. An agreement on border demarcation was signed with Greece. In general, diplomatic contacts increased with Western European and Third World countries.

On the other hand, the *Albanian Labor Party* continued to reject party–to–party relations with other communist countries during this period and the only ones represented by an ambassador in Tirana were Romania, North Korea, and the People's Republic of China. Albania did sign a major trade agreement with the German Democratic Republic, however. Under the terms of the agreement, the GDR agreed to provide Albania with industrial technology, including agricultural machinery, in return for Albanian chrome ore.

A further, if still cautious, breakthrough then occurred in September 1987 when Albania reestablished diplomatic relations with Canada. One week later, the Albanian Government followed this up by agreeing to establish diplomatic relations with the Federal Republic of Germany. The near simultaneity of the announcements appears to be coincidence, however, for talks with West Germany had actually been going on for three years.

A further interesting development occurred in January 1988 when Albania and Bulgaria agreed to raise diplomatic relations between the two countries to the ambassadorial level. Albania also agreed to attend a foreign ministers conference on the Balkans hosted by Yugoslavia. The six foreign ministers (of Albania, Yugoslavia, Romania, Bulgaria, Greece and Turkey) met in Belgrade in February 1988. Their talks covered a number of issues, including trade, regional economic interests, communications, and creation of a nuclear–free and chemical weapons–free Balkans. Not much of a concrete nature was accomplished, but they did agree to meet again. For Albania, of course, the very fact of its participation represented a breakthrough of sorts. There have been two follow–up meetings of Balkans foreign ministers, the last in Tirana in the spring of 1991.

The wave of political change sweeping across Eastern Europe in the last months of 1989 did not affect Albania directly, but it did change the world in which it operated. Prefacing his remarks with a specific reference to recent international developments, Alia told the Central Committee in April 1990 that "the problem of the reestablishment of diplomatic relations with the United States of America and the Soviet Union is on the agenda." Albania resumed diplomatic relations with the Soviet Union soon afterwards. The first contacts between American and Albanian diplomats occurred in May 1990, but the United States Government was concerned about internal Albanian developments and the discussions continued for some time before they were successfully concluded. Diplomatic relations were officially renewed in March 1991.

After a government of national unity in which half of the cabinet seats were held by members of the political opposition was installed in early June, Albania found additional doors opening to it. It was admitted to the European Bank for Reconstruction and Development in September and the IMF and World Bank in October. Membership in these organizations made Albania eligible for technical assistance and also loans.

Albania's relations with the United States also improved after the change in government in June 1991. The U.S. Government supported Albania's membership applications to international organizations and promised it humanitarian economic assistance. Ylli Bufi, Chairman of the Council of Ministers, traveled to the United States in November, the first Albania leader to come to Washington. Although the visit was technically private, Bufi did meet with Arnold Kanter, U.S. Undersecretary of State for Political Affairs.

The main purpose of the visit was economic, however. In addition to an agreement which he signed with the

Overseas Private Investment Corporation to guarantee American investments in Albania, Bufi met with officials of the Treasury. Commerce, and Agriculture Departments, and with members of the House Foreign Affairs and Senate Foreign Relations committees. He also met with officials of the World Bank.

Since the election of Sali Berisha as President in March 1992, relations with the United States have undergone a major chance. Flora Lewis, who visited Albania in the spring of 1993, reported that there's "a constant flow of American military personnel coming and going to give advice and check the situation." With Albanians fearful that the Yugoslav war might spread first to Kosovo and then to Albania, "America is seen as a protector." The United States has, in fact, made no commitments to Albania, though the Clinton Administration, worried about the war spreading to Kosovo, has expressed its disquiet to the Serbian Government. Albania has said that it would resist any attack from across the border, but its weapons, almost entirely Soviet or Chinese–made versions of Soviet weapons from the 1950's and early 1960's, would be almost useless against well–armed Serbian forces. This is probably one reason why President Berisha, visiting NATO headquarters in Brussels in December 1992, said that Albania would like to join the western alliance.

In another change, John Paul II became the first pope to visit Albania since the middle ages when he arrived there in April 1993. Only about ten percent of the population is Roman Catholic, but the Pope got a warm welcome. President Berisha welcomed the Pope and the two speeches made an interesting dialogue about the Balkans. John Paul II, addressing a rally in Tirana, advised:

"Do not let the sense of nation that you feel strongly at this moment degenerate into the kind of intolerant and agressive nationalism that claims its victims still today and fuels ferocious hatreds in several parts of the world, some not far from here."

President Berisha's speech touched on the same theme. "The Holy Father," he said:

"has come to the Balkans today at a time when not far from us, in Bosnia–Herzegovina, criminal demons are committing massacres and ethnic cleansing, are exterminating an entire people. We can never permit the ethnic cleansing of Albanians from their territory, and we insist that the region's crisis will never be resolved without a solution of the question of Albanians in Kosovo."

NATURE OF THE REGIME

The Albanian Government

The "supreme organ of state power" is a 140–member People's Assembly, which is elected for a four–year term. In the latest elections, which took place on March 22–29, 1992 the *Democratic Party* won 92 seats while the *Socialist Party* (the renamed communists) took 38. The remaining seats were shared by the *Republicans* and *Social Democrats*.

Under the new multiparty democracy that has resulted from this election, the Assembly is the fulcrum of power, with the authority to elect the President, confirm the Chairman of the Council of Ministers, and approve the budget and all legislation.

The Assembly has played this role to some extent ever since the first multiparty elections took place in March 1991. But the fact that the *Party of Labor* won two–thirds of the seats in that election, while the opposition, organized as the *Democratic Party*, was able to win only 75 of the 250 seats, negated that to some extent. Now the promise will become the reality.

Executive authority within the government is shared by the President of the Republic, who is viewed as spokesman for the nation and therefore the individ-

In the past an ever–present bust of Stalin.

Albania

ual who sets general policy, and the Chairman of the Council of Ministers, who carries out the functions of a prime minister. He oversees the actions of his ministers and maintains liaison with the People's Assembly.

There also is a Supreme Court, though its duties and functions are likely to change in the future. Under the old system which has not been completely changed, justices were elected by the People's Assembly for a four–year term. The Supreme Court operates as a court of appeal from decisions of local People's Courts. In May 1990, the People's Assembly created the office of Justice Minister and instructed him to draw up a plan for creation of a new system of courts and defense attorneys.

The Economy

Before Enver Hoxha's death in 1985, Albania always billed itself as the world's first "true socialist economy." One reason for this claim was that 100% of the "means of production" had been nationalized under Hoxha. Until 1990, this extended even to motor vehicles, which could be owned only by the state. Citizens were permitted to own bicycles, however. That proud boast lost all of its glitter long before the defeat of the *Socialist Party of Albania* in the May 1992 elections, but the truth behind that boast continues to give government ministers headaches as they work to privatize the economy and move Albania toward a market economy.

Albania launched its first Five Year Plan in 1951 with a goal of a rapid development of industry and national self–sufficiency in both industrial and agricultural products. Growth during the first two Five Year Plans was fairly rapid, since Albania was starting from literally nothing. It slowed thereafter, but this can largely be blamed on the halt in Soviet economic aid after the break in relations in 1961. There was fairly rapid growth between 1966 and 1970—reflecting the assistance that the country got from China—but there has been a slowdown since 1970 which some blame on a breakdown in labor discipline in the early 1970's. It may be connected with the fact that Albania achieved full collectivization of agriculture in 1967 and followed this up by a reduction in the size of peasants' private plots. Albanian agriculture regularly achieved only about 50% of its assigned production targets in the late 1960's and early 1970's. This sector also suffered from the loss of Chinese assistance after the Albanian–Chinese diplomatic break in that year. As a result, the government abandoned its long–term goal of self–sufficiency and began to develop foreign trade.

Albania is still the least developed country in Europe, but the regime's policy of industrialization did produce substantial changes in a number of areas. For example, Albania has significant resources of chrome, iron, coal, copper and petroleum, and these have been developed over the past 40 years or so. Albania has the capacity to produce over 800,000 tons a year, which makes it the world's third–largest producer of that vital metal. In the 1970s, Albania constructed an oil refinery with an annual capacity of one million tons and began exporting crude oil and refined petroleum products to Italy, Greece, the Federal Republic of Germany, Switzerland and Romania.

Other exports included electric power, copper, coal, textiles and food industry products. Albania's exports began dropping drastically beginning in 1989, partly as a result of a severe drought that didn't leave the government enough money to import spare parts or raw materials

The severe drought that began in the late 1980s had a devastating effect on agriculture, but the overall economy was having difficulties even before that. Red tape and too much control from Tirana had created a situation of slow growth that the bureaucrats were unable to reverse. Severe shortages developed, particularly of raw materials, modern machinery and consumer goods. Food items such as meat and cheese had to be rationed, though staples such as bread, sugar and milk remained adequate until 1990. Fruits and vegetables were still freely available at that time.

In March 1990, however, Ramiz Alia promised to institute a number of economic reforms aimed at decentralizing decision–making and creating some economic incentives in industry and agriculture. Though developments elsewhere in Eastern Europe were an important influencing factor, the state of the Albanian economy played the more important role in the political developments in 1990–91. A common complaint, both of people demonstrating in the cities and of others who fled the country was the lack of any hope as far as their own futures was concerned. Part of that pessimism was caused by the failure of the communist system itself but not all of it.

The other serious, long–term problem is that of Albania's rate of population growth, which was higher than its rate of economic growth even before three years of drought in 1989–91 exacerbated that situation further. The Albanian Government obviously has its hands full dealing with immediate economic problems, but it will have to address this problem eventually or see its gains in the economic area negated by continued increases in population.

The new democratic government is committed to the privatization of state–owned industry and the creation of a market economy, but it hasn't been able to make much progress in the area of privatization because of the dire state of the economy by the time it took power. When the previous coalition government removed subsidies on state industry in November 1991, about half of industry closed down or laid off workers and went on short hours. With social discipline breaking down, Albania entered a period of effective anarchy. The new democratic government managed to reverse that trend and to restore order in the cities, though roving bands of robbers are still reported in parts of the countryside. Meanwhile, industrial production continued to drop with many plants working at five percent capacity by November 1992.

Things look bleak for Albania for the foreseeable future, but Albania has an unusual source of assistance that it has only begun to exploit. Because of past

James V. Elias, president of the Albanian–American Trade Association (left) with President Sali Berisha of the Republic of Albania

migrations from this poor land, about 600,000 persons of Albanian descent live in America. Reports indicate that they were heavy contributors to the *Democratic Party* in the run up to the March 1992 elections. If a significant number of them can be persuaded to invest in their old homeland, or return with their foreign skills, they could make a significant difference in how quickly Albania develops. Some Albanian–Americans have already provided capital to Albanian relatives to set up or buy businesses and more assistance of this nature is likely.

Albania has also begun to receive some foreign assistance and this will eventually make some difference. The United States, for example, provided $83 million in aid in 1992. In an innovative program, $15 million of this assistance was in the form of raw cotton for an Albanian cotton mill in Berat, which had had to lay off its 15,000 workers for lack of raw materials. The supply of cotton was expected to keep the mill going for a period of five months.

The news from the countryside is a little better. First of all, the old collective form of farming has almost disappeared as a result of the legislature's 1991 decision to allow peasants to obtain their own parcels of land. Most of the implementation of that decision was carried out by the peasants themselves, however, and they did so in a haphazard manner. Basically, the peasants were unable to agree among themselves about who owned what lands. As a result, only about half the agricultural land was planted in 1991. Most of the quarrels over land ownership were resolved by 1992, and the harvest was much better. Albania is still receiving international humanitarian assistance from several countries, but the threat of a famine is over.

Culture

The two elements that defined traditional Albanian culture were religion—primarily Islam—and the way of life associated with the peasantry of the Balkans. After 1945, the *Albanian Party of Labor* introduced its own double agenda, an economic goal of industrialization and a social goal of creating the "new socialist person." Industrialization increased the urban population and led to increased mechanization of the countryside. In addition, because of its need for trained technicians, the regime set up many new technical schools that eventually produced an educated, urban elite. Albania is still basically a rural and peasant society, however, with 63% of the people living in villages in the countryside where clan or feudal relationships tend to persist.

In 1964, Hoxha launched an ideological and cultural revolution aimed at eliminating religion, the influence of family and sectional loyalties, and prejudices toward women. All churches and mosques were closed and most religious leaders were imprisoned. In addition, a major effort was made to end the traditional Islamic seclusion of women and to bring them into the workplace. Three years later, Albania became the world's first officially atheist country.

The party relaxed some of its controls beginning in 1970, but the cultural revolution resumed again in 1973. Now the targets were young people, the military and the technicians. The party reorganized the education system to make it stricter. Party officials who had advocated a moderate line were purged. Intellectuals were sent to factories and collective farms to do manual labor.

This cultural revolution didn't actually succeed in changing the basic culture of the country, but it did enforce a surface conformity. It is not even clear that closing all of the mosques and churches reduced the number of believers—though it did succeed in driving religion underground.

The prohibition against all public religious rituals left a void, however, and the regime attempted to fill this by creating a new calendar of secular festivals. National holidays such as Albanian Independence Day (November 28) formed the core of the new calendar, but there are also days set aside for honoring the worker and a number of agricultural festivals.

In April 1990, the regime rescinded laws prohibiting the practice of religion. In November, the party voted to return all houses of worship to their respective religious communities. Most churches and mosques had been converted into things like gymnasiums, movie theaters and warehouses or had been allowed to fall into disrepair, however, so implementation has been slow. About 40 churches had been turned over to religious authorities by April 1991. A much more serious problem in rebuilding the church is the shortage of priests, however. There were fewer than 10 Greek Orthodox priests in the country in April 1991 and only 32 Catholic priests. All were elderly and most had spent long years in prison. The head of Albanian Catholics, the Apostolic Administrator of Durres, was a 76–old man who lived in total retirement in a small village in the north of the country.

On March 21, 1991, a symbolic mass was said in Shkodër Cathedral, though the building was not really in a condition to be used. Its two towers had been demolished in 1967, its portal was boarded up, and inside the yellow plaster was peeling everywhere. In another symbolic act, Mother Theresa, an ethnic Albanian born in nearby Macedonia, came to Shkodër in March 1991. She attended the first mass at Shkodër Cathedral and opened a convent nearby. The three nuns in residence opened an orphanage for unwanted Albanian children.

The Islamic community has taken back perhaps 10–15 mosques but they are, like the churches, in a dilapidated condition. One mosque, the Xhamia e Plumbit, an eighteenth century mosque that stands before the gates of Shkodër, had been rehabilitated somewhat and is currently in use. Moslem clerics suffered a treatment similar to Christians and they are also elderly men who have served long terms in prison. In many ways, in fact, they are even more badly off. There are between 10 and 15 Moslem dignitaries in the country and most of them have had no theological training.

The new constitution drawn up in 1991 recognizes freedom of religion and conscience as fundamental human rights. The victory of the *Democratic Party* in the March 1992 elections—and the poor showing of the *Socialist Party*—gives promise that a genuinely pluralistic society may now develop in Albania.

The Future

Things look extremely bleak for this country for the foreseeable future, but Albania has an unusual source of assistance that it has only begun to exploit. Because of past migrations from this poor land, about 600,000 persons of Albanian descent live in America. Reports indicate that they were heavy contributors to the *Democratic Party* before the recent elections. If a significant number of them can be persuaded to invest in their old homeland, or return with their foreign skills, they could make a significant difference in how quickly Albania develops. Some Albanian–Americans have already provided capital to Albanian relatives to set up or buy businesses and more assistance of this nature is likely.

The Baltic Republics

Due to their shared histories as well as frequent geographical and cultural similarities, there is necessarily some repetition from one entry to the other.

to 17th centuries, and extensive Russian influence as a result of being part of the Russian Empire 1709–1918. Estonians currently make up about 61.5% of the population.

Other Ethnic Groups: Russians (30.3%); Ukrainians (3.1%); Belarusians (1.8%); Finns (1.1%).

Principal Religions: Lutheranism, Russian Orthodox Christianity.

Chief Commercial Products: Ships, mineral fertilizers, paper products, peat, agricultural products, fish.

Currency: Krona.

Former Political Status: Conquered by German and Danish Knights in the 13th century, it came under Swedish control in the 17th century. Peter the Great annexed it in 1709 and it remained part of the Russian Empire until 1918. Independent state, 1918–1940. Annexed to the Soviet Union by Stalin in 1940; declared its independence in August 1991.

Independence Day: February 24.

Chief of State: Lennart Meri, President.

Head of Government: Mart Laar, Prime Minister.

National Flag: tricolor—blue, black and white.

The Republic of Estonia

Area: 18,370 square miles (47,549 sq. km.).

Population: 1.6 million.

Capital City: Tallinn (506,000).

Climate: Temperate with cool summers and cold winters, somewhat tempered by an arm of the gulf stream that reaches into the Baltic.

Neighboring Countries: Russia (east); Latvia (south).

Official Language: Estonian.

Other Principal Tongue: Russian.

Ethnic Background: Estonian is linguisticly close to Finnish. There is some German influence as a result of being ruled by German Knights from the 13th

**Lennart Meri
The President of Estonia**

The Republic of Latvia

Area: 25,400 square miles (65,786 sq. km.).
Population: 2.7 Million.
Capital City: Riga (Pop. 915,000).
Climate: Temperate with cool summers and cold winters, somewhat tempered by an arm of the gulf stream that reaches into the Baltic.
Neighboring Countries: Estonia (north); Russia (east); Belarus (southeast); Lithuania (south).
Official Language: Latvian.
Other Principal Tongues: Russian.
Ethnic Background: Latvian belongs to the Letto–Lithuanian family of Indo-European languages. It is closely related to Lithuanian, but contains words taken over from Swedish, German and Russian, the languages of peoples that controlled the country at various times in the past. Letts currently make up about 52% of the population.
Other Ethnic Groups: Russians (33%); Ukrainians, Belarusians, Others (14%).
Principal Religions: Lutheran, Russian Orthodox Christianity.
Chief Commercial Products: Machinery, electrical equipment, agricultural engineering, paper products, timber, building materials, chemicals, pharmaceuticals, dairy products.
Currency: Latvian Ruble. The currency may eventually become the "Lat."
Former Political Status: The Latvian lands were part of the territory governmed by the Teutonic Knights from the 13th to the 16th century. They were subsequently ruled by Poland, then Sweden. Peter the Great annexed Riga in 1710; the remainder of the country fell to Russian rule in the 18th century. With the collapse of the Russian Empire, Latvia declared its independence in 1920. Occupied by Soviet forces in June 1940, it was annexed by Stalin in August 1940; declared its independence May 4, 1990.
Independence Day: November 18.
Chief of State: Anatoly Gorbunovs, Chairman of the Latvian Parliament (informally, President).
Head of Government: Ivars Godmanis, Chairman, Council of Ministers (informally, Prime Minister).
National Flag: Three vertical stripes—dark red, white (half as thick), dark red.

Anatoly Gorbunovs
The President of Latvia

Algirdas Brazauskas
The President of Lithuania

The Republic of Lithuania

Area: 25,174 square miles (64,445 sq. km.).
Population: 3,690,000.
Capital City: Vilnius (Pop. 582,000).
Climate: Temperate with cool summers and cold winters, somewhat tempered by an arm of the gulf stream that reaches into the Baltic.
Neighboring Countries: Latvia (north); Belarus (southeast); Poland (southwest); Russia (Kaliningrad Enclave) (west).
Official Language: Lithuanian.
Other Principal Tongues: Polish, Russian.
Ethnic Background: Lithuanian belongs to the Letto–Lithuanian family of Indo-European languages. It is closely related to Latvian, but contains heavy influences from the Polish language. Lithuanians, mentioned in Tacitus's *Germania* as excellent farmers, have occupied the southern shores of the Baltic for over two thousand years. A dynastic union with Poland in the 14th century brought a Polanization of the Lithuanian upper classes. Russian influence began in the 18th century when Lithuania became part of the Russian Empire. Lithuanians currently make up 80% of the population.
Other Ethnic Groups: Russians (8.6%); Poles (7%); Other (4.3%).
Principal Religion: Roman Catholic Christianity.
Chief Commercial Products: Agricultural products, timber, paper, ships, textiles, synthetic fibers, leather, cellulose, metal goods, tape recorders, televisions.
Currency: Talon.
Former Political Status: An independent Principality in the 13th century; A dynastic union with Poland in 1385 led to an increasing closeness between the two countries until they were merged in 1569. Lithuania became part of the Russian Empire in the 18th century and remained so until 1918. Independent state 1918–1940; annexed to the Soviet Union in 1940; declared its independence again in March 1990; took control of its borders on August 26, 1991.
National Day: February 16 (Independence Day).
Chief of State: Algirdas Brazauskas, President of the Republic.
Head of Government: Bronislovas Lubys, Prime Minister.
National Flag: Three horizontal stripes—yellow, green, red.

The Baltic Republics

Lachemaa National Park, Estonia

NOVOSTI photo

The Baltic Republics

THE LAND AND THE PEOPLE

The three republics of Estonia, Latvia, and Lithuania are located along the eastern shores of the Baltic Sea. Finland lies to the north, separated from Estonia by the Gulf of Finland, while Sweden lies to the west, across the Baltic Sea.

Estonia, the most northern of the three republics, borders on Russia to the east, though the two countries are physically separated along most of the border by a series of lakes that stretch from just north of Pskov to the Baltic Sea. Tallinn, the capital, major port and largest city, lies on the Gulf of Finland, directly across from Helsinki, the capital of Finland. Latvia, to the south of Estonia, shares borders with Belarus and Russia on the east. Its capital, Riga—located on the Gulf of Riga at the mouth of the Daugava [Western Dvina] River—is at the same time its largest city and best port.

Lithuania, the most southern of the three republics, borders on the Kaliningrad enclave of the Russian Republic to the south and the Republic of Belarus on the east. Its shoreline, only 99 kilometers long, is relatively narrow and it has only one good port, the city of Klaipeda. Vilnius and Kaunas, its two major cities, lie considerably inland, Kaunas along the upper reaches of the Nemunas [Niemen] River and Vilnius on the Neris River, a tributary of the Nemunas. Vilnius, the current capital and the ancient capital of the Grand Principality of Lithuania, lies quite close to the current border of Belarus and was actually part of Poland between the first and second world wars.

The entire Baltic coastal area is a plain with occasional higher elevations, particularly as one moves away from the sea, but the highest of these elevations are never more than about 900 feet in height. Nevertheless, they are the reason why a number of small rivers flow through the Baltic Republics and into the Baltic Sea. The shoreline itself consists mostly of low dunes running along the beaches. There are plenty of sandy beaches, but the water tends to be extremely shallow for a good distance into the sea, making swimming difficult. Pine forests, which predominate throughout the Baltic coastal area, often come down almost to the shore.

It is these pines that help to explain amber, the symbol of the Baltic. Fifty million years ago, the Baltic Sea was a vast marshland covered by pine trees. The resin oozed out of the pine trunks and dripped into the silt of the marsh where it eventually hardened, then petrified over succeeding millenia. Today, amber is often found along the shore, washed up by the sea.

Most of the area was originally a combination of marsh and forest and even today farms give the appearance of having been cut out of the forest. Small lakes are very common, with an estimated 3,000 in Lithuania alone. Soils, which are usually gray, tend to be relatively poor, and most farming is dairy farming. One arm of the Gulf Stream reaches into the Baltic, making the climate milder than it would otherwise be. Summers tend to be cool with frequent light rains. Winters are cold and damp.

Languages

The Estonian language belongs to the Finnish branch of the Ural–Altaic family, though it contains words taken from Swedish, German and Russian. The Estonians, along with the Finns, are the remnants of tribes which once lightly peopled much of the northern two–thirds of what is today European Russia. Although still existing in some places in small pockets in Russia, particularly in the Karelian Peninsula, most were absorbed into the larger Slavic population over the centuries.

The Lithuanian and Latvian languages belong to the Letto–Lithuanian family of Indo–European languages. Lithuanian was heavily influenced by the Polish language, however, while Latvian shows influences from Swedish, German and Russian, the languages of peoples that controlled the country at various times in the past.

HISTORY

The peoples living along the southern shores of the Baltic have had a relatively long history, and have occupied this same area for over two thousand years. The first historical reference to be found is in Tacitus's *Germania*, where he praises the Lithuanians for their talents in farming. At that time, the Baltic area had some contact with the civilizations to the south because of amber, which occurs along the Baltic coast and became the basis for a trade route which actually came into existence as early as the second millennium B.C. The decline of the Roman Empire turned this area once more into a backwater, however, and nothing more was heard for several centuries.

The next historical reference dates from the seventh century, when Viking raiders swept down out of Scandinavia and launched a series of raids along the coast and up the rivers. These invasions, continuing for the next two hundred years, eventually resulted in some Viking settlements along the rivers and, in 862, the beginning of the Kievan Rus State at Novgorod when Riurik established himself as ruler at Novgorod. Most of the Baltic Sea area was under the control of the Vikings at this time, but their main interest was on expansion of the trade route across Russia down to Constantinople. Accordingly, they only levied an annual tribute on the Baltic peoples and otherwise left them alone.

Remaining on the periphery, the Baltic peoples all remained pagan even as their neighbors to the west and the south embraced Christianity. That led, at the beginning of the thirteenth century, to a Christianizing effort by German missionaries. These first efforts were peaceful, and a bishopric was actually established at Riga in 1201. This peaceful penetration was soon followed by an invasion of crusading knights, the most significant being the Knights of the Sword and the Order of Teutonic Knights. The Teutonic Knights conquered the area of present–day Latvia in 1225. Gradually, the area of Estonia was also brought under the control of the Knights of the Sword, who subsequently turned it over to the Order of Teutonic Knights. The Latvians and Estonians were enserfed and converted to Christianity, but managed to retain many of their customs and their own languages.

Meanwhile the Lithuanians, who up to this time had been organized into separate tribes, formed a federation under the Grand Duke Ringaudas. His successor, Mindaugas, defended the federation against the Russians, Poles and the Teutonic Knights and even converted to Christianity in an attempt to put an end to the outside pressure. He was assassinated, however, and his successor, Vitenis, continued the struggle against the Teutonic Knights. It was Vitenis' brother and successor, Gediminas [1316–1341], who, building on the victories won by his brother, founded the Jogaila [Jagellon] dynasty and laid the basis of the Grand Duchy of Lithuania. During his lifetime, Gediminas extended his conquests southward, fighting both Russians and Tatars until his kingdom extended from the Baltic to the Black Sea. He thus freed the western part of Kievan Rus from the control of the Tatars, including the city of Kiev itself. At this time, a majority of his subjects were either White Russians or Ukrainians, and Russian became the official language of the realm. Although Gediminas was himself still a pagan, most of his subjects were Orthodox Christians.

Gediminas was slain in 1341 while once again attempting to drive back the Teutonic Knights. He was succeeded by his son, Jagellon [Jogaila], who married Hedwige, Queen of Poland. Jagellon, having converted to Roman Catholicism, took over as ruler of Poland and turned over the Grand Duchy of Lithuania to his cousin, Vytautas. Vytautas died without an heir in 1430, however, so the crown reverted back to the Jogaila line. From that time, the Grand Duchy of Lithuania was increasingly tied to Poland until, in

The Baltic Republics

Baltic Area – 15th to Early 18th Centuries

Swedish Possessions

Teutonic Order (about 1400) / Prussia (1561, 1660 and 1721)

Republic of Novgorod (about 1400) / Muscovy (1561) / Russia (1660 and 1721)

Lithuania (about 1400) / Poland-Lithuania (1561, 1660 and 1721)

Duchy of Courland: Dependency of Poland-Lithuania (1660 and 1721)

The Baltic Republics

Mindaugas

1569, the two kingdoms were merged in the Union of Lublin.

Lithuania continued to have its own laws and army, but the upper classes became increasingly Polanized and most of them became Roman Catholic. Polish replaced Russian as the language of administration in the 16th century.

In the last half of the 18th century, Poland–Lithuania was partitioned among its neighbors, in 1772, 1793 and 1795. As a result, Russia obtained the Ukrainian and White Russian territories plus all of Lithuania proper up to the Nemunas River. Russia obtained the remaining Lithuanian territories in 1815.

The spread of the Protestant Reformation in the 16th century led to the creation of the two secular states of Courland and Livonia and the dissolution of the Teutonic Knights in 1560. The former knights converted to Lutheranism and became a secular nobility. Their Estonian and Latvian serfs were also converted at this same time.

Courland and Livonia also became takeover targets of their neighbors at this time. The Russian Tsar, Ivan IV, wanting to gain control of ports along the Baltic, launched his Livonian War in 1558. He was successful in the beginning but, when the Teutonic Knights collapsed in 1560, Poland stepped in and stole his conquests, annexing Livonia and Courland to Poland–Lithuania. Then, at the beginning of the 17th century, the Swedish King, Gustavus Adolphus, intervened and seized most of Livonia in 1626. The Swedish territory, which included most of modern day Estonia, was given a relatively liberal regime. The privileges of the German nobility—the so–called Baltic Barons—were curtailed somewhat and a university was established at Dorpat. It was also as a result of Swedish rule that

the Lutheran Church continued as the established church in Estonia.

Then, at the end of the 17th century, Peter the Great came to the throne in Russia and launched his Great Northern War against Sweden in 1700. The war lasted until 1721, but Riga fell to Russia in 1710 and Tallinn [Revel] soon afterwards. Russia obtained Livonia and Estonia by the Peace of Nystadt. Courland gradually became a Russian protectorate during the 18th century, and was formally annexed in 1795.

The Baltics Under Russian Rule

Peter the Great allowed his new Baltic subjects to retain their own laws and the autonomous status which they had enjoyed under the Swedes. There was no attempt to introduce Russian institutions or to encourage the spread of the Orthodox religion to the area. Peter's second wife, Catherine, was actually a Baltic peasant girl whom he took as a mistress during the Baltic campaign and later married. On the other hand, it was basically the German–speaking nobility that benefited from this autonomy; the Letts and Estonians were at this time still mainly serfs. There were some economic benefits to the area, however; in the 18th century, Riga became Russia's second major port after St. Petersburg, a position it would continue to hold in the 19th century.

A major change occurred at the beginning of the 19th century when Alexander I became Tsar. Alexander detested serfdom and as early as 1803 issued a decree permitting the voluntary emancipation of the serfs. Later in his reign, Alexander abolished serfdom in the Baltic Provinces, in Estonia in 1816, Courland in 1817, and Livonia in 1819. In Lithuania, which was under a separate administration, serfdom continued. It was abolished there in 1861, as part of the general serf emancipation throughout the Russian Empire.

In the Baltic Provinces, the short–term consequences of emancipation were mainly negative. The Baltic serfs were freed without land and, with no alternate means of employment, found themselves working as day laborers for the same large landowners who had been their masters before emancipation. On the other hand, the long–term consequences were both positive and far–reaching. The presence of free labor made Estonia and Latvia logical places to locate manufacturing plants when foreign capital began pouring into Russia after Alexander II launched his great reforms in the 1850s.

Russian rule also had its negative aspects in the 19th century. In Lithuania, in particular, the Russian Government resented the role of the Roman Catholic Church and actively fostered the spread

On the way to church, Estonia (19th century)

187

The Baltic Republics

of the Orthodox Church in this area. It did not help that Lithuania participated, along with Poland, in the uprisings of 1830 and 1863. The University of Vilnius was closed down after the 1830 uprising and the Russian language was introduced in all schools. After the 1863 uprising, land ownership was limited to adherents of the Orthodox faith.

Perhaps the greatest sustained effort at Russification came during the reign of Alexander III [1881–1894]. Alexander III, a Slavophil and strong adherent of Russian Orthodoxy, extended previous Russification efforts to the areas of Estonia and Latvia and even applied them to the previously exempt German–speaking upper classes.

On the other hand, the industrialization process, begun by Alexander II, was continued by his son, Alexander III, and one result was the creation of both an urban working class and a middle class, including professionals and intellectuals, in the Baltic provinces. All of this provided the basis for the beginning of Estonian and Latvian national movements.

In Lithuania, a similar development occurred, though on the basis of a different class, the peasant landholders who emerged as a result of serf emancipation in 1861. Many of these peasant proprietors sent their sons off to be educated in Russian universities and they came back as doctors, lawyers, teachers and engineers. This led to the creation of the first specifically Lithuanian nationalist movement in the 1890s.

By 1905, illegal nationalist political parties existed in Estonia, Latvia and Lithuania and took an active part in the Revolution of 1905. The Lithuanians were perhaps the best organized, having suffered longer from repression, but similar activities were carried in all three areas. A provisional revolutionary government was established in Riga and two separate congresses met in Vilnius in December 1905. With the collapse of the revolution, widespread arrests were carried out, but government repression only succeeded in forcing the more prominent nationalist leaders to emigrate while the nationalist movements themselves went underground.

The beginning of World War I provided a new opportunity for the nationalists, however. Although the majority of the Baltic peoples loyally supported the war effort in the beginning, the subsequent course of the war brought disaffection here as it did in other parts of the Russian Empire. After March 1917, the Baltic nationalists supported the democratic aspirations of the first Russian Revolution of 1917, but began pressing for their own governments. The Bolshevik Revolution of November 1917 further alienated the Bal-

tic peoples for the vast majority favored the creation of democratic states.

The Bolsheviks wanted to retain the Baltic provinces but one of the results of the Bolshevik seizure of power was disintegration of the Russian army. Unable to stop the German advance, the new Communist government signed the Treaty of Brest–Litovsk with Imperial Germany in March 1918, thereby giving up all claims to the Baltic provinces. The entire Baltic coastal area was at this time occupied by the German army. Now the threat which the Baltic nationalists faced was annexation by Germany. The collapse of the German Empire in November 1918 put an end to that threat but, as the German armies began to pull out the Bolsheviks poured back in, and the Baltic peoples had to fight another round with the Bolsheviks in order to establish their independence. The last Bolshevik forces finally withdrew from the Baltic area at the beginning of 1920 and the Soviet Government then signed agreements with the governments of the three Baltic States recognizing their independence. The treaty with Estonia was signed on February 20, 1920; that with Lithuania was signed on July 12 and that with Latvia on August 11.

Creation of the New Baltic Governments

Developments in the Baltic provinces followed a fairly similar pattern after March 1917, though the fact that almost all of Lithuania and the southern half of Latvia were occupied by German troops obviously made for differences. The most important factor between March and November 1917 was the attitude of the Russian Provisional Government. Although not sympathetic to independence movements, it actually authorized establishment of an autonomous Estonian Government in April 1917, which led to elections for an Estonian National Council in July.

A group of middle class parties plus the allied Labor Party won 60 percent of the seats. Konstantin Paets, leader of the Farmers' Union, was installed as President of the National Council on July 14.

Lettish delegates to the Russian Duma had organized a Latvian Refugees' Committee even before the March Revolution. After March 1917, they began urging the Provisional Government to establish an autonomous administrative district for the part of Latvia still under Russian control. Local elections were held in the north, but the fact of German occupation of the south militated against any further developments at this time.

The situation with regard to Lithuania was even worse, for almost the entire country was under occupation. Nevertheless, Lithuanian deputies to the Duma

organized a Lithuanian National Council in Petrograd and began to demand political autonomy from the Provisional Government. This was the situation in November 1917.

The Bolshevik seizure of power in November 1917 proved to be a turning point, for the national movements rejected Bolshevism and tried to break away from the new Communist government. The Bolsheviks, in turn, rejected the national movements and tried to suppress them.

A Latvian National Council, established after the November Revolution, declared Latvian autonomy on November 16 and called for election of a constituent assembly to form a Latvian government. The Estonian government proclaimed its independence on November 28 and also called for elections to a constituent assembly.

The Bolsheviks not only refused to recognize the Latvian National Council; they also abolished the local government bodies set up by the Provisional Government. In Estonia, they arrested President Paets and dispersed the National Council. The Bolsheviks did permit elections to a new constituent assembly but, when the parties of the old government won a majority of the seats in the January 1918, the Bolsheviks moved to suppress the winners. A civil war now broke out and lasted about a month before German troops moved into Estonia and the Bolsheviks were forced to flee. The Lithuanian National Council, split between radicals and moderates, did not take a specific stand against the Bolsheviks, but the Bolsheviks moved to suppress the Lithuanian National Council anyway.

The Bolsheviks soon lost control of the Baltic provinces, however, first, because of advances of the German army, then, through agreement to the Treaty of Brest–Litovsk. Now the nationalists had to contend with the desire of the Germans to annex the Baltic provinces and make them part of the German Empire. Once again, the Baltic nationalist movement found itself suppressed and its leaders imprisoned. This phase ended in November 1918 with the collapse of the Imperial German Government.

The armistice called for the German army to begin evacuating the Baltic provinces, a process that eventually stretched over several months. In the meantime, the nationalist leaders began organizing independent governments. Estonia, which had an operating government once before, began reconstituting itself immediately after the armistice. The Estonian National Council met on November 20, President Paets was released from prison soon afterwards, and the new government began operating on February 24, 1919. Two months later, Paets was re-

Newspapers (top to bottom) from Estonia, Latvia, and Lithuania

placed by Otto Strandman, a member of the leftist *Workers' Party*. A few months later, Strandman was replaced by Jaan Tonisson, the leader of the *People's Party*, who served until 1920.

Governments had to be created in Latvia and Lithuania, but the nationalist leaders had been active for some time and so were well known. An All–Latvian Council of State met at Riga on November 18, 1918, formed a Provisional Government and appointed a president and prime minister. Karlis Ulmanis, leader of the *Peasants' League*, became the first president. He held this office until 1920.

In Lithuania, a Provisional Government was also set up in November. A provisional National Assembly met in Kaunas in January 1919. The first Lithua-

nian president was elected on April 4. Even as they were organizing their governments, however, the nationalists found themselves again under attack as *Bolshevik* armies reopened the war following the German surrender. By February 1919, Latvia had been completely overrun and most of Lithuania was under occupation by *Bolshevik* forces. Estonia, which had begun to form its own army, was a little luckier. It had to defend itself, but managed to drive the *Bolsheviks* back to the border.

The situation in Latvia was more complicated. A Latvian army was created and began driving back the *Bolsheviks*, with some assistance from German army units still in the country. Once they had regained control of most of the country, however, the German army supported a

coup d'etat against the Latvian government, installing a new government controlled by Baltic Germans. The Estonian and Latvian armies first joined to drive out the *Bolsheviks*, then turned on the puppet Baltic German government and overthrew it. The Latvian government was reinstated on July 7. Riga, the Latvian capital, came under attack again by German forces in October, but managed to hold out. Meanwhile, part of Latvia was still held by *Bolshevik* forces, but they were driven out in January 1920. Lenin, finally recognizing that the Baltic provinces had been lost, agreed now to recognize the independence of the Baltic States. International recognition soon followed and all three states were admitted to the League of Nations in 1922.

The Baltic Republics

Tallinn's harbor with its sign: The Baltic Sea—The Sea of Peace

ESTONIA SINCE WORLD WAR I

Independent Estonia, 1919–1939

Estonia had elected a constituent assembly charged with drawing up a constitution for the country in April 1919. The assembly was dominated by the left, so that the constitution that was eventually produced was what might be called "radical liberal" in orientation. Approved by the assembly in June 1920, it went into effect on December 21, 1920. All power was vested in a single–body legislature of 100 members called the *Riigikogu*. This was a parliamentary system. The "commission of the legislature" was essentially a cabinet, while the presiding officer, called the "Senior Statesman" [*Riigivanem*], performed the functions of a premier. There was no separate head of state, however, so the "Senior Statesman" performed all ceremonial functions as well. Another unusual feature of the constitution is that it provided for popular participation in decision–making by means of the referendum and the initiative.

Although early elections had produced leftist majorities, new elections held in 1921 produced a swing to the right with the *Farmers' Union* emerging as the dominant party.

A survey taken in 1922 gives us a good picture of the country. The total popula-

tion was 1,107,300 with Estonians making up 87.6 percent of the total. Another 8.2 percent of the population spoke Russian, while 1.7 percent spoke German. Estonia was thus the most homogeneous of the Baltic states at this time. It was also religiously homogeneous, with 78.3 percent of the population declaring themselves to be Protestant, with another 19 percent professing Russian Orthodoxy. And it was rural, with 58.5 percent of the

population earning their living from agriculture.

In 1918, two–thirds of the rural population had owned no land whatsoever but, instead, supported themselves by working as day laborers for the large estates which made up 58 percent of the land. Land reform legislation, passed in October 1919, expropriated nearly all of the estates and provided for distribution of the land to the landless rural laborers. An additional 56,000 small holdings were created as a result of the land reform law. This undoubtedly made political sense, since a majority of the estates had been owned by Baltic Germans, but the small holdings turned out to be too small, so that a majority of the new owners were unable to make a go of it without extensive governmental assistance. The eventual answer found by the Estonians was to organize the small holders into cooperative societies, which were able to buy modern machinery which could be used on several farms.

Although the land reform was pushed through by the left, it resulted in additional support for the *Farmers' Union*, a more or less conservative agrarian party. Its support grew from 8 delegates in the constituent assembly to 21 in 1920 and 24 in 1929. Between 1919 and 1934, it also produced ten of the twenty premiers.

The *Farmers' Union* was opposed on the left by the *Social Democratic Party*, with the space in between filled in by the *Independent Socialists*, the *Radical Democratic Workers' Party*, the *People's Party*, the *Christian People's Party*, and the *Settlers' Party*.

The *Communist Party* maintained an organization in Estonia until 1924 and its candidates did well in places like Tallinn and Tardu. It was driven completely underground after a communist insurrection in Tallinn in December 1924, though individual communists continued to stand for the legislature using an assumed party name.

The relative strength of the parties can be seen from the number of premiers each produced through 1934. The *Social Democrats* produced one, the *Workers' Party* four, the *People's Party* four and the *Christian People's Party* two.

Because of the number of political parties, governments were invariably coalitions. The most centrist of the parties was the *People's Party*, which participated in seventeen of the twenty coalitions between 1919 and 1933. Over time, there was some merging of the parties. In 1923, the *Independent Socialists* merged with the *Social Democrats* to form the *Socialist Workers' Party*. In 1931, the *Christian People's Party* merged with the *People's Party*; one year later, the *Workers' Party* also merged with the *People's Party*. In 1933, this became the *National Center Party*. In 1932, the *Farmers' Union* joined with the *Settlers' Party* to form the *United Agrarian Party*.

Most of these mergers were the result of the economic crisis that had begun in 1929 and then turned into what the Americans called the "Great Depression." Estonia was heavily dependent on agricultural exports, and the sharp drop in the international price of these products led to great distress in Estonia, particularly in the countryside. People were seeking answers which none of the political parties was competent to provide. The result was a drop in support for all of the established parties and their partial collapse. In 1933, eleven percent of the parliamentary delegates either changed their party or dropped all affiliation whatsoever.

It was at this time that a new political grouping, the *Association of Estonian Freedom Fighters*, began to grow in significance and power. Organized in 1929 as a veterans' organization espousing patriotism, nationalism and anti–communism, by 1932 it was beginning to show increasing tendencies toward anti–parliamentarianism and anti–liberalism. The *Freedom Fighters*, organized into paramilitary organizations, wore grey–green shirts, with black and white arm bands bearing a hand grasping a sword and the dates 1918–1920.

Their most important demand was for the creation of a separate executive power that would be independent of the legislature. Such ideas had already been proposed by the *Peoples' Party*—and defeated in a referendum—in 1926 and again in 1932. The *Freedom Fighters* proposal for constitutional reform was submitted to referendum in October 1933—and passed. This constitutional change created the office of President of the Republic, to be popularly elected for a term of five years. It also vested executive power in the President rather than the legislature. The President could appoint and dismiss governments, declare states of emergency and dissolve the legislature. The revised constitution went into effect on January 24, 1934, and elections were set to fill the new presidency. Among the candidates was General Andreas Larka, president of the *Freedom Fighters*. Another candidate was Konstantin Paets, then serving as premier. The *Freedom Fighters* swept urban local elections at the beginning of 1934 and it appeared that their man would win the presidency as well.

Paets decided to take preemptive action by pulling off his own *coup* before elections could occur. He therefore gave the commander–in–chief of the army special powers to maintain law and order and then banned the *Freedom Fighters* as a "threat to the security of the state." He also banned all political assemblies. The Estonian legislature met, approved Paets' emergency legislation, then was dismissed. Paets next issued a decree postponing presidential elections indefinitely. The legislature met for a short time in September 1934, but it was dissolved when it did not prove to be completely pliant. Paets continued to rule by decree. In February 1935, another decree dissolved the political parties. In their stead, a number of "corporations" representing various interest groups were formed to represent the interests of the people.

In February 1936, Paets began moving to "legitimatize" his authoritarian regime by submitting a referendum to the people asking them to approve calling a new constituent assembly to draft a new constitution. This passed and the new assembly met in February 1937 to ratify a new constitution drafted by the Paets government. This constitution, which went into effect on January 1, 1938, provided for a strong presidency on the order of the one approved in 1933, except that the president was to be elected by a special electoral chamber, not by popular vote. The new parliament also consisted now of two chambers, with the upper chamber partially appointed by the president. The electoral chamber met in April 1938 and confirmed Paets in office.

A small oppositional group was permitted to exist in the lower body of the legislature, but it held only seven out of eighty seats. This was the structure that was still in operation in 1939–40 when Stalin signed his pact with Hitler putting the Baltic States in the Soviet sphere of influence.

Hitler launched his invasion of Poland on September 1 and Soviet troops entered to occupy the eastern third of Poland on September 17. With Poland settled, Stalin moved to cash in his other chips. On September 19, the Estonian Government was informed that the Soviet fleet had extended its defense perimeter to include the Estonian coastline. Six days later, the Soviet Foreign Ministry presented the Estonian Government with a treaty for a military alliance between the two countries, which included the establishment of Soviet bases in Estonia. Left with no alternative, the Estonian Government signed the agreement. On September 28, the first Soviet troops entered Estonia.

Nothing happened for several months, probably because the Soviet Union was tied down in its "Winter War" with Finland. Once that was resolved, the Soviet Union turned its attention back to the Baltic States. Toward the end of May 1940, the Soviet Foreign Ministry accused all three states of violating the 1939 mutual assistance pacts with the Soviet Union. Then all three were were pressured into installing popular front governments. The popular front governments did not last long, however. In July, all political parties other than the *Communist Party* were banned and most non–communists were dismissed from office. This was followed by a wave of arrests in all three countries. Then, with only communists, organized as the *Working People's League*, standing for office, new elections were held on July 14. The newly elected legislatures met on July 21. Their only piece of business was to vote on whether to join the Soviet Union, which they did by acclamation. The following month, the USSR Supreme Soviet acceded to their request. They thus became Soviet Socialist Republics.

Nazi Germany's invasion of the Soviet Union beginning on June 22, 1941 reversed this situation somewhat, for German troops overran and occupied the three Baltic Republics later in 1941. They remained under German occupation until 1944. However, with the German retreat, the Baltic Republics once again fell under Soviet control. Guerrilla movements in the three republics continued to oppose Soviet control for some time after the end of the war in 1945, but such efforts were, of course, ineffectual. The movements got no outside assistance, and they were eventually suppressed.

Many changes occurred in the three republics over the next thirty–five years. Soviet policy was to integrate the republics so thoroughly that there would be no

The Baltic Republics

question of their ever leaving the union. To that end, the Soviet Government first carried out policies of nationalization and collectivization. Next it sought to bind the Baltic Republics to the rest of the Soviet Union economically by locating branch factories of Soviet industry in the three republics. Such factories received most or all of their raw materials from other parts of the Soviet Union, and delivered most of their finished products to customers in the other republics. This economic integration was so successful that the three Baltic Republics became more integrated into the Soviet economy than any other republic. Between 1945 and 1959, approximately 250,000 non–Estonians were resettled in the republic, some as employees of the Soviet Government, particularly its security agencies, but most as part of a project to develop Estonia's lignite and brown coal fields. Another wave began arriving in the 1960s when the Soviet Government began developing a branch of its military–industrial complex in the Narva area. As a result, the population in areas such as Narva was eventually 90 percent non–Estonian.

This program of economic integration was accompanied by a program of "Soviet Russification," aimed at transforming the cultures of the three republics. All students received Russian language training in the schools, plus general indoctrination lectures on the nature of Soviet culture. In addition, there was a systematic effort made to settle non–Baltic nationals in the republics. When a new factory was built, most of the workers would be transferred there from elsewhere in the Soviet Union.

The effects of this policy can be seen by examining the figures of the 1989 Soviet census. Ethnic Estonians by this time made up only 61.5 percent of the population of the republic. These overall figures also masked the fact that, in certain industrial regions near the border, Estonians had become a tiny minority. On the positive side, the heavy industrialization carried out since 1945 meant that the standard of living in Estonia was above that of any part of the Soviet Union.

Estonia Regains its Independence

The Estonian people accommodated themselves to Soviet rule, but they were never happy with it. When, therefore, Gorbachëv launched his programs of *glasnost* and restructuring after coming to power in 1985, Estonians were among the first to take advantage of them.

In enunciating his policy of *glasnost*, Gorbachëv called on the Soviet peoples to speak out against negative tendencies in the society, and to support his reforms. This became a manifesto which led to the creation of thousands of "unofficial" organizations all over the Soviet Union. Formed originally in support of Gorbachëv's policy of reform, many of them soon began to push their own agendas. For Estonians, Gorbachëv's policies were a welcome breath of fresh air, and they were among the first to throw their enthusiastic support to him. At the same time, and almost from the beginning, the Estonian people used *glasnost* for their own purposes.

The first unofficial Baltic organization was the *Estonian Heritage Society* (*EHS*), founded in December 1987. Ostensibly aimed at preserving the national heritage, the *EHS* very quickly became a vehicle for

The 13th century City Hall, Tallinn

Celebrating Independence Day, Tallinn

NOVOSTI photo

specifically catering to it. He reduced the size of the Central Committee, purging mainly non–Estonians, and he carried out a similar purge of the Estonian Supreme Soviet, increasing the number of Estonians to two–thirds of the membership.

Meanwhile, the goals of the *Popular Front of Estonia* were shifting. The original emphasis had been on breaking the control of the "centralized administrative–bureaucratic system" and establishing the right of Estonians to decide their own affairs without outside interference. This had been symbolized by the call for sovereignty. Increasingly, however, the argument was made that these goals could not be achieved without political pluralism and that political pluralism was not possible without a break from the communist system. For people who accepted this argument, independence became the necessary goal.

The elections to the USSR Congress of People's Deputies in March 1989 gave the *PFE* the chance to test its strength, though the results were somewhat obscured by the fact that many *PFE*–endorsed candidates were also members of the *Communist Party*. Nevertheless, *PFE* candidates basically swept the slate, winning 18 out of 21 seats that they contested.

A new test came in February 1990, when republic elections were scheduled. The *Popular Front of Estonia* adopted a platform in October 1989 calling for sovereignty and independence. Thus the *PFE* went on record for the first time as publicly favoring independence.

Meanwhile, the *Communist Party of Estonia* was moving in the same direction. In February 1990, Prime Minister Indrek Toome, a former head of ideology for the CPE, founded the *Free Estonia Group* as his vehicle for reelection. He ran on a platform of experience and competence. Arnold Ruutel, President of the Supreme Soviet, also maneuvered to assure his reelection. As presiding officer for the Full Assembly of People's Deputies—a meeting of deputies at the local, republic and union level—he squired through a resolution declaring that Estonia's independence should be restored on the basis of the 1920 Tartu Treaty (with Soviet Russia). Thus Ruutel was also on record as supporting Estonian independence.

Reform communists who had endorsed Estonian independence did well in the February 1990 elections, but it was the candidates endorsed by the *Popular Front of Estonia* who made the best showing, winning a clear majority of the seats. When the new Supreme Soviet met at the end of March, it first passed a resolution declaring that it did "not recognize the legality of state authority of the USSR on the territory of Estonia." The next day, it elected Edgar Savisaar—head of the *Pop-*

Estonian nationalism. It stressed Estonian history; it honored Estonian heroes killed while fighting for Estonian independence; and it resurrected the old Estonian blue–black–white flag. Opposed by the government at first, its programs proved to be so popular that the Estonian Government eventually endorsed some of its positions. For example, the Presidium of the Estonian Supreme Soviet legalized the pre-revolutionary flag in June 1988.

An organization destined to play a much larger role than the *EHS* was the *Popular Front of Estonia* (*PFE*), first suggested by Edgar Savisaar, a sociologist and planning official, in April 1988. Many communists quickly threw their support to the idea so that the *PFE* quickly won preliminary approval both from the *Estonian Communist Party* Central Committee and the Estonian Government. This gave the *PFE* access to the public media, and it quickly began to build up public support.

This led to a split in the *Estonian Communist Party* for Karl Vaino, Party Secretary since 1978, began to fear the challenge raised by the *PFE* and sought to limit its influence. He was challenged by reformers within the party, however. Moscow sided with the reformers and Vaino was replaced as Party Secretary by Vaino Valjas.

Valjas officially addressed the first congress of the *PFE*, held in October 1988, and expressed his support for the goals of the *PFE*. With some 22 percent of the delegates also belonging to the *Estonian*

Communist Party, it appeared that the *PFE* was merely a popular arm of the party. That was misleading, however; although communists made up a significant percentage of the membership, it was overwhelmingly reform communists who joined the *PFE* and, increasingly, the *PFE* was used to allow reform communists to take control of the *Estonian Communist Party* and the Estonian Government. For example, Savisaar, head of the *PFE*, was appointed deputy chairman of the Estonian Council of Ministers and head of the state planning committee.

Another Estonian unofficial organization was the *Estonian National Independence Party* (*ENIP*), established in August 1988. Political parties other than the *Communist Party* were illegal at this time, so the *ENIP* was given a hard time by the government in the beginning, and it was undoubtedly the existence of the *ENIP* that helps explain the significant communist support for the *PFE*. Other unofficial organizations that came into existence in 1988–89 were the *Estonian Green Movement*, the *Estonian Council of Churches* and a *Rural Movement*. In addition, the *Social Democratic Party* was revived in 1989 and a *Christian Democrat* movement came into being.

Meanwhile, there was a further split in the *Estonian Communist Party*. Faced with a choice between nationalism and communism, more and more Estonian communists were opting for nationalism. Valjas tried to control this tendency by

The Baltic Republics

Arnold Ruutel

ular Front of Estonia—as the new Prime Minister. Since he had resigned his membership in the *Communist Party* some months earlier, he became the first non–Communist to be elected head of Estonia's government since 1940.

Savisaar's government now began taking on many of the trappings of independence. Postage stamps were issued and plans were announced to issue an Estonian currency, the Kroon. The government also launched a campaign aimed at privatizing service industries and state distribution networks. The Estonian Supreme Soviet also passed a law prohibiting the drafting of Estonian youths into the Soviet military.

Then, on May 8, 1990, Estonia became the third of the Baltic republics to declare its independence. Six days later, Gorbachëv issued a decree invalidating the declaration. Vadim Bakatin, Soviet Minister of the Interior, ordered troops into Estonia to enforce Gorbachëv's decree. However, Prime Minister Savisaar telephoned Bakatin and got the order reversed. Bakatin later signed an order guaranteeing the Estonian Government control over law enforcement in Estonia. Bakatin's leniency toward the Baltic republics was probably an important reason why he was later dismissed as Interior Minister and replaced by a hardliner, Boris K. Pugo, one of the plotters of the August 1991 *coup*. Estonia was to remain in a sort of state of suspended animation for another year before its independence would be recognized.

Periodically, Gorbachëv would con-

demn Baltic demands for independence and he continued to insist that the Baltic States could only obtain their independence by complying with legislation passed by the Supreme Soviet on the question. This was out of the question for the Baltic States, since their legal position was that they were reasserting an independence which, under international law, had never been lost. Meanwhile, the Communist Party of Estonia, which had voted the previous March to separate from the Communist Party of the Soviet Union, actually carried through its break in September 1990. One more connection was thus severed.

During the fall of 1990, Gorbachëv, surrounding himself with more and more conservative officials, sought to enforce a more hardline position. This lasted until May 1991, when it finally became clear to Gorbachëv that his policy had alienated reform–minded individuals without producing anything positive. Moreover, Gorbachëv now began to realize that he could not achieve a new union treaty without reaching a new accommodation with reformers—which would include accepting a major transfer of power and authority to the individual republics. Boris Yeltsin's election as President of the Russian Republic in May 1991 was another factor. Negotiations for a new union treaty went on during the summer and it was due to be signed on August 17, 1991.

Hardliners opposed to the new union treaty launched their *coup d'etat* against Gorbachëv on August 16. The failure of that *coup* finally broke the logjam on recognition. Estonia and Latvia actually declared their independence while the *coup* was still in progress. After the *coup* failed, most of the world rushed to extend recognition to all three Baltic Republics. The post–coup Soviet Government extended its own recognition in September.

Edgar Savisaar remained as Prime Minister of an independent Estonia for approximately 5 months. In January 1992, he came increasingly under attack for the state of the economy and he proposed a state of emergency to strengthen his hand in dealing with the situation. The parliament voted to impose a state of emergency, but criticism of Savisaar continued. He submitted his resignation after the parliament failed to agree on the membership of an anticrisis commission being set up under the state of emergency ruling and the *Coalition Party*, which controlled 5 seats in the cabinet, called for Savisaar's resignation. Tiit Vahi was selected as the new Prime Minister of a government of experts. Individuals entering the cabinet dropped their party membership for the duration of their time in the cabinet. Vahi himself had been Minister of Transport and Communica-

tions in the previous cabinet. One of his first acts as Prime Minister was to repeal the state of emergency and to promise to work closely with the parliament. He said that he expected to remain in office only about 6 months. His political agenda included a new constitution and a new law on Estonian citizenship, to be followed by new elections to the parliament. The Supreme Council approved the new citizenship law on February 26 1992. Automatic citizenship was granted only to those persons—and their descendants—who were Estonian citizens prior to June 16, 1940—the date of Estonia's incorporation into the Soviet Union.

The 600,000 persons who moved to Estonia after 1940—and their descendants—thus became aliens. The law turned approximately 38 percent of the population into "resident aliens" and excluded them from the scheduled parliamentary elections. These individuals could become Estonian citizens through a process of naturalization, whose requirements included three years residence in Estonia, ability to speak Estonian, and a loyalty oath. As an exception, persons who had resided in Estonia for more than ten years were not required to take the language test, but still had to qualify for naturalization. The government also decided not to accept applications for citizenship until after legislative elections. All of this became even more important when a new law on the privatization of land stipulated that one had to be a citizen in order to purchase land.

In April 1992, another law restructured the government by replacing the Supreme Council by the *Riigikogu*, a single-chamber assembly consisting of 101 members. The same law created a President of the Republic to replace the Chairman of the Supreme Council.

The new constitution was submitted to a referendum in June 1992. The question of denying citizenship to individuals who had moved to Estonia after 1940 was also included on the ballot. Both measures were approved overwhelmingly. The new legislative elections that took place in September were therefore limited almost exclusively to ethnic Estonians. That helps explain why the new legislature is dominated by the right–wing *Fatherland Alliance*. The September elections also included a popular vote to fill the office of President of the Republic. Arnold Ruutel, who had steered Estonia to independence as head of the *Estonian Communist Party*, actually came in first with 43 percent of the vote. Because he failed to win an absolute majority, however, the new President was elected by the *Riigikogu* when it convened on October 5. Their choice was Lennart Meri, candidate of the *Fatherland Alliance*, even though he came in a poor second in

Prime Minister Mart Laar

September with only 29 percent of the popular vote.

Meri is a former foreign minister and Ambassador to Finland. His family, which comes from the city of Tallinn, was also among those deported to Siberia in 1941. They were permitted to return to Estonia in 1946.

Estonia's Prime Minister is Mart Laar. He heads a coalition government made up of the *Fatherland Alliance*, the *Moderate Bloc*, and the *National Independence Party*. These three groups together control 53 out of the 101 seats in the *Riigikogu*.

Even though Estonia has a rightist government, it is outflanked on the right by the *Eesti Kodanik*, a rightist–nationalist movement headed by Juri Toomepan, a U.S. citizen and retired U.S. Army colonel. Toomepan considers the government to be too lenient toward residents who are not ethnic Estonians. He has proposed a citizenship law which would deny permanent residence status to any person who had not entered the country on a residence permit issued by the Estonian Republic "in compliance with the legislation of 1940 replicated in 1992."

NATURE OF THE REGIME

Estonia is a multiparty, parliamentary democracy in transition from the earlier communistic system. Most of the forms of government have recently been changed, with the legislature reassuming the name of *Riigikogu*. In a departure from the past, a new executive President of the Republic has been created, modeled somewhat on the French Fifth Republic. Estonia remains essentially a parliamentary system, however.

The Estonian Government

Under the new constitution, executive power is shared by the President of the Republic and the Prime Minister. The President, as head of state, is responsible for general domestic policy. He is also considered to be the chief spokesman for the nation internationally.

There is a popular vote to fill the office of President but, if as happened in September 1992, no candidate wins a majority of the vote, then the President is elected by a vote of the *Riigikogu*. The current President, Lennart Meri, was elected by the *Riigikogu* in October 1992.

The Prime Minister presides over the cabinet and oversees day–to–day operations as head of government. Although appointed by the President, he must be approved by, and maintain the support of, a majority in the *Riigikogu* in order to remain in office. The Prime Minister's cabinet must also be approved by the legislature. The legislature is made up of numerous political parties, none of whom controls a majority of the seats, so the government is a coalition. The largest grouping in the coalition is the *Fatherland Alliance*, itself a coalition of four parties (*Christian Democratic Union*, *Unified Party of Republicans*, *Conservative People's Party*, and *Liberal Democratic Party*). Mart Laar, the current Prime Minister, was appointed to that office by President Meri in October 1992. He was born on April 22, 1960.

Economy

Estonia is an overwhelmingly urban society, with approximately 72 percent of the population living in cities or towns. One of the problems which the current government is facing, however, is that Estonians actually constitute a minority of workers in industrial concerns. Most of the workers are Russians, Belarusians and Ukrainians brought in to staff new factories built during the Soviet era. Because of the strong antipathy toward such workers, the Estonian Government has been promoting economic policies that stress privatization, policies likely to affect these factories the most. Thus far, factory managers have resisted government efforts to bring their expenses in line with costs, but many of the factories are in desperate shape because of the collapse of Russian demand for their products. Unemployment, still low, is growing.

The *Fatherland Alliance*, main component of the government coalition, is obviously hoping that, given bad enough economic circumstances, many Russians and others will choose to leave and go back to their home republics. As Klara Hallik, Minister for National Minorities phrased it, the Estonian Government

Dockers at the port, Tallinn

NOVOSTI photo

The Baltic Republics

would be delighted if the Russians in Estonia would leave voluntarily—"in a civilized manner, of course."

This is particularly true with regard to the area of Narva, located in the northeastern part of Estonia. Narva is inhabited almost entirely by Russians, the result of the fact that the Soviet Government decided in the 1960s to build a branch of its industrial–military complex there. Almost no Russian in the Narva area has bothered to learn Estonian. As one said, "Why should I bother, when everybody here speaks Russian?"

According to Yuri Mishin, a deputy in the Narva city council, about 12,000 Estonian Russians have applied for Russian citizenship under the terms of a new law passed by the Russian parliament making it easier for Russians living abroad to obtain Russian citizenship. Many of these are undoubtedly thinking of emigrating, but almost none have actually done so. The fact that living conditions in Estonia are still better than those in Russia continues to act as a limiting factor.

In spite of the numerous factories built in the 1960s and 1970s to serve as suppliers of the Soviet arms industry, Estonia's largest industry is still that of primary extraction, the production of oil from oil shale. Two other major industries are the manufacturing of mineral fertilizers and shipbuilding. It also has consumer industries such as textiles and medium industry such as electrical and mechanical equipment. Most of the rest of the republic's industry is concerned with the processing of forest products (timber, wood pulp for paper manufacturing, peat) or food processing. Fishing is another major industry. Estonia has established its own currency, the *krona*, and it has taken a number of other measures aimed at asserting its political independence. It has, however, not proceeded very fast or very far in dismantling the command economy inherited from the Soviet Union. A market economy is coming into being, however. In December 1992, Prime Minister Laar announced that private enterprise

Lecture in Tartu University's physics department

had provided 64.3 percent of all tax income over the preceding eleven months.

Agriculture and the processing of agricultural products still employ about 28 percent of the population. The legislature has passed a law on land privatization, but this has gotten bogged down in the politics of nationalism. Only individuals who can trace Estonian citizenship prior to 1940 may buy land. Most agricultural land is still organized into collective and state farms, but they are expected to be broken up in the near future. Progress in this area has been slow because of the problem of restitution for land nationalized after 1940.

The Estonian Department of Statistics reported in December 1992 that the volume of production was 39.5 percent less than for the comparable period of 1991. This was largely the result of a near collapse of production in certain areas—building materials, glass works, metal processing and chemical production. At the same time, production actually increased in areas such as dry goods, concentrated foods, starch, butter and a few other foodstuffs. The Estonian economy is expected to continue to contract in 1993, but to begin bottoming out in 1994.

Culture

Estonia's culture is very much associated with its historic cities, the most important of which are Tallinn (the capital), Narva and Tartu. Tallinn, historically known as Reval or Revel, was founded by King Waldemar II of Denmark in 1219 on the site of an earlier fortress and it has played an important role in Estonian history ever since. The city became a member of the Hanseatic League in 1284 and a major trading center. Over the centuries, it belonged to the Danes, the Teutonic Knights, the Swedes and, from 1710 onward, Russia. The old city was surrounded by a city wall, about two–thirds of which still stands. Most of the guard towers and some of the gates are also still extant. Medieval buildings include the Dom Castle and the Long Hermann Watchtower.

The oldest of the churches is the Domkirk, which dates from 1232. Other churches of interest are St. Nicholas, built in the fourteenth century, St. Olaf's, built in the thirteenth but with a Gothic spire from the seventeenth century, and the Bremer Chapel of St. Mary, built in the sixteenth century. Most Estonians are Lutherans, but there is also a Russian Orthodox Cathedral, St. Alexander Nevsky's, built in the late nineteenth century. Other cultural treasures include the Town Hall, built in 1371–74, and the Blackheads' Club, which dates from the fourteenth century.

Being the capital, Tallinn also has Estonia's Academy of Sciences, established in 1946, an Art Institute and Conservatoire, founded in 1919, the Vilde Pedagogical Institute, a Polytechnical Institute, the Estonian State Opera House and numerous theaters.

Narva, known historically as Dorpat, was founded in 1030 by Grand Prince Yaroslav of Kievan Rus. Then called Yuriev, it was built at the site of an earlier Estonian settlement, Tarpatu. Yuriev was conquered by the Teutonic Knights in 1212 and it later became the seat of the Livonian bishops. The Germans gave it the name of Dorpat. Fought over numerous times over the centuries, it passed back under Russian control in 1710 when Peter the Great took it from Sweden. The modern name dates from the first period of Estonian independence following World War I.

Tartu, also a member of the Hanseatic League, was a major trading center; its chief claim to fame is its university, founded in 1632 by King Gustav II of Sweden. Transferred for a time to the city of Parnu during the eighteenth century, it was returned to Tartu in 1802. Today Tartu University has seven faculties and 4,000 students. The university library, most of which is housed in the Cathedral of Peter and Paul, contains over two million volumes. The cathedral, in ruins in 1802 when it was reconstructed as a library, is probably the oldest building in Tartu. Most of the other university buildings date from the nineteenth century.

Although the ancient Estonians had an oral literature, very little of that survived the centuries of domination by other cultures. The roots of modern Estonian culture should probably be traced to the formation of the University of Tartu in 1632, for that marked the beginning of a small educated Estonian elite. The first book of Estonian grammar appeared in 1637, followed by an Estonian translation of the Bible in 1739.

Little more happened until the nineteenth century when an attempt was made to revive a folklorist tradition. Many songs, sayings and fairy tales were eventually collected, most strongly reminiscent of Finnish folklorist survivals. Somewhat later, Friedrich Reinhold Kreutzwald used many of these oral works to create an artificial epic which he called Kalevipoeg [The Son of Kalev]. It was published by the Estonian Learned Society in 1857–1861.

Kreutzwald's epic marked the beginning of an Estonian national literature, exemplified by the appearance of poets such as Lydia Koidula, Friedrich Kuhlbars and Jacob Tamm, novelists such as Eduard Vilde and Juhan Liiv and Ernst Scrgava, and the playwright August Kitzberg. Estonian writers worked under a great handicap, however, for the Russian Government enforced a censorship down to 1905 that attempted to suppress themes that might encourage Estonian nationalism.

The Revolution of 1905 forced a number of writers to flee abroad, but the constitutional regime established in 1906 led to the abolition of most censorship and the appearance of a vigorous Estonian press. It also marked the birth of a new literary movement called Young Estonia, whose chief representative was the poet Gustav Suits. But Suits, who had fled to Finland in 1905, continued to live abroad until after the Russian Revolution of 1917. Suits eventually became a professor of Estonian Literature at Tartu University. Another figure from this period was Friebert Tuglas, a writer of short stories and novels. Suits and Tuglas, along with a third writer, Ernst Enno, and the poet Marie Under, became the dominant figures in Estonian literature during the period of independence down to 1940. Tuglas, a member of the Social Democratic Party prior to 1917, succeeded Suits as Professor of Estonian Literature at Tartu in 1944, after Estonia had come under Soviet domination. However, Tuglas made no literary contribution after that time except for a travelogue, The First Trip Abroad, which appeared in 1945 except for a volume of musings called Thoughts and Moods, published in 1960.

A number of Estonian writers made their way abroad during World War II. These included Marie Under, Karl Rumor, Artur Adson, August Mclk, and August Gailit. These and other writers kept Estonian literature alive as an emigre literature even as the Soviet occupation regime was imprisoning figures such as Hugo Raudsepp, Estonia's greatest playwright, and exiling others, such as the poet Heiti Talvik, to Siberia. Most of these figures are too well integrated into their new environments to resettle in Estonia, but their influence on the new generation of emerging Estonian writers is likely to be great.

The Future

Estonia is a small state with a well–educated population and its long–term prospects are probably rather bright, if its neighbors will leave it alone. After the general problem of how to make the transition from a command to a market economy, a problem shared by all of the successor republics to the now defunct Soviet Union, Estonia's greatest problem is how to deal with the large Slavic minorities that make up so much of the industrial work force. How Estonia resolves this problem will essentially determine its relations with its neighbors, in particular Russia, and its own domestic tranquility. Developments thus far have not been encouraging.

The Baltic Republics

Dressed for a festival on a street in Riga

NOVOSTI photo

LATVIA SINCE WORLD WAR I

Latvia's history as an independent state after World War I bears many similarities to that of Estonia. That is not surprising, since the two countries were alike in many respects. Like Estonia, Latvia created a 100 member single–chamber parliament (called the *Saeima*) based on proportional representation. The Latvian constitution, approved in February 1922, did provide for the election of a President of the Republic to a fixed five–year term, however. The President, who was made commander–in–chief of the military, was also authorized to issue decrees when parliament was not in session, subject to parliamentary confirmation when it reconvened.

The first President of the Republic elected under terms of the new constitution was Janis Cakste. A lawyer and early nationalist leader, he had headed the Latvian delegation to the Paris Peace Talks.

Latvia's population at this time was approximately 1.9 million, with Latvians making up about 75 percent of the popu-

lation. The largest single minority was Russian, which made up about 7.8 percent of the population. Another 8.1 percent were other Slavs, mainly White Russians and Poles. Other minorities

included Jews (5.2 percent), Baltic Germans and Lithuanians.

Like Estonia, Latvia had an agrarian–based economy, with 66.2 percent of the population supporting themselves through agriculture. One difference is that Latvia had significantly more industry, particularly in and around the city of Riga. The majority of the population was Protestant (57.2 percent), but there were significant Russian Orthodox (13 percent) and Roman Catholic (22.6 percent) populations.

Latvia also began its existence with a land reform which expropriated the old landed estates and provided for their distribution to landless peasants. As a result of the reform, 22.2 percent of the land was held by small holders who had obtained their land at this time. In general, Latvia had better luck with its land reform than Estonia and food production, particularly of beef and dairy cattle, continued to grow through the 1920's and 1930's.

With the same kind of legislative system and similar type of population, it is not surprising that Latvia's political parties were similar to those in Estonia. There was, for example, a *Peasants' League* on the right with the *Social Democratic Party* on the left, with the *Democratic Party*, the *Radical Democratic Party* and the *People's Party* filing up the middle. In 1922, these three centrist parties merged to form the *Democratic Center*. Thereafter it was to be found in every coalition, for neither the left nor the right was able to obtain a majority on its own.

Latvia's use of proportional representation also made it more difficult to form stable governments, since it increased the number of political groups vying for seats. In the 1931 elections, for example, 27 different political groupings won representation in the legislature. Twelve of the groups managed to elect only a single member, however. At the other end, only two groups had more than ten members. To be sure, this proliferation of political parties was partly a reaction to the bad economic conditions since 1929—characterized by a drop in exports, especially agricultural products, and a rise in unemployment—which had led to a loss of confidence in the older political parties.

Latvia's Move Toward Authoritarianism

The bad economic situation also led to a growth of anti–parliamentarianism in Latvia, mainly led by right–wing, nationalist forces. The resurgence of a nationalist movement can be traced back as far as 1926, but the first proposals for a change in the nature of the regime came after the major economic crisis began in 1929. It was at this time that the *Nationalist Association*, then a small and relatively insignificant right–wing party, proposed giving additional political powers to the President of the Republic. A number of fascist or semi–fascist groupings also emerged at this time, and began pushing anti–communist, anti–socialist, anti–Jewish and anti–foreign policies. The Latvian Government proscribed most of these, but the mainline political parties began to take a more nationalist and anti–foreign stance as well.

In August 1933, Karlis Ulmanis, leader of the *Peasants' League* and one of the founders of modern Latvia—he served as first provisional president from 1918 to 1920—proposed a number of constitutional changes to strengthen the executive. He could not get sufficient support from among the other members of the legislature, however, so his constitutional proposals were tabled at this time. Then, on March 16, 1934, Ulmanis was made Premier. Four days earlier, President Paets had asserted authoritarian control in Estonia. Although there is no evidence of any direct connection, the program which Ulmanis implemented as Premier was strikingly similar to the Paets program in Estonia.

Claiming that he had discovered a communist plot to overthrow the government, Ulmanis declared a state of emergency, suspended the parliament, banned party political activities, and proscribed the *Thunder Cross Association*, a fascist organization. Two months later, Ulmanis organized a separate government committee to take on certain of the functions of the parliament, that is, to handle matters which would normally require legislation. President Kviesis gave his approval to this new arrangement in June.

Most Latvians quietly accepted this new authoritarian regime, apparently convinced by Ulmanis' argument that he needed the additional powers to defend Latvian democracy. Two years later, when President Kviesis' term came to an end, he stepped down and was succeeded by Ulmanis. Since Ulmanis continued to hold the office of Premier, the effect was to merge the two offices from this point onward.

Latvia under Soviet Rule, 1939–1991

The authoritarian direction of the Latvian Government after 1934 weakened it internationally, especially insofar as the Western democracies was concerned. When the leaders of Nazi Germany and the Soviet Union got together to negotiate a "non–aggression" pact in August 1939, therefore, their stipulation that Latvia fell within the Soviet sphere of influence caused less of a reaction than it might otherwise have done.

Hitler launched his invasion of Poland on September 1 and Soviet troops entered to occupy the eastern third of Poland on September 17. With Poland settled, Stalin moved to bring the remaining areas of the Soviet "sphere of influence" under his control. Latvia was forced to sign a mutual assistance pact with the Soviet Union on October 5.

Nothing happened for several months, probably because the Soviet Union was tied down in its "Winter War" with Finland. Once that was resolved, the Soviet Union turned its attention back to the Baltic. Toward the end of May 1940, the Soviet Foreign Ministry accused the Latvian Government of violating the 1939 mutual assistance pact signed with the Soviet Union. Almost immediately thereafter, the Latvian Government was forced to resign and a popular front government was installed in its place.

But Latvia's popular front government had a remarkably short life. In July, all political parties other than the *Communist Party* were banned and most non–communists were dismissed from office. This was followed by a wave of arrests. Then, with only communists standing for office, new elections were held on July 14. The newly elected legislature met on July 21.

Its only piece of business was to vote on a resolution asking to join the Soviet Union. The resolution was passed by acclamation. The following month, the USSR Supreme Soviet acceded to the Latvian request. Latvia thus became a Soviet Socialist Republic.

During the period from August 1940 to June 1941, the new communist government nationalized the land, then launched a program of "land reform" whereby larger estates were turned into state farms while smaller parcels were distributed to landless laborers. Nazi Germany's invasion of the Soviet Union beginning on June 22, 1941 reversed this situation somewhat, for German troops overran and occupied Latvia later in 1941. Latvia remained under German occupation until 1944. With the German retreat, however, Latvia once again fell under Soviet control. A guerrilla movement arose to oppose Soviet control after the end of the war in 1945, but such efforts were, of course, ineffectual. Latvia got no outside assistance, and the opposition was eventually suppressed.

Many changes occurred in Latvia over the next thirty–five years. Soviet policy was to integrate the Baltic Republics so thoroughly that there would be no question of their ever leaving the union. To that end, the reestablished Latvian communist government reinstated its 1941 nationalization decree, then followed this up by carrying through a general collectivization of agriculture. Meanwhile, the Soviet Government sought to bind Latvia and the other two Baltic Republics to the rest of the Soviet Union economically by locating branch factories of Soviet industry in the three republics. The first factories in the 1950s emphasized primary extraction, but a much larger range of factories was built there in the 1960s and 1970s. Such factories received most or all of their raw materials from other parts of the Soviet Union, and delivered most of their finished products to customers in the other republics. This economic integration was so successful that Latvia and the other two Baltic Republics became more integrated into the Soviet economy than any other area of the Soviet Union.

This program of economic integration was accompanied by a program of "Soviet Russification," aimed at transforming the cultures of the Baltic Republics. All students received Russian language training in the schools, plus general indoctrination lectures on the nature of Soviet culture. In addition, there was a systematic effort made to settle non–Baltic nationals in the republics. When a new factory was built, most of the workers would be transferred there from elsewhere in the Soviet Union.

The effects of this policy can be seen by

The Baltic Republics

examining the figures of the 1989 Soviet census. Ethnic Latvians made up only 52 percent of the population of the republic. Latvians had nearly become a minority in their own country. These overall figures also masked the fact that, in certain industrial regions near the border, Latvians had become a tiny minority. In many urban areas, it was more common to hear Russian spoken than it was to hear Latvian. Russians also tended to monopolize many types of jobs, particularly in management and in parts of government. Everywhere, the Russian way of doing things became the acceptable way. On the positive side, the heavy industrialization carried out after 1945 meant that the standard of living in Latvia was above that of any other part of the Soviet Union.

Latvia Regains Its Independence

The Latvian people accommodated themselves to Soviet rule, but they could not forget their brief period of independence between the wars. When Gorbachëv launched his programs of *glasnost* and restructuring after coming to power in 1985, Latvians were therefore among the first to take advantage of them. In enunciating his policy of *glasnost*, Gorbachëv called on the Soviet peoples to speak out against negative tendencies in the society, and to support his reforms. This became a manifesto which led to the creation of thousands of "unofficial" organizations all over the Soviet Union. Formed originally in support of Gorbachëv's policy of reform, many of them soon began to push their own agendas.

Latvians were among the early supporters of Gorbachëv's policy of *glasnost* and restructuring, and Latvian unofficial organizations also sprang up, taking advantage of the new atmosphere. One of the first such organizations was *Renaissance and Renewal*, a religious rights organization. The *Popular Front of Latvia* (PFL), organized in October 1988, incorporated many of these earlier unofficial organizations into its overall structure. The leader of the *PFL* was Dainis Ivans, a journalist. Within a year its membership had grown to 250,000, about 85 percent of whom were Latvians. This provided an important contrast with the *Latvian Communist Party*, which had a membership of 184,000, only 39.7 percent of whom were Latvians.

The ethnic issue was a greater one in Latvia than in either of the other two Baltic republics, because of the much larger percentages of non–Latvians in the republic. Conservatives were particularly disturbed by what the front represented and managed to get the *PFL* decertified in January 1989.

This did not stop the front from continuing to operate, however. In the March 1989 elections to the USSR Con-gress of People's Deputies, front–supported candidates won three–fourth of the seats.

Like Estonia, Latvia had a political party specifically committed to independence, the *Latvian National Independence Movement* (LNIM). Labeled an extremist organization, it nevertheless exercised influence on the *PFL*. Under the prodding of the *LNIM*, the *Popular Front of Latvia* went on record in June 1989 as favoring "Latvia's independent statehood."

Russians and other non–Latvians had become very concerned about Latvian nationalism, and there were rising fears of ethnic strife. The *Popular Front of Latvia* sought to alleviate these anxieties by advocating equal rights for all persons living in Latvia, regardless of nationality or other affiliation. The front specifically supported the right of other nationalities either to receive instruction in their own language in the public schools or to set up their own schools. It also advocated political pluralism. This defused a lot of the opposition and helped to win additional support for independence from among the non–Latvian sections of the population.

The *Latvian Communist Party*, with more Russians than Latvians among its membership, proved to be the most conservative of the Baltic communist parties, but even it came under pressure from its Latvian members to take a more nationalistic stance. In September 1989, Janis Vagris, the First Secretary, endorsed the concept of a sovereign Latvia, including republican economic autonomy.

The overlap between the *Latvian Communist Party* and the *Popular Front of Latvia* can be seen in the list of delegates to the second congress of the *PFL*, held in October 1989. Twenty–four percent of the delegates were members of the *Latvian Communist Party*, while 45 out of 100 of the members of the steering committee were *LCP* members. They obviously represented members of the reform wing of the party, however, for the Congress not only endorsed Latvian independence and creation of a multiparty political system,

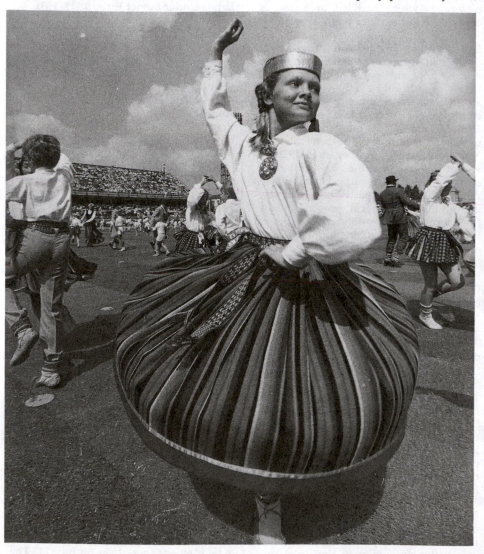

Latvian folk dancer

NOVOSTI photo

200

but called upon the Latvian Supreme Soviet to declare illegal Latvia's 1940 incorporation into the Soviet Union.

New elections to the Latvian Supreme Soviet were scheduled to take place in March 1990. Hoping to co–opt the nationalism issue, the communist members of the old Supreme Soviet adopted a declaration, on February 15, endorsing an independent Latvia. That statement proved to be too weak for the new delegates elected in March. On May 4, the new Supreme Soviet proclaimed Latvian independence, though with a transition period before implementation. Although the declaration got 138 positive votes, 57 deputies refused to participate in the vote, claiming that the declaration was unconstitutional. Most of the delegates abstaining had been elected by the large non–Latvian element within the population. Nothing happened for ten days, probably because the Soviet Government was preoccupied by its economic war against Lithuania. On May 14, however, Gorbachëv issued a decree invalidating Latvia's declaration of independence. The Soviet military also became involved in the issue when it began dropping leaflets on Riga, accusing the Latvian Government of counter revolution. The next day, several hundred Soviet army soldiers, accompanied by cadets from an officers' training school in Riga, joined a protest march against Latvian independence.

By June, however, the Soviet Government had begun ignoring the situation in Latvia, even as it began easing off on its pressure on Lithuania and Estonia. The negative international reaction to the Soviet moves in the Baltic was clearly a factor in this change of policy. Thereafter, Moscow virtually ignored what was happening in Latvia until January 1991, when hardliners launched another intervention. Once again there was an international protest, however, and Moscow eased off.

By May 1991, Gorbachëv apparently decided that his conservative policies of the past several months had been a failure and threatened the new union treaty which he wanted to get negotiated and signed over the summer. He began a rapprochement with Boris Yeltsin, which led to nine of the republics agreeing to sign a new union treaty on August 17. This became the signal for conservative hardliners to organize a *coup* with the aim of overthrowing Gorbachëv and reasserting centralized control.

The *coup* failed but, even as it was going on, the Latvian Government declared its independence. The post–*coup* Soviet Government temporized for two weeks but it soon found the number of states granting recognition to Latvia and the other Baltic Republics to be irresist-

ible. In early September, it, too, recognized the independence of the Baltic Republics. Latvia was admitted to the United Nations in October 1991.

A major preoccupation of the Latvian Government since that time has been the continuing presence of ex–Soviet troops in the Republic, plus the problem of an extremely large non–Latvian population. These troops were originally under the jurisdiction of the Commonwealth of Independent States, but the Russian Government assumed responsibility for Russian troops stationed in the ex–Soviet Republics in the summer of 1992 after establishing its own Ministry of Defense. Subsequent negotiations between the Latvian and Russian Governments elicited a Russian promise to have all troops out of Latvia by the summer of 1993; however, President Yeltsin rescinded this agreement in September 1992 after the Latvian Government stripped non–Latvians of citizenship.

The Latvian Government took this action because it was under pressure from Latvian nationalists within its ranks concerned with the extremely large non–Latvian element in the population. It should be remembered that the current government was elected in March 1990 and that its leaders are essentially the leaders of the *Popular Front of Latvia*. Most of the *Popular Front's* leadership were originally reform communists who eventually broke with the party. One of the problems of the *Latvian Communist Party*, in fact, was that it was dominated by Russians and only about 40 percent of its membership was Latvian. Although most of the support for the *Popular Front of Latvia* came from ethnic Latvians, the government pursued moderate policies toward minorities and attempted to win them over to support of the government. It was fairly successful until 1992.

A new citizenship law was discussed in the legislature, but the legislature was badly divided over the issue. It was then decided to handle the matter administratively. Under new government regulations issued at this time, automatic citizenship could be claimed only by persons who were Latvian citizens—or their direct descendants—prior to Latvia's incorporation into the Soviet Union in 1940. This rendered about 48 percent of the population of the Republic "stateless." These regulations were subsequently incorporated into a new electoral law passed in October 1992. Under the terms of this new law, non–Latvians may qualify for naturalization if they can establish a fluency in the Lettish language and have been permanently residing in the republic for at least 16 years. Since the government is currently not processing citizenship applications, how-

ever, almost all residents who are not ethnic Latvians were excluded from the elections, which took place in early June 1993.

In December 1992, the government announced the first partial results of a citizen registration that it had begun carrying out. About 67 percent of the inhabitants of the republic had been registered by that time. Of those registered, 1,339,530 were classified as Latvian citizens, while an additional 452,378 persons were classified as non–citizens. However, the government also announced that 405,124 of these non–citizens—or 89.5 percent—had expressed a desire to become Latvian citizens. This is undoubtedly good news, for it indicates that government actions thus far have not yet alienated any significant portion of the non–Latvian population. The problem is that the government has not yet come up with a formula that will be acceptable to both the non–Latvians and the Latvian nationalists.

The October 1992 electoral law also gave the government the right to pass laws "within the limits of the laws and resolutions adopted by the Latvian parliament." Since that time, the government has essentially ruled by decree.

A significant part of retail trade had already been privatized by that time in the cities, but the government has used its new powers to complete the process throughout the republic. Many shops have since either been sold at auction, leased to individual entrepreneurs, or turned into retail outlets of individual manufacturing plants.

NATURE OF THE REGIME

Latvia is a multiparty, parliamentary democracy in transition from the earlier communistic system. Although the Latvian Government has not yet been able to agree on a new constitution, a new electoral law, originally passed by the legislature in March 1992 and then modified in October 1992, began the process of remaking the governmental structure. According to the terms of this new law, the legislature, formerly known as the Supreme Soviet or Supreme Council, will be replaced by a single–chamber legislature, the *Sejm*. Elections are to be conducted on a proportional basis. For this purpose, the country has been divided into five constituencies and party representation in the *Sejm* will be on the basis of the percentage of votes won in each constituency. The *Sejm* itself will have 100 members; however, the number of deputies per constituency will be based on the number of voters per constituency. Elections to the *Sejm* are expected to take place in the spring of 1993.

The Baltic Republics

Enjoying their work: Chimney-sweeps, Riga

NOVOSTI photo

The Latvian Government

The ceremonial head of state, formerly the Chairman of the Presidium of the Supreme Soviet, is now formally referred to as Chairman of the Supreme Council and, informally, as President. The current incumbent is Anatolijs Gorbunovs, an ex–communist and one of the founders of the *Popular Front of Latvia*.

The chief political official is the Chairman of the Council of Ministers, or Prime Minister, who leads the government on the basis of majority support in the legislature. The current Chairman, Ivars Godmanis, was a reform communist who became an early supporter of the *Popular Front of Latvia*, which won the 1990 elections.

The Economy

Latvia is the most industrialized of the Baltic republics. Its major industries include machinery, metalworking, electrical equipment, light industry, agricultural equipment, chemicals, and pharmaceuticals. Forestry products and extractive industry are also important, including things like timber, paper, peat, limestone, dolomite and clay. Riga, a major center for industry, manufactures consumer goods like radios and other electrical appliances, cars and trucks, and agricultural equipment. Light industry,

including food processing and woodworking, is also important. In the past, about 80 percent of Latvia's exports went to other parts of the Soviet Union. The Government is now attempting to reorient its trade to other countries.

Latvian agriculture is still organized into collective and state farms. Privatization, originally expected to begin sometime in 1992, has been put off, at least partly because the Supreme Council has not been able to pass the necessary legislation. The government had been using its decree–issuing authority to denationalize domestic retail trade, but that process was slowed in November 1992 when the government announced that it would not sell any more state–owned facilities for Latvian rubles. Although agriculture has lost most of its former importance, Latvia still has an important dairy industry. Dairy products, one of Latvia's important exports, have been mainly shipped to other parts of the Soviet Union in the past. Attempts to redirect part of this trade to the west has run into the problem of a world–wide surplus in dairy products.

Latvia has been granted $18.75 million by the European Community to assist the government in carrying out "privatization, for transforming the structure of enterprises, for reforms to the banking

and finance system, and also for education."

There has been relatively little foreign private investment in Latvia so far, but the government has worked at establishing ties with the Scandinavian countries and this is beginning to pay off. The first private bank in Latvia has been established by the Parex Finance Company with collaboration of the Swedish company Kungsorden AB Foretags. The bank has a capitalization of 100 million rubles.

Overall, the economic situation deteriorated in 1992, with gross domestic product decreasing by perhaps 30 percent. The main cause for this massive drop was a collapse of exports to Russia, which dropped by 70 percent over 1991. A second cause is that Russia began to charge world prices in hard currency for its oil exports outside the CIS area as of July 1992 and Latvia can't afford to pay the new price.

Culture

Latvian culture was historically the culture of the peasantry, the upper classes being mainly German. The same was also true of the cities, for that was where the German and Jewish merchants and tradesmen lived. Thus a great deal of Latvia's historical culture is not Latvian at all, though as Latvians became educated and entered the middle class in the nineteenth century, they tended to adopt elements of that earlier culture. Modern Latvian culture is no longer a peasant culture and it is, in fact, mainly an urban culture.

Approximately a third of the population lives in the city of Riga, Latvia's capital, its chief port, and its largest industrial center. In the twelfth century, German merchants of the Hanseatic League began trading with Latvian tribes living along the Daugava [Western Dvina] River. In 1201, Bishop Albert of Bremen, who had been given the title of Bishop of Livonia by the Pope and dispatched to the area accompanied by the Teutonic Knights, built a fortress along the right bank of the river. Bishop Albert also founded his own militant Order of the Brethren of the Sword and he used it to spread Christianity among the Latvians. A town grew up around the fortress and the town, Riga, quickly became a major center for trade. It became a member of the Hanseatic League in 1282. But Bishop Albert's religious order controlled the city until the Reformation. Riga became an independent merchant city–state in 1561, but it was soon taken over by the Polish king. It passed back and forth between Poland and Sweden until 1710, when Peter the Great captured it and it became part of the Russian Empire.

Riga remained mainly a city of foreigners until the late nineteenth century, when it gradually became a Latvian city. Today it is not only the political and cultural center of the republic, but the industrial center as well. Riga University, founded in 1861, is the main university of the country, though there are a number of colleges and technical schools as well. The Latvian Academy of Sciences and its 14 affiliated research institutes is also located here. The city has an Opera and Ballet Theater, numerous other theaters for plays, and four concert halls. It is therefore the center for higher Latvian culture.

The city itself is full of historic buildings, including guild halls, medieval warehouses and private residences, dating back as far as the fourteenth century. One of the oldest buildings is the Riga Castle itself, headquarters of the Livonian Order in Riga, which dates from 1330. There are also many churches, a few of which date from this same period, though most of them were at least partially rebuilt in subsequent centuries. The oldest of these is the Domkirk, a brick church consecrated in 1211. For centuries the seat of the archbishop of Livonia and Prussia, it has been rebuilt or remodeled many times and shows evidence of many architectural styles, stretching from the Romanesque to the Baroque. The Reformation reached Riga in the middle of the

sixteenth century and the Domkirk became a Lutheran Church at that time. Today it is a museum. The city also has many operating churches representing many denominations—Roman Catholic, Russian Orthodox, Baptist, and, of course, Lutheran. There is also one remaining synagogue.

Latvia has a strong folklorist tradition, but because most Latvians lived historically in the countryside, most of the early collections of Latvian folk tales were made by Germans resident in the cities and most of these were translated into German before being published. A written literature by Lettish writers first appeared in the nineteenth century as the number of educated Latvians began to grow. The man usually given credit for laying the foundations stones for a Lettish literature was Juris Neikens, a nineteenth century author of numerous short stories. A contemporary, Juris Alumans, was the first Latvian poet, but he helped to start a school of poetry, represented by Krisjanis Barons, Fricis Brivzemnieks, and Atis Kronvalds. Another nineteenth century figure, Adolfs Alunans, is considered to be the father of Latvian drama. The novel was given Latvian form by two brothers, Reinis and Matiss Kaudzites, who jointly wrote *The Times of Land–Surveyors*, published in 1879.

Two novelists of the early twentieth century were Augusts Deglavs, author of *Riga*, a three volume work published between 1912 and 1921, and Jekabs Jansevskis, author of *The Native Land*, a six volume work published in 1924–25. Realism is represented by the dramas and short stories of Rudolfs Blaumanis and the poems of Vilis Pludonis. Romanticism is represented by the dramas of Janis Rainis, whose greatest work, written in 1905, is a epic tragedy dealing with early Latvian history entitled *Fire and Night*.

Rainis was also a social reformer who spent several years in tsarist prisons before 1905. He participated in the 1905 revolution and subsequently had to escape to Switzerland, where he lived until 1920. *Fire and Night* became the basis for an opera written in 1921 by the composer Janis Medins.

Literary figures of the period of Latvian independence include the novelist Janis Akuraters, the poets Karlis Skalbe and Edvards Virza, the short story writer Janis Ezerins, and the novelist Janis Jaunsudrabins. Jaunsudrabins is unusual in that he also made a reputation for himself as a painter.

A novelist of the Soviet period is Jonas Miesnieks, whose historical novel, *The Judge of the Livonian District*, was published in 1948. Most other better writers of this period belong, however to that group of individuals who managed to make their way abroad. These include the playwright Martins Ziverts, the essayist and novelist Zenta Maurina, and the novelists Anslavs Eglitis, Girts Salnais, and Antons Rupainis.

The Future

Latvia will have to undergo several lean years as it makes the transition from a communist command economy to a market economy. This process is underway, but so far the speed has been slow. On the plus side, Latvia has a well educated work force, and a fairly disciplined populace. The chief negative is the extremely large non–Latvian population, which may turn against the government at some point if economic conditions get too bad or Latvian nationalism becomes too virulent. The government is operating on an extremely thin edge and the consequences for failure are rather high. It will need a lot of luck and good sense to survive and succeed.

A performance of Swan Lake at the Academic Opera and Ballet Theatre, Riga
NOVOSTI photo

The Baltic Republics

Wedding Day, Vilnius

LITHUANIA SINCE WORLD WAR I

Independent Lithuania, 1919–1939

Elections to the Lithuanian Constituent Assembly took place in April 1920. A provisional constitution was adopted two months later, though the permanent constitution did not go into effect until August 1, 1922.

This constitution created a parliamentary system with a single–body legislature, called the *Seimas*. It also created a ceremonial President of the Republic, elected for a five–year term. Aleksandras Stulginskis became the first president under the new constitution.

Lithuania was overwhelmingly rural at this time with 79 percent of the population earning their living from agriculture. It was also relatively backward; according to the 1923 census, approximately a third of the population was illiterate. There was no individual agriculture among the peasants, since their holdings were organized into communes similar to the *mirs*

of Russia and farmed in common. The large estates were mainly in the hands of either Poles or Russians, though the

Poles were mainly descendants of individuals of Lithuanian extraction who had been Polanized in the 16th to 18th centuries, when the Polish monarchy and Polish culture dominated the united Poland–Lithuania.

A 1922 land reform program expropriated the land of Russian estate owners and limited the size of other estates to 375 acres. These lands were subsequently redistributed to peasant small holders. The land reform also provided for the break up of the peasant communes and the distribution of the land to the peasants to create private farms. Turning the peasants into individual farmers brought increased prosperity to the countryside. However, the plots of land given out after the breakup of the large estates were so small that the peasant small holders thus created had great difficulty making a go of it on their own. In the 1930's, many either sold or abandoned their land, and then sought employment in the cities or emigrated.

Lithuania was the most densely populated of the three Baltic States. With a population of 2,035,121 in 1923, it also had the largest population of the three. Its population was rather mixed ethnically, with approximately 80 percent speaking Lithuanian.

Jews were the single largest minority [7.6 percent], followed by Poles [3.2 percent], Russians [2.5 percent] and Germans [1.4 percent]. There were also a few White Russians and Latvians. Religiously, Lithuania was rather homogeneous, with 85.7 percent professing Roman Catholicism. The remainder were either Jewish or Protestant.

The party system that developed in Lithuania bore some similarity to the pattern already seen in Estonia and Latvia, except that the dominant right–wing party was the *Christian Democratic Party*. The *Christian Democrats*, allied with the *Lithuanian Peasants League* and the *Workers' Federation*, was a broad–based party with its main base among the peasants of the countryside, but with an urban wing of industrial workers who rejected Marxism. Its broad base made it the majority party in the period up to 1926.

The *Social Democratic Party* was the principal left–wing party, though Lithuania, with its smaller urban population, proved to have a less congenial climate for Marxism than either Estonia or Latvia. The *Social Democrats* were also unable to make any inroads into the countryside because of the existence of a leftist liberal party, called the *Peasant Populists* [literally, Party of Rural People], which espoused a sort of agrarian populism similar to the *Socialist Revolutionaries* of Russia. The other political party, the *National Party*, had played a role in formation of the republic—Antanas Smetona, leader of the *Nationalists*, served as the president of the country in 1919–20—but remained insignificant during the 1920's down to 1926.

Lithuania's Border Disputes

Lithuania's chief problem in the period of the 1920's was in securing acceptable international borders. Although there were a number of border disputes, its most significant problem by far was with regard to the city of Vilnius, the historic capital of Lithuania. The problem was that a number of the leaders associated with the new Polish State, including Joseph Pilsudski—sometimes called the father of modern Poland—had strong ties to the Vilnius area. Pilsudski, descendant of a Polonized Lithuanian noble family, had been born in Vilnius. These Polish leaders wanted to recreate the old Polish–Lithuanian union. When the Lithuanian leadership opted for a separate, independent Lithuania, Pilsudski, in particular, decided that the Vilnius area ought to be

part of Poland. His real aim, of course, was to recreate the old Polish–Lithuanian Empire.

But here it is necessary to provide a little background in order to understand just what happened and why. The original Lithuanian proclamation of independence had been made in the city of Vilnius, but the newly–proclaimed Lithuanian Government was forced to abandon that city in January 1919 as *Bolshevik* forces approached the city. They fled to Kaunas, which became the provisional capital. The *Bolsheviks* were forced out in April 1919 by Polish forces, who then occupied the city. In the summer of 1920, the *Bolsheviks* launched a counter–offensive, driving the Poles back.

Now Soviet Russia and Lithuania signed a peace treaty on July 12, under which the *Bolsheviks* recognized Lithuanian independence. Three days later, they offered to restore Vilnius to Lithuania, if Lithuania would ally itself with Soviet Russia against Poland. Basically, this required Lithuania to allow Soviet troops to pass through Lithuania during their invasion of Poland. In the process, they took and occupied Vilnius. The Soviet invasion force continued westward toward Warsaw and was only stopped by a major battle at the Vistula River in August. As the Soviet forces retreated, they turned Vilnius over to the Lithuanian Government, which took possession of the city on August 26, proclaiming it once again the national capital.

Meanwhile, the Polish armed forces pressed further and further eastward, hoping to fulfill Pilsudski's dream of restoring the ancient borders of Poland–Lithuania. Since the Polish Government was desirous of Allied support against Soviet Russia, it gave in to Allied pressure to end its border dispute with Lithuania. On October 7, therefore, Poland signed the treaty of Suwalki granting Lithuania the city of Vilnius and the surrounding district.

By this time, however, the Polish invasion force, defeated by a Soviet force, was beginning its retreat westward. Two days later, a Polish force under General Lucjan Zeligowski broke away from the main Polish force and advanced into Lithuania, apparently acting under secret instructions from Pilsudski. Vilnius was quickly occupied and then General Zeligowski moved further into Lithuania, apparently intending to conquer the entire country. Lithuanian forces counter–attacked, however, and General Zeligowski was forced to withdraw to Vilnius.

The Polish Government disavowed Zeligowski, but that was only for international consumption. Zeligowski, acting on orders from Pilsudski, now proceeded to create a Central Lithuanian Republic, supposedly independent of both Poland

and Lithuania. There were a number of attempts to solve the matter diplomatically, but all failed. Then General Zeligowski arranged for "elections" to take place in January 1922, which were won by pro–Polish candidates. The puppet legislature then voted for union with Poland. The Polish *Sejm* now proceeded to annex the Vilnius area. The Allied ambassadors, tired of the whole thing, accepted the annexation, thereby recognizing the existing line as the final frontier. Lithuania, refusing to accept the annexation, broke diplomatic relations with Poland. These were not resumed until 1938. In the case of Vilnius, therefore, Lithuania never did achieve an acceptable international frontier.

The second boundary question was with regard to Memel, located on the Lithuanian coast a short distance from the mouth of the Nemunas, Lithuania's largest river. Memel had been part of Prussia since the 18th century, but was taken from Germany by the Treaty of Versailles. The Allies had intended that Memel go to a reconstituted Poland–Lithuania. Although Lithuania's decision to seek its separate independence ended that possibility, the Allies, refusing to recognize Lithuanian independence because of its border dispute with Poland over Vilnius, could not bring themselves to turn Memel over to Lithuania. Instead, Memel was placed under French military administration and the matter was put on hold.

Memel itself was a town of only about twenty thousand, most of whose citizens were German nationals. Lithuania's interest in the city was that it needed a seaport, and Memel was the only good seaport along the entire Lithuanian coast. Its interest in Vilnius was much greater, however, so it did nothing until it had become clear that the international community had recognized Poland's annexation of Vilnius. With nothing further to lose, the Lithuanian Government decided to seize Memel by force. On January 7, 1923, days after the French had begun their own occupation of the German Ruhr, Lithuania sent troops accompanied by a large number of Lithuanian "volunteers" to invade and occupy Memel. The Lithuanians lost twenty men, while two Frenchmen and a German policeman were killed on the other side. With the French tied down in Germany and the German and Soviet Governments supporting Lithuania, the Allies decided that nothing could be done and agreed, in February 1923, to formally transfer Memel to Lithuanian sovereignty.

Thus in the Memel dispute, Lithuania got both the desired seaport and international recognition of that fact. The government immediately gave the Lithua-

The Baltic Republics

nian name of Klaipeda to the city and the region, and established it as an autonomous province with its own government. Klaipeda, with all of Lithuania as its hinterland, flourished in subsequent years, though it continued to have a significant German population, and that would become a diplomatic issue between Germany and Lithuania after Hitler came to power.

Lithuania's Move Away From Democracy

The May 1926 elections resulted in a political transformation when the *Christian Democrats*, who had dominated every government up to this time, were defeated. A new coalition government under the premiership of Mykolas Slezevicius now took power, composed of the *Social Democrats* and the *Peasant Populists*. One month later, in June 1926, the coalition's candidate, Dr. Kazys Grinius, a prominent leader of the *Peasant Populists*, was installed as President.

Among the changes introduced by the new government was a change in the attitude toward the Soviet Union, symbolized by a non–aggression pact which the two countries signed in September 1926.

The *Christian Democrats* and the *Nationalists* had opposed an agreement with the Soviet Union from the beginning, and they now began planning a counter–stroke. On the night of December 16, with the support of the army, they carried out their *coup d'etat* against the government. Entering the parliament building accompanied by a group of officers, they seized control, then dismissed the cabinet, adjourned the session of parliament, and deposed the President of the Republic. Antanas Smetona, leader of the *Nationalists* and first President in 1919–20, was appointed President of the Republic.

The *coup* having succeeded, the left decided to cooperate to save what they could of Lithuanian democracy. Grinius submitted his resignation as President, and Slezevicius resigned as Premier. The parliament then met and elected Antanas Smetona as President of the Republic. The *coup* had been legalized. One of Smetona's first acts as President was to name Augustinas Voldemaras, a prominent *Nationalist*, as the new Premier. Voldemaras formed a cabinet composed of *Christian Democrats*, *Nationalists* and members of parties of the center.

The *Social Democrats* and *Peasant Populists* continued to control a majority in the legislature, however, and when, after a period of cooperation, they challenged the government in April 1927, the government dissolved the legislature. Smetona ruled for approximately a year by decree, then proclaimed a new constitution in May 1928 which formalized the new structure. From that time onward, Smetona and his Premier, Augustinas Voldemaras, ruled the country by decree. Lithuania was thus the first of the Baltic countries to abandon democracy and replace it with a form of authoritarianism.

The Lithuanian Authoritarian Regime

Lithuania differed from its two Baltic neighbors in that its authoritarian regime involved two figures, Smetona and Voldemaras, in the beginning and because some political organizations continued to operate. The *Nationalist Party* was the most significant of the political groups at this time, though a semi–fascist group, *Iron Wolf*, was created by Voldemaras at this time. Voldemaras was forced out in September 1929, however, after he came under clerical criticism and became the target of a failed assassination attempt by three Lithuanian students. He was succeeded as premier by J. Tubelis, President Smetona's brother–in–law. Tubelis remained premier until 1939.

In 1934, spurred on by worsening economic conditions, a number of military officers attempted a *coup* to restore Voldemaras to power. When the *coup* failed, Voldemaras was arrested and sentenced to several years in prison. Released in 1938, he left the country and settled in southern France.

There were also a number of peasant revolts in 1934 which were put down by force. Believing that the revolts were the

Ornamental cats

NOVOSTI photo

206

result of political agitation, Smetona banned all political parties other than the *Nationalists*. The government permitted the election of a new legislature in 1935, but this was largely meaningless, since the government nominated all electoral candidates. A new constitution was also approved in 1936. In essence, it legalized the authoritarian Presidency which had existed since 1926. In one innovation, Smetona was henceforth to be addressed as *Tautos Vados*, or "Leader of the People."

Lithuania Under Soviet Rule, 1939–1991

Although the Lithuanian people had failed in some respects with regard to domestic policies, their greatest mistake was internationally. Perhaps nothing they could have done would have made any difference, but it is nevertheless true that they were at odds with almost all of their neighbors and had no international friends. Thus when Nazi Germany and the Soviet Union got together to negotiate their "non–aggression" pact in August 1939, Lithuania was among their victims. Dividing eastern Europe into spheres of influence, the original agreement assigned Estonia and Latvia to the Soviet Union; Lithuania to Germany. A September 23, 1939 protocol assigned Lithuania to the Soviet Union, while Nazi Germany got an extra piece of Poland.

Hitler launched his invasion of Poland on September 1 and Soviet troops entered to occupy the eastern third of Poland on September 17. With Poland settled, Stalin moved to cash in his other chips. During the month of October all three Baltic States were forced to sign mutual assistance pacts with the Soviet Union. As an aside, Lithuania was the only one to get anything out of the agreements. The Soviet Union transferred the city of Vilnius and surrounding area, which it had just taken from Poland, to Lithuania.

Nothing happened for several months, probably because the Soviet Union was tied down in its "Winter War" with Finland. Once that was resolved, the Soviet Union turned its attention back to the Baltic States. Toward the end of May 1940, the Soviet Foreign Ministry accused Lithuania of violating the 1939 mutual assistance pact. Then, on June 14, Soviet Foreign Minister Molotov demanded the arrest of the Lithuanian interior and security ministers and the creation of a new Lithuanian Government capable of supporting the 1939 treaty. In addition, Molotov demanded that Soviet troops be authorized to enter the country and to occupy "the most important centers."

Lithuania had no choice but to give in to the Soviet request. After the Red Army had entered the country, Molotov demanded the right to name a new premier. A popular front government was now

The old part of Vilnius, the Lithuanian capital whose "sister" city is Madison, Wisconsin
NOVOSTI photo

established. The *Social Democrats* and *Peasant Populists* were given ministerial seats, but all the important ministries were controlled by the *Communists*.

But the popular front government had a remarkably short life. In July, all political parties other than the *Communist Party* were banned and most non–communists were dismissed from office. This was followed by a wave of arrests. Then, with only communists, organized as the *Working People's League*, standing for office, new elections were held on July 14. The newly elected legislature met on July 21.

Its only piece of business was to vote on whether to join the Soviet Union, which it did by acclamation. The following month, the USSR Supreme Soviet acceded to this request. Lithuania thus became a Soviet Socialist Republic.

The new communist government immediately began to implement general Soviet policies. A government decree nationalized all of the land. Larger estates were taken over directly and turned into state farms, but there was also a promise of land to landless laborers. Smaller farmers were permitted to retain up to 75

The Baltic Republics

acres, though technically they did not own it any longer. Nationalist elements now began to organize opposition to the new policies. In retaliation, the communists began rounding up oppositional elements and deporting them to Siberia.

Nazi Germany's invasion of the Soviet Union beginning on June 22, 1941 reversed this situation, for German troops overran and occupied Lithuania later in 1941. It remained under German occupation until 1944. With the German retreat, however, Lithuania once again fell under Soviet control. A anti–communist resistance movement once again arose, often consisting of individuals who had been active in guerrilla actions against the Germans. By the summer of 1945, this movement had approximately 50,000 members and was operating throughout Lithuania. Units tended to operate in rural parts of the country, with their encampments in the middle of a forest. Guerrilla units would move out to attack centers of communist control while, back at the encampment, others worked to organize popular resistance. The reconstituted Lithuanian Communist Government countered the resistance movement by creating its own "People's Defenders," though the main struggle against the guerrillas was carried out by the NKVD. This war between the Lithuanian resistance and the NKVD went on until 1947. Such efforts were, of course, ineffectual. Lithuania got no outside assistance, and the resistance movement was eventually suppressed.

Many changes occurred in Lithuania over the next thirty–five years. Soviet policy was to integrate the Baltic Republics so thoroughly into the Soviet system that there would be no question of their ever leaving the union. To that end, the Soviet Government first carried out policies of nationalization and collectivization. Next it sought to bind the Republics to the rest of the Soviet Union economically by locating branch factories of Soviet industry there. Such factories received most or all of their raw materials from other parts of the Soviet Union, and delivered most of their finished products to customers in the other republics. This economic integration was so successful that the three Baltic Republics became more integrated into the Soviet economy than any other republic.

This program of economic integration was accompanied by a program of "Soviet Russification," aimed at transforming the cultures of the three republics. All students received Russian language training in the schools, plus general indoctrination lectures on the nature of Soviet culture. In addition, there was a systematic effort made to settle non–Baltic nationals in the republics. When a new

factory was built, most of the workers would be transferred there from elsewhere in the Soviet Union.

It was Estonia and Latvia that became the chief victims of this policy, however. According to the figures of the 1989 Soviet census, Lithuania is still 80 percent ethnic Lithuanian. By comparison, ethnic Estonians by this time made up only 61.5 percent of the population of the republic, while in Latvia the figure was only 52 percent. On the positive side, the heavy industrialization carried out since 1945 meant that the standard of living in the three Baltic Republics was above that of any part of the Soviet Union.

Lithuania Moves Toward Independence

The Lithuanian people accommodated themselves to Soviet rule, but they were never happy with it. Thus when Gorbachëv launched his programs of *glasnost* and restructuring after coming to power in 1985, Lithuanians were among the first to take advantage of them. In enunciating his policy of *glasnost*, Gorbachëv called on the Soviet peoples to speak out against negative tendencies in the society, and to support his reforms. This became a manifesto which led to the creation of thousands of "unofficial" organizations all over the Soviet Union. Formed originally in support of Gorbachëv's policy of reform, many of them soon began to push their own agendas. For the Baltic peoples, Gorbachëv's policies were a welcome breath of fresh air, and they were among the first to throw their enthusiastic support to him. At the same time, and almost from the beginning, the Baltic peoples used *glasnost* for their own purposes.

The Lithuanian people were a little slower to get organized than the Estonians and Latvians but, once organized, they proved to be even more determined to split with Moscow than either Estonia or Latvia. *Sajudis*, the Lithuanian Popular Front, traces its origins to a commission established by the Lithuanian Academy of Sciences on May 23, 1988 to propose changes to the Lithuanian constitution to accommodate Gorbachëv's policies of *glasnost*, *perestroika*, and democratization. The commission brought together party and non–party intellectuals and professionals who, in turn, decided that the times demanded something more. On June 3, they created an "initiative group" which subsequently took the name of *Sajudis*. Over the summer, *Sajudis* organized mass meetings and demonstrations on issues such as the 1939 Molotov–Ribbentrop Pact, the status of the Lithuanian language and the possibility of some form of economic autonomy. From the beginning, the animating spirit behind *Sajudis* was a non–party intellectual, a

Vytautas Landsbergis

musicologist by the name of Vytautas Landsbergis.

Sajudis held its founding congress in October. Here a resolution was passed calling on the republic government to issue an assertion of Lithuanian sovereignty. Algirdas Brazauskas, who had just been appointed First Secretary of the *Lithuanian Communist Party*, was one of the invited speakers at the congress. He supported the measure initially, but was then forced to reverse himself on orders from Moscow. The *Lithuanian Communist Party* lost a great deal of its credibility as a result, as can be seen by looking at the results of the March 1989 elections to the USSR Congress of People's Deputies.

Sajudis candidates won 36 out of 42 seats to the Congress and might have won even more had they not deliberately refrained from challenging certain top communists, including First Secretary Brazauskas, who was liked personally, in spite of his having toed Moscow's line on the sovereignty issue. In fact, there was a tremendous overlap in the electoral positions of *Sajudis* and the *Lithuanian Communist Party*, for the latter advocated economic autonomy, pluralism of opinions, democracy and *glasnost*.

The *Lithuanian Communist Party* came under tremendous pressure after it had lost to *Sajudis* in the spring elections. In an attempt to create nationalist credentials, the party began discussing a split with the *Communist Party of the Soviet Union* in mid–1989. Another indication of the way opinion within the party was evolving came on August 22, 1989 when a commission of the Lithuanian Supreme

Soviet, at that time still controlled by communists, voted to condemn the 1940 Soviet annexation of Lithuania and to declare it invalid. The party's formal split with Moscow came in December, at the *Lithuanian Communist Party* Congress. The *Lithuanian Communist Party* became the first republic party to split with the *CPSU*.

Even so, the *Lithuanian Communist Party* still found itself following along in *Sajudis's* wake. On August 23, 1989, the governing council of *Sajudis* voted unanimously that Lithuania should "take the peaceful course to becoming an independent democratic republic once again." In December 1989, Brazauskas, going further than he had ever gone before, could only bring himself to advocate a "sovereign Lithuanian state in a new union of free republics."

And even that position caused a split in the *Lithuanian Communist Party*, when a faction claiming to represent one–fourth of the membership broke away and reaffirmed its ties with Moscow.

It was against this background that elections were held to elect a new Lithuanian Supreme Soviet. The elections took place on February 24, 1990 with run–off elections on March 10. The *Sajudis* slate, which included reform communists as well as representatives of the newly legalized *Christian Democrat*, *Social Democrat* and *Green* parties, won an overwhelming majority.

When the newly installed parliament met to elect its Chairman of the Presidium, it chose Vytautas Landsbergis, head of *Sajudis* and a non–communist. Lithuania had its first non–communist government since 1940. On March 11, the Lithuanian Supreme Soviet adopted a declaration of Lithuanian independence.

The Soviet Union not only did not recognize Lithuanian independence; it also organized a partial economic boycott against the republic. Orders went out to all state enterprises in the republic to obey only orders from Moscow. There was also public discussion about presenting Lithuania with a bill for Soviet capital investments over the years—estimated at 21 billion rubles—payable in hard currency. There were also Soviet military maneuvers held in March 1990 in and around the city of Vilnius, though Gorbachëv claimed at the same time that force would not be used except to prevent bloodshed.

The Lithuanian response to the Soviet demand for indemnities was to raise counterclaims for goods and services extracted from the republic, environmental damage and for the tens of thousands of Lithuanians killed by Soviet officials over the years. The rhetoric escalated still further in April when Gorbachëv threatened to sharply reduce the flow of gas and oil to Lithuania if it did not immediately retract its declaration of independence. The Lithuanian Government offered to discuss the question of the effective date of independence but not the question of independence itself. Oil shipments to Lithuania's sole refinery were then cut off and cuts were made in the delivery of other raw materials.

Meanwhile, Lithuania got some support of sorts when the Estonian and Latvian Governments joined Lithuania in issuing their own declarations of independence, though the declarations were not to take force immediately. In addition, the United States Government threatened to withhold most–favored–nation trading status from the Soviet Union if it blockaded Lithuania. As a result, after some further threats, the Soviet Union lifted its partial embargo on Lithuania. Things remained quiet for several months, but there was a new move against Lithuania by Moscow hardliners in January 1991. Gorbachëv claimed no advance knowledge when USSR Ministry of Interior troops seized a television tower in Vilnius, but he did not repudiate the action.

The issue of Baltic independence was one of the issues that precipitated the *coup* against Gorbachëv in August 1991. The failure of that *coup* led most of the world to extend recognition to the Baltic States and led the post–*coup* Soviet Government to extend its own recognition in September 1991. Lithuania was admitted to the United Nations in October 1991.

The newly–independent Lithuanian

Weaving wicker baskets

NOVOSTI photo

The Baltic Republics

Government concentrated mainly on domestic problems at first, although it also pressed for the removal of Soviet troops from Lithuania as soon as possible. That presented a particular problem so long as the troops remained under the aegis of the Commonwealth of Independent States, but the Russian Government set up its own Ministry of Defense in the summer of 1992 and subsequently negotiated an agreement with Lithuania for the removal of the troops as soon as possible.

There were approximately 20,500 troops in Lithuania at this time. Some small token force withdrawals began in September, and Russia promised that all would be out by sometime in 1993. President Yeltsin suspended the troop withdrawals in October, however, asserting a "profound concern" over the treatment of ethnic Russians in the Baltic Republics. Since Lithuania, unlike the Estonians and Latvians, had extended citizenship to all persons who were resident prior to mid–1990, it is not certain why Lithuania was included in the decree. The decree appears to have been a gesture toward Yeltsin's domestic opposition; in fact, there have been indications that troop withdrawals have been continuing on their old timetable.

Lithuania has also had some problems with minorities within the country, mainly Poles and Russians. District governments in and around Vilnius where Poles were in a majority were suspended, apparently because the Poles elected communists to office. In spite of nationalist demands to the contrary, however, the Government eventually ended up extending citizenship rights to its minorities.

A new constitution was adopted in 1992 and new parliamentary elections were subsequently held in October, with a run–off election in November. In a surprise, the electorate gave *Sajudis*, the party of President Landsbergis, only about 22 percent of the vote. The winner was the *Democratic Labor Party*, the successor party to the *Lithuanian Communist Party*, led by Algirdas Brazauskas, which got over 40 percent of the vote and a majority of the seats in the *Seimas*. Thus it might appear that the Lithuanians have returned the communists to power.

In fact, Brazauskas is a nationalist who was responsible for the *Lithuanian Communist Party's* split with Moscow and subsequently supported Lithuanian independence. Brazauskas also maintains that the *Democratic Labor Party* is a new party and that only about five percent of its current membership were formerly members of the *Lithuanian Communist Party*.

In actuality, it is not politics but economics that is responsible for Brazauskas' victory. The Lithuanian economy is in relatively poor shape. Salaries have been frozen and many people are paid up to three months late. Moreover, Lithuania began restricting its imports of oil and gas in July 1992, in response to Russia's decision to begin charging world prices payable in hard currency for exports to areas outside the ruble zone. As a result, Lithuania did not have sufficient fuel to heat most buildings. As one commentator explained the vote, "the simple people know only that before it was warm, and now it is cold."

Brazauskas supports Lithuania's transition to a market economy but he did urge a slower pace of change during the campaign. As he commented after his victory, "we support the idea that there can be no sharp turns, that we cannot do anything at any price. We have already done that. We have frozen salaries and removed subsidies. Can you imagine how a person receiving a small salary can survive, with world prices coming down upon their heads? A government has to reply to the people's cries."

Brazauskas is expected to cooperate more closely with factory managers in working out a transition to private enterprise. In foreign policy, he is likely to encourage a closer working relationship with Russia, particularly in the economic area. He has, however, insisted that Russia remove the last of its troops by September 1993.

NATURE OF THE REGIME

Lithuania completed its transition from the earlier communistic system in October 1992 when the Lithuanian people approved a new constitution in a national referendum and is now a multiparty, parliamentary democracy. Under the terms of a new constitution, transition titles adopted after Lithuania became independent in September 1991 have been replaced by permanent titles, some of which reflect titles current during the earlier Lithuanian Republic. For example, the legislature, known as the Supreme Soviet when Lithuania was a Soviet Republic, became the Supreme Council after September 1991. Under the new constitution, it reverted to its previous name, the *Seimas*. The head of state, formerly known as the Chairman of the Presidium of the Supreme Council, is now the President of the Republic. The head of government, formerly referred to as the Chairman of the Council of Ministers, is the Prime Minister.

The Lithuanian Government

The most important political figure within the new governmental system is the President of the Republic. Popularly elected, he is expected to represent the country internationally and to provide general political leadership domestically.

The current President of the Republic is Algirdas Brazauskas, leader of the *Democratic Labor Party*, who was elected to that office on February 14, 1993. Brazauskas was originally named Chairman of the Presidium and Acting President by the *Seimas* in November 1992, following the victory of the *Democratic Labor Party* in the Fall elections. Brazauskas's February victory thus confirmed the results of the Fall 1992 parliamentary elections. The *Democratic Labor Party* is the renamed *Lithuanian Communist Party*, though it has been transformed by Brazauskas into a "left of center," democratic party.

The official next in importance to the President is the Prime Minister. As the constitutionally–designated head of government, the Prime Minister is responsible for the day–to–day operations of government. Appointed by the President, the Prime Minister must be confirmed by the *Seimas*—and must retain the support of a majority of that body to remain in office. Thus, among his other functions, the Prime Minister is expected to maintain a close working relationship with the *Seimas*.

The current Prime Minister, Bronislovas Lubys, was appointed by President Brazauskas on December 2, 1992. An engineer by profession, Lubys does not belong to any political party, though he was associated with the liberal group in the previous legislature and held the office of Deputy Prime Minister in the former government.

The current cabinet is essentially a coalition, though it might also be labeled a government of specialists. Of the 17 ministers, only three portfolios are in the hands of *Democratic Labor Party* members. The rest are held by representatives of other parties, six of whom have led ministries in the past. All are locally recognized as "eminent specialists and professionals in their fields."

The *Seimas* is a single body legislature with a total of 141 members. Under Lithuania's voting system, 71 of the seats are filled by direct vote; the remaining 70 seats are awarded on a proportional basis, each political party being assigned seats on the basis of its share of the popular vote. In the current *Seimas*, 73 seats are held by the *Democratic Labor Party*, while 52 seats are held by *Sajudis* and its allies.

Culture

Lithuanian culture was essentially a rural, peasant culture until the end of the nineteenth century. After that, it developed an urban culture, based on the rising professional and middle classes, though the population of most Lithuanian cities remained largely non–Lithuanian until fairly late in this century. Vilnius, the current capital and largest city, continues to have a large Polish population. It was, in fact, part of Poland until 1939, and only became Lithuanian shortly before Lithuania itself was incorporated into the Soviet Union. In one sense, then, Kaunas, the second city and the capital of Lithuania in the inter–war period, is more Lithuanian than Vilnius.

Vilnius does have Gediminas Castle, the fortress–residence of the Grand Dukes of Lithuania, the Gothic Church of St. Anne that dates from the fourteenth century, the University building in the oldest part of the city, and the "Medininku vartai," all that is left of the nine gates in the former wall that surrounded the city when it was the capital of the Grand Duchy. There are also some houses that date from the fifteenth–seventeenth centuries. But the city became Polanized after the Union with Poland in 1569. Vilnius University, the republic's

greatest center of learning, was originally founded in 1579, but it was closed by the Russian Government in 1832. When it reopened in 1919, Vilnius was part of Poland, so it was located in Kaunas until after World War II. Today, of course, Vilnius is home to the Lithuanian State Opera and Ballet Company and to numerous theaters for the presentation of plays, as well as the republic's main philharmonic orchestra.

Kaunas also has its own philharmonic and numerous theaters, though it lacks an opera and ballet company. It also has numerous churches and museums. There are five institutes of higher education in the city, including a medical college. Another is Kaunas' Polytechnical Institute, founded in 1951 after the university was shifted to Vilnius. There are also a number of scientific research institutes.

Lithuanian Literature

Although the Lithuanian people had a

strong oral folklorist tradition, a written literature was rather late in developing. In fact, the first book published in the Lithuanian language was a religious text, *Simple Words of the Catechism*, published in 1547. The religious controversy associated with the reformation led to the translation of the *Bible* into Lithuanian in 1590 but, as a result of the triumph of Catholicism in Poland–Lithuania, it was never published but remained in manuscript form in the library of Koenigsberg University. The Jesuits, who were primarily responsible for the triumph of Catholicism, did produce several things in Lithuanian, including a catechism, a collection of sermons, and a dictionary, the latter published in 1629.

The first example of secular literature in the Lithuanian language, a translation of ten of Aesop's fables, appeared in 1706. The first Lithuanian author, the poet Kristijonas Donelaitis, lived in the eighteenth century, though his epic poem,

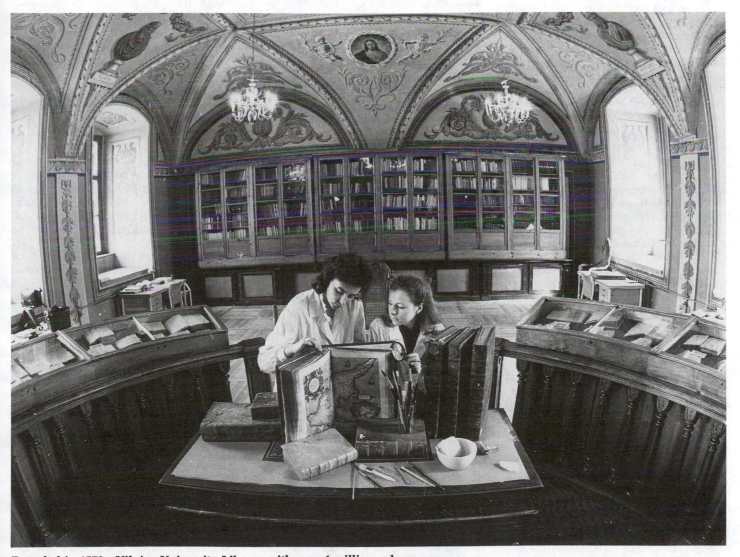

Founded in 1570—Vilnius University Library with over 4 million volumes

NOVOSTI photo

The Baltic Republics

The Seasons, circulated only in manuscript form during his lifetime and was not published until 1818. Donelaitis was a Protestant pastor in the town of Tolminkiemis and parts of his poem appear to be paraphrases of his sermons. Yet the poem also presents a realistic portrayal of the life of the peasants, at that time still struggling serfs. The German poet Goethe, who was familiar with the poem, compared Donelaitis to Homer.

A second poet, Antanas Baranauskas, who lived and wrote in the nineteenth century, had a background similar to that of Donelaitis in that he also followed a religious avocation, and in later life became the Catholic bishop in Seinai. Baranauskas actually wrote his poems during his youth, however, before being ordained as a priest. His most important poem, written during summer vacations at home in 1858–59, was *The Forest of Anykščiai*. Baranauskas projects a mystic oneness with nature that is almost pagan in its orientation:

"Forest and peasant knew no discord,
Grew up together, aged in accord.
To the Lithuanian, caveman of yore,
The forest gave a strong wooden door;
And since he never would hew the wood,
Till aged it fell, the dry trees still stood."

Lithuania became a part of the Russian Empire at the end of the eighteenth century, along with parts of eastern Poland. At that time, there was no separate Lithuanian nationalism, but Lithuanians supported Polish attempts—in 1831 and again in 1863—to throw off the Russian yoke. As a result, the Russian Government attempted to stamp out Polish–Lithuanian nationalism by Russifying the people and the culture. The University of Vilnius was closed after the 1831 uprising; then the Latin alphabet was replaced by the Cyrillic alphabet after the 1863 uprising. These efforts to stamp out the local culture were unavailing, however.

Instead, Lithuanian political and cultural leaders arranged to have Lithuanian–language books and newspapers published in East Prussia, then smuggled them across the border. The first Lithuanian–language newspaper, *The Dawn* began publishing in Tilset in 1883. In addition, increasing numbers of Lithuanians entered universities either in Russia or abroad and subsequently added their literary output to the stream. Jonas Maironis–Mačiulis studied at Kiev and St. Petersburg and later became a professor and a priest. His collection, *The Voices of Spring*, published in 1895, glorified the Lithuanian countryside. He also wrote ballads and satires and even a drama in verse, *The Death of Kestutis*,

which, however, was not published until 1921. Another dramatist, Vilius Storasta, who wrote under the name of Vydūnas, produced *The Shadows of Ancestors* in 1908, *The Eternal Flame* in 1912, and *Bells of the Sea* in 1914. A fourth play, *The World on Fire* was produced in 1928.

Vincas Krēvē, another playwright, produced his first dramas before World War I, but his most important plays appeared in independent Lithuania. Important plays include *Skirgaila* (1922), *On the Roads of Destiny* (1926), *The Death of Mindaugas* (1930), and *The Son–in–Law* (1939). Kreve served for a short time as Minister of Foreign Affairs in the new Soviet–dominated government in 1940, then went into hiding before fleeing abroad. In 1947, he became a member of the faculty of the University of Pennsylvania and remained there until his death in 1954.

The second major figure of the period of Lithuanian independence was Vincas Mykolaitis, who wrote under the *nom de plume* of Putinas. Extremely versatile, Putinas, who was also an ordained priest, produced poetry, novels, and plays. His two best novels are probably the autobiographical trilogy, *In the Shadow of Altars* and *The Crisis*, both written in the 1930's. Putinas, who died in 1967, continued to write after the Soviet occupation of the country in 1940, but these works, favorable to the new regime, are lesser works.

There is also a body of works done by Lithuanians in emigration. Antanas Vaičiulaitis taught at several American universities after World War II, then joined the Voice of America. His books include three volumes of short stories, legends and myths. Jurgis Gliauda, who also made his way to America after World War II, is the author of *House Upon the Sand* (1951), *Ora pro nobis* (1952), and *The Sonata of Icarus*. Other writers in emigration include Nēlē Mazalaitē, Alfonsas Šešplaukis, Henrikas Radauskas, and Stepas Zobarskas.

Economy

Lithuania is the least industrialized of the Baltic Republics, with only about 40 percent of the work force involved in industry. Even so, industry contributes more to the overall economy than agriculture.

Most of Lithuania's industry is located in or near its major cities. Kaunas, Lithuania's second largest city, has metal and woodworking industries as well as light and food industries. Kleipeda, Lithuania's third largest city and its major seaport, is home to a large deep-sea fishing fleet, and it has one of the largest shipyards in the Baltic. The main local industry is fish processing. The town also has a pulp and paper mill, a

woodworking factory, textile mills, plus a large plant that manufactures radios and telephones. In addition, it is a traditional center for the working of amber. Vilnius, Lithuania's largest city and its capital, is a center for computer manufacturing, machine tools, electric meters, drills, farm machinery, building materials and food processing. There is also a small amount of industry located in smaller towns.

A large part of Lithuania's agricultural land is still organized into collective and state farms, even though the previous government supported the privatization of agriculture. That government did manage to create some private farms, though a major problem was that individual peasants had to be persuaded to accept the responsibility of private farming. The process may slow down somewhat under the new government. President Brazauskas said in December 1992 that it was "a mistake to get rid of the remaining collective farms . . . by giving their property to individuals." Brazauskas said that farmers who "wished and were able to keep their private farms should be provided with all the necessary facilities for it" but that those still on collective farms should be allowed to choose their own form of privatization.

Forestry products are another source of income for persons residing in the countryside. With approximately 25 percent of the land covered by trees, Lithuania produces both timber and pulp wood. There are also considerable deposits of peat plus materials used in construction such as limestone, chalk, dolomites, clays and gravel, whose exploitation provides additional jobs in the countryside.

In the past, about 55 percent of Lithuania's exports went to other parts of the Soviet Union. Negotiations with Russian and some of the other republics have extended those arrangements, but the *Sajudis* government was committed to reorienting its trade more toward the west. President Brazauskas has said that he would like to improve economic relations with the ex–Soviet republics, but the collapse of inter–regional trade in 1991–92 will make that difficult.

Approximately one–third of the republic's industrial workers work in engineering or metal–working factories created during the Soviet period. These factories, which were built to serve customers located mainly in the other republics, have been particularly hard pressed recently. Overall, the Lithuanian economy has suffered fairly steep declines over the past two–three years, but these declines have been similar to developments elsewhere in the former Soviet Union and less than in some republics. One of Lithuania's

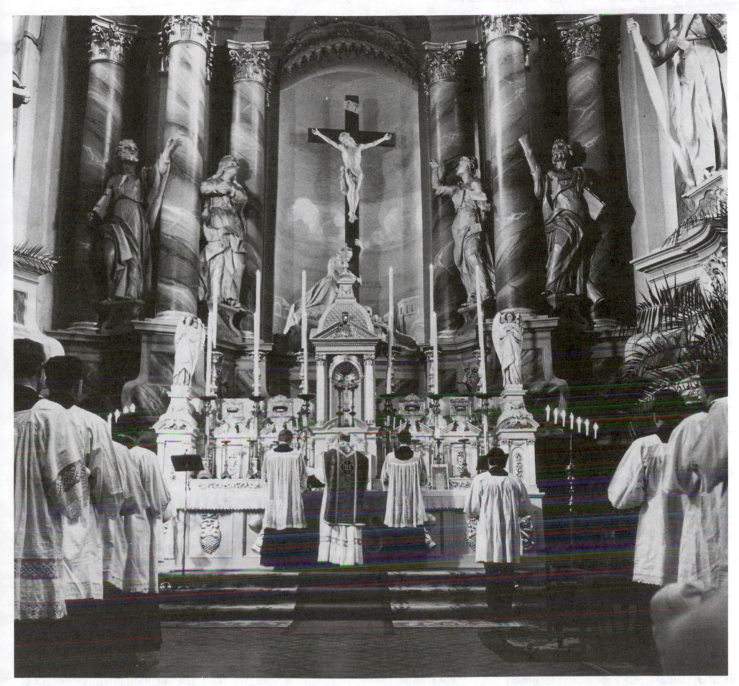

Mass is celebrated in Kaunas

NOVOSTI Photo

major problems has been obtaining energy supplies from Russia.

The Lithuanian economy is still declining and no one is predicting a turnaround in the near future. According to the Lithuanian Department for Statistics, industrial output for the period January–October 1992 was 47.5 percent less than output for the comparable period in 1991. According the World Bank, it will be the turn of the century before the Lithuanian economy again reaches its 1989 level.

The Future

Lithuania's larger agricultural population probably gives it a cushion that the other two Baltic states lack. Its greater ethnic unity and the strong unifying role of the Roman Catholic Church are other pluses. It has also shown that it can have a peaceful change of government. On the negative side, it is the poorest of the Baltic republics, so its reserves are that much less. Its transition to a market economy may be somewhat slowed down as a result of its recent change of government, but President Brazauskas appears to share most of the goals of the previous government.

The Republic of Bulgaria

An expensive purchase in Sofia: costume jeweley

Area: 111,852 sq. km. = 42,729 sq. mi.

Population: 9.6 million (projected).

Capital City Sofia: (Pop. 1,064,000, projected).

Climate: Mediterranean in the South, cooler in the North.

Neighboring Countries: Romania (North); Turkey, Greece (South); Serbia, SFRY (formerly Yugoslavia), Macedonia (West).

Official Language: Bulgarian.

Other Principal Tongue: Turkish.

Ethnic Background: Slav, Turkish.

Principal Religions: Bulgarian Orthodox, Islam.

Chief Commercial Products: Machinery and equipment, agricultural and forest products, fuels, minerals, metals, rose oil, wine.

Currency: Leva.

Former Political Status: Part of Ottoman Empire, 1393–1878; Autonomous Principality, 1878–1908; Independent, 1908–1944; Communist State, part of Soviet Empire, 1945–1990.

National Day: Undetermined.

Chief of State: Zhelyu Zhelev, President.

Head of Government: Lyuben Berov, Prime Minister.

National Flag: Horizontal stripes of white, green and crimson, with a coat of arms of the Republic.

THE LAND AND THE PEOPLE

The Republic of Bulgaria is a relatively small, square–shaped country bordering on the Black Sea to the east and bounded by the Danube River to the north. The Black Sea coast has not only beautiful sandy beaches which are now being developed, but it is also the site of the major industrial center of Varna. Stretching from west to east is the Balkan Range (Stara Planina) separating the fertile Danubian Plain in the north from the Thracian Plain in the south.

In the exact center of the country there is the Kazanlik "Valley of Roses" where fragrance and beauty combine with commercial value in the production of rose oil. The southwest is dominated by the rugged Rila Mountains—which include Mount Musala, the highest peak in the Balkans—and by the snow–capped Pirin Mountains. South of Plovdiv, Bulgaria's second largest city built on a cliff overlooking the Maritsa River, lie the Rhodope Mountains, where hundreds of mineral springs can be found.

In the 7th century an Asiatic people called the Bulgars crossed the Danube River and settled in the area which is known today as the People's Republic of Bulgaria. Within two centuries after their conquest of the region, the Bulgars had become completely absorbed into the native Slav population, adopting their language and culture. The Bulgarians were converted to Orthodox Christianity during the 9th century by Cyril and Methodius, two missionaries, who devised a Slav alphabet in order to translate the Bible and religious writings into the language of the people. The conversion of the Bulgarians thus brought them their first literary language and early contact with the Byzantine Empire.

HISTORY

The rise of Bulgarian power began when they challenged the Byzantine Empire, which had become a powerful Greek super–state of the medieval period that grew with and through the eastern Orthodox Church. On two occasions, the Bulgarians were able to seize and control substantial lands in what are now Bulgaria, Greece, Turkey, Russia, Yugoslavia and Romania. The swirling tides of battles during this period are complicated, involving both the eastern Orthodox Church and the Roman Church. The expanding Ottoman Turks conquered Bulgaria in 1393 and remained in control until 1878. The inhabitants of the Ottoman Empire were organized into administrative units on the basis of their faith,

214

with a religious leader as head of each unit. The Orthodox Church was thus used by the Turks to administer the Bulgarians.

The Birth of Modern Bulgaria

The liberation of Bulgaria from Turkish control was the product of a war between Russia and Turkey which ended in Turkish defeat. The Russians had envisioned a single, large Bulgarian state and this was stipulated in the resulting Treaty of San Stefano. The Austrians and British objected, however, and Russia was forced to permit a rewriting of the treaty at the Congress of Berlin. The result, signed in 1878, was that the southern portion of Bulgaria was returned to Turkey while the remaining area was divided into two parts, separated by the Balkan Mountains. The northern part became Bulgaria and was established as a self–governing territory with the right to select its own Prince. The portion south of the mountains became the autonomous Turkish territory of East Rumelia. The division did not last, however; in 1885, the East Rumelians voted to merge with the rest of Bulgaria. The nation as a whole remained a self–governing autonomous principality until it declared its complete independence from the Ottoman Empire in 1908.

There were three main problems that Bulgaria inherited from the period following Ottoman rule. The first concerned territory—the Great Bulgaria envisioned in the Treaty of San Stefano had included much of the territory the Bulgarians had lived in at the time of their greatness in the 10th century. The Treaty of Berlin had reduced those territories by nearly two–thirds. The Union of East Rumelia and Bulgaria in 1885 partially cured the situation, but still left Bulgaria with claims to additional territory. It was this question that led to Bulgarian participation in the two Balkan Wars of 1912–13, to an alliance with Germany and Austria in World War I and to an alliance with Germany in World War II.

The second problem was the status of neighboring Macedonia. The majority of the people of Macedonia are Slavs (not necessarily Bulgarians, however) and there is no genuinely reasonable way to determine whether the area should be in Bulgaria, Yugoslavia (Serbia) or Greece. The Greek influence is strong; it dates from the medieval period and persists to this day. In the late 19th century, Greek–Serbian–Bulgarian rivalry was intense, with each trying to increase its influence through a variety of means including political propaganda, school subsidies, Orthodox Church authority and, worst of all, terrorism.

The third problem was the nature of Bulgaria's relationship with Russia. On one hand, there had been a great deal of popular affection for Russia as the liberator of Bulgaria from Turkish rule. On the other hand, this affection had been mingled with a fear that the price of Russian friendship may be Bulgarian servitude.

This was the only nation in the Balkans to join the Central Powers (Germany-Austria) in World War I; this not only resulted in defeat in 1918, but a loss of even more territory. The terms of the treaty settling the war and the boundaries of the southern Balkans were denounced by Bulgaria as harsh during the interwar period.

From 1919 to 1939, Bulgarian history was troubled. There were political plots from left and right–wing groups, assassinations, mass murders and constant acts of individual terrorism. One of the most

important groups in the country, especially in the years between 1923 and 1934 was the *Internal Macedonian Revolutionary Organization (IMRO)*. This was a terrorist group fighting for Macedonian self–government and undermining any political leaders who pursued policies inconsistent with this goal.

The early post–World War I period years were dominated by Alexander Stambuliski, a colorful, strong–willed leader of the *Agrarian Party*. During the period he was premier, which lasted until 1923, reforms in the tax structure, legal system and land ownership were carried out. The land reforms were not as drastic as they were elsewhere in the Balkans since Bulgaria was basically a peasant society with few large landholdings.

While Stambuliski was in office, the *Communist Party of Bulgaria* was the second–largest party in the country. After a right–wing military regime came to power in 1923, the party was banned, and its leaders, such as Georgi Dimitrov, had to go into exile.

After ten years of *IMRO* terrorism and government inefficiency, a military *coup* was engineered in 1934. Colonel Kimon Georgiev, the leader of the *Zveno* group—an organization of reform–minded intellectuals and politicians—became premier. In less that a year he was out of office; his powers went to King Boris, who ruled Bulgaria as a royal dictator from 1935 until his death in 1943.

Bulgaria joined the Axis in 1941, but refused to declare war on the Soviet Union when that nation was invaded by Germany. During 1941, as a by–product

Bulgaria

of a German attack on Yugoslavia, Bulgaria occupied the Yugoslav portion of Macedonia, part of Serbia and also took over Western Thrace, a part of Greece.

Boris was succeeded in 1943 by his six–year–old son, Simeon. A three–man regency exercised state power. Under the administration of Premier Ivan Bagrianov, a less pro–Axis policy was soon adopted. Thousands of political prisoners were released and persecution of Jews decreased.

Bulgaria announced in 1944 that it was ready to seek a separate peace with the Allies. However, the Soviet Union declared war on Bulgaria within a few days and the Soviet army entered the country.

Bulgaria Becomes a People's Republic

Technically, the government was overthrown at this time by a native resistance group calling itself the *Fatherland Front*. This was a "popular front" grouping which had come into existence during World War II with the assistance and under the sponsorship of the Communist International (Comintern). An undoubted factor in this sponsorship was that Georgi Dimitrov, the Bulgarian communist who had fled the country in 1923, was now Secretary General of the Comintern.

The communist role in the *Fatherland Front* was very strong, but it was a genuine "popular front," encompassing the Agrarian Union, one wing of the Social Democrats, and Zveno. In fact, the premier of the new government was Colonel Kimon Georgiev, a member of Zveno. The communists were a minority in the cabinet, but they controlled the key ministries of Justice and Interior. This gave them control over both the police and the courts, and they used this to institute a systematic purge of opposition figures.

Since all the parties of the *Fatherland Front* were pro–Russian and united in their hatred of the "German collaborators" who had frozen them out of power in the past, there was strong support among the other parties for these actions. Those executed included the three regents, former premiers Bagrianov and Bozhilov, twenty–six former cabinet ministers and sixty–eight deputies from the wartime Assemblies. In addition, special "People's Courts" were set up throughout the country and thousands of additional individuals were sentenced to death and executed.

Having eliminated the "German collaborators," however, the communists next turned to their partners in the *Fatherland Front*. Under the terms of the Yalta Declaration of February 1945, free elections were to be held throughout eastern Europe. The communists, determined to establish their own political dominance, demanded a common *Fatherland Front* list of candidates with a prearranged ratio giving them half the seats in the new Assembly. *Zveno*, more a military faction than a political party, accepted these terms. The *Agrarian Union* and the *Social Democrats* did not. The communists thereupon produced their own Agrarian

collaborator, Alexander Obhov, and, by packing the congress of the *Agrarian Union*, managed to get him elected head of the party. Similar tactics were used against the *Social Democrats*. The elections, which took place in November 1945, produced an 86% majority for the *Fatherland Front*.

Georgi Dimitrov, who had been elected President of the Central Committee of the *Bulgarian Communist Party* at a Party Congress in March 1945, returned to Sofia in the midst of the election campaign. Although clearly the preeminent leader of the party that dominated the government, he did not enter the government at this time. One reason may have been that the American and British governments challenged the validity of the November elections and demanded that the true leaders of the *Agrarian Front* and *Social Democrats* be brought back into the government. This became the subject of the Moscow Conference of December 1945, but American and British pressure was of no effect.

By the summer of 1946, in fact, the communists felt strong enough to campaign against *Zveno*, the remaining independent element in the *Fatherland Front*. An attack was launched in the communist press against the founder of *Zveno*, General Velchev, who held the position of Minister of War. Velchev eventually was forced to resign from the cabinet. Colonel Georgiev remained on as premier until the autumn when he, too, was forced out.

Bulgaria was still technically a monarchy up to this point; however, a plebiscite, held in September 1946, resulted in a vote in favor of a republic. A month later, new elections were held for a Grand National Assembly which was charged with preparing a new constitution.

The *Fatherland Front* won those elections and Georgi Dimitrov took the office of premier in the new government. Some legal opposition continued for awhile, however, since the independent factions of the *Agrarian Union* and the *Social Democrats* had both run candidates in the elections and had managed to get a few of their candidates elected. For awhile, they were permitted to make speeches in the Assembly, but this was soon replaced by a campaign of intimidation. Things came to a head in June 1947 when Nikola Petkov, leader of the independent faction of the *Agrarian Union*, was arrested on the floor of the Assembly—even though his parliamentary immunity should have protected him. Charged with preparing for a *coup d'etat*, he was found guilty and sentenced to death.

Somewhat later, Georgi Dimitrov addressed a specific warning to the few Social Democrats remaining in the Assembly. "As you remember," Dimitrov

The old part of Plovdiv

Bulgaria

Пролетарии от всички страни, съединявайте се!

РАБОТНИЧЕСКО ДЕЛО

Вестник „Работническо дело" започва да излиза на 5 март 1927 година. Той е продължител на „Работнически вестник", основан на 17 септември 1897 година.

Год. LIX брой 168 София, понеделник, 17 юни 1985 г. Цена 6 ст.

ОРГАН НА ЦЕНТРАЛНИЯ КОМИТЕТ НА БЪЛГАРСКАТА КОМУНИСТИЧЕСКА ПАРТИЯ

ДНЕС В БРОЯ:
- 17 ЮНИ — МЕЖДУНАРОДЕН ДЕН НА РАЗОРЪЖА-ВАНЕТО: милиони хора издигат глас за мир
- Социалистическите страни осъществяват своята перспективна политика с развитието на новите технологии, микроелектрониката, роботиката
- Стари проблеми в подготовката на тазгодишното БРИГАДИРСКО ЛЯТО
- ДОБРАТА ОРГАНИЗАЦИЯ Е РЕШАВАЩОТО УСЛОВИЕ ЗА СПОРНА ЖЪТВА, за прибиране на реколтата в срок и без загуби

ПРЕД ТРИНАДЕСЕТИЯ КОНГРЕС НА ПАРТИЯТА

РЕВОЛЮЦИОННО МИСЛЕНЕ, РЕВОЛЮЦИОННО ДЕЙСТВИЕ!

ЧОВЕКЪТ И НАУЧНО-ТЕХНИЧЕСКИЯТ ПРОГРЕС

Социолози и общественици участвуват в дискусия: СПОСОБНОСТТА ДА ТВОРИ НОСИ ВСЕКИ ОТ НАС — КАК ДА РАЗПАЛВАМЕ ТОЗИ ПЛАМЪК!

ЗАДОЧНА НАУЧНО-ПРАКТИЧЕСКА КОНФЕРЕНЦИЯ

ПОСЛЕДНИ НОВИНИ — Ле Зуан ще посети СССР

АКТ НА НАСИЛИЕ — Светът осъжда нападението срещу Ботсвана

Rabotnichesko Delo ("Workers' Cause"), the former Bulgarian Communist Party daily

informed them, "from this rostrum I many times warned your political allies from Nikola Petkov's group. They did not listen to me. They took no notice of all my warnings. They broke their heads, and their leader is now under the ground. You should now think it over, lest you share their fate . . ."

The following July, Kosta Lulchev, head of the *Social Democrats*, was arrested, along with six of the nine remaining deputies from that party, and was subsequently sentenced to fifteen years imprisonment.

The Dimitrov government presented Bulgaria with a new constitution in December 1947. As might have been expected, it was modeled closely after the 1936 "Stalin Constitution" of the U.S.S.R. Bulgaria now became a "people's republic" while its government became almost a carbon copy of the Soviet model, except that the legislature consisted of one house only, since Bulgaria had no need for a separate house representing different nationalities such as existed in Russia and Yugoslavia. Like the Soviet Union, theoretical sovereignty rested with the legislature, but the actual decision-making was carried out by a Presidium and a separate Council of Ministers. Reflecting the fulcrum of power, Georgi Dimitrov took the position of President of the Council of Ministers for himself.

Internecine Struggles

Having eliminated the opposition, the communists turned against each other. The charge was "nationalist deviation" and the ostensive cause was Tito's break with the Soviet Union. It tended to turn into a struggle between communists who had served an apprenticeship in the Soviet Union and those who had remained behind. It appears to have been largely directed from Moscow, for Stalin apparently became convinced that he couldn't trust any of the "native" communists.

The most significant of that group was Traicho Kostov, who had risen to the position of Vice-President of the Council of Ministers in charge of economic affairs and who was widely considered to be Dimitrov's probable successor. The list of charges eventually filed against him was rather extensive, but the most serious charge was that he had kept secret information on Bulgarian economic matters from Soviet representatives, not realizing, as *Rabotnichesko Delo*, the communist party newspaper phrased it, that "secrets and commercialism do not exist in our dealings with the Soviet Union." Kostov was sentenced to death and executed in late 1949. Several of his associates, including the Finance Minister, the Foreign Trade Minister, the Director of the National Bank and the Commercial Attaché in Moscow, were sentenced to long terms in prison. Other leading native communists were tried, sentenced and eliminated. In addition, a purge of the party ranks resulted in about 20% of the membership being expelled from the party.

In the midst of the purge, Georgi Dimitrov died while on a trip to the Soviet Union. His immediate successor was Vasil Kolarov, but he died six months later in 1950, and was in turn replaced by Vulko Chervenkov. The latter was Dimitrov's brother-in-law and had spent many years in the Soviet Union. Known as an arch-Stalinist, he was almost certainly responsible for the severity of the purge of the "native" communists. By using the weapon of "nationalist deviation," he eliminated all possible rivals and consolidated his own power position.

The purges had one final result. At the Kostov trial, an attempt was made to portray the defendant as an American agent who had been encouraged in his actions by U.S. Minister Donald Heath. This was followed by the arrest of five Bulgarians employed by the U.S. Mission and a subsequent "spy trial" of other alleged U.S. agents. Finally, the U.S. had enough, and in early 1950 it broke off diplomatic relations with the Bulgarians.

Chervenkov was the most ruthless of Bulgaria's post-war rulers, but he did not get to enjoy his power for very long. Stalin's death in 1953 was the first change, for now his old patron was dead. Khrushchev's rise to power threatened Chervenkov's position, for Khrushchëv was determined to heal the breach with Tito of Yugoslavia, and Chervenkov had distinguished himself as an enemy of Tito. In 1954 he gave up the position of General Secretary of the Central Committee—the leading Party position—although he managed to retain the leading state position, that of premier. Chervenkov actually managed to hold on to most of his power for another two years, but he was never able to overcome his Stalinist past. And when Khrushchëv launched his attack against Stalin in 1956, Chervenkov found himself accused of Stalin's chief crime—promoting a "cult of person-

Bulgaria

Cleaning the streets of Sofia

AP/Wide World Photo

ality"—and was again forced to accept a demotion, this time to Deputy Chairman of the Council of Ministers.

The Beginning of the Zhivkov Era

The man who got Chervenkov's party position in 1954—changed at this time from General Secretary to First Secretary—was Todor Zhivkov. His first membership in the Bulgarian Communist Party dates back to 1932 and he had been one of the organizers of the partisan underground in the Sofia area during World War II; he commanded the partisan regiments in and around Sofia at the time of the 1944 *Fatherland Front* seizure of power. Lacking close ties to the "Moscow" communists, who had returned to Bulgaria to take charge of the party, Zhivkov spent the next four years in various subordinate positions. His breakthrough came in 1948 when he became First Secretary of the Sofia City Committee, and simultaneously, a member of the party Central Committee. From this time, his rise was more rapid. He became an alternate member of the Politburo in 1950 and a member of the Secretariat. A year later, he was admitted to full Politburo membership. Thus, when Chervenkov came under attack in 1954 as a Stalinist, Zhivkov was able to move into the position of First Secretary of the Central Committee, a position he held until November 1989.

Zhivkov's rapid rise after 1948 would indicate that he got his start as Chervenkov's protégé, and his actions after 1954 would bear that out. It was not until

Chervenkov had been further demoted in 1956 that Zhivkov made his own bid for greater power: in 1957 he increased his control by removing some of his opponents, but it was not until 1962 that he consolidated his position by taking the additional title of Chairman of the Council of Ministers (Premier). At the same time, he severed his last connection with Chervenkov and had him dismissed from the government. The break apparently was over foreign policy—Zhivkov favored closer relations with Yugoslavia and, in general, wanted to bring Bulgarian foreign policy closer into alignment with Soviet foreign policy under Khrushchëv. After Chervenkov's dismissal, Zhivkov publicly endorsed Soviet policies in the Cuban missile crisis of 1961, made moves toward establishment of better relations with Yugoslavia and totally supported the Soviet Union in its disputes with China.

One of the problems Zhivkov also had to face was the trend toward a more relaxed and liberal leadership which had started prior to the time he became Premier. Detention camps had been closed, and limits were placed on the secret police. Writers and scholars were given more freedom to express their views—in some cases this new freedom was used to criticize the government. But Zhivkov's position was not secure enough to tolerate such criticism. He had eliminated his rivals from the top level of the party, but was still faced with the opposition of lesser members who had been supporters of Chervenkov.

Other problems were created by popular discontent with a shortage of food, consumer goods and housing. Economic reform was needed to stifle criticism, but it would have met with opposition from the "dogmatists" and those who profited from the present set-up. Zhivkov's only alternative was to end the brief period of liberalization and to reimpose restrictions. Even though this was a step backwards, it was not a return to the repressive atmosphere of the Stalinist days. Meanwhile, Zhivkov tried to shore up his own position by tying himself closely to his Soviet benefactor, Khrushchëv. When Khrushchëv lost power in November 1964, Zhivkov's position became precarious and his gestures of loyalty toward the new Soviet leadership could not disguise the loss of support which he experienced at this time.

A few months later the inner turmoil of Bulgaria was underlined by the most unusual event in its postwar history. In April 1965 a plot to overthrow the government was discovered in Sofia. The *coup* had been planned for the April 14 meeting of the Politburo, at which time the plotters intended to arrest leading party members and to occupy important areas to prevent Soviet military action within Bulgaria.

The plot was discovered by Soviet military spies and the *coup* was quickly prevented. It was not until mid–May, however, that the Bulgarians received their first official explanation of the plot. It was declared to be an unimportant event caused by a small group of pro–Chinese plotters. This was not the case—the conspirators were not insignificant people but were former World War II freedom fighters, Bulgarian communists, high-ranking army officers and top-level party members. It is probable that they wanted to remove Zhivkov in the hope that a new leadership would bring a new course of independence for Bulgaria in its relations with the Soviet Union.

After the attempt failed, one member of the Central Committee of the party committed suicide, others were tried secretly and there was the usual purge of anyone with questionable loyalty. There was a renewed pledge of allegiance to the Soviet Union.

Perhaps shaken by the events of 1965, Zhivkov initiated a series of reforms, particularly in the area of the economy. These were designed to allow some decentralization of decision-making, but they were so strenuously opposed by the entrenched bureaucracy and conservatives they were phased out in mid-1968. Although he had initiated them, Zhivkov's support was never more than half-hearted, so it did not reflect adversely on him when they were discontinued.

Zhivkov continued as Chairman of the Council of Ministers until 1971 when a new constitution created the position of President of the State Council. When Zhivkov gave up his previous position, it went to Stanko Todorov and Zhivkov was named *President of the State Council*. This relieved Zhivkov of many day-to-day duties connected with running the government, but still gave him a government post as titular head of state. Todorov was subsequently replaced as Chairman of the Council of Ministers by Grisha Filipov, who continued to hold that position until 1986.

By this time, Zhivkov was 75 and the Bulgarian Politburo had gotten old along with the Secretary General. The example of Gorbachëv's significant personnel changes since coming to power a year earlier began to create strong pressure on Zhivkov to step down and allow a new generation of leadership to take over. As a result, a significant reshuffle occurred among Bulgaria's senior government and party leaders, though Zhivkov managed to retain his own hold on power.

Grisha Filipov retired as Chairman of the Council of Ministers and was replaced by Georgi Atanasov. One Politburo member and one candidate member were retired and four younger men—all combining strong party credentials with technical backgrounds—were added. This was accompanied by a streamlining of the government, including the elimination of six ministries.

Atanasov, the new Chairman of the Council of Ministers, was still in his for-ties and the government which he then headed was both distinctly younger and better-educated than the previous regime.

The Party Congress which took place in April 1986 was a low-keyed affair with no significant additional changes. Zhivkov was reelected to another five-year term. There were no changes made in either the Politburo or Secretariat, though there was a fairly significant turnover in membership on the Central Committee. About 80 out of 250 members were retired and replaced by younger individuals from the city and regional party organizations.

The Congress also created a new "Economic Council," with the delegated authority to make decisions which would have the force of actions decreed by the Council of Ministers. This Economic Council apparently took the place of the six recently abolished ministries. It was thus a part of the streamlining of government that Zhivkov began emphasizing in January 1986.

In January 1988, the *Bulgarian Communist Party* held a special party conference whose purpose, according to advance reports, was to discuss the progress of *perestroika* in Bulgaria. What was outlined was a relatively cautious approach to reform modeled closely on developments in the Soviet Union. Enterprises were to operate under a form of self-management with the right to set prices, salaries and production goals, but all of this would be within general guidelines set in Sofia. There was also a suggestion that terms of office of higher party officials might be limited, though implementation was not to begin until the next party congress in 1991.

A new political shake-up of sorts occurred in July 1988 when Zhivkov ousted three men from the Politburo who had been strong supporters of reform. It appears that Zhivkov might also have been concerned about his own political survival, however, for one of those removed, Chudomir Alexandrov, a young technocrat in the mold of Gorbachëv, had been tipped by many as the next leader of the party. In any case, the result, according to Stephen Ashley, head of Bulgarian research at Radio Free Europe, was "to reduce the Politburo to a tight clique of former partisans and Zhivkov's long-standing proteges."

In spite of Zhivkov's purge, pressure for change continued to build within the country. Domestically, Bulgarian industrialization had brought into existence a significant and growing "middle" class—of technicians, engineers, teachers, doctors, and other better educated individuals—who wanted a larger role in decision-making and resented the interference of political operatives in their areas of expertise. Internationally, the Bulgarians had always looked to the Soviet Union for leadership and so were inevitably affected by the wave of changes occurring there. Actually, Zhivkov's own first reaction was to go along with Moscow's reforms and for a while *glasnost* and *perestroika* became the new watchwords in Bulgaria. Local newspapers were suddenly filled with unprecedented debates and "independent associations" were authorized by law.

But when a human-rights group was formed to monitor rights abuses, Zhivkov considered this to be too great a challenge. Moving to isolate the group, he expelled those who happened also to be members of the *Bulgarian Communist Party*. Another leading communist, Svetlin Rusev, lost his seat on the Central Committee when he organized and independent environmental committee to protest pollution in the city of Ruse.

Perhaps the greatest challenge came in November 1988 when a group of 100 leading intellectuals formed the "Club for the Support of *Perestroika* and *Glasnost*." Once again, Zhivkov reacted by arresting the leaders and expelling them from the party. In effect, Zhivkov had rejected *glasnost* and *perestroika* and opted for repression and the status quo. While pleasing some people, such actions alienated intellectuals and set the stage for Zhivkov's own eventual departure.

That came in November 1989 in a palace coup organized by Zhivkov's Foreign and Defense Ministers, in a sort of counterpoint to the revolutionary ferment then sweeping across Eastern Europe. Petar Mladenov, the man who engineered the coup, had been Zhivkov's Foreign Minister for the previous 19 years. Over the years, he had kept his mouth shut and was awarded by promo-

President Zhelyu Zhelev

Bulgaria

tions that eventually put him in the Politburo. After Gorbachëv launched his policy of *perestroika*, however, Mladenov became attracted to the new ideas, and in particular as they applied in the international arena.

Increasingly, however, he found his efforts frustrated by actions Zhivkov was taking for domestic reasons. Thus, in May 1989, only four months after Mladenov had signed a new international human rights accord in Vienna, Zhivkov launched a new campaign encouraging the emigration of ethnic Turks. Then when Mladenov organized a 35–nation environmental conference in Sofia in October and invited an independent Bulgarian group, *Eco–Glasnost*, to participate, Zhivkov had his secret police rough up *Eco–Glasnost* members in a Sofia park. Mladenov was embarrassed and his attempt to polish up Bulgaria's image was largely negated.

Mladenov first submitted his resignation and, when it was not accepted, he decided that Zhivkov had to go. Cautiously, he began sounding out other Politburo members. This brought a promise of support from Dobri Dzhurov, the Defense Minister. Dzhurov, a World War II partisan colleague of Zhivkov and longtime Politburo member, had been revolted for years by Zhivkov's behavior and incessant efforts to advance the career of his son, Vladimir. His support was particularly important because he could guarantee the loyalty of the army. Mladenov also got promises of support from Georgi Atanasov, the Chairman of the Council of Ministers, and Andrei Lukanov, the Minister for Foreign Economic Relations.

Meanwhile, a wave of change was beginning to sweep across Eastern Europe and this strengthened Mladenov's case even further. Even Zhivkov realized by this time that some concessions were necessary. In a statement published in the party newspaper on October 29, Zhivkov conceded the failure of earlier Bulgarian reform efforts and promised to introduce changes along Soviet lines. He had very little credibility left by that time, however.

The pivotal Politburo meeting took place on November 9. Mladenov made a motion calling for Zhivkov's resignation and proposing himself as General Secretary. He won on a vote of five to four. The next day, Gorbachëv put his stamp of approval on the change by sending Mladenov a highly complimentary, congratulatory message.

One of Mladenov's first actions as General Secretary was to reinstate 11 former party members who had been purged because of their membership in a dissident organization called the *Independent Discussion Club for the Support of Glasnost and Perestroika*. He followed this up with a

statement pledging support for greater diversity and promising that, in the future, street rallies by anti–Government groups would be allowed. That same week, *Eco–Glasnost* was granted official recognition, making it a legal organization.

Mladenov next called a meeting of the Central Committee for November 16. Here, Zhivkov and three of his supporters were removed from the Politburo, while a fourth was dropped as a Central Committee secretary. Half a dozen other men were also dismissed, including two non–voting members of the Politburo. In addition, the Central Committee recommended that Mladenov take over Zhivkov's other post as head of state.

The next day, the National Assembly met to implement the recommendation of the Central Committee. At the same time, it also repealed a law making it a crime to say anything likely "to create dissatisfaction with the government and its undertakings" and declared an amnesty for persons convicted under the old legislation. Speaking afterwards, Mladenov told the legislature that he favored political and economic restructuring and that the National Assembly "should play a democratic alternative to the administrative command system that reigned before."

The monument to the Soviet Army in Sofia

Later, he told journalists "personally, I am for free elections." Another interesting aspect of the proceedings was that a number of the members of the Assembly rose to give anti–Zhivkov speeches. All of this was broadcast to the nation via live television.

Mladenov clearly wanted controlled change but news of the events happening elsewhere in Eastern Europe reverberated through Bulgaria and popular demands began to mount. Mladenov visited Moscow at the beginning of December. Asked there by journalists what his reaction was to the decisions of the Czechoslovak and East German *Communist Parties* to give up their constitutional monopoly of power, he first suggested that he would leave that up to the Bulgarian people to decide, then that, though he couldn't predict how the issue would be resolved, "I foresee changes in the Constitution."

Back in Bulgaria, popular demonstrations, which had begun occurring on an almost daily basis, grew larger in size and their demands became more far–reaching. A new, umbrella organization, the *Union for Democratic Reform*, was also formed to coordinate the actions of the opposition. Responding to these pressures, Mladenov called another meeting of the Central Committee on December 8. Six more members of the Politburo were ousted, plus 27 members of the Central Committee.

This second purge in a month only seemed to whet the appetite of the opposition. Two days later, 50,000 of them gathered for another pro–democracy rally in the middle of Sofia. All of this was fully covered by the controlled press and state television. The next day, Mladenov went on television to promise that the Communist Party's monopoly on power would be abolished and that there would be free elections in the spring. "We need to adopt the principle of a multiparty system," he said.

Mladenov's promises did not placate the opposition. On December 14, when the National Assembly took up a bill to scrap Article I of the Constitution, which guaranteed the party's leading role, 20,000 demonstrators surrounded the legislature and began shouting for an immediate end to the party's monopoly on power. When Stanko Todorov, the assembly's chairman, told them that Article I had already been suspended but could not be repealed for a month because of another constitutional provision, he was met by cries of "we do not believe you," "resign," and "Berlin, Prague, Sofia." The next day, the Assembly unanimously passed a declaration affirming that Article I would be stricken from the constitution at its next session in January. Mladenov also announced that round–

Bulgaria

table discussions with opposition leaders would begin the following week.

In a new development, thousands of ethnics organized a mass rally against government persecution at the end of December. That same day, the Party Central Committee met and voted to reverse Zhivkov's policy of assimilation, calling it "a grave political error." Under the new policy, ethnic Turks could take back their old names and speak Turkish in public. This policy was subsequently adopted by the government. For the first time, this led to a demonstration of another sort, as thousands of anti–Turkish Bulgarian nationalists gathered outside the National Assembly chanting "Bulgaria for the Bulgarians" and demanding that the government's action be rescinded. In a curious reversal of past developments, the communists and the democratic opposition now came together to reaffirm the new policy.

When the National Assembly met on January 15, 1990 and voted to delete Article I from the constitution, the action came as a sort of anticlimax. Roundtable discussions between the communists and the opposition, a coalition of 13 new parties, movements and groups collectively referred to as the *Union of Democratic Forces*, began in January. At the beginning of February, Mladenov offered to form a coalition government with the opposition. When this offer was refused, Georgi Atanasov was replaced as Chairman of the Council of Ministers by Andrei Lukanov.

At a hastily called party congress, the party voted to change its name and to become the *Bulgarian Socialist Party*. This was accompanied by a general restructuring of the party. The old power position of General Secretary was abolished, replaced by a Chairman. In another change, the congress also endorsed the creation of an executive presidency.

These changes were voted into law by the National Assembly at the beginning of April. Mladenov was then elected President. Alexander Lilov then became the new Chairman of the *Bulgarian Socialist Party*.

Multiparty elections took place in June and they were won by the *Bulgarian Socialist Party* with almost 53% of the vote. The *UDF* got only about a third of the seats in the Assembly, with the rest going to a third party, the *Movement for Rights and Freedoms*, which represents the one million or so Turkish– speakers, plus independents. Although the socialists won in the overall vote, their main support came from the countryside. The *UDF* actually won in the urban areas. For this reason, the *UDF* thought of themselves as having won the election, and they refused to cooperate with the socialists.

Before the socialists could get their new

Bulgarian sheepherders

government installed, President Petar Mladenov came under attack for remarks he had made in December 1989 about ordering tanks to be used against the Bulgarian people. Mladenov resigned on July 6. After almost a month of stalemate, Zhelyu Zhelev, who had led the democratic opposition in the June elections, was named President by the Bulgarian Assembly. Zhelev, who had spent 17 years under house arrest under the former regime, was a compromise candidate backed by all the parties.

Meanwhile the socialists, divided between conservatives and reformers, were having difficulty getting a government organized. They first offered to form a coalition government with the *UDF*. When the opposition refused, it took the socialists three months to get their new government chosen and approved. Andrei Lukanov was reappointed Chairman of the Council of Ministers in September but his tenure turned out to be short. By November, thousands of Bulgarians were demanding his resignation. Lukanov won a vote of confidence in the Assembly, but the demonstrations continued. One issue was an unpopular austerity plan put into effect by the government and widespread shortages of food, gasoline and consumer goods, but a greater issue was a lack of confidence in a government led by an ex–communist. Lukanov finally stepped down on November 29, 1990 after the Confederation of Independent Trade Unions began a general strike aimed at forcing him out of office. His successor, Dimitar Popov, was chosen on December 7.

Popov, a non–politician who had been head of Sofia's municipal court before becoming Chairman of the Council of Ministers, was apparently selected to stand above the parties and lead a coalition government that could be supported by all factions.

Although originally considered to be a caretaker government, Popov submitted a far–reaching program in January 1991 that began moving Bulgaria toward a free

market. Price controls were loosened, interest rates were increased, a new land ownership law was passed and proposals were submitted to reform the banking and tax laws and begin the privatization of state–owned enterprises. Prices rose ten–fold, interest rates soared to about 50% and unemployment began edging up. On the positive side, shop windows and market stands began filling up and food became plentiful, though things like medicines, fertilizers, toilet paper, sugar, petroleum products and pesticides remained scarce. Polls indicated that Bulgarians had become more optimistic, apparently convinced that their present sacrifices would pay dividends later.

New parliamentary elections were set for October 1991. In the lead up to the elections, the *Union of Democratic Forces* broke down into four factions and numerous new political parties came into being. The number of seats in the National Assembly was reduced from 400 to 240, so each candidate had to campaign in a larger constituency. A form of proportional voting was utilized, but an attempt was made to keep out fringe parties by establishing a threshold of 4% before a party would become eligible for a seat.

When the election was over, only three parties had crossed that threshold, the *UDF* with 34.36% of the vote, the *Bulgarian Socialist Party*, with 33.14% and the *Movement for Rights and Freedoms* with 7.54%. This gave the *UDF* 111 seats, the *BSP* 106 seats, and the *MDR* 23 seats. President Zhelev designated Filip Dimitrov, head of the *UDF*, to form a cabinet on November 5. Since it lacked a parliamentary majority, Dimitrov offered to form a coalition with the *MDR*. The *MDR*, an ethnic Turkish party that represents Bulgaria's Moslem population, refused to enter the cabinet but agreed to support the government in the National Assembly. In the end, the 14–member cabinet contained a number of "technicians" chosen for their expertise and belonging to no party.

Bulgaria

The Kliment Ohridski University, Sofia.

Only 8 of the 14 were members of the parliament. For example, Yordan Sokolov, a Sofia lawyer with no political affiliation, was appointed Minister of the Interior.

In his beginning policy statement, Prime Minister Dimitrov set forth long and short–term goals. His long–term goal would be to replace the previous system; his short–term goal would be to stabilize the country's economy and curb inflation. His specific policies included amending the Foreign Investment Act passed by the previous government, privatization, the reform of banking, tax reform, and amending the Land Act. The prime minister will probably be able to carry out most of his program, though he may have trouble with his long–term goal of replacing the previous system. Any change which would require a constitutional amendment would require the co-operation of the *Bulgarian Socialist Party*, since constitutional amendments require a two–thirds majority and the *BSP* controls just over a third of the seats in the National Assembly.

Popular elections for the presidency took place in January 1992. President Zhelyu Zhelev, who had been elected by the National Assembly in January 1990, was a candidate, while the *Socialists* supported Velko Vulkanov. A third candidate was George Ganchev, a former fencing champion who had lived for a number of years in the United States. Zhelev got 45% of the vote, Vulkanov 30% and Ganchev 17%. In the run–off, Zhelev got just under 53% while Vulkanov polled 47%. The electorate is thus very closely divided and the *Socialists* have clearly established themselves as the political opposition. Should the liberals falter in their program, the *Socialists* can expect to be back in power.

Foreign Policy

Bulgarians have always admired the Russian people and looked to Russia for assistance and leadership. Even after the Bulgarian Government banned a domestic communist party in 1923, it continued to maintain good diplomatic relations with the Soviet Union. When Bulgaria became a communist state after 1945, therefore, it was not surprising that the first principle of Bulgarian foreign policy became loyalty to the Soviet Union. This would probably have happened regardless, because Georgi Dimitrov, the new Bulgarian leader, had been a loyal servant of Stalin since the 1920s.

After 1948, Bulgaria's traditional rivalry with Yugoslavia reinforced this orientation. Following Tito's quarrel with Stalin, Bulgaria replaced Yugoslavia as the principal country through which Soviet influence was projected in the area of the southern Balkans.

This relationship with the Soviet Union was reflected not only in Bulgaria's relations with its neighbors, but in its relations with the United States as well. As the Cold War began, Bulgaria joined the Soviet Union in making extravagant attacks on the United States. As a result, relations broken by the U.S. in 1950 were not renewed until 1959. Formal, but cool, relations continued until the 1970's, when Bulgaria became interested in exports to the United States.

The government agreed to end jamming of Voice of America radio broadcasts and also signed a consular convention which accorded greater protection for Americans in Bulgaria. Deputy Premier Ivan Popov then paid a visit to the United States in 1974 and it appeared that U.S.–Bulgarian relations would continue to improve. Then the Soviet Union renounced its trade agreement with the United States in 1975 over the issue of Jewish emigration, and the Bulgarians followed suit, abandoning their efforts to expand trade. Thereafter, American–Bulgarian relations simply mirrored the state of American–Soviet relations. For example, when the Soviets announced a boycott of the 1984 Olympic contests in Los Angeles, Bulgaria was the very first country to indicate that it would not participate either.

The country had no diplomatic relations whatsoever with Greece until 1964. Relations then remained cool for another ten years, becoming cordial only after 1974. They were particularly good during the years of the left–wing Papandreou government.

Relations with Yugoslavia followed the pattern of Soviet–Yugoslav affairs. There has been one additional complication, however—the traditional rivalry over Macedonia. The Bulgarian Government has never recognized Macedonian as a separate nationality and on occasion it has felt called upon to speak out on behalf of "Bulgarians" living in the Yugoslav republic of Macedonia. The death of Tito in 1980 brought no change, for better or worse. The collapse of Yugoslavia in 1991 when Croatia and Slovenia seceded, coupled with the subsequent decision of the Republic of Macedonia to seek recognition as an independent country, has changed that situation. However, Bulgaria is one of four states that has extended diplomatic recognition to the Republic of Macedonia. The Bulgarian Government still does not recognize that there is such a thing as a Macedonian "nationality", but it has recognized the existence of a Macedonian "state."

Romania is the one nation with which Bulgaria has maintained consistently friendly relations over the years. Of course, Romania was the only one of Bulgaria's neighbors that was also a member of the communist bloc. The two nations have continued to cooperate since 1989, however. At first, one factor may have been that ex–communists continued to play important political roles in both societies and both were at first denied economic assistance by the EC and the United States. Today, the important factor is that the two nations are involved in a number of joint economic projects dealing with hydroelectric works on the Danube River.

There was an evolution toward greater independence in Bulgaria's relations with the Soviet Union in the 1980s, particularly after the death of Brezhnev in November 1982. The first signs came in 1984–85 when the Soviet Union instituted a political–economic boycott of Western Europe after arms negotiation talks had failed to resolve the issue of intermediate range ballistic missiles in Europe. The Bulgarian Government, interested in obtaining new technology from Western Europe to reverse several years of declining growth rates, was unwilling to go along at first. After some pressure from the Soviet Government, it went along with a political freeze, but did everything it could to maintain its economic ties to Western Europe.

Gorbachëv's rise to power was welcomed in Bulgaria and his foreign policy of cooperation with the West found particular support. Bulgaria's Zhivkov instituted his own political opening to the West in June 1987, when he paid an official visit to the Federal Republic of Germany. Bulgaria, he told his hosts, wanted to expand its economic relations with West Germany and the European Community.

Even then, West Germany was Bulgaria's largest trading partner outside of the CMEA. Since that time, Germany has been unified, the CMEA and the Soviet Union have collapsed, and Bulgaria has lost most of its markets in eastern Europe and the former Soviet Union. Bulgaria has applied for associate membership in the European Community and it is looking to Germany and the EC as major trading partners in the future. At the same time, Bulgaria is working to create closer economic relations with the successor states to the old Soviet Union, in particular Russia and Ukraine.

The Nature of the Regime

The Bulgarian Government is of a presidential–parliamentary type. A popularly elected president presides over the executive branch, assisted by a prime minister who is nominated by the president and confirmed by the 240 member National Assembly. The president, who is considered to be the spokesman for the nation, is responsible for general policy. He is also commander–in–chief of the armed forces. The prime minister presides over the cabinet and oversees day–to–day affairs of government. He thus is responsible for implementation of policy.

The current president, Zhelyu Zhelev, was originally elected president in 1990 by the National Assembly. He won reelection in a popular election that took place in January 1992. The current prime minister, Lyuben Berov, took office in December 1992 after a period of political instability in which two previous nominees for the office failed to win a vote of confidence in the National Assembly. His selection represents a widening of the governing coalition for he was nominated by the *Movement for Rights and Freedoms*, which represents the nation's one million ethnic Turks. Mr. Berov, who belongs to no party and had previously served as an economic adviser to President Zhelev, is not an ethnic Turk, but his Deputy Prime Minister, Yevgeny Matinchev, is a member of the *Movement for Rights and Freedoms*. The government coalition thus now consists of the *Union of Democratic Forces*, which controls 110 out of 240 seats plus The *Movement for Rights and Freedoms*, which controls 24 seats. The *MRF* had previously refused to enter the cabinet, though it had supported the government in the Assembly. The third party in the Assembly is the *Bulgarian Socialist Party* (the ex–communists), which holds 106 seats.

Frigid in the valleys, hikers find the sun warm enough to run bare-chested across the snow-covered Rhodope Mountains in southern Bulgaria. AP/Wide World Photo

Bulgaria

Bar America in Roussé, Bulgaria's fourth largest city

Photo by Rasho V. Rashkov

The Economy

Bulgaria was still predominantly an agricultural society at the end of World War II. Using the Stalinist model, the government started the first of its Five Year Plans in 1949. The emphasis has always been on the industrial sector, and this has resulted in a transformation of the Bulgarian economy. Today, over three–quarters of the gross national product is attributable to either industry or construction.

In spite of this significant shift, agriculture continues to play an important role in the Bulgarian economy. Although the population has become predominantly urban, nearly one–fourth of the people are still employed in agriculture–related jobs.

Bulgaria placed a heavier emphasis on the development of agriculture than did the other Eastern European countries. Collectivization, begun in 1948, was carried out more quickly than elsewhere. By 1950, 43% of the land had been collectivized; by 1960 this figure reached 100%. This is even more surprising when one considers that Bulgaria is a mountainous country and much of the land is not suitable for intensive cultivation. Extensive wineries have been established in the hills, however, and produce good wines which are reasonably priced by western standards.

Originally some 3,200 collective farms were set up, roughly corresponding to the number of villages in the country. These were then merged into 930 economic units beginning in 1960. A further consolidation began in 1969 when Bulgaria launched what it termed Agro–industrial complexes *(AICS)*. The *AICs* became the model for subsequent Soviet experiments of this same nature. There are 281 such *AICs* in the country and they have their own factories for the processing of the harvests. Although the new regime is committed to the development of a market economy, the *AICS* still exist at the moment and remain responsible for most agricultural production.

The private plots assigned to peasant families are the one exception. Today, about 13% of the land is held in this form. As elsewhere in Eastern Europe and the Soviet Union, they are much more productive than the collectivized lands, producing about 28% of total output. Since peasants already sell the excess production from the private plots in local markets, a quick way to increase market influences would be to increase the size of the private plots. This may be what the government has in mind, for it announced in December 1992 that a land reform it had begun to implement would result in 20% of the land being transferred to private ownership.

The situation in industry is in many ways worse than that of agriculture. Almost all of Bulgaria's industry was created after World War II and it consists mainly of large monopoly units which have always operated on the basis of orders from Sofia. Many were created specifically to produce goods for export to the Soviet Union or other members of the Council for Mutual Economic Assistance (CMEA). In 1989, over 80 percent of Bulgaria's foreign trade was carried on with other member states of the CMEA. Most of those markets have since evaporated with the collapse of communism in Eastern Europe and the disintegration of the CMEA. The disarray in the Soviet economy has been particularly painful for Bulgaria, since over 50 percent of Bulgaria's foreign trade was with that country alone. The situation has become even worse since January 1, 1991, when all CMEA trade began to be expressed in dollars. The Soviet Union, short of hard currency, canceled 70 percent of its Bulgarian orders. One example of how these events effected the Bulgarian economy can be seen by looking at the individual case of Balkancar, a manufacturer of electric fork lift trucks. In 1990, the company manufactured 50,000 trucks, almost all of which were exported to the Soviet Union. In 1991, it produced 29,000 trucks, and 20,000 in 1992. The company is exploring new markets in Argentina and the United States, but it is also attempting to win back its markets in the former Soviet Union by creating dealer networks in the CIS. Bankancar's recent history is typical of Bulgarian enterprises that depended on the Soviet market.

Meanwhile, although the government has said that it is committed to creating a market economy in the country, it has managed to do so only in the area of retail trade. State enterprises still account for more than 90% of economic activity. Privatization is finally at the top of the agenda, however, and plans now call for profitable state enterprises to be turned into joint stock companies, with stock then sold to the public. Unprofitable state enterprises are to be broken up and absorbed as part of other groups. Current plans call for 25% of all state enterprises, comprising 70% of all assets held by the state, to be privatized by the end of 1995.

Bulgaria is now having difficulty financing its foreign debt of about $11 billion. The government submitted a request $3 billion in assistance from the International Monetary Fund and it is also eligible for assistance from the European Bank for Recovery and Development. It is likely, however, that the situation will grow worse before it starts to improve.

Culture

Bulgaria was still mainly a peasant society when the communists came to power in 1945 and began to transform it. They got rid of the private farms and herded the peasants into either collective or state farms. Some of the traditional peasant culture died as a result, but much of it survived and is starting to reemerge. The *Bulgarian Communist Party* had greater success in the cities, though not in the way it had hoped. The workers who came to the cities to work in the new industry did abandon most of their traditional peasant ways, but the party's attempts to create communist intellectuals through its emphasis on education actually produced the new elite that overthrew the communists in 1990–91.

The *Bulgarian Communist Party* is gone now, and its successor, the *Bulgarian Socialist Party,* has the support of about a third of Bulgarian voters. Bulgaria has a long tradition of peasant radicalism that is anti–capitalist rather than pro–communist, however, and the *Socialists* drew most of their support in the October 1991 elections from peasants rather than workers. The *Union for Democratic Reform* has the support of most of the workers and the urban elite and they are committed to a transformation of the society in a liberal democratic direction.

This is the struggle that is currently going on in Bulgaria, a struggle between those who favor an evolution toward a market society and private enterprise and those who seek a "third way" between capitalism and communism. While neither force has a majority, a genuine pluralism has taken hold in the country. Bulgaria is still a society in the process of change, however, and its past history is not such as to make one optimistic about the outcome.

Religion is being accorded a greater role, and the government has become officially neutral. Anti–Turkish legislation has been withdrawn and the Turkish–speaking minority may now use Turkish in public. They have also been permitted to take back their old Turkish names. There are about a million ethnic Turks in the country, about 800,000 of whom are Moslem.

The Bulgarian Orthodox Church, which was accorded a special position even under the old regime, has begun to speak out and take a more active role. Its membership is estimated at three million. There are about 60,000 Roman Catholics in the country, plus an extremely small number of Protestants, divided up into Pentecostals, Congregationalists, Seventh–Day Adventists, Methodists and Baptists. There are also several other identifiable minority groups—about 250,000 Macedonians with smaller numbers of Gypsies, Armenians and Albanians.

The Future

Bulgaria is beginning to evolve into a genuine multiparty democracy and the government has taken the first steps toward creating a market economy. Transforming a command economy into a market economy is not easy, however, and it probably can't be accomplished without considerable pain. That will require a degree of political sophistication which the Bulgarian people may not have. The next two or three years will be crucial. Bulgaria is enjoying a boom in tourism from western Europe because of the strife in Yugoslavia.

Picking roses near Karlovo—which starts before dawn. Some 2,000 rose petals are needed to produce a single gram of attar, an essential oil in making perfume.

The Czech Republic

Area: 78,742 sq. km. = 30,441 sq. mi.
Population: 10.4 million.
Capital City: Prague (Pop. 1,206,098).
Climate: Continental, with lower temperatures in the higher elevations of the north.
Neighboring Countries: The Federal Republic of Germany (West); Poland (North); Republic of Slovakia (East); Austria (South).
Official Language: Czech.
Other Principal Tongues: Slovak, German.
Ethnic Background: Slav.
Principal Religions: Roman Catholic (39%), Protestant (4.6%), Orthodox (3%), Atheist (37%), Other (16.2%).
Chief Commercial Products: Machinery and equipment, coal, aromatic oils, energy ores, metals, consumer goods.
Currency: Czech Kroner.
Former Status: Part of the Austro–Hungarian Empire until 1918 (ruled from Vienna); Part of Czechoslovakian Republic, 1918–1938; Part of Nazi Germany, 1939–45 (incorporated into the Third Reich as Bohemia and Moravia); Part of Communist–influenced Czechoslovakian Republic, 1945–48; Communist State, 1948–89; Part of democratic Czech and Slovak Federal Republic, 1990–1992.
National Day: May 9 (Liberation Day).
Chief of State: Vaclav Havel, President of the Republic.
Head of Government: Vaclav Klaus, Prime Minister.
National Flag: White and red horizontal stripes with a blue triangle extending from the staff to the center of the flag.

THE COLLAPSE OF THE CZECH AND SLOVAK FEDERAL REPUBLIC

The Czech and Slovak Federal Republic, a federal state encompassing the Czech Republic with 10.4 million inhabitants and the Slovak Republic with a population of 5.3 million, ceased to exist on January 1, 1993. Having agreed to a peaceful separation into two independent nations, the Czechs and Slovaks nevertheless recognized that their economies would be tightly bound to each other for some time and that it would be wise to retain certain elements of the former union if they could. These would include a common currency and a customs union which would allow for the free movement of goods. In addition, Czechs and Slovaks would not required to show passports to pass from one country to another. Although the common currency collapsed after less than two months, the customs union is likely to last. Trade between the two new republics fell off considerably in the first three months following separation, but it cannot yet be said whether that was a shortlived phenomenon engendered by the political and economic instability created by the separation, or part of a continuing trend. In any case, it has had negative results for both economies.

In light of the fact that they have existed as a single entity throughout most of the twentieth century and that, in view of the recentness of their separation, they have not had time to create new identities as separate nations, we have chosen to continue to treat them as a single entity for this edition.

The Slovak Republic

Area: 49,000 sq. km. = 18,819 sq. mi.
Population: 5.3 million.
Capital City: Brataslava (Pop. 429,743).
Climate: Continental, with lower temperatures in the higher elevations of the north.
Neighboring Countries: The Czech Republic (West); Poland (North); Republic of Ukraine (East); Hungary (South); Austria (West).
Official Language: Slovak.
Other Principal Tongues: Magyar, Czech, German.
Ethnic Background: Slav.
Principal Religions: Roman Catholic (60.3%), Protestant 8.4%), Orthodox (4.1%), Atheist (9.7%), Other (17.5%).
Chief Commercial Products: Machinery and equipment, coal, aromatic oils, energy ores, metals, consumer goods, arms.
Currency: Slovak Kroner.
Former Status: Part of the Hungarian Kingdom of the Austro–Hungarian Empire until 1918; Part of Czechoslovakian Republic 1918–1938; Part of Nazi Germany, 1939–45 (organized as a separate protectorate state); Part of Communist–influenced Czechoslovakian Republic, 1945–48; Communist State, 1948–89; Part of Czech and Slovak Federal Republic, 1990–1992.
National Day: May 9 (Liberation Day).
Chief of State: Michal Kovac, President of the Republic.
Head of Government: Vladimir Meciar, Prime Minister.
National Flag: Three equal horizontal stripes—white, blue, red—with a shield on the left showing a two–armed white cross on a red field with a blue base.

THE LAND AND THE PEOPLE

Czechoslovakia was a federal state consisting of the Czech Republic with 10 million plus inhabitants and the Slovak Republic with a population of more than 5 million. Most of the country consists of rolling hills—approximately 55% of the country is farmland—but individual peaks of the Sudeten Mountains in the north and the Carpathian Mountains in the east rise to over 5,000 feet. The only high mountains in the country are the High Tatras, in the northeast along the border with Poland; here steep, rugged peaks, the tallest of which is 8,620 foot–high Mount Gerlach, tower over deep valleys dotted with numerous lakes. Most of this territory is now part of Tatra National Park, which has been a popular place for vacationing since the 19th century—it is full of spas and holiday resorts. About 35% of the country is covered by forest. The largest of these areas, the Bohemian Forest, is in the west along the border with the Federal Republic of Germany. The only extensive plain in the country is in the area of Bratislava, the capital of Slovakia. It is also here that the Danube River forms the border for some distance between Czechoslovakia and Hungary.

As its name implies, Czechoslovakia is essentially a land of two nations, the Czechs and the Slovaks. But there are four minorities making up 5.2% of the population which have the status of "nationalities;" these include Hungarians, mainly in the southeast, Germans in the west, Poles in the northeast and Ukrainians in the east. The Hungarians, who number about 600,000, are the largest minority.

The Czech and Slovak Republics

HISTORY

Ancient Kingdoms

In the early centuries of the Christian era, a sub–group of the Slavs, subsequently to be known as the West Slavs, settled in what is now Czechoslovakia. According to the Frankish chronicle of Fredegar, they were organized into a unified state at the beginning of the 7th century by a Frankish trader named Samo. This state collapsed at Samo's death in 658, however, and it was not until the 9th century that the Moravian Empire came into being, taking its place.

Christianity was introduced into the Moravian Empire in both its western and eastern forms. The Roman church sent missionaries into Moravia first—they were principally Germanic. The Moravian ruler requested missionaries from the eastern church and in response, Cyril and Methodius, two young men, came and taught the Slavs in their own language. They used a script they had devised to write the language of the people, which came to be known as the Cyrillic alphabet. Although the two brothers were successful in converting the people, they were unable to end the influence of western missionaries backed by the Pope. When Methodius died in 885, the Slav worship he had urged all his life was banned, and before long the Roman Church became predominant.

Neighboring Magyar (Hungarian) people embarked on a series of conquests at the end of the 9th century which disintegrated the Moravian Empire. According to Czech historians, the Magyars "drove a wedge" between the Western Slavs and the Southern Slavs, and also separated the Czechs from the Slovaks. By the beginning of the 10th century, the center of Czech development moved westward into what is called Bohemia, while the Slovak lands began a thousand–year period under the Hungarian crown.

The old Moravian Empire was replaced by the Kingdom of Bohemia, ruled by the Princes of the Premyslid Dynasty who became powerful in the tenth century. One of the members of this family was the legendary "Good King Wenceslas" (later named St. Wenceslas)—he was

Moravia and Bohemia ca. 1360

The Czech and Slovak Republics

murdered by his brother, Boleslav I who then brought much of the former Moravian Empire under his rule. He also joined with the Germans in containing the Magyars.

The German Emperors recognized the right of the Bohemian nobles to elect their own ruler who would be the highest authority in his own realm, but would also acknowledge the supremacy of the Holy Roman Emperor. The Kingdom of Bohemia grew briefly in the mid–13th century, but this gave way to a rise in German authority around and within Bohemia. There was substantial German migration into Bohemia and parts of Moravia.

By the mid–14th century, a new line of Czech rulers was able to assert growing influence over neighboring states. The "golden age" of Czech history occurred under Charles IV, King of Bohemia and also Holy Roman Emperor. He founded a university in the city of Prague which he had rebuilt and in which he established his Imperial Court.

The 14th century also saw the beginnings of a desire for church reform in Bohemia; this prepared the way for the great upheaval, the Hussite Movement, in the 15th century. Opposition was directed against the power of the Roman Church that was exercised through extensive land ownership, and in opposition to German supremacy in religious and political matters. The movement was led by a young preacher, John Hus, who criticized the papacy and the corruption of the clergy. He maintained that the sole authority for Christians is the Bible rather than the teachings of the Church. The Roman Church regarded this as heresy and excommunicated Hus and his followers. In an effort to defend his views, Hus obtained a promise of safe conduct from the German Emperor Sigismund and traveled to Constance where the church council was meeting. Upon his arrival he was condemned to death by the Council and was burned at the stake in 1415. He became a martyr even to those Czechs who had not been his followers—a national hero who died at the hands of the Germans.

Sigismund tried to succeed to the Bohemian crown when the Czech king died in 1419; this led to the Hussite Wars from 1420 to 1436. Although the wars were fought in the name of religion, they also had great political and social overtones, and were a form of expression of Czech nationalism. The conflict was extremely complicated by the fact that the Hussites were divided among themselves to the extent that they waged war against each other in 1434.

Part of the Multi–National Hapsburg Empire

Moderate Hussites negotiated an end

The Austrian monarchy ca. 1793 (showing present-day Czechoslovakia)

to the war with the Catholics. This agreement failed to endure because the more radical Hussites were repressed and Czech Catholic nobility resisted the treaty terms during the following decades. The Pope declared the agreement invalid in 1462 and sent troops under King Mathias of Hungary to enforce his decision. With the support of Czech Catholics, the Hungarian king extended his domain to include Bohemia; Hungarian rule continued until 1526 when Ferdinand of Hapsburg was elected to the Crown of St. Wenceslas. This was proclaimed to be hereditary property of the House of Hapsburg after 1547.

Conflict between the predominantly Protestant Czechs and their Catholic kings continued during the next decades. Although the Protestants were able to obtain promises from the kings allowing freedom of worship, they continued to fear persecution—this was a time when the Catholics were trying to end the Protestant separation not only in Bohemia, but in Germany itself.

Conflict erupted in May 1618 after two Protestant churches were closed. The angry Protestant leaders bodily threw two royal governors through a window of Prague Castle in an act since known as the "Defenestration (window–breaking) of Prague." The *Thirty Years' War* followed.

The Czechs deposed the Catholic king and elected the head of the Protestant Union of German Princes, Frederick of the Palatinate, as their king. The Protes-

tants were defeated in 1620 at the battle of White Mountain, and the Catholics again possessed the Bohemian Crown. This was a disaster for the Czechs—the leaders of the revolution were executed, suspects had their property confiscated and more than 30,000 families fled from the terror that gripped Bohemia. Among those fleeing were members of Czech nobility; this deprived the Czechs of a source of national leadership. Roman Catholicism was imposed and the German language was given equal status with the Czech; publications were censored and books were burned. The hereditary claim of the Hapsburgs to the Bohemian Crown was confirmed and the Bohemian lands were administered from Vienna until 1749.

The Thirty Years' War ended with the Peace of Westphalia in 1648. It had gravely damaged Czech culture and devastated the economy. During the century that followed there was a large–scale German peasant immigration into traditionally Czech lands, and a gradual process of Germanization in education, cultural and urban life.

Under Empress Maria–Theresa (1740–1780) Bohemia and Austria were joined into a single state; a subsequent tariff union between Bohemia, Moravia (to the east) and Austria enabled Bohemia to become the most industrially developed part of the Empire. Joseph II (1765–90) tried to impose other reforms, which resulted in a larger system of German government officials and the creation of a

228

secret police. In spite of this, the influence of the Catholic Church decreased and there was evidence of the start of a period of Czech cultural revival.

Central Europe lapsed into what appeared to be a period of relative tranquility after the Napoleonic period. The Czechs were controlled by the Austrian Hapsburgs, as were the Hungarians, Slovaks and other nearby people in spite of their nationalistic feelings. In reality, the Austrian Hapsburg Empire was seething with discontent. The Hapsburg rulers devoted their energies principally to maintaining themselves and other royalty in power throughout Europe, including France, the seat of revolutionary spirit in the late 18th century.

Paris erupted in rioting in early 1848; in turn, Berlin, Vienna, Prague and Budapest exploded in turmoil. On March 11, an assembly in Prague demanded freedom of the press, equality of languages, a legislature to represent the Czech people and release of the peasants from feudal serfdom. The first Pan–Slav Congress assembled in Prague in June, dominated by Francis Palacky, a Bohemian historian who believed the Czechs could find freedom and remain within the empire at the same time.

While the Congress was meeting, riots broke out against the commander of the Austrian forces in Prague. He suppressed the revolutionary movement firmly, and set up a military dictatorship. Further efforts of moderate Czechs to obtain a new constitution failed and order was restored throughout the empire under a centralized, absolutist regime.

Prior to World War I, Czech national ambitions were limited to demands for self–government within the Austro–Hungarian Empire. The goal of independence was not actively pursued until the fortunes of the war presented the opportunity to sever the centuries–old domination of Austria. Attainment of this goal was helped by the extensive propaganda campaign carried on by Czech and Slovak people living in Paris and in the United States.

Birth of an Independent Czecho–Slovak State

The first direct contribution to independence was made by the thousands of Czech and Slovak soldiers who refused to fight with the armies of the Central Powers, choosing instead to surrender to the Russians. These prisoners of war formed a special force, the Czecho–Slovak Legion, which then fought on the side of the Russians against Germany and Austria.

The position of the Czech Legions became complicated when the Bolsheviks (communists) signed the Treaty of Brest–Litovsk taking Russia out of the war with Germany. The decision of the western allies to transfer the legions to the western front by way of Siberia and Japan resulted in a historic journey during which these troops became involved in the Russian Civil War that had erupted, fighting on the side of the anti–Bolshevik forces.

Although Bohemia remained under Austrian control during World War I, a Czech National Council started to function in early 1916. Located in Paris and composed of such leading personalities as Thomas G. Masaryk, Eduard Benes and Milan Stefanik, it maintained contact with a resistance organization, the "Mafia," back in Bohemia.

The Council's goal which was close to being achieved by mid–1918, was to win support for the creation of an independent Czechoslovak state. T.G. Masaryk was instrumental in gaining American support for this cause—he had married an American girl, Charlotte Garrigue, and took her family name as his middle name. He was able to organize and gather together the Slovak people and their descendants in the U.S. to sign the Pittsburgh Agreement on June 30, 1918. This document expressed their support for the union of Czech and Slovak lands in return for the promise that Slovakia would have considerable independence

From the heights above Prague's Vltava River, the Czech capital's medieval heritage comes into full splendor

Photo by Jon Markham Morrow

The Czech and Slovak Republics

within the new state. A similar document, the Philadelphia Agreement, was signed in October by Masaryk and the leader of American Ruthenians, promising autonomy for Ruthenia (a region in the easternmost part of pre–war Czechoslovakia that is now a part of the Ukraine).

A National Committee headed by Karel Kramar, which represented three parties, the *National Democrats*, *Agrarians* and *National Socialists*, was set up in Prague in July 1918. It was this Committee which proclaimed the Independent Czechoslovak State on October 28, 1918. Two days later the Slovak *National Council* voted at Turciansky Svaty Martin, a town in eastern Czechoslovakia, to be part of the proclaimed state. The two groups were joined on May 8, 1919 by the *Central National Council of the Ruthenians*, which indicated its desire to be a part of the state as a semi–independent region.

The First Czechoslovak Republic 1918–1939

The frontiers of the Czechoslovakian state were drawn during 1918–1919 partly as a result of military action and partly by by the decisions of the post–war peace conference between the major powers. The borders between the Czechs and Poles, and between the Slovaks and Hungarians were contested; the final settlements resulted in confusing and potentially troublesome borders. A large number of Hungarians were included in Slovak territory and a number of Slovaks resided in Hungary.

The result of Czechoslovakia's borderlines was a state of several ethnic groups. It included minorities of Poles and Hungarians as well as about three million Germans living in northern (Sudeten) Czechoslovakia. The Germans were culturally identified with Germany during the period that followed World War I; they were represented in the Parliament and Cabinet by several political parties.

Ruthenia was never granted the self–government it had been promised. This small area was backward and inhabited by poverty–stricken peasants—it was economically a drain on Czechoslovakia, but it enabled the nation to have a border with Romania, considered to be an important ally.

Throughout the interwar period there were a number of differences that divided the Czechs and the Slovaks. The conflicts between the groups centered on the form and concept of the Czechoslovakian nation. The Czechs were more advanced industrially than the Slovaks and being in the majority, Czech civil servants dominated the government. The Slovaks insisted that the term "Czechoslovak nation" was no more than a cover–up for

Czechoslovakia, 1918–1938, encircled by hungry neighbors

Czech–dominated centralization of government.

However, the problem was even more complex—Slovak political leaders who favored a decentralized government joined with Czechs in urging a single Czechoslo-

President Thomas G. Masaryk

vak nation. Slovaks opposed to this even asserted that they had the right to secede from Czechoslovakia.

The Czechoslovak Republic which lasted from 1918 to 1938 was an economically developed country with a democratic pattern of government. Political parties represented a wide range of outlooks. The *Communist Party* was legal throughout the years of the republic and claimed a substantial following among Czech workers, Slovak and Ruthenian peasants. Although the government was by a coalition of parties throughout the two decades, the *Agrarian Party* was continuously a part of the government after 1922.

Stability was also provided by the top political leadership. Thomas G. Masaryk, Czechoslovakia's first president, was re-elected in 1927 and 1934. When he died in 1935, he was succeeded by Eduard Benes, who had been Foreign Minister since 1918.

Benes realized that Czechoslovakia had land and people which other nations claimed. For this reason, his policy was directed toward encouraging strict observance of the Treaty of Versailles; he formed alliances with other nations having similar interests. He found willing allies in Romania and Yugoslavia and turned first to France and later to the Soviet Union among the major powers.

Czech–German relations within the Republic of Czechoslovakia worsened seriously during 1938 when efforts at compromise between the Prague government and the German minority failed. In a bold move, Hitler demanded that the area inhabited by the Sudeten Germans be ceded to Germany; a four-power conference was summoned. It included Germany, Italy, France and Great Britain, but excluded Czechoslovakia and the Soviet Union and met at Munich, Germany. Seeking a solution short of war, the powers agreed on September 30, 1938 that the German army could occupy the Sudetenland of Czechoslovakia.

This decision was made despite the fact that France had guaranteed Czechoslovakia's borders by a treaty of alliance in 1924, and the Soviet Union had concluded a mutual assistance pact with Czechoslovakia in 1935. This latter agreement promised armed assistance if France also fulfilled its commitment. As a result of the Munich Pact, Germany occupied some 10,000 square miles of territory inhabited by three and one-half million people, one-quarter of whom were Czechs.

The Czechs were forced to accept the pact in order that the major powers could gain what the British Prime Minister Neville Chamberlain weakly prophesied to be "peace in our time." The result only whetted the Nazi appetite, and on March 15, 1939, the remainder of Czechoslovakia was occupied by German troops. Bohemia and Moravia were proclaimed a German Protectorate; Slovakia was made a nominally independent state and Ruthenia was occupied by Hungary.

Czechoslovakia: "Divided and Reconstructed, 1939–1948"

Although there were some isolated attempts to resist the German occupation, one of which resulted in the destruction of two villages and the mass murder of their people, the Czechs had to await the Soviet army for liberation. In June 1945 as the war drew to an end, there was an uprising in Prague against the Germans which badly needed outside help if it was to succeed. However, the nearest Allied force, U.S. General George Patton's Third Army, stood back—the Allied political leaders had agreed that the Soviet "Red" Army was to liberate Prague. This decision was to have a tremendous effect on postwar Czechoslovakia.

During World War II, many of Czechoslovakia's leaders left the country. Eduard Benes, who had resigned on October 5, 1938, became the head of the Provisional Government organized in London in 1940. Klement Gottwald and other important Czech communists sought support in Moscow. Negotiations in March 1945 between Benes, Gottwald and Joseph Stalin of the Soviet Union laid the basis for a post-war government. This was formed in Kosice in April 1945 and moved to Prague the following month.

The government was drawn exclusively from the parties belonging to the *National Front*, consisting of four Czech and two Slovak parties. Their outlook under the Kosice program was that Czechoslovakia's future foreign policy would have an "all-Slav" foundation and would be based on an alliance with the Soviet Union. This declaration was even more meaningful because of the territorial closeness of the Soviet Union to Czechoslovakia, particularly after Ruthenia was made a part of the Soviet Ukraine.

President Eduard Benes

For three years after the end of World War II, Czechoslovakia was governed by the *National Front*, and functioned as a democratic nation. During this period, the Soviet Union was willing to tolerate parliamentary politics so long as the communists held the upper hand on matters of importance. Although they seized power altogether in 1948, they could have done this in 1945 since they were the strongest party of post-war Czechoslovakia. They occupied key positions within the *National Front*, such as Deputy Premier and the Ministries of Information, Interior, Agriculture and Education.

In free elections held in 1946 the communists received by far the largest number of votes. However, by the winter of 1947–48 there were signs that their electoral strength was declining. It appeared that the communists were headed for defeat in an election set for May 1948.

The circumstances leading up to a communist *coup* in 1948 began with the dismissal of eight police officers in Prague and their replacement by communists. When the Minister of Interior refused to reinstate the non-communist officers, twelve non-communist ministers resigned in the hope that this would force new elections in which the communists would be defeated.

Instead of submitting to elections, the communists threatened to use force—a threat strengthened by the arrival of Soviet Deputy Foreign Minister Valerian Zorin in Prague. Communists "action committees" took control of newspapers and occupied the headquarters of non-communist parties. Faced with this show of strength and organization, coupled with the fear of a possible civil war, President Benes accepted a new government formed by Klement Gottwald. When Benes resigned in June 1948, Gottwald succeeded to the presidency and Antonin Zapotocky became premier.

Jan Masaryk, son of Thomas G. Masaryk, had been Foreign Minister under Benes. At the time of the *coup* he was reported to have committed suicide by leaping from a high window of a government building to a stone courtyard below. This was widely disputed; it was officially confirmed in 1989 that he was pushed.

Czechoslovakia Becomes a People's Republic

After the 1948 *coup*, Czechoslovakia was a faithful ally of the Soviet Union, imitating the Stalinist pattern of rule at home and supporting Soviet policies abroad. As in other East European communist countries, a series of purges occurred between 1949 and 1954, aimed at cleansing the party of individuals who might have a greater loyalty to nationalism than to communism. Both Vladimir Clementis, Foreign Minister, and Rudolf Slansky, Secretary General of the Czechoslovak Communist Party, were among eleven victims hanged in 1952 after having been found guilty of "Titoism" and "nationalist deviation."

The death of Joseph Stalin in the Soviet Union in 1953, followed by Gottwald's a few days later, brought no visible change to the government. This was because the domestic scene was stable—economic growth and an increase in the standard of living kept the population relatively settled. No single individual was able to assume all of Gottwald's authority, however; there thus began a period of collective rule within the party. Antonin Zapotocky, who had held the office of Premier since 1948, succeeded to the Presidency—the dominant political position within the Czechoslovak system—while Antonin Novotny became party leader. Reflecting a change also carried out in the Soviet Union at this time, Novotny's title was downgraded to First Secretary. There was a brief period of rioting at Pilsen which brought some minor changes, but the

The Czech and Slovak Republics

communist leadership of Czechoslovakia, strengthened by purges, remained Stalinist (completely authoritarian) even after the end of Stalin.

The denunciation of Stalin by Soviet leader Nikita Khrushchev in 1956 and the neighboring Hungarian revolution of the same year also failed to bring any substantial changes, but the communist leadership of Czechoslovakia, rendered more monolithic by purges, remained Stalinist even after his death.

President Zapotocky died in 1957 and was succeeded by Antonin Novotny who, however, retained his position as First Secretary of the *Czechoslovak Communist Party*. Novotny's succession to the Presidency thus marked the beginning of his political ascendancy and, since Novotny was no reformer, a further period of Stalinist rule in Czechoslovakia.

Khrushchev had launched his de-Stalinization campaign in 1956, but Novotny distinguished himself by opposing nearly every proposal for political innovation and resisting any move toward de-Stalinization within Czechoslovakia. Almost alone among the members of the Communist bloc, Czechoslovakia continued to have political prisoners left over from the Stalinist purges of the early 1950s.

One symbol of the Novotny era became a huge statue of Stalin, erected in 1955 on an embankment overlooking the Vitava River in Prague. The statue survived Khrushchev's 1956 de-Stalinization campaign and even the 1961 decision of the 21st Party Congress to remove Stalin's body from the mausoleum on Red Square. It was finally taken down in October 1962.

Perhaps Novotny's proudest achievement was the new constitution which he pushed through in 1960. According to its terms, Czechoslovakia had become the second country—after the USSR—to make the transition to "Socialist Republic." Since the name was identical to that of the individual Soviet republics, it has even been suggested that Novotny had in mind the incorporation of Czechoslovakia into the USSR.

Novotny's troubles began after 1960. Domestically, there was a growing intellectual ferment that was pressing for greater cultural freedom while, in the economic field, industry began to show the strains of the Stalinist command model. By 1962, the situation had reached crisis proportions. The government was forced to abandon its third five–year plan and to rely on make-shift annual plans for the next three years. Internationally, there was Khrushchev's continuing de–Stalinization campaign.

The events in the USSR reinforced the more liberal, reform elements in the Czech party. Rudolf Barak, Minister of the Interior and a member of this faction,

was an obvious challenger to Novotny's leadership. However, fortunately for Novotny, even the influence of events in Moscow was not sufficient to boost Barak to power as long as he lacked firmer support within the party. In early 1962 Barak was removed from all positions, arrested and sentenced to fifteen years in jail for embezzlement and "conspicuous consumption," which probably meant that he had been living too luxuriously.

The removal of Barak did not end Novotny's troubles—at a party congress in Prague in 1962 the Central Committee decided to conduct an inquiry into the purges of 1949–1954. The result was a declaration that Clementis and Slansky had been wrongfully convicted. The desire for reform also encouraged Slovak agitation, especially among writers and scholars, for the restoration rights of two Slovaks who had been thrown into prison for "bourgeois nationalism." One of these men, Gustav Husak, would himself become leader of the party in 1969.

Novotny had no choice but to yield to pressure—in addition, he was pressed to the extent that he dismissed some of the most unpopular party and government officials. Karol Bacilek, the immensely unpopular First Secretary of the *Slovak Communist Party*, and Viliam Siroky, Premier since 1953 were removed. Both men had aroused Slovak hatred by a consistent policy of cooperating with the Prague government's policies of centralization. Even in the post–World War II period the age–old problem of lack of cooperation between the Czechs and the Slovaks was evident. Siroky was replaced by the more popular Slovak, Josef Lenart, and Bacilek was succeeded by Alexander Dubček (pronounced *Doob-chek*). These changes enabled Novotny to save himself—by 1964 the danger of his loss of power seemed to have passed. He was unanimously selected for another seven–year term as President of the Republic.

However, long before Novotny's term of office expired, he fell from power. Plans for economic reform intended to relieve the conditions which had led to popular complaints in 1962–63 were slow in taking effect. In time, it became apparent that if there was to be economic reform, there also had to be political reform. Disagreement within the party over the progress of reform as well as a number of other issues, including the national thorn–in–the–side, Czech–Slovak relations, resulted in a challenge to Novotny's authority.

At a meeting of the party Central Committee in late 1967, Dubček accused Novotny of undermining the program of economic reform and of refusing to meet Slovak demands for more self–government. These accusations, coming at the

same time there were protests from the Czechoslovak Writers' Union and demonstrations by students in Prague, led to a visit by Soviet party chief Brezhnev as a gesture of support for Novotny.

The visit was not enough to save the falling president; this was made clear by a sharpening division in the higher party ranks between Novotny's supporters and those of Dubček. When the Central Committee convened again two months later, it was decided that the functions of the presidency should be separated from those of the First Secretary of the Communist Party. On January 5, 1968, Alexander Dubček became the first Slovak to assume the top post in the Communist Party of Czechoslovakia. An unsuccessful attempt at a *coup* showed that not even the army could help Novotny. The plot was discovered and the participants were removed from office by Dubček. One army general committed suicide while a second fled the country, eventually making his way to the U.S.

"Socialism With a Human Face": An Experiment and its Consequences

The change in party leadership generated even greater hope that wider political, economic and social changes would follow. When Novotny finally resigned from the presidency in March 1968, it was clear that Czechoslovakia was proceeding in a new direction. A popular national military hero who had been decorated by both Tsarist and Soviet Russia, General Ludvik Svoboda (pronounced Sfo–*boh*–dah) was chosen president. Oldrich Cernik (pronounced *Chur-nik*) became Premier, and formed a cabinet of moderate and liberal membership which supported Dubček.

The party's plans for the future were adopted in April under the general title of "Czechoslovak Road to Socialism," also known as the "Action Program." Important changes in domestic policies were included, such as the virtual end of censorship, limitations on the powers of the secret police, and guarantees for minority views. There was nothing in the program to suggest that Czechoslovakia's policies either toward the Soviet Union or the Warsaw Pact (military alliance) would change. Dubček also repeatedly declared that the Communist Party had the leading role in the government and that his administration was committed to socialist democracy.

Liberalization moved relatively rapidly—a "Two Thousand Words" statement signed by more than seventy writers was published in mid–1968 calling for "pressure from below" for further liberalization and democratic reform. The overall purpose of the entire reform movement was to create what Dubček called "socialism with a human face"—

Curious youngsters mill around a Soviet tank and armored personnel carrier in downtown Prague on the morning of August 21, 1968.

AP/Wide World Photo

Czechoslovakia's own special road to communism.

The leadership of some of the neighboring communist countries of Eastern Europe viewed these developments with great anxiety—they felt that once liberalization was set in motion there could be no assurance it would be controlled. Visits to and from Moscow during May 1968 were occasions on which the Czechs were given "friendly" advice concerning the threat of counter–revolutionary (non–communist) forces to the leading role of the party. When the "Two Thousand Words" appeared, the Soviet press regarded it as proof that such forces existed in Czechoslovakia. Verbal criticism was also accompanied by a lengthy presence of Soviet forces close to and within Czechoslovakia long after scheduled Warsaw Pact maneuvers had ended.

At the beginning of July, neighboring communist nations urged that a joint meeting be held between themselves and Czechoslovakia, but the Czechs were willing only to talk with them one at a time. This resulted in a meeting held in Warsaw in mid–1968 at which the Czechs were not present. It produced a document of great significance, known as the "Warsaw Letter"—a warning was given that the Czechs could maintain their independence only as a socialist (communist) country; reactionary (non–communist) forces were diverting them from socialism and, finally, that this was of concern to all nations of the Warsaw Pact. A demand was made that the Czechs take immediate action to muffle the press and radio and to clamp down on anti–socialist political movements.

Prague's reply to this was that the party was in complete control, but that its authority was secure only so long as it was responsive to the will of the people, who desired more freedom of expression. The exchange of letters settled nothing, and was followed by a Soviet request for a special meeting with the Czech leadership. Two meetings were held in late July and early August 1968; at the second meeting, other Warsaw Pact nations attended with the exception of Romania. The result was a joint statement which spoke vaguely about the need to strengthen the forces of socialism against imperial aggression. In reality, the meeting ended in total disagreement.

Invasion And Its Aftermath

On the night of August 20–21, military units of the Soviet Union, Hungary, East Germany, Poland and Bulgaria swiftly invaded Czechoslovakia, occupying the leading cities within a few hours. The official Soviet news agency, Tass, issued a statement that the occupation was in response to a request for assistance against "counter–revolutionary" forces made by a group of Czech Central Committee, Government and National Assembly members. The military operation was an obvious success, but the political performance of the Soviets was not equally as smooth. The fact of the matter is that there had been no request for occupation by any of the Czech leadership.

Immediate problems arose over the fate of the Czechoslovak leadership—Dubček, Cernik, and Josef Smrkovsky, President of the National Assembly—who had been placed under arrest. There was a dire need to find Czech collaborators who would confirm the Soviet explanation of the invasion. This was made more difficult by the Czech Foreign Ministry which denounced the invasion as a violation of the Warsaw Pact. President Svoboda flatly refused to participate in the formation of a Soviet–dominated government, but the deadlock was broken when he agreed to go to Moscow for direct talks with the Soviet leaders.

At Svoboda's insistence, Dubček and the other leaders also participated in the Moscow talks, which resulted in a Soviet agreement to accept the return of the Dubček administration to office. But it was at the same time made clear that Czech leaders would have to change their political outlook. A treaty was signed in October providing for the stationing of

The Czech and Slovak Republics

Wenceslaus Square, central Prague

Soviet troops within Czechoslovakia for an unlimited time. A Czech party congress which had been quickly convened during the first week of the invasion was declared invalid—it had selected a strongly liberal Central Committee. Finally, a new party group, the Executive Committee of the Presidium was created to counteract liberals in the Presidium itself.

Retreat From Reform

At midnight on December 31, 1968, Czechoslovakia became a federal state comprised of the Czech Socialist Republic and the Slovak Socialist Republic. Cernik remained Premier in the federal government and Svoboda continued as President. During 1969 there was a gradual replacing of the pre–invasion reform leadership through demotion, resignation or dismissal. Josef Smrkovsky was elected President of the People's Chamber of the Federal Assembly, although his rank and experience qualified him for a higher post. Dubček's position became very complicated—he wanted to prove to the liberals that there had been no surrender to the Soviet Union and that reform was still possible. He also wanted to reassure the conservatives that there was no danger in reform and to convince the Soviet Union that he would not be the source of additional political strife.

Dubček found it difficult to be in favor of so many conflicting political views at the same time. Unable to withstand conservative pressures within the party and outside it, he criticized anti–Soviet attitudes, denounced student demonstrations and reimposed censorship. He was ultimately replaced in April by Gustáv Husák, who had initially supported reform, but later took the position that it was paramount for Czechoslovakia to live in harmony with the Soviet Union.

A little more than a year after the invasions, a purge of liberals was carried out in the federal as well as in the regional government and party organizations. Dubček had been "Chairman of the Federal Assembly" since April 1969, but he was removed, ultimately to be sent to Turkey as ambassador. Smrkovsky was ousted from the Central Committee and from his post in the People's Chamber. With the pro–Moscow conservatives dominating the party leadership, the Central Committee issued a declaration that the resolution condemning the Warsaw Pact invasion was annulled. It was termed an act in defense of socialism. Thus, Czechoslovakia was, for the time being, back in line. In May 1970 a new friendship treaty was signed with the Soviet Union.

It was also in early 1970 that Cernik was dismissed as Premier and replaced by Lubomir Strougal. The general assumption at the time was that Strougal, then known as a conservative, had been installed as a counter–weight to Husak and a possible rival for power. The expulsion of Dubček from the communist party in June 1970 was a victory for the party's "hardliners," leaving Husák in the isolated position of being a moderate surrounded by conservatives. In the general elections of 1971, over 99% of the votes were cast for the party–approved list of candidates.

An extensive purge of the party was carried out between 1970 and 1975 which resulted in the dismissal of about 450,000 members—nearly one–third of the total membership. In general, it was the more liberal members and, in particular, those who could be identified as Dubcek supporters, who were purged. It was also during this time—in 1972—that Husak's party title was changed from First Secretary to General Secretary, thereby mirroring the change Brezhnev had pushed through for the CPSU in 1966.

Having consolidated his power, Husak announced in 1976 that he was ready to begin a policy of reconciliation. Purged members were invited to apply for readmission to the party and he estimated that up to thirds of them might be taken back. There was one major stipulation, however; applicants for readmission had to formally repudiate the policies and leaders of the Prague Spring. In spite of this rather harsh precondition, some ex–

members did apply and were accepted back into the party, and the party began to grow again.

The government was again reorganized in early 1971 at both the federal and national levels. The powers of the Federal Cabinet were increased at the expense of the Czech and Slovak cabinets. The central body then had the right to veto decisions of either national unit.

In May 1975, Husak replaced the ailing Svoboda as President of the Republic, retaining his position as head of the party. The Czechoslovak power structure thus reverted to the pattern that had existed prior to Dubcek's replacement of Novotny as First Secretary of the Communist Party in January 1968. Husak would continue to occupy both positions for another 12 years. Thus the man who had once been thrown into prison for "bourgeois nationalism" became both the symbol and instrument of Soviet domination of Czechoslovakia.

Western newspapers published in early January 1977 a declaration by a group within Czechoslovakia. Entitled "Charter 77," it outlined in great detail human rights violations, among them that young people were denied the opportunity for higher education because of their political views—or even those of their parents—and that there was almost a total lack of freedom for public expression, specifically guaranteed by the constitution. Those who signed the charter were immediately harassed, and some given prison sentences on trumped–up charges. This group was not silenced.

Because of the way in which the Czechoslovak leadership had been installed, it was probably unrealistic to expect any policy other than that which was carried out after 1969. But it is precisely for this reason that recent political changes in the Soviet Union had an unsettling effect in Czechoslovakia.

Gorbachëv's campaigns for *glasnost*, *perestroika* and *democracy* led to a debate within the Czechoslovak Presidium as individual leaders more or less publicly debated whether loyalty to the USSR required them to support a similar program in Czechoslovakia. It soon became clear that the top leadership was sharply divided over the issue. Vasil Bilak became the chief spokesman for the hardliners, while Premier Strougal spoke out in favor of Prague's own restructuring.

Meanwhile, Husak remained silent until March 1987, when he finally endorsed a general program of reform. But Husak remained a reluctant reformer; no changes were to be implemented until the beginning of the next five–year plan on January 1, 1991. Gorbachëv visited Czechoslovakia in April 1987 and used his public speeches to set forth the rationale for reform. While he did not insist that the Czechoslovak leadership implement a similar program, he also, significantly, had no praise for them. It was, in fact, becoming clear that Husak, at 74, was no longer able to provide any clear leadership and that the issue of reform was becoming a vehicle to determine the succession.

The issue was resolved in December 1987 when Husak announced that he was retiring as General Secretary and that his successor would be Milos Jakes [pronounced Ya–kesh]. Jakes, then 65, and a member of the ruling Presidium since 1981, was an obvious compromise choice, a man not associated with either of the two factions within the Presidium.

Although he had been a member of the party secretariat for over 20 years by this time, he had never developed a strong political profile and, in fact, his record was a rather ambivalent one. Originally appointed head of the Party Control and Auditing Commission by Dubcek in 1968, he transferred his loyalty to the new leadership installed after the Soviet invasion. He then supervised the post–1968 purge of the party that resulted in the expulsion of most liberals and moderates. Many of these same people, who consti-

Shoppers look with skeptical amusement at relaxing skateboarders

Photo by Jon Markham Morrow

The Czech and Slovak Republics

tuted an important part of the country's cultural and technological elite, were also fired from their state jobs and forced either to take menial jobs or emigrate. Given this background, Jakes had a problem establishing credibility in his new job.

Jakes' own public statements after becoming General Secretary were rather unconciliatory and, on at least one occasion, he characterized the Prague Spring as an attempt "to destroy the socialist system." At the same time, his speeches included references to the need for a "fundamental restructuring of all spheres of public life."

Jakes' promotion to General Secretary did not put an end to the Bilak–Strougal struggle and may even have intensified it, since they were now trying to influence a man of untried qualities. Strougal's speeches in favor of Gorbachëv–style reform apparently became embarrassing to the party, however, for he was forced out as Premier in October 1988. Ladislav Adamec, who succeeded Strougal was, like Jakes, a man of the middle. During a trip to Moscow in February 1989, he spoke of the need for political as well as economic reforms. He was also responsible for a Presidium decision to begin implementation of the economic reform as of January 1, 1991, one year earlier than previously announced. At the same time, Adamec remained willing to carry out the will of the conservative majority on the Presidium. All of this began to change in the late summer of 1989. As the change sweeping across Eastern Europe reached the German Democratic Republic, the West German Embassy in Prague became a refuge center for East Germans attempting to get to West Germany. This proved to be embarrassing to the Czechoslovakian government and it began putting pressure on the GDR regime to do something about it. Eventually the GDR government caved in and arranged for trains to carry the refugees to West Germany. As the GDR was forced to give in more to the demands of its people, disaffected Czechoslovakians began to organize their own demonstrations demanding greater rights.

It all came to a head on the evening of November 17, when a crowd of about 3,000 young people gathered at the entrance of Wenceslas Square (Vaclavske Namesti) and began a chant calling for free elections. They were met by a line of riot police plus an anti–terrorist squad called the Red Berets who attacked them and bludgeoned them to the ground. The attack, personally ordered by the party leader, Jakes, was a fatal error. It ignited the emotions of the Czechoslovakian people, who responded with ten days of singing, chanting and non–stop organiz-

ing. This was Prague's so–called "velvet revolution," and at its end the communists had been elbowed from power. On November 24, with 300,000 people in the streets, Jakes called a meeting of the Central Committee and submitted his and the entire Presidium's resignations.

Jakes' resignation was accepted and he was replaced by Karel Urbanek, who issued an unequivocal condemnation of the violence of November 17. But it was Ladislav Adamec, the Premier, who now stepped into the power vacuum and began discussions with the opposition, since November 19 organized as the *Civic Forum*. He continued to play that role for perhaps two weeks. During that time, the party agreed to give up its monopoly of power and to form a coalition government with the opposition. But Adamec wanted to keep a majority of the seats in the hands of the communists. When *Civic Forum* rejected his proposed cabinet on December 3, Adamec resigned and was replaced by Marian Calfa. The new cabinet, installed on December 10, contained a majority of non–communists. Perhaps more important, Jiri Dienstbier, a founder–member of *Charter 77*, became Foreign Minister while Vaclav Klaus, an economist committed to creation of a market economy, became Finance Minister.

As an added benefit, Gustav Husak now submitted his resignation as President, thus opening the question as to who his successor should be. Alexander Dubcek, leader of the Prague Spring in 1968, was first mentioned, but was eventually ruled out because he is a Slovak. That seemed to leave the other prominent leader of the opposition, Vaclav Havel, longtime dissident, founder of *Charter 77*,

President Vaclav Havel

and prominent playwright. On December 29, he was elected President by acclamation. Alexander Dubcek was elected leader of the national assembly.

With the new leaders all in place, the country settled in for a period of consolidation that included some dismantling of the old system. In the political and social arenas, the secret police were dissolved, and required courses in Marxism–Leninism were abolished in the universities. In the area of religion, *Pacem in Terris* was dissolved and the government dropped its system of licensing priests and ministers. Fewer changes were made in the economic sphere, though one reason for this is that everybody seemed to be waiting for new elections scheduled for June 6 in order to have a popular mandate.

One other domestic issue, the rivalry between Czechs and Slovaks, resulted in a change in the name of the country. Upon Slovak insistence, the name of the country was changed to the Czech and Slovak Federal Republic.

Czechoslovakia's first democratic elections since 1946 finally took place in June 1990 and resulted in a victory for *Civic Forum* and its Slovak partner, *Public Against Violence*. An astonishing 96% of Czechoslovakia's voters participated in the election. After the election, Vaclav Haval was reelected President and Marian Calfa was reappointed Premier.

After the June elections, there was a struggle of sorts between free marketers and advocates for a "third way" between communism and capitalism within the leadership of the *Civic Forum*. The spokesman for the free marketers was the Finance Minister, Vaclav Klaus, while Foreign Minister Jiri Dienstbier was a major spokesman for the opposing viewpoint, which also included most of the 1968 communists. President Haval tried to stay above the fray. Klaus won the first round in October 1990 when he was elected chairman of *Civic Forum*. In February 1991, however, the two factions decided to divide into two separate organizations, though they would continue to be associated on a coordinating committee of *Civic Forum* chaired by President Haval.

One other issue that emerged after the June 1990 elections was the issue of Slovak separatism. Slovaks were from the beginning concerned about their separate identity, but then Slovak nationalists began demanding a breakup of the Czechoslovak federation and the creation of a separate, independent Slovak state.

In December 1990, the Federal Assembly attempted to defuse the situation by passing new legislation outlining the powers of the Czech and Slovak regional governments. The legislation also gave President Haval special powers to deal with the threat of Slovak separatism.

236

Everybody likes to polka on Sunday afternoons in Julius Fucik Park, Prague.

Although both Slovak and Czech deputies afterwards expressed their satisfaction with the legislation, the situation continued to simmer and President Haval was rushed by thousands of Slovaks shouting abuse when he visited Bratislava, the capital of Slovakia, in March 1991. Part of the problem was that the Slovak Premier, Vladimir Meciar, had taken up the Slovak nationalist cause—at least partly because he feared the effect of Prague's privatization policies on Slovak industry. Things improved somewhat after Meciar was replaced in April 1991 by Jan Carnogursky, head of Slovakia's *Christian Democratic Movement*. His position was somewhat ambiguous, however; although he supported continuation of the federation for the time being, he also said that he favored an independent Slovakia in principle.

Slovak nationalism continued to be the dominant factor in Czechoslovak politics throughout the rest of 1991 and into 1992. President Haval spent more and more of his time on this issue as he tried to act as a mediator between the Czechs and Slovaks, bringing the two sides together for discussions and, at one point, calling for a referendum on the issue. Public polls showed that a small majority of Slovaks supported a continuation of the federation, however, so the Slovak political leadership eventually rejected that suggestion.

Haval also proposed some changes in the nature of the federal government, and these were presented to the Federal Assembly by the Czechoslovak Government in December 1991 in the form of three draft laws. The first of the draft laws would have abolished one of the houses of the bicameral Federal Assembly and created a Federal Council in its stead consisting of representatives of the Czech and Slovak legislatures. A second draft law would have given the president special powers to issue decrees, should the Federal Assembly be dissolved. The third draft law would have allowed the president to call a plebiscite if he had the concurrence of the federal government.

The three draft laws were not passed, but they may have acted as a catalyst. An *ad hoc* commission of the Czech and Slovak National Councils (i.e.,legislatures) announced on February 9, 1992 that its members had drawn up a draft agreement on a future common state which would be submitted to their respective legislatures. The draft agreement listed foreign policy, defense, monetary, credit, interest and currency policies and budgetary regulations as falling within the powers of the federation. Czechs and Slovaks would be equally represented in the federal bodies. The agreement also specified that either republic could withdraw from the common state "only on the basis of the will of the majority of its citizens expressed in a referendum."

What appeared as a breakthrough fell to pieces when the Presidium of the Slovak National Council met on February 12 to consider the draft, however; a majority opposed it and it was turned down. Then another partial reversal occurred two weeks later when the Slovak National Council passed a resolution on the draft treaty, in effect asking the Presidium to reconsider. The resolu-

tion requested Slovak National Council deputies to submit their views on the draft to the Presidium and instructed the Presidium to compile a comprehensive report on the comments that the deputies submitted. The resolution further recommended that the Presidium meet with the Presidium of the Czech National Council "to jointly assess . . . the possibility of concluding the treaty."

These maneuvers failed to produce an agreement, however, so it was decided to hold new federal elections on June 5–6 to resolve the general issue. Slovakia decided to hold its own elections to the National Council on the same days. The *Christian Democratic Movement*, the party of Slovak Premier Jan Carnogursky, then split into two factions. The more radical faction that had been pushing for an independent Slovakia formed a new party, the *Slovak Christian Democratic Movement*, and announced that they would run a separate slate of candidates in the June elections. With the radicals gone, the *Christian Democratic Movement* reaffirmed its support for a common state.

In the June 1992 elections, the vote split along national and ideological lines, with the Czechs voting for reform and anti–communist candidates and the Slovaks casting their ballots for nationalists and leftists. In the Slovak Republic, Vladimir Meciar and his *Movement for a Democratic Slovakia*, won with their blend of statism, socialism and nationalism. In the Czech Republic, Vaclav Klaus and his *Civic Democratic Party* won an equally convincing victory on a program of anti–communism and reform.

The Czech and Slovak Republics

Prague: wedding couple receives gifts following ceremony

Meciar and Klaus met after the election to discuss the formation of a new federal government. Here, Meciar made it clear that he would not accept a federal state that could dictate policy to Slovakia. He demanded that the Slovak Republic be authorized to establish its own army, its own currency–issuing central bank and that it be permitted the independent right to borrow. He also indicated that he intended to reverse some of the recent national policies as they applied to Slovakia, including restoring subsidies to state industry, increasing social benefits, and slowing privatization. None of these positions were acceptable to the free market Klaus and the talks collapsed after six and a half hours.

Because a new federal government had to be formed, Klaus suggested giving a new, temporary federal government the power to act until a referendum could be held to ask citizens whether they wanted to live in a federal state. After further talks, Czech and Slovak negotiators agreed to establish a weak interim federal government whose task would be to facilitate bringing the union to a close. The actual constitutional questions relating to

the separation would be resolved in the legislatures of the two republics.

Vaclav Haval, still trying to save the federal state, agreed to stand for reelection to the federal presidency. Slovak nationalists blocked his reelection, however. Haval could have stayed on in a caretaker capacity until October, since the dominant Czech party, the *Civic Democratic Party*, had vowed to block any other candidate for the presidency. But he was unwilling to remain under those circumstances and submitted his resignation instead. Most people saw that as a further step in the dissolution of the federal government. As Haval said, had he stayed, he would have been committed by the constitution to defending a common state that no longer had much purpose.

Further negotiations now produced an agreement, signed on August 26, calling for a split into two independent states by January 1. The process suffered a set–back on October 1, when the federal parliament rejected a bill legalizing the end of the federation. After further negotiations, however, the federal parliament voted itself out of existence on November 25.

By that time, the two national legislatures had begun acting like the federation had already disappeared. This was particularly true in the case of the Slovak legislature. Meciar had said in June that he wanted to slow down privatization and he began submitting bills to the Slovak legislature to accomplish that purpose. The Slovak government called for the renegotiation of several privatization agreements and stopped the privatization of a number of companies. As a result, only 5.3% of Slovak industry had been privatized by the end of 1992 as compared to 25.2% for the Czech Republic.

On January 1, 1993, The Czech and Slovak Federal Republic disappeared and in its place there emerged an independent Slovak Republic and an independent Czech Republic. The separation was peaceful, but all of the celebrations were in Brataslava, the capital of Slovakia. There was no ceremony to make the occasion in Prague. In the speech he gave to mark the occasion, Prime Minister Meciar attempted a note of conciliation. "Two states have been established," he said. "Living together in one state is over. Living together in two states continues."

THE INDEPENDENT SLOVAK REPUBLIC

In July 1992, the Slovak legislature had issued a declaration of sovereignty, then adopted a constitution for an independent Slovakia, to go into effect on January 1. In the constitution, the country is formally designated as the Slovak Republic. The constitution also created a 150 seat assembly as the nation's legislature and bestowed on the assembly the right to elect the head of state, to be known as the President of the Republic. In January, Prime Minister Meciar proposed his deputy prime minister, Roman Kovac, for the post of President. Although Meciar's *Movement for a Democratic Slovakia* dominates the assembly, he was not able to put together the three–fifths majority necessary to elect his candidate. After two votes, therefore, he was required to withdraw his candidate and submit another name. He then nominated Michal Kovac, who won on the first ballot. Michel Kovac, expelled from the communist party in 1970 as a supporter of Dubcek, served as Slovakia's Finance Minister from the end of 1989 to the beginning of 1992, then served as the last chairman of Czechoslovakia's federal parliament.

Since achieving independence for Slovakia, Prime Minister Meciar has reiterated the positions he enunciated in 1992. In his New Year's Day address, he rejected both free market economics and a ban on former communists in top government positions. And he has surrounded himself with individuals who were active in the Prague Spring. Meciar's commitment to democracy and pluralism is also not very firm. For example, the government has tightened its control on the press and on television since January 1, dismissing individuals suspected of oppositionist tendencies, and there have been accusations that Slovakia is sliding toward one party rule. The Slovak Government also recently began taking moves to restrict the language rights of its 600,000–strong Hungarian minority. For example, in October 1992, the government began taking down Hungarian–language signs in border areas. It also formally announced that Hungarian names for Slovak towns may not be used in Hungarian–language broadcasts.

Meciar's greatest changes are likely to be in the area of economics, however. Privatization has already effectively come to an end, at least for the moment. In addition, increased credits to state industry have enlarged budget deficits and contributed to the collapse of the common currency arrangement with the Czech Republic. Exports to the Czech Republic are down by half since the first of the year, while Czech exports to Slovakia are down by 60%. There have also been reports that significant deposits

have been switched from Slovak to Czech banks. These developments threaten both republics, of course, but of the two Slovakia appears to be more vulnerable—and more culpable.

THE INDEPENDENT CZECH REPUBLIC

The Czech legislature adopted a new constitution for an independent Czech Republic in December 1992. It provides for an 81 member senate and a 200 member lower house, or parliament. In lieu of elections, the Czech members of the Czechoslovak federal parliament will fill the Senate seats until the next regularly scheduled elections.

On January 26, the 200–member Czech Parliament elected Vaclav Haval President of the Republic. His inaugural speech of February 2, given from a balcony of Hradcany Castle, was rather somber in tone, in contrast to his first inaugural speech. "The revolutionary times are over," he said. "This is the time of every day, common and hard work. To cultivate our best traditions today is infinitely harder than in times of great historical change and the euphoria that came with it."

On the same day, and almost as a counterpoint to his speech, the Czech and Slovak parliaments announced the end of the common currency agreement between their two republics and that each republic would be issuing its own currency.

The Czech Republic is far more prosperous than its Slovak counterpart. Its unemployment rate is much lower and it has received the lion's share of foreign investment. Yet the break–up of the federal republic has had a significant negative effect on Czech morale and self–confidence. It's hard to say how long the mood will last.

Foreign Policy

While Czechoslovakia was controlled by the *Communist Party*, it had no independent foreign policy. Or, as the Czechoslovakian Ambassador to the United States told this writer several years ago, "the foreign policy of Czechoslovakia is the foreign policy of the Soviet Union."

That all changed in December 1989. Since that time, the Czechoslovakian government has established relations with Israel and the Vatican, President Havel has given orders for the curtailment of worldwide arms exports, and the country carried out successful negotiations with the Soviet Union to get Soviet troops withdrawn from Czechoslovakia. The last of the troops left in June 1991.

In other signs of change, both Alexander Dubcek and Vaclav Havel have made trips to the United States and Havel

gave a major address before a combined session of Congress. Czechoslovakia was also among those nations urging the Soviet Union to drop its insistence that a united Germany either be neutral or hold simultaneous membership in both military alliances; Czechoslovakia wanted a united Germany to be part of NATO.

The demise of both the Warsaw Pact and the Council for Mutual Economic Assistance had some effect on Czechoslovakia's international relations, though Czechoslovakia's participation in both memberships had become increasingly nominal. Czechoslovakia was among those nations insisting that all CMEA accounts be settled in dollar or other convertible currencies as of 1991.

The demise of the Soviet Union in 1991 changed that relationship even further as Czechoslovakia extended diplomatic recognition to the successor republics and opened separate relations with them. Czechoslovakia has sought good relations with the newly imdependent Republic of Ukraine, but the Czechoslovakian leadership is more attuned to the new Russian political leadership in Moscow. Its relations with the remaining successor republics are likely to be more nominal.

Czechoslovakia was admitted to Associate Membership in the European Community in December 1991, along with Hungary and Poland, and this is likely to be the major focus of its foreign policy in the future. Czechoslovakia wants to become a full member of the European Community as soon as possible and it has already begun aligning its foreign policy to that of the EC. In the case of the break up of Yugoslavia, for example, Czechoslovakia extended diplomatic recognition to the successor republics only after the EC had done so.

American–Czechoslovakian relations remain good and the Czechoslovakian Government would welcome greater American investment in Czechoslovakian industry, partly to offset the strong investment drive from Germany but partly also because they would like to see a greater American economic presence. Over the past two years, Czechoslovakia has received, after Hungary, the largest amount of foreign investment in Eastern Europe.

The foreign policies of the newly independent Czech and Slovak Republics are not likely to differ very much from each other, though Prime Minister Meciar of Slovakia has indicated that he intends to particularly cultivate relations with Russia and Ukraine. Slovakia inherited Associate Membership in the European Community, however, as one of the two successor states to the Czech and Slovak Federal Republic. This ought to give him reason to cultivate ties with the west.

The Czech and Slovak Republics

Slovakia intends to increase its efforts to sell the products of its large armaments industry abroad, but it was already trying to do that before independence. Its reasons for doing so are economic, not ideological.

The Economy

Czechoslovakia was already an industrialized nation when the communists took over in 1948. The coalition government installed in office in 1945 had nationalized about 60% of all industry and instituted a land reform aimed at breaking up all large land holdings. Major steps had also been taken toward institutionalizing socialism and state planning. With half their work done for them, the communists only had to complete the nationalization of industry and adapt state planning to the command model developed by the Soviet Union in the 1930's. This was accompanied by a gradual collectivization of agriculture.

Czechoslovakia's first Five Year Plan was launched on January 1, 1949, and it, and the following two subsequent Five Year Plans, placed a major stress on the creation of heavy industry—again a slavish following of the Soviet model. The relative neglect of consumer industries and agriculture produced a lop-sided economy which began to resemble more and more an industrialized copy of the Soviet economy. Certain food items such as meat became scarce, a severe housing shortage developed in the cities, and the quality of consumer goods declined as well. These developments obviously had an effect on ordinary morale, and, as the third Five Year Plan progressed, even heavy industry began to fall short of its targets. In 1962, with the economy in a severe recession, the third Five Year Plan was simply abandoned.

A number of Czech economists associated with the Institute of Economics of the Czechoslovak Academy of Sciences had been critical of Stalinist concepts of command planning for a number of years. One of the most prominent and outspoken of these proposed a plan for reordering the economy which became known as the "New Economic Model." The Czech economist had been influenced by a Soviet counterpart, Yevsei Liberman, and his plan, like the Liberman Plan, called for greatly limiting the role of the central planners. Individual enterprises were to be managed on the basis of *profitability;* worker salaries were to be based in part on individual skills and there was to be a major stress on upgrading technology.

President Novotny initially opposed the plan. The economy continued to flounder, however, and at the beginning of 1967 Novotny gave a grudging approval for initiation of the plan—with the important condition that it leave the Party's central policy–making authority intact. But it was a start in name only; as a result of continued opposition by conservatives involved in central planning, it failed to have any significant effect.

A similar effort in the Soviet Union resulted in a victory for the conservatives there. In Czechoslovakia, the reformers decided to challenge the conservative leadership and were instrumental in securing the resignation of Novotny as head of the *CPCz.* Dubček, his successor, fully supported the reform measures and the economist who initially wrote the plan became deputy prime minister.

A start in the direction of the "New Economic Model" was made in 1968, but the arrival of Soviet troops abruptly ended it. It was later abandoned by the Husák regime as a "romantic notion." The central planners again assumed control of the economy.

Czechoslovakia's problems remained, however, and the new Husák regime had to face them. An injection of Soviet aid plus a vigorous investment effort got the economy back on a positive course, but in 1975 the regime introduced its own economic reform, based on some ideas developed in East Germany in the 1960's. Essentially a bureaucratic solution, a new "middle level" of managers between the central planners and the individual managers was created—a sort of regional level of managers whose function was to coordinate the working of the plan within their sub–areas.

There might have been some decentralization in this cautious reform, but it was insufficient to have a noticeable effect on the economy. As a result, the Husák regime continued to tinker with the central planning mechanism, but always in a cautious manner. The frame of reference within which Czech central planners work is perhaps best illustrated by the title of a 1980 proposal: "Set of Measures for Improvement of the System of Planned Management in the National Economy After 1980." This concept, put into action in 1981, developed what might be called the concept of the conglomerate. Twenty to 40 enterprises were to be organized under a single management which was then to be given a certain amount of independence from the central state planning bureaucracy. A similar system was introduced in the German Democratic Republic in the 1970s, but there the companies are referred to as *kombinate.*

This reform did not prevent a slowing of the economy, however, nor was it able to reverse an increasing shortage of certain types of consumer goods, particularly pork and beef. The government raised the prices of meat, milk and bread by as much as 150% in February 1982, but when shortages persisted, new price rises were instituted the following year.

Official statistics reported a 3 percent average growth rate during most of the 1980's, but industry continued to be plagued by outdated technology, declining productivity and low–level products. Proposals for economic reform were never really put into effect or, if they were, had no effect.

All of that is now changing. The revolution of 1989 put a new set of leaders in power and, although there was some floundering about in the first year, the government has now begun to take the necessary steps to create a market economy. In February 1991, the Federal Assembly passed a broad privatization law which commits the government to denationalize all industry. Companies nationalized after 1948 will be returned to their original owners or their descendants, while remaining companies will be privatized through a complex system of government–issued coupons or sold to foreign investors. The key individual responsible for the government's plans is Vaclav Klaus, the Finance Minister.

The political debate between Czechs and Slovaks over the future of the common state grew in intensity through most of 1991, however, and Klaus's plans for economic reform were thrust partially aside. As a result, the government's plans to begin privatization of large–scale industry through its coupon program was pushed off to March 1992.

Privatization is actually being implemented by the Czech and Slovak governments rather than the national government. In November 1991, the Czech Government announced that it had made significant progress in its small–scale privatization program, having sold 12,333 out of 20,786 business units included in the program. Less progress had been made in large–scale privatization, but the government had held seven auctions, approved five direct sales, and prepared two public tenders. Much more of Slovak industry is large–scale and much of it is uncompetitive. Privatization has, accordingly, been much slower there.

The Federal Government has also launched a program to transform the country's agriculture. In earlier legislation, collective farms had been legally transformed into cooperatives and employees were given the right to ask for their own land. Only 1,120 of those who applied for land took more than 25 acres, however. Most wanted only a couple of acres to work for themselves. This was disturbing from the government's point of view, for the large agricultural subsidies which the cooperatives require to make them competitive act as a drain on the national budget. The government sought to deal with this problem by pass-

A Slovak peasant woman shows off her daughters after church on a Sunday morning

ing a "transformation" law which reduced government oversight over the cooperatives and made the elective bodies of the cooperatives responsible for management and decision–making. The government is hoping that, given the responsibility, the cooperatives will transform themselves. To encourage them in this direction, the government cut agricultural subsidies by one–quarter in December 1991.

The Czechoslovak Arms Industry

In the decade from 1978 to 1988, Czechoslovakia was the world's eighth largest weapons exporter and the global leader in per capita terms. More than 100 plants produced various types of weaponry ranging from Skorpion machine pistols to L–39 jet trainers, exported to Czechoslovakia's Warsaw Pact partners and Third World countries. Most of these plants were located in central Slovakia, which became the center of Czechoslovakia's heavy–arms industry in the early days of the cold war. "These plants were put up

in green meadows," says Josef Fucik, head of the department for conversion of military production in the federal Ministry of Economics in Prague. "It was a quick fix in the '50s to give modern jobs to Slovakia. Now the bill has come due." The town of Martin, 230 km north of Bratislava, was the site of a tank plant that employed 11,000; nearby Dubnica built armored personnel carriers, while Povazska Bystrica, down the road, produced jet engines.

Two months after the November 1989 revolution, Foreign Minister Jiri Dienstbier announced that Prague would "simply end its trade in arms" without regard to economic consequences. That turned out to be impossible. With 80,000 jobs dependent on arms production, the bulk of them in a depressed region of Slovakia, the government had to modify its plans. It pledged to cut the output of weapons plants to 25% of 1988 levels by 1993, but Slovak politicians opposed the cuts.

Exacerbating the situation is Czecho-

slovakia's own commitment under the Conventional Forces in Europe agreement to destroy 1,600 of its tanks. Thus, domestic demand for tanks has disappeared completely. Sales to Warsaw Pact members also dried up. The Soviet Union, once Czechoslovakia's largest customer, had begun to cut arms purchases in 1990 and cancelled almost all purchase orders in 1991 when it would have been required to pay for such purchases in hard currency. The subsequent collapse of the Soviet Union had a psychological effect in Czechoslovakia, but it had already ceased to be a major arms purchaser prior to its collapse.

Sales to the Third World have thus become even more important. Two such sales are affecting Czechoslovakia's foreign relations—an agreement to sell up to 300 T–72 tanks to Syria in a deal worth $200 million and an oil–for–arms barter with Iran. U.S. officials joined Israel in condemning the projected sale to Syria. Czechoslovak Prime Minister Marian Calfa said that "Czechoslovakia is not

The Czech and Slovak Republics

interested in producing tanks. But we don't want to break the economy of a region." Slovak Premier Jan Carnogursky said that "We've asked the federal government to clear up the matter and persuade complaining governments that the deal is harmless."

The Syrian sale may not be that beneficial economically. Syria already owes Czechoslovakia the equivalent of $1 billion for previous arms shipments, according to Fucik. The new sale would also be on the basis of long–term government credit.

Meanwhile, conversion has made some headway. ZTS Martin (Factory Turcanske Strojarne Martin), the tank manufacturer, has an agreement with the German firm Hanomag to manufacture earthmoving equipment. The company has also begun working under license from the Italian manufacturer Lombardini to produce tractor engines and other machinery. The firm eventually plans to turn out 40,000 engines annually. Military production has already dropped from three–quarters of total output in 1988 to less than one–quarter in 1991.

Culture

Because of the historic separation of the two peoples, there have always been two separate Czech and Slovak cultures. The latter, part of the Hungarian Kingdom from the 11th century, were a peasant people heavily influenced by Hungarian culture. That part of the country is particularly known for its unique and lively folk music and dances, performed in brightly–colored traditional dress. Slovakia has changed greatly in recent years, however, and it is now nearly as urbanized and industrialized as the rest of the country. On the other hand, much of Slovakia's industry, built during the communist era, is precisely the sort of industry that will have difficulty competing during the transition to a market economy. Most of Czechoslovakia's arms industry is, for example, located in Slovakia. Fears about the fate of its heavily subsidized plants has helped fuel a Slovak separatist movement. Slovaks also tend to be somewhat defensive about the level of their culture, but the truth is that the work of individual Slovak artists and craftsmen compares favorably with that of other Europeans.

Prague, the center of Czech culture, is an achingly beautiful city full of carefully preserved ancient churches with gold–tipped spires, plus baroque, romanesque and art nouveau buildings untouched by the bombs of World War II. On the hill above the Vltava River stands Hradcany Castle, residence of the President. St. Vitus Cathedral, Prague's great Gothic cathedral, is part of that same complex and its spires stand out against the sky. Down the hill from Hradcany and St. Vitus, the 14th century Charles IV bridge—now a pedestrian walkway closed to traffic—leads across to the old city center. Here, in the old residence quarter of the city, one finds Wenceslas Square (Vaclavske Namesti) and Old Town (Stare Mesto) Square, with its Jan Hus Memorial.

One must give the old communist government credit; they did put a great deal of money and effort into fixing up the older buildings of Prague in their last years in power. It seemed at the time that scaffolding surrounded half of the city's architectural, historical and religious structures, but visitors to Prague have the benefit of that effort today. Incidently, soon after it took over, the new Czechoslovakian Government abolished all visa requirements for Americans planning to stay less than 30 days. It is also now possible to rent a room in a private home or apartment and the arriving visitor is likely to receive many such offers. That is particularly important,

A mountain village in Slovakia in the late 1900's

242

since hotel space is still extremely limited.

Czechoslovakia has contributed substantially to the world of music and literature. One needs only to recall such persons as Anton Dvorak, composer of the *New World Symphony*, Vilém Blodek, famous for his comic operas, such figures as Smetana, Janácek and, of course, Franz Kafka. Restrictions imposed on creative artists reduced their output during the Communist era, but the government did keep alive the tradition of older Czechoslovak culture. Czech musicians continued to enjoy quite a reputation around the world, and classical music records were an important export product.

Czechoslovaks must have been very pleased when one of their poets, Jaroslav Seifert, was awarded the Nobel Prize for Literature in 1984. The government was not as happy. Mr. Seifert was one of the founders of Charter 77, the civil rights group organized to monitor the government's implementation of the Helsinki Accords. His poetry had not been published in Czechoslovakia for a number of years and was not generally available inside the country. Mr. Seifert's poetry is not really political, however. A typical example is his "Spring in the Fisherman's Net," a translation of which follows:

"In the fisherman's cork–fringed net
is spring. Young bulbs abound
on the trees and smile at us
when we look round.

In the fisherman's cork–fringed net
spaced out in three
are the stars; we are acquainted,
one always remembers me
and lights up the pathway home
in the dark at journey's end.
Not so many have the luck
to find in the stars their true girl friend.

In the fisherman's cork–fringed net
the wind is caught. Its laughter is the
laugh all women know
when they talk about men together.

In the fisherman's cork–fringed net
the claws are caught of tender fear. The
same fear that men know
when they talk about women
together."

(Tr, by ORBIS; used with permission)

Religion

The old communist regime was extremely hostile to religion and it went out of its way to make its practice difficult. It

Peace and quiet reign in the Krkonoše mountains   AP/Wide World Photo

was the Czechoslovakian Government, for example, which sponsored the creation of *Pacem in Terris*, whose essential purpose was to co–opt the church.

The Catholic Church was particularly restricted by the regime, probably because it is part of an international organization. Since the 1989 revolution, the Catholic Church has revealed that it maintained an underground church in Czechoslovakia during those years. This involved such things as secretly providing theological training in private apartments and homes, and ordaining hundreds of individuals as priests who then continued to work in their regular jobs while performing their priestly functions in secret.

As this underground church has emerged, people were surprised to learn of the double lives some of these individuals had been living. As an example, five faculty members at the communist–run Kosice University were actually Jesuit priests, including the Dean of the School of Civil Engineering. It also turns out that 1,200 of the approximately 3,000 priests in the country belong to religious orders like the Dominicans, Jesuits and Silesians, all of which were banned by the communists.

There were even some married men ordained as priests, plus some women

who became deacons. The newly appointed papal nuncio and the re–established Czech Bishops Conference are now attempting to sort all of these anomalies out.

The Future

The break–up of the Czech and Slovak Federal Republic, accomplished peacefully, has created a new political situation in the center of eastern Europe. It is not just that there are two nations where formerly there had been only one. It is rather that the reasons that drove them apart will continue to pull them farther apart in the future. Some people speak of a dividing line that runs north to south through eastern Europe. Slovakia lies east of that line, with a culture more akin to those of Ukraine and Romania than to the Czechs and Hungarians. The Czech Republic, by this reasoning, belongs to the west. If this thought has any validity, it is not good news for Slovakia, which will find itself falling ever farther behind its western Slavic neighbor. Change is, it is true, painful, but Slovakians may wish someday that they had stayed and paid the price.

The Republic of Hungary

View from Buda across the Danube to Pest, with Parliament building on the right.

Courtesy: Jon Markham Morrow

Area: 92,981 sq. km. = 35,900 sq. mi.
Population: 10,750,000 (projected).
Capital City Budapest (Pop. 3 million, projected).
Climate: Continental, with long, dry summers and severe winters.
Neighboring Countries: Czechoslovakia (North); Ukraine (East); Romania (Southeast); Serbia, Croatia (South); Slovenia, Austria (West).
Official Language: Hungarian (Magyar), a Finno–Ugrian language related to Finnish.
Other Principal Tongues: Languages of small minorities, German, Serbo–Croat, Slovak, Romanian.
Ethnic Background: Magyar (92.4%) Gypsy (3.3%); German (2.5%), Jewish (0.7%) other (1.1%).
Principal Religions: Roman Catholic and Protestant Christianity.
Chief Commercial Products: Machinery and equipment, agricultural and forest products, fuels, minerals, metals, consumer goods.
Currency: Forint.
Former Political Status: Independent,

1918–1945; Communist State, part of Soviet Bloc, 1945–1990.
National Day: April 4, Liberation Day.
Chief of State: Arpad Goncz, President.
Head of Government: Joszef Antall, Chairman, Council of Ministers.
National Flag: Horizontal stripes of red, white and green.

THE LAND AND THE PEOPLE

The Republic of Hungary, second smallest country in Eastern Europe, lies in the Middle Danube Basin. Two great rivers, the Danube and the Tisza, cross the rolling plains which cover most of the country. The Danube—one of Hungary's few natural frontiers—provides part of the border between Hungary and Czechoslovakia, then turns sharply southward, passes through Budapest, and divides Hungary. Contrary to legend, just like most rivers, its waters are not blue, but are usually brown because of the presence of silt from upstream areas.

To the east of the river lies the great fertile plain, a vast rangeland used for cattle grazing. The northeast section along the Slovak border is covered with forested mountains, abundant with wildlife. Here one can find limestone caverns and Europe's largest stalactite caves. Most importantly, the northeast contains Hungary's famous wine–producing centers, Eger and Tokaj. West of the Danube, plains turn into hills where the easternmost part of the Alps reach into western Hungary.

Although there are several theories concerning the origins of the Hungarian people, it is generally agreed that they are a Finno–Ugrian people, that is, they speak a language related to Finnish. In early historic times, they were first found inhabiting a part of the Russian Plain west of the Ural Mountains. Apparently suffering attacks from even more aggressive neighbors, several Hungarian tribes migrated westward, crossed the Carpathian Mountains and settled the broad plain that speads out from the Danube River east and south of the present–day city of Budapest.

244

HISTORY

Origins of the Hungarian State

Initially led by Arpad, for whom the first dynasty of Hungary was named, the Hungarians did not immediately settle down in central Europe. They terrorized most of the surrounding people until the tenth century when they were defeated by the German Emperor Otto I. Although there was earlier Christian missionary work among the Hungarians, Stephen I of the Arpad Dynasty "converted" the whole nation on Christmas Day, 1000 A.D. when he accepted a cross and crown sent by Pope Sylvester II. After his death, he was proclaimed a Saint by the Church in 1083.

At a later time in the history of Hungary, the Crown of St. Stephen became the symbol of highest authority. It represented the "unity" of all lands claimed by Hungary, including those not inhabited solely by Hungarians. During the 10th century, Slovakia was conquered; by 1003 Transylvania was under the Crown and a century later, Croatia, Slavonia and Dalmatia were united with Hungary. By the late 14th century, the Kingdom of Hungary contained extensive areas inhabited by Saxons (Germans), Slavs, Vlachs (Romanians of Wallachia, and Szecklers (Transylvanian Magyars living in the Carpathian Mountains).

During the Middle Ages, Hungary was not isolated from the rest of Europe. At the end of the 12th century a dynastic connection with France was established when King Bela III married the daughter of the French king; the marriage settlement showed that Hungary's national treasury equalled that of France. Hungary's early constitutional development resembled England's; the Hungarian king was forced to sign a document called the Golden Bull in 1222 which guaranteed the rights of the nobility, similar to the English *Magna Charta*.

A Mongol invasion in 1241 devastated Hungary and resulted in the loss of one-half of the population. However, the Mongols remained only for a year, so their occupation did not influence Hungary as it did Russia.

The Arpad Dynasty ended in 1301 and for two centuries Hungary was ruled by foreign nobility. In the 15th century one of Hungary's greatest kings, Mathias Corvinus, ascended the throne. An enlightened Renaissance monarch, he reformed the country's administrative and judicial systems, reorganized the army, founded universities and preserved Hungary's position as an important European power.

A Part of the Multi–National Hapsburg Empire

Hungary's defeat by the Ottoman

Turks in 1526 was a turning point in the nation's history. After a period of civil war, Hungary was partitioned between the Turks and the Hapsburgs; the central part was controlled by the Turks, the western part was controlled by the Hapsburgs. A third region consisting of Transylvania and sixteen neighboring counties was declared to be a self–governing principality. This area became the center of Hungarian culture during the next two centuries and gave Hungary such heroes as Stephen Bocskay and Gabor Bethlen. Transylvania was a model of religious tolerance among the states of Europe. Its princes, backed by armies, spread the principle throughout the rest of Hungary, forcing its adoption as the law of the land.

The country was the easternmost one to participate in the Protestant Reformation—the great spiritual movement of the 16th century. By the end of that century, 90% of the Hungarians were Protestant, but this figure was reduced later by the Counter–Reformation in the 17th century. However, the Protestant population of Hungary and Transylvania is now still the most significant of that group in Eastern Europe.

By the Peace of Karlowitz in 1699, most of Hungary, Transylvania and Croatia passed from Turkish to Austrian hands. This led to the suppression of protestantism, which had been tolerated by the Turks as a protection against the influence of the Roman Catholic Hapsburgs, and also to a weakening of the traditional Magyar aristocracy and the end of an elected monarchy in Hungary.

Francis Rakoczy led a rebellion in 1703 against Hapsburg domination. Although

Hungary c. 1350

Hungary

it was suppressed, it was a foretaste of the nationalist movement which shook the Empire a century later. During the 18th century, Hungary was tied to Austria by the *Pragmatic Sanction*, although it had its own *Diet* (assembly) composed of a Table of Magnates and a Table of Deputies.

The political climate of Hungary in the 1830's and 1840's was infected with the spirit of nationalism and reform. Radicals, such as Louis Kossuth, advocated independence from Austria; other more moderate leaders wanted Hungarian self–government within the Empire. A program known as the March Laws was adopted in 1848 which made Hungary practically independent, connected with Austria only through a unified monarchy.

This didn't last long—the various non–Magyar people, who numbered half of the population, soon realized that Hungary's independence simply meant that the Magyars could mistreat the minorities within the borders—independence for Hungary meant "Magyarization" for the rest of the people.

Louis Kossuth declared Hungary's complete independence in 1849, but within a few months, the revolution was suppressed by Austria with the aid of Russian troops. A highly centralized system of government was adopted. Many Magyars came to realize that a change in Hungary's status could only come within the limits of Austrian imperial government. The events that followed were largely the result of efforts of a moderate leader, Francis Deak, who constructed a plan of government which was the basis for the *Compromise of 1867*. This created the Dual Monarchy—Austria and Hungary were separated, each had its own constitution and parliament, but there were common ministries set up for finance, foreign affairs and war. The *Compromise* was important because it provided the basis for relations between Austria and Hungary until 1918.

It was natural that Hungary sided with the Central Powers (Germany–Austria) in World War I. Although some leaders favored negotiation of differences which led to the war, they agreed to refrain from quarreling over domestic issues in the so–called "Truce of God" (1914) after Hungary had entered the war. By 1916, opposition to the war had increased; the truce was broken and extremists began a propaganda campaign against the war. Two years later, one of these leaders, Michael Karolyi, became head of the government in a war–weary defeated country. This government proclaimed Hungary a republic in 1918 which lasted only five months; the immediate cause of its downfall was an ultimatum from the allies, demanding that Hungary surrender

Budapest: March 22, 1919. The pouring rain does not deter the celebration of Hungary's communist revolutionaries.

part of its territory. Unable to accept the demand, Karolyi resigned and the next day, March 21, 1919, the communists were in power.

The communist leadership of Hungary consisted of soldiers who learned of Marxism while prisoners of war in Russia. They had no political experience nor had any of them held any important post in the Hungarian labor movement of the prewar period. Upon their return, they formed the *Communist Party* of Hungary in November 1918 and spread propaganda of peace and prosperity among the mass of unemployed workers and soldiers, undermining the support that the moderates had. The government had attempted for the first time in February 1919 to suppress the activities of the young *Communist Party* by imprisoning its local leadership. Among these was Bela Kun, who had been a prisoner of war in Russia, fought in the Russian Civil War on the communist side, then organized the Hungarian section of the *Russian Communist Party* and played a leading role in founding the *Hungarian Communist Party*.

While in prison, the communists and some prominent members of the *Social Democratic Party*, the strongest political group in the country, decided to merge the two. This gave the communists the political strength with which to come to power without a violent revolution and without a popular following. Actually, their success was also because of nation-

alist sentiment—the ultimatum of the allies to the Karolyi government put it in an impossible position and gave the communists a national issue to use against the government.

Bela Kun became head of the *Hungarian Soviet Republic*. The government nationalized all banks and all enterprises which had more than 20 workers. All titles and ranks of the nobility were abolished. Private property was also ended, but the land from the great estates was not given to the peasants. The failure to carry out land reform had been one of the biggest mistakes of the ruling class and of the Karolyi government, and it eventually was one of the principal causes of the downfall of Bela Kun.

The young Soviet Republic collapsed because of Kun's inability to deal either with internal problems or with the threat of advancing Romanian troops. He resigned in 1919 and fled the country; the Romanian army occupied Budapest until November, when its western allies persuaded it to withdraw.

A number of pre–war politicians who had been loyal to the old regime had set up an opposition government during the time Kun held power. They raised a small army which, under the command of Admiral Nicholas Horthy, moved into the capital in late 1919, set up an anti–Bolshevik government and asked to be recognized by the allies. However, the response was a demand for a provisional government that would hold elections.

246

A coalition provisional government including the *Smallholder Party*, the *National Democratic Party* and the *Social Democrat Party* was formed; it announced elections to be held in January 1920. During the months before the elections, bands of terrorists roamed the country, attacking Jews, Social Democrats, members of trade unions and anyone they suspected had communist sympathies, or opposed the return of the conservatives to power.

The first post–war parliament was not representative of the country because of the terrorism which had prevailed during the campaign. The *Social Democrats* decided to boycott the elections because of the attacks on them. The new parliament, as it first order of business, took up the question of whether Hungary was still a monarchy; King Charles had renounced all power in 1918, but had not abdicated. The parliament's decision was that Hungary would continue to be a kingdom, but without a king—a Regent would be elected to act as head of state. From March 1920 to October 1944, Admiral Nicholas Horthy was Regent of Hungary. The question of Charles' claim to the throne ended in 1922 when he died.

Admiral Horthy

The *Treaty of Trianon*, signed on June 4, 1920, legalized the loss of territory which had been taking place since 1918. By its terms, a weakened Hungary had to submit to immense losses of territory. Slovakia and Ruthenia went to the recently–created Czechoslovakia; Croatia and Slavonia went to Yugoslavia; most of the Voivodina also went to that country. Transylvania and part of the Banat went to Romania. Hungary thus emerged from World War I losing almost three–fourths of its prewar territory and about two–thirds of its population. Since boundary lines could not follow ethnic divisions, a large Hungarian population was left in each of the lost areas.

Arguments during and after the Paris Peace Conference, which ended World War I, about which nation was "rightful" claimant to a piece of territory were not only unresolved, but were also largely very irrelevant. As in all wars, the victor took the spoils. After 1920, Hungarians used the word "dismembered" to describe Trianon Hungary. This was intended to produce the image of a broken state which for a thousand years had been held together under the legal and patriotic symbol of the Crown of St. Stephen.

The interwar period was one that appeared to be peaceful. A Conservative government led by Stephen Bethlen, a Protestant aristocrat from Transylvania, held power from 1921 to 1931. Desiring a return to the "good old days," but without the Hapsburgs, he ignored the need for land reform and had no understanding of the worker's and peasants' problems. Hungary was internationally isolated by the "Little Entente" consisting of Czechoslovakia, Romania and Yugoslavia, which wished to retain Hungarian lands gained by the Treaty of Trianon.

The world–wide economic depression of the 1930's and Hungary's continuing desire to regain lost lands led the nation down a disastrous path to alliance with Nazi Germany in World War II. Government leadership changed five times between 1931 and 1939, but the conservatives remained in control. Anti–Jewish measures were enacted which affected even the political leadership. The last of the five premiers, the patriotic statesman Count Paul Teleki, committed suicide as a dramatic protest against the invasion of Yugoslavia by Germans crossing Hungarian soil.

Diplomatic activity preceding World War II resulted in Hungary's regaining southern Slovakia and Ruthenia; northern Transylvania was recovered in 1940. Hungary signed the *Tripartite Pact* of the Axis powers in November 1940 and in spite of a treaty of friendship between Yugoslavia and Hungary, German troops crossed Hungary to invade Yugoslavia. The next question was whether Hungary should join in the war on Russia launched by the Germans. On the pretext that Russian planes had bombed Kosice, Premier Laslo Bardossy, siding with the military, published a declaration of war against Russia in mid–1941 without the consent of the Parliament. It is probable that the Russian aircraft were really German planes on which Russian markings had been painted.

Parliamentary institutions and political parties functioned until late in the war; there was no German occupation until March 1944 when this was prompted by the advance of the Red Army. A pro–German government dissolved political parties and increased the persecution of Jews to a level not previously experienced in Hungary.

The Regent, Admiral Horthy, and his advisers came to the conclusion in the fall of 1944 that the Axis powers could not win the war. Seeking a separate armistice, Hungary sent a diplomatic team to Moscow and, on October 15, 1944, announced that an armistice with Russia had been requested. Horthy's proclamation was poorly timed—the Germans had time to take control of the capital, seize him and force him to retract his proclamation; he was then forced to abdicate.

General Bela Miklos, the Hungarian Commander–in–Chief, joined with the Russian army when it crossed Hungary's borders. With Russian support, Committees of National Liberation were set up in the Russian–held areas, and a Provisional Government was formed in Debrecen. When Russian forces besieged Budapest, the pro–German puppet government fled, and in January 1945 the Provisional Government concluded an armistice in Moscow. The government of Hungary was based on a coalition of political parties which included three major ones: the *Hungarian Independence Front*, the *Social Democratic Party*, the *Communist Party*, and two smaller ones, the *Smallholder's Party* and the *National Peasant Party*.

According to the terms of the armistice, Hungary was directed to return to its 1938 frontiers; this provision was contained in the Peace Treaty of February 10, 1947. The agreement also provided for an Allied Control Commission with Soviet Marshal K. E. Voroshilov as its chairman.

Hungary Becomes a People's Republic

By a decree of March 1945, the Provisional Government started an extensive land reform program which was accomplished under the direction of Imre Nagy, the communist Minister of Agriculture. In probably what were the freest popular elections Hungarians had ever experienced, held in late 1945, the *Smallholders Party* received 57% of the vote. The *Communist Party* and the *Social Democratic Party* each received 17%. Zoltan Tildy, the leader of the *Smallholders* became Prime Minister and later President of the Hungarian Republic after the National Assembly proclaimed Hungary a republic in early 1946. Ferenc Nagy succeeded Tildy in the office of Prime Minister. Although the *Smallholders Party* had won a majority of the vote in the election, the government consisted of a coalition; Imre Nagy became Minister of the Interior.

It is inaccurate to describe the process by which the communists came to dominate the Hungarian government as a "seizure" of power. In reality, this was

Hungary

achieved quite slowly and cautiously over a three–year period. The leadership of the *Smallholders Party* was picked off individually in a variety of ways. Bela Kovacs, secretary of the party, was arrested by the Russians on charges of conspiracy. Ferenc Nagy was blackmailed into resigning by a threat of physical harm to his son. Losses of leadership and continued attacks on members weakened the *Smallholders Party* to the point it could not provide any real opposition to the communists.

The *Communist Party* and the *Social Democratic Party* merged in mid–1948 to form the *Hungarian Workers' Party*. Tildy was replaced by a communist sympathizer in that year, and communists dominated the cabinet. The final move was made in February 1949 with the establishment of the *Hungarian Independent People's Front*, a combination of all parties and mass organizations. It presented a single-list of candidates which received 96.5% of the vote in May 1949. The newly elected National Assembly proclaimed Hungary a *People's Republic* and adopted a constitution reflecting Hungary's official position as a member of the Soviet bloc.

The Stalinist Period

The years from 1949 to 1953 have been called the "Stalinist period" in Hungary and other East European nations. Political control of the party, and through the party, over Hungary, was wielded by Mathias Rakosi, a dedicated communist since 1918. He had been a prisoner of war in Russia during World War I, returned to Hungary in 1918 and helped Bela Kun form the *Hungarian Communist Party*, held office in the Hungarian Soviet Republic, left Hungary when the republic collapsed and worked for the *Communist International (Comintern)* for a number of years.

Rakosi tried to reorganize the outlawed *Communist Party* in 1924, but was arrested and spent most of the next 15 years in prison until 1940. He was then traded to the Soviet Union for some Hungarian flags that the Russian army had captured in 1849. He returned to his homeland in 1944 and became Secretary General of the *Communist Party*, Deputy Prime Minister until 1952 and Prime Minister from 1952 until 1953.

Under his supervision, a reorganized secret police conducted a purge of the party, attacked rich landowners, undermined the churches and kept a close watch over social life in general. The most dramatic event of this period was the trial of Laszlo Rajk, a "home communist" and one–time Minister of the Interior and Foreign Affairs. He was accused on falsified evidence of conspiring with Yugoslavia's Tito and was executed in 1949. This was followed by a purge of the party membership which eliminated from it all

those suspected of having nationalist or anti–Rakosi sentiments. In the process, several thousand party members were also imprisoned.

By 1949 the new regime had introduced the Stalin model of economic planning with its emphasis on central decision–making and heavy industry. All industry employing more than ten workers had been nationalized and a program for the collectivization of agriculture had been initiated.

Lacking most raw materials, Hungary had never placed any great stress on heavy industry, but had concentrated on the development of agriculture based on the processing of its products and the manufacture of consumer goods. The new emphasis on heavy industry of the first Five–Year Plan accordingly produced spectacular growth totals in the beginning. Heavy industrial production increased fivefold and the engineering industry showed a sevenfold increase in productivity over 1938.

By 1953, however, serious shortages had begun to appear in both raw materials and fuel supplies, and a serious disproportion had begun to appear between heavy and light industry. Agriculture was beginning to stagnate under the combination of the policy of collectivization accompanied by a decline in investment. Wages and salaries had risen less rapidly than consumer prices, with the result that there was a 20% decline in the general standard of living between 1948 and 1953.

The New Course and Revolution

There had been some muted criticism of these developments even before March 1953, but Stalin's death at the time brought these out into the open. The lead was taken by Imre Nagy, who challenged Rakosi's handling of the economy, accusing him of forcing the tempo of industrialization all out of proportion to the country's resources. Rakosi was forced to step down as Chairman of the Council of Ministers—though he retained his position as head of the *Hungarian Workers' Party*—and Nagy was named in his place.

In his first speech to the Parliament in 1953, Nagy presented a program which later became known as the "New Course." It included an emphasis on consumer goods instead of heavy industry, abolition of collective farms when such was desired by a majority of the workers, and the release of many political prisoners. Among those released was Janos Kadar.

Continued disputes over these new policies, particularly in agriculture, coupled with a failure to gain support of important party members, led to Nagy's resignation in 1955. He was replaced by Andras Hegedus and Hungary returned

to the old policies of heavy industrialization and collectivization. After the unkept promises of the New Course and a disappointing return to earlier policies, protests from writers and scholars began to be heard in the autumn of 1955. The following summer, the *Petofi Circle*, named after a revolutionary poet killed in 1849, was formed, providing a forum for debate among those who were critical of government.

In an effort to appease the critics, the Soviet Union brought increased pressure on the Hungarian party to dismiss Rakosi. He resigned in mid–1956 and was replaced by Erno Gero. This did not quiet the discord. A number of party leaders who had been executed in the purges of 1949 were reburied with honor, the funerals turned into a mass demonstration against the government. A few weeks later, the students of Szeged University in the city of that name organized a non–communist youth organization.

By late 1956 news of the Szeged students and of the anti–government activities in neighboring Poland reached Budapest. This prompted students and writers to draw up a resolution and to hold a public demonstration expressing sympathy for the Polish cause. Their plan was to march to a statue of General Joseph Bem, a Polish soldier who had fought with the Hungarians against the Austrians and Russians in 1848–49. The resolution demanded the evacuation of Soviet troops from Hungary, the return of Nagy as Prime Minister, free elections and freedom of speech and press. This was not so much in opposition to communism as it was in favor of the development of some form of socialist democracy.

Although planned only as a demonstration, the October 23 events turned swiftly into a mass revolution. This was due to poor judgment of officials and the emotions generated by the mass activity. The Minister of the Interior responded to news of the planned demonstration by banning it, and then agreeing not to interfere. The demonstrators, joined by members of the communist youth movement, marched reading the immensely patriotic poem "Arise, Magyars" and the resolution. By evening a huge crowd had gathered in front of Parliament calling for Nagy, who addressed them briefly and asked them to disperse.

Later in the evening, two specific events triggered an uprising; an untactful and accusing speech by First Secretary Erno Gero which denounced the demonstrators, and the refusal of the radio station director to broadcast the resolution. Fighting which first broke out between the demonstrators and the secret police, quickly spread into the working class districts. A gigantic statue of Stalin in the

Soviet tanks guard the street intersection leading to the Danube Bridge in Budapest on November 5, 1956.　　AP/Wide World Photo

center of Budapest was toppled; because only the boots remained, the site is now popularly called "Boot Square."

During the night, Soviet tanks appeared and fighting erupted between Soviet troops and revolutionaries who were by then supported by parts of the Hungarian army. The fighting spread even further into the countryside, where Workers' Councils and Revolutionary Councils were organized to replace the local communist administrations.

On October 24, Nagy replaced Hegedus as Chairman of the Council of Ministers and the next day Janos Kadar replaced Erno Gero as First Secretary of the *Hungarian Workers' Party*. Anastas Mikoyen was in Budapest at the time as a representative of the Soviet Politburo. He accepted political changes and negotiated an agreement with Nagy and Kadar for the withdrawal of the Soviet army from Hungary.

Mikoyan's agreement was obviously based on the premise that Nagy and Kadar, as communists, were committed to the maintenance of communist control in Hungary. However, Nagy, in announcing the Soviet troop withdrawal agreement, also promised to abolish the secret police and to bring representatives of non–communist parties into the government.

Reports reached Budapest on November 1 that Soviet troops had stopped their withdrawal and, reinforced now by additional Soviet tanks of the latest design,

were heading back toward Budapest. Nagy responded by announcing Hungary's withdrawal from the Warsaw Pact (the military organization of Eastern Europe presided over by the Soviets), committing Hungary to a policy of neutrality and appealing for help from the United Nations.

Soviet troops attacked Budapest on November 4, 1956. At the same time, Kadar, now in eastern Hungary, having left Budapest on the evening of November 1–2, proclaimed the establishment of a "revolutionary government of peasants and workers" to replace the "fascist" Nagy government. Although there was a great deal of resistance by the Hungarian people, a basically unarmed people were no match for Soviet tanks, and the revolution was ruthlessly suppressed. Janos Kadar, First Secretary of the Communist Party, was back in power with the backing of Soviet troops.

Politics Since 1956

Kadar was in a difficult position after 1956 because he lacked party support and general popular support. Within the party, he was opposed by those who favored internal reform, who accused him of selling out the revolution. The Stalinists in the party wanted to return to the style of the Rakosi era.

Large segments of the population, including students, writers and workers who had played such a large role in the revolution, viewed Kadar as a Soviet

puppet. He was in power only because he had the support of the man who had suppressed the revolution, Nikita Khrushchëv, leader of the Soviet Union.

During the two years after the uprising, Kadar repressed various social groups and political parties which opposed his government. Hundreds of people associated with the revolution were imprisoned.

In 1959–1960 there were signs that the government was willing to allow a relaxation of its tight control. Partial amnesty was declared and several hundred political prisoners were released. After 1961, Kadar adopted policies intended to win popular support. The "People's Courts" that had convicted the revolutionaries were abolished and in 1962 Rakosi and Gero were expelled from the party, demonstrating Kadar's desire to break completely with the Stalinist policies of the past. Although he became Prime Minister in addition to First Secretary of the party, there was no return to the so–called "personality cult" of which Stalin had been accused after his death.

Kadar reported to a party congress in 1962 that collectivization had been completed the previous year, with 90% of the farmland in cooperative and state farms. Most industrial products were from socialist enterprises. In foreign policy, he expressed complete support for the Soviet policy of peaceful coexistence, for its actions in the Cuban missile

Hungary

crisis and its position in the disputes with China.

The congress, in turn, adopted Kadar's "one nation" policy, which declared in effect that the government was willing to cooperate with anyone who was not actively opposed to the communist party. In this respect, it was willing, he said, to recruit competent, non–party members for government service. Further liberalization was evident by 1963, when a general amnesty was declared, freeing additional political prisoners numbered in the thousands. Travel restrictions were lowered and tourism increased.

Kadar's popularity greatly increased as a result of these changes and that was a considerable help when Nikita Khrushchëv fell from power in November 1964. Although now "on his own," Kadar managed to hold on to power, though he did have to relinquish the office of Chairman of the Council of Ministers in mid–1965. Julius Kallai got that position,

while Kadar remained First Secretary of the party.

Kallai was Chairman of the Council of Ministers until 1967. He was replaced by Jeno Fock, who held the position until 1975. Fock's resignation came shortly after the Eleventh Congress of the *Hungarian Socialist Workers Party*, where he took personal responsibility for his government's failure in its "Leninist duty" to adequately supervise the functioning of the national economy. His resignation "for reasons of health" almost certainly reflected the Soviet leadership's dissatisfaction with the relatively freewheeling style of economic management in Hungary under the "New Mechanism." His successor as Chairman of the Council of Ministers was Gyorgy Lazar, who held the position until 1987.

The Eleventh Congress of the *HSWP* tightened party regulations by introducing a ban on "propagating dissent," almost certainly a gesture meant to appease

their Soviet comrades. In another gesture, this time aimed at Hungarian workers, the congress also endorsed the reduction of the work week to 44 hours by 1980.

Although he held no state office after 1965, Kadar continued to be the key leader in the political system. As such, he tended to run a rather collegial Politburo, though he did not hesitate to dismiss those members who got too far out of line. In general, he tended to prefer technocrats rather than political types. This may have been because he recognized that they were needed to carry out his economic reforms, but he could not have been blind to the fact that they were also less likely to be rivals for power.

Kadar, in fact, always tried to limit the personal power of his associates. In 1978, for example, he dismissed his deputy, Bela Biscku, because the latter had ambitiously extended his personal control over the party apparatus, the military and the security forces. It was the purge of Biscku which opened the way for Karoly Nemeth, who became Kadar's deputy for the party apparatus at this time. Nemeth, although not particularly liked either within the party or by the Hungarian public, was officially designated as Kadar's deputy at the 13th Congress of the Hungarian Workers' Party in March 1985. Nemeth was considered by many to be a likely Kadar successor. In June 1987, however, he was promoted to the largely ceremonial post of President of the Presidential Council instead.

It was also at this time that Karoly Grosz replaced the ailing Gyorgy Lazar as Chairman of the Council of Ministers. Grosz, former party boss in Budapest, had often been mentioned as a potential Kadar successor, but he was only one of three potential candidates at this time. The other two were Janos Berecz, former editor of the party newspaper, *Nepszabadag*, and Laszlo Marothy. Berecz, party chief ideologist, was promoted to the Politburo in June 1987. Marothy, Deputy Chairman of the Council of Ministers, had been a member of the Politburo since 1976. Although Berecz often took conservative positions on issues, he appealed to many party intellectuals because of the quality of his arguments. Marothy was supported by those who were attracted by his reputation for moderation and pragmatism.

The matter came to a head in May 1988 at a special Hungarian Socialist Workers' Party Conference. It had become clear in the months leading up to the conference that Kadar intended to retire and so, for the first time, there was something of a campaign for the office of party leader. Grosz, who had previously had a reputation as a hard–liner, put himself forward as an aggressive and energetic pragmatist

Peasant girls in native costume in the courtyard of Parliament.

Courtesy: Jon Markham Morrow

who supported further reform. He also adopted an open style reminiscent of that of Gorbachëv.

It was Grosz who was selected by the party conference to succeed Kadar as General Secretary. As it turned out, however, this was not just a succession but, rather, something approaching a revolution in the party. In addition to the appointment of Grosz, eight of the 13 members of the Politburo were dropped, along with 40 percent of the Central Committee. Kadar was among those dropped from the Politburo, though he was given the honorary title of party president. Marothy was also dropped, though Berecz kept his seat.

Six persons were added to the Politburo, including two well-known advocates of radical reform, Rezso Nyers and Imre Poszgay. Both had previously been Politburo members, but had been dropped because of their political positions.

Nyers, a member of the Economic Institute of the Hungarian Academy of Sciences and a former Minister of Finance, was one of the principal authors of the 1968 reform. Several years ago, he wrote an article for the Budapest daily (Magyar Hirlap) in which he advocated a larger political role for the Hungarian parliament. In 1985, when the party established multiple candidacies and moved to give a larger role to parliament, it was implementing most of what Nyers had advocated in his article. Imre Pozsgay, Chairman of the Patriotic Peoples' Front since 1982, attempted to give this umbrella organization new life and more influence. He had also argued that the party ought "to withdraw from its present relationship with the state and society—and to establish a new relationship." In addition, he was on record as supporting the creation of autonomous interest groups, including, under certain circumstances, independent trade unions.

Grosz, speaking to the party conference following his election as General Secretary, promised that he would seek "to expand democratic procedures within the party to match some of the 'practical advantages' of western multiparty systems." Later, in an televised address to the Hungarian people, he admitted past mistakes on behalf of the party and promised a new approach "in public life, in production, in human sectors and other fields."

Gorbachëv was quick to put his stamp of approval on the new General Secretary, calling him "a principled communist and authoritative leader" and wishing him "big successes . . . in tackling the task of improving and renovating his socialist society on Hungarian soil." Grosz continued as Chairman of the Council of Ministers until November 1988, when he turned the office over to Miklos Nemeth. Nemeth, a 40–year–old economist, had been added to the Politburo in May 1988. Known as a strong advocate of change, he was described by Janos Lukacs, another Politburo member, as a "young, dynamic workhorse."

His biography indicates that, after graduating from Karl Marx University in Budapest, he studied at Harvard University. He began working for the party's economic department in 1981. In 1987, he became a member of the Central Committee and, simultaneously, party secretary for economic policy. Mark Palmer, American Ambassador to Hungary in 1988, characterized Nemeth as an affable man who would be easy for the West to work with. "He has," Ambassador Palmer went on to say,

"very rich experience in the area of economic reform. He clearly has the strong backing of Grosz and a great deal of experience in the West. We believe he is committed to reform and will push ahead."

Nemeth's appointment was, in fact, further evidence that the reformers were in more or less complete charge, though they still retained their alliance with the moderate Grosz. And having placed their supporters in all of the key positions, they turned their attention to the subject of institutional reform.

There was some question about where all of this was leading and the situation became even more muddled in December 1988, when Imre Pozsgay spoke out publicly in favor of a multi–party system. One week later, Karoly Grosz rejected Pozsgay's suggestion, but that actually marked the beginning of a struggle within the party over the issue. The matter was largely resolved in February 1989, when the party announced further details of proposed constitutional changes. A multi–party system was to be formally established and additional political parties were to be permitted to operate freely. The draft also provided for the creation of a new executive Presidency. Among other things, the President would be commander–in–chief of the armed forces. Free elections were also scheduled for 1990.

Although the program had not formally gone into effect, independent political groups immediately began to form. In March 1989 the first of those, the Democratic Forum, had its first convention in Budapest. In addition, the Smallholders Party and the Hungarian Socialist Party— both of which had been part of the first government coalition (along with the Communist Party) in 1945—were revived and began to operate as independent groups.

However, the HSWP's commitment to multi–party elections was too much for conservatives still within the party and they opposed it. To resolve the issue, Grosz proposed at a plenum of the Central Committee in April 1989 that the Politburo "lay down its powers and hold a new secret ballot on its composition." In the subsequent voting, four remaining conservatives were removed from the Politburo, including Janos Berecz. Two persons, Mihaly Jasso and Pal Vastag, were added. The size of the Politburo was thus reduced from 11 to 9. In a separate move, Janos Kadar was dropped from the Central Committee and his title of honorary president was abolished. He died soon afterwards.

Two months later, the party went through yet another leadership shake–up. In June, the Politburo and the office of General Secretary were both abolished. They were replaced by a four–member Presidium, with Rezso Nyers as President. Karoly Grosz was made a member of the Presidium but lost most of his power.

The winds of change continued to blow strongly in 1989. In October, the party dropped its old name and became the Hungarian Socialist Party. Somewhat later, a group of party stalwarts resurrected the old party. As other parties had begun to operate, it became clear that it had little chance of winning in the upcoming free elections, but it still hoped to install its man as president while the HSWP controlled the legislature. That hope was dashed in November when opposition parties forced a referendum to postpone election of the president until after free elections; the referendum favored this move.

In March 1990, in the first free elections since 1945, the Hungarian people repudiated both the communist–reformist Hungarian Socialist Party and the communist Hungarian United Workers Party. No single party received a majority but it was the centrist Democratic Forum that came in first with approximately 42% of the vote and therefore won the right to organize the new government. A coalition was formed with two smaller parties, the Independent Smallholders and the Christian Democrats with Jozsef Antall, leader of Democratic Forum, as Chairman of the Council of Ministers. Together the three parties control more than 60% of the seats in the new Parliament. The main opposition party is the left–liberal Alliance of Free Democrats, with the Hungarian Socialist Party reduced to a tiny remnant on the left.

The greatest problems faced by the new government were all related to the state of the economy. As a result, most of its efforts have focused on establishing policies that would move Hungary more rapidly toward a market economy. It was

Hungary

President and Mrs. Arpad Goncz

already the furthest along this path of all the Eastern European nations, but state–owned enterprises still constituted 90 percent of the productive sector of the economy.

Thus far, the government has drawn up a long list of laws and regulations aimed at fostering private initiative, encouraging direct foreign investment, and developing private capital markets, and it has committed itself to reducing the state sector to less than 50% by 1995. Foreign investment is up and a number of companies have been partly or wholly privatized. But the process is really only at the beginning.

Meanwhile, the government is being criticized by some who argue that it is moving too slowly and by others who fear that it is dissipating the nation's wealth. Some of this showed up in the local elections in October 1990, when the parties of the government coalition lost badly. In Budapest, the two major opposition parties won over 50 percent of the vote. In most places, independents won, however, possibly indicating a distaste for the political partisanship that has recently dominated debate. None of this threatened the coalition's majority in parliament, however. In fact, the government had regained much of its popularity in the country by the beginning of 1992 and Prime Minister Antall, though still not overwhelmingly popular, was conceded to be the most effective leader in eastern Europe.

Foreign Policy

With the installation of Hungary's first non–communist government since 1945, Hungary's foreign policy will change but perhaps not all that much. The most important change will come in its altered attitude toward the former

The Crown of St. Stephen returned

Soviet Union. Relations are expected to remain friendly, but Hungary will no longer look to Russia for its lead.

Under the communists, alignment with the Soviet Union was a basic component of foreign policy. For example, Hungary followed the lead of the USSR in breaking relations with Israel in 1967 and it joined the Soviet boycott of the 1984 Los Angeles Summer Olympics. It also tended to support the Soviets in quarrels with the People's Republic of China.

On the other hand, Hungary always maintained a more independent position vis–à–vis the Soviet Union than either Bulgaria or Czechoslovakia. Hungarians were frank about their desire for better relations with the West. Although they participated fully in the CMEA, and the Soviet Union remained their single largest trading partner, they also pushed to increase their trade with the west and were the first to call for reform of the CMEA.

Trade between Hungary and the Federal Republic of Germany grew greatly, exceeding 5.2 billion Deutsche Marks (about $2.3 billion) by 1985. This was roughly 30% of all Hungarian trade with the west, making the Federal Republic Hungary's second largest trading partner after the Soviet Union. There was also extensive cooperation between the two countries designed to facilitate the transfer of technology. Approximately 350 cooperative agreements were signed between West German and Hungarian firms before 1989.

Austrian entrepreneurs have also been active investors recently. According to the Hungarian Government, approximately 1880 joint ventures were established between foreign investors and local partners in the first eighteen months of the new democratic regime. More than 60% percent of the investors were either Austrian or German. US–Hungarian relations have been relatively good since 1973, when the two countries signed an agreement settling claims for damages to American property during World War ll. The U.S. government also returned the St. Stephen's Crown, in American custody since World War ll, to Hungary in 1978. It also granted Hungary "most–favored nation" trade status at about the same time.

Relations, already very good even under the reform communist leadership, have become even warmer since 1989. Arpad Goncz, the new Hungarian President, paid an unofficial visit to the United States in September 1990, followed by an official visit by Prime Minister Jozsef Antall in October. During the visit, President Bush publicly called on the IMF to lend up to $5 billion to the new democracies of Eastern Europe, including Hungary. The United States has, in general, been a strong supporter of multilateral economic assistance to Hungary. One problem that Hungary has with its neighbors is over minorities. Significant Magyar–speaking populations are to be found in Romania, Czechoslovakia and Yugoslavia. Romania, with between 1.7 and 2 million ethnic Hungarians, has the most, but there are also at least 600,000 in Czechoslovakia, mainly in the area of the plain in southern Slovakia. There are fewer in Yugoslavia, and they are mainly to be found in the area of the autonomous province of Voivodina. The "Yugo" Magyars have become a particular problem for Hungary since 1989, however. Serbia's destruction of the government of the autonomous province of the Voivodina has put these Magyars directly under Belgrade. With the withdrawal of Croatia and Slovenia from the collapsing Yugoslavia in 1991–92, these Magyars became hostages to Hungary's actions as Serbia accused Hungary of assisting the Croatians. On a number of occasions, Yugoslav People's Army troops or military aircraft carried out incursions across the border into Hungary. As a current member of the UN Security Council, Hungary has supported sending in UN peacekeeping troops and has argued that the UN ought to be given a greater role in protecting human and minority rights. In his address to the Security Council in January 1992, Geza Jeszenszky, the Hungarian Foreign Minister, argued that:

"protecting human and minority rights is more than a legal and humanitarian issue: It is an integral part of international security. Therefore, a firm assertion of these rights by the UN Security Council is indispensable."

Hungary had a running controversy with Romania concerning Romanian treatment of ethnic Magyars during the latter years of the Ceausescu regime, but the matter has become more low–key since the fall of Ceaucescu. Hungarians fear that the Romanians are attempting to "denationalize" the Hungarians of Transylvania. The situation in Czechoslovakia is similar, with Slovak Magyars claiming discrimination. This has become an issue from the Slovak side as well as nationalists, campaigning for Slovak independence, object to the lack of Magyar support. The Magyars support a common Czechoslovak state because they feel their rights would be better guaranteed in a common state than a Slovak one.

Although the new non–communist government has only been in power since May 1990, it has already established diplomatic relations with Israel and the Vatican and signed an agreement with the Soviet Union that resulted in the removal of all Soviet troops by July 1991. Hungary was also instrumental in the demise of

the Warsaw Pact. When the Hungarian Government announced that it intended to leave the Warsaw Pact, Moscow, apparently fearing that other members would join the exodus, proposed that the military aspects of the organization be terminated as of April 1, 1991. The Warsaw Pact plus the CMEA, Hungary's other formal tie to Moscow, were formally dissolved on July 1, 1991.

Hungary was admitted to membership in the 23–nation Council of Europe in November 1990, the first East European nation to seek and receive admittance. Hungary became an associate member of the European Community in December 1991, along with Poland and Czechoslovakia. This will give most Hungarian industrial goods duty– free entry to the EC. It hopes to achieve full membership by the year 2000.

The Nature of the Regime

Hungary is a multiparty democracy in transition to a free market economy. A new constitution was adopted in 1990 which created a parliamentary form of government with a ceremonial President of the Republic as chief of state. The President is elected by the National Assembly for a term of four years. The National Assembly is the new fulcrum of power, with the Chairman of the Council of Ministers as the country's political leader.

The Hungarian Government

The President of the Republic is Arpad Goncz, a well–known writer and dissident. He was jailed for six years after the Hungarian Revolution of 1956. A founding member of the *Alliance for Free Democrats*, he became the head of the National Writers Association in 1989, then was

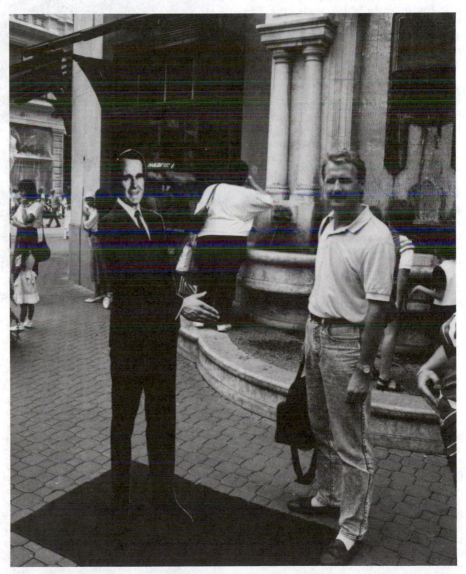

On a Budapest square, a German tourist wonders whether or not he should be photographed with a cardboard likeness of President Bush

Photo by Jon Markham Morrow

Hungary

elected President of the National Assembly (interim President) in May 1990. He was elected President of the Republic on August 3, 1990.

The Chairman of the Council of Ministers is the head of government and the individual responsible for government policy. He is nominated by the President and confirmed by the National Assembly. He can be removed if he loses a vote of confidence in the National Assembly.

Hungary's first non–communist Chairman of the Council of Ministers is Jozsef Antall, who assumed office in May 1990. Leader of the Democratic Forum, he heads a coalition government consisting of his own party plus *Independent Smallholders* and the *Christian Democrats.*

The National Assembly is a single chamber parliament with a total of 386 seats. Its members are elected for a four year term in an election that is part proportional, part constituency. The *Democratic Forum* controls 165 seats, the *Free Democrats* 92 and the *Independent Smallholders* 43. The remaining 86 seats are divided up among a number of smaller parties and independents.

The Economy

The economy which the Antall Government inherited when it took power in May 1990 was one which had been moving away from an orthodox communist command economy for a good number of years, though it still retained and retains many aspects of that original pattern. The deviation began in the 1960's under the leadership of Janos Kadar. For the first six years after he became First Secretary of the communist *Hungarian Workers' Party* after the Soviet intervention to put down the Hungarian Revolution, Kadar enforced the old policies of heavy industrialization and collectivization which the regime had tried to get away from after the death of Stalin in 1953. The results were predictably unsatisfactory.

In 1963, with the economy in extreme stress and performing badly, Kadar came across a reform proposal by a Professor Liberman at the University of Kiev. Intrigued, Kadar decided to try out some of Professor Liberman's ideas. To encourage individual enterprise, the Hungarian government granted a one–year tax exemption to new artisan–type enterprises and guaranteed them access to supplies of raw materials. The result was an immediate increase in the number of working artisans in the villages, a welcome reversal of the long–time trend of migration to the cities. The reform also led to increased service facilities in the cities as tailors and repairmen and mechanics set themselves up in their own shops.

In 1966, a more extensive economic reform began to be discussed. This program, which eventually became known

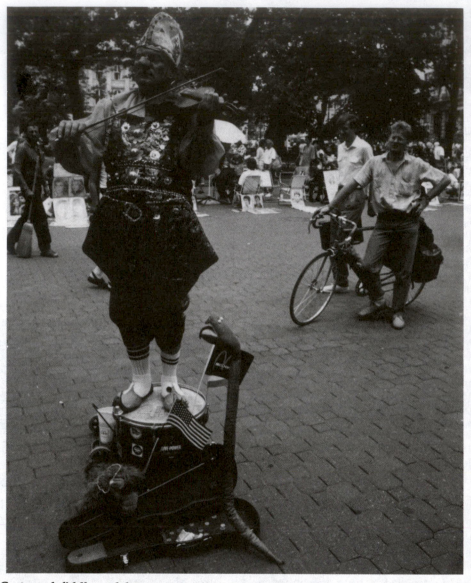

Costumed fiddler celebrates two significant events of 1989—President Bush's official visit and the opening of Budapest's McDonald's restaurant (note U.S. and McDonald's flags below)

Photo by Jon Markham Morrow

as the "New Economic Mechanism," went into effect in 1968. The New Economic Mechanism postulated the continuation of central planning but proposed a change in the nature of that planning. Instead of concentrating on a minute, day–to–day control over the economy, central planning experts would concentrate on long–range goals.

Day–to–day management of the economy was delegated to the managers of individual enterprises, who were enjoined to go forward with the plan based on market demand. Although industry would remain state–owned, the state's control would be exercised indirectly, by general credit and interest policies and, in the case of individual enterprises, by means of loans provided to finance technological innovations. Wages were to be established by individual factories,

though within guidelines set out by the central planners. Most important of all, the government gradually relinquished its control over prices. Before the reform began, there were over one million administered prices; by mid–1970, the figure had dropped to just over one thousand.

The New Economic Mechanism differed from Czech economic proposals of the same time period in envisioning a continued positive role for the central planners. It was also not accompanied by a parallel discussion of possible political reforms. It therefore managed to survive the Soviet invasion of Czechoslovakia. Kadar's condemnation of the Czech experiments and his participation in the invasion of Czechoslovakia were additional significant factors.

The plan had beneficial effects

throughout the economy, but this was particularly true with regard to agriculture. The end of artificially low prices for agricultural products and the accompanying increase in average earnings in the countryside increased incentives and led to greatly increased production. The change was spectacular. In the mid–1960's, Hungary was a net importer of agricultural products. By the end of the 1960's, it had become a net exporter. In 1990, approximately 30 percent of exports were agricultural products.

The Hungarian Government instituted some further economic changes in 1984 which amounted to a strengthening of the New Economic Mechanism. As of January 1, 1985, approximately three–quarters of all enterprises became eligible for a new type of management system which gave them almost complete autonomy. In addition, a new set of financial rules was issued whereby efficient companies were permitted to pay higher wages and were actually encouraged to get rid of unnecessary employees.

The plan called for state subsidies to be eliminated and those inefficient enterprises which couldn't make it on their own were to be allowed to go bankrupt. Only one major company was permitted to go bankrupt at this time, however, and all of its viable parts, along with

Hungarian children at the library

employees, were taken over by other companies.

Following the change in political leadership in May 1988, a further change in the economic program was adopted by the party in July. Essentially, this extended and intensified the reform program of the government, continuing an austerity program begun in 1987. Submitted by Miklos Nemeth, the new Chairman of the Council of Ministers, its object was to create "a genuine commodity,

monetary, capital and labor market." A long–range plan, it contemplated several years of austerity and at least 2–3 years of little or growth before a turn–round would occur.

The most important change had to do with Hungary's small private sector. This sector, which constituted only 4–5% of the overall economy in 1988, was to be encouraged to grow until it became approximately 30%. Hungary also joined the International Monetary Fund, the

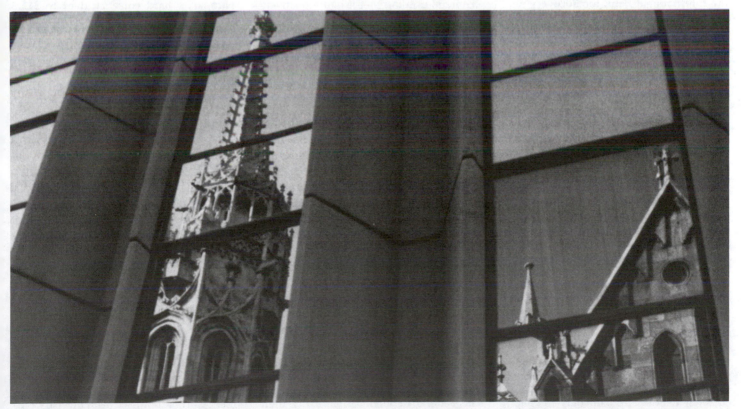

The Hilton Hotel's mirrored facade reflects the Gothic spires of Matthias Church in Old Budapest, site of the coronation of Charles II as King of Hungary in 1916.

Courtesy: Jon Markham Morrow

Hungary

Harvesting corn on a collective farm

Bank for International Settlements, and the International Bank for Recovery and Development (The World Bank) while the communists were still in control. That same government also established a realistic exchange rate for the Forint, its national currency.

Reorientation toward world markets was undertaken. In the 1970's, it began negotiating with western companies for the opening of manufacturing facilities in Hungary. The most famous of the products is probably Levi jeans, which Hungary exports throughout Eastern Europe and the Soviet Union. In the 1980's, a number of other western companies began operating in Hungary. Among those was McDonald's, which opened its first store in downtown Budapest in 1987. Although fast food restaurants are still pretty much a foreign concept in Eastern Europe, the Hungarian government began opening its own fast food outlets in 1984 under the English name of "City Grill." They proved to be so popular that a state catering firm signed a contract with McDonald's to franchise the real thing.

On the negative side, Hungarian borrowings to finance the importation of Western technology had raised its hard–currency debt to approximately $8 billion by 1981. When the Polish economy collapsed, Western bankers began to worry about Hungary's debt as well. The government, arguing that it had a relatively well–managed, market–oriented economy, managed to retain its access to Western credit. For example, between 1982 and 1984, it received a $596 million medium–term credit from the International Monetary Fund, negotiated a $200 million loan from a West German bank and was awarded a mandate for a $250 million six–year loan.

Nevertheless, the regime also instituted austerity measures designed to produce a positive balance of trade with Western nations. Between 1981 and 1984 the government managed to reduce its hard currency debt by about $1 billion. Then the government began easing off its austerity program and this, combined with a drop in the prices of its major exports caused its hard currency debt to begin growing again. Hungary's export situation worsened in 1986 with the country actually running a deficit in its convertible currency trade, instead of an expected surplus. This led the government to opt for a new austerity program at the beginning of 1987.

Hungary's adverse trade balance worried foreign bankers and it came under international financial pressure again. The Federal Republic of Germany then came to Hungary's rescue with a credit of a billion marks ($526 million). Additional borrowing since that time has raised Hungary's hard currency debt to $17.3 billion. This is potentially a very serious situation for Hungary. In 1989, debt servicing consumed 38.5% of Hungary's hard–currency earnings. The ratio has dropped since that time, however. Hungary is currently running a favorable balance of trade, tourism receipts are up, and foreign direct investments, some $1.46 billion in 1991, had grown by another $1.08 billion by September 1992. It is estimated that Hungary has been the recipient of more foreign investment than the rest of eastern Europe combined.

General Motors has invested $193 million in a joint venture project with Hungary's Raba Factory to produce 200,000 engines and assemble an estimated 15,000 Opel Astra automobiles a year. The first Opel Astra rolled off the assembly line in March 1992. Suzuki, a Japanese automobile company, will begin manufacturing Suzuki Swifts at its plant in the town of Esztergom in the fall of 1992. Ford has paid $80 million for a plant to produce electronic components for cars. General Electric purchased Tungsram, Hungary's lighting manufacturer, in 1989. Other American companies investing in Hungary include the Digital Equipment Corporation, Schwinn Bicycle Company, Cartier, Apple Computer, and US West.

In addition, the Swiss have entered into joint ventures in pharmaceuticals and food, and Ikea, the Swedish–based furniture group, has opened its first store in Budapest. Austrian and German firms have also been large investors, with more than 60% of all joint ventures in 1990 being sponsored by nationals of these two countries.

Hungary is also a major recipient of loans from the new European Bank for Reconstruction and Development, formally established in April 1991 with an initial capitalization of 12.4 billion.

Its greatest problem is that of privatization of industry, of course. Foreign investment, particularly joint ventures, has made a contribution, but it could become a political issue if a significant percentage of Hungarian industry were to pass into foreign hands. That is not yet a major problem, since foreign investments currently constitute only 4% of the gross domestic product. In addition, the number of Hungarian–owned small firms continues to grow rapidly even as the state sector contracts. A senior official of the European Bank for Reconstruction and Development has argued, in fact, that the private sector already accounts for over 50% of the gross domestic product. The government is committed to reducing state ownership from the present 90% down to 21%. It is identifying those enterprises which it wants to remain under state ownership and has set up a new state holding agency, the State Property Company, to operate these firms. It is expected that the State Property Company will issue stock, some of which will be sold to the public.

Tourists enjoy ice cream on a street in Budapest.

AP/Wide World Photo

257

Hungary

Joszef Antall, Chairman, Council of Ministers

Natural Resources

Hungary is relatively short of natural resources, which means that it is heavily dependent on imports. In the past, the Soviet Union has provided it with approximately 90% of its oil, iron ore and timber needs, plus a high proportion of other raw materials. The CMEA's conversion to dollar prices as of January 1, 1991, plus domestic economic problems the Soviet Union is experiencing, have disrupted CMEA trading patterns and left their future in doubt. Soviet oil exports to Eastern Europe dropped somewhat in 1990–91, but this has become less important since Eastern European countries now have to pay in dollars in any case.

Hungary's main domestic fuel source is a low–quality brown coal. Unfortunately, the country's reserves are not extensive, and coal production has started to decline. For this reason, the Government several years ago made a commitment to the development of nuclear energy and it currently has three plants in operation, two of which were completed in 1987. Twenty–five percent of Hungary's electricity comes from nuclear energy. The old communist government had committed itself to build four additional reactors by the year 2000—raising the amount of the nation's electricity generated by nuclear plants to 40% but that probably won't occur.

The Soviet nuclear accident at Chernobyl is one factor, but not necessarily the most important one. The Hungarian plants are of a different design than that which exploded at Chernobyl—they make use of pressurized water in their design to slow down the neutrons in the fuel instead of graphite as at Chernobyl. In addition, as Joszef Bognar, director of the World Economics Institute insisted, the Hungarian government has "taken many more security steps than in the Soviet Union and incorporated many Western design elements."

Culture

Because the Magyar language is not related to any of Europe's major languages, Hungarian culture is rather distinct from that of its neighbors. There tends to be a strong international culture also, since most educated Hungarians are fluent in at least one foreign language. Hungarian plays have to be translated before they can go abroad, but one such play, *Cats Play*, was extremely popular when it was produced in the United States in the 1970's.

Hungarians are also noted for their films, many of which would be classified as new wave or art films. Only about 20 Hungarian films are made in a year, however, so Hungarian theaters show many foreign films. One particularly successful Hungarian producer in recent years, made the films *Colonel Redl* and *Hanussen*, both of which have been released in the United States. Incidently, both deal with the cultural area of the old Austro–Hungarian Empire and were released with a German soundtrack.

The old communist Hungarian Government was strongly supportive of cultural activities and in the 1980's spent an estimated $27 million to renovate the State Opera House in Budapest. Cultural activities were heavily subsidized, with the average ticket to a full opera or first–class concert costing about $2. The government also sponsored numerous "folk festivals" throughout the country. That is not expected to change significantly under the new regime, though subsidies may be reduced somewhat.

A crisis of sorts broke out in 1986 between the Hungarian government and the Writers' Union. In recent times, many Hungarian writers had begun testing the limits of the permissible and this led to the suspension of a cultural monthly, *Tiszataj*, and pressure on a sociological journal, *Medvetancs*, to close down. When the Writers' Union held its general assembly in late 1986, therefore, trouble was already brewing.

When Janos Berecz, the party's chief ideologist, delivered a scathing attack on the writers during his opening address, several writers took the floor to answer the attack. Then, in a gesture of defiance, the Writers' Union elected—by secret ballot—a new 71–member executive board which contained almost no party members. In retaliation, the government "de-recognized" the Writers' Union and sponsored the creation of a new association for poets, translators and other writers under the auspices of the trade union. Although the government made no attempt to close down the Writers' Union, writers were under clear pressure to come to terms with it. In retrospect, however, this can be seen as another step toward the repudiation of the communist leadership which finally came in 1990.

Religion

Church–state relations were quite bad for many years but they began to improve after Cardinal Mindszenty, who had been residing in the American Embassy since 1956, agreed to go into exile; he died in Vienna in 1975. His successor, Laszlo Lekai, was named a cardinal in 1976. Janos Kadar summed up his position on religion at a press conference in Paris in 1978:

"We have ever considered it most important that honest religious citizens, doing a fair day's work building our country, should not be faced with irreconcilable problems of conscience by the confrontation of state and church. As the result of protracted, patient work settling the relationship between the state and the churches, a religious citizen can now, at the same time, be committed to social progress and socialism, and be a faithful son of his church" . . .

Cardinal Lekai died in the summer of 1986. Negotiations for appointment of his successor and new bishops dragged on for some time before the government finally gave its approval to the appointment of Laszlo Cardinal Paskai. The Hungarian Government had insisted that the Church take action against one of its priests, Father Gyorgy Bulanyi, who was preaching the incompatibility of Christianity and service in the Hungarian military. The Church, which had its own problems with Father Bulanyi, was nevertheless unwilling to repudiate him completely.

Church–State relations improved dramatically after Grosz became General Secretary. It was under Grosz, for example, that the government rehabilitated Joszef Cardinal Mindszenty and extended an invitation for the Pope to visit Hungary. One of the first acts of the new non–communist government, installed in office in May 1990, was to reopen diplomatic relations with the Vatican. It followed this up by dismantling all government controls over religion. The *Christian Democrats* are, of course, part of the current government coalition.

Hungary also has about 80,000 Jews, a tiny remnant of the estimated 600,000

Jews who lived in Hungary prior to World War II. Under the communists, Jews kept a low profile, though the government permitted them to run a school and the only rabbinical seminary in eastern Europe. Since the fall of communism, however, the local Jewish population has opened two Jewish schools, Jewish publications, cultural associations, and youth groups are expanding, and work is currently underway to renovate Budapest's 4,000 seat synagogue. As Peter Maass of the *Washington Post* reported, "it all amounts to the revival of what was one of Europe's largest and most prolific Jewish communities."

The Future

Hungary, which has been pursuing its own reform program for a number of years, was one of the few quiet places in Eastern Europe in 1989–92. Even so, it has continued on its path of reform, electing its own non–communist government in March 1990. That government has been in power for a little more than three years and, although there was been some political dissent, continues to have the confidence of the Hungarian people.

Hungary has economic problems in common with all the countries of Eastern Europe, but its progress has been more rapid than any other country because of the reforms it had already made under the communists. There will be more pain, but the future is basically optimistic.

Father and son on the way to market. Courtesy: Jon Markham Morrow

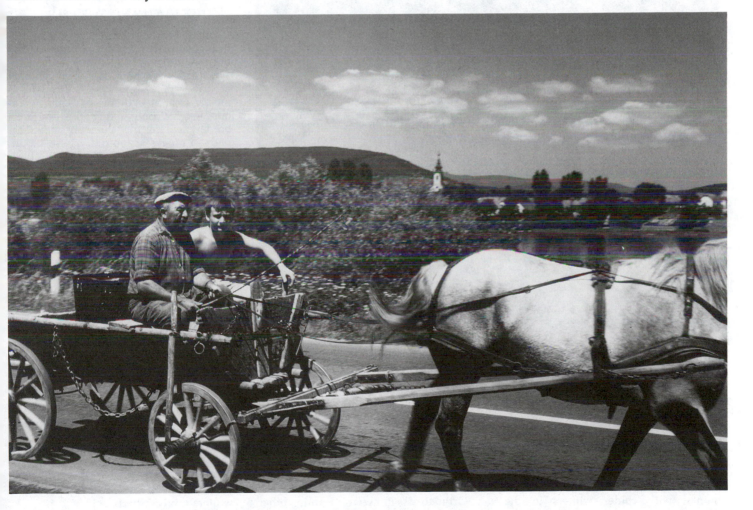

The Republic of Poland

Confident candidate Lech Walesa after the second round of voting in the presidential election, December 9, 1990.

AP/Wide World Photo

kingdom from the 10th century; joined with Lithuania in the 14th century, decline in power in the 17th century leading to partitions of Poland by Russia, Prussia and Austria at the end of the 18th century; independent from 1918 until German conquest in 1939; "People's Republic" within the Soviet sphere 1947–1989.

National Day: May 3 (marking the day in 1791 when Poland adopted the first democratic constitution in Europe).

Chief of State: Lech Walesa, President.

Head of Government: Hanna Suchocka, Prime Minister (in caretaker status as of May 28, 1993, when she lost a vote of confidence in the Sejm).

Type of Government: Multiparty democracy.

National Flag: Red and white horizontal bars.

THE LAND AND THE PEOPLE

Poland, formerly the largest communist–governed country of east–central Europe, is shaped in an uneven circle as a result of the boundary changes that occurred after World War II. The land is mostly a flat plain that rises to mountainous heights only along the southern border, where the Sudeten and Carpathian ranges are found. These mountains seldom exceed 2,000 feet in elevation within Poland.

The soil is not very rich, and for this reason, agricultural yields are rather modest except in relatively small areas of black soil and wind–driven topsoil found in the center and south of the country.

Poland is bordered on the north by the waters of the Baltic Sea. The province of Olsztyn has a number of scenic lakes which form about ten per cent of the land area. Almost 26% of the total land is covered by forests. The longest river is the Vistula (*Wisla*) which stretches for 664 miles northward to the Baltic Sea, exiting in the Gulf of Danzig (*Gdansk* in Polish).

The climate reflects the middle position of Poland between Western Europe, with its moist oceanic climate and Eastern Europe with a dry, continental climate. There is slow change between the seasons because of the distinctive features of early spring and early winter. The summers are warm and permit the cultivation of fairly good crops except during the years when there is not enough rain. The winters can be bitterly cold.

Although Poland prior to World War II had significant Ukrainian, White Russian, Jewish and German minorities, because of events associated with that war, Poland is ethnically and religiously now quite unified—almost every citizen is both an ethnic Pole and a Roman Catholic.

Area: 312,354. sq. km. = 120,533 sq. mi.
Population: 37.5 million
Capital City: Warsaw (Pop. 1,641,300)
Climate: Temperate in the West; continental with colder winters in the East.
Neighboring Countries: Ukraine, Belarus (East); Lithuania (Northeast); Russia (Kaliningrad Enclave, North); Czechoslovakia (South); Germany (West).
Official Language: Polish.
Other Principal Tongues: Belarusian, Ukrainian, Russian, German.

Ethnic Background: Polish (98.7%) other (2.3%).
Principal Religions: Roman Catholic (95%; 75% practicing), Uniate, Greek Orthodox, Protestant and other (5%).
Chief Commercial Products: Machinery and equipment, fuels, raw materials, partially manufactured goods, light industrial goods, agricultural and food products.
Currency: Zloty.
Former Political Status: Independent

Poland

HISTORY

The Early Polish Kingdoms

In 1966 Poland officially celebrated its millennium—a thousand years of existence as a state. This date, observed with much pomp by the communist government, is actually the thousandth anniversary of the introduction of Christianity into the area; Roman Catholicism was established in 966.

The Piast ruling dynasty, named after its semi–legendary founder Piast, established itself in control of a number of Slav tribes living in the area between the rivers Vistula and Oder. The most important of these were the *Polanie*, which means "inhabitants of the plains"—they gave their name to the nation and the country. In Polish, Poland is *Polska*. Prince Mieszko I (Mee–*ehs*–ko) adopted Roman Catholicism and was joined by those he ruled.

The adoption of Christianity and the submission to the protection of the Virgin Mary, officially called "Queen of the

Polish Crown," had a political purpose. One thousand years ago it was an insurance policy against continued pressure of German rulers who justified their incursions into Polish lands as a movement to convert the pagans. The fact that Christianity was adopted in its western form has been of great and lasting influence. With Roman Catholicism came the introduction of the Latin, or Roman alphabet, to which were added letters designed to render some specific Slavic sounds. This was in contrast to the Cyrillic alphabet, developed from the Greek alphabet, adopted by the Russians and other eastern and southern sub–branches of the Slav family.

Because of the split between the Roman Catholic and the Eastern Orthodox churches, the Poles developed the notion that they were an outpost and frontier of Catholicism and western culture. The Russians, professing what they regarded as orthodox ("correct") religion, viewed the Poles as "intruding Roman heretics." The mixture of political claims and conflicting spiritual values caused a lasting hostility between the two leading Slav nations.

The consequences of this split did not fully appear for several centuries.

During this time the Polish state, later combined with the much larger Grand Duchy of Lithuania, was one of the most important European realms. What later became known as Russia slowly dragged itself out of isolation, backwardness and a long period of Tartar rule which all but severed its contacts with Europe.

The early history of Poland was

Shifting borders: c. 1150 . . .

and c. 1350

Poland

marked by attempts to create a solid national state with an independent existence against eastward pressures by the Germans and contests for territory and power with "Russian" princes. There was also competition with the early Bohemian (Czech) rulers whose claims to certain areas overlapped with those held by the Polish rulers.

Early successes by the Piast rulers included the brief occupation of Kiev (now the capital of the Ukraine) and an extension of control toward the Black Sea by Boleslaw the Brave. Important trade routes were also brought under Polish control. These successes were soon followed by a disintegration caused primarily by the so–called *appanage* system of inheritance by which the territory of a ruling prince was subdivided among all his sons, causing endless clashes among brothers and cousins for the position of leadership. The development was similar to what prevailed in the early "Russian" state of Kiev. The competition forced the contenders to rely for support on combinations of fighting men and also of the higher clergy. Support in the battle was paid for with land grants and with political power given to the landed gentry (*szlachta*). This became the basis for the development of the political power of the gentry which hampered the growth of a strong, centralized monarchy. It also led later to a concept of liberty almost bordering on anarchy, thus making orderly government almost impossible.

The most famous—or infamous—example of this development in later centuries was the concept of the *liberum veto*, where a *single* member of the national assembly could block legislation and force the assembly to be dissolved by speaking the words *nie pozwalam*—"I do not allow." In practice, these obstructive votes of minor gentry could be controlled or purchased by powerful magnates, or even by agents of foreign powers meddling in Poland's affairs. Although praised as a "democratic system, the constitutional freedoms and privileges actually were extended almost exclusively to the gentry, which was about 10% of the population. The cities enjoyed some rights, but the peasants were reduced to serfdom. This oppressive system continued with little change during the existence of the Polish–Lithuanian "commonwealth."

The unity of the state was restored in the 14th century under Casimir (Kazimierz) the Great; substantial reforms were introduced. The cities, which had lain neglected were developed, often settled by German artisans and Jewish traders. Culture advanced—the University of Krakow, a distinguished seat of learning and *alma mater* of the astronomer Copernicus, was established in 1364.

In spite of Casimir's wisdom and great contributions to government, law and culture, his rule was characterized by a further retreat of Polish control in the West and Southwest. The province of Silesia was ceded to semi–Germanized Czech rulers; the order of the Teutonic Knights, a Germanic religious group, was allowed to extend its control over areas adjacent to the Baltic Sea. Polish expansion was eastward, bringing closer a future clash with the Russian state once Tartar domination ceased there. For awhile, however, it seemed that the Polish state was safely launched on a course of greatness with its power embracing territory from the Baltic to the Black Sea.

The Jagiellonians

Casimir the Great was the last of the Piast dynasty—he had no male heir. The throne passed to his nephew, Louis of Anjou, who was also the King of Hungary, and then to the latter's daughter, Jadwiga. A new era in the history of Poland opened when Jadwiga married the Duke of neighboring pagan Lithuania, Jagiello. He adopted Christianity and became king of Poland in 1386, founding a dynasty that lasted until 1572. During this period, in theory, the kings were elected, thus earning Poland the name "royal republic."

One of the reasons for the union of Poland and Lithuania was joint defense against the pressure of the Teutonic Knights along the Baltic Sea. Although the Knights were soundly defeated in 1410 at Tannenberg (Grunwald) and were forced to accept the authority of the Polish kings, they were never fully dislodged from their positions. With the advent of the Reformation in the sixteenth century, the Knights discontinued their role as a pseudo–religious organization and eventually became the nucleus of the kingdom of Prussia, thus establishing a standing menace to Poland's access to the sea. The Reformation also resulted in the adoption of Protestantism by some distinguished Polish families, but the bulk of the people remained stalwart Roman Catholics. Their faith was bolstered by the vigorous activity of the Jesuits during the counter-reformation.

Decline and Fall

The previously loose organization of Poland–Lithuania was changed in 1569 into a more centralized state. However, soon thereafter, with the end of the Jagiellonians, the process of decline began, Until a final collapse at the end of the 18th century, there was a succession of elected kings, most of whom were foreign.

One of these monarchs, Sigismund III of the Swedish royal house of Vasa, involved Poland in the troubles that raged in Russia following the death of Ivan the Terrible; Polish troops occupied Moscow in 1610 and used false pretenders to the Russian throne to advance Polish policy. These attempts to profit from Russia's weakness were unsuccessful, but they created lasting resentment and distrust.

The rest of the 17th century was one of much misery for Poland. The Cossacks of the Ukraine, whose territory was mostly under Polish control, staged a bloody uprising in 1648, devastating much of the country. The Swedes "deluged" and almost destroyed Poland in 1655—tradition

Shrine to the Virgin Mary, Czestochowa

places the reason for the rescue of the country to the miraculous intervention of the Virgin Mary. The invaders were stopped near a shrine to the Virgin Mary at Czestochowa. Soon, Poland was forced to give the eastern part of the Ukraine to Russia in 1667.

The decline of Poland was briefly interrupted by the brilliant performance of Polish forces under the native king, Jan Sobieski, which contributed greatly to the defeat of the Ottoman Turks at the gates of Vienna, Austria in 1683. This victory bolstered the self–image of the Poles as a strong Christian power, but in reality the weakening of Turkey opened the door to the strengthening of neighboring Russia and Austria. They began to plan the partition and destruction of the declining commonwealth.

Throughout much of the 18th century, Russian and other foreign troops occasionally occupied the territory of Poland; foreign ambassadors frequently dictated who was to sit on the throne. The last king of Poland was Stanislaw August Poniatowski, a former favorite of Catherine the Great, Empress of Russia. He was a man of great culture and charm, but possessed only limited talents for governing a country which was in a state of disintegration. Partitions of Poland were carried out in 1772, 1793 and 1795 by neighboring Russia, Prussia and Austria;

POLAND: A land devoured

they diminished and finally ended the independent existence of the once–glorious commonwealth.

Before the final partition, there were tardy expressions of patriotism in Poland. The youthful leader of one movement, Casimir Pulaski, eventually came to the United States and died while fighting the English in the War of Independence. Another Pole, Tadeusz Kosciuszko (Kos–chewsh–ko) led an unsuccessful uprising in Poland after fighting in the U.S. Revolutionary War. There was a last–ditch effort to reform the political structure which resulted in a proposed constitution, referred to with reverence even today as the May 3 Constitution (1791), though it was never actually put into effect.

"Not Yet Lost"

After the collapse of the old commonwealth, the struggle for the revival of Poland was carried on mainly through efforts to interest foreign powers in sponsoring restoration of an independent Poland. Poles also flocked to various armies involved in fighting or preparing to fight one or another of the partitioners. Many were attracted by the high–sounding and seemingly universal slogans of the French Revolution; a Polish legion was created by Napoleon in the Italian province of Lombardy. Their official song began with the words "Poland is not yet lost as long as we live." It became the national anthem in later years and still is today. Actually, although glad to see Poles join his armies, Napoleon had little concern for the cause of Polish independence. He revived a symbolic "Polish" state in 1807—the Duchy of Warsaw—which collapsed with the defeat of Napoleon's troops in the historic battles of 1812.

At the Congress of Vienna, Alexander I, the Russian Emperor, demanded that the historic Polish lands be brought together in a Kingdom of Poland. One of Alexander's advisers was a Pole by the name of Adam Czartoryski and he had suggested the idea to the Russian Tsar. Neither Austria nor Prussia was eager to give up their claims to Polish territories obtained as a result of the partitions, but they eventually agreed to Alexander's demands. The Kingdom of Poland thus came into existence in 1815 as a separate

Poland

possession of the Russian Emperor; Alexander took the title of King of Poland and not only granted the Poles a constitution, but also set up a separate Polish army. The actual ruler of Poland was the Russian Grand Duke Constantine, regent.

Many Poles were dissatisfied with this arrangement which implied Russian domination, and in 1830 they rebelled, attempting to expel the Russians. The attempt was a failure and Nicholas I, who had in the meanwhile become Tsar, punished the Poles by abolishing the constitution and making Poland a state within the Russian Empire. In spite of another Polish uprising in 1862–63, it remained part of Russia until World War I.

There were, throughout the nineteenth century, many expressions of sympathy for the cause of an independent Poland, especially whenever there occurred spectacular, but unsuccessful, uprisings in 1830 and 1863. Russia had earned the name "gendarme (policeman) of Europe." But there was no occasion for outside intervention in "The Polish Problem" until the first World War, which involved the partitioning powers in a fatal struggle ending with the defeat of Germany, the collapse of the Austro–Hungarian Empire and the weakening of Russia by revolution and civil war. President Woodrow Wilson of the U.S. advocated the rebirth of an independent Poland, saying that "statesmen everywhere are agreed" that an independent Poland would become necessary with the collapse of the partitioners.

Poland After World War I

The "new" Poland was officially reborn on November 11, 1918, and it enjoyed an independent existence for a little more than twenty years. The Treaty of Versailles which ended the war granted Poland access to the Baltic Sea through a narrow corridor which separated East Prussia from the main body of Germany. The area around the port city of Danzig (Gdansk) was organized as a Free City with a League of Nations high commissioner, Polish control over its foreign relations and internal self–government by a largely German–speaking population. The demand for its return to Germany would later be used to "justify" the Nazi invasion of Poland.

The reborn Polish state consisted of provinces which had been governed and neglected by foreign rulers for over a century. There was much wartime destruction and hunger, alleviated to some extent by a U.S. relief program. Politically, the nation was divided into a number of parties competing for power. An important outlet for the pressure of a rapidly growing population was formerly provided by emigration, especially to the U.S. This was virtually stopped after World War I, thus making the economic situation even more difficult.

One of the first prime ministers, the world–famous pianist Ignacy Paderewski (Pad–er–*ev*–ski), left the country after a few months, disgusted with the constant political squabbles. The provisional chief of state, Marshal Jozef Pilsudski, a former socialist who had fought for awhile on the side of Germany and Austria in World War I, temporarily retired from politics. However, he returned to power in May 1926, to rescue the country from disaster due, in his opinion, to the political bickering that was ever present. From that time until the end again came in 1939, the country was governed first by Pilsudski, who died in 1935, and then by his associates, especially a group known as "the colonels."

Parliamentary government was never fully abolished, but the system was "streamlined." Political parties were permitted to continue in existence, but only the candidates which had the approval of the administration could be elected to the parliament (*Sejm*).

In addition to continuing economic problems, the country was beset by activities of ethnic minorities of doubtful loyalty to Poland. Many Germans turned out to be Nazis. The Ukrainians had a strong revolutionary movement, with some terrorist groups.

Many alienated young people joined the illegal *Communist Party;* filling the prisons with these disaffected youngsters only turned the jails into "prison universities where the inmates received thorough indoctrination from fellow–prisoners who had sometimes been deliberately planted by the party. The fear of communism and the bitter relations with Soviet Russia against which a war was waged in 1920 in another attempt to profit from Soviet weakness, forced Poland to maintain a large, but poorly equipped army; this force proved unable to resist the massive attack launched by Hitler in September 1939.

Aware of their dangerous location between Germany and Russia, the Poles tried to maneuver between the two powerful neighbors. Although they signed a non–aggression agreement with Hitler in January 1934, they refused to enter into a closer, anti–Soviet association with the Nazis. In the end, the Poles aroused the suspicions of Germans and Russians alike. They also alienated western public opinion by participating in the division of Czechoslovakia with Germany that followed the Munich Conference in 1938.

Poland During World War II

Undeterred by a guarantee given to Poland by the government of Great Britain, Hitler made a series of brash demands on Poland which were rejected as "impossible" by the Polish foreign minister. A week before the Germans launched their attack on Poland, Hitler scored a diplomatic success by reaching an agreement

Signing the German-Russian Pact (August 23, 1939) which divided Poland between them. L. to r.: German's Ribbentrop with Stalin, Molotov

Poland

with the Soviet Union. The secret portions of the pact provided for a new partition of Poland, with the Soviet Union receiving the eastern part of the country with its heavily non–Polish population. Soviet troops marched into Polish territory on September 17, after the last members of the government had left the national territory to seek refuge in neighboring Romania.

The heroic, but futile Polish resistance to the German armies came to an end in mid–September 1939. Soviet troops marched into the eastern part of the country and stopped along an agreed–upon line, called the Ribbentrop–Molotov Line after the names of the German and Soviet foreign ministers. Between September 1939 and June 1941 when the short–lived "friendship" between Hitler and Stalin came to an end, the partitioning powers energetically tried to wipe out all traces of an independent Poland. A large part of the German share of the land was directly incorporated into Germany; the remainder was formed into a "General Government" under a Nazi governor, Hans Frank.

A systematic policy of exterminating Poland's political and intellectual leaders reflected a Nazi plan to make the Poles a source of manual labor, working for the benefit of the "master race." The Jews were first herded into enclosed ghettos and later subjected to the "final solution"—death in gas chambers that operated around the clock. The eastern portions of Poland that were held by the Russians until they were overrun by Hitler in 1941 were declared to be parts of the Soviet Union. Massive transfers of people occurred in these regions.

Symbolically, an independent Poland continued to exist in the form of a government in exile, located first in France and later in England. Many thousands of Poland's fighting men managed to make their way west and formed military detachments pledged to fight side–by–side with the western Allies. Polish airmen distinguished themselves during the massive German air assault on England.

The position of the Poles was complicated by the fact that while the West was fighting Hitler's forces, the Poles were in conflict also with the Russians, who had joined in the partition of their land. On the surface the situation changed when Hitler launched an attack on Russia in mid–1941. Through British mediation, an agreement was signed restoring relations between the USSR and Poland. This made possible the formation of Polish fighting units from among the prisoners taken by the Russians in 1939 and from the many Polish citizens who had sought refuge in Russia. Because of the serious rifts between

Warsaw in ruins, 1944

the Polish forces and the Soviet leadership, the troops under the command of General Wladyslaw Anders, left the territory of the Soviet Union. They fought gallantly in North African and Italy, especially at Monte Cassino, under British command.

As the war fortunes of the Soviet Union began to improve, the Russians showed increasing dissatisfaction with the insistence of the Poles in exile on regaining the prewar frontiers of Poland in the East. When the Germans announced in 1943 the discovery in the Katyn Forest of a mass grave of Polish officers apparently slaughtered by the Russians, a new break between the Russians and the "London" Poles occurred. Pressured by his military staff, the Polish prime minister in exile, General Wladyslaw Sikorski, asked for an impartial inquiry by the International Red Cross. This was used by the Russians as a pretext to break diplomatic relations with the Poles in exile. A *Union of Polish Patriots* emerged as spokesman for the Poles in the Soviet Union; a Polish "army" was formed as a auxiliary of the Soviet troops.

These front organizations became the nucleus of a government set up when the Soviet Red Army in its westward drive reached what the Russians were willing to consider Polish territory. In August 1944, when it looked as if the Germans were withdrawing from Warsaw, the underground loyal to the London leadership staged an uprising, in the hope of obtaining control of the city before it was captured by the Russians. At the last moment, Hitler issued orders for his troops to make a stand, and the

uprising was brutally crushed. The city was almost completely destroyed by the Nazis and many thousands perished in the ruins. Russian troops, although they were at one point very close to the suffering city, but across the Vistula, for political reasons, showed little desire to come to the assistance of the Poles.

This attitude, although possibly justified in part by the fact that Soviet forces had run out of steam after a successful westward push in the summer, added another lasting element of bitterness and resentment to the relations between the two nations. Stalin was determined that no group of Poles not under his control would make a political comeback. At one point, sixteen leaders of the pro–London underground were lured into the open supposedly for the purpose of negotiation with the Soviets, but they were unceremoniously arrested and sentenced to jail.

After the Yalta Agreement of February 1945, the government–in–exile located in London was eventually "de–recognized" by the U.S. and the British; a lame compromise was worked out in the spring of 1945 which led to the creation of a government of "national unity," built around the Russian–sponsored group, with the addition of a few non–communist leaders, the most prominent of whom was the peasant leader Stanislaw Mikolajczyk (Mee–koh–*lie*–chik).

Stalin's vague promises of "free and unfettered elections" offered little protection to non–communist groups which tried to resume their political activities after the war. The fiction of "national unity" came to an end once the illusion of

Poland

BALTIC SEA · Kaliningrad · U.S.S.R. · Vilnius
Gdansk · U.S.S.R.
Szczecin · Bialystok · U.S.S.R.
E. GERM. · WARSAW · Brest · Pinsk
Wroclaw · Jelenia Gora
Krakow · L'vov · U.S.S.R.
CZECHOSLOVAKIA · U.S.S.R.
ROMANIA

Annexed to Russia, 1939 — 1939 Boundary
Annexed from Germany, 1945 — 1945 to present
— Curzon line

0   60   120 mi
0   60   120 km
N
Jan 85

postwar accord between East and West was ended by the opening of the "Cold War." Mikolajczyk had to flee the country in 1947.

From "People's Democracy" to "People's Republic"

Postwar Poland was and still is, in many respects, an almost entirely new country. It is about 185 miles farther to the west than it had been in 1939. At the expense of Germany, it gained a 325–mile–long coast on the Baltic Sea—a large coastline when compared to the narrow corridor of the interwar period. What had been East Prussia prior to the war was divided between Poland and the Soviet Union, eliminating what many Poles viewed as a "dagger pointed at the heart of Poland."

The frontier line with Germany was substantially shortened. The "recovered" lands taken from the Germans are economically more valuable than those surrendered to the USSR. Another basic change was in the composition of the population. Instead of having over 30% of its people ethnically non–Polish, the

country is now inhabited by 37 million people, of whom only a little more than 2.3% are ethnic minorities. The Ukrainians and Byelorussians that had lived in Poland were taken into the Soviet Union; the bulk of the more than three million Jewish population was exterminated by the Germans and most who managed to survive chose to leave the country. Most Germans were expelled or moved westward. Thus, Poland is more Polish and, incidentally, more Roman Catholic than it has been for many centuries.

Until mid–1947, during the period of "national unity," the official claim was that the system established in Poland was to be different from both the capitalist model of the west and the communist one of the Soviet Union. This claim could not survive the beginning of the Cold War with its divisive effect. While the United States proclaimed a policy of "containment" of communism, the founding of the Communist Information Bureau (*Cominform*) at a con ference held in western Poland in 1947, symbolized the beginning of a

new era. Under the circumstances, Poland was compelled by Moscow to reject an offer of Marshall Plan aid extended by the U.S. Soon thereafter, the rift between Stalin and the Yugoslav communists made the Russians exert still more pressure to hold the line in the governments of other eastern European states. In one country after another, communist leaders identified with the "national" road to socialism were removed from office, jailed and sometimes executed.

For a variety of reasons, events in Poland did not lead to such extreme measures against leaders accused of "nationalist deviationism," but there were drastic changes. Wladislaw Gomulka, who had been active in the pro–Soviet underground during the years of German occupation and who presided over the absorption of the territories "recovered" from Germany, was removed from office and eventually imprisoned. He was never tried and was later able to reemerge as a leader in 1956. Communist control over all aspects of social life and Soviet direction of Polish internal affairs were substantially strengthened in the late 1940's.

Pressure was brought against political parties that had kept their prewar names and occasionally some of the pre–1945 non–communist leaders were induced to merge either with the communists or with the communist–front groups. Thus, the *Polish Socialist Party (PPS)* was forced to merge with the communists, who had been using the name *Polish Workers Party*, to form the *Polish United Workers Party*.

In spite of all of the changes of the wartime and early postwar period, the communists could not compete for the support of the workers against the traditional *Polish Socialist Party*, which had to be merged out of existence largely with the help of one of its younger leaders, Jozef Cyrankiewicz (Tsee–*ran*–kay–vich). He was rewarded with the job of Premier; some years later, he was appointed Chairman of the Council of State (1970–1972). The *Peasant Party*, which had retained a large following under its prewar leadership, was forced to combine with a communist–front group to form the *United Peasant Party*. Independent social organizations were also herded together into "united" groups controlled by the communists.

The high point of Soviet meddling in Polish affairs was reached when Konstantin Rokossowski, a Soviet army marshal, was made commander–in–chief of Poland's armed forces, minister of defense and a deputy premier in the government. Important positions in the army were given to Russian officers, not all of whom could claim, as did Rokossowski, to be of Polish descent. Economic transformation was reflected in stepped-up industrialization plans, and an almost complete elimination of private enterprise in industry and commerce. There was an attempt to shift land ownership from individual peasant holdings to a form of collectivized farms. However, in comparison with other countries of the area, the results of collectivization remained rather limited. Poland is to this day agriculturally the least collectivized of the communist–governed states.

In the years following 1947, increasing pressure was brought to bear on the Catholic Church, directed principally at educational efforts. Church schools were secularized, Church lands were confiscated and restrictions were placed on religious activities. This pressure reached its peak in 1953 when Cardinal Wyszynski (Vee–*shin*–skee) was placed under house arrest in a monastery and forbidden to carry out his functions as primate of Poland. However, the confiscation of Church lands and the general persecution probably had an effect opposite to that intended. The fact that the Church was no longer a landowner probably increased its hold over the rural population and the general persecution mainly served to increase its hold over the masses, which remains remarkably strong.

The Catholic educational system was topped by the Catholic University of Lublin and the Theological Academy in Warsaw. The communists looked upon the Church as a rival organization which competed for the allegiance of the people, and no efforts were spared to make the position of the Church difficult. At the same time, the regime had great respect for the traditional power of the Church in Poland and it was this which protected the Church from an all–out frontal assault. This also produced some anomalies as when, for example, the communist leadership publicized the endorsement of Cardinal Wyszynski in the 1956 elections, even though they had kept him under house arrest since 1953.

The Polish Struggle of October 1956

Following the death of Josef Stalin in 1953, the Polish government launched a "New Course" which involved some relaxation of the old Stalinist norms. Workers were little affected, but there was a cut in taxes for the peasantry and a slowdown in the process of collectivization. Intellectuals found they could be a little more critical in their comments about Polish life.

Then an event occurred that had widespread repercussions. Jozef Swiatlo, a high official of the Polish secret police, fled westward soon after Stalin's death. In 1954, Radio Free Europe in Munich began a series of broadcasts of Swiatlo's memoirs. His well–documented disclosures of the terroristic activities of the *UB*, the political police organization, became widely known in Poland and led to the abolition of the Ministry of Public Security. This was followed later by the arrest of some leading secret police officials.

Several economic reforms were also introduced, especially in the field of labor discipline. Critical voices began to be heard, first among writers and students and then among the rank and file membership of the party. In the field of communist political theory, "revisionist" views came to the fore, accompanied by a tendency to question some of the most basic tenets of Marxism–Leninism. Students and recent graduates began to organize discussion clubs in which pointed questions embarrassing to the government were raised in lengthy debates.

Poland was thus in a state of political turmoil when Khrushchev made his famous "secret" speech denouncing the evil deeds of Stalin at the 20th Congress of the party in the Soviet Union in 1956.

As luck would have it, Boleslaw Bierut, First Secretary of the Polish Communist Party, died in Moscow two weeks after Khrushchev's speech. He was succeeded by Edward Ochab, a shrewd politician who recognized the need for reform. It was Ochab who freed Gomulka, at that time under house arrest in a villa on the outskirts of Warsaw, and facilitated his reentry into the party; this occurred in August.

A wave of strikes by industrial workers broke out in June 1956, topped by clashes in Poznan between workers and troops. The regime at first tried to blame the outbreaks on "capitalist provocation," but soon came to the conclusion that the entire structure of communist rule might tumble unless there was a dramatic change of direction in government.

The logical choice to accomplish this was Gomulka, who because of his insistence on a "Polish road to socialism" became a symbol of independence from the Soviet Union. He was thought likely to satisfy the "revisionist" elements within the party, but also the masses of workers and ordinary citizens. Amid

First Secretary Wladyslaw Gomulka (left) chats with President Aleksander Zawardski
AP/Wide World Photo

Poland

preparations to put Gomulka in the position of First Secretary of the party in mid–October 1956, an impressive delegation of top Soviet leaders suddenly appeared in Warsaw and there were rumors of Soviet troops on the march toward the Polish capital. However, Khrushchev and his comrades, reassured about continued Polish–Soviet ties and possibly impressed by the resolute stand of factory workers who had obtained arms and were converging on the airport, departed.

The Soviet delegation flew back to Moscow, grudgingly, accepting changes in the Polish communist leadership, which included the elimination of Marshal Rokossowsky, a visible symbol of Soviet interference in the internal affairs of a neighboring and friendly country. In this way, a tragic clash such as occurred about the same time in the Hungarian capital of Budapest was avoided. Because of the role he played in the unseasonal "spring in October," Gomulka was thought by many to be a "liberal" who favored popular control of government. Actually he was rather an austere, conservative communist with a political sense for what could be done in Poland and with the Polish people; this sense failed him in later years, however. As the "thaw" of 1956 passed into history, many of the more visionary hopes of the intellectuals were disappointed.

However, the Polish regime continued to differ from those in neighboring communist–ruled countries. There was a reversal of the trend toward collectivization of agriculture. Prior to 1956, progress toward this goal had at all times been slower in Poland, and when Gomulka returned to power, there was a massive abandonment of even the token collectivization that had occurred.

Agricultural Circles were about the only form of cooperative organization in the farmlands. Their main function was the joint purchase and use of farm machinery. This was a far cry from the practice of totally controlling agricultural production through a system of collective farms. Gomulka apparently decided that the Polish peasant had to be left to discover for himself the blessings of socialism rather than be forced into it.

In other branches of the national economy, especially in industry, Gomulka saw less room for non–communist management. Workers Councils, organized during the 1956 upheaval, were later discouraged, and industry once again ran in a centralized manner. There were, however, some attempts to make central planning of the economy less rigid. For a number of reasons, Polish industry continued to suffer from serious shortcomings; various emergency measures occasionally resulted in unemployment and a halt in the movement of people from the overcrowded countryside to the cities.

In commerce, a degree of private enterprise was permitted, although it was overburdened by state controls and taxation. Individual craftsmen were also permitted to work alone or in small groups.

In the cultural sphere, there was a tremendous outburst of creative activity after 1956 as the rigid rules of "socialist realism" were relaxed and it became possible to experiment with new and nonconformist forms of artistic expression. Access to the Western press and literature was relatively free and travel permits to areas outside the communist bloc were issued more generously than elsewhere in Eastern Europe.

In political life, an effort was also made to create a real function for the parliament (Sejm). The habit of debating proposed legislation in committee and attempts to critically evaluate the efficiency of government changed the legislature from a rubber stamp completely controlled by the leadership to a reasonably authentic voice of some parts of public opinion. Polls and other studies of public attitudes also came into use. Polish sociologists point with pride to the fact that, under their influence, a revised interest in the social sciences spread to other nations of Eastern Europe and to the Soviet Union. The relatively tolerant Khrushchëv was dismissed from office in 1964 and his successors began a retightening of control. These Soviet events were mirrored in Poland, where the "spring" of 1956 was followed by a new freeze. Although the people continued in various ways to have "little freedoms," a sense of disappointment and distrust characterized the attitude of intellectuals, who had high hopes of basic changes under Gomulka.

Dissatisfaction with the regime came into the open in early 1968 when students and intellectuals clashed with the police. The reasons for the conflict was the suppression of a theatrical performance of a work by Poland's greatest poet, Adam Mickiewicz (Mits–kay-witch). The work, Dziady (Forefathers), contained anti–Russian themes which were lustily applauded by audiences. There also was dissatisfaction with the official attitude of the government, which (following the lead of the Soviet Union) came out in support of the Arabs in their conflict with Israel. This policy enabled one of the groups within the leadership, the so–called Partisans led by the ambitious General Mieczyslaw Moczar (Mo–char) to open an attack on "Zionist" elements supposed to be in the government and the party.

These charges appealed to a deeply–rooted anti–Semitism of the Poles; Gomulka, although himself married to a Jewess, decided to go along with what turned out to be a massive purge of Jews within the government, universities and cultural organizations. Many had to leave the country practically overnight because they could not make a living in Poland.

They had to renounce their Polish citizenship and leave most of their belongings. Thus, the once–flourishing Jewish community of Poland, reduced by Hitler's destruction and postwar emigration from over 3 million to less than 30,000, has by now almost ceased to exist.

Gomulka's political maneuvering and his obedience to the Soviet Union demonstrated in his support for the invasion of Czechoslovakia in 1968 saved him temporarily from political defeat. He was reelected leader of the Party in 1968 in spite of pressure from Moczar and his Partisans, with the support of Edward Gierek, boss since 1957 of the Party organization in the important mining and industrial province of Upper Silesia. But Gomulka (aptly described as a "spent force" by one observer) could no longer control the conflicting trends within the party leadership. Differences were not only over the direction of leadership, but reflected a generation gap between old timers such as Gomulka and younger, better educated, technically–minded elements demanding a share of power.

Edward Gierek

The final downfall of Gomulka was triggered by an apparently spontaneous outbreak of protests by workers expressing dissatisfaction over increased food prices on the eve of the Christmas holidays of 1970. A coalition of competing factions within the Party leadership agreed to dismiss Gomulka and elected Edward Gierek as First Secretary. Some of the ex–leader's closest colleagues also lost their positions.

Swientojanska Street in Krakow—the city's Archbishop became Pope John Paul II

Under the leadership of the initially popular ex–miner Edward Gierek, Poland embarked on an ambitious plan of rapid industrialization and economic growth, financed by heavy borrowing of capital from the Soviet Union as well as from a number of Western governments, international financial institutions and private banks.

Until about the mid–seventies the results seemed impressive; there was a substantial rise of the gross national product and a striking improvement in the standard of living. However, this economic "miracle" came to an end, in part, because of a dramatic change for the worse in the international economy, but also because of widespread graft and mismanagement within the government.

To service the foreign debt, Poland had to resort to increased export of food, thus cutting into the supply of food for consumption at home. While workers' wages had increased, less and less was available

for purchase. An attempt in 1976 to raise prices on basic food articles led to the outbreak of strikes as well as looting and attacks on communist party headquarters in many localities. The decision of the government to *cancel* price increases a bare 24 hours after they had been announced, undermined the prestige of the ruling party. Legal measures taken against workers who had incited strikes led to the creation of an organization for the defense of arrested and dismissed workers known by the initials *KOR*. Another organization came into being in 1977 called *Movement of Defense of Human and Civil Rights (ROPCIO)*.

The new Gierek leadership also expressed a desire to "improve communication with the working masses" and sought a further normalization of relations with the Roman Catholic Church. Several anti–Church measures were dropped, permission was given to construct churches in the new industrial

towns and the Church's debts to the state were cancelled.

The election of a Polish Pope in 1978 was another factor in this development. The election of Karol Wojtyla (*Voi*–chla), Archbishop of Krakow—who took the name of John Paul II—brought an outburst of national pride which extended even to many members of the Communist Party. Gierek sent a handsome message of congratulations to Rome and negotiations began immediately for a papal visit to Poland. It occurred in June 1979 and included a nationally–televised meeting between the Pope and Edward Gierek and other leaders of Party and state.

Gierek was more successful in his relations with the Catholic Church than he was in his second goal of improving communication with the masses. He promised that workers would be consulted and that intellectuals would be heard. He also declared that the Party could not possibly

Poland

regulate *everything*. The political thaw did not last long.

By 1973 censorship had been fully restored and it soon became clear that the Party, instead of reducing its intervention in national life, was in practice carrying through a further centralization in the name of reform.

Moreover, while claiming to be the "leading political force in society in constructing socialism," the Party was granting its own members special pay and privileges that set them off from, and aroused the hate of, the masses. Isolated and filled with bureaucrats, the Party became more and more a hollow stem willing to "stonewall" just about anything.

Strikers and Dissidents

Dissatisfaction with the communist system had been simmering in Poland for a number of years. It brought about the emergence of various dissident groups on the political and intellectual level, ranging from barely legal to illegal organizations; some of these groups claimed belief in the basic tenets of communism, but advocated reform of the system and removal of those who mismanaged it, while others, on the extreme right, advocated abandonment or overthrow of the system.

Illegal publications, study circles and "flying universities," often holding classes in church buildings, proliferated over the years. However, the decisive change came when the small intellectual groups identified themselves with the plight of the workers who had resorted to strikes to protest oppressive conditions in the factories and the undercutting of their living standards by a hike in the prices of food.

Opposition in Poland derived substantial support from the outspoken position of the Catholic Church under the leadership of Cardinal Wyszynski (d. 1981). The election of a Polish prelate to be Pope was also a source of moral support. Nevertheless, it was the spectacular collapse of the economy after a decade of what looked like successful development that set off Poland's latest crisis in 1980–81. One could hardly imagine the dramatic and potentially catastrophic pressures for reform without the spectacular collapse of the economy after several years of what looked like successful development.

The government, facing a rapidly deteriorating economic situation and a crushing debt to foreign lenders (estimated at some $28 billion) tried to appease the workers as well as the political dissidents by a number of half–measures and promises of improvements which could not always be kept. Matters came to a head when thousands of workers in the Gdansk (Danzig) shipyard went on strike and occupied the premises of the enterprise.

December 1980: Lech Walesa with supporters

"Confrontation," Confusion and Clumsiness

Under the leadership of Lech Walesa (Vah–*len*–sa), an unemployed electrician who emerged from nowhere to a position of prominence, the workers refused to vacate the factory and insisted that the government send a negotiator to deal with the *Twenty–one Demands* posted by the workers' strike committee.

The main point of the demands was permission to establish independent trade unions *in competition with the party–controlled official trade union organization*. When this demand was accepted by the government, a new institution was born: *Solidarity*, which claimed a membership of ten million workers. An extension of the protest movement to the countryside resulted in the creation of a rural branch of *Solidarity*. Whether intended or not, there was underway a confrontation between the Polish workers in association with the Church and, ultimately, the Soviet Union.

What followed was a drastic shake–up of the Party–State leadership. Gierek and his close associates were ousted and the relatively unknown Stanislaw Kania became leader of the Party. The post of Chairman of the Council of Ministers was taken over by the man who already held the post of Defense Minister, a career

military officer, General Wojciech Jaruzelski (*Voy*–check Ya–roo–*zel*–skee). For awhile, negotiations involving the communist government, the independent *Solidarity* movement and the Catholic Church raised the hope that Poland might enter a new phase of its history under a rather unusual triangular arrangement between the formal, but discredited communist authorities (with the Soviets lurking in the shadows), the independent trade union movement and the Church (now led by Cardinal Wyszynski's successor, Cardinal Glemp). However, a worker movement independent of the Polish United Workers' Party was, by its very existence, a challenge to the communist claim to be the party of the workers, and it soon became clear that an independent *Solidarity* was unacceptable not only to significant elements in the *PUWP* but to the Soviet leadership.

The true picture became clear in October 1981 when Kania resigned as Party Secretary and was replaced by General Jaruzelski, who, significantly, was not only Chairman of the Council of Ministers (prime minister) but also Defense Minister and therefore head of the Polish armed forces.

During previous periods of unrest, the armed forces had not been used to restore order. On December 31, 1981, however, General Jaruzelski declared martial law throughout the country and ordered the armed forces to begin a roundup of trade union activists and intellectual dissidents. Thousands were rounded up, including Lech Walesa and most of the other *Solidarity* leaders. A curfew was enforced throughout the country and telephone communications between cities were restricted.

The Polish government also sought to discredit *Solidarity* by attempting to show that the trade union was not merely seeking an improvement in the economic situation as it claimed, but that it was interested in sharing political power with the communists, or taking it away from them. Secret tapes made by the government at a national conference of *Solidarity* in the city of Radom had Lech Walesa and others stating that the time had come for "confrontation" with the government rather than "compromise." The tapes were probably altered. In late 1982 *Solidarity*—and the discredited old official trade unions—were banned and new official trade unions replaced them. According to the government, the new official unions currently have a membership of about 7 million, of which 60% are former members of *Solidarity*. If correct, that figure would represent slightly less than half of the total labor force.

Solidarity may have been banned, but it was by no means dead. Lech Walesa, after being held in custody for several months, was eventually released without any charges being filed against him. His receipt of the Nobel Prize for Peace also strengthened his hand. As a result, he was permitted to continue to speak out publicly, though his actions were closely monitored by the government and he was continuously under the threat of harassment or worse. An amnesty of mid–1984 resulted in the release of the last 652 *Solidarity* detainees. A few were rearrested after meeting with Walesa. They were subsequently released, but remained subject to government harassment when they attempted to speak out publicly.

While there were those within the leadership of the *PUWP* who opposed the independent *Solidarity* movement, the decisive factor that led the Polish government to declare martial law and ban the movement was the strong pressure being exerted at this time by the Soviets.

Yet another concern of the Soviet leadership under Brezhnev was the still–important position of the Roman Catholic Church in Polish life, and that concern appears to have increased after John Paul II, the former Karol Wojtyla, Archbishop of Krakow, was elected Pope in 1978. It is for this reason that scholars are inclined to accept a connection between the Soviet

General Wojciech Jaruzelski

KGB and a subsequent attempt on John Paul II's life while he was officiating at a ceremony in St. Peter's Square in Rome. The connection is indirect because the man who actually fired the shot was a Turkish national who, the Italian government charged, was an agent of the Bulgarian secret police. The Soviet connection derives from the fact that the Bulgarian secret police would almost cer-

His Holiness Pope John Paul II

tainly not have been operating in such an important matter without the knowledge of the Soviet KGB.

The most important connection between the attempted assassination of the Pope and the government of Poland is that John Paul II is a Pole; there is absolutely no evidence that it knew anything whatsoever about the plan to kill the pontiff. At least up to 1985, the Polish Government was under pressure from the Soviets to reduce the influence of the Church. The government was divided on the issue, with moderates arguing the value of cooperation with the Church and "hard–liners" arguing the danger of such an accommodation. While the internal struggle was still going on, three members of the Polish security police, acting under orders of their superior officer, a colonel, brutally murdered Father Jerzy Popieluszko, a priest. He had become a target because he was an ardent and public supporter of *Solidarity*. Eleven days after he had been reported missing, his body was found, weighted, at the bottom of a reservoir. An autopsy showed that he had been beaten to death before being thrown into the water.

This forced General Jaruzelski's hand. Disassociating himself and his regime completely from the killing, he ordered that the four implicated individuals be put on public trial and that it be televised nationwide. All four were convicted and received long prison sentences. In addition, their superior in the Ministry of the Interior was fired. Jaruzelski himself took the further step of assuming direct responsibility for the police and the internal security forces, replacing two members of the Party secretariat who had formerly been in charge of those activities.

In spite of Jaruzelski's actions, State–Church relations reached a new low, charged with emotion arising out of the revelations during the trial of the dirty war waged by the security police against the Church. Responding to these emotions, Cardinal Glemp began to take a more militant line, and Jaruzelski answered in kind. In a 1985 press interview, speaking about differences with the Church, the general was quoted as saying somewhat defensively:

"In Poland the church has a vast, favorable opportunity to carry out its priestly mission. Regrettably, certain priests abuse this freedom to stage unlawful acts. We talk about it openly."

Church–state relations began to improve again in 1986. They climaxed in January 1987, when General Jaruzelski paid a state visit to Italy and was received by Pope John Paul II. The 70–minute private talk was described by a Vatican

Poland

spokesman as "earnest, clear and profound." Symbolically, Jaruzelski's daughter, Monika, who accompanied him, was given a rosary and took another home to her mother. Equally symbolically, Jaruzelski invited the Pope to visit Poland and the visit took place in June 1987. According to press reports at the time, Jaruzelski also promised to grant the Church full legal status—a move that would allow the Church's youth organization and its various professional bodies to operate publicly—but nothing was done to put this into effect before the June arrival of the Pope.

When the pontiff arrived, the fireworks began. *Solidarity* banners appeared widely everywhere he went. Crowds ultimately numbering into the millions attended the many masses he said, cheering him with wild enthusiasm. At each mass or appearance he praised *Solidarity* with warm enthusiasm to show his disapproval of the government. Jaruzelski tried to talk him into silence midway during the visit, but to no avail. He kissed the tomb of Father Popieluszko, reviving all of the old emotions surrounding his death. Upon his departure, the General appeared at the airport to say relatively harsh words to the highly respected Pope. Jaruzelski, usually "unflappable," had visibly been disturbed and was shaking with undisguised anger. The damage had been done.

Although Jaruzelski had not gotten what he wanted from the Pope's visit, he was evidently impressed by the response of the Polish people to the Pope. From this, he concluded that some accommodation with the Church was necessary if he wanted to reconcile the Polish people to continued communist rule. As a result, the government began permitting the Church to enlarge its area of activities and to become, in the words of one Pole associated with the movement, "the most interesting independent intellectual and social center in Poland."

As in East Germany, the Church became a refuge for dissident artists. In September 1987, Wroclaw's large Gothic "Church of the Holy Cross" arranged an exhibit of the works of 151 artists from all over Poland under the title "National Biennial of Young Artists." The Government permitted the exhibit, even though many of the 423 works of art on display had secular themes and, according to Polish law, could not legally be exhibited inside a church.

The Church was also permitted to expand its educational role. Church schools teaching secular subjects were established throughout the country and the Catholic University in Lublin added faculties in law, economics, psychology and sociology. In addition, the Church established publishing facilities where it began printing its own textbooks. Many of the activities originally sponsored by *Solidarity* were thus given new life under the patronage of the Church.

But Jaruzelski did not want the Church to be the sole intellectual alternative, and he accordingly moved to grant more freedom generally. This led the government to give approval to *Res Publica*, a privately owned magazine, to begin publishing in July 1987. Although allowed only 25,000 copies, it was important as the first of Poland's many underground magazines to achieve legal status. An even more important move came in January 1988 when the government stopped jamming the broadcasts of Voice of America, Radio Free Europe and the Polish language broadcasts of the BBC.

Although Jaruzelski made the final decision himself, it was reportedly on the advice of Mieczyslaw Rakowski, then Deputy Chairman of the Council of Ministers and an ex–journalist. Rakowski had been editor of *Politika*, Poland's most important journal of politics, before joining the government.

All of this provided background for Jaruzelski's greatest gamble—his attempt to implement an economic reform that had much in common with what Gorbachëv was trying to do in the Soviet Union at this same time. In an attempt to obtain public backing, Jaruzelski submitted the plan to a public referendum in November 1987. Although the three–year program contained elements such as increased private enterprise and a decentralization that was supposed to cut the number of government jobs by a quarter, it also included a cut in subsidies that would have brought an immediate, significant increase in prices. Whether for that reason or because they simply did not trust the communists, voters rejected the reform.

Stung by its defeat, the government decided to begin implementing the reform anyway, although more slowly than originally planned. The first price rises went into effect at the beginning of 1988 with food, rent, and fuel increasing by an average of 45 percent.

It was the official party unions that protested first, and this led to a strike among transport workers in the city of Bydgoscz. The government granted a 60 percent pay increase to the transport workers but, in the meantime, the strike began spreading to other parts of Poland. Among those joining the strike were the workers at the Lenin Shipyard in Gdansk.

The strike now became explicitly political, for this was the birthplace of *Solidarity* and Lech Welesa once again emerged as a local leader. Occupying the Lenin Shipyard and refusing to leave, the Gdansk workers demanded that, in addition to a pay increase, *Solidarity* activists dismissed in 1981 should be reinstated in their jobs. The government agreed to a wage increase but refused to bargain over the political issue. When the government held firm, it soon became clear that this was not to be a replay of 1980–81. There was no national ground–swell of support for the Gdansk workers, and after eight days they were forced to end their strike.

The government thus won a victory of sorts, but not one of much value. For its economic reform to have any chance of success, it had to have the active support of the workers, and this it did not have. In fact, a public opinion poll taken in early 1988 indicated that only 7% of those polled believed that the economic reform had any chance of success.

That is not surprising. After all, the political leadership had been pursuing a program of economic reform since 1980, all without tangible results. This bred a sense of pessimism exemplified by the comment of one Polish journalist in July 1988 that Poland had already been through reform, "and it did not work."

Inflation, already bad, grew worse as the summer progressed and there were increasing shortages of all kinds of consumer goods. In August, a new wave of strikes swept across Poland, spreading for the first time to the Silesian coal fields. Because coal exports were one of Poland's major sources of hard–currency earnings, the government had always gone out of its way to keep the miners happy. But even the miners had seen their standard of living drop in the preceding months, and they were now demanding action.

In a final irony, it was the official trade unions, not the outlawed *Solidarity*, that declared a lack of confidence in the government and demanded that it resign. The government stepped down in September and General Jaruzelski appointed Mieczyslaw Rakowski (*Myek–cis–lav Ra-Kov–skee*) as the new Chairman of the Council of Ministers (Premier).

Rakowski, determined to break the political–economic deadlock, introduced a new phrase into the communist lexicon—the "constructive opposition"—and offered four cabinet seats to *Solidarity* supporters. He also called for roundtable negotiations with the opposition. But what he offered the opposition was the chance to participate in the economic reform; there were to be no political reforms. *Solidarity* was not to be legalized and, in fact, *Solidarity* supporters were urged to repudiate their leadership, since "it is impossible to compromise with Walesa." Under the circumstances, no one in the opposition was willing to join the government, and the proposed roundtable negotiations never got started.

Poland

WIARA DZI...
WIARA N...
WIARA DZIECI
WNUKÓW NASYCH BĘDZIE...
P.P. 1938

SOLIDARNOŚĆ

A church courtyard's fence displays a banned *Solidarity* sign

Rakowski was left with the alternative of either dealing with Walesa or of somehow discrediting him. The party decided to assign that task to Alfred Miodowicz (*Meeo–doe–vitz*), leader of the official trade unions and a member of the party Politburo. Miodowicz challenged Walesa to a television debate, which took place in November. With 70% of the nation watching, it was Walesa who came across as the statesmanlike leader. This point was conceded even in the USSR. *Komsomolskaya Pravda*, reporting on the debate, said that some of Walesa's "recent speeches have been distinguished by a certain political balance and reasonableness. It would also be possible to agree with a number of his assertions made directly during the debate." The party next tried to co–opt Walesa personally by offering to make him a deputy premier, but Walesa held out for formal negotiations and "laws, rights, positions offered by law, not by privilege."

By December, it had become clear that all of Rakowski's efforts to push through economic reform while ignoring *Solidarity* had been a failure, as were the party's efforts to discredit Walesa. Yet conservatives in the top leadership of the party continued to oppose any compromise with the opposition.

To clear the way, General Jaruzelski called a Central Committee meeting just before Christmas. Six hard–liners were removed from the Politburo and eight persons were added. This was followed by a second two–day meeting of the Central Committee in January 1989, which ended with a communique supporting the legalization of *Solidarity*.

Even at the January meeting, conservatives attacked the leadership decision to deal with Walesa, but Jaruzelski pushed through the decision against their opposition. Among those who opposed the decision was Alfred Miodowicz.

Roundtable Discussions Begin with *Solidarity*

Roundtable negotiations between the government and *Solidarity* opened on February 6. Once the two sides began talking, they quickly carried their discussions beyond the question of the legalization of *Solidarity* and began to put together an historic compromise. As Tadeusz Mazowiecki, a leading *Solidarity* negotiator, commented, "both the communists and we crossed the Rubicon. It's really surprising how far things went."

In addition to the legalization of *Solidarity*, the April agreement called for creation of a Senate as a second legislative body, all of whose members were to be chosen by popular election. That election took place in June. New elections to the *Sejm*, the old legislative body, also took place at the same time. In the latter case, however, the communists and their allies were guaranteed 65% of the seats, with the remaining 35% to be freely contested.

To provide executive authority and to act as a counter–weight to a more powerful legislature, the post of President was also created. The President was to be chosen by the newly elected legislature.

Most of those in leading positions in the *Solidarity* movement decided to stand for either the *Sejm* or the Senate. Walesa declined, saying that he did not want to compromise his credentials as a trade unionist. He did, however, create a Citizens' Committee of approximately 100 opposition figures which took over management of the campaign for the opposition, and he actively campaigned for *Solidarity* candidates.

In the June elections, the *Polish United Workers' Party* suffered a crushing defeat. *Solidarity* took 99 out of 100 seats in the Senate, plus all of the open seats in the *Sejm*. In addition, most of the top communist leadership, running unopposed for *Sejm* seats, were rejected because they failed to get 50% of the valid votes. These seats, reserved for communists, were filled in a second round of voting only because *Solidarity* instructed its supporters to support the new candidates.

The newly elected legislature managed to agree to install Jaruzelski as President but the failure of the communists at the polls meant that they were in practice unable to form a government. Their allies, the *United Peasants' Party* and the *Democratic Party*, refused to support the PUWP candidate for Chairman of the Council of Ministers and opened discussions with *Solidarity*. This led Lech Walesa to propose a *Solidarity*–led coalition government which would include representatives of the PUWP. Now came a second decisive Soviet intervention. After Mieczyslaw Rakowski, the new head of the *Polish United Workers' Party*, announced his opposition to such a coalition, he got a 40 minute telephone call from Gorbachëv, the essence of which was that Gorbachëv expected the Polish party to accept a *Solidarity*–led coalition

Poland

Native costumes in Gdansk

government. Tadeusz Mazowiecki, Lech Walesa's hand–picked candidate, was installed as Chairman of the Council of Ministers at the end of August.

Poland's First Post–War Non–Communist Government

In December 1989, the legislature made several changes in the constitution. The adjective "People's" was dropped from the official name of the country and it is henceforth to be known as the Republic of Poland. All references to Socialism and the leading role of the *People's United Workers' Party* were also deleted from the document.

On January 1, 1990, the government instituted its plan to bring about Poland's transition to a free–market economy. In general, prices were freed, subsidies to industry were canceled, the currency was essentially set free to float, and there is a planned surplus in the budget. The plan produced hardships throughout the society, but it also began the process of

transforming the economy. Unemployment rose as inefficient state industries lost their subsidies and had to begin laying off employees in order to cut their costs, but individual Poles began establishing thousands of small businesses and small amounts of foreign investment began to pour into the country. For the year, foreign investment was estimated at $100 million.

As the year progressed, a split became evident in the *Solidarity* ranks. Walesa began to issue public statements more and more critical of the Mazowiecki government. Although he supported the government's program of economic reform in general, he argued that it was being implemented in a way that made it harder on the Polish people than it needed to be. That was a minor criticism, however. His main objection was that the government was not moving fast enough in clearing communists out of key positions. Poland was, by this time, the only country in Eastern Europe other than

Albania which still had a communist as head of state. Communists also held 45% of the seats in the *Sejm*, though the results of the June 1990 elections suggested that they would not be able to retain most of those seats in a genuinely free election.

When Walesa first raised the issue of his becoming President, many of his supporters in *Solidarity* tried to persuade him not to run. Walesa backed down at first, then changed his mind and declared his candidacy for the Presidency on September 17. Two days later, astute General Jaruzelski, sensing the direction of political winds in Poland, elected to a six year term as President in July 1989, agreed to step down because of his "concern to prevent undesirable public sentiment" and to "promote democracy."

The Polish Parliament then modified the office of the Presidency, setting a 5–year term of office and specifying that the President was to be elected by popular vote. The election was set for November 25. Prime Minister Mazowiecki then announced that he would stand for the Presidency himself.

It was never clear why Walesa and Mazowiecki had their falling out. Perhaps Mazowiecki feared that Walesa as President would repudiate his economic program. Or perhaps it was related to the fact that Mazowiecki was a university graduate and had a reputation as a learned theorist, while Walesa had only a trade–school education and a background as a shipyard electrician. Adam Michnik, editor of the *Solidarity*–founded newspaper *Gazeta Wyborcka*, added another reason when he accused Walesa of having dictatorial tendencies. Whatever the reasons, Mazowiecki's candidacy represented the end of *Solidarity* as the unifying umbrella organization of the non-communist forces.

Walesa, though still the head of *Solidarity*, did not attempt to use that organization in his presidential campaign. His supporters were organized as the *Center Alliance*. Mazowiecki's political organization was known by the acronym *ROAD*. Later in the campaign, a third candidate emerged as a contender based on his promise to bring western business know–how to Poland. This was Stanislaw Tyminski, a Pole who had emigrated to Canada and whose qualification was that he was a successful businessman.

Tyminski, the only one to attack the government's economic reform program, edged Mazowiecki out for second place, taking 23% of the vote to Mazowiecki's 16%. Walesa came in first with about 40% of the vote, but since he did not get a majority, there had to be a second round of voting on December 9. This time, Walesa got an overwhelming 75% of the vote and was sworn in as President on December 21, 1990. Mazowiecki had submitted his resignation as Prime Minister after his defeat in the first round of voting. Walesa asked him to continue to serve until new parliamentary elections. He refused but remained on in a caretaker capacity. Walesa offered the position to several people, including Leszek Balcerowicz, Finance Minister in the Mazowiecki government. Balcerowicz declined, saying he wanted to stay on as Finance Minister, so Walesa eventually offered the position to Jan Krzysztof Bielecki.

Before becoming Prime Minister, Bielecki was leader of a small free enterprise political party in the parliament, the *Liberal–Democratic Congress*, and head of a consulting company. From Gdansk, he had also been involved in the *Solidarity* underground. The *Liberal–Democratic Congress* is strongly committed to the development of private enterprise in Poland, and Walesa's selection of Bielecki was seen as his way of underscoring his commitment to Poland's program of economic reform.

Walesa was also anxious that new elections to the *Sejm* take place as soon as possible in order to remove the influence of the communist deputies still sitting there. Under the compact negotiated with the communists in 1989, however, new elections were not required until 1993. In March, Walesa urged the legislature to ignore the 1989 deal with the communists. "I am convinced that Poland today needs instant elections," Walesa told the legislature. "One has to put an end to growing disillusion and mistrust of political institutions, including Parliament." Parliament did schedule a debate on Walesa's appeal, but it ultimately decided to postpone new elections until October 1991.

Before the elections occurred, however, the *Sejm* passed a new electoral law that instituted an extreme form of proportional representation in an apparent attempt to protect as many seats as possible held by the communists and their allies. President Walesa vetoed the legislation on the basis that it would produce a too fragmented legislature, but the communists and their allies, with control of 65% of the seats, passed it over his veto.

The election results were more or less what Walesa predicted. Twenty–nine parties won seats in the *Sejm*, with the largest of the parties winning only 12.2% of the vote. The *Democratic Left Alliance*—the renamed communists—came in second with 12.1% of the vote, while their ally, the communist *Peasant Party*, got 8.9%. Creating a coalition government that could count on a stabile majority in the *Sejm* was no easy task and it was not accomplished until the end of December. Walesa even offered to lead a gov-

ernment of national unity himself, but there was no significant support for that idea.

Eventually, however, Jan Olszewski managed to put together a coalition of seven parties and his government was approved by the *Sejm*. Over the next three months, the new government worked on a new economic program that, if enacted, would have negated most of the gains of the preceding two years. Olszewski wanted to put off privatization and increase subsidies to state–owned companies so they wouldn't have to lay off more employees. He would have also increased spending on social welfare. With the Polish budget deficit already running more than 5% of GDP, that would have forced the government to print more money and destroyed the value of the currency. Olswzewski continued to push the policy even after his Finance Minister resigned over the issue, and it was not until after the *Sejm* had voted down his economic program and the IMF threatened to cancel future lending that he abandoned this approach. In late March, he went back to the budget worked out by the previous government and already approved by the IMF.

That opened the possibility of broader support in the *Sejm* and led to discussions in early April between the government coalition and three additional parties about enlarging the coalition. Significantly, two of the parties, the *Democratic Union* and the *Liberal Democratic Congress*, were the parties of the two previous non–communist Prime Ministers, Tadeusz Mazowiecki and Jan Krzysztof Bielecki. A programmic document was actually agreed on by the two groups on April 11, but the talks subsequently collapsed.

Mr. Mazowiecki later remarked that "conditions are not right to form a big coalition and reshuffle the government." It is likely that Mazowiecki and Bielecki were unable to get the guarantees they wanted that Olszewski would not revert to his earlier economic program.

Olszewski's government lasted for another two months. In that time, he lost his finance minister over the issue of the size of the deficit, then his defense minister over that individual's charges that President Walesa was planning a coup against the government. Finally, on June 5, Parliament voted to oust Olszewski himself. President Walesa then proposed Waldemar Pawlak, 33–year old leader of the *Peasant Party* as Prime Minister. Pawlak was never able to put together a majority coalition, however, and he submitted his resignation to parliament on July 2.

Meanwhile a coalition of seven parties with ties to *Solidarity* proposed Hanna Suchocka as Prime Minister. Suchocka, a

46–year old law professor and member of the *Democratic Union*, one of the parties strongly supportive of economic reform, was confirmed as Prime Minister on July 11. Prime Minister Suchocka has been adamant that Poland would continue its austerity regime and that the budget deficit would be kept under 5% of GNP, the figure set by the IMF which Poland must meet if it wants IMF aid. She has twice had to take a firm stand against strikes whose demands would have increased social spending. She even had to defy the *Sejm* in February 1993 when it adopted social spending bills that would have raised the budget deficit. But she faced them all down, even the *Sejm*, which finally agreed to pass the government's proposed budget on February 12.

Making her task somewhat easier, recent economic reports indicate that Poland's economic decline has stopped and that industrial production has actually been growing since April 1992. Unemployment, on the other hand, is still at 13.8%.

Prime Minister Suchocka still occasionally loses an important bill in the *Sejm*, but when she does she just comes back and continues fighting. An example is the government's privatization bill, which the *Sejm* rejected on March 18. The bill would have authorized the privatization of 600 state companies through the mech-

Solidarity **Chairman Lech Walesa addresses Congress, November 1990.**

Poland

Young Poles waiting to begin a march to the Black Madonna.

anism of 20 different investment funds. Prime Minister Suchocka rfused to accept defeat, however, and on April 30 finally got the bill through the *Sejm*. Recent statistics indicate that more than 50% of Polish workers are now employed in private enterprise. This mass privatization bill will significantly increase that figure.

Prime Minister Suchocka suffered another defeat on May 28, 1993 when she lost a vote of confidence by a single ballot. At issue was Suchocka's refusal to grant pay raises to striking health workers and teachers and increases in pensions. Suchocka's position was that there was no money in the treasury to pay for the raises. President Walesa then announced that he would dissolve parliament and schedule new elections in the fall. In the meanwhile, Suchocka has remained on in her former capacity but in a caretaker status. Since recent polls indicate that she is still immensely popular with the Polish people, it is still too early to say that her tenure as Prime Minister is over.

Foreign Policy

The installation of Poland's first non–Communist Government since World War II did not bring about a significant change in Poland' foreign policy. The new Government remained in the Warsaw Pact and the CMEA and fulfilled its obligations to these two organizations so long as they continued to exist. Relations with the West improved, of course, but predecessor communist governments had also attempted to have good relations with the West. This was particularly true after 1970 when Gierek launched his economic modernization

program based on the importation of foreign technology.

The beginning of the *Solidarity* era in 1980 greatly complicated the situation. The government found itself under increasing pressure from the Soviet Union to take action against the populist union, but was constantly reminded by the West that giving in to the Soviet demands would mean an end to normal relations with the West (and, of course, an end to western credits). The Soviet pressure proved to be irresistible, however, and on December 13, 1981 the government declared martial law, denounced its former recognition of *Solidarity* and ordered the arrest of thousands of its members.

The various western nations then suspended normal relations with Poland and cancelled outstanding negotiations over the terms of repayment of Poland's foreign debt. The United States also took a number of additional measures, including a suspension of fishing rights for Polish ships in U.S. waters, suspension of landing rights for *LOT*, the Polish national airline, cancelled scientific exchanges, cancelled the "most–favored–nation" status for Polish exports and opposed Poland's application for membership in the International Monetary Fund (IMF).

The United States offered to drop these measures in return for an end to martial law and further liberalization, including a release of all political prisoners. As Jaruzelski dismantled his martial law regime, one after another of the above measures was dropped. This had little official effect on U.S.–Polish relations, however, for the Polish government took the position

that economic sanctions were both unjustified and illegal.

It must be pointed out that U.S. economic policy toward Poland during this period was somewhat more of a two–way street than might be thought from the foregoing. For example, the United States continued to distribute surplus food to the Polish people through various voluntary charity organizations even during the period of martial law. Still, this had little official effect on U.S.–Polish relations, which General Jaruzelski characterized in 1984 as being "the worst since 1919." While U.S.–Polish relations remained on hold, the Polish did manage to break out of their earlier diplomatic isolation. During 1984 the Polish government received as official visitors the British under secretary of state, the Prime Minister of Greece, and the foreign ministers of Austria, Finland and Italy.

In 1985 Jaruzelski paid official visits to India, Libya, Algeria, Tunisia and—in December—a semi–official visit to France, where he met with President Mitterrand. The French visit was by far the most important, for it marked the first time that a Western leader had met with Jaruzelski since the declaration of martial law in 1981.

In addition, in another gesture only slightly less significant, Willy Brandt—ex–Chancellor of the Federal Republic of Germany and currently chairman of the Social Democratic Party—visited Poland at the invitation of the Polish Government to celebrate the 15th anniversary of the Polish–West German normalization treaty. There was an official commemoration of the treaty in the Federal Republic as well.

A breakthrough in U.S.–Polish relations came in the fall of 1986 when the regime released 250 political prisoners. The U.S. responded by dispatching John Whitehead, Deputy Secretary of State, on a visit to Poland in early 1987. Three days of discussions produced an agreement to begin negotiations for a new scientific–technical accord, a decision to revive the activities of the U.S.–Polish trade mission and an invitation for a Polish parliamentary delegation to visit Washington. Whitehead's report upon his return must have been favorable also, for a month later the U.S. announced the lifting of the last of its economic sanctions. Poland thus regained "most favored nation" trading status and again became eligible for new U.S. Government guaranteed credits.

The U.S. government welcomed the re–legalization of *Solidarity* and the evolution toward a multiparty democracy implied in the 1989 agreement. President Bush, in a major speech, also threw his support behind a program of economic aid for Poland, including an IMF loan for $300 million which Poland has applied for and a rescheduling of other loans. In addition, President Bush accepted an invitation to visit Poland in July 1989.

Americans were even more pleased at the installation of the first non–communist government in Poland since World War II. When Lech Walesa paid a six day visit to the United States in March, President Bush used the opportunity to announce that the United States was cancelling 70 percent of the $3.8 billion debt that Poland's owed to Washington. By going beyond the action of the Paris Club, the consortium of western creditor nations, to forgive 50% of Poland's debt, the United States was, according to the administration, not only signaling its approval of the changes occurring in Poland, but was also attempting to encourage the American business community to invest in Poland.

Poland's official relations with the USSR were always good so long as the communists were in power in Warsaw, but Polish public opinion also became less anti–Soviet after Gorbachëv came to power in 1985. Gorbachëv's policy of *glasnost* and *perestroika* appealed to many Poles tired of the failure of their own government's attempts to institute economic reforms.

Gorbachëv's 1988 visit to Poland did not go over well, however, partly because the Soviet Government was still supporting the Polish Government's continuing attempts to stamp out *Solidarity* at that time. But another issue that may have been even more important for ordinary Poles was the position of the Soviet Government toward the Nazi–Soviet Non-Aggression Pact of 1939 and the Katyn Forest massacre of 4,000 captive Polish officers during World War II.

A year earlier, Gorbachëv and President Jaruzelski had agreed to set up a joint commission to address issues such as these, which Gorbachëv referred to as "blank spots" in history. The commission decided not to deal with the Katyn Forrest massacre, however. This became public shortly before Gorbachëv's visit to Poland. As a result, Polish reporters tried to get Gorbachëv to comment on the matter, but he refused.

Gorbachëv did change his position on both of these matters later, however. For example, when a group of Polish intellectuals submitted a list of questions to him dealing with these subjects, Gorbachëv sent answers in which he conceded that "many Poles are convinced that Katyn is a work of Stalin and (NKVD—predecessor of the KGB—head) Beria." The Soviet press also reported factually on the matter in 1989, though the Soviet Government did not formally assign blame to Stalin until 1990.

After Gorbachëv's trip to Poland, the Soviet press began publishing a series of articles on Lech Walesa and *Solidarity* which treated the leader and the movement in an objective, and relatively favorable manner. Gorbachëv thus made it impossible for Polish conservatives to argue against coming to terms with *Solidarity* on the basis of Moscow's opposition. This led to the round table talks that eventually allowed *Solidarity* to come to power in 1989.

The final repudiation of communism in the Soviet Union following the failed *coup* against Gorbachëv in August 1991, and the subsequent disintegration of the Soviet Union into its constituent republics created another situation for Poland. Although the collapse of the Soviet Union had negative economic consequences for Poland, the government welcomed it for political reasons and attempted to address the economic aspects by quickly establishing relations with the successor republics. It has negotiated new economic agreements with Russia, Ukraine, Belarus, and several others and is now hoping that they will be able to keep the agreements.

One left over problem from the Soviet era was the 50,000 Soviet troops in Poland. The Soviet Government had not wanted to withdraw the troops until it had withdrawn all of its troops from Germany. The Russian Government has promised to have the troops withdrawn as soon as possible, and some have already left.

Nature of the Regime

Poland is a multiparty democracy with a presidential–parliamentary system of government. The fulcrum of power within the system lies with the prime minister, who is responsible to the *Sejm*. Decommunization—purging the system

Selling bananas at a Warsaw market

Poland

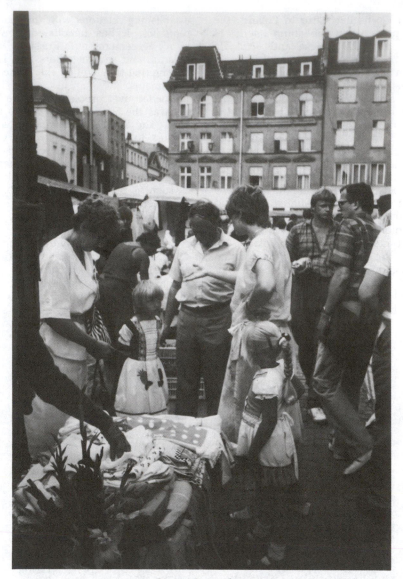

Open-air market

of communist elements and getting rid of communist bureaucrats—was an issue in the October 1991 elections and the new government has promised to move quickly in this area. Numerous laws have to be rewritten, however, and the process could take years.

The Polish Government

When the office of President was created in 1989, it was spoken of as an executive presidency, and the President was given extensive powers, particularly in the areas of foreign affairs and defense. He is, for example, commander–in–chief of the military. Under President Jaruzelski, however, the office was largely ceremonial. President Walesa has attempted to use the powers of the office more broadly, but not always successfully. For example, he attempted to get the *Sejm* to dissolve itself in the spring of 1991 and to call for new elections, but it refused and he was unable to do anything about it.

Part of the problem is historical. Over the centuries, Polish governments have always had either a strong executive or a dominating legislature. A strong legislature is considered to be more democratic, but less able to defend the country's interests. The communist era represented a period in which all decision–making was centered in the executive, and, in fact, in the leadership of the *Communist Party*. Most democrats are therefore chary of supporting the growth of a strong executive under President Walesa. Should the legislature prove incapable of handling Poland's pressing problems, however, there will be growing pressure to bestow more power on the office of the President.

The legislature consists of two bodies, an upper house called the *Senate*, which was created in 1989, and a lower house, called the *Sejm*. The term of office is four years. The *Senate* has 100 members, while the *Sejm* has 460 members. Both are elected by a complex system of proportional representation which has resulted in 29 parties being represented in the legislature, the largest controlling only 12.2% of the seats.

The Prime Minister is nominated by the President, but must have the confidence of a majority in the *Sejm*. She is the political leader of the country and is in charge of the government. She has overlapping responsibilities with the President in the area of foreign affairs and the military.

The Economy

The pattern of economic development in Poland since World War II has been similar in many respects to that in other countries of the area under Soviet domination. Limited natural resources and the resistance of the population to measures of forced savings resulting in fewer consumer goods have slowed the drive to change from a predominantly agricultural economy to one based on industry.

Centralized industrial and economic planning was adopted when the communist regime came to power. Although there were attempts between 1980 and 1989 to reduce the rigidity of central planning, they failed because of the lack of a political alternative and because of the opposition of the entrenched bureaucracy. As a result, Poland continued to suffer from a severe housing shortage, high inflation and the shortage of many consumer goods.

Non–agricultural employment accounts for about 73% of the national work force. Though the government is committed to privatization, a majority of industrial establishments are still state–owned. Private enterprise is growing rapidly, but the lack of local capital has largely limited it thus far to retail trade, services and handicrafts. Poland's coal mines, which are all state–run, are its most significant industry. They meet most of Poland's energy needs and provide an additional 20 million tons each year for export. Other state–owned industries include metal production, heavy industrial equipment, and ship–building. There is also a chemical industry which produces chemical fertilizers and artificial fibers.

Economic reforms introduced in January 1982 were supposed to be a mixture of Hungarian decentralization and Yugoslavian self–management with the Central Planning Commission limited to forecasting, rather than directing the economy. Because of the shortage of raw materials, however, government planners began allocating them to enterprises, and in that way. Because of the shortage of raw materials, the government planners began allocating them to enterprises, and in that way retained their centralized control. The economy did begin to grow again in ate 1982 and Poland began to run trade surpluses with the West, though only as a result of a drastic decline in imports, causing serious shortages throughout the economy and leading to a lower standard of living for the Polish people. And even that effort began to falter after 1986.

In March 1987, the government launched what it called "the second stage of the economic reform," aimed at modernizing the economy. The reform, a furtherance of the 1982 efforts, called for introduction of economic accountability and was accompanied by extensive price increases on food, fuel, transportation and postal services. Prices for gasoline, natural gas and electricity rose by 25% and coal by 50%. After complaints from the official trade unions, food price increases were held to 9.6%. The purpose of the increases, to reduce the level of subsidies found throughout the economy, was thus frustrated. This put the government in a bind. It needed the support of the official trade unions in implementing the second stage of economic reform but they publicly opposed the elimination of food and other subsidies.

The government attempted to win public backing for its economic reform by submitting the issue to a referendum in November 1987. Although it offered certain political concessions, it lost that referendum. Refusing to accept defeat, it began implementing the reform in January 1988 and this included a 45 percent increase in the price of most basic goods.

At first, there was sullen acceptance of the increases but, in April 1988, one of the official unions launched a strike among transport workers in the city of Bydgoscsz. Strikes spread quickly to Kracow and Gdansk, but there was, significantly, no national groundswell of support. The government was eventually able to bring an end to the strikes by promising to raise wages.

The country was in deep economic difficulties. By its own estimates the economy would not reach the point where it was in 1978 until the year 2000. A major problem was with agriculture. Although about 85% of all land was privately owned, government policy had always discriminated against the private peasants in an effort to persuade them to join collective farms. There was some modification of this policy under the new reform, but the government did not have large funds it could pour into agriculture, even if it wanted to. The Catholic Church had talks with the government on a plan to funnel money in from abroad to assist the private landowners, but this evaporated as Church–state tensions grew.

The installation of a new non–communist government in 1989 led to a major change in economic policy and a firm commitment to institute a market economy, but that transition, launched as of January 1, 1990, will take time. Some estimates have been overly pessimistic, however. For example, the government estimated that it would take three years for the country to be self–sufficient in agriculture, but this was achieved by the spring of 1991.

Poland's economic reform program became an issue in the presidential elections, but not a significant one. Still, a lot of Poles had mixed feelings about the reform by the fall of 1990. Clearly, there were some successes. Poland's currency, the *zloty*, had been stabilized, bringing an end to the currency black market, and all over Warsaw, thousands of stalls had been set up at which individuals sold a variety of products from farm produce to cassette tapes. In general, store shelves were again full and people no longer had to stand in line or pay bribes to obtain certain products. The other side is that official statistics, which admittedly covered only the state–owned sector, showed that production had plunged by 25%. Strict wage controls had also cut the purchasing power of ordinary Poles. On balance, however, Poles continued to support the reform program, because they expected to benefit eventually, even if there was some current pain.

Some Poles criticized the reform because it was going so slow. Ten months after it was initiated, not a single large state–owned company had been privatized. Parliament debated such issues as the rights of employees in private companies and whether shares ought to be made available at a discount to employees. Many Poles were also concerned about foreigners coming in and buying everything up.

In September, the government announced that it would issue shares in seven state–owned companies and make them available to the public for purchase. It took the government four months to prepare the shares. By that time, the

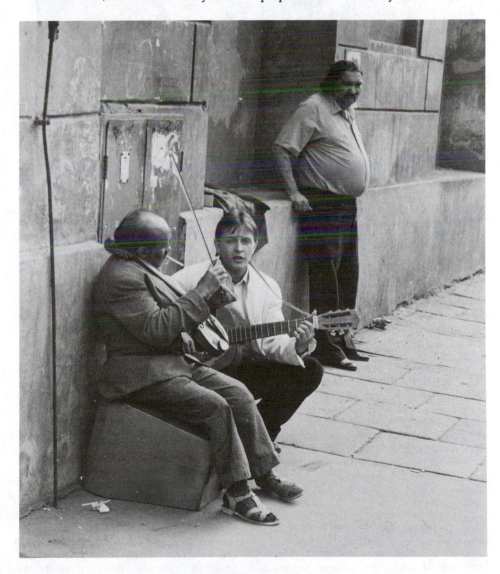

Gypsy musicians in Krakow

279

Poland

President Lech Walesa

government had reduced the number of companies being sold to five. And when the shares were offered in January 1991, the deadline for purchase had to be extended because there weren't enough takers. Another approach to privatization being discussed would be to issue script or coupons to all Polish citizens, who could use them to purchase shares in companies that were being privatized. There are more than 8,000 companies, however. The process is obviously going to take quite a bit of time.

Poland got some international assistance in March 1991, when western nations agreed to forgive 50 percent of the $33 billion that Poland has borrowed from foreign governments. The United States was even more generous, forgiving 70 percent of the $3.8 billion debt held by it. Poland also reached an agreement with the IMF in April 1991 which made it eligible for $2.48 billion in loans over the next three years.

And in a turn–about from the situation just 18 months ago, when Poles faced long lines for food, Poland, in April 1991, offered to sell the Soviet Union 1.5 million tons of grain, 300 tons of sugar, 2 million tons of potatoes, 10,000 tons of meat, plus an unspecified amount of vegetable oil.

The news was not all good, however. By late summer, it has become apparent that the budget deficit was running at a much higher rate than the target negotiated with the IMF. As a result, the IMF suspended Poland's borrowing authority until new targets were agreed to and met. This was even more serious than the loss of the IMF loan, however, for the governments of the "Paris Club" which had agreed to forgive 50% of loans owed them by Poland had stipulated that the offer only held if Poland fulfilled the stabilization program negotiated with the IMF. The stabilization program will run through March 1994.

The legislative elections of October 1991 played an important role in all this, for economic reform was probably the most important issue in the elections. As it turned out, no party did well in the elections, but the *Liberal Democratic Congress*, the party of Prime Minister Bielecki, won only 7.2% of the vote, dooming his chances of staying on as Prime Minister. The *Democratic Union*, the party of Tadeusz Mazowiecki, his predecessor as Prime Minister, made the best showing with 12.2% of the vote, but his challenge of Lech Walesa for the presidency argued against their being able to work together in the future. Thus the mantle fell to Jan Olszewski, who had criticized the reforms for causing too much unnecessary pain. He wanted to reflate the economy and do something for growing unemployment. He also spoke of putting off privatization of major state companies even further into the future. He was nevertheless confirmed as Prime Minister at the end of December.

Prime Minister Olszewski is a lawyer, not an economist, and his economic program reflected "political realities" as he saw them rather than any particular economic viewpoint. When he set about to implement his plans, however, he found that he did not have the freedom that he thought he had. On February 17, his Finance Minister, Karol Lutkowski, resigned, citing "major differences of opinion" on socio–economic strategy. Next, the *Sejm* rejected a resolution on the government's socioeconomic guidelines for 1992. Finally, the IMF made it clear that future loans would depend on the government's adherence to its agreement with the IMF.

Olszewski finally realized that he had misunderstood the "political realities" and announced on March 23 that the government would "stick to the 1992 draft budget already approved by the IMF. A programmic statement was actually approved on April 11 and it appeared that the government would soon consist of a 10–party "grand coalition." The talks subsequently failed, however. Olszewski himself lost a vote of confidence in the *Sejm* in early June. After five weeks, Hanna Suchocka was confirmed as Prime Minister. Supported by a seven—later nine—party coalition, Prime Minister Suchocka has been a strong proponent of reform and she has shown her ability by facing down strikers and persuading the *Sejm* to accept her budget. In April 1993, she also got a major privatization bill through the *Sejm*.

Recent economic statistics have been somewhat heartening. The number of companies in the private sector grew from 29,000 to about 50,000 in 1991. Moreover, the private section had created about a million new jobs in the 18 months up to July 1991. Other statistics indicate that the state sector is still pursuing dangerous and illusory policies. Here, real wages rose by 3% in 1991 and pensions shot up by 15%, even while productivity was falling drastically. The problem here is that management of state companies can be dismissed by elected workers' councils. What is needed is a way to make the workers' councils responsive to market forces. Making them co–owners might be a step in the right direction.

Culture

Since Poland regained its independence in 1918, successive governments have always accorded respect, sometimes positive and at other times grudging, to cultural endeavors. This tradition may have its roots in the fact that, in the 19th century when there was no independent Poland, culture, particularly literary works, provided an important bond of national unity in spite of the partition of the country among several empires. The communists, eager to win the support of intellectuals, provided lavish government subsidies for various cultural programs.

Rigid insistence on "socialist realism" was never as strong in Poland as it was in the Soviet Union, even during the dictatorship of Stalin; this permitted greater intellectual experimentation than elsewhere in the Soviet orbit. In the post–Stalin period, a cry for greater freedom and a more humane form of socialism originated in Polish literary circles— among writers who considered themselves to be loyal communists but who insisted they had the right to describe things as they were, sordid and often heartbreaking. This was in stark contrast to the cheerful distortions of fact by Party propaganda.

The *Poem for Adults* by the communist writer Adam Wazyk, published in 1955, heralded the beginning of the "thaw" in cultural as well as in political relations in Poland. This wave of writing was denounced as "revisionist" by the Party and eventually suppressed, as were the publications and free discussion groups created by students. No literary works of

great value appeared in later years under the communists.

On the other hand, the politically less controversial fields of graphic arts and music continued to flourish. At least one composer of the younger generation, Krzysztof Penderecki, achieved international fame with his "Passion According to St. Luke."

Under the Communist regime, official statistics stressed the numerical growth of cultural institutions; Poland boasted ten philharmonic orchestras, nine symphony orchestras and three musical ensembles associated with the state–run radio network. The theater also continued to enjoy official support, though the quality of plays tended to be poor, with a few significant exceptions such as the plays of Slawomir Mrozek, now better known in the West than in Poland.

Polish education is based on a system of 8 years of compulsory primary schooling, followed by secondary general and technical schools, which about 75 per cent of the elementary school graduates attend. Access to universities and specialized institutes of higher learning is controlled by entrance examinations. According to official figures, the number of students in universities and similar schools rose from 14.4 per 10,000 population in 1937–1938 to 85.9 in 1966–67. As in the Soviet Union and other communist–governed nations, there was particular stress on the exact sciences and less on humanistic subjects which apparently are considered less "relevant" to the efforts of the regime. About half of the students are children of white collar

workers; only 17.7% are the sons and daughters of peasants.

One development arising out of the declaration of martial law in December 1981 was the growth of an underground culture. Many cultural workers refused to collaborate with the regime and turned to underground publishing. Novels and short–story collections were published unofficially during this period and then hawked from door to door. Some became underground best–sellers. Art shows were held in apartment houses and churches. There were even underground cabarets. Some mediums, such as film, do not lend themselves to such a culture, however, and they suffered.

With the installation of Poland's first non–communist government in 1989, all of this began to change. The old proscriptions and prohibitions were removed and artists became free to write and publish what they liked, at least insofar as the government was concerned. Commercial considerations have now become important, however, and not everybody likes the new literature catering to popular tastes that has begun to appear. Almost no one wants to go back to the old system of state control, however.

Religion

Religion has always played an important role in Polish life, usually as a unifying force, since over 90% of all Poles classify themselves as Roman Catholics. Under communism, the church actually prospered and Poland was one of the few countries in the world where the number of persons becoming priests and nuns

Heroes of the Warsaw Ghetto Memorial

Poland

new medical code in May 1992 which effectively prohibited physicians from performing abortions. This was written into law in January 1993 when the *Sejm* passed a bill setting restrictions on abortion.

Other potential church–state controversies are over anti–pornography censorship, divorce, contraception and homosexuality, all areas where the church's position is considerably more conservative and restrictive than what actually exists today in Poland.

Since approximately 95% of all Poles are Roman Catholic, even if only about 75% percent are practicing Catholics, all of this is essentially a quarrel "within the family." In that sense, it is a societal quarrel, rather than a state–church quarrel.

The Future

Poland has made further political progress over the past year as it carried out its first completely free legislative elections. The result—29 parties with the largest party controlling only 12.2% of the vote—was not very promising, but the Poles have once again shown they can deal with imperfect circumstances and the ten–party coalition that recently came into being promises a stable government. The private sector is also growing rapidly and creating new jobs. Latest statistics show that the overall economy is now growing, fueled almost exclusively by private enterprise, and that over 50% of all employment is in the private sector. Poland has also obtained a strong Prime Minister in Hanna Suchocka. Unemployment is still unacceptably high, but things are definitely looking up.

actually increased. Today Poland has 24,678 priests, up from 20,234 in 1980. That gives a ratio of one priest for every 1,280 church members, compared to one priest for every 1,650 church members in the United States. In addition, nearly 1,000 church and other religious buildings have been constructed in Poland since 1985.

Undoubtedly the fact that Pope John Paul II is Polish plays a role in this. His photograph is to be seen almost everywhere, over shop doors, on placards hanging from rearview mirrors in automobiles, and on keychains. There was a close identity between *Solidarity* and the Catholic Church during the period of the 1980's, so it was not surprising that almost one of the first things the new Mazowiecki government did was to reinstate religious instruction in the schools.

The church is finding that its positions are not shared by the government in every case, however. The most important

one of these is the matter of abortion, long legal in Poland. In the fall of 1990, the church launched a campaign to ban all abortions, and this has severely divided the country. In spite of Pope John Paul II's personal intervention, polls continue to show that a majority of Poles favor continuation of abortion, at least under specific circumstances. One result of all this is that, for the first time since World War II, polls show a drop in the approval rating of the church.

The Polish legislature began debate on the issue of abortion in May 1991. Before it was a bill which would have barred abortion in all cases and set a jail term for anyone who performed an abortion or had one. That was too strong for Parliament, and it refused to take any action on the issue. When Pope John Paul II visited Poland again in June 1991, therefore, he brought up the issue again. Because of this continued church pressure, the Polish Congress of Physicians adopted a

Dziś dodatek **tele**

RZECZPOSPOLITA

Poland

Nr 111 (3455) wydanie 3

Warszawa, piątek 14 maja 1993 r.

nakład 235 657 egz. cena 5000 zł

Nr indeksu 35063 X

Po decyzji Komisji Krajowej „S"

Cisza przed burzą

Skończył się strajk generalny w Wałbrzyskiem. Strajk budżetówki trwa już ósmy dzień. W piątek odbędzie się półgodzinny strajk poparcia dla „budżetówki" w Regionie Śląsko-Dąbrowskim „S". Tego dnia zapadnie decyzja o miejscu i zakresie strajku solidarnościowego kolejowej „S". Według Komitetu Strajkowego „budżetówki" protest nasila się i jest niewiele odzewów z regionalnych komitetów strajkowych na środową sugestie, by złagodzić formy protestu. Jak się wydaje w wielu rejonach zaproponowany przez „S" drugi termin matur — 19 i 20 maja — został przyjęty przez kuratoria (np. w Łodzi, Warszawie, Lublinie i Bydgoszczy). We Wrocławiu w demonstracji „S" udział wzięło pięć tysięcy osób.

Według danych MEN, 13 maja strajkowało 15,8 proc. szkół w całej Polsce. W niektórych regionach strajk przygasa, np. na Podkarpaciu. W Koninie i Białej Podlaskiej nie strajkuje żadna placówka, w Lesznie, Pile, Su- walkach w proteście bierze udział mniej niż 1 proc. szkół. Największy zasięg ma strajk w województwach: legnickim, szczecińskim, tam także zorganizował swój strajk ZNP, elbląskim, słupskim, gdańskim i krakowskim.

Od piątku 14 maja rozpocznie się bezterminowy strajk w Łodzi, organizowany przez ZNP. Podczas obrad 13 maja Prezydium ZG ZNP zdecydowało, że ponieważ ostatnie rozmowy z rządem nie przyniosły satysfakcjonujących rezultatów, a główny postulat — zwiększenie nakładów na oświatę — nie został spełniony, dlatego od 14

maja ZNP rozpocznie strajk rotacyjny, prowadzony w poszczególnych okręgach w imieniu całego Związku. Strajk w Łodzi rozpoczyna tę akcję, a o dalszych formach protestu Ogólnopolski Komitet Protestacyjny ZNP zdecyduje 18 maja. Prezes ZG ZNP Jan Zaciura zapewnił, że strajkujący nauczyciele w Łodzi nie będą czynić przeszkód w przeprowadzeniu matur.

Mazowsze: Rząd jest skreślony

— Pani premier jest czarująca ko- bietą i trudno ją skreślić, ale rząd jest skreślony — powiedział na konferencji prasowej szef Regionu Mazowsze Maciej Jankowski. Jankowski jest pewny na 95 proc., że dojdzie do strajku generalnego „S". Stwierdził, że po przegłosowaniu w Sejmie wotum nieufności dla rządu, parlament powinien powołać nowy rząd do wyko-

nania określonych zadań. Powodzenie tego wariantu szef Mazowsza określił na 20 do 30 proc. — Jeśli to się nie uda, prezydent powinien utworzyć swój rząd — stwierdził Jankowski. Przyznał, że nie konsultował tej propozycji z Lechem Wałęsą. Jankowski jest przekonany, że cały Klub „S" nie poprze wniosku o wotum nieufności dla rządu, gdyż niektórzy jego członkowie (Jankowski wymienił posłów Rulewskiego i Arkuszewskiego) zachowują się jak urzędnicy koalicji. Dodał, że nie liczy na poparcie żadnych klubów parlamentarnych w sprawie wotum nieufności, choć przyznał, że „S" wiele łączy z Unią Pracy i KPN. 18 maja Region Mazowsze zakończy przygotowania do strajku generalnego.

Dokończenie ☞ 2

...ektów ustaw realizujących ...enia „Paktu o przedsiębior... w czwartek przedmio... ego czytania w Sejmie. ...iesione przez rząd sa roz... m trybie pilnym. ☞ 2

...cunkowych obliczeń, na ...ało w ubiegłym roku ... osób. Ok. 1000 osób ... w Legii Cudzoziem... ☞ 7

...we tempo napływu ka- ...icznego do Polski jest — tak odpowiedziała ...a trzecia (37 proc.) spo... ...łych obywateli ankie- ...wietniu przez Demo... ☞ 7

...osłów powinni skła... ☞ 7

ŻYCIE WARSZAWY

PISMO CODZIENNE • ISTNIEJE OD 1944 ROKU

NR 123

PIĄTE... 28 MAJA

CENA 200...
NR INDEKSU 35...

DZIŚ W NUM...

...zanse rządu 50:50

...gabinetu zależny od ...y posłów PSL i SLD

...vartek nie mógł przewidzieć wyników ...a na votum nieufności. Przeciw rzą- ...ować będzie PC, RdR, SLD, PSL, KPN, ...większość „S" i może UP. Wstrzyma ...R. Koalicja zabiegała o poparcie ca... ...o pojedynczych posłów opozycji.

...R ZALEWSKI, PIOTR ZAREMBA

...ł obalony, za ...wołanie musi ...1 biorących ...niu. Nieobec- ...wstrzymanie ...więc na ko-

...liczeń wyni- ...pewne gło- ...Konwencja ...Niemiecka). ...a kilkuna- ...ych — po- ...i Czajka ...im Świtka ...dziewać, ...sież prze- ...ądu. ...głosu za- ...niedaw- ...zto w ...Łącz- ...zieważ, ...0) opo- ...za rzą-

...alicja uzyskała też podobno wstępne obietnice kilku PSL- owców, że w ogóle nie będą głosować. Jednak władze tej partii postanowiły surowo karać tych, którzy złamią uchwaloną dyscyplinę i niektórzy kompromisowi ludowcy zaczęli się wycofywać.

Unia Pracy dysponująca 6 głosami zapowiedziała, że będzie głosować przeciw odwołaniu gabinetu tylko w przypadku, gdy koalicja zgodzi się na przyspieszone wybory. W związku z tym klub Unii Demokratycznej opowiedział się za ustaleniem kalendarza wyborczego. Również czteroosobowe koło UPR — głosząc, że ten rząd to „mniejsze zło" — być może wyjdzie z sali.

„, CZYTAJ NA STR. 3

Premier Hanna Suchocka wychodzi z sali obrad Sejm...

Rekord obrotów padł na giełdzie

Wczorajsza sesja na Warszawskiej Giełdzie Papierów Wartościowych sypnęła rekordami. Warszawski Indeks Giełdowy osiągnął wartość 3674 punktów. Za jedną akcję „Mostostalu" płacono 1 mln 340 tys. zł.

JB, KW

Rekordowe w historii giełdy obroty, które przekroczyły wczoraj 397 mld złotych to wynik względnej równowagi między popytem a podażą. Ceny akcji rosły o 9-10%, lecz tym razem redukcja kupna były bardziej łagodne niż na kilku poprzednich sesjach. Niewykluczone, że uczestnicy gry giełdowej zbliżają się do stanu nowej równowagi.

O 10% staniał wczoraj „Żywiec". Wielu posiadaczy tego waloru po nabyciu prawa do dywidendy postanowiło pozbyć się piwnych akcji. Krakowska korporacja Efekt" ...notowana...

tyd...

Bezpłatny dodatek telewizyjny „Życia"

FORUM

Miał być Eichmannem

Pokazowy proces Johna Demianiuka trwa od 1975 roku

8-...

625.37.07

CZYTELNICY-REDAKCJA

RELAKS

Krzyżówka na wyspie

12-dniowe wczasy na Grado do rozlosowania wśród zwycięzców

14

ŚRODOWISKO

Słońce z umiarem

Nasz poradnik...

Two important Polish newspapers: Rzeczpospolita and Życie Warszawy (photo shows Prime Minister Suchocka leaving Parliament).

The Republic of Romania

After work in Bucharest—time for a slow beer and catching up on the day's gossip

Area: 237,503 sq. km. = 91,699 sq. mi.

Population: 22,680,000 (projected).

Capital City Bucharest (Pop. 2.24 million (projected).

Climate: Continental, with moderate rainfall.

Neighboring Countries: Moldova, Ukraine (Northeast); Bulgaria (South; Serbia, SFRY (West); Hungary (Northwest).

Official Language: Romanian.

Other Principal Tongues: Hungarian, German.

Ethnic Background: Ancestry rooted in Dacian and Roman heritage, with some Slav intermixture.

Principal Religion: Romanian Orthodox Christianity.

Chief Commercial Products: Machinery and equipment, petroleum, minerals and metals, manufactured goods, agricultural products and foodstuffs.

Currency: Lei.

Former Political Status: Independent states in the east and south from the 13th century; Turkish control from the 15th and 16th centuries in the south and east; increasing Russian influence in the 19th century; independent in 1878 after Russian–Turkish conflict. The western sector was under the Hungarian Crown in the Middle Ages, under independent princes in the 16th century, and under Hapsburg control and later part of Hungary until 1918, when it became a part of Romania. Commu-nist state, part of Soviet bloc, 1945-1990.

National Day: December 1 (Date in 1918 when Transylvania became part of Romania).

Chief of State: Ion Iliescu, President.

Head of Government: Nicolae Vacaroiu, Prime Minister (Appointed November 1992).

Type of Government: Multiparty democracy (in transition).

National Flag: Vertical stripes of blue, yellow and red.

THE LAND AND THE PEOPLE

The dominant feature of Romania's geography is the system of mountains which separate Moldavia and Wallachia from Transylvania in the West. This system has been most commonly described as a giant reverse "S" composed of the Eastern Carpathians and the Southern Carpathians, the latter of which are also called the Transylvanian Alps. They extend westward as far as the magnificent cliffs of the Iron Gate, located on the banks of the Danube River, where it flows through the Alps. This mountain range continues through Bulgaria, where the bottom of the "S" forms the massive Balkan Range. About one–fourth of Romania is covered by forests which are an important source of timber and timber products.

The Danube flows eastward for more than 200 miles from the Iron Gates, forming the border between Romania and Bulgaria. One hundred miles from the Black Sea the river turns north and eventually east again, flowing through Romania to the Black Sea. The area between the river and the sea in this region is known as Dobruja and has been the object of many disputes in the past. Romania's only seaport, Constanta, lies on the Black Sea.

Recently canals have been completed through Dobruja and Bulgaria making transit along the Danube to the Black Sea shorter by more than 100 miles.

The other geographical feature is a plain which begins in the southwest, just south of the Iron Gate, and broadens as one travels eastward. By the time one gets to Bucharest, the "valley"—for it is actually the northern side of the Danube River Valley—has widened to about 80 miles. East of Bucharest, it widens out into a broad plain which becomes the delta of the Danube River. This plain is the chief grain–growing region of Romania. Although mountains dominate the center and north of the country, much of this area actually consists of mountain valleys or plateaus, and so is also productive for purposes of agriculture.

Although most of the population is ethnic Romanian, minorities do make up approximately 12 per cent of the population. The two historic provinces of Moldavia and Wallachia are over-whelmingly ethnic Romanian, but Tran-

Romania

Dacia c. 110 A.D.

Wallachia, Moldavia, Transylvania, c. 1555

Adrianople signed in 1829 in which the Turkish sultan agreed that rulers elected by the two states could not be removed without Russian consent. It further provided that Russia could occupy the area for a period of time. During this occupation, from 1829 to 1834, the principalities were governed by a Russian commander, Count Paul Kisselev, who helped prepare the "Organic Statutes" which became the basic law of Moldavia and Wallachia.

According to the statutes, the two principalities would be separate, each with its own assembly of wealthy land owners who would in turn elect a prince. This system of separation was soon undermined by the forces of nationalism and revolution. The European revolutions of

sylvania has significant Hungarian and German minorities. Latest estimates put the number of Hungarians at 1.7 million, or nearly 8% of the population; the number of ethnic Germans is about 350,000, or about 1.6%. Other minorities includes Jews, Armenians, Gypsies, Serbs, Turks, Bulgarians and Greeks.

HISTORY

Origins of the Romanian State

The Romanians trace their earliest history back to an unknown time when their ancestors, the Dacians, formed a state in Transylvania. Conquered by the Roman Emperor Trajan in 106 A.D., Dacia became a province of Rome, remaining under its rule until the Emperor Aurelian withdraw Roman forces in 271. Although the Latin heritage of the present–day Romanians is reflected in their name and in the character of their language, they are not completely distinct from their Slavic neighbors—this is because the Dacians were subjected to Slavic influence during the centuries that followed the Roman withdrawal.

Not much is known about the life of the Slavic Dacians until the 13th century. Possibly they found safety from the invasions of the barbarians from Central Asia by moving high into the Carpathian Mountains, living in pastoral isolation.

There are three major areas which constitute Romania today—Wallachia, Moldavia and Transylvania. The first two became independent states in the 13th century. Transylvania, which had been inhabited by the ancient Dacians, was under the Hungarian Crown during the middle ages, under independent princes during the time the surrounding area was part of the Turkish Ottoman Empire in the 16th and 17th centuries, under the Hapsburgs after 1699 and under Hungarian (Magyar) control after 1867. It finally became part of Romania after World War I.

The Turkish Ottoman Empire gained control of Wallachia and later Moldavia in the 15th and 16th centuries. They were not incorporated into the Empire, but were allowed a measure of independence in choosing their princes, called *Hospodars*.

At the beginning of the 18th century, the Turkish rulers started to select puppet Greek princes. Until the 19th century, Wallachia and Moldavia were nominally under Ottoman rule, which was not always rigid and was often shared with other powers. In addition to Turkish control of their internal affairs, the Romanians were also subjected to the cultural influence of the French, economic domination by the Greeks and political intervention of the Russians.

Russian interest in the two principalities was recognized by the Treaty of

Romania

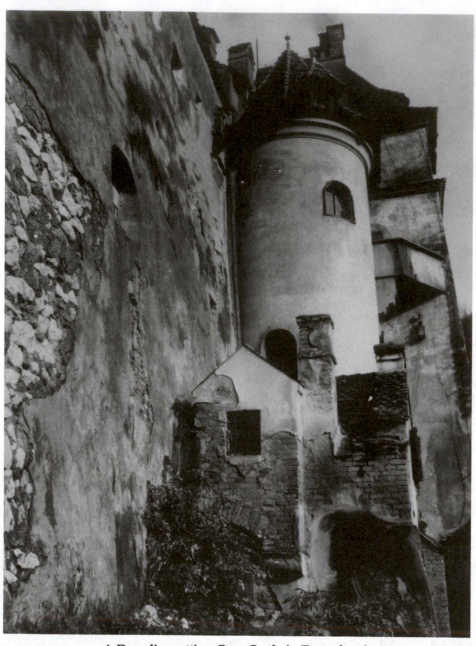

A Draculian setting: Bran Castle in Transylvania

Charles of Hohenzollern–Sigmaringen (Germany) was selected prince, and he ruled until 1881 using that title. From 1881 to 1914, he ruled as King Carol I of Romania. A new constitution was adopted shortly after he arrived, and two political parties alternated in power during his reign—the *Liberal Party* represented the middle class and the *Conservative Party* represented the landowners. The large peasant class had no voice in government.

After another round of Russian–Turkish conflict, the Treaty of Berlin in 1878 recognized Romania's independence. Under the direction of the major powers, Romania was forced to cede the province of Bessarabia to Russia, receiving in turn the region of Northern Dobruja from Turkey.

Romania avoided involvement in the First Balkan War (1912) but battled against Bulgaria in the Second Balkan War of 1913. It remained neutral during the first two years of World War I. The promise of Bukovina, Transylvania and other Hungarian lands was enough bait to bring Romania into the war on the allied side. Its troops entered Transylvania, but were badly beaten by a German counterattack, which resulted in the fall of Bucharest on December 6, 1916. In early 1918 Romania sued for peace, but as the tide turned against Germany, it reentered the war. Romania was thus on the winning side at the peace conference, and in a particularly good position to press territorial demands because its troops had occupied Transylvania and Bessarabia.

Romania After World War I

With Romanian troops on the scene, the councils of Bessarabia and Transylvania voted to unite with Romania. In the peace settlement, Romania was awarded Bukovina (formerly part of Austria), as well as Transylvania and part of the Banat from Hungary. It kept Southern Dobruja which had been seized from Bulgaria in the Second Balkan War.

The areas of Transylvania and Bessarabia were the greatest problems. The first had a large Szeckler population related to the Magyars of Hungary. The Hungarians rejected Romania's claim to the area on the ground that the Daco–Romans had been exterminated or removed from Transylvania by the end of the 3rd century. It was argued that the Romanians made no attempt to re–enter the region until the 13th century while Hungarian settlements dated from the 9th century, therefore Transylvania should belong to Hungary.

The region of Bessarabia had been the subject of disputes involving Russia and the Ottoman Turks in the past. Russia had acquired this territory in 1812 from the Ottoman Empire; Moldavia took southern Bessarabia in 1856 and Russia

1848 spread into Romania—in Wallachia revolutionaries forced the ruler to abdicate and set up a provisional government, which proclaimed as its goal the unification of all Romanians into a single state. This goal was not accomplished for another 13 years because Russia suppressed the revolution.

Russian occupation of Moldavia and Wallachia in 1853 was one of the causes of the Crimean War involving Russia and Turkey which followed in 1854–1856. Under the terms of the Treaty of Paris which ended the conflict, Moldavia and Wallachia were placed under the joint protection of the so–called great powers—France, England and Austria. The great powers decided after the Paris Peace Conference that each of the Romanian principalities was to have a separate assembly and prince. On matters of common concern, the parliaments could meet together.

The effect of this decision was overcome in 1859 when both principalities chose Alexander Cuza to be their prince. Two years later, he proclaimed the unified Romanian state, with Bucharest as the capital. He made efforts toward land reform, freeing the peasants from their feudal obligations. But the peasants were not given enough land to live on, and they remained indebted to the landlords. Cuza was ousted in a military *coup* staged in 1866 by both conservatives and liberals, who favored installation of a member of European royalty as ruler in Romania.

took it back in 1878. The annexation of Bessarabia by Romania after World War I was recognized by the western allies in 1920.

Untroubled by losses of territory as were many of its neighbors, Romania had the opportunity to deal with its fundamental problem: the need for greater land reform. But its governments during the interwar period were inefficient and corrupt. There were land reforms that resulted in the taking of large tracts and distributing them to the peasants, which temporarily appeased them. But it did not provide a real solution to the poverty of the peasants, who then constituted almost 80% of the population.

An important consequence of the land reform was that it reduced the class of wealthy landowners and thereby weakened their representatives from the *Conservative Party*. The *National Liberal Party* came to power in 1922, and except for a brief period from 1926–1927, remained in power. Despite great opposition from Transylvania, a new constitution was adopted which made Romania a centralized state. The government embarked on a program of industrialization for which the peasants had to bear the burden.

The *National Peasants' Party*, organized in opposition to the *Liberal Party*, came to power in 1928 as a result of what was probably the most free election of the interwar period. The government of Iuliu Maniu which had promised to help the peasants did not improve their condition. Instead, it concentrated on attracting foreign investment to boost the industrialization program.

Ferdinand, who had succeeded his father to the throne in 1914, reigned until 1927; his son, Carol II did not take the throne immediately because of a scandal involving an attractive woman, Madame Lupescu, with whom he preferred to live in Paris. The youthful Michael, Carol's son, was nominal ruler from 1927 to 1930 with Nicholas, Carol's brother, as regent. Carol returned to Bucharest in 1930 and persuaded parliament to revoke the law excluding him from the throne.

From 1930 to 1940, King Carol actively promoted the disintegration of the traditional political parties by playing off party leaders against each other and, in the process, strengthening his own power. By 1938 Romania was a royal dictatorship. During the late 1920's a group was organized called *The League of the Archangel Michael*, which, in accordance with its Biblical name, was supposed to do battle with the Devil.

In Romania, the Devil turned out to be anyone who opposed the League, which was fascist and anti–Jewish in outlook. Its name was later changed to the *Iron Guard*. After his return, King Carol subsidized

the group and it became the largest fascist party in the Balkans.

In elections of 1937, the *National Peasants' Party* received the largest vote, but the King refused to ask its leader, Maniu, to form a government. Instead, the leader of the fascist *National Christian Party* was named premier. The dismissal of the premier in 1938 marked the beginning of Carol's dictatorship; a new constitution was drafted, the *Iron Guard* was outlawed and political parties were replaced by the *Front of National Rebirth*—Romania's fascist party.

The country had supported the League of Nations and a system of regional treaties to preserve the balance of power in the Balkans after World War I. However, from 1936 onward, closer ties were established with Hitler's Germany. Despite this, in the first year of the war Romania lost the territories acquired after the First World War. Russia got Bessarabia back, as well as Northern Bukovina; Hungary got Northern Transylvania and Bulgaria took back Southern Dobruja.

An Ally of Nazi Germany

Carol II abdicated and fled Romania in September 1940. General Ion Antonescu, backed by the *Iron Guard*, formed a government and on November 23, 1940, Romania joined the Axis powers. The cooperation between General Antonescu and the *Iron Guard* didn't last long—with Hitler's blessing, he suppressed an attempted revolt by the *Guard* in January 1941. Hitler's concern over stability in Romania was greater than his support for the "like–minded" terrorists whose activities disrupted the country.

From early 1941 until mid 1944 the country was governed by Antonescu's military dictatorship, with the backing of German troops. Romania participated in military operations against the Soviet Union after Germany invaded that country, and it made heavy contributions to the Axis war effort. Although there was only a very weak anti–Nazi movement in Romania, it was the first Axis satellite to defect at the close of the war. On August 23, 1944, King Michael (Carol's son), backed by the *National Peasants' Party*, the *Liberal Party*, the *Socialist Party* and the *Communist Party*, ousted the Antonescu government. Romania then declared war on Germany. Negotiations which had started in Cairo were ended in September in Moscow with the signing of an armistice.

The Romanian People's Republic is Born

Prior to World War II, the *Romanian Communist Party* had been weak and unpopular. It had been outlawed by the government in 1924; further, its pro–Russian attitude and advocacy of self–deter-

mination for Bessarabia and Transylvania were contrary to the prevailing spirit. A communist–sponsored railroad strike in 1933 was quickly suppressed by the government and was followed by the arrest of dozens of party members.

During the 1930's and 1940's there were two groups of Romanian communists—the "home" communists who were behind bars in Romania and the "Muscovites" who had fled to the Soviet Union to avoid being jailed and persecuted. In the early postwar period, the power struggle between the two groups became the most significant feature in domestic politics. The "Muscovite" communists—Ana Pauker ("Red Ana"), Vasile Luca, Teohari Georgescu and Emil Bodnaras—returned to Romania in 1944.

In October the communists joined with the *Social Democratic Party*, the *Union of Patriots* and the *Ploughmen's Front* to form the *National Democratic Front*. The first objective of this union of parties was to launch an attack on the leadership of the *National Peasants' Party* which controlled important posts in the government, headed by General Constantin Sanatescu. He was replaced by Nicolae Radescu.

Early in 1945 the communists started a campaign to publicize a program which they hoped would bring them to power—agrarian reform, a new government and the return of that part of Transylvania transferred to Hungary during World War II to Romanian administration. There was a communist–supported demonstration in early 1945 in which several people were killed. A few days later, Andrei Vyshinsky of the Soviet Foreign Ministry demanded the resignation of the Radescu government. He further specified that a *National Democratic Front* government, led by Petru Groza should be put in power. Radescu could offer no resistance, since Romanian troops had been ordered out of Bucharest.

The new government included noncommunists as well as communists, but the important Ministry of the Interior was given to Teohari Georgescu, one of the "Muscovite" communists. Northern Transylvania was returned and a land reform program was started. General Ion Antonescu was executed in mid–1945.

The Soviet Union recognized the new government headed by Groza. The United States and Britain, however, did not. It was decided that a special commission should advise King Michael, titular head of state, to include representatives of the *National Peasants' Party* and the *Liberal Party* in the government. The new "broadened" government should then call for elections.

The enlarged government took office in early 1946 and was recognized by the western powers the following month.

Romania

The abdicated King Michael with his bride, Princess Anne of Bourbon-Parma, at their June 1948 wedding in Athens

Elections, in which women could vote for the first time, were not held until November 1946. In the months before the elections, the communists pressured some of the other parties into running a common list of "Government" candidates; the result was a victory at the polls for this bloc.

A peace treaty was signed on February 10, 1947, formally returning Transylvania to Romania; the other frontiers were to follow the line of January 1, 1941, which meant that Bessarabia and Northern Bukovina remained part of the Soviet Union and Southern Dobruja stayed with Bulgaria.

The communists eliminated opposition from other political parties outside the *National Democratic Front* in 1947. Ion Mihalache, Iuliu Maniu and other leaders of the *National Peasants' Party* were arrested and sentenced to life imprisonment on charges of conspiring with U.S. intelligence officers. The *National Peasants' Party* was outlawed, and government officials from the *Liberal Party* who had agreed to a common list of candidates in the elections were dismissed in late 1947. The left–wing *Social Democrats* who had also joined in the common list of candidates were absorbed into the *Communist Party*, which was given the name *United Workers Party*. (The name was changed back to *Communist Party of Romania* in 1965).

Having eliminated and neutralized all

opposition, they removed the last remnant of the old system by forcing King Michael to abdicate at the end of 1947. The monarchy had been retained for more than two years after communist–approved Groza became premier.

A new constitution was adopted in 1948 and the Romanian People's Republic was officially born. The story of internal politics in the following years is concerned with a struggle for power between the "home" communists and the "Muscovite" communists. Initially the government was controlled by the "Muskovite" group—Ana Pauker was Foreign Minister, Vasile Luca was Minister of Finance and General Emil Bodnaras was Minister of War.

A "home" communist, Gheorghe Gheorghe-Dej, had helped organize the railroad strike in 1933 and was arrested and sentenced to twelve years in prison. He escaped in August 1944 and in October 1945 became Secretary General of the *Communist Party*, which meant that he was titular head of the party while Ana Pauker and her associates were in control of the government. During the postwar years he consolidated his power and gained support from within party ranks to the extent that he was able in 1952 to remove Pauker, Luca and Georgescu from their party and government posts.

The current official Romanian explanation of this purge is an example of rewritten history. The move has been described

as the beginning of Romania's independence from foreign domination. The fact is that there was no real change in Romanian foreign policy or in Romania's relations with Russia until the late 1950's–early 1960's. Also of significance was the execution in 1954 of Lucretiu Patrascanu, a moderate national communist who had been removed from office in 1948. This event took place two years after the supposed beginning of Romania's new national course.

A more probable explanation of the 1952 purge was that the victory of the "home" communists was the result of an internal power struggle in which Gheorghe-Dej had the support of General Bodnaras and probably Moscow. The reason for dismissal of Pauker and her followers was their supposed responsibility for economic failures.

In addition to his party post, Gheorghe-Dej assumed the post of Chairman of the Council of Ministers in 1952. Holding the highest party and government offices, he had become the real ruler of Romania. The death of Stalin in 1953 would bring upheavals in the communist world and Gheorghe-Dej would adapt to these changes, but he would continue to exercise the primary power in Romania until his death in 1965.

Following the death of Stalin, the Soviet leadership adopted the principle of collective leadership. Gheorghe-Dej obediently resigned his party post, retaining for himself the position of Chairman of the Council of Ministers. Gheorghe Apostal, the trade union chief, became First Secretary of the Communist Party. Gheorghe-Dej soon realized that the party post was more important than the government position, however, so he took it back in October 1955, giving up his government position instead. Chivu Stoica became the new Chairman of the Council of Ministers. Two further changes occurred in 1961. Gheorghe–Dej decided that it would be convenient for him to have a government post, so he added the title of President of the Council of State (ceremonial head of state). He also decided that Stoica was becoming too ambitious, so he replaced him as Chairman of the Council of Ministers with Ion Gheorghe Maurer.

The Ceausescu Era Beginning

This was the situation when in 1965 Gheorghe-Dej died unexpectedly at the age of 63. There was no designated successor so his offices were divided among his subordinates. Nicolae Ceausescu (Cha–*shes*–koo) was Gheorghe-Dej's deputy in the party secretariat and he managed to obtain the top party post. (The title of the office, formerly First Secretary, now became Secretary General.) Maurer remained on as Chairman of the Council of Ministers while Chivu Stoica got the title of President of the Council of State.

Ceausescu, the new Secretary General, had joined the Romanian Communist Party in the 1930's through its youth organization. A protégé of Gheorghe-Dej, he became a full member of the party Politburo in 1955, at the age of 37. Over the next ten years, he occupied himself as a member of the Central Committee Secretariat. His special area of responsibility was party organizations and cadres, a position which allowed him to exercise extensive control over party appointments. In 1965, however, he was only one of three individuals who exercised power in a collective leadership.

It was under these circumstances that the Ninth Congress of the Romanian Communist Party met in July 1965. The congress approved a new constitution—the one in force until the revolution of 1989—and a new set of party laws. The adoption of a new constitution was largely symbolic. It did not change the general system in any important respect, though it did announce that Romania was no longer a "People's Republic" and that it would be known as the "Socialist People's Republic of Romania." It also made explicit that it was the *Romanian Communist Party* that exercised all leadership within the state.

The constitution increased guarantees of civil liberties and a general emphasis on national independence. At the same time, it abolished the Szeckler autonomous region, which had originally been set up in Transylvania to give the Hungarian-speaking minority a modicum of self-government.

The most formidable opponent of the new Secretary General was probably Alexandru Draghici, Minister of the Interior, who controlled the secret police. Ceausescu invoked one of his new party laws which provided that government and party functions could not be combined in one man. When the party Congress elected Draghici to the Secretariat, he had to give up his post as Minister of the Interior.

Following this move, Ceausescu had a national party conference in late 1967 reverse the policy of the separation of party and government offices. Instead, plans were made for reorganization of the government on all levels based on the principle of combining state and party offices; this was supposed to avoid duplication of functions between party and state. This principle was immediately carried out at the highest level—Ceausescu was elected by the National Assembly to succeed Chivu Stoica as President of the Council of State; he was on his way toward establishing his preeminent authority within the country.

Over the next several years Ceausescu

President Nicolae Ceausescu

also became Chairman of the National Defense Council, Supreme Commander of the Armed Forces and chairman, or honorary chairman, of any number of party and state commissions and committees. The culmination of all this came in mid-1974 when the constitution was amended to create the position of President of the Republic—the position was, of course, filled by Ceausescu.

This accumulation of offices was accompanied by the development of a full-blown "cult of personality" around Ceausescu. In speeches and in the press, he began to be referred to as the "hero of heroes" and the years of his rule as "the years of light." In later years, he was given credit for everything that happened in the country. In fact, he often intervened to resolve petty matters at the local level.

More ominously, he also placed his family in important positions of power in the government and party. Three of his brothers held senior posts in the govern-

ment, one on the Council of Ministers, while his wife, Elena, was First Deputy Chairman of the Council of Ministers, member of the Permanent Bureau of the Political Executive Committee (Romania's equivalent of a Politburo), and Chairman of the National Council for Science and Technology. Finally, his son, Nicu, was First Secretary of the Union of Communist Youth and a candidate member of the Political Executive Committee. Nicu's wife was also a member of the Central Committee.

Ceaucescu's Fall

All of this was swept away at the end of 1989 in a violent uprising that ended in Ceausescu's death by firing-squad on December 25. Ceausescu, who was proud of his independence from Moscow, had rejected Gorbachëv's policy of reform and made every effort to isolate his countrymen from events going on elsewhere in Eastern Europe. In November 1989, he had reaffirmed his policies at a Party Congress and had been reelected head of the party for a further five-year term. It was probably this act of reaffirmation that was responsible for his downfall, for those same policies had been responsible for a significant decline in the standard of living of Romanians over the previous nine years.

The revolt, which actually began as an ethnic dispute in the city of Timisoara, in the western part of Romania, spread to Bucharest, the capital, when Ceausescu called a mass meeting for December 21 to denounce the events in Timisoara. Instead, the people began shouting "freedom" and "democracy" and Ceausescu stalked off. That afternoon, the streets were full of people demonstrating against Ceausescu. That evening, Ceausescu ordered the secret police to begin firing on the people. A similar order to the army brought a refusal from General Milea, the Defense Minister. General Milea was executed the next morning,

TV picture shows the Ceausescus upon their capture

Romania

President Ion Iliescu

but the army now joined the revolution. Ceausescu and his wife fled the capital, but they were captured, brought back to Bucharest, tried, and summarily executed.

The *Securitate*, Ceausescu's secret police, fought on for a few days more but the army gradually managed to restore order. In the meantime, a group calling itself the *National Salvation Front* emerged as the new political leadership in the country.

The New Government

The *Front*, at first made up almost exclusively of former establishment figures who had fallen out with Ceausescu, was enlarged within a few days to take in various non–communist elements. It then began referring to itself as the *Council of National Salvation*. In the third week of January, the Council announced that multi–party elections would take place in May and that it intended to run its own candidates. This brought a condemnation from the leaders of the three largest opposition parties. After a series of negotiations, the *Council* agreed to make room for representatives of other parties. On February 1, the Council brought the representatives of 29 other political parties into the government coalition. By this time, it had grown to approximately 180 members. It also underwent a name change at this time and became the *Provisional Council for National Unity*. A new ten member Executive Committee,

headed by Acting President Ion Iliescu, also came into existence at this time.

Meanwhile, the original *National Salvation Front* reorganized itself as a political party, announced that it, not the Council, would field candidates in the upcoming May 20 elections. As its candidate for President, it nominated Ion Iliescu. Most of the leadership of the *Front* had been members of the old *Romanian Communist Party* and the local branches of the *National Salvation Front* set up at the time of the revolution were largely made up of ex–officials. Thus, while the old *Communist Party* structure had collapsed, a large percentage of its membership transferred their loyalties to the *National Salvation Front*.

Eventually, some 80 political parties came into existence, though only three of them had any significant political support in the country. Two of these, both parties that were outlawed when the communists took over, are the *Liberals* and the *Peasant Party*. The third, the Hungarian Democratic Union, represents the interests of ethnic Hungarians. Although the opposition attacked the *National Salvation Front* because of its high component of ex–communists, there was, in fact, little to differentiate between them as far as programs were concerned. All said that they were committed to the creation of a multiparty democracy and a market economy.

In the May elections, Ion Iliescu was

elected President with approximately 83 percent of the vote while the *National Salvation Front* took 66 percent of the seats in the National Assembly. Election observers announced that there had been some irregularities in the voting but that, overall, the election was free.

For approximately six months, the policies of the new government remained unclear as factions within the Front debated whether Romania would move toward a free market or attempt to develop some sort of mixed economy with the government continuing to play an important role. Petre Roman, the new Chairman of the Council of Ministers, called for a transformation to a market economy within two years. Others talked about a gradual transition that would safeguard jobs and wages. The *Peasants Party* and the *National Liberal Party* the two main opposition parties, had argued for a rapid transition to a market economy and privatization of land and industry. Their showing in the May 1990 elections strengthened the hand of those who argued for a mixed economy.

Still some progress was made. Over the summer, legislation was passed encouraging the creation of small businesses and authorizing the government to turn state enterprises into privately owned companies. Other legislation authorized the government to sell apartment houses built after 1948. These laws were permissive in nature, however, and longtime bureaucrats found it easy to frustrate their intent.

A larger issue is that the democratic credentials of the government came into question after the government encouraged miners to attack a group of anti–government demonstrators on University Square in Bucharest in June. Six individuals were killed in the resulting violence and the headquarters of some of the opposition political parties were ransacked. Anti–government rallies continued over the summer. As a result, the Romanian government found itself boycotted by potential donor countries, in spite of its desperate need for economic assistance.

In October, Petre Roman submitted another package of land, banking and tax proposals to the Assembly which he said were intended to speed Romania's transition to a market economy. Among the proposals was that prices of nonessential goods and services would be freed, though the government would continue to subsidize the price of energy, fuel and rent for another year and control the price of basic foods and services. Although Romanians were talking about these proposals as radical and likely to contribute further to the spiral of inflation that had hit the country, they were actually yet another example of gradualism which would leave the underlying problems unsolved.

The government did take one set of actions of a positive nature. It redistributed almost a third of the country's arable land to private farmers, and the result was an unusually good grain harvest and an increase in meat and fresh products in the unregulated farmers' areas. The government got some more good news in Janaury 1991, when it was finally admitted to the economic aid program set up a year earlier to provide economic assistance to the emerging democracies of eastern Europe. Separate discussions with the International Monetary Fund resulted in an agreement in April 1991, under which Romania became eligible for up to $1 billion in financial support. In return, Romania agreed to phase out subsidies on basic food products. This led to major increases in the prices of bread, eggs and meat.

The government began converting the National Bank into a western-style central bank in December 1990. The bank was to give up all of its retail operations and confine itself to issuing currency and controlling monetary policy. The Foreign Trade Bank, which formerly performed certain central bank functions, gave up its monopoly over foreign exchange. Private banks were also authorized at this same time. Eight private banks came into existence within the next six months, the first being the Banka Comerciale Ion Tiriac SA, founded by a Romanian expatriate, the ex-tennis player Ion Tiriac.

In January 1991, the government learned that it had finally been admitted to the economic aid program set up a year earlier to provide economic assistance to the emerging democracies of eastern Europe. Separate discussions with the International Monetary Fund resulted in an agreement in April 1991, under which

Romania became eligible for up to $1 billion in financial support. In return, Romania agreed to phase out subsidies on basic food products. This led to major increases in the prices of bread, eggs and meat. In a separate move, the World Bank approved a $175 million loan to Romania in June 1991. The loan was to be used for technical assistance and for financing imports of critically needed spare parts.

Although Roman's economic reforms had the support of international economists, their implementation was causing a drop in the standard of living of most Romanians as inflation outpaced wage increases. The matter became political in September 1991 when 52,000 coal miners in western Romania went on strike over pay and prices. Several thousand of the miners made their way to Bucharest, where they demanded the resignation of Petre Roman. The demonstrations soon turned violent and before they were

A group of young folk dancers from the provinces

AP/Wide World Photo

Romania

over three persons had been killed and hundreds had been wounded. President Iliescu, whose relations with his prime minister hadn't been very good for some time, fired Mr. Roman and promised the miners that he would form a new "government of national openness."

Roman afterwards charged that Iliescu and his allies had called in the miners and that it was all a communist plot to remove him and reverse his economic reform. There is no evidence of that. It appears, rather, that President Iliescu took advantage of the miners' protest to get rid of Mr. Roman. It does not appear to have been a policy matter either, for the man Iliescu named as Roman's replacement, Theodor Stolojan, had been at one point Minister of Finance in Roman's government and later was his Minister for Privatization. A strong believer in reform, he pledged his new government to a continuation of Roman's economic policies. His cabinet, a government of national unity, included seven technicians not associated with any political party, four ministers, plus the Prime Minister, from the *National Salvation Front*, three from the *National Liberal Party*, and one from the *Agrarian Democratic Party*.

Economic reform has, in fact, continued and perhaps even speeded up a little under Stolojan. He has been no more successful than Roman in perking up the economy, however, and dissatisfaction is inevitably growing. This showed up in February 1992, when local elections were held throughout Romania. The *National Salvation Front* proved its strong organizational structure by winning more mayoral elections overall, but still lost in Bucharest and in many smaller cities. The second largest total was won by independent candidates, however, so support for opposition political parties is not yet significant.

According to the constitution, new elections for the presidency and the national legislature were scheduled to take place in the summer of 1992. These would obviously be a larger test for the government than the local elections and it appears that President Iliescu at one point considered not standing for reelection. One problem was that Iliescu was not sure that he could obtain the backing of a political party in the campaign. Although a founding member of the *National Salvation Front*, he had resigned his membership after he was elected president. The party subsequently came under the control of Petre Roman, Iliescu's first Prime Minister. However, the two had had a political falling out after Roman was forced to step down as Prime Minister in September 1991.

The elections took place on September. The *National Salvation Front* had split over the issue of supporting Iliescu. One wing, supporting Iliescu, split off and formed the *Democratic National Salvation Front*. Mr. Roman's wing, which opposed Iliescu, organized itself as the *Front For National Salvation*. It fielded no opposition candidate, but did run a separate slate of candidates for seats in the parliament. There were five other candidates for the office of President. Iliescu came in first with 48% of the votes. Emil Constantinescu, candidate of the *Democratic Convention Alliance*, came second with 33%. Gheorghe Funar, an ultra–nationalist candidate came in third with 10%.

Because Iliescu had not obtained a majority of the votes, there had to be a second, runoff election, which was scheduled for October 11. The runoff was between Iliescu and Constantinescu. Iliescu won, this time taking 61.4% of the votes.

The results of the parliamentary elections were far less decisive. The *Democratic National Salvation Front* became the largest of the parties with 28% of the seats. The *Democratic Convention Alliance* (which is actually a coalition of political parties) won approximately 20% of the seats, followed by the *Front For National Salvation* with about 10%. Five other parties also won representation. With no party or coalition controlling a majority of the seats, it took five weeks to put together a majority willing to support a new Prime Minister. The selection finally fell on Nicolae Vacaroiu, a 49–year old economist who had been head of a tax department in the Economics Ministry of the previous government. Vacaroiu, a technocrat without close political ties, has since loyally implemented President Iliescu's policy of slow reform.

Foreign Policy

Romania first obtained the ability to develop its own independent foreign policy in 1958, when Soviet troops were withdrawn from the country, but the issue over which it split with the Soviet Union, its desire to industrialize, first became an issue in 1961–62. It was at this time that the Soviet Union proposed the creation of a supranational planning group within the Council for Mutual Economic Assistance (CMEA) to decide which country should produce how much of what. The Soviets wanted an international division of labor which would allow some countries to emphasize industrial production while others (notably Romania and Bulgaria) were intended to be a source of raw materials and agricultural products. The Soviet–Chinese dispute gave Romania the chance to defy Moscow. The first sign of opposition came in March 1963 when Romania refused to support the creation of the CMEA group.

In April 1964, the Romanian Central Committee issued a statement which has been described as a "Declaration of Independence" in economic as well as in political matters. In the economic area, they asserted the right to develop their own natural resources. In political affairs they rejected the idea that any communist party was superior to another, claiming the right of each party to develop its own policies. Their attitude toward the Warsaw Pact military alliance has been similar to their attitude on CMEA. Soviet attempts in 1966 to strengthen the Warsaw Pact Organization by creating a permanent East European political authority and by increasing the integration of the various military units from each country were successfully resisted by the Romanians. And when the Soviet Union intervened in Czechoslovakia in 1968, Ceausescu criticized the Soviet actions and coupled it with a statement that Romania would resist any Soviet incursion into Romanian territory. Romania maintained this critical attitude toward the Soviet Union from that time onward. It always refused to permit Warsaw Pact maneuvers on Romanian soil and refused even to attend the annual meeting of Warsaw Pact nations in 1971. Relations improved somewhat in the middle of the 1970's but Ceausescu publicly aired his differences with the Soviet Union in November 1979, following the Warsaw Pact meeting in Moscow, over Soviet Middle Eastern policy and Soviet demands that the East European members of the Warsaw Pact increase their military expenditures.

In early 1980, Romania publicly, if indirectly, criticized the Soviet invasion of Afghanistan when Ceausescu attacked countries that "gravely threaten the cause of people's independence." The Romanian position became even clearer in January 1981 when it abstained on a United Nations vote demanding the withdrawal of foreign troops from Afghanistan. All of the Soviet Union's Eastern European client states voted against the resolution.

Ceausescu also took an independent position with regard to Soviet SS–20 missiles and Theater Nuclear Force negotiations. In December 1983, after the Soviets withdrew from the TNF talks in Geneva, Ceausescu issued a public call for both the Soviet Union and the United States to stop deploying nuclear missiles and to resume arms control negotiations. Another example of Romania's independence was the Soviet decision to boycott the 1984 Summer Olympics. Every other Soviet "ally" joined in the move, but Romania sent its athletes to Los Angeles—and brought back 32 medals, including 20 golds, to place third in the total number of medals won.

Romania's relations with the Soviet

Street intersection in Bucharest

Union became more complex after the Soviet Communist Party's 27th Congress in early 1986. Ceausescu forthrightly condemned Gorbachëv's programs for economic reform, but, at the same time, Romania's economic ties to the Soviet Union actually increased. Gorbachëv finally paid a visit to Romania in May 1987. The Soviet press gave the visit a rather low–key treatment, but the Romanian press was far more enthusiastic. Several economic agreements were signed, but it was clear that political differences remained.

Under Ceausescu, relations with other countries were basically determined by the relations of those countries with the Soviet Union. Thus the primary thrust of Romanian foreign policy in those years was to establish close relations with those countries opposed to an expansion of Soviet power. A second, related interest was Romania's desire to expand its trade with the West. Neither of these principles involved a turning away from communism. Domestically, Romania remained among the most orthodox of communist nations.

During those years, it maintained its closest relations with the People's Republic of China. The reasons for this are clear. In addition to a common ideology, the two nations strongly opposed Soviet domination of the communist world. Romania consistently supported the Chinese arguments in the Sino–Soviet quarrels. In addition, there was a regular exchange of high–level diplomatic missions between the two countries and an extensive promotion of cultural contacts and trade.

Relations with Western Europe and the United States developed on another basis during those years, with trade, perhaps being the most important factor. Romania never made the mistake of thinking it could ignore its geopolitical position entirely, or that it could depend on any country other than itself in case of extreme Soviet displeasure. It was nevertheless the first East European nation to establish diplomatic relations with the Federal Republic of Germany and until about 1985 it went out of its way to encourage better relations with the United States. The breakthrough may be said to date from 1967 when Richard Nixon, visiting various European capitals, stopped in Bucharest and was personally received by Ceausescu. Two years later, then President Nixon decided to pay a state visit to Romania as part of a round–the–world trip. He thus became the first American President to pay a state visit to a communist country. Nixon suggested the visit to "needle our Moscow friends" but he evidently wanted to show his appreciation for the way he had been treated in 1967. The visit took on a symbolic importance beyond that, however.

First of all, a Romanian Communist Party conference, to which the Soviet leadership had been invited, had to be rescheduled in order to make the visit possible. However, Brezhnev and Kosygin, originally scheduled to attend the conference, cancelled out of the rescheduled conference. Secondly, as reported by a New York newspaper, Nixon received "a warm reception from hundreds of thousands of flag–waving Romanians in the largest and most genuinely friendly welcome of his global tour." It also was during this visit that President Nixon asked Ceausescu to act as a channel of communication to the Chinese. The subsequent breakthrough in U.S.–Chinese relations therefore owed something to the Ceausescu connection.

The Nixon visit to Romania was fol-

Romania

lowed up by a Ceausescu visit to the United States the following year. This visit, which lasted two weeks, had an obvious political component, but its major emphasis was economic. Ceausescu met with a number of American businessmen, signed a contract for a $10 million aluminum sheet–rolling mill and signed an agreement for an exchange of researchers and university teaching staff. Ceausescu had been to the United States twice since that time, in 1973 and again in 1978. On the American side, President Ford stopped in Bucharest in mid–1975 and at that time the U.S. accorded Romania the "most favored nation" trade status. The United States also sponsored Romanian applications for membership in international organizations such as the International Bank for Reconstruction and Development (World Bank) and the International Monetary Fund (IMF).

Beginning in the 1980's, the United States became increasingly critical of Romanian internal developments. This was accompanied by occasional threats to withdraw "most favored nation" status unless the Romanian Government made certain internal changes. One instance was a tax on Jewish emigration which Romania had instituted. Under the Reagan Administration, it focused increasingly on Romanian treatment of Christian evangelicals.

The matter came to a head in June 1987 when the U.S. Senate voted to suspend Romania's "most favored nation" status for six months to indicate that it disapproved of Romania's human rights record. To put an end to such recriminations, the Romanian Government responded by voluntarily renouncing all such trade concessions.

Romania's actions did not put an end to U.S. criticism of Romania's human rights record, however. In the last two years of Ceausescu's rule, the U.S. Government several times criticized his program to transform the countryside by razing villages and replacing them with high–rise "agro–industrial" complexes. The basis for the criticism was that the program, although billed as an economic measure, was being implemented almost exclusively in areas where there were Hungarian and German ethnic minorities and a major goal of the program appeared to be to destroy these centers of non–Romanian culture so that their inhabitants could be assimilated into the majority Romanian culture.

Romania's foreign policy changed after the overthrow of Ceausescu in December 1989 and the creation of a new government committed to democracy and a market economy, but less than one might have thought. The new leadership has attempted to establish a friendly relationship with all nations and thus far it has largely succeeded. The only exceptions would be the People's Republic of China and such hard–line Communist nations as Vietnam and Cuba, who, generally speaking, have condemned the events of 1989 in Eastern Europe. On the other hand, the Soviet Union welcomed the overthrow of Ceausescu and followed this up with friendly gestures such as opening the border between Moldova and Romania for a day so relatives could visit back and forth. The repudiation of communism following failure of the August 1991 *coup* against Gorbachëv, followed by the subsequent collapse of the Soviet Union, obviously changed that relationship as Romania quickly moved to establish diplomatic relations with the successor republics, but the changes have been more in form than in substance. In any case, with the notable exception of the newly independent Republic of Moldova, Romania's main interest in the successor republics is economic as it struggles to hold on to export markets there.

Romania's relations with Moldova are complicated. This area, except for that part east of the Dniester River, had been part of Romania prior to 1940 and a majority of the people living there speak Romanian. On the other hand, President Snegur of Moldova favors an independent Moldova and he was elected to the presidency of that republic by a large majority in December 1991.

His opposition, the *Moldova National Front*, favors union with Romania, but their call to boycott the December 1991 elections was ignored by the vast majority of the Moldovan people. The Romanian Government has been careful to remain neutral in this internal quarrel.

The United States welcomed the overthrow of the Ceausescu regime and our early attitude toward the new government was extremely favorable. Among other things, Secretary of State Baker arranged a short visit to Bucharest in the spring of 1990. But the United States was also critical of some of the actions of the new government, and decided after the death of six demonstrators in June 1990 that all assistance to Romania would be put on hold. The United States went along with inclusion of Romania in the aid consortium for eastern Europe, but it was not until Petre Roman visited Washington in April 1991 that one could speak of a noticeable thawing of relations. Relations have probably warmed up somewhat further in the past year.

The Revolution of 1989 overthrew the old Communist regime and installed a revolutionary regime whose stated goals were the creation of a multiparty democracy and a market economy. Free elections occurred in May 1990. The new Government gave itself 18 months to draw up a new constitution and it accomplished that when the new constitution was submitted to the people for approval in a popular referendum on December 8, 1991. The new constitution got the support of 77 percent of those going to the polls, but a majority of ethnic Hungarians voted against the constitution, since the constitution lacks the specific guarantee of rights for minorities that they had demanded.

Whether this becomes a problem in the future will depend on how local governments treat ethnic Hungarians. New national elections must take place by December 1992, but will probably be held earlier. There had been discussion of holding them in May 1992, but parliament had not yet passed a new electoral law as of the beginning of April. The draft bill drawn up by the upper house, the Senate, called for a 147–member Senate and a 310–member lower house.

The Government

Romania held its second set of presidential and parliamentary elections in September 1992 and may be said to have made the transition to a multi–party democracy. Many of the people in leading positions are ex–communists, but they have won their positions in democratic elections. No single party or coalition commands a majority in the Grand National Assembly. The current Prime Minister, essentially a technocrat, is more of an implementer than a maker of policy.

The President, who is popularly elected, exercises overall executive power. He is expected to set general policy and act as spokesman for the nation. In addition, he has specific responsibilities in the areas of foreign affairs and defense. He nominates the Prime Minister, who must be confirmed by the Grand National Assembly. The Prime Minister, in turn, chooses his cabinet, who must also be confirmed by the Assembly. The Prime Minister articulates specific policies, maintains liaison with the legislature, and oversees the day–to–day operations of government.

The Economy

At the end of World War II, Romania was still an overwhelmingly agricultural economy with over three–quarters of the workforce employed in farming. Bucharest, center of what industry there was, was large and relatively modern; but there were only three other cities in the country with populations of over 100,000 persons. The political elites who had dominated the government during the interwar period had been committed to a policy of industrialization but, except for the petroleum industry, they were not notably successful.

Immediately following World War II, a land reform act set an upper limit of 123 acres (50 hectares) on all individuals. This act also provided for the expropriation of all real property of individuals held to be fascist collaborators. The collectivization of agriculture was begun in 1949. It was in theory voluntary, but peasants who refused to join a collective found themselves required to deliver a set amount of produce to the state at an artificially low price.

Collectivization was completed in 1962, although there was a subsequent further amalgamation of collective farms that brought together single villages into new multi–village cooperatives. Under the Communist regime, the state purchased, processed, and distributed most agricultural products. It did, however, run town and city markets where individuals and also state and collective farms could market some of their produce. Agricultural output increased considerably during the period 1970–1977 but largely stagnated after that. This was particularly true in the area of animal production. From 1979 onward, Romanians had trouble finding beef and pork in the markets. Perhaps the largest reason for this was the government's decision to place a greater emphasis on the export of agricultural products as part of its program to pay off the foreign debt.

There were some problems with the overall level of production as well, however, for cattle herds were a million below planned levels by 1980 and President Ceausescu publicly complained that exports had to be reduced "year after year" in order to maintain domestic levels of consumption.

One problem appears to have been organizational—state and collective farms fairly efficiently produce grain and fodder crops but perform badly in the production of meat, milk, eggs, fruits and vegetables. Thus, although all but 9.4% if the land was controlled by the state, it was this privately–held land (nearly all located in mountainous areas deemed unsuitable for extensive cultivation) plus the private plots of individual collective farmers which provided over half the country's production of potatoes, fruit, meat, milk and eggs. In fact, these two sectors produced an estimated one–third of Romania's total agricultural production during this period.

Although under communism nearly all capital flowed into state and collective farms and the machine–tractor stations serving them (plus other state units such as experimental stations) their use of capital was actually very inefficient. Between 1962 and the early 1980's, output per unit of fixed capital on state and collective farms was filled by about one–half.

In spite of its shortcomings, however, collectivization, with its emphasis on mechanization, did bring about major changes in the countryside. The old, traditional farming methods were largely supplanted and productivity accordingly increased, so that only 32% of the workforce was still engaged in agriculture by the 1980's. Most of these excess agricultural workers were drawn into the industrial workforce. Starting from a relatively low base in 1948, Romania began an industrialization program using the Stalinist command model which resulted in one of the fastest growth rates in the world. The driving force behind the Stalinist command model is the very high investment level—up to 35% of gross national product—which is determined by the state. This will result in a very rapid growth rate if one is dealing with a situation in which there is a surplus of labor and adequate raw materials—as was the situation in Romania in the 1950's and 1960's. On the other hand, a high investment level means that there is less left over for consumption, and living standards will necessarily remain low. This has also been the case insofar as postwar Romania has been concerned.

Under communism, Romania's industrialization program also concentrated on the creation of heavy industry rather than consumer goods. The major industries built or expanded during this period include oil refineries, chemical plants and various sorts of metal–working and machine–building enterprises. In later years, a major area of emphasis was electric power generation.

Two huge hydroelectric stations, the Iron Gate II project with Yugoslavia and the Trunu–Magurrele project with Bulgaria, were constructed during the 1980's. Its first nuclear power plant was completed in the second half of the 1980's. These new sources of energy were designed to allow for a continued growth in industry in general and the metallurgical industry in particular. Two other projects pursued by the government in the 1980's were an expansion of the Galati steel complex and construction of a new steel complex at Calarasi.

In the last several years under Ceausescu, however, Romania had largely exhausted the possibilities of the Stalinist demand model and had reached the point where both labor and raw materials

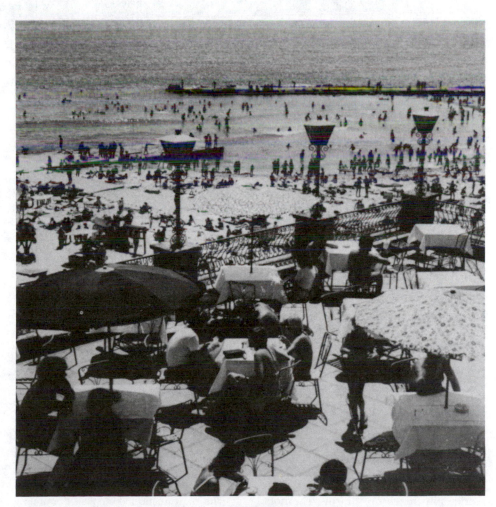

The seaside resort of Eforia

Romania

The Trade Union Cultural Home in Slatina, southern Romania

were scarce—and in fact many of the raw materials had to be imported. Instead of moving toward decentralized decision–making and placing greater emphasis on quality as opposed to quantity, however, Ceausescu stubbornly clung to the command model.

The situation was also exacerbated by Ceausescu's determination to pay back the foreign debt of approximately \$13 billion which he had run up during his industrialization spree in the 1970's. To accomplish that, Ceaucescu instituted a harsh austerity program and cut Romania's hard currency imports by more than two–thirds. Romania also began to reorient its trade toward the CMEA countries, in particular with the Soviet Union. Between 1980 and 1989, the proportion of Romania's trade with other members of the CMEA grew from a third to just over a half. The government was also able to pay off its hard currency debt by the beginning of 1989 but only by dropping Romania's standard of living to the lowest in Europe. During Ceausescu's last years, food was rationed, cities were unlighted at night, and gas and electricity were available only on a limited basis.

The first sign that the Romanian people were losing their patience came in November 1987 when riots broke out among workers in the city of Brasov. The riots, triggered by a new government decree

announcing additional penalties for workers who failed to fulfill production quotas, were met by tanks, police dogs and tear gas. For several days, Brasov was off–limits to all foreigners.

The government did not, in the end, have any great difficulty putting down the riots, but the blows to Ceausescu's credibility and to the regime's legitimacy were more severe. Once again, workers had risen up in protest against a so–called workers' state. One indication of this loss of credibility was that, for the first time in memory, a number of prominent Romanians dared to criticize the regime publicly. One such was Silviu Brucan, former Ambassador to the United States and the United Nations, who urged the government to recognize the legitimacy of the workers' grievances. Several government ministers also dared to defend themselves against charges that they were responsible for the widespread shortages.

In spite of these signs of growing domestic opposition, Ceausescu held to his policy of austerity and used the funds thus accumulated to pay off Romania's foreign debt. As a result, Romania announced in April 1989 that it had paid off the last of its foreign loans and was debt–free.

The big question then was Romania's future economic policy. Its 1989 current–

account surplus was expected to be around \$3.5 billion, and Ceausescu could have eased off on his austerity program and allowed some increase in imports. Instead, he used the funds to finance such grandiose schemes such as his creation of a grand avenue and Presidential Palace, which he had been building in the middle of Bucharest over the previous five years. Ceausescu also continued the grand program, launched in 1988, of transforming the countryside by razing half of Romania's villages by the year 2000 and moving the inhabitants into new high–rise buildings in "Agro–industrial" centers.

The answer of the Romanian people came in December 1989, when they rose up and brought the entire regime down. Romania has now had a non-Communist government committed to multiparty democracy and a market economy since the beginning of 1990. But the individuals making up the new government were badly divided among themselves as to the proper path to follow and they had been in power for about a year before taking any action to begin transforming the economy. They also took certain decisions during that first year that temporarily eased the lot of the Romanian people, but which had negative longer-term consequences.

One of those decisions was to use part

of Romania's foreign currency reserves, then about $1.8 billion, to import food for domestic consumption. The government continued the policy in 1991 but, by that time, it had used up most of its foreign currency reserves and so turned to financing consumption through an enlarged budget deficit. In effect, then, Romania has been living beyond its means since 1989 and can't afford to do it any longer. International aid may help to close the gap, but it is likely that the standard of living will have to drop in 1992.

Economic statistics also look awful. For example, industrial production has decreased by over 40 percent since 1989. Part of this drop can probably be blamed on the disruptions of the revolution itself, but there are larger causes as well. Domestically, shortages of energy and raw materials play an important role. Internationally, Romania lost a significant part of its market for exports when the Soviet Union collapsed. It also lost a major source of raw material imports.

The Romanian working class is naturally unhappy about the economic situation. Freeing prices has produced a virulent inflation that has eroded wages, while talk of privatization of state firms promises future unemployment. Surprisingly, polls indicate that a majority of the Romanian people continue to favor both privatization and the development of a market economy. Yet the *National Salvation Front* has lost a lot of its popularity in recent months, as witness the fact that it lost in most cities and towns in the February 1992 local elections. That's not necessarily bad, since the political opposition also supports economic reform and some parties favor a speeded up temporary scheme.

The news from the countryside is also somewhat more negative than it was in 1991. The break up of the collective and state farms has given land to the peasants, but most of them can't afford farm machinery to work the land. Energy shortages are another problem. Farm production may drop in 1992. How soon before Romania turns the corner? It is difficult to say and it will partly depend on the amount of international assistance Romania qualifies for. But the government ought to be able to stabilize the economy by the end of 1992. The beginning of new growth is probably 3–5 years away.

Culture

The Romanians take great pride in their Latin origin, although over the centuries they have also been subject to Hungarian, Slav and Turkish cultural influence. Romania has a large Hungarian minority located primarily in the Tisa Plain and in Transylvania. The Szecklers,

though they speak a Magyar dialect, are distinguishable from the Hungarians on historic grounds. They have been in Transylvania since the Middle Ages when they were frontier guards for the Magyar settlements. The Hungarian Magyars recognized them as a free people of noble birth and as one of the privileged nations of Transylvania, along with the Saxons (Germans) and the Magyars.

The Romanian Orthodox Church has the largest following, but Roman Catholicism and Calvinism are strong among the Hungarian population. The old communist constitution guaranteed freedom of religion with qualifications—for instance, the organization of "religious cults" was regulated by law. Schools other than seminaries could not be operated by the Church; the Church budget was under state control and the Church officials had to be acceptable to the state. The new revolutionary government pledged a "hands–off" attitude toward religion, so most of that will probably change, though it is still too early to say for sure.

There has been considerable movement from rural to urban areas since World War II, but Bucharest is still by far the largest city, containing more than 1/5 of the city dwellers of Romania. It is modern and a center of cultural expression. In the countryside, the folk music, art and colorful costumes prevail.

Free primary education is compulsory for eight years, and there are universities in Bucharest and in four other major cities.

The Future

Romania held new elections for President and legislature in September 1992. President Iliescu was reelected but no party won a majority in the legislature. The government continues to support a policy of transition to a market economy, though at a relatively slow pace.

Romania is an extremely poor country today, largely because of the policies of the Ceausescu regime and the sort of policies it pursued. Some progress has been made in the area of agriculture. Peasants now have their own land, although they often have very little in the way of equipment or farm animals to work the land. It is not unusual to see milk cows hitched to a plow. In spite of this, agricultural production appears to be up.

The government has not yet begun any major reforms in industry, though it has permitted considerable privatization in the area of retail trade. Converting an inefficient industrial base that has been constructed largely on Stalinist command lines is a task so large, and one which will require so much capital, that the government appears not to be sure how to begin. Moreover, a large part of Romania is an ecological disaster area. Romania's economic progress will be slow and painful.

Piatra Neamt City in Romania's Moldavia region

The Former Yugoslavia

Montenegro: Police hold back demonstrators protesting the deteriorating economic conditions

AP/Wide World Photo

On April 27, 1992, after four of the six republics which had been integral parts of *The Socialist Federal Republic of Yugoslavia* had declared their independence, the remaining two, Serbia and Montenegro—the largest and the smallest in the former union—proclaimed themselves the successor nation as the "new" *Federal Republic of Yugoslavia*, a rump state which has not been accorded diplomatic recognition by any nation. Its naked aggression against Bosnia–Herzegovina has seen 70% of that republic's land fall into the hands of the Serbs' "Yugoslav People's Army" and Serb irregulars living within that nation. After fourteen months, during which the United Nations has attempted to bring the war to an end, the conflict continues. Nothing has helped. A UN embargo hurt Serbia economically but not enough to get it to end its support for the war in Bosnia. UN relief efforts have also been frustrated by Serbian opposition and manipulation. The embargo was strengthened in May 1993 and President Milosevic of Serbia, the real power in rump Yugoslavia, says he is now for peace. The self–styled Serb assembly in Bosnia recently rejected peace, however.

The basic facts listed immediately below relate only to the new Serbia/Montenegro "marriage" followed by a general history of that area of the Balkans and of the now disintegrated *republic* born on November 26, 1945.

Area: 39,408 square miles (102,261 sq. km.).

Population: 10,406,742 (April 1991 census).

Capital City: Belgrade (Pop. 1.3 million, metropolitan area, projected).

Climate: Continental, with marked contrasts between summer and winter, with lowest temperatures in the high elevations. The summers are hot.

Neighboring Countries: Hungary (north); Romania, Bulgaria (east); Macedonia (south); Albania, Bosnia– Herzegovina, Croatia (west), but this may change.

Official Language: Serbo–Croatian.

Other Principal Tongues: Albanian, Hungarian, and Romanian.

Ethnic Background: Slav, with Albanian ancestry in the southwest, Hungarian in the Voivodina.

Principal Religions: Serbian Orthodox Christianity, Islam.

Chief Commercial Products: Chemicals, farm equipment, paper, glass, textiles, sugar, flour, wheat, corn, tobacco, fruits and vegetables, lead, zinc, copper, silver, gold, chromium, coal, and consumer goods.

Currency: New Dinar (This may soon change).

Former Colonial Status: Yugoslavia did not exist as a state prior to World War I; it was created around the core of old Serbia by adding the Kingdom of Montenegro and territories taken from the Austro–Hungarian Empire.

Yugoslavia

National Day: April 27 (1992), the date on which Serbia and Montenegro declared themselves the successor nation as the "new" Yugoslavia.

Chief of State: (vacant) Dobrica Cosic, who had held the position of "President of the Republic," was ousted on June 1, 1993.

National Flag: Horizontal stripes of blue, white and red, with a five–pointed red star in the center, outlined in gold.

The Land

With the collapse of the Yugoslavian Federal Government in 1991 following the withdrawal of four of the six republics, Yugoslavia has shrunk to a rump of its former self and now consists of the two republics of Serbia and Montenegro. Serbia has two "autonomous" regions, the Voivodina (Vojvodina) and Kosovo–Metohija, the latter of which now seeks its own independence or affiliation with Albania.

The Voivodina is that part of Serbia north of the Danube River. It is a rich, flat plain, divided by tributaries of the Danube flowing across it from the north. The Voivodina borders on Hungary to the north, Croatia to the west, and Romania on the east. It was granted an autonomous status because a majority of the population is ethnically Hungarian.

Kosovo–Metohija, the second "autonomous" region, is located in the southwestern part of Serbia. About 90 percent of this area is ethnically Albanian. This is a mountainous region, with the highest ones, the Albanian Alps (in Serbian the *Mokra Mountains*), located in the northeastern part of the province. A second mountain, the Sar, arises in the southwest. There is a plateau region in the center, with lower mountains rising again to the east. Northern Serbia is mostly the lowland area of the Danube River Valley. As one travels south away from the river valley, however, the land becomes rolling hills, then mountain ridges cut by river

Yugoslavia

valleys open to the north. Mountains also predominate along the western border with Montenegro, in the south along the border with Macedonia, and in the east along the border with Bulgaria.

Montenegro means "Black Mountain" and that describes most of this mountainous land. The Dinarian Alps extend into the republic from the north. In the south, the Albanian Alps run west–east along the border with Albania. Montenegro also has a fairly long coastline on the Adriatic Sea. Skhoder Lake, also located here, forms part of the border with Albania. The northern half of the lake belongs to Montenegro.

The People

The rump Yugoslavia of 1992 consists almost entirely of Serbs and the linguistically and culturally closely related Montenegrins, except for the two autonomous regions of Serbia, where Hungarians predominate in the Voivodina and Albanians in Kosovo–Metohija. In 1990–91, the Serbian Government destroyed the autonomous status of both these regions, so today the governments in these areas are appointed by Belgrade. The people of the Voivodina have quietly accepted the situation, but the Albanians of Kosovo held a referendum on independence and declared their own republic in 1991. The area is still occupied by Serbian troops and the situation is far from stable.

History

The Slavic–speaking peoples of the Balkan Peninsula are classified as South Slavs and they are one of three branches of the Slavic peoples, the other two being the East Slavs (Russians, Ukrainians, Belarusians) and the West Slavs (Poles, Czechs, Slovaks). The Slavic language is, in turn, a branch of the Indo–European family of languages. When the Slavic peoples first appeared in history, they were found mostly in the area of the Pripet Swamps in what is now the republics of Belarus and Ukraine.

The South Slavs began migrating into the area of the Balkans sometime in the sixth century. At first, the Slavs were dominated by two Turkic peoples also present in what became the Balkans, the Avars and Bulgars. When the Avar and Bulgar khanates crumbled in the first quarter of the seventh century, however, the Byzantine Emperor signed an alliance with two of the stronger Slavic tribes, the Serbs and Croats. Supported by this alliance, the Slavic peoples either pushed the Turkic peoples out of the Balkans or submerged them in their greater numbers. By the end of the seventh century, Slavic language and culture was dominant throughout most of the northern Balkans, except for the east where the Vlach (ancestors of modern Romanians)

were in a majority and in mountainous areas of the west where the native Illyrian people (ancestors of the modern Albanians) managed to keep their culture alive.

The Serbs and Croats eventually gave their names to the areas of the Balkans they now occupy, while a third tribe, the Slovenes, who had actually been the first of the Slavic tribes to enter the Balkans, settled further west. In 748, the Slovenes were incorporated into the Carolingian Empire and converted to Roman Catholicism. They remained a part of western culture from that time onward. The Croats were also incorporated into the Carolingian Empire for a short time at the beginning of the ninth century and converted to Roman Catholicism. It was not until the end of the eleventh century that they came under the control of the Kingdom of Hungary, however.

The first Serb state rose about the middle of the ninth century when a number of south Serbian tribes united to oppose expansion from the Bulgar state to the southeast. Vlastimir, the ruler of this state, sought the support of the Byzantine Emperor against the Bulgars; in the process, he submitted himself to the over–lordship of the Byzantine Emperor. One effect of this is that Serbia became open to Byzantine cultural influences, the most important of which was Orthodox Christianity. In addition, the two missionaries from Thessalonica, Cyril and Methodius, had created a script for the Slavic language based on Greek letters. The Cyrillic alphabet was adopted by Serbia along with Orthodox Christianity, and in the process a great cultural divide was created in the Balkans that ran through the middle of the Slavic settlements. Henceforth, Serbs (along with Bulgarians, Montenegrins and Macedonians) were on one side of that divide and the Croats and Slovenes on the other.

In spite of Byzantine assistance, Vlastimir's kingdom eventually fell under Bulgarian control. As a result, the Serb church became a part of the Bulgarian Orthodox Church. The area of Serbia next came under the control of a Macedonian kingdom created at the beginning of the eleventh century. Then the Byzantine Empire overthrew the Macedonian kingdom in 1018 and tried to extend its control over the area of the eastern Balkans. This led to short–lived kingdoms arising in Herzegovina and Montenegro to challenge the Byzantine control. Toward the end of the eleventh century, yet another kingdom rose in the area of Novi Bazar, only to be supplanted by a revived Bulgarian kingdom after the capture of Constantinople by soldiers of the fourth crusade in 1204.

A new Serbian kingdom rose in the area of Skopje ("j" is almost always pro-

nounced "y") beginning in 1282, called the Nemanjid Empire after the name of the dynasty. The founder of this dynasty was Stefan Nemanja. This kingdom reached its height under its ninth ruler, Stefan Dusan, who ruled from 1331 to 1355. Although this kingdom eventually extended its control over a large part of the northern Balkans, its greatest significance was probably cultural. The Nemanjids were committed to the Orthodox Church and it was during this time that the Serbs managed to separate from the Bulgarian Orthodox Church and establish an autonomous *Serbian* Orthodox Church. The seat of the church was later moved to Pec; In 1375, it was raised to a patriarchate.

Equally important, the Nemanjids managed to create a Serbian "high culture" based on religious cohesion. They fought the influence of Roman Catholicism and worked to suppress Bogomilism, a religious heresy centered in Bosnia. They were also responsible for construction of many churches and monasteries, which have come to signify the essence of medieval Serbian Orthodoxy. Among the most renowned of these churches are the Milesevo (c. 1235), Pec (1250), Moraca (1252), Sopocani (c. 1260), and the Decani (1327). Many of these churches are decorated by frescoes, the most important being those of the Rasko school.

In addition, this period produced a number of literary works, including a biography of Stefan Nemanja. A close partnership between church and state produced a courtly culture which was at the same time a religious culture. This continued to define the best of what it meant to be a Serbian long after the kingdom itself was no more. This kingdom came to an end in the fourteenth century, when Turkish armies defeated the Serbs in the Battle of Kosovo which took place on June 15, 1389. The leader of the Serbian forces was Prince Lazar. The Turkish Sultan, Murad I, was actually killed early in the day by a Serbian assassin, Milosh Obilic, who made his way into the Turkish camp pretending to be a deserter. He stabbed the sultan with a poisoned dagger.

Murad's son managed to rally his forces and defeat the Serbians. Prince Lazar, taken prisoner during the battle, was beheaded. For seventy years, Serbs were required to pay an annual tribute and to serve in the Turkish armies, but were allowed domestic autonomy. Then, in 1459, the sultan placed all of Serbia under Turkish rule. All lands became the property of the sultan and all Serbs became bond slaves of the land. The patriarchate of Pec was also suppressed for a time, but was restored in 1557. Henceforth, Serbian culture lived on only within the Serbian Orthodox Church.

WESTERN BALKANS 1560–1680

REPUBLIC OF VENICE

Venice

HUNGARY

CROATIA

OTTOMAN

EMPIRE

PAPAL STATES

REP. OF RAGUSA

MONTENEGRO

Rome

KINGDOM OF NAPLES (to Spain)

—— Boundary of the Holy Roman Empire ⬚ Austrian Possessions

OTTOMAN (Turkish) EMPIRE at its greatest extent.

MONTENEGRO, an area of virtually inaccessible mountains, never conquered by the Turks.

REPUBLIC OF VENICE, ruled by an elite of wealthy merchant families. Dominated the Adriatic Sea from bases in Dalmatia.

REPUBLIC OF RAGUSA (Dubrovnik), a small city–state which flourished as an important cultural center, developing distinctive local styles of architure and sculpture, and establishing Croatian as a modern literary language.

These boundaries were essentially stable for over a century as the Austrian Hapsburgs resisted further Turkish advances into Central Europe.

KINGDOM OF NAPLES, ruled by the Spanish Hapsburgs as a separate kingdom.

PAPAL STATES—In these territories the Pope was the secular ruler. Other Church territories were ruled by bishops or abbots who were princes of the Holy Roman Empire.

AUSTRIAN POSSESSIONS—A collection of separate kingdoms, duchies and counties, ruled by the Austrian branch of the House of Hapsburg.

HOLY ROMAN EMPIRE—During this period all emperors were from the Austrian Hapsburgs.

——— 1680–1740 ———

The Ottoman Empire attempted to expand into Central Europe, but the Turkish army was held at the gates of Vienna in 1683, and then forced back, liberating the entire central basin of the Danube River; the new Austro–Turkish border stabilized in 1739.

AUSTRIAN MILITARY FRONTIER—Refugee Serbian communities were settled along the border in Croatia and Slavonia (not to be confused with the present republic of SLOVENIA) by the Austrian government. A military constitution to defend the Slavonian borderland was granted in 1702 and later extended to Croatia and Transylvania.

KINGDOM OF THE TWO SICILIES—After changing hands several times, the Kingdom of Naples and the Kingdom of Sicily were combined in 1735 under a junior branch of the House of Bourbon.

Yugoslavia

WESTERN BALKANS 1740–1797

- Boundary of the Holy Roman Empire ▢▨▨ Austrian Military Frontier ▢⋯⋯ Austrian Possessions

The Ottoman Empire was no longer a threat, and Austria was occupied in central Europe with the rise of Prussia and the partition of Poland. Boundaries were basically stable during this period.

─────────── 1797–1815 ───────────

During the Napoleonic wars political boundaries and country names changed frequently.

The Venetian territories were carved up in 1797, the largest part going temporarily to Austria.

The Holy Roman Empire became extinct in 1806.

In 1809 France briefly annexed all of the eastern Adriatic coast as well as Ragusa and nearly all of present–day Slovenia.

By 1809 all territories ruled by the Roman Catholic Church had been acquired by secular states.

Meanwhile, Montenegro won a small expansion of its boundaries.

WESTERN BALKANS 1815–1860

Boundary of the German Confederation   ▧▧▧ Austrian Military Frontier   ▦▦▦ Austrian Possessions

In the post–Napoleonic settlements, Austria (re)gained all of the Venetian territories plus Ragusa as well as those Church territories within its borders. The Military Frontier was maintained, becoming a separate crownland in 1849 with special privileges for the Serbian settlers.

GERMAN CONFEDERATION—Created to replace the Holy Roman Empire with the same eastern and southern boundaries.

The Pope was restored as ruler of central Italy, but all other former Church territories remained secularized.

SERBIA—The Serbs had been fighting for their independence since 1804, achieving in 1817 recognition as an autonomous principality under Ottoman overlordship.

These boundaries were essentially stable during this period.

See the text and map of this area (c. 1350) on page 245. Also, note the map on page 305 for later pre–World War I boundaries.

Yugoslavia

THE ETHNIC/RELIGIOUS MIXTURE WITH RESULTING AGE–OLD TENSIONS

As of the 1980 census

- Slovenes
- Croats
- Serbs
- Bosnians (Moslems)
- Montenegrins
- Macedonians
- Hungarians
- Albanians
- Ethnic mixture

Alexander of Bulgaria and it was only Austria's threat to enter the war on Serbia's side that produced an armistice. Serbia then recognized the union of Bulgaria and Eastern Rumelia.

In 1903, a palace revolution led by forces loyal to the Karageorgevic family led to the murder of the Obrenovic family and the Karageorgevic dynasty to the throne. In a change of foreign policy, the Karageorgevic king set out in earnest to create a Greater Serbia by bringing as much of the Balkans as he could under his control. This brought Serbia into conflict with the Austrian Empire, since Serbia also laid claim to Austrian lands occupied by South Slavs. Relations worsened after Austria formally annexed Bosnia-Herzegovina in 1908. Austria had obtained these lands in 1878 as part of the Treaty of Berlin, but had not formally annexed them. Serbia, supported by Russia, threatened to go to war against Austria in 1908, but Russia was forced to back down in 1909 and Serbia was left in a lurch.

The last King of Serbia, Peter I

It then began putting together an alliance of Balkan countries that led to the First and Second Balkan Wars in 1912–13. Serbia obtained additional territories as a result of these wars, but Austria frustrated Serbia's attempts to gain access to the Adriatic Sea coast, among other things by sponsoring creation of an independent Albania. In 1914, Serbia played an important role in the origins of World War I by sponsoring the Black Hand, the Serbian revolutionary group which carried out the assassination of Archduke Franz Ferdinand, heir to the Austrian throne, while he was paying a state visit to Sarajevo, capital city of Bosnia–Herzegovina.

Turkish rule continued for another five centuries before the Serbs raised the banner of revolt. Under the leadership of Karageorge (Black George), the Serbs revolted against the rule of the Turks in 1804. The revolt was suppressed in 1813, but a more successful revolt broke out two years later under the leadership of Milosh Obrenovic. In 1817, Serbia won

the right to have its own national assembly. Milosh became Prince of Serbia and promptly had his great rival, Karageorge, murdered. This was a beginning of a feud between the Obrenovic and Karageorgevic families which continued into the twentieth century, frequently disrupting the political life of the country.

After the Russo–Turkish War of 1828–29, Serbia was given the status of an autonomous principality, technically still under Turkish suzerainty but effectively a Russian protectorate.

In 1876, Serbia became the cause of another war between Russia and Turkey when it declared war on Turkey. When it became clear that Serbia would not be able to stand against the Turks, Russia intervened in 1877. Russia defeated the Turks and forced Turkey to recognize the independence of Serbia (and Romania) in the Treaty of San Stefano. The Treaty was revised by the great powers at the Congress of Berlin in 1878, but the resulting Treaty of Berlin included recognition of Serbian independence.

In 1885–86, Serbia fought a war against Bulgaria after that nation and Eastern Rumelia united in 1885. The war began when Prince Milan demanded that Bulgaria cede some of its territory to Serbia. Serbian forces were defeated by Prince

The last King of Montenegro, Nicholas I

Austrian armies reached Belgrade by December 1914, but were repelled by a counter–attack. Bulgaria's entry in 1915 helped shift the equation against Serbia. The Serbian army retreated to the Adriatic coast and then to the island of Corfu. In 1918, Allied forces made their way into the Balkan Peninsula. The Serbian army joined with the Allies in defeating Bulgaria, then liberated Serbia.

A New Nation is Born

During the war, discussions were held on creating a separate state for South Slavs who had been part of the Austro–Hungarian Empire. Serb leaders hesitated at first because their long–time vision was of a single Greater Serbian Kingdom which would include all areas inhabited by Serbs. The remaining South Slavic leaders had in mind a different vision. They wanted a decentralized South Slavic state organized along federal lines, which would allow a large amount of autonomy to the individual ethnic groups. Representatives of the two points of view signed the Corfu Pact in 1917 in which they agreed to create a South Slav state under the Karageorgevic dynasty after the war.

Although basically South Slav, what became Yugoslavia consisted literally of what was left over after France, Great Britain and the U.S. redrew a new map of eastern Europe after World War I. On December 4, 1918, the Kingdom of the Serbs, Croats and Slovenes was proclaimed in Belgrade with Prince Alexander of Serbia as Regent. Serbia (including Macedonia and Kosovo), which had been independent before the war, formed the core of this new kingdom. The Kingdom of Montenegro, also independent before the war, was added when

Montenegro

Montenegro experienced centuries of independence while the surrounding areas seethed under Turkish control. The almost impassable mountains allowed the Montenegrins to resist repeated Turkish attempts to conquer the area; although they and later the Venetians did occupy parts, it was never completely controlled. Its independence was recognized by the Congress of Berlin in 1878. During the years before World War I, the Montenegrins, like some of their neighbors, were advocates of South Slav nationalism, lending military support to the cause in 1878 against the Turks and during the Balkan Wars of 1912–13.

World War I

A Bosnian student assassinated Archduke Franz Ferdinand, heir to the Hapsburg throne, in Sarajevo on June 28, 1914. He belonged to the "Black Hand," which was formed in Serbia in 1911 with a goal of the union of all Serbs.

Austria responded to the murder with an ultimatum to Serbia, demanding in part that Austrian officials be permitted to participate in the investigation of the crime. When the Serbian government accepted only part of the terms of the ultimatum, Austria–Hungary declared war on Serbia. Because of a multitude of cross–alliances, France and Russia came into the war on the side of Serbia, while Germany entered as an ally of Austria–Hungary. England entered when Germany violated Belgian neutrality and World War I began. Bulgaria and Turkey later entered on the side of Germany and Austria–Hungary, while Romania entered as an ally of France, England and Russia. Thus almost all of the Balkans became involved in the war.

The combatants at the start of World War I, 1914

305

Yugoslavia

the King of Montenegro resigned his throne in favor of the new South Slavic State. To this was added territories from the former Austro–Hungarian Empire—Croatia, the Voivodina, Bosnia–Herzegovina, and Slovenia—plus strategic points taken from Bulgaria along the Serbian–Bulgarian border.

Politics of the Interwar Period

The question of the political structure of this new kingdom was supposed to be decided by the Constituent Assembly which was elected in 1920. The parties represented in the Constituent Assembly included the *Democratic Party*, the *Radical Party*, the *Croatian Peasant Party*, the *Agrarian Party*, the *Slovene People's Party*, the *Moslem Party*, and the *Communist Party*. Of these, the *Radical Party* was the largest. Led by Nikola Pashich, they were in power almost continuously until 1926. The *Croatian Peasant Party* was the most important in Croatia and its leader, Stepjan Radick, was the most prominent Croatian political figure until his death in 1928.

In 1921, the Constituent Assembly adopted a constitution which created a centralized government. The necessary votes came from the Serbian parties and smaller ones which had "sold" their votes in return for promises of special favors. The *Croatian Peasant Party* boycotted the Assembly because of its opposition to the centralized system outlined by the constitution.

The period 1921–1928 was one of conflict between the Serbs and Croats over the question of centralism vs. federalism. The Serbs prevailed by using increasingly harsh tactics, including the arrest of the Croat opposition leader and dissolving his party. Outraged, the Croatian deputies withdrew from the body, swearing not to return until they had been granted a federal system in which Croatia would no longer be controlled from Belgrade. The demands of the Croats were unacceptable to the Serbian leaders, and also King Alexander. Taking advantage of a decade of disagreement between the Serbs and Croats, the king abolished the constitution and proclaimed a royal dictatorship, later changing the name of the country to the Kingdom of Yugoslavia. The change in name did not alter the fact that Serbs, Croats and Slovenes lived and fought with each other within the boundaries of the kingdom. Alexander's mistake was in thinking he could create a Yugoslav nationalism by decree. He was assassinated in 1934 by a Macedonian terrorist.

From 1934 to 1941 a three–man regency ruled the country with Prince Paul as First Regent. Internal affairs were left to the Premier, who governed with the support of a specially organized party, the

Assassination: King Alexander of Yugoslavia at Marseilles, France, October 1934

Yugoslav Radical Union. Parties in opposition formed an alliance and demanded a new constitution which would set up a government capable of dealing with the discontented Croats. When the extent of the Serb–Croat split was revealed in 1938 elections, the government sought talks with the Croatian leadership. The result was an agreement which created an internally self–governing Croatia.

Prince Paul of Yugoslavia

In international relations during the interwar period, Yugoslavia was most concerned about the protection of its borders against the ambitions of neighboring states and against the Great Powers who wanted to use the conflicts among the Balkan states to extend their own influence. Both the "Little Entente" and the "Balkan Entente" were supposed to serve these purposes. In 1920–21 Yugoslavia formed an alliance with Romania and Czechoslovakia, the "Little Entente," which was directed primarily against Hungarian ambitions to revise the Treaty of Trianon. The "Little Entente" was backed by France through treaties with Czechoslovakia (1924), Romania (1926) and Yugoslavia (1927).

After a series of conferences between 1930–1933, Greece, Turkey, Romania and Yugoslavia signed the Balkan Pact (February 1934) guaranteeing the territorial status quo against aggression by any Balkan state. In practice, this meant that the Pact was directed against Bulgaria. Several months later, the signatories adopted the Statutes of the Balkan Entente which set up a Permanent Council, provided for regular meetings and for extensive economic and political cooperation. Both alliance systems disintegrated by the end of the 1930's. The rise of Germany and Italy, the inability of the League of Nations to deal with acts of aggression, and the appeasement policy of Britain and France made Yugoslavia search for new means of ensuring her security. Accordingly, it signed a pact of friendship with Bulgaria (1937) and a non–aggression and arbitration pact with Italy in the same year, which moved Yugoslavia closer to the Axis powers.

World War II

The decision of the government to sign the Tripartite Pact and thus join the Axis side in 1941 was bitterly opposed by many Yugoslav government officials and army officers. A military *coup* deposed Prince Paul and the army announced a policy of neutrality. However, Germany's Hitler had already decided that Yugoslavia could not be left in the hands of an "unreliable" government. An invasion by Nazi troops resulted in an Axis victory within two weeks, after which Yugoslavia was divided.

Croatia was enlarged and placed in the hands of a fascist dictator, Ante Pavelich. Slovenia was divided between Germany and Italy, Macedonia was occupied by Bulgaria, parts of Bosnia and Dalmatia went to Italy, a small piece in the north was given to Hungary, and German administration was imposed on Serbia. A puppet government was established in Belgrade.

From 1941 to 1944 Yugoslavia was ravaged not only by struggles against the Nazi occupation, but also by civil war between the *Chetnik* and *Partisan* resistance forces. The Chetniks were bands of officers and men drawn from the remnants of the Royal Yugoslav Army; they were loosely organized and generally undisciplined, pro–Serbian and anti–communist. The Partisans, led by Tito and the *Yugoslav Communist Party*, tried to form an organization with a broader, national following.

The *Communist Party* had been one of the largest in the Constituent Assembly elected in 1920. Its goal was the establishment of a Yugoslav Soviet Republic. In 1921, however, the government banned the party after the murder of the Minister of the Interior, although there was no evidence linking the party to the assassination. The party remained illegal throughout the interwar period, which meant that its members were forced to operate underground. One of its early members was Josip Broz, whose revolutionary *nom de guerre* was Tito. The son of a Croatian peasant who had been inducted into the Austrian army, he was taken prisoner of war by a Russian detachment at the age of 23. He escaped from prison in Russia and joined the Bolsheviks, fighting with them in the Russian civil war. After he returned to Yugoslavia, he became the secretary of the Zagreb branch of the *Communist Party of Yugoslavia*. When the party was declared illegal, Broz was

arrested and sentenced to five years at hard labor.

By 1937 he was the Secretary General of the *Yugoslav Communist Party*, which he reorganized and purged in accordance with the latest dictates from Moscow. After the country was occupied by the Germans, he used his control of the party organization to create guerrilla units called "Partisans" for use against the Germans.

At first, Partisans and Chetniks attempted to fight side–by–side, but it soon became evident that while they were both

Marshal Josip Broz-Tito, leader of the *Partisans* in World War II

fighting to free Yugoslavia from Axis control, their image of the future of the country was totally different. The Chetniks were fighting for the return of the monarch and Serb–dominated government. The Partisans were fighting for a federally–organized, socialist republic. There also was a disagreement on general military strategy—the Partisans wanted all–out resistance while the Chetniks, afraid of German reprisals, wanted to wait for the arrival of the Allies.

Eventually the Chetniks and Partisans were fighting each other as hard as they

fought the common enemy. In order to combat the Partisans and to prevent the Germans from killing Serbs, the Chetniks began to collaborate with the enemy. Evidence of collaboration resulted in a loss of Allied support for them. The British sent a military mission to aid the Partisans several months before there was a similar move by the Soviets. The contribution of the Partisans to the war effort and the leadership of Tito were thus formally recognized by the Western Powers.

Under Tito's direction, the *Anti–Fascist Council for National Liberation of Yugoslavia (AVNOJ)* was formed in 1942 to function as a government in liberated territories. A year later at Jajce in Bosnia, the *AVNOJ* elected a provisional government which made Tito Marshal of Yugoslavia and Premier. The AVNOJ thus replaced the nominal authority of the government–in–exile, located in London, and forbade King Peter, successor to Prince Paul, to return.

The British prevailed on the king to appoint as premier of the exiled government a man who could negotiate with the

Yugoslavia

Partisans, and Dr. Ivan Shubashich, who had been governor of Croatia until 1941, was selected.

In October 1944 Russian and Partisan forces liberated Belgrade. It is significant that by the time Russian forces arrived in Belgrade the Partisans were in firm control of large parts of Yugoslavia. After the liberation of Belgrade, Tito and Shubashich signed an agreement providing for a Regency Council to act in the king's name, free elections within three months of liberation and a legislature consisting of the *AVNOJ* until an assembly could be convened. This arrangement was approved by the "Big Three"—the U.S., the U.S.S.R. and Great Britain—at the Yalta Conference in 1945, and the king was thus forced to accept it also. Three Regents were chosen in March 1945—a Serb, a Croat and a Slovene, none of whom were communists but all of whom had Tito's approval.

Tito then formed a new government in which he was Premier and Shubashich was Foreign Minister; the cabinet included representatives from each of the six areas of Yugoslavia and of the government–in–exile. Before the elections for a Constituent Assembly took place, Shubashich resigned, protesting the government's refusal to allow "collaborators" to vote—this term was loosely applied to anyone who opposed the government. The elections were boycotted by the opposition parties, the *Serbian Radical Party*, *Agrarian Party*, *Democratic Party* and *Croat Peasant Party* in protest against the atmosphere of intimidation created by what had become a very active secret police. As a result, the people could vote only for the *Communist People's Front* list of candidates.

Yugoslavia Becomes a Federal People's Republic

The Constituent Assembly which was elected declared Yugoslavia to be a Federal People's Republic; when a new constitution was adopted in early 1946, the Assembly changed its name to the People's Assembly. This body consisted of two houses, a Chamber of Nationalities and a Federal Chamber. The Chamber of Nationalities had 30 representatives from each of the six federal republics, plus 15 from the autonomous province of Kosovo and 20 from the autonomous region of the Voivodina. In theory, therefore, it served a function somewhat similar to that of the U. S. Senate. The Federal Chamber was the "popular body", with one representative for every 50,000 inhabitants.

The People's Assembly was not designed as a deliberative body, however. It met only twice a year, on April and October 15th, then only to rubber–stamp decisions of the government. More power resided with the Presidium of the People's Assembly, since the Presidium appointed and dismissed cabinet ministers and had law–making authority when the Assembly was not in session. As with all communist regimes, however, real power rested with the Communist Party.

Although the government remained in theory a "People's Front," the policies which it instituted during this period were based on Soviet models. Larger estates were expropriated and a beginning was made on the establishment of collective farms. In 1947, the government launched its first Five–Year Plan. In industry, emphasis was placed on electrification, chemicals and metallurgy. Foreign trade was oriented toward the eastern bloc nations.

The Soviet–Yugoslav Dispute of 1948

Yugoslavia had been considered such a loyal satellite that the new Communist Information Bureau, or *Cominform*, set up in September 1947, had established its headquarters in Belgrade. But now a quarrel began over the issue of joint Yugoslav–Soviet companies. Two joint companies were actually set up, for air transport and for river shipping, but the way they were operated appeared so disadvantageous to the Yugoslavs that they refused to allow any further joint companies to be formed. This led to a bitter quarrel between Tito and Stalin and resulted in the curtailment of Russian aid and a reduction of trade between Yugoslavia and the rest of the eastern bloc nations.

The dispute marked the first time a ruling communist party defied the authority of Moscow and still remained in power. The disagreement arose over the question of the power relations between the two countries. Tito's challenge to Moscow was possible because his political survival did not depend on Stalin's support. Unlike the communist leaders of other East European countries, Tito had not come to power by the might of the Soviet army, but because of his personal following in the Partisan movement which had the leading role in liberating Yugoslavia at the end of the war.

After the war, the Yugoslav communists thought of themselves as Moscow's most faithful followers. Tito's desire to follow the correct line was evident in the enthusiasm with which he modeled Yugoslavia's economy and constitution on those of the Soviet Union. It was probably in recognition of Tito's importance that Stalin set up the *Cominform* headquarters in Belgrade.

In light of this background, the real issue in the dispute was not Yugoslav departure from the official Moscow communist line, but the refusal to be controlled by Moscow in matters which affected the interests of Yugoslavia. The question was one of how two communist parties and their leaders should conduct their relations with each other when each was also responsible for the interests of his own state.

Stalin's opposition to any communist power that was not under his personal control was shown by his attitude toward the plans for a Balkan federation authorized by Tito and supported by the Bulgarian communist, Dmitrov. The Bulgarians even agreed that after federation, Yugoslavia should annex the part of Macedonia that lies within Bulgaria. By 1947 the plans included the possibility of also bringing Albania, Romania and Greece into some kind of union and there were hints of a Balkan–Danubian Federation involving Hungary.

Sensing an increase in Tito's power if there were federation, Stalin abruptly reversed his early support for the plan. When the Bulgarian leadership expressed hope for a customs union as a step towards federation, *Pravda*, the Moscow official newspaper, responded with an article stating that the Balkan states did not need any kind of customs union or federation.

At a meeting in the Kremlin in 1948, Yugoslavian and Bulgarian representatives were scolded by Stalin and Soviet Foreign Minister Vyacheslav Molotov. The Bulgarian communists were criticized for planning a customs union with Romania and the Yugoslavs were denounced for helping Greek communists and for sending troops into Albania without Moscow's approval.

There were other issues involved in the break between the two nations. The Yugoslavs were critical of the Soviet failure to send aid to the Partisans during the war and Stalin's instructions to play down the role of the *Communist Party* in the resistance movement. They recalled that Stalin had opposed setting up the AVNOJ as the supreme authority in 1943. Further charges included the failure of the Soviet Union to press Yugoslavia's claim to Trieste against Italy at the close of the war because Stalin did not want to antagonize the Allies by bringing up the claim.

The Soviets accused the Yugoslavs of directing propaganda against the Soviet Union and of having an "unduly large" peasant membership in their communist party; there were also accusations charging that the party was being run "undemocratically." The treatment of Soviet military advisors and civilian experts as foreigners was also a target.

The Yugoslavs requested that the dispute be settled by two–party discussions. Instead, the Soviets called a meeting of the *Cominform* and issued a statement in

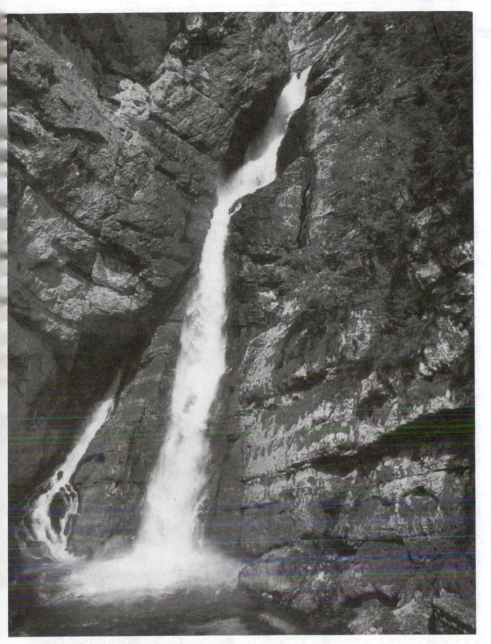

The Savica waterfall, source of the Sava River.

Photo by Prof. Janko Ravnik

each of the republics. Thus, the central directive role of the state was reduced while, at the same time, the participatory role of the workers was enhanced at the local level.

In 1953, the constitution was modified to incorporate the concept of workers' self–management. Beginning in 1952, producers' councils had been created at the local and republic levels. In 1953, a national Council of Producers was created as a second national legislative body to replace the Chamber of Nationalities. The Chamber of Nationalities was not abolished, however, but was partially amalgamated into the Federal Chamber. What was different about the national Council of Producers as well as the local and republic producers' councils was that representation was on the basis of occupation and that persons voted where they worked. It was, in effect, an attempt to give political expression to the term "economic democracy."

On the other hand, decentralization was considered to apply primarily to economic decision–making. In the political arena, other constitutional changes made at this time had as their purpose to create a more obvious central political authority. To this end, the old executive structure of a "Presidium of the National Assembly" and a Council of Ministers were abolished and replaced by a "President of the Republic" with true executive powers, assisted by a Federal Executive Council. Needless to say, Marshal Tito became the new President.

The Communist Party also changed its name at this time and became the "League of Communists of Yugoslavia," the name by which it still goes today. But the League of Communists was not willing to give up its monopoly of political power. When Milovan Djilas, a Vice–Premier and President of the National Assembly, late in 1953 began a series of articles in the communist newspaper *Borba*, in which he argued, among other things, that:

> "No class or political movement can claim the exclusive right to represent society as a whole or to proclaim their ideas as objective truth . . . ,"

he was expelled from the Politburo and Central Committee and forced to resign his government offices. Later he would be imprisoned, but that would be for more critical things he would write, in particular, such things as his study of the new Communist elite, which he entitled *The New Class.*

A new constitution was adopted in 1963 which extended the concept of worker's self–management to that of "social self–management." In a move toward greater economic democracy, more authority was given to local communes, to the govern-

mid–1948 which indicated that the member parties backed the Soviet position. The *Yugoslav Communist Party* was expelled from the *Cominform,* Tito was denounced by Stalin and his name became a symbol of hatred among communist leaders who courted Moscow's favor. Despite economic and diplomatic isolation, Yugoslavia survived and set a precedent for other challenges to Soviet authority which followed after Stalin's death.

Relations with the U.S. warmed, but didn't boil over. U.S. President Harry S. Truman is reliably rumored to have privately commented that although Tito was a "son–of–a–bitch, at least he's *our* son–of–a–bitch."

Politics Since 1950

After 1949, Yugoslavia began to search for new trading partners, for a new foreign policy which would demonstrate its independence, and for a new statement of principles which would explain the changes introduced in the Yugoslav system *after* the break with Moscow.

In domestic politics, the two themes which were developed were decentralization and economic democracy. The first step came in 1950 with the creation of "workers' councils" in all state–owned economic enterprises. At the same time, the former economic ministries which had directed the economy were abolished and replaced by national coordinating councils made up of representatives from

Yugoslavia

ments of the republics and to the organs of self–management in the economy. These changes compounded Yugoslavia's problems with regionalism, however, and re-opened conflict between the so–called liberals and conservatives as well as between the wealthier and poorer republics. The less–developed republics, such as Serbia and Montenegro, argued that the changes benefited only the developed republics. Croatia and Slovenia, on the other hand, argued that the changes didn't go far enough and that they were still subsidizing the rest of the country.

One of the foremost opponents of the reforms was Alexander Rankovich, then Vice–President of Yugoslavia, strong– man of the Serbian party organization, influential in the security police and once considered a likely successor to Tito. The decision to expel him from the Central Committee of the Party in 1966 was a decisive victory for the reformists, this time backed by Tito. Although the decision was a blow to Serb nationalists, it did not eliminate the basic anxiety of the remaining republics over Serbian domination of Yugoslavia. In order to give the individual republics a greater stake in the general affairs of the country, a group of amendments was adopted in 1967 giving a stronger voice to the Chamber of Nationalities and in general increasing the role of the individual republics in decision–making at the center.

There was another series of amendments in 1971 which, in addition to establishing a collective presidency to handle the matter of the succession after Tito, made a number of economic changes. Worker councils were given greater authority to determine how the surplus funds of their enterprises were to be allocated, and private individuals were guaranteed the right to work with their own "means of production" and to employ workers on a contractual basis.

In 1974, a new constitution introduced a system of elections to the various legislative assemblies based on delegations drawn from occupational and interest groups. It also provided that the federal legislature—the Assembly of the Socialist Federal Republic of Yugoslavia—be made up of an equal number of delegates from each of Yugoslavia's six republics. Elections to the federal legislature were indirect. Delegates to the assemblies of the individual republics, themselves representing local occupation and interest groups, selected delegates to the federal legislature.

One purpose of the new system was to give the League of Communists of Yugoslavia (LCY) greater control over the elected representatives. Under its self–managing socialism, Yugoslavia had created a degree of economic democracy;

The May 5, 1980, edition of *Politika* announces Tito's death

politically, however, the LCY retained its monopoly of power.

The period of the 1970's saw a number of purges within the party, the most prominent of which was the more or less mass purge of the Croatian wing of the LCY in 1971–72 because of alleged nationalistic deviations. Between 1972 and 1974, there were additional purges within the Serbian wing, this time be-cause of an over–liberal attitude toward dissent within *LCY* ranks. Despite these purges, there remained a large core of veterans, both in the LCY and the government who had remained more or less continuously in office since 1945.

The core of the problem was that the LCY attempted to withdraw from direct control of the economy while retaining an overall political ascendancy. The eco-

310

omic reforms devolved considerable authority to the republic level, to regional banks and to individual enterprises and the result was to create a tremendous stake in control over local economic activity. This often encouraged local decisions which were at variance with national political policy, in particular the commitment at the national level to redistribute funds to poorer areas of the country for the purpose of financing industrialization. After Tito's death in 1980, it also acted to frustrate attempts of the new national leadership to control growing inflation through a national austerity program. What Yugoslavians discovered was that, control over the economy having been shifted to the Republic/Autonomous Province level, the federal government no longer had the tools to manipulate the economy. This chiefly explains the continued high inflation of the 1980s.

The "Republic of Kosovo:"

Nationalism in the Autonomous Province of Kosovo

The interest of the political leadership of the individual republics to retain the maximum amount of scarce investment funds for local use also led to grievances upon which local nationalism then fed. The Autonomous Province of Kosovo in the Republic of Serbia was one area that became particularly disaffected. The homeland of almost all of Serbia's ethnic Albanians, who constitute approximately 90% of the population of the province, is primarily an agricultural area with little industry. It was always one of the poorest parts of Yugoslavia. Its unemployment rate is also the highest and it also has an extremely high birthrate. In the 1970s, its per capita income actually dropped.

At the beginning of the 1980s, dissatisfaction with the local situation produced a wave of nationalist agitation. Riots began in Kosovo in March–April 1981, led by youths from the University of Pristina (in mid–1981 renamed "Kosovo University"). Eventually thousands of demonstrators joined in clashes with police and openly propounded nationalistic slogans. Originally limited to the city of Pristina, the demonstrations spread to other parts of Kosovo and then to the neighboring Republic of Macedonia (where another 374,000 ethnic Albanians live).

The University was closed on April 2, 1981, and the Yugoslav regime began a policy of "rooting out Albanian nationalism" and purging the local wing of the LCY of Albanian nationalist elements. The University had undoubtedly become a hotbed of Albanian nationalist sentiment, but the underlying cause of the agitation was almost certainly economic. While there were demands for creation of a separate Albanian Republic, there was no strong sentiment to merge the province with Albania. It is generally conceded that the standard of living of the people of Kosovo was higher than that of Albanians in Albania and they also had a freer life and were permitted to practice their religion. Only a tiny minority supported union with Albania at that time.

The effective abolition of Kosovo's autonomous status in early 1989 and the subsequent fall of communism in Albania changed that situation, however. Reports out of Kosovo indicate that the ethnic Albanians are completely disaffected, feeling that they have been relegated to second–class status. Serbia's reestablishment of control over Kosovo left a sullen populace that boded ill for the future. This led the displaced Albanian leadership to declare an independent Republic of Kosovo in 1991 and to confirm popular support for the idea by carrying out a referendum in the province. Serbia still controls the province, but it is a powder–keg waiting to blow up.

Speculation about the internal and international outlook for Yugoslavia were understandably centered in recent years on the question of what would happen to the country if and when President Tito would disappear from the scene. The aging leader and his associates were certainly aware of the problem, and they decided to establish a system of post–Tito government hopefully designed to keep the country together in spite of deep–seated animosities kept alive among the various nationalities.

The Constitution of 1974, while making Tito president for life, provided for several collective bodies—including a rotating presidency of the supreme governing council—representative of the major national units. This body began to function when Tito, struggling for months against a terminal illness, gave up his position as chief of state.

The collective leadership thus gained experience in running the state without Tito at the helm. When the aged leader finally died in May 1980, his funeral became the occasion for a glittering assembly of heads of state and other dignitaries, ranging from kings to leaders of communist states.

The new leadership functioned with modest success until 1988, although it was unable to reverse growing economic difficulties. The government actually attempted to bring inflation under control, but soon found that the mandate of the 1974 constitution that all federal decisions of significance required the consensus of all six republics and two provinces meant it was powerless to do so. Unfortunately, there was no consensus and the result was a stalemate at the center. The government was thus reduced to the policy of muddling through.

By 1988, the annual rate of inflation was 200% and growing, and workers, worried about their dropping standard of living, launched a series of strikes. Intellectuals, losing confidence in the system, began to demand changes. In less–developed areas of the country, there was also growing dissatisfaction among individual ethnic groups who had come to believe that the system was treating them unfairly. Among the most disaffected were the ethnic Albanians of the autonomous province of Kosovo.

Greater Serbian Domination Threatens the Union

Up to that moment, one might have described the situation as serious but not threatening. What turned it into a crisis was the emergence of a new Serbian leader, Slobodan Milosevic, who launched a broad movement to reassert Serbian leadership. Arguing that the promotion of regionalism was the root cause of Yugoslavia's problems, Milosevic demanded control over the police, judiciary and economy in the two autonomous provinces of the Voivodina and Kosovo. In addition, Milosevic demanded a radical increase in Serbia's power within the Yugoslav Federation.

To achieve these goals, Milosevic began mobilizing the Serbian masses. In the Voivodina, 100,000 Serbs besieged the provincial parliament in September 1988, forcing the resignation of the entire Voivodina leadership and their replacement by Milosevic loyalists. The same tactics were also tried against Kosovo, and demonstrations and counter–demonstrations continued over the next several months.

Meanwhile, inflation continued to grow and the worsening economic situation, coupled with the growing ethnic problems, led to a collapse of the Yugoslav Government on December 30, 1988.

Yugoslavia

Branko Mikulic

Branko Mikulic, President of the Federal Executive Council, submitted his resignation when he could not get his budget through the Yugoslav parliament. Yugoslavia remained without a government for almost three months before agreement was reached on a successor to Mikulic. Before agreement was reached, Stipe Suvar, the LCY Party President, also resigned his position and one–third of the membership of the party Central Committee was replaced. Ante Markovic was appointed President of the Federal Executive Council in March 1989. In May, Milan Pancevski was elected President of the *League of Communists*. Originally scheduled to serve only until a special party congress met, he was subsequently confirmed in that office.

The remainder of 1989 was characterized by a steadily worsening inflation and a seeming inability of anybody to do anything about it. Finally, it was Ante Markovic, President of the Federal Executive Council, who decided to take advantage of loopholes in the law and propose an economic stabilization program himself. Markovic's program, approved by the federal parliament on December 20, went into effect on January 1, 1990. The program consisted of making the Yugoslavian dinar convertible by pegging it to the West German Deutsche Mark, allowing interest to rise to market levels, and removing price–controls from most goods. Certain goods, including various raw materials and energy, were frozen. The program worked. By March, inflation had sunk from over 2,000 percent to 8.4 percent. In addition, the government had managed to reduce the foreign debt by $3 billion and build up currency reserves of $7.5 billion. Unem-

ployment was expected to rise and some state–subsidized businesses were expected to go bankrupt, but the government was determined to stick with its economic program.

This was the good news, however. Political developments continued to move in a direction that threatened the future of the united Yugoslav state. In January, an emergency congress of the *League of Communists* was held, among other things to discuss a move toward creation of a multiparty system. There was a serious split, on one side the hardliners, led by Slobodan Milosevic of Serbia, and on the other those pushing for a multiparty system, led by Ciril Ribicic of Slovenia. The Congress actually passed a resolution favoring creation of a multiparty system, but the Slovenian delegation walked out of the Congress, thus bringing it to a halt. They were particularly incensed about an economic boycott against Slovenia that Serbia had instituted at the end of November.

Thus, while in Serbia, Milosevic was threatening to colonize the province of Kosovo, Slovenia was moving toward creation of a multi–party democracy and suggesting that there was no future for Yugoslavia. In April elections, the people split their votes, electing Milan Kucan, candidate of the communists, as President while giving the *Demos*, a coalition of conservative political parties that had campaigned on a platform of independence within a year, control of the legislature. A month later, Croatia held its own multiparty elections, which were won by the *Croatian Democratic Union*, which campaigned on a platform of making a confederation of sovereign states out of Yugoslavia.

Macedonia and Bosnia–Herzegovina held their own free, multiparty elections in November 1990. Montenegro and Serbia were scheduled to hold their own multiparty elections for December. In Serbia, Milosevic decided to further consolidate his control within Serbia by transforming the Serbian branch of the *League of Communists of Yugoslavia* into the *Serbian Socialist Party*. Thus the old *LCY*, already in a minority status in all the republics other than Montenegro and Serbia, lost out in its largest remaining base. Effectively it ceased to exist as a national party except in the Yugoslav army, where the leadership remained communist. This was a strange action by someone who claimed to stand for a strong, unified country. In fact, Milosevic is a Serbian nationalist who wanted to hold Yugoslavia together only if he could dominate it completely. Otherwise he would tear it apart and seize what other pieces of Yugoslavia he could.

A look at the policies he has pursued over the past few years bears that out.

Appealing to Serbian nationalism, he demanded greater control in the two autonomous provinces of Kosovo and the Voivodina, eventually destroying their autonomy completely. In 1990, his agents began organizing Serbian nationals living in the other republics, fomenting them to demand secession of their areas from their republics and union with Serbia. He personally declared that he would demand a rectification of boundaries so as to reclaim Serbian lands if the federation broke up. The other republics have always reacted negatively to the idea of a Serbian–dominated Yugoslav government, for they are thereby reminded of the period after World War I when Serbs dominated the new Yugoslavia. Milosevic's Serbian chauvinism, and his destruction of the autonomy of Kosovo and the Vojvodina, convinced many non-Serbs that he intended to once again assert Serbia's control over all of Yugoslavia. And at least three separate actions taken by Milosevic in 1990–91 contributed to that perception.

In December 1990, in the lead–up to Serbian elections, Milosevic undermined the financial stability of the national government by illegally siphoning off $1.5 billion from the Yugoslav National Bank. The money was taken in the form of a "loan" on the authority of a vote by the Serbian assembly. Both the Serbian assembly session and the removal of the money were kept secret from Yugoslavia's federal government. Milosevic then used the money to pay for pensions and salaries, which he had raised in the run-up to Serbian elections. The salary and pension increases were undoubtedly a factor in the elections, which Milosevic

Slobodan Milosevic

and his *Serbian Socialist Party* won handily. The other republics were outraged when they learned of Milosevic's actions. Since the $1.5 billion was half of the new money the Yugoslav National Bank had assigned for circulation in 1991 in *all six republics*, Milosevic's action seriously undermined the federal government's economic stabilization program.

Milosevic's second action was to organize a boycott of Slovenian products and to begin levying a tariff on all items brought into Serbia from that republic, effectively negating the concept of a *united* Yugoslavia. Milosevic's third action in his program of rule or ruin was to block election of a new Federal President in May 1991. The outgoing President was Borisav Jovic, a Serb. Under Yugoslavia's system of rotating Presidencies, the incoming President was the man who had held the Vice–Presidency for the past year, Stipe Mesic, a Croat.

To be sure, Milosevic was not the sole offender in this regard. In 1990, when the leaders of Slovenia and Croatia began pushing for a change in the structure of the Yugoslav Federation to allow for greater autonomy for the individual republics, they passed laws declaring their laws to be superior to federal law and also created republic militias.

The sad thing is that this quarreling completely undermined the economic stabilization program of the federal government. Only the Yugoslav People's Army remained united at this point, though there were clear signs that this unity was very frail and depended in the army's not getting involved in the quarrels between the individual republics.

The army also had its own problems, the most important of which is that there was strong sentiment in the army to preserve a united Yugoslavia, even if it meant using force against a part of the Yugoslav people. A second problem was that 70% of the officers were Serbians and a good percentage of them were attracted to Milosevic's program. A third factor was that the army was the one remaining place where the *LCY* continued to exist. A final factor was that, while the officers were mainly Serbian, ordinary soldiers were conscripts who came from throughout Yugoslavia. Many feared, therefore, that the army would begin to disintegrate if it intervened against an individual republic and was perceived as doing so on behalf either of Serbia or the *LCY*.

Yugoslavia Comes Apart

On May 19, 1991, the Croatian Government held a referendum on the question of independence for the republic. After a favorable vote, the Croatian Assembly adopted a declaration of independence on June 25. The Slovene Government adopted its own declaration on the same day. Both Governments did reiterate, however, that they remained willing to join a looser Yugoslav confederation in which the central government would handle foreign policy, defense and economic matters such as a common currency.

In economically-torn Montenegro, a youngster holds up a sign "We wait for you, Slovo" (Serbian leader Slobodan Milosevic) during an anti-government demonstration in Titograd

Yugoslavia

Meanwhile, the Yugoslav People's Army reacted to the declarations of independence by sending an invasion force into Slovenia. That republic was selected because it had moved to take control of its international border with Italy and Austria. The YPA was apparently not expecting much opposition, but the Slovenians fought back valiantly. Meanwhile, the rest of the world, which had encouraged the army action by asserting that they would not support a separate Slovenia or Croatia "under any circumstances," began calling for a ceasefire. At the same time, army desertions by non–Serbs began to be a problem. This led to an agreement with Slovenia that it could man the control posts if it would turn the revenues over to the central government. The YPA also agreed to return its forces to the barracks. Slovenia and Croatia also agreed to suspend their declarations of independence for three months. Serbia, in turn, agreed to allow Stipe Mesic to be elected President. The latter agreement was important in a military as well as a political sense because the President has also been the Commander–in–Chief of the Yugoslav People's Army.

The agreement brought peace to Slovenia, but not to Yugoslavia. One of the first actions of President Mesic was to arrange a cease–fire–the third–on July 2. That same day, General Blagoje Adzic, chief of the YPA General Staff, angrily repudiated the ceasefire—and thereby his own Commander–in–Chief—in an interview that appeared on Belgrade television and added that the army "accepted the challenge of total war that had been imposed on it" and would soon end it with a complete victory. The next day, an armored column left Belgrade for Croatia.

When Slovenia and Croatia began moving toward independence, President Milosevic called upon Serbs in other republics to remain loyal and not allow the Yugoslav union to be broken up. In Croatia, Serbs organized Serbian governments in two different parts of Croatia and declared these regions *independent* of Croatia. Hoping to conciliate the Serb leaders, the Croatian legislature passed a law guaranteeing protection for minority ethnic groups within the republic. Arguing that Serbs could secede from Croatia if Croatia could secede from Yugoslavia, Croatian Serbs held a referendum on July 7 affirming their intention to remain a part of the Socialist Federal Republic of Yugoslavia.

Meanwhile, President Milosevic of Serbia gave a speech on July 6 in which he told Serbs to be ready to defend themselves. He also gave Serb leaders in Croatia generous access to Serbian radio and television. The first fighting in Croatia began on July 7–the same day as the referendum–when Croatian Serbs attacked Croatian territorial defense forces near the town of Tenja.

As soon as fighting broke out, the Yugoslav People's Army sent in its own units "to keep the peace." It seemed, however, that its targets were always Croatian territorial units. There were, in fact, no reports whatsoever of any Serbian territorial units being in conflict with YPA forces.

The fighting remained small–scale for some time, since President Tudjman had ordered Croatian units not to attack the Yugoslav People's Army. On its part, the YPA had received instructions from its Serb (but moderate) Defense Minister, General Veljko Kadijevic, that it should not initiate battles but only intervene when new fighting occurred. Gradually, however, the YPA's control of Croatian territory spread as Serb territorial forces launched new battles in area after area.

Croatia's Serbian problem existed because Serbs insisted on living in a state *controlled by Serbs*. But Croatians were not entirely free of this mentality of imperialism. The Republic of Bosnia–Herzegovina, which lies between Serbia and Croatia, has an extremely mixed population, with 31% Serbs and about 17% Croats. President Tudjman admitted in July that members of his government had held secret talks with Serbian leaders about carving up Bosnia between Serbia and Croatia, leaving a small Moslem rump that neither wanted. Word of these talks did not help Croatia internationally.

Croatia was "saved" by the fact that Serbia and the YPA were even more bloody–minded. In August, Milosevic revealed his plans for a reconstituted Yugoslavia which called for carving up Croatia and incorporating about a third of the territory into the new state. Serbs actually constitute only 12 percent of Croatia's population. Even more revealing, on August 20, 1991, Milosevic's chief ideologist praised the Moscow *coup* leaders as "tough men but not dogmatics" and accused Gorbachëv of pushing the Soviet Union toward a break–up by his attempt to create a union of sovereign states. Neither event made it easy for other countries to continue to defend the Serb side of the argument.

Meanwhile the YPA, which up to this time had contended that it was acting as a neutral buffer between the two sides, began bombarding Croatian cities with artillery and aircraft. In late August, much of the city of Vukovar was destroyed. By this time, perhaps twenty percent of the republic had fallen under YPA or Serb militia control. On September 18, Zagreb, the capital, came under fire from aircraft and artillery. At about the same time, the Yugoslav navy instituted a blockade of Croatia's Dalmatian ports. Soon it began attacking them, beginning with the city of Split. Up to this moment, the Croatian Government had been carrying out a "passive defense" and refusing to challenge the YPA directly. But it then cut oil lines across Croatia to Serbia and laid siege to Yugoslav army barracks in Croatia. The Yugoslav military retaliated by laying a naval siege around the Croatian city of Dubrovnik and later bombarding it with artillery shells and missiles. Today this historic and once beautiful city has been reported to be in shambles.

Croatia got some indirect assistance from other republics when Bosnia–Herzegovina and Macedonia publicly declared the neutrality of their governments and ordered their citizens to ignore conscription notices from the YPA. The Serbian and Montenegrin political response was to order general mobilization in both those republics. Even in Serbia, however, many young men went into hiding rather than serve. The European Community had put itself forth as a peacemaker even before the war began, and subsequently negotiated cease–fire after cease–fire, only to see each new one broken.

They threatened Serbia with an economic embargo without effect. They arranged for a peace conference to begin at The Hague on September 7, 1991. This was also supposed to be accompanied by a cease–fire agreement, though that one fell through as well. The EC then appointed Lord Carrington as chairman of the European peace conference and sent him to Yugoslavia. He met with Presidents Milosevic and Tudjman plus Yugoslav Defense Minister Kadijevic. The three agreed that the YPA ought to return to its barracks, that the Croatian national guard should be demobilized, and that all irregular militias should be disbanded. *Nothing actually happened, however, and the war went on.* Kadijevic had apparently been ignored by his chief of staff, the radical General Adzic.

Meanwhile the three–month moratorium on the independence declarations of Croatia and Slovenia–agreed to at Brioni–expired on October 7, 1991. Freed of that limitation, the Croatian and Slovenian governments severed all ties with the Socialist Federal Republic of Yugoslavia. By this time, approximately a third of Croatia was occupied by the YPA and Serb militias. The Yugoslav air force marked the day with an attack on the presidential palace in Zagreb at the very moment that President Tudjman was in conference with Stipe Mesic, the Federal President, and Ante Markovic, the Federal Prime Minister. As the *Economist* put it, "the attack put to rest any pretense that there is real life left in the Yugoslav federation."

Four days earlier, the Serbs had taken control of the Federal Presidency. On

A scarecrow original.

Photo by Prof. Janko Ravnik

October 3, Branko Kostic, Montenegrin representative to the SFRY Presidency and Vice President, called a meeting of the Presidency and submitted a declaration of a state of emergency. With President Mesic absent and the Slovenian representative to the Presidency boycotting the meeting, the proposal was passed with Kostic's own vote plus the three votes controlled by Serbia (plus its two formerly autonomous regions).

By this time, it had become clear to almost everyone just what Serbia was attempting to do. After the October 3, 1991 meeting of the Presidency, characterized by President Gligorov of Macedonia as "illegitimate and unconstitutional," both Macedonia and Bosnia–Herzegovina withdrew their representatives to the Presidency. Macedonia's representatives to the Federal legislature also withdrew from that body as well.

Up to this time, Montenegrin troops had not been directly involved in the war. Now, however, they entered Croatia from the south, conquering the area up to Dubrovnik and establishing a land siege around that city. They were joined by troops of the Yugoslav People's Army

who had pushed their way down from the north.

As the siege continued, the EC drew up yet another plan for peace. Serbia was given until November 5 to accept a ceasefire and enter serious negotiations or face economic sanctions. In this new peace plan, the EC proposed that Yugoslavia become a loose association of sovereign republics with a currency union. Internal border changes would be by mutual consent only and disputed areas where minorities lived would be demilitarized under international peacekeepers. Kosovo and the Voivodina would also regain their autonomous status. Serbia, rejecting the plan, insisted that it could not abandon Serb minorities outside Serbia.

It would not agree to any plan that did not be permit minorities to switch the regions where they were in a majority from one republic to another. The exasperated EC instituted economic sanctions against Serbia and Montenegro after the deadline had expired. The United States Government, for its own reasons, instituted economic sanctions against all of Yugoslavia, including Croatia and Slovenia.

Serbia then took the EC proposal for an international force to police disputed areas where minorities lived and expanded it, suggesting that all areas occupied by the YPA should be so policed. Serbia still insisted that minorities be given the right to vote on whether to remain under Croatian jurisdiction, however.

Meanwhile, the last vestige of a united Yugoslavian Government disappeared in December 1991 when Ante Markovic, the prime minister, resigned. The Yugoslav legislature, dominated by Serbia after representatives of Slovenia, Croatia and Macedonia had withdrawn, had already expressed its lack of confidence in Markovic, a Croat from Bosnia–Herzegovina. However, the reason Markovic gave for his resignation was that 81% of the proposed budget for 1992 was earmarked for the army.

By this time, Germany and Austria had begun to make a public case for recognition of Slovenia and Croatia. Some of the other members of the EC, in particular France and Britain, continued to oppose recognition until Germany announced that it would proceed unilaterally if the EC took no action. Prime Minister Major of Britain then threw his support to Germany, and France grudgingly gave in. In December, the EC announced that its members would implement recognition of those Yugoslav republics that requested it and deserved it on January 15, 1992.

General Veljko Kadijevic, the Yugoslav Defense Minister, resigned on January 8, citing ill health. That gave Serb radicals control of the YPA, but Slobodan Milosevic, President of Serbia, had by this time switched positions somewhat and he and the EC had reached agreement on a new ceasefire and peacekeeping plan modeled on the suggestions he had put forth in November. Under the plan, the YPA would pull out of the three Serb enclaves in Croatia and be replaced by a peace force from the United Nations. The UN force would disarm local militias and organize a local police force. Croatia would not have control over the enclaves, but neither would Serbia. The future of the enclaves would have to be determined at subsequent talks. The cease-fire—the fifteenth—went into effect on January 3. Five days later, the UN Security Council voted to send 50 UN observers to Croatia to report on the feasibility of the plan.

By January 15, 1992 four republics—Slovenia, Croatia, Macedonia and Bosnia–Herzegovina—had requested recognition by the EC. The EC actually recognized only the first two, largely out of political considerations. The various governments of the EC were worried that recognition of Bosnia–Herzegovina

Yugoslavia

would cause the war to be expanded to that republic. The *Serbian Democratic Party*, the main spokesman for Serbs in Bosnia–Herzegovina, opposed separation of it from Yugoslavia and threatened to lead a secession of Serb–dominated areas. The Serbs formed their own "Serbian Republic of Bosnia–Herzegovina" and began arming themselves.

Because of this development, the EC advised the government of Bosnia–Herzegovina to hold a referendum on independence to establish that a majority actually wanted to break free from Yugoslavia. The referendum was held on March 1 and produced a two–thirds manority in favor of independence. Serbs, who had boycotted the referendum, threw up barricades throughout the capital city of Sarajevo that evening and it appeared that a major civil war was ready to break out. President Alija Izetbegovic managed to get the leaders of the Serbs to meet with him and the major Croat leaders and thereby defused the situation. The Serbs agreed to dismantle their barricades and the other two political factions agreed to joint patrols by the Yugoslav People's Army and the Bosnian police.

On March 18, the leaders of the three communities agreed on a plan for restructuring the state, creating "three constituent units, based on national principles and taking into account economic, geographic and other criteria."

The plan would have created three autonomous units within the governmental structure, one for Moslems, one for Croats and one for Serbs. Control in each municipality would have been by that national group which was in an "absolute or relative majority." Since the three communities have always lived side by side and many families are mixed, the agreement would have been difficult to implement. In any case, it was never given a chance. The radical Serb leaders who wanted a single Greater Serbia forestalled that possibility by launching a war of conquest in April.

In essence, the Yugoslav army, overwhelmingly dominated by Serbs, split itself into two parts, those with any ties to Bosnia or other non–Serb lands remaining in Bosnia with the rest of the army removing itself to Serbia and Montenegro. Units left behind in Bosnia were provided with tanks, artillery and all the equipment of a modern army. General Ratko Mladic became the military commander of this force, while political leadership was exercised by Radovan Karadzic. The Yugoslav army has continued to provide support and resupply from Serbia, however. Thus the Yugoslav army, having learned from its involvement in Croatia that it could not afford to be seen as being present itself, created a proxy to continue its war for a Greater Serbia. Within three months, this Serbian army in Bosnia had managed to capture approximately 70 percent of the territory of Bosnia. They have also laid siege to the capital, Sarajevo, in the process directing an unceasing bombardment into this once-beautiful medieval city in an effort to crush resistance. The siege has now continued for 14 months and large parts of the city are in ruins.

Meanwhile, Serbs have used their control of the Yugoslav legislature to pass new laws establishing customs zones in

A ploughman.

Photo by Prof. Janko Ravnik

Serb–inhabited areas of Croatia and parts of Bosnia–Herzegovina. In the case of Croatia, they have also decreed that Yugoslavian, not Croatian, law would apply in Serb areas occupied by the UN peacekeeping force. In addition, the legislature passed a law on the new Yugoslavia which states that the "new community be made up nations and republics which want to remain in Yugoslavia." They have implemented this by giving Serbs living outside Serbia representation in the Yugoslav legislature.

Montenegro held its own referendum in March and the people voted overwhelmingly to remain in a Yugoslav Federation. A union of two nations, one with a population of ten million and the other with only half a million, is rather odd, but that is what exists at the moment. The autonomous province of Kosovo remains a real question mark in this equation. Having been stripped of their autonomy, the Albanians, who make up 90 percent of the population of the province, have declared their own "Republic of Kosovo." Their actions remain theoretical, however, since a large number of Yugoslav army units now occupy the province.

Serbia, the main component of rump Yugoslavia, has been badly hurt economically by the UN embargo, but not to such an extent that it has been willing to end its war of conquest for a Greater Serbia. When the UN tightened the embargo in May 1993 after the Bosnian Serbs rejected a UN peace plan, President Milosevic appeared to change his tune. He promised to cut off all except humanitarian support to the Bosnian Serbs unless they agreed to accept the plan. It is hard to believe that he has had a real change of heart, however.

In fact, the Yugoslav Government subsequently stated that it would not agree to allow UN monitors on its border with Bosnia to verify that aid to Bosnian Serbs had actually stopped. As a further indication of Milosevic's actual position, Yugoslav President Dobrica Cosic was ousted on June 1, 1993 after Milosevic's *Socialist Party* joined with the ultranationalist *Radical Party* in calling for Cosic's removal. Milosevic apparently decided to get rid of Cosic after the latter had appealed to Bosnian Serbs to accept the UN's peace plan.

Cosic's ouster did not come without consequences. That night, there were violent demonstrations in Belgrade by Milosevic's political opposition that left 32 people injured and most of the opposition leaders in custody. It does not appear to have shaken Milosevic's hold on power, but it might yet have consequences for any future international recognition of "Yugoslavia." As Cosic said after his dismissal,

"The federal state, if it is a state at all, is practically under the protectorate of Slobodan Milosevic and the Serbian Government."

Foreign Policy

Yugoslavia has been a "friend" of the west so long that it was always easy to forget that Yugoslav's leaders remained communists and that its relations with the west were the result of its having been expelled from the communist bloc by Stalin, not because they had ceased being communists. Nevertheless, this led Yugoslavia to sign a five–year Treaty of Friendship and Assistance with Turkey and Greece in 1953 which was subsequently known as the Balkan Pact. The following year, it was converted into a full defensive alliance. Yugoslavia also settled an outstanding issue with Italy that had been left over from World War II, the disposition of Trieste, by agreeing to divide the disputed land.

It also built up its international prestige by actively courting the non–aligned nations of Africa and Asia. These nations accepted Yugoslavian leadership in the non–aligned movement because Tito had given Yugoslavia what they thought of as the best of all possible worlds—following a course of socialist development, though free of Soviet control, and receiving aid from the west, but without becoming an economic adjunct to capitalism. As communism–socialism has crumbled throughout the world, this dream has evaporated.

Yugoslavia thus positioned itself between the two blocs. It was never an ally of the United States and it welcomed the resumption of diplomatic relations with the Soviet Union in June 1953, after the death of Stalin. Thereafter, Yugoslav–Soviet relations alternated between periods of calm and storm, depending on the extent of control Moscow was attempting to exercise over Yugoslavia.

Bulganin and Khrushchëv of Russia visited Belgrade in 1955. Syrupy words flowed as the Soviets acknowledged that what the Yugoslavs were doing was their own business. In turn, Tito agreed to support Soviet policy on arms limitation, the division of Germany and the then Soviet cause of getting Red China admitted to the UN.

Following Khrushchëv's denunciations of Stalin in 1956, the dissolution of the *Cominform* in the same year, and the dismissal of Vyacheslav Molotov from the Soviet Foreign Ministry, there were further improvements in Yugoslav–Soviet relations. All of these moves indicated a Soviet acceptance of the possibility of different paths toward socialism. By June 1956 the two sides announced that they had achieved a "complete

normalization" of relations on party and state levels.

But this was only a brief interlude. The actions of the Soviets and the apparent willingness to deal with Yugoslavia on an independent basis created false hopes of liberalization in Poland and Hungary. Hungary embarked upon a liberal and more independent course and the result was a harsh Soviet military invasion in the fall of 1956. Subsequent Soviet attacks on "revisionism" reopened the old conflict between Tito and Moscow. It was not until 1960–61 that a new attempt to smooth relations was made, probably to counteract the effect of increasing difficulties between the Soviet Union and China.

In 1968–69, Soviet–Yugoslav relations suffered once again under the impact of an international crisis. Tito had spoken out in favor of programs of liberalization that were taking place in Czechoslovakia; when the Soviet Union intervened militarily in that country, Tito voiced his condemnation of this move in the strongest terms. He rejected the *Brezhnev Doctrine*, the Soviet explanation for the move, as no more than an attempt to justify a violation of the sovereignty of a communist state by invoking the higher interests of socialism.

Brezhnev paid a visit to Yugoslavia in 1971 for the first time since the invasion of Czechoslovakia. During the meeting with Tito, the Soviet leader disavowed the existence of any doctrine of limited sovereignty and, to Tito's satisfaction, endorsed the view that each country has the right to develop socialism according to its own experience. The reaffirmation of the 1955 Belgrade Declaration opened the door to better relations between the two countries.

One major issue between Yugoslavia and the Soviet Union in the 1970's was the latter's desire for a European Communist Conference. Yugoslavian participation in it was extremely important, for without it several of the Western European communist parties would probably have refused to attend.

Yugoslavia's price, exacted at a 1974 preparatory meeting in Warsaw, was that the meeting be open to the public, that it would not become a forum for attacking parties that had declined to attend, and that all decisions be by con census. Yugoslavia was supported in this stand by Romania and by the delegates representing the Italian, Spanish and French parties.

The conference finally took place in the summer of 1976 in Berlin. Although the meeting endorsed the main lines of Soviet foreign policy, the Soviets could not have been happy with other parts of the concluding document, which reiterated the Yugoslav–Romanian formula for in-

Yugoslavia

The rapids on the Kira River.

Photo by Prof. Janko Ravnik

terparty relations of "voluntary cooperation" based on the principles of equality, sovereignty, noninterference in internal affairs, and the respect for different roads to socialism.

Soviet–Yugoslav relations remained at about the same level until December 1979. Then the Yugoslavs condemned the Soviet invasion of Afghanistan and political relations turned cool. Yugoslavia did sign a ten–year economic agreement with the Soviet Union in 1980; however, the reasons were almost certainly economic. As a result of the second oil crisis in 1979, Yugoslavia was finding it harder and harder to compete in western markets. The economic agreement with the Soviet Union seemed to offer the promise of a long–term market for Yugoslav goods. The Soviets paid in convertible rubles, however. As the Yugoslav Government eventually learned, convertible rubles were of little value if the Soviet Union was not producing the things Yugoslavia was willing to import. Yugoslavia eventually built up a huge credit

of several billion rubles which it was unable to use.

Yugoslav relations with the Soviet Union improved after Gorbachëv came to power in 1985. The Yugoslavian people welcomed him when he visited in March 1988. Gorbachëv traveled to various parts of the country, making speeches wherever he went. In retrospect, the visit took on a greater significance because of Gorbachëv's assertion, in the agreed joint statement at the conclusion of the visit, that every country had a right to pursue the variant of communism that it chose. This statement, which was essentially a repudiation of the Brezhnev Doctrine, paved the way for the 1989 revolutions in eastern Europe.

U.S.–Yugoslav relations were always based on the premise that Yugoslavia espoused a non–expansionist and therefore more benign form of communism and that it therefore offered an alternate pattern of development that might influence other communist countries in eastern Europe. Because of this strategic role

assigned to it, the U.S. supported a unified, federal Yugoslavia.

The collapse of communism in eastern Europe in 1989 ended this strategic role for Yugoslavia and, in fact, exposed it as being a badly run communist state. Reformers in the western part of the country argued first for radical reforms, only to have their projects blocked by the Serb leadership. They then abandoned communism and carried out democratic elections. In Serbia, however, the communists changed the name of the party but managed to keep political control. Since they continued to obstruct real reform at the federal level, the democrats eventually opted for independence.

The U.S. Government never understood the dynamics of what was going on in Yugoslavia and continued to support a *unified* Yugoslavia even after it had become clear that such a Yugoslavia would be dominated by Serbia and neo–communist in its policies. In the summer of 1991, for example, even after President Milosevic of Serbia had destroyed the autonomy of Kosovo and the Voivodina, had instituted a boycott of goods from Slovenia, had organized Serbs in other republics to oppose their republic's policies, and undermined the economic policy of the Yugoslav government at the national level, Secretary of State Baker announced that the United States would not support a break–up of Yugoslavia "under any circumstances."

Thus encouraged, Milosevic, supported by the Yugoslav People's Army— the last stronghold of communism at the national level—launched his war against Croatia and threatened one against Bosnia–Herzegovina. Even in November 1991, when Serbia's aims had become clear to the world and the EC had decided to institute economic sanctions against Serbia and Montenegro, the two aggressors, the U.S. decided to institute economic sanctions against both sides, *aggressors and victims.*

This was a classic case of a policy outliving its usefulness. The EC extended recognition to Slovenia and Croatia on January 15, 1992. The U.S. waited another three months before following suit. Ambassador Warren Zimmerman remained in Belgrade, however, and the U.S. Government continued to maintain good relations with the Serb–dominated Yugoslav Government. All of this ended when, with U.S. backing, the UN voted to impose economic sanctions against Serbia and Montenegro in late May 1992. The U.S. Government had begun to press Serbia on its treatment of Albanians in Kosovo, however. On March 23, Ambassador Zimmermann traveled to Pristina to open an exhibition organized to mark

318

the 50th anniversary of the *Voice of America*. While there, he held talks with representatives of Albanian parties.

Nature of the Regime

The collapse of Yugoslavia in 1991–92 as a result of the withdrawal of four of the six republics has left behind a rump Yugoslavia composed of the two remaining republics of Serbia and Montenegro. Serbia has organized Serbs outside of Serbia into a separate political force and has arranged for their continued representation in the Yugoslav legislature. It has taken control of the national institutions—the presidency, the legislature—but it is not suitable for a union composed of two republics, and there are plans to modify them.

The political problem of the Serbian enclaves in Croatia and Bosnia–Hezegovina will have to be resolved before this new "Yugoslavia" takes its final form, however. Meanwhile, the Serb and Montenegrin contingents of the national government continue to meet and speak on behalf of the presidency and the legislature. The Yugoslav People's Army has always been dominated by Serbs, with approximately 70% of the officer corps being Serbian. In March 1992, a purge of most remaining non–Serb ranking officers reinforced that control. Because of desertions on the part of soldiers and orders from the various republics that their citizens should ignore conscription notices, the army has shrunk to about 50% of its size a year ago. That will help with one other problem facing the army—the fact that over 60% percent of all national revenues came from Slovenia and Croatia in the past. Clearly the army will have to make do with a much smaller budget.

The Economy

Rump Yugoslavia or the "new" Yugoslavia which is supposed to emerge—in either case the two republics of Serbia and Montenegro—still has what must be called a socialist market economy. This means that it is neither a capitalist nor a totally government–directed economy. Although most industry is publicly owned, there is a significant private sector. In agriculture, 84% of the land is in private hands, the private purchase and sale of land is permitted, and there exists a free market in agricultural products. The government still encourages peasant work cooperatives and there still exist a few state farms. There is also a maximum limit of 10 hectares (about 25 acres) on the amount of land an individual peasant may own.

In the public sector, the government introduced the concept of worker self–management in 1952 and that system continues today. In each enterprise, a workers' council is elected by all the members of the facility; the management is then selected by the council and both take part in hiring a director.

Yugoslavia was a leader among the socialist states in economic decentralization, but it remained a *socialist* state. Fast economic growth in the period of the 1970's brought better living conditions, but a multitude of problems as well. Mounting inflation became more and more of a problem and the foreign trade deficit began to grow as well. Not wishing to put an end to the economic growth, the leadership rather reluctantly responded with things like import restrictions and a ceiling on wage increases. Eventually it was also forced to begin devaluating the currency as well. The great increase in energy prices in 1973–74 and again in 1979 eventually proved too much for the Yugoslav economy and it, like most of the world, slipped into recession.

While Yugoslavia's economy drifted during the 1980's, inflation grew year after year until, by the end of 1988, it had gotten out of control completely, soaring to an annual rate of 2,500%. The situation frightened the political leadership and in desperation they turned to Ante Markovic, an exponent of the free market. He was installed as President of the Federal Executive Council in March 1989.

Even then, there was stiff opposition to his stabilization program, but he managed to get it adopted after several months and it went into effect on January 1, 1990. Within three months, the dinar had been stabilized and inflation had been brought down to single digits. In addition, currency reserves were up and the foreign debt had been reduced to $16 billion. Foreign investment also began pouring into the country and several thousand privately–owned businesses were started by individual Yugoslavs.

With the stabilization program so successful, politics reasserted itself. The second phase of Markovic's program called for beginning the privatization of state–owned industry, instituting radical changes in the federal tax structure and making banks more independent of the government. But elections were scheduled in the various republics, so the pol-

Photo by Prof. Janko Ravnik

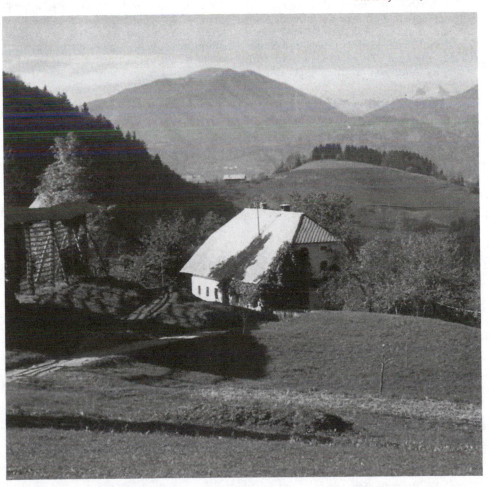

Yugoslavia

iticians demanded that the national wage freeze be lifted instead. It was Slobodan Milosevic, President of Serbia, who most strongly opposed the privatization policy. Lacking support in the republics, the national stabilization program was put on hold.

Meanwhile, free elections in Slovenia and Croatia brought a repudiation of the old communist leadership and their replacement by nationalist leaders who began talking of the need to replace the federation by a loose confederation of sovereign nations. Domestically, these new leaders adopted free market economic policies. This contrasted with the position of Slobodan Milosevic, the Serbian President and head of the Serbian branch of the League of Communists, who argued for a strong centralized Yugoslavia and against free market economic policies.

Caught between the two forces, the economic stabilization program of the Markovic government collapsed. By the beginning of 1991, inflation was again running at an annual rate of 120% and the dinar had to be devalued by 30%. In addition, internal convertibility was suspended when local banks were barred from access to hard currency. By April 1991, strikes were breaking out all over the country as thousands of enterprises were unable to meet their payrolls. Things were bad all over the country, but Serbian industry, the largest and most inefficient in the country, was worst off. Unemployment was at 15% percent and rising as industrial production continued

to plummet. Thus an economic stabilization plan that had been working was completely destroyed by national and political rivalries.

The secession of Slovenia and Croatia in June 1991, followed by an attempt by the Serbs and the Yugoslav People's Army to keep the two republics in the federation *by force*, actually resulted in international recognition of those two republics and the withdrawal of two further republics, Macedonia and Bosnia–Herzegovina, from the federation. Since the war was fought almost exclusively on Croatian soil, Serbia and Montenegro, the two remaining republics in the SFRY, suffered no direct war damage. On the other hand, the EC eventually instituted an economic embargo against the two offending republics. In addition, the very existence of the war meant that the tourist industry, normally a large earner of foreign exchange, was dead.

According to statistics published by the Federal Institute of Statistics, "Yugoslavia" saw its GDP fall by 15% percent in 1991, which dropped the level of production to what it had been in 1976. The reason for this was a 20.7% decline in industry. Agriculture actually grew by 7.6%. Tourism was 61% percent lower than in 1990 and now virtually nonexistant. At the same time, inflation ran at 235% for the year. Serbia reported a 236% increase in retail prices during the year and Montenegro reported a similar amount. Most of these statistics apply to all of Yugoslavia, but it is clear that the economy of *rump* Yugoslavia is in dread-

ful shape. The UN imposed economic sanctions are the prelude to tremendous change.

Culture

The withdrawal of Croatia, Slovenia, Bosnia–Herzegovina and Macedonia from the Socialist Federal Republic of Yugoslavia has left behind a rump Yugoslavia consisting of the republics of Serbia and Montenegro. That has not eliminated all of the differences in cultures which have fascinated foreign visitors, but it has reduced them considerably. Now what is left is essentially Serbian culture, characterized by the Serbian language, written in a 38–character Cyrillic alphabet, the Serbian Orthodox religion, and the remnants of a communist political–economic system which the current political leaders—all ex–communists—have thus far preserved. This "federation" still includes approximately half a million Montenegrins, but they speak a language that is almost identical to Serbian and they use the Cyrillic alphabet. They also are Orthodox Christians.

The Republic of Serbia does have two formerly autonomous provinces, the Voivodina and Kosovo, where Serbs are in a minority. Hungarians are the dominant group in the Voivodina, while Albanians make up approximately 90% of the population of Kosovo. Hungarians are usually Roman Catholic or Protestant. Most Albanians are Moslem, though there is a small minority that is Roman Catholic and even a few who are Orthodox.

There are also differences in the art and temperament of the people. Dalmatian coastal architecture displays the gracefully ornate Italian influence, while in Bosnia Islamic domes and minarets are more common. The mild–tempered Slovenes contrast with the more emotional Serbs and the proudly independent Montenegrins. The unevenness of economic development throughout the country has also contributed to cultural differences. The levels of urbanization and literacy are higher in Slovenia and Croatia than in the mountainous regions of Serbia, Montenegro and Macedonia. In music, energetic melodies of Slav derivation are heard in Serbia and Croatia, played on a number of different *tamboura*, a high stylized stringed instrument that is plucked. In Macedonia, traditionally costumed peasants dance to the more plaintive melodies common to the eastern Mediterranean.

We often attempt to characterize peoples by using adjectives. Words that have been used to describe Serbs include "emotional," "hot–tempered," and "proud." Their enemies tend to use words like "hegemonic" and "bullying."

Passersby in Belgrade look at the new technology

HAMBURGER

HAMBURGER SA SIROM

DUPLI HAMBURGER SA SIROM

BIG MAC

POMFRIT standard/veliki

SLADOLED SA PRELIVOM

MLEČNI ŠEJK

BIG MAC MEAL

GENEX McDONALD'S
McDONALD'S „SLAVIJA", DELIGRADSKA 2 BEOGRAD

McDonald's je restoran za Vas, vašu porodicu i prijatelje. Uslužićemo Vas brzo sa toplom i kvalitetnom hranom. Naši proizvodi se prave od najkvalitetnijeg goveđeg mesa, mleka i krompira.

Cene su za Vas!

Dođite i uživajte u čistom i lepo opremljenom restoranu, ili, ako se žurite ponesite hranu sa sobom — upakovana je tako, da je uvek spremna za pokret.

Dođite ponovo i ne zaboravite — McDonald's ima vremena za Vas!

A *McDonald's* "tray-liner"—Belgrade, Yugoslavia

Montenegrins are usually described as "proudly independent" by admirers, "rural rustics" by detractors. Both Serbs and Montenegrins are also described as "fierce fighters." Such adjectives should not be taken too seriously, for they are more a reflection of Serbia's and Montenegro's relations with their neighbors than any underlying reality.

Serbs can be justly proud of the beautiful Serbian Orthodox churches and monasteries that date from that one great blossoming of culture during the middle ages. Modern Belgrade is in its own way a beautiful city, and an attractive city to visit because of its many sidewalk cafes, where one can order Turkish coffee and linger as long as one wants drinking it. Serbs are also, individually, a friendly people with a grace and charm all their own. Unfortunately, they can be easily stirred by appeals to Serbian nationalism, whereupon they lose their individual personalities and become, in effect, a mob.

They have been badly misled by their government in recent years, but there are signs that they are beginning to wake up to reality. Let us all hope so, for the sake of Serbia itself as well as the rest of the Balkans.

The Future

Serbs have been on a nationalistic binge for the past several years that has led to the collapse of the Socialist Federal Republic of Yugoslavia and a civil war that has left large parts of Croatia and Bosnia–Herzegovina in ruins. United Nations peacekeeping forces have not been able to either prevent a renewed outbreak of the civil war or to bring it to a close. The UN has also not been able to produce a peace plan acceptable to all sides. The basic problem is that Serb leaders insist that Serbs should not have to live under any government that they do not control. Thus the Serb leadership in Serbia supports the right of Serbs in

Croatia and Bosnia–Herzegovina to secede from their republics and remain a part of a federal Yugoslavia. Yet they deny this same principle to minorities in Serbia. Neither Croatia nor Bosnia–Herzegovina has been willing to agree to the partition of their republics. Serbs have attempted to break this political stalemate by destroying as many of the Moslem–inhabited parts of Bosnia as they could. In the process, they have instituted a process of "ethnic cleansing," driving the Moslems out of areas where they have traditionally lived.

From the standpoint of an outsider, the cultural differences between Serbs and other Yugoslavs are not too great to be bridged—with a little restraint on all sides and a willingness to compromise. Yet it is becoming increasingly unlikely that the sides will be willing to make the necessary compromises. Rump Yugoslavia's future must, therefore, be considered as very bleak indeed.

AND NOW THE NEWLY–ESTABLISHED REPUBLICS . . .

The Republic of Slovenia

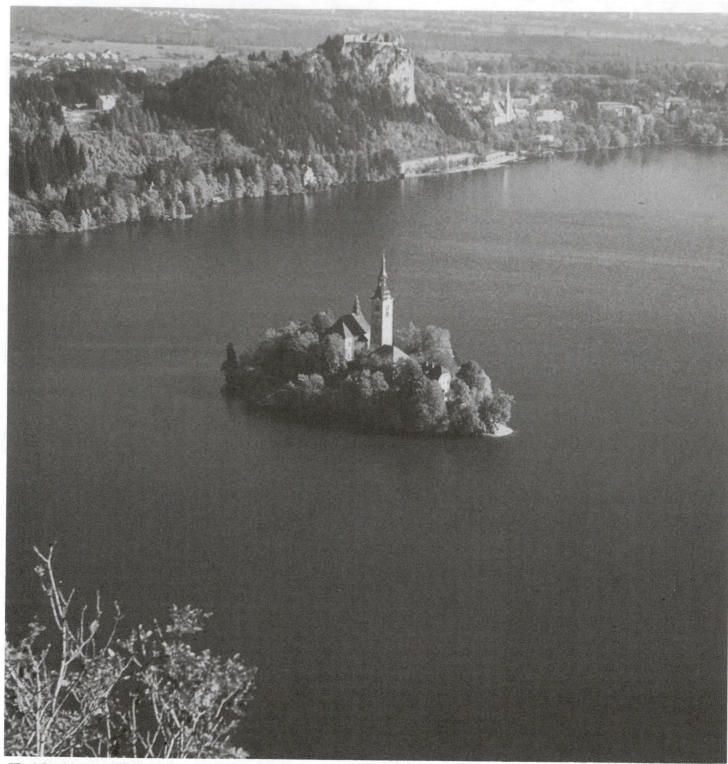

The island in Lake Bled with its ancient church.

Photo by Prof. Janko Ravnik

Area: 7,819 square miles (20,251 sq. km.).

Population: 1,940,000 (estimated).

Capital City: Ljubljana (255,000, estimated. (Pronounced Lube–lee–anna).

Climate: Mediterranean west of Ljubljana; continental in the rest of the republic.

Neighboring Countries: Italy (west); Austria (north); Hungary (east); Croatia (south).

Official Language: Slovenian.

Other Principal Tongue: Serbo–Croatian.

Ethnic Background: South Slavic with strong Germanic influences.

Principal Religion: Roman Catholicism.

Chief Commercial Products: Agricultural products and processed foods, dairy products, metals, machinery.

Currency: Tolar (issued on October 8, 1991).

Recent Political Status: Part of the Austro–Hungarian Empire until 1919, part of Yugoslavia since 1929.

Slovenia

Independence Day: June 25, 1991.

Chief of State: Milan Kucan, President (pronounced *Cooch*–an).

Head of Government: Janez Drnovsek (pronounced Der–no–sheck), Prime Minister.

National Flag: Equal horizontal stripes of white, blue, and red, with the nation's coat–of–arms on the left over the white and blue stripes.

The Land

The newly independent Republic of Slovenia was until 1991 known as the Socialist Republic of Slovenia and was part of the Socialist Federal Republic of Yugoslavia. It is located in the northwestern part of the Balkans.

The Julian Alps run along most of the border with Italy, while the Karavanke Mountains mark the border with Austria. Somewhat further south and southeast are the Kamnik Mountains. The Sava River forms a wide valley between the Julian Alps and the Karavanke Mountains, then flows across the republic in a southeastern direction. A second major river, the Drava, forms in Austria (where it is known as the Drau), then enters the republic north of the Kamnik Mountains. It then flows in a southeastern direction across the republic before crossing into Croatia. Except for the mountainous area, most of Slovenia is covered by often steep, heavily forested rolling hills, with the exception of the plateau area of gray karst limestone east of Trieste.

Slovenia also takes in the northeastern part of the Istrian Peninsula, which gives it a coastline on the Adriatic Sea. Its major port is, however, the one–time Italian city of Trieste.

The People

The Republic of Slovenia has a population about 88% of whom belong to the majority ethnic group. Except for some Italians living in the western part of the republic, most of the "minorities" are people who came to the republic from other parts of former Yugoslavia in search of work. However, a flood of Moslems fleeing Bosnia–Herzegovina as a result of Serbian aggression, was entering Slovenia in mid–1992.

History

The Slovenes migrated into the area of the western Balkans in the sixth century, the first of the Slavic peoples to enter the region. In 627, a Slavic kingdom came into existence in the Sava River Valley. It lasted for about 120 years, then was incorporated into the Carolingian Empire in 748. It was at this time that the Slovenians were converted to Roman Christianity.

In the ninth century, the Carolingian Empire was divided, and Slovenia passed to Germans; in the tenth century it became part of the Holy Roman Empire. This area remained within the Holy Roman Empire through several changes of rulers and eventually passed to the Hapsburgs, who established their capital at Vienna. Periodic attempts at Germanization shrunk the area of Slovenian culture, but not most of the Slovenian heartland, through the efforts of native Roman Catholic priests.

Slovenian peasants were eventually enserfed, along with the peasantry in other parts of the empire. This produced a number of uprisings in the fifteenth and sixteenth centuries, but things remained very much the same until the eighteenth century, when Maria Theresa and her son, Joseph II, attempted to ameliorate the lot of the people by granting them personal freedom.

After the collapse of the Austrian Empire in 1918, Slovenian leaders supported creation of the Kingdom of Serbs, Croats and Slovenes. This became the Kingdom of Yugoslavia in 1929. Slovenia was partitioned during World War I, with Italy taking the southwest, Hungary a small piece of land north of the Mura River called Prekomurje, and Germany took the northeast. This led to a Slovenian resistance movement, the most significant of which was the communist–led *Liberation Front.*

After the defeat of Germany in World War II, Slovenia became one of the constituent republics of the People's Republic of Yugoslavia. In 1947, the republic received some additional territory from Italy as part of the Paris Peace Treaty. In 1954, some of the former Free Territory of Trieste was transferred to Slovenia.

Slovenians are a hard–working people with a good republic leadership; they did well economically up through about 1980. Yugoslavia never recovered from the oil shock of 1979, however, and the wealthier parts of the country found themselves

President Milan Kucan

called upon to provide more assistance to badly run and failing large–scale industry in the eastern part of the country. By the middle of the 1980s, political leaders in Slovenia and Croatia were pushing for a change in the economic system, but they were opposed, particularly, by the leadership of Serbia; Slovenia and Croatia then proposed a loosened form of federation that would give them economic independence. This was unacceptable to Serbia.

Faced with this stalemate at the national level, Slovenia and Croatia began to push for internal changes. By the spring of 1990, Slovenia had ended the political monopoly formerly held by the *Slovenian Communist Party* and created a *de facto* pluralistic system. In April 1990, multi–party elections resulted in a legislature dominated by the six–party *Democratic United Opposition*, or *Demos*.

The *Demos*, a coalition of conservative political parties, had campaigned on a platform of independence within a year. At the same time, Milan Kucan, candidate of the communists, was elected President. Shortly thereafter, the communists became the *Party of Democratic Renewal* and endorsed independence as well.

On July 2, 1990, the Assembly adopted a "declaration of sovereignty" by an overwhelming 187 votes to 3. In September, the Assembly took control of the "territorial defense force." A referendum on independence was held on December 23, 1990. Of those voting, 88.5% opted for independence, "unless it proved possible to negotiate a looser Yugoslav confederation." The Assembly then adopted its own endorsement of the declaration on December 26. The Assembly voted in February 1991 that republic law would

Slovenia

henceforth take precedence over laws of the Yugoslav Federation.

Meanwhile, all attempts to negotiate a new union proved unavailing, as Serbia stonewalled. After Slovenia has passed its legislation establishing the paramountcy of republic legislation, Serbia went further and instituted a boycott of goods from Slovenia. Then it took another step in May when it refused to accept the election of the Croatian Vice President to the Yugoslav Presidency. For two months, the office of President remained vacant. Finally, Slovenia and Croatia declared their independence on June 25, 1991.

On June 27, the Yugoslav People's Army moved against Slovenia, probably selecting Slovenia because the republic had taken charge of some border posts with Austria and Italy. The Slovenes fought back, however, and even managed to capture some tanks.

Meanwhile, the West, which had attempted to dissuade the Slovenians and Croatians by refusing, as Secretary of Baker put it, to recognize their independence "under any circumstances," was appalled by the bloodshed and began to offer mediating services.

Some of the European nations even began talking about extending recognition to Slovenia and Croatia. This led to a break in the stalemate at the center and the installation of Stipe Mesic as President. Finally, after two cease–fires had broken down, the third held. In a compromise imposed by negotiators from the EC, Slovene agents were authorized to collect federal customs duties at the disputed custom posts, while Slovenia agreed to suspend application of its declaration of independence for three months.

This brought an end to the war in Slovenia, but it actually only moved the

venue of the war to Croatia. Three months later, the Yugoslavian People's Army was still trying to conquer Croatia and nothing had been settled. Slovenia thereupon activated its declaration of independence as of October 7.

By December, with the war in Croatia still going on, most European nations were fed up with Serbia and the leadership of the Yugoslav People's Army. Germany now pressed the EC to recognize the two republics and this was finally agreed to, effective as of January 15, 1992. Secretary of State Baker refused to follow suit, however, in effect continuing support for the hardline, Serbian nationalist and ex–communist leadership of Serbia and the Yugoslavia People's Army. Apparently anything was better to Secretary Baker than to see one more part of Europe falling apart. This changed only after the Yugoslav army began to spread its destruction throughout most of the rest

Slovenia's capital, Ljubljana, as seen from the Castle.

324

Slovenia

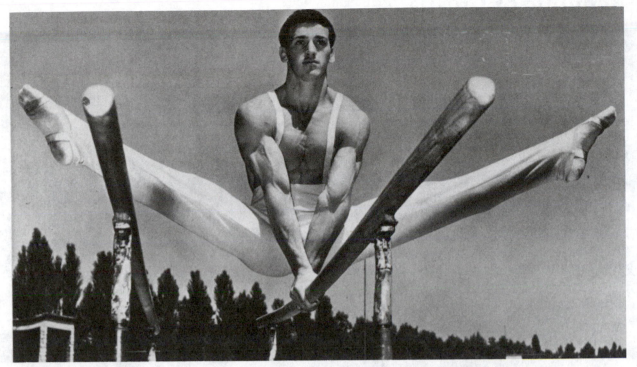

Slovenia's Miro Cerar, world champion on parallels and horizontal bars, European gymnastics champion, prepares for the Olympics.

of former Yugoslavia. The United States then changed its mind and sponsored UN economic sanctions against Serbia and Montenegro.

Slovenia held new elections to its parliament in December 1992. The elections essentially confirmed the previous political situation. In January, Janez Drnovsek was reappointed Prime Minister. The key members of the cabinet are all ex–communists, with the exception of Lojze Peterle, the Foreign Minister, who is a *Christian Democrat*. The government's program is essentially the same as it was three years ago, prior to the country's independence.

Nature of the Regime

Slovenia has been a multiparty democracy since 1990, when a six–party *Democratic United Opposition*, also known as the *Demos*, won 55% of the vote. The *Slovenian Communist Party*, which had changed its name to the *Party of Democratic Renewal*, won 18% of the vote, but the former communist leader, Milan Kucan, won the presidency with 52% of the vote. Kucan and the *Demos* have since established that they can work together.

The prime minister is the leader of the *Demos*. Slovenia adopted a new constitution in 1991.

Culture

Slovenian culture reflects the fact that this is an overwhelmingly Roman Catholic country, but it differs from Croatia, which is also Roman Catholic, in that it is much more western in its orientation. Driving through the beautiful countryside, it is impossible to differentiate this area from those of Austria across the border. Towns and cities are clean and prosperous–looking and the people dress much as they do elsewhere in Europe. Only the signs in Slovenian make it clear what country you are in.

There is not a great deal of literature in Slovenian and much of what exists is religious in nature. The Freising manuscripts, dating from about the year 1000, are the earliest works available. Slovenian came into wider use during the reformation, when Protestants translated the Bible and also produced some tracts in the language. The Slovenians eventually rejected Protestantism, however. In the eighteenth century, a Roman Catholic version of the Bible appeared in Slovenian and this was followed by grammars in the early nineteenth century. Slovenian came into common use only after the middle of the nineteenth century, however.

Economy

Slovenia is still primarily agricultural, though the harvesting of forestry products provides an additional income for many rural inhabitants. Crops include wheat, corn, rye, oats, potatoes, rape-

seed, sugar beets, and fruit. Livestock raising (cattle, sheep, pigs, poultry) is also carried on throughout the republic. Agriculture is highly mechanized and the standard of living in the countryside approximates that of its neighbor, Austria.

It has a significant steel industry that produces approximately three–quarters of a million tons of steel annually. It also manufactures trucks and automobiles. It produces its own coal and has some hydroelectric stations, but all other energy must be imported. Other industrial products include cement, sulphuric acid, cotton and woolen fabrics, plus processed agricultural products such as sugar.

The Future

The Republic of Slovenia is basically a prosperous land, made so by a hard–working citizenry. Continuing bitterness in Serbia and Montenegro may mean that these markets are more or less permanently lost to Slovenian business, but that should prove no long–term hardship, since Slovenian manufactures are, in general, of good quality and competitive. Most industry is still state–owned, but the government is committed to a policy of privatization. Most people, in any case, make their living from agriculture, which was never collectivized. The transition should, therefore, not be a difficult one.

The Republic of Croatia

The picturesque medieval city of Dubrovnik on the Adriatic Coast before its bombardment by the *Serbs*

Area: 21,829 square miles (56,538 sq. km.).

Population: 4,760,344 (April 1991).

Capital City: Zagreb (765,000).

Climate: Mediterranean in the west; Mild continental east of Zagreb.

Neighboring Countries: Slovenia (north); Hungary (northeast); Serbia, SFRY (east); Bosnia (east and south); Montenegro (southwest).

Official Language: Croatian.

Other Principal Tongues: Serbo–Croatian.

Ethnic Background: South Slavic.

Principal Religions: Roman Catholicism, Serbian Orthodox.

Chief Commercial Products: Agricultural products, lumber, coal, steel, plastics, cement, cotton fabrics.

Currency: Croatian Dinar (Introduced December 1991).

Former Political Status: Constituent republic of SFRY.

National Day: June 25, 1991.

Chief of State: Franjo Tudjman, President.

Head of Government: Nikica Valentic, Prime Minister (April 1993).

National Flag: Three horizontal stripes from the top—red, white, blue, with a checkered crest of the country imposed on the white stripe.

The Land

The Republic of Croatia is the independent successor state to the *Socialist Republic of Croatia*, one of the six republics of the now defunct Socialist Federal Republic of Yugoslavia. Croatia declared its independence in June 1991. After a bitter six month war fought against it by Serbia and the Yugoslav People's Army, it received international recognition by the members of the European Community in January 1992.

Croatia, has a long coastline on the Adriatic Sea. In the north and east, the chief topographical features are the Sava and Drava River valleys, plus the Croatian–Slavonian Mountains, a mountainous ridge that separates the two river valleys. The Drava River forms the border with Hungary while the Sava forms the border with Bosnia–Herzegovina. Most of the rest of Croatia consists of either mountains or uplands.

The Great Kapela Chain crosses the republic in the northwest. Somewhat further south, the Velebit Range begins, followed by the Dinarian Alps, which run along the border with Bosnia–Herzegovina. The long Croatian coastline consists of the Dalmatian Islands plus a fairly narrow strip of the mainland reaching down as far as Montenegro. This is essentially a coastal plain backed by mountains. This, plus the Dalmatian Islands, became a major summer resort area for West Europeans.

This region was once the ancient Greek Kingdom of Dalmatia and includes such

326

Croatia

historic cities as Split, where the Emperor Diocletian lived after his retirement from 305 to 313. The nucleus of the town is actually the Palace of Diocletian. Another important city is Dubrovnik, a town founded in the seventh century and famous for its late–Renaissance buildings. The city's former picturesque streets, which are narrow and winding (and now in ruins) are closed to motor vehicles. Dubrovnik was badly damaged when it was shelled by the Yugoslav People's Army in the fall of 1991 and early 1992.

The People

Croats represent 77.9% of the total. Serbs, the largest minority, account for 12.2% of the population. A further 2.2 percent identified themselves as "Yugoslavs," and 1% Moslems.

History

The Croatians entered the Balkan Peninsula from the area of the western Carpathian Mountains in the 7th century. Even at this time they were separate from the Serbs, constituting, along with the Slavonians, the western division of the Serbo–Croatian migration, while the Serbs formed the eastern portion. At this time, the Croats were ruled by tribal institutions. While the Slovenians were being incorporated into the Carolingian Empire, however, the Croats fell under the domination of the Byzantine Empire beginning in 877.

Rebelling against this outside control, they formed the first united Croatian Kingdom in 910. The ruler of this first Croatian kingdom was Tomislav and the kingdom he founded lasted for about two centuries. During this time, Croatia waged war against Bulgaria and managed to extend its control over part of the Dalmatian coast. This period of history is, in fact, looked on by many Croatian nationalists as the golden age of their country. They did build up a large navy and for a time at the end of the tenth century even exacted tribute from Venice.

Croatia was included in the new Kingdom of Serbs, Croats and Slovenes which was formed on December 4, 1918. In 1921, a constitution was adopted which created a unitary central government. Since Serbs made up about 40% of the overall population, their party, the *Radical Party*, tended to dominate this new kingdom. When Stepjan Radic, leader of the *Croatian Peasant Party*, protested the Serbian domination, the government responded by arresting him and banning his party. The period from 1921 to 1928 was one of constant conflict over the issue of centralism versus federalism, with Croatian nationalists advocating creation of a federal state.

When Radic was assassinated within the parliament building by a Montenegrin in 1928, the Croatian deputies withdrew from the body, threatening not to return until a federal state had been created in which Croatians were not dominated by Serbs. King Alexander I (see Yugoslavia) opposed the idea of a federal state so, in 1929, he abolished the constitution and took power himself. After he had proclaimed his royal dictatorship, he changed the name of the country to Yugoslavia.

Alexander was assassinated in 1934 by a Macedonian associated with the Croatian dissidents. Since Alexander's son, Peter, was then only a child, Alexander's cousin, Prince Paul, was named regent; he ruled until 1941. In 1939, he attempted to solve the problem of nationalist dissent by creating an internally self–governing Croatia.

Paul was deposed in March 1941 after he allied Yugoslavia with Germany. The denunciation of the alliance brought a German invasion in April 1941 and German occupation of the country between 1941 and 1945. Hitler permitted an "independent" Croatia to be proclaimed in April 1941, however. The head of this entity was Ante Pavelic, head of a fascist organization called *Ustasha*. The Pavelic regime was characterized by brutality and violence, much of it targeted against local Serbs. One of the problems the Croatian Government has today with Serbs is that they remember the actions of a previous Croatian Government and are unwilling to trust the current one.

There were lots of Croats who opposed this Ustasha Government, however, one of whom was Josef Broz Tito, leader of the *Partisan Forces* against the Germans. During the war, Tito and his Communist Partisans organized local committees throughout Croatia as they liberated individual areas from German or Ustasha control. Toward the end of the war, these local committees were organized into a council of national liberation and after Zagreb was liberated, this council proclaimed itself the People's Government of Croatia. When the country was reconstituted as the People's Republic of Yugoslavia in 1945, the People's Republic of Croatia joined as one of the six constituent republics.

The self–promoted Marshal Tito, who ruled Yugoslavia from 1945 to 1980, ruthlessly suppressed all nationalist agitation within the country. Franjo Tudjman, now President of the Republic of Croatia, was one of Tito's generals. In the early 1970s, he and Stipe Mesic, the last President of Yugoslavia, were among Croatian Communist leaders imprisoned on charges of nationalistic deviations.

Croatian nationalist groups began to reemerge in the late 1980s. Most of these eventually joined to form the *Croatian Democratic Union*. This political party won the republic elections in April 1990. Franjo Tudjman, leader of the party, was elected President at the same time. The political program of the movement only called for increased autonomy within a more confederal Yugoslavia.

It was Yugoslavia's tragedy that a Serbian dominist, Slobodan Milosevic, rose to power within the *League of Communists of Serbia* at this same time. Milosevic not only opposed all political concessions to Croatia; he also deliberately sabotaged economic reform as well. He therefore created a political stalemate which was also destroying the economy.

On May 19, 1991, the Croatian Government held a referendum on the question of independence for the republic. After a favorable vote, the Croatian Assembly adopted a declaration of independence on June 25. The Croatian Government did reiterate, however, that it was willing to continue discussions on a looser Yugoslav confederation, with the central government confined to foreign policy, defense and a common currency.

When the Government of Croatia began moving toward independence, the Serbs within the republic, egged on by Milosevic and a press dominated by Serbs, organized two autonomous regions. Despite a new law passed by the Croatian legislature guaranteeing protection for minority ethnic groups, the Croatian Serbs held their own referendum on July 7 reaffirming their loyalty to the Socialist Federal Republic of Yugoslavia.

Meanwhile, the Yugoslav People's Army (YPA) reacted to the declarations of independence by sending an invasion force into Slovenia. That republic was selected instead of Croatia because it moved to take control of its international

President Franjo Tudjman

Croatia

border with Italy and Austria. The YPA was apparently not expecting much opposition, but the Slovenians fought back valiantly.

Meanwhile, the rest of the world, which had encouraged the army action by asserting that they would not support a separate Slovenia or Croatia "under any circumstances," began calling for a cease-fire. At the same time, army desertions by non–Serbs began to be a problem. This led to an agreement with Slovenia that it could man the control posts if it would turn the revenues over to the central government. The YPA also agreed to return its forces to the barracks.

Slavonia and Croatia also agreed to suspend their declarations of independence for three months. Serbia, in turn, agreed to allow Stipe Mesic to be elected President. The latter agreement was important in a military as well as a political sense because the President was also the Commander–in–Chief of the Yugoslav People's Army.

The agreement brought peace to Slovenia, but not to Yugoslavia. One of the first actions of President Mesic was to arrange a ceasefire—the third—on July 2. That same day, General Blagoje Adzic, chief of the YPA General Staff, angrily repudiated the ceasefire—and thereby his own Commander–in–Chief—in an interview that appeared on Belgrade television and added that the army "accepted the challenge of total war that had been imposed on it" and would soon

end it with a complete victory. The next day, an armored column left Belgrade for Croatia.

On July 6, 1991, Milosevic gave a speech in which he told Serbs to be ready to defend themselves. He also gave Serb leaders in Croatia generous access to Serbian radio and television. The first fighting in Croatia began on July 7 when Croatian Serbs allied with Milosevic attacked Croatian territorial defense forces near the town of Tenja. Once the fighting had begun, the Yugoslav People's Army intervened "to keep the peace," though its targets were always Croatian territorial units. Since President Tudjman ordered Croatian units not to attack the YPA, the fighting remained small scale for some time. In addition, the YPA did not initiate battles at this time and only advanced when new fighting would break out. Gradually, however, the YPA's control of Croatian territory spread as Serb territorial forces launched new battles in area after area.

The Serbian problem existed because Serbs insisted on living in a state controlled by Serbs. But the Croatians were not entirely free of this empire mentality themselves. The Republic of Bosnia–Herzegovina, which lies between Serbia and Croatia, has an extremely mixed population, with 31% Serbs and about 17% Croats. In July, President Tudjman admitted that members of his government had held secret talks with Serbian leaders about carving up Bosnia between the

two, leaving a small Moslem rump that neither wanted. Word of these talks did not help Croatia internationally.

Croatia was "saved" by the fact that Serbia and the YPA were even more bloody–minded. In August, Milosevic revealed his plans for a reconstituted Yugoslavia which called for carving up Croatia and incorporating about a third of the territory into the new state, although Serbs constitute only 12% of Croatia's population. Even more revealing, on August 20, Milosevic's chief ideologist praised the Moscow *coup* leaders as "tough men but not dogmatics" and accused Gorbachëv of pushing the Soviet Union toward a break–up by his attempt to create a union of sovereign states.

Meanwhile the YPA, which up to this time had contended that it was acting as a neutral buffer between the two sides, began bombarding Croatian cities with artillery and aircraft. In late August, much of the city of Vukovar was destroyed. By this time, perhaps twenty percent of the republic had fallen under YPA or Serb militia control.

On September 18, 1991, Zagreb, the capital, came under fire from aircraft and artillery. At about the same time, the Yugoslav navy instituted a blockade of Croatia's Dalmatian ports. Soon it began attacking them, beginning with the city of Split. Up to this moment, the Croatian Government had been carrying out a "passive defense" and refusing to challenge the YPA directly. Now it cut oil lines across Croatia to Serbia and laid siege to Yugoslav army barracks in Croatia. Croatia also began getting some indirect assistance from other republics when Bosnia–Herzegovina and Macedonia adopted a position of neutrality and ordered their citizens to ignore conscription notices from the YPA. Even in Serbia, however, many young men went into hiding rather than serve.

The three–month moratorium on Croatia and Slovenia's independence declarations—agreed to at Brioni—was set to expire on October 7. Freed of that limitation, the Croatian Assembly approved a resolution severing all ties with the Socialist Federal Republic of Yugoslavia. By this time, approximately a third of the country was occupied by the YPA and the Serbs. The Yugoslav air force marked the day with an attack on the presidential palace in Zagreb at the very moment that President Tudjman was in conference with Stipe Mesic, the Federal President, and Ante Markovic, the Federal Prime Minister. As the *Economist* put it, "the attack put to rest any pretense that there is real life left in the Yugoslav federation."

Four days earlier, the Serbs showed that they realized this when they instituted a maneuver to take control of the

The Tudjman family occupies the front pew in Zagreb Cathedral

328

Federal Presidency. On October 3, Branko Kostic, Montenegrin representative to the SFRY Presidency and Vice President, called a meeting of the Presidency in President Mesic's absence and proposed declaring a state of emergency. The resolution was passed with the support of the three votes controlled by Serbia (Serbia plus its two formerly autonomous regions), plus Kostic's own vote.

By this time, it had become clear to almost everyone just what Serbia was attempting to do. But it took almost three months more before Britain and France could be persuaded to abandon the ideal of a united Yugoslavia. And even then, the American Government refused to abandon that ideal. But the European Community announced in December that they would recognize Slovenia and Croatia as of January 15. The fighting continued up to that date, but tapered off afterwards.

As of early July 1992, about a third of Croatia is controlled by either the YPA or Serb militias. A UN effort to replace them with peacekeeping troops has had mixed success. Many of Croatia's cities are badly damaged with Vukovar in ruins. For Croatia, the cost of independence has come extremely high.

Culture

The Croatian people have a dominant Roman Catholic religious tradition which permeates and largely defines the culture. For example, it was Bishop Josip Juraj Strossmayer who carried out a reorganization of the University of Zagreb in 1874. A secular tradition tended to develop in the nineteenth century. One such cultural figure was Franjo Rachki, the Croatian historian.

Linguistically, Croatian does not differ greatly from Serbian, though borrowed-words in the vocabulary tend to come from German or Latin rather than from Greek or Turkish as in the case of Serbia. Another difference is that Croatian uses the Roman alphabet, while Serbian uses the Cyrillic alphabet. There are, of course, differences in pronunciation as well. There is a significant Serbian influence in Croatia, however, since 12% of the population is Serb.

Economy

About half of Croatia's work force is engaged in industry, while the other half support themselves from agriculture. Croatia has a great deal of excellent farmland in the northeastern part of the country, but farming is carried on throughout the republic. Corn is the chief grain crop, followed by wheat. Other commercial crops include plums, used in the production of slivovitz (a dry, usually colorless brandy), grapes, which are processed

The rugged, mountainous Croatian terrain on the road to Karlovac

into wine and other brandies, sugarbeets, flax, hemp, and fruits.

The raising of livestock also plays a significant role, with it about equally divided between cattle and sheep. Pigs and poultry are also important farm products. Croatia still has significant forest areas, so timber products provide employment to many rural inhabitants.

Manufacturing is better developed in Croatia than in any of the other republics. Most of this is light industry which concentrates on manufacturing goods for sale to consumers, though Croatia also produces extractive products such as petroleum, coal, and bauxite. Fishing is also a major industry for people along the Dalmatian coast. Perhaps the greatest

money-maker of all used to be tourism, particularly along the Dalmatian coast, famous for its many resorts.

The Future

Although Croatia strived for its goal of independence, the republic is still partially occupied and its largest minority, the Serbs, are determined to bring the republic into Yugoslavia. United Nations peacekeeping forces can police a truce, but they can not produce a political solution. But until its ethnic-political problems are solved, Croatia faces a bleak future.

The Republic of Bosnia–Herzegovina

(pronounced Hairs–eh–govena)

A column of Bosnian policemen, Sarajevo.

Area: 19,696 square miles (51,129 sq. km.; almost 3/4 of its area (as of July 1992) is under control of the Yugoslav People's Army plus Serbian irregulars).

Population: 4.4 million (April 1991 census).

Capital City: Sarajevo (380,000).

Ethnic Background: South Slavic. Moslem (44%), Serb (33%), Croat (17%).

Climate: Continental in the north; Mediterranean in the southwest.

Neighboring Countries: Serbia, SFRY (east); Montenegro, SFRY (southeast); Croatia (west and north).

Official Language: Serbo–Croatian.

Other Principal Tongues: Albanian.

Principal Religions: Islam, Serbian Orthodox, Roman Catholicism.

Chief Commercial Products: Grains, potatoes, plums, livestock, timber, coal, iron ore, bauxite, cement, cotton fabrics, cars.

Currency: Dinar.

Former Political Status: Constituent republic of SFRY.

Chief of State: Alija Izetbegovic (pronounced *Ease–et–behgo–vich*), President.

Head of Government: Jure Pelivan, Prime Minister.

National Flag: In the center of a white base is imposed a blue shield divided diagonally by a white stripe with 3 golden lilies in each of the two parts.

The Land

The Republic of Bosnia–Herzegovina is the independent successor state to the Socialist Republic of Bosnia–Herzegovina which was until 1991 part of the Socialist Federal Republic of Yugoslavia. The republic is roughly triangular. It also has a tiny, 13 mile section of coastline on the Adriatic Sea, but no harbor. It has an area of 19,741 square miles (51,129 sq. km.), almost all of which is mountainous. Herzegovina, the name which applies to the southern part of the republic, is derived from *Herzog*, a Germanic title meaning duke taken by a local ruler in the fifteenth century. The name Bosnia is derived from the Bosna River, a tributary of the Sava River. The course of the 168–mile long river is almost entirely within the republic. It begins in Herzegovina in the south and then flows north-ward through Bosnia and enters the Sava River at the border. The Sava River, in turn, forms the western border with Croatia.

A second river, the Drina, forms a large part of the border with Serbia. The Drina

...s also a tributary of the Sava. Two further rivers flow from south to north across the republic, the Vrbas to the west of the Bosna and the Una in the extreme northwest part of the republic. The source of all of these rivers is the mountain chain known as the Dinarian Alps, which runs in a northwest–southeastern direction across the western part of the republic.

Individual peaks soar to over 7,500 feet, though wide valleys running in the same direction separate the ridges. The center of the republic is a piedmont region with an average height of 1500 feet, while the Sava and Drina River valleys produce lowlands in the east. About half the land of the republic is arable, with most of the remainder covered by forests of pine, beech and oak. The exception is the area of Herzegovina in the south. A native proverb says that "Bosnia begins with the forest, Herzegovina with the rock." The mountains of Herzegovina are of gray Karst limestone, filled with crevices, sinkholes and pits, and they overwhelm the viewer with their barren desolation. Most of this area has very little population. It is only possible to live in the fertile river valleys that cut through the mountains and in some upland hollows where there is arable soil. Bosnia's weather is generally mild with cold winters. In Herzegovina, on the other hand, summers are often oppressively hot.

The People

The population of the Republic of Bosnia–Herzegovina is just over 4.6 million and it is the most diverse of the republics of the old Yugoslav Federation. No single group is in a majority, but Moslems have been the largest grouping with 44% percent of the population. Serbs account for 33% percent of the population, while Croats constitute a further 17% percent. The basis of the three "nations" of Bosnia–Herzegovina is religion, not language. The Moslems of Bosnia–Herzegovina are a Slavic people who converted to Islam and the language they speak is Serbo–Croatian. Serbs are adherants of the Serbian Orthodox Church, while Croats are Roman Catholics.

History

Although the present–day area of Bosnia–Herzegovina was settled by Slavic–speaking peoples as early as the seventh century, it first emerged as a separate political entity toward the end of the twelfth century when a nobleman by the name of Kulin managed to gain control of most of the lands along the Bosna River, which became known as the Ban of Bosnia. Kulin's principality did not last long, but one of the things he did was to convert to Bogomilism and make it the state religion.

Bogomilism had originated two centuries earlier, further to the east in Bulgaria, but by the twelfth century it had become well established in Bosnia. Its distinguishing characteristic was it taught that the world was governed by two principles, good and evil, the first spiritual and the second material. The physical world, being material, is the realm of the devil. This Manichaean dualism was condemned as heretical by both the Roman Catholic and Greek Orthodox churches, so Bogomils found themselves rejected by both the west and the east.

Early in the thirteenth century, the Roman Catholic Church dispatched a papal legate to the area to institute a purge of the local clergy. Somewhat later, Dominican missionaries were sent in to fight the heresy. They came with military might provided by the Hungarian monarchy. These military forces brought Bosnia under Hungarian control. In 1299, The Hungarian king granted Bosnia as a fief to a Croatian aristocrat by the name of Paul Subic. After he took over, Subic brought in Franciscan missionaries to help stamp out the Bogomils.

Subic passed the principality on to his son, Mladen, but the latter was overthrown by the local nobility in 1322. He was replaced as *Ban* by Stephen Kotromanic, a native Bosnian. Kotromanic was succeeded by his nephew, Stephen Tvrtko, who expanded the principality greatly during his lifetime, annexing part of Dalmatia to the west and part of the area of modern–day Montenegro to the south. Tvrtko eventually took the title "Stephen I, King of Serbia, Bosnia, Dalmatia, Croatia, and the Primorje."

Tvrtko was succeeded by his younger brother, who was crowned as Stephen II in 1391. By the time of his death seven years later, the Turks had launched an invasion of Bosnia and the kingdom began to disintegrate. The kingdom soon broke down into several principalities, most of them paying a yearly tribute to the Turks. The ruler of one of these principalities opted to become a vassal of the Holy Roman Emperor instead, however, and for this had bestowed on him the title of *Herzog* (duke) of St. Sava. Over time, this title became attached to the land instead of the ruler, and in its modern form is Herzegovina.

After the fall of Constantinople in 1453, the Turks decided to take control of the Balkan Peninsula directly. The new invasion of Bosnia began in 1460. Some parts tried to hold out against the Turks, but many of the Bogomil leaders apparently saw the Moslem Turks as being preferable to the Hungarian Roman Catholics, still trying to stamp out Bogomilism, and allied themselves with the Turks. Afterwards, most of these Bogomils converted to Islam.

These new converts adopted the dress, titles, and etiquette of the Turkish court, while retaining their lands, their language, and most of their old customs. They also became the local military caste, which gave them a rank just below that the Turkish governor. They remained loyal to the Ottoman Empire and some of them even rose to the highest offices in the empire. One such was Ali Pasha, who became grand vizier in 1570. His successor, Mahomet Beg Sokolovic, also came from Bosnia. Meanwhile, most of the peasants remained Orthodox Christians.

Little changed until the seventeenth century, when the Austrian Empire, then still known as the Holy Roman Empire, began to push down into the Balkans. Prince Eugene of Savoy burned Sarajevo in 1697. Part of the sea coast area of Herzegovina plus a part of Bosnia that bordered on the Sava River passed to Austria in 1718. Turkey took the Bosnian territory back in 1739, but it passed back under Austrian control 1791.

In the first half of the nineteenth century, an estrangement began to grow between the Moslem aristocrats of Bosnia and the Ottoman government, primarily over the issue of traditional privileges. There were several revolts between 1820 and 1850 that led the regime to strip the aristocracy of most of its privileges. The peasantry were also growing dissatisfied as a result of increasing tax obligations and this led to other revolts.

Things came to a head in July 1875 when a revolt among Christian peasants soon spread throughout the country and turned into a war specifically against Turks. The revolt next spread to Herzegovina, then to Bulgaria. Serbia and Montenegro then declared war against the Ottoman Empire in July 1876. Russia entered the war in July 1877.

Russia and Austria–Hungary had been rivals in the Balkans throughout the nineteenth century, so Alexander II, the Russian Tsar, opened negotiations with the Austro–Hungarian Government immediately after Serbia entered the war against Turkey. The agreement the two sides signed at Reichstadt stipulated among other things that Austria–Hungary would receive territorial concessions in case of a change in the *status quo* in the Balkans.

After Russia had won its war against Turkey, the Austro–Hungarian regime was outraged when it learned of the terms of the treaty. The creation of a large Bulgarian state clearly constituted a change in the *status quo*, but the treaty made no mention of corresponding territorial concessions to Austria–Hungary. It then threatened Russia with war and Bismarck, the German Chancellor, had to step in to preserve the peace. He suggested a congress of European nations to

Bosnia–Herzegovina

meet at Berlin. A Congress, among other things, awarded Austria–Hungary administrative control of Bosnia–Herzegovina. The territory was not formally annexed at this time because the Austro–Hungarian Prime Minister, a Hungarian, did not want any more Slavs in the empire. This was a technicality, however. From this moment onward, Bosnia–Herzegovina became a part of the Austro–Hungarian Empire. And in 1908, after a successful revolt of the Young Turks against the Ottoman Empire, Austria–Hungary annexed Bosnia–Herzegovina formally.

Ten years later, the Austro–Hungarian Empire was in collapse as a result of its defeat in World War I. The Serbs, with Allied blessing, claimed all of the South Slavic lands for a new Kingdom of Serbs, Croats and Slovenes, which was proclaimed on December 4, 1918. In 1929, this new state changed its name to Yugoslavia. The area of Bosnia–Herzegovina was submerged within this centralized state of South Slavs. Bosnia–Herzegovina was at this time both poor and rural, with no strong local political leaders. Serbs tended to look to Serbia, while Croats looked to Croatian leaders outside of Bosnia.

Bosnia did produce one outstanding leader during this time, Josef Broz, better known by his revolutionary *nom de guerre*, Tito. But he was head of the *Communist Party of Yugoslavia*, and had to work underground, since the party was illegal during the interwar period. After World War II, however, Tito became the ruler of the reconstituted Yugoslavia and he saw to it that Bosnia–Herzegovina became one of the six constituent republics of the new state.

The people of the republic were satisfied to be part of the Socialist Federal Republic of Yugoslavia, even though the republic remained primarily rural where even today approximately two thirds of the people make their living from agriculture. It did develop its own republic leadership, however, and when things began falling apart in the late 1980s, the political leadership of Bosnia–Herzegovina had its own ideas about what should be done.

The political discussions remained within the *League of Communists of Bosnia–Herzegovina*—the monopoly party—until 1990, when new elections were set to occur. When the party authorized the formation of additional political parties,

however, the old system collapsed. The November 1990 elections were won by three new parties, the Moslem *Party of Democratic Action*, which gained 86 assembly seats, the *Serbian Democratic Party*, which won 70 seats, and the *Croat Democratic Union*, which got 45 seats. These three political parties subsequently formed a coalition and in December they elected Alija Izetbegovic, leader of the *Party of Democratic Action*, as President of the republic.

The political leadership of Bosnia–Herzegovina mainly stood aside as the quarrel between the Serbs on one side and the Croats and Slovenes on the other grew more heated in 1990–91. They favored continuation of a united Yugoslavia, but also wanted economic reforms, repudiation of the communist leaders, and a more decentralized political structure. When Croatia and Slovenia declared their independence on June 25, 1991, the political leaders of Bosnia–Herzegovina once again urged calm on both sides, but to no avail. After the Serbs and Yugoslav People's Army began their war against Croatia, however, the Bosnian leadership began to prepare for the break–up of the country. They wanted a united Yugoslavia, but were unwilling to remain in a truncated Yugoslavia—dominated by Serbia.

Bosnian representatives stopped participating in the institutions of the Yugoslav Federal Government on October 3, 1991 after Serbian and Montenegrin leaders pulled off a *coup*, and took control of the Yugoslav Presidency. On December 20, the Bosnian Government voted to ask the EC for recognition as an independent state. The Government split on the issue, with the Moslems and Croats voting for independence and the Serbs insisting that Bosnia–Herzegovina ought to remain part of the Federal State of Yugoslavia. The Serbs then threatened to form their own "Serbian Republic of Bosnia–Herzegovina" encompassing those territories where Serbs are in a majority.

On March 18, 1992 the leaders of the three communities agreed in principle to restructure the state, creating "three constituent units, based on national principles and taking into account economic, geographic and other criteria." The effect would be to create three autonomous units within the governmental structure, one for Moslems, one for Croats and one for Serbs. Control in each municipality would be by that national group which was in an "absolute or relative majority." The agreement would be extremely difficult to implement, since the three communities live side by side and many families are mixed. Its main value, therefore, was more as a way to forestall a civil war rather than as a practical blueprint.

A group of Moslems mourn a fallen comrade.

AP/Wide World Photo

Bosnia–Herzegovina

Its other value was that it allowed Serb leaders to back down from their policy of confrontation while protecting them from charges of betrayal from the radicals who argue for a single Greater Serbia.

In early April, the European Community and the United States recognized the independence of Bosnia–Herzegovina. Although gratifying in the abstract, it had a negative side, for the *Serbian Democratic Party* then withdrew from the coalition, the two Serbian members of the Presidency resigned, and Serb leaders announced the formation of a "Serbian Republic of Bosnia–Herzegovina" which intended to remain part of Yugoslavia.

President Alija Izetbegovic

The Yugoslav Army was also still stationed in Bosnia at that time. It announced that it would withdraw from Bosnia, moving its forces to Serbia and Montenegro. In fact, it divided its forces, leaving in Bosnia all those who had any connection with Bosnia or other non–Serb states. These forces, provided with tanks, artillery and all the equipment needed to fight a modern war, became the army of the Bosnian Serbs. With a UN arms embargo making it impossible for the Bosnian Government to obtain any significant number of weapons, the forces supporting an independent Bosnia found themselves completely outclassed. Within three months, the Bosnian Serbs controlled 70% of the territory of Bosnia (with Bosnian Croatians who were receiving military assistance from Croatia controlling most of the rest) and they surrounded the capital of Sarajevo, holding that city under siege. Fourteen months later, the Bosnian Serbs control an even

larger part of Bosnia. Over the past several months, they have also instituted a policy of "ethnic cleansing," in the areas under their control, destroying the homes of Moslems and forcing them to flee these areas. A UN peace plan which would have allowed Serbs to retain most but not all of the land they occupy was rejected by the Bosnian Serb leadership in May 1993.

Nature of the Regime

Bosnia–Herzegovina formerly had a seven–member collective presidency. The last President is nominally a Moslem, but anarchy prevails. The government was a coalition representing the three major national groupings within the republic, but has evaporated.

Culture

One of the more interesting cultural elements in Bosnia–Herzegovina is that approximately 44 percent of the population are Moslems. These Moslems speak Serbo–Croatian, however, and they are a Slavic people who converted to Islam.

Economy

Though industry contributes over half the GDP, Bosnia–Herzegovina is still overwhelmingly agricultural. Herzegovina, with its warmer climate specializes in semitropical crops like pomegranates,

lemons, olives, rice and tobacco. Further north, cereal grains and soybeans are widely grown, but other crops include potatos, melons, grapes, plums, mulberries and figs. Cattle, sheep, pigs, and poultry are raised throughout the republic.

Most of Bosnia–Herzegovina's industry is extractive in nature. Bosnia produces coal, iron, copper, manganese, lead, mercury, bauxite and silver, as well as things like marble and building stone. Asphalt and lignite are found in the southern part of Herzegovina. Timber is another major industry. There is also some textile manufacturing in the larger cities.

The Future

The question the world must ask is whether Bosnia–Herzegovina has a future. Although it has received international recognition as an independent state by the EC and the United States, the most important entities, Serbia and the Yugoslavia People's Army, refuse to concede the point. A Serb plan to seize up to two–thirds of the territory of the republic for incorporation in a Serbian Republic of Bosnia–Herzegovina, published in early 1992, has since been more than realized. And with Sarajevo under siege and most of the rest of Bosnia actually controlled by Croatian forces, any future for an independent Bosnia seems rather divorced from reality.

333

The Republic of Macedonia

The covered marketplace and the Isac Mosque in Bitola, southern Macedonia

Area: 9,928 square miles (25,713 sq. km.).

Population: 2,033,964 (April 1991).

Capital City: Skopje, pronounced *Scope–yeh* (505,000).

Climate: Mediterranean in the south; mild, temperate elsewhere.

Neighboring Countries: Albania (west); Greece (south); Bulgaria (east); Serbia, (north).

Official Language: Macedonian.

Other Principal Tongues: Albanian, Turkic, Serbo–Croatian.

Ethnic Background: South Slavic.

Principal Religions: Orthodox Christianity; Islam.

Chief Commercial Products: Agricultural products, chemicals, steel, textiles.

Currency: SFRY New Dinar.

Former Political Status: Constituent Republic of SFRY.

National Day: Not available.

Chief of State: Kiro Gligorov, President.

Head of Government: Branko Crvenkovski, Prime Minister.

National Flag: A golden sun is centered on a plain red field.

The Land

The Republic of Macedonia is the independent successor of the Socialist Republic of Macedonia, a constituent republic of the Socialist Federal Republic of Yugoslavia. It declared its independence in September 1991 after a referendum on independence had won the support of the Macedonian population. Bulgaria extended its recognition and Turkey has indicated its intention to do so. It has not yet received recognition from the European Community, however, because of Greek opposition. Greece has demanded that Macedonia change its name because, otherwise, it will seem to be claiming the Greek province of Macedonia.

The center of the republic is dominated by the Vardar River Valley. The Vardar River begins in the northwestern part of the republic, in the Plakenska Chain, and flows north and east until it reaches Skopje, the capital. It then continues southeastward down through the republic, hemmed in by mountains to the west and east.

Macedonia's one area of lowlands is along the lower reaches of the Vardar River, just before it crosses the border nto Greece. At the Greek border, it becomes the Axios River. Flowing down through Greek Macedonia, it empties nto the Gulf of Salonica. Macedonia thus has a natural outlet toward the south, though this is dependent on the status of relations with the government of Greece.

The Plakenska Chain, which dominates the western part of Macedonia, is a series of ridges that run in a southwest–northeast direction, and fairly wide valleys are to be found between the ridges. A second chain of mountains, the Sar, runs west–east along the border with Serbia. In the center, the Black Mountains reach down into Macedonia from Serbia, stopping just north of Skopje. Another mountain, the Osogovske Chain, marks most of the border with Bulgaria.

The People

Macedonia's population as of the April 1991 census was 2,033,964; Macedonians represent 64.6 percent of this total. The language is closely related to Bulgarian and is also spoken in adjacent areas of Greek Macedonia and in western Bulgaria and is written in the Cyrillic alphabet. Albanians, the largest minority, are 21 percent of the total. Albanians live mainly in the western part of the republic. Other minorities include Turks (4.8%), Romanies (Gypsies, 2.7%), and Serbs (2.2%). Almost all Serbs live in the northeastern part of Macedonia, near the city of Kumanovo and villages on Mount Skopska Crna Gora near the capital of Skopje.

History

The name Macedonia is an ancient one, going back to the fourth century B.C. and earlier. Modern Macedonia has little, if anything, to do with that particular past, however.

There was also a larger Macedonia that was part of the Ottoman Empire from 1371 to 1912. It was probably always an area of mixed populations, but the Turks ruled non–Islamic peoples through their religious structures and most Macedonians are Orthodox Christians. Thus the Turks made no differentiation beyond this point.

In 1913, this historic Macedonia was divided up Greece, Bulgaria and Serbia after they had wrestled it from the Ottoman Empire in the First Balkan War. Greece carried out a Hellenization of the territories it obtained, so today Macedonian speakers are only found in the northern part of the province. Bulgaria always treated Macedonians as Bulgarians and so they tended to become amalgamated to the larger Bulgarian population, though Macedonia continues to be spoken in western Bulgaria. Serbia treated the Macedonians as Serbs until World War II. During the war, Marshal Tito, the communist leader, created a

separate Macedonian section of his *Partisan Movement*. After the war, he turned Yugoslavia into a Federal Republic and the Socialist Republic of Macedonia became one of the six constituent republics.

Macedonians were not unhappy as part of a federal Yugoslavia, but the failure of the *League of Communists of Yugoslavia* to solve the country's economic problems led to a slow disintegration. Macedonians never took the lead in this process but they, like the Slovenians and Croatians, supported abandonment of communist economic policies. In 1990, the legislature passed legislation asserting Macedonia's sovereignty and new elections resulted in the first non–communist government.

By the beginning of 1991, they supported a major reformation of the SFRY, though they continued to favor some continued form of union. When Serbia and Montenegro kept their communist leaders in their own republic elections, the stage was set for a confrontation. It was the new Slovenian and Croatian leaders who made the strongest case for change, but it was the Serbian stonewalling that eventually convinced Macedonians that they could not remain part of a Yugoslavia dominated by Serbia. In September 1991, therefore, Macedonians followed the lead of Slovenia and Croatia and voted in a referendum for a "sovereign and independent" republic.

On October 3, Branko Kostic, Montenegrin representative to the SFRY Presidency, called a meeting of the Presidency in his role as Vice President and proposed declaring a state of emergency in the country. Since the president, Stipe Mesic, was not present and the Slovenian delegate was boycotting the meeting, Kostic got his resolution passed with the support of the three votes controlled by Serbia (Serbia plus its two formerly autonomous regions). As a result, the Macedonian delegate to the Presidency withdrew from subsequent meetings of the Presidency and the Macedonian Assembly condemned Kostic's actions as unconstitutional and invalid. The Macedonian Government then condemned the war against Croatia, declared its neutrality, called upon Macedonian soldiers to return to Macedonia, and requested the Yugoslavia People's Army to withdraw its local forces. The YPA, apparently not wanting to drive Macedonia into an alliance with Croatia, agreed to have all of its troops out of Macedonia by April 15. The Macedonian delegates to the SFRY legislature also stopped attending the sessions of the legislature in November.

In January 1992, the Macedonian Assembly passed two amendments to the constitution demanded by the EC as a price for recognition. The first amendment stated that Macedonia does not

have any territorial claims toward its neighbors. The second amendment states that Macedonia will not interfere in the internal affairs of the neighboring sovereign countries. Other related actions by the Assembly included repealing the two sections of the constitution that provided for participation in federal organs, terminating the term of the representative to the Presidency, and recalling all Macedonians in the diplomatic staff. In addition, the Assembly approved the formation of a Macedonian national army of 25,000–30,000 troops.

The EC did not extend recognition to Macedonia at the time it recognized Slovenia and Bosnia–Herzegovina because the Greek Government had objected. It insisted that Macedonia had to change its name before it could be recognized, apparently fearing that an independent Macedonia could exert some influence on its own Macedonian–speaking citizens in *Greek* Macedonia. Bulgaria and Turkey did recognize Macedonia's independence at this time, however. Greece finally abandoned its attempt to get Macedonia to choose a different name in April 1993. On that basis, Macedonia received general recognition and was admitted to the United Nations under the name of the "Former Yugoslav Republic of Macedonia." It was also understood that Macedonia's flag, whose 16–point star has an association with the ancient kings of Macedonia, may not be flown at the United Nations.

Nature of the Regime

The President of Macedonia is Kiro Gligorov. The government is technically a "government of experts," though it normally receives the support of the largest party in the Assembly, the *Internal Macedonian Revolutionary Organization*, usually identified by its Macedonian ini-

President Kiro Gligorov

Macedonia

tials, *VMRO*. A second party that usually supports the government is the Democratic Party for Macedonian Unity. These two political parties are, in fact, so closely associated that they are often spoken of as a single political party. The *VMRO* is often accused of being pro–Bulgarian.

The second strongest party in the republic is the *Social Democratic Alliance of Macedonia,* successor of the former communist party. It supports Macedonian independence. When Branko Kostic, the Yugoslav Vice President and the Montenegrin representative to the Presidency, began calling meetings of the presidency and making decisions in the name of the presidency with only four individuals present, the *Social Democratic Alliance* accused the Yugoslav People's Army of having carried out a *coup*. It also accurately accused the Serbian authorities of having ideas of a "Greater Serbia and Serbian hegemony, directly threatening its neighbors, primarily Macedonia."

The third largest of the political parties represented in the Assembly is the *Party for Democratic Prosperity*, which held its first congress in February 1992. This is

essentially an Albanian party. The chairman of the party is Nevzat Halili. The main plank of the party is a demand for political and territorial autonomy for Albanians in Macedonia. Another is that the party recognizes the Republic of Kosovo. Albanians make up some twenty percent of the republic's population. There is also a second "Albanian" political party, the *National Democratic Party*. It also supports demands for political and territorial autonomy.

The other two political parties sitting in the Assembly are the *Movement for Pan-Macedonian Action* and the *People's Democratic Party*.

Culture

There is a separate Macedonian culture, but it is very similar to that of Bulgaria and Serbia. The chief element that defines the culture is that most people live in villages in the countryside and make their living from agriculture. There also is a more middle class and cosmopolitan culture associated with the city of Skopje.

Religion is the second defining influence. Most Macedonians are Orthodox

Christians. The Church was part of the Serbian Orthodox Church until 1967 when it broke away and formed the Macedonian Orthodox Church. The Serbian Orthodox Church has never accepted the split, however, and does not recognize the Macedonian Church. Approximately 21% of the population is Moslem. Most of these speak Albanian as their first language.

Economy

Macedonia is overwhelmingly an agricultural area, with most people living in the Vardar River Valley or the valleys interspersed between ridges of the Plakenska Chain in the west. Because of the limited farmland available, many young workers live and work in northern Serbia or in Germany. The per capita income of Macedonia trails that of Serbia.

The chief crops are wheat, barley, corn, tobacco, cotton, rice, sunflowers and sugar beets. Cattle raising is also important.

Almost all industry is concentrated in the Skopje area. Heavy industry consists of steel and chemicals. Light industry includes textiles, furniture, porcelain, and chinaware.

The Future

The Macedonians were willing to remain inside a united Yugoslavia until it had become clear that such a Yugoslavia would be dominated by the former communist–turned–nationalist Serbian leadership. It then opted for independence. It wants to maintain good economic relations with Serbia, however, and has said that it would continue to use the Yugo Dinar as its currency. It also favors retention of a common market among the former republics.

Macedonia has been very lucky so far. The Yugoslav People's Army agreed to pull out all of its troops and the small number of Serbs in the republic has meant that it is not faced with a Serb rebellion such as has occurred in Croatia and Bosnia–Herzegovina.

Still, it is a poor republic and the standard of living has been dropping over the past two years because of the unstable political situation. The likelihood is that Macedonians are in for a couple difficult years before they can expect any improvement.

In July 1993, after consultations with the Macedonian government, the United States sent a special 300–troop contingent to be stationed in northern Macedonia; they will reinforce the 800–man Scandinavian battalion sent to the republic in early 1993 in an apparent effort to keep the struggle in the war–torn former Yugoslavia from spreading.

On the way to a marketplace

336

BIBLIOGRAPHY OF KEY
ENGLISH LANGUAGE BOOKS

SOVIET UNION
GENERAL
Kaiser, Robert G. *Russia: The People and the Power.* New York: Pocket Books, 1974, 557 p. (pb).
Smith, Hedrick *The Russians* New York: Ballantine Books, 1976, 706 p. (pb).

HISTORY
Chamberlin, Willliam Henry *The Russian Revolution* 2 vols., New York: Macmillan, 1952.
Daniels, Robert Vincent. *The Conscience of the Revolution: Communist Opposition in Soviet Russia.* Cambridge: Harvard U. Press, 1960. 524 p.
Dmytryshin, Basil *A History of Russia* Englewood Cliffs, N.J.: Prentice Hall, 1977, 648. p.
Dmytryshyn, Basil. *U.S.S.R. A Concise History* (3rd Ed.) New York: Charles Scribner's Sons, 1978, 620 p.
Florinsky, Michael T. *Russia: A History and an Interpretation.* 2 vols. New York: Macmillan, 1954.
Pipes, Richard. *Russian Under the Old Regime.* New York: Charles Scribner's Sons, 1974, 361 p.
Riasanovsky, Nicholas. *A History of Russia* 4th Ed. New York. Oxford University Press, 1984. 695 p.
Treadgold, Donald W. *Twentieth Century Russia.* (3rd ed); Chicago: Rand McNally & Co. 1972, 563 p.
Ulam, Adam B. *The Bolsheviks: The Intellectual and Political History of the Triumph of Communism in Russia.* New York: Macmillan, 1965, 598 p.
Wolfe, Bertram. *Three Who Made a Revolution.* New York: Dial Press, 1948; 661 p.

POLITICS
Bailer, Seweryn. *Stalin's Successors: Leadership, Stability, and Change in the Soviet Union.* Cambridge, Eng.: Cambridge Univ. Press, 1980; 312 p. (pb).
Balzer, Harley D., ed. *Five Years That Shook the World: Gorbachëv's Unfinished Revolution.* Boulder, CO: Westview Press, 1991; 267 p. (pb).
Bialer, Seweryn, ed. *Politics, Society and Nationality inside Gorbachëv's Russia.* Boulder CO: Westview Press, 1988, 180 p.
Breslauer, George W. *Khrushchev and Brezhnev as Leaders: Building Authority in Soviet Politics.* London: Allen & Unwin, 1982; 318 p. (pb).
Brzezinski, Zbigniew. *The Grand Failure: The Birth and Death of Communism in the 20th Century.* New York, Charles Scribner's Sons, 1989.
Daniels, Robert Vincent. *Stalin Revolution: Foundations of Soviet Totalitarianism.* (2d ed.) Boston: Heath, 1973; 106 p.
Djilas, Milovan. *Conversations with Stalin.* New York: Harcourt Brace & World, 1962; 211 p.
d'Encausse, Helen Careere. *Decline of an Empire: The Soviet Socialist Republics in Revolt.* (trans); Martin Sokolinsky and Henry A. La Farge, New York: Newsweek Books, 1978; 304 p.
Gorbachëv, Mikhail. *Perestroika: New Thinking for Our Country and the World.* New York:Harpers & Rowe, 1987. (pb)
Hosking, Geoffrey. *The Awakening of the Soviet Union.* Cambridge: Harvard University Press, 1990; 182 p.
Linden, Carl. *Khrushchev and the Soviet Leadership, 1957–1964.* Baltimore: The Johns Hopkins Press, 1966; 270 p. (pb).
Medvedev, Zhores A. *Gorbachëv.* Norton, 1986; 272 p.
Olcott, Martha, ed. The Soviet Multinational State. Armonk, NY: M.E. Sharpe, Inc., 1989; 400p.
Salvadore, Massimo. *The Rise of Modern Communism.* (3d ed) Hinsdale, Ill.: The Dryden Press, 1975; 203 p. (pb).
Schapiro, Leonard. *The Communist Party of the Soviet Union.* (rev. ed.) New York: Random House, 1971; 631 p. (pb).
Steeves, Paul D. *Keeping the Faiths: Religion and Ideology in the Soviet Union. New York: Holmes and Meier, 1988. (pb)*
Tucker, Robert C. *The Marxian Revolutionary Idea.* New York: W.W. Norton, 1969; 240 p. (pb).
Volkogonov, Dmitri. *Stalin: Triumph and Tragedy.* Grove Weidenfeld, 1991: 642 p.
Yeltsin, Boris. *Against the Grain.* New York: Summit, 1990; 225 p.

ECONOMY

Aganbegyan, Abel. *Perestroika Revolution.* New York: Harper & Rowe, 1990; 248 p.

Goldman, Marshal I. *Gorbachëv's Challenge: Economic Reform in the Age of High Technology.* New York: W.W. Norton & Company, 1987, 296 p. (pb)

Goldman, Marshal I. *USSR in Crisis: the Failure of an Economic System.* New York: W.W. Norton, 1983. 210 p. (pb).

Karcz, Jerzy F. *The Economics of Communist Agriculture: Selected Papers.* Bloomington, Ind.: International Development Institute, 1979, 494 p.

Millar, James R. *The Soviet Economic Experiment.* Champaign, IL: University of Illinois Press, 1990. 352 p.

Shmelev Nikolai and Vladimir Popov. *The Turning Point: Revitalizing the Soviet Economy.* New York: Doubleday, 1990; 352 p.

FOREIGN POLICY

Bialer, Seweryn. *The Soviet Paradox–External Expansion, Internal Decline* New York: Alfred Knopf, 1986; 391 p.

Brzezinski, Zbigniew. *Game Plan–A Geostrategic Framework for the Conduct of the U.S.–Soviet Contest* Atlantic Monthly Press, 1986; 288 p.

Fischer, Louis. *Russia's Road from Peace to War.* New York: Harper & Rowe, 1969; 499 p.

Graziani, Giovanni. *Gorbachëv's Economic Strategy in the Third World.* New York: Praeger, 1990; 136 p. (pb)

Harriman, W. Averill. *Special Envoy to Churchill and Stalin, 1941–1946.* New York: Random House, 1975; 595 p.

Kennan, George F. *Russia and the West under Lenin and Stalin.* Boston: Little, Brown, 1961; 411 p.

Staar, Richard F. *USSR Foreign Policies after Detente.* Stanford, CA: The Hoover Institution Press, 1988; 308 p.

Ulam, Adam B. *Expansion and Coexistence.* New York: Praeger, 1968; 797 p.

Ulam, Adam B. *The Rivals: America and Russia Since World War II.* New York: Viking Preass, 1971; 405 p.

CULTURAL

Bailes, Kendall E. *Technology and Society under Lenin and Stalin: Origins of the Soviet Technical Intelligentsia.* Princeton: Princeton Univ. Press, 1978; 472 p.

Boiter, Albert. *Religion in the Soviet Union.* Beverly Hills: Sage Publications, 1980; 88 p.

Conquest, Robert. *Religion in the U.S.S.R.* New York: Praeger, 1968; 135 p.

Hosking, Geoffrey A. *Beyond Socialist Realism: Soviet Fiction Since Ivan Denisovich.* New York: Holmes & Meier Publishers, 1980; 260 p.

Inkeles, Alex. *Social Change in Soviet Russia.* Cambridge: Harvard U. Press, 1968; 475 p.

Kolarz, Walter. *Religion in the Soviet Union.* New York: St. Martin's Press, 1961; 518 p.

Rand, Robert. *Comrade Lawyer: Inside Soviet Justice in an Era of Reform.* Boulder, CO: Westview Press, 1991; 166 p. (pb)

Segal, Harold B. *Twentieth–century Russian Drama: From Gorky to the Present.* New York: Columbia Univ. Press, 1979; 502 p.

Shneidman, N.N. *Soviet Literature in the 1970's: Artistic Diversity and Ideological Conformity.* Toronto: Univ. of Toronto Press, 1979; 128 p.

Solzhenitsyn, Alexander et al. *From Under the Rubble.* (trans. A.M. Brock) Boston: Little, Brown, 1975; 308 p.

Solzhenitsyn, Alexander. *The Gulag Archipelago: 1918–1956.* (trans. Thomas R. Whitney) New York: Harper & Rowe, 1974, 640 p. (pb).

EASTERN EUROPE
GENERAL

Bahro, Rusolf. *The Alternative in Eastern Europe* (trans. David Fernbach) Norfolk, Eng.: NLB, 1978; Distributed in the U.S. by Schocken Books; 463 p.

Brzezinski, Zbigniew. *The Soviet Bloc.* New York, Praeger: 1967. 467 p.

Bukowski, Charles and J. Richard Walsh, eds. *Glasnost, Perestroika and the Socialist Community.* New York: Praeger, 1990; 187 p.

Carrere d'Encausse, Helene. *Big Brother: The Soviet Union and Soviet Europe.* New York: Holmes and Meier, 1988; 336 p. (pb)

Connor, Walter D. *Socialism's Dilemmas: State and Society in the Soviet Bloc.* New York: Columbia University Press, 1988; 320 p.

Fischer–Galati, Stephen (ed). *The Communist Parties of Eastern Europe.* New York: Columbia Univ. Press, 1979; 393 p.

Fischer–Galati, Stephen (ed). *Eastern Europe in the 1980s.* Boulder, Colo.: West-view Press, 1981; 291 p. (pb).

Kuhlman, James A. *The Foreign Policy of Eastern Europe.* Leyden: Sijhoff, 1978; 302 p.

McInnes, Simon et al (eds.). *The Soviet Union and East Europe in the 1980s.* Oakville, On.: Mosaic Press, 1978; 340 p.

Palmer, Alan. *The Lands Between: A History of East–Central Europe Since the Congress of Vienna.* New York: Macmillan, 1970; 405 p.

Schnitzer, Martin. *U.S. Business Involvement in Eastern Eruope: Case Studies of Hungary, Poland and Romania.* New York: Praeger, 1981; 155 p.

Seton–Watson, Hugh. *Communist Regimes in Eastern Europe.* (4th ed., Stanford, Cal.: Hoover Institution Press, 1982; 375 p. (pb).

Staar, Richard F. *Communist Regimes in Eastern Europe.* (5th ed.) Stanford, CA: The Hoover Institution Press, 1988; 369 p. (pb)

Triska, Jan F. and Charles Gati (eds.) *Blue Collar Workers in Eastern Europe.* Winchester, Mass: Allen and Unwin, 1981; 320 p (pb).

Winiecki, Jan. *The Distorted World of Soviet–Type Economics.* Pittsburgh, PA: University of Pittsburgh Press, 1989. 241 p.

Wolff, Robert Lee. *The Balkans in Our Time.* New York: W.W. Norton, 1967; 618 p. (pb).

ALBANIA

Hamm, Harry. *Albania: China's Beachhead in Europe.* London: Victor Gollancz, 1977; 230 p. Marmullaku, Ramadan. *Albania and the Albanians.* London: Hurst, 1975; 178 p.

Pano, Nicholas C. *Albania.* New York: Columbia University Press, 1989; 220 p. (pb)

Prifti, Peter R. *Albania Since 1944.* Cambridge: MIT Press, 1978; 311 p.

BULGARIA

Crampton, Richard *A Short History of Modern Bulgaria.* Cambridge, ENG: Cambridge University Press, 1987; 224 p. (pb)

Dellin, L.A.D. (ed.) *Bulgaria.* New York: Praeger, 1957.

Feiwel, George R. *Growth and Reforms in Centrally Planned Economies: The Lessons of the Bulgarian Experience.* New York: Praeger, 1977; 345 p.

Zhivkov, Todor. *Modern Bulgaria: Problems and Tasks in Building an Advanced Socialist Society.* New York, International Publishers, 1974; 238 p. (pb).

CZECHOSLOVAKIA

Benes, Edward. *Memoirs of Dr. Edward Benes.* London: Allen & Unwin, 1954; 364 p.

Golan, Galia. *Reform Rule in Czechoslovakia: The Dubcek Era, 1968–1969.* Cambridge, Eng.: Cambridge U. Press, 1975; 349 p.

Kusin, Vladimir V. *From Dubcek to Charter 77.* New York: St. Martin's Press, 1978; 353 p.

Journalist M. *A Year is Eight Months.* Garden City, N.Y.: Doubleday & Co., 1971; 260 p.

Paul, David W. *Czechoslovakia: Profile of a Socialist Republic at the Crossroads of Europe.* Boulder, Col.: Westview Press, 1981; 196 p.

GERMAN DEMOCRATIC REPUBLIC

Childs, David. *The GDR: Moscow's German Ally.* London: Allen & Unwin, 1983; 346 p. (pb).

Hanhardt, Arthur M. Jr.. *The German Democratic Republic.* Baltimore: The Johns Hopkins Press, 1968; 126 p.

Klein, Margarete Siebert *The Challenge of Communist Education: A Look at the German Democratic Republic.* New York: Columbia Univ. Press, 1980; 174 p.

Legters, Lyman H. (ed.) *The German Democratic Republic: A Developed Socialist Society.* Boulder, Col.: Westview Press, 1978; 304 p.

Leptin, Gert and Manfred Melzer. *Economic Reform in East German Industry.* Oxford: Oxford Univ. Press, 1978; 200 p.

Schneider, Eberhard. *The GDR: The History, Politics, Economy and the Society of East Germany.* London: Hurst, 1978; 121 p.

HUNGARY

Felkay, Andrew. *Hungary and the USSR, 1956–1988.* Westport, CT: Greenwood Press, 1989; 343 p.

Ferge, Zsursa. *A Society in the Making: Hungarian Social and Societal Polities, 1945–75.* White Plains, N.Y.: E.M. Sharpe, 1980; 288 p.

Hare, Paul et al. (eds.) *Hungary: A Decade of Economic Reform*. Winchester, Mass: Allen & Unwin, 1981; 257 p.

Held, Joseph (ed.) *The Modernization of Agriculture: Rural Transformation in Hungary*. New York: Columbia Univ. Press, 1980; 508 p.

Kourig, Bennett. *Communism in Hungary: From Kun to Kadar*. Stanford, Cal.: Hoover Institution Press, 1979; 525 p.

Toth, Zoltan (ed). *Some Issues of the Political System in Hungary*. Budapest: Institute of the Social Sciences, 1979; 179 p.

POLAND

Bethell, Nicholas. *Gomulka, His Poland and His Communism*. Harmondsworth, Eng.: Penguin Books, 1972; 307 p. (pb).

Bromke, Adam. *Poland's Politics: Idealism vs. Realism*. Cambridge: Harvard Univ. Press, 1967; 316 p.

Brumberg, Abraham, (ed). *Poland, Genesis of a Revolution*. New York: Random House, 1983; 322 p.

Groth, Alexander J. *People's Poland: Government and Politics*. San Francisco: Chandler Publ Co., 1972; 155 p.

Kanet, Roger E. and Maurice D. Simons (eds.) *Policy and Politics in Gierek's Poland*. Boulder, Colo.: Westview Press, 1980; 418 p.

Karpinski, Jakub. *Countdown: The Polish Upheavals of 1956, 1970, 1976, 1980*. (trans. Olaga Amsterdamska & Gene M. Moore), New York: Karz–Cohl, 1982; 214 p.

Kaufman, Michael. *Mad Dreams, Saving Graces*. New York: Random House, 1990; 270 p.

Schaufele, William E. *Polish Paradox: Communism and National Renewal*. New York: Foreign Policy Association, 1981; 72 p.

Szymanski, Leszek. *Candle for Poland: 469 Days of Solidarity*. San Bernardino, Cal.: Borgo Press, 1982; 128 p.

Weschler, Lawrence. *The Passion of Poland: From Solidarity to the State of War*. New York: Pantheon Books, 1984; 288 p.

Woodall, Jean (ed.) *Policy and Politics in Contemporary Poland*. London: Frances Pinter, 1982; 200 p. (pb).

Woods, William H. *Poland: Eagle in the East; a Survey of Modern Times*. New York: Hill and Wang, 1968; 272 p.

ROMANIA

Braun, Aurel. *Romanian Foreign Policy Since 1965*. New York: Praeger, 1978; 218 p.

Graham, Lawrence S. *Romania: A Developing Socialist State*. Boulder, Colo.: Westview Press, 1982; 136 p.

King, Robert R. *History of the Romanian Communist Party*. Stanford, Cal.: Hoover Institution Press, 1980; 190 p.

Nelson, Daniel N. (ed.) *Romania in the 1980s*. Boulder, Colo.: Westview Press, 1981; 313 p.

Tsantis, Andreas C. and Roy Pepper. *Romania, the Industrialization of an Agrarian Economy Under Socialist Planning*. Washington, D.C.: World Bank, 1979; 707 p.

YUGOSLAVIA

Banac, Ivo. *The Nationality Question in Yugoslavia*. Ithaca, NY: Cornell University Press, 1984; 456 p. (pb)

Borowiec, Andrew. *Yugoslavia After Tito*. New York: Praeger, 1977; 177 p.

Dunn, William N. & Josip Obradovic. *Workers' Self–Management and Organizational Power in Yugoslavia*. Pittsburgh: Univ. of Pittsburgh Press, 1978; 448 p.

Gapinski, James H., Borislav Skegko and Thomas W. Zuehlka. *Modeling the Economic Performance of Yugoslavia*. New York: Praeger, 1989; 311 p.

Macesich, George, ed. *Essays on the Yugoslav Economic Model*. New York: Praeger, 1989; 261 p.

Shrenk, Martin et al. *Yugoslavia: Self Management Socialism and the Challenges of Development*. Baltimore: Johns Hopkins Univ. Press, 1979; 329 p.

Sher, Gerson S. *Praxis: Marxism Criticism and Dissent in Socialist Yugoslavia*. Bloomington, Ind.: Indiana Univ. Press, 1977; 360 p.

Sirc, Ljubo. *The Yugoslav Economy Under Self–Management*. New York: St. Martin's Press, 1979; 270 p.

Stankovic, Slobodan. *The End of the Tito Era*. Stanford, Cal: Hoover Institution Press, 1981; 168p.